Evolutionary Computation

Edited by

Wellington Pinheiro dos Santos

Evolutionary Computation
Edited by Wellington Pinheiro dos Santos

This is a reprint of the book published in 2009 by In-Teh

Republished by InTech
Janeza Trdine 9, 51000 Rijeka, Croatia

Technical Editor Teodora Smiljanic

Additional hard copies can be obtained from orders@intechopen.com

Evolutionary Computation, Edited by Wellington Pinheiro dos Santos
p. cm.
ISBN 978-953-307-008-7

For EU product safety concerns:
IN TECH d.o.o., Prolaz Marije Krucifikse Kozulić 3, 51000 Rijeka, Croatia,
info@intechopen.com or visit our website at intechopen.com.

Meet the editor

Wellington Pinheiro dos Santos holds a degree in Electrical and Electronics Engineering (2001) and MS in Electrical Engineering (2003) from the Federal University of Pernambuco, and Ph.D. in Electrical Engineering from the Federal University of Campina Grande (2009). He is currently a Professor (exclusive devotion) of the Department of Biomedical Engineering at the Center of Technology and Geosciences - Engineering School of Pernambuco, Federal University of Pernambuco, acting in Undergraduate Biomedical Engineering and Graduate Program in Biomedical Engineering, which was one of the founders (2011). He founded the Center for Social Technologies and Bioengineering, at the Federal University of Pernambuco, NETBio-UFPE (2012). He is member of the Graduate Program in Computer Engineering from the Polytechnic School of Pernambuco, University of Pernambuco, since 2009. He also has experience in the area of Computer Science, with an emphasis on Graphic Processing (Graphics), acting on the following themes: digital image processing, pattern recognition, computer vision, evolutionary computation, numerical methods of optimization, computational intelligence, computer graphics, virtual reality, game design and applications of Computing and Engineering in Medicine and Biology. He is a member of the Brazilian Society of Biomedical Engineering (SBEB), the Brazilian Society of Computational Intelligence, the Institute of Electrical and Electronic Engineers (IEEE) and the International Federation of Medical and Biological Engineering (IFMBE).

Preface

This book presents several recent advances on Evolutionary Computation, specially evolution-based optimization methods and hybrid algorithms for several applications, from optimization and learning to pattern recognition and bioinformatics. Concerning evolution-based optimization methods, this book presents diverse versions of genetic algorithms, genetic programming, and performance studies and analyses, as well as several particle swarm optimizers and hybrid approaches using neural networks and artificial immunological systems for multi-objective optimization. This book also presents new algorithms based on several analogies and metafores, where one of them is based on philosophy, specifically on the philosophy of praxis and dialectics. In this book it is also presented interesting applications on bioinformatics, specially the use of particle swarms to discover gene expression patterns in DNA microarrays. Therefore, this book features representative work on the field of evolutionary computation and applied sciences. The intended audience is graduate, undergraduate, researchers, and anyone who wishes to become familiar with he latest research work on this field. The contents of this book allow the reader to know more both theoretical and technical aspects and applications of evolutionary computation.

Editor

Wellington Pinheiro dos Santos

Escola Politécnica de Pernambuco,

Universidade de Pernambuco

Brazil

Contents

1

Study of Genetic Algorithms Behavior for High Epitasis and High Dimensional Deceptive Functions

Gras Robin
University of Windsor
Canada

1. Introduction

Optimization is a widespread notion: a large number of concrete problems require, during the solving process, optimizing a set of parameters (or variables) with respect to a given objective function (or fitness function). These variables can take integer or real values. Such problems for which variables can only take integer values, are called *combinatorial optimization* problems. This paper focuses on combinatorial optimization problems. The set of all possible combinations of values for the variables of the problem represents the *search space* of the problem. *Constraint combinatorial optimization* problems - that is problems which define a set of constraints on the variables enabling a part of the search space - are not considered here. *Global combinatorial optimization* problems - for which the whole search space is available – are the main focus. In a large number of real problems, in particular in bioinformatics, the objective function is partially or entirely unknown. In this contest, it is however possible to calculate the value of the function in each point of the search space. This kind of problem is called a "black box" problem. Classical techniques of operations research are weakly or not at all fitted to black box problems. Consequently, evolutionist approaches of heuristic exploration strategies, have been developed specifically for black box problems. We are particularly interested in the complexity of such problems and in the efficiency of evolutionist methods to solve them.

1.1 Definitions and notations

Let $X = \{x_1, x_2,\dots, x_n\}$ be a set of n binary variables and $C = 2^X$ the set of parts of X. X denotes an element of C. Let F be a function from C to R. A combinatorial optimization problem O is a problem of discovery of maxima, for every possible point X of the search space C, of the objective function $F(X)$. Such a problem is said to be of size n. Its complexity is the minimum number of X of C for which $F(X)$ has to be calculated in order to guarantee the discovery of maxima. This number obviously depends on n but also on a large number of other parameters which influence can be greater than the influence of n.

Let $M = \{X_m \in C \mid \forall X_i \in C,\ F(X_m) \geq F(X_i)\}$ the set of all the solutions of O (also called global maximums), that is the set of points C for which F is maximal.

Exploration algorithms parse C using one or more operators which, from one or several points of C, will lead to one or several points of C. Let Ec be a subset (or sample) of C. We define an operator o as a function from Ec_1 to Ec_2. Ec_2 is said to be the set of points of C, which are neighboring points of Ec_1 for operator o. We define a function Vo, called neighborhood function of operator o, such as $Vo(Ec_1) = Ec_2$. $P = \{C,F, Vo\}$ is called a landscape of O for operator o. Therefore, a landscape depends on the neighborhood associated to an operator.

It is now possible to define the notion of local maximum which depends on a neighborhood and consequently on an operator. The set of local maximums for a given operator o is the set $Mo = \{X_m \in C \mid \forall X_i \in Vo(X_m), F(X_m) \geq F(X_i)\}$.

We define the basin of attraction of a maximum according to an operator as the set $Bo(X_m) = \{X_0 \in C \mid \exists X_1,\ldots, X_n , X_n = X_m \in Mo$ and $X_{i+1} \in Vo(X_i) \ \forall\, 0 \leq i \leq n\}$, that is the set of points from which it is possible to reach the maximum repetitively applying the operator o.

We call *strict hill-climber* a kind of exploration method that only uses operators of the form o: $Ec_1 \rightarrow Ec_2$ with $\forall X_i \in Ec_1$ and $X_j = o(X_i)$, $F(X_j) \geq F(X_i)$ and $X_j \in Vo(X_i)$. We call stochastic hill-climber a kind of exploration method that only uses operators of the form o: $Ec_1 \rightarrow Ec_2$ with $\forall X_i \in Ec_1$, $X_j \in Vo(X_i)$ and $X_j = o(X_i)$, $P(F(X_j) \geq F(X_i)) = g(Vo(X_i))$ where g is a non-uniformly distributed function on [0..1] with a bias towards high values. In general, we also have $|Ec_1| = |o(Ec_1)| = 1$. The most used neighborhood for hill-climbers is the Hamming neighborhood. In this case, the neighborhood of a point $X_i \in C$ is $Vo(X_i) = \{X_j \in C \mid H(X_i,X_j) = 1\}$ with $H(X_i,X_j)$ the Hamming distance between X_i and X_j.

We call *evolutionary algorithm* an exploration algorithm which maintains a sample Ec (called *population*) of points of C and uses an operator os, called *selection operator*, which, from Ec, produces another bias sample Ec' such as $Vos(Ec) = Ec$ and $\forall X_j \in Ec' = os(Ec)$ and $\forall X_i \in Ec$, $X_j \in Vos(Ec)$ and $P(F(X_j) \geq F(X_i)) = g(Vos(Ec))$ where g is a non-uniformly distributed function on [0..1] with a bias towards high values. Then, 0, 1 or several operators are probabilistically applied to each point of Ec' leading to a new population. The same process is recursively reapplied to this new population until the end of the algorithm.

1.2 Complexity of problems

The complexity of combinatorial optimization problems has been extensively studied. Mostly, NP-completion proofs were first realized for classical problems - such as that of the knapsack, graph coloring, search of a clique of size k…- (Garey & Johnson, 1979; Papadimitriou & Steiglitz, 1998). These proofs are however not very informative indices. Indeed, it is well known that for a problem with NP-complete proof, there are, in most cases, instances of the problem that can be solved in polynomial time. Unfortunately, the problem properties that contribute to its complexity are not clearly known in most cases. This information worth discovering since it is often the key to design an efficient solving algorithm. Notions like the breaking in subproblems or the number of solutions of the problem have important consequences on its complexity. The complexity of a problem is also obviously directly linked to the efficiency of the algorithms applied to solve it and to the capacity of these algorithms to exploit the properties of this problem (Jones, 1995).

The first property influencing the complexity is the number of maxima of F (Kallel et al., 2001). For example, when $|M|$ is large compared with $|C|$, an algorithm that evaluates points of C randomly and which has therefore an average complexity of $|M|/|C|$, is very efficient. In the extreme, the problem of "needle-in-a-haystack" (Forrest & Mitchell, 1993; Goldberg, 1989), in which $F(X)$ is identical for 2^n-1 points of C and has a higher value for the last point, is a problem of maximal complexity since no property can be exploited. A

landscape property that is more precise than the number of maxima is the number and the size of the basins of attraction. The higher the size of a basin of attraction of a maximum given an operator o is, the higher the probability of discovering this maximum from a random point of C and using an algorithm based on o is. Thus, the respective size of the basins of attraction of local and global maxima in a given landscape strongly influences the complexity of the exploration of this landscape.
A second property is the epistasie level of a problem. It corresponds to the maximum number of other variables each of the n variables depends on. For example, a problem with zero epistasie is a problem in which all variables are independent[1]. The epistasie is a more general concept than that of decomposability. Indeed, an epistasie level of k does not imply that the problem is decomposable into n/k completely independent sub-problems. The sub-problems can share variables, and there can be, for example, n sub-problems of size k. k dependent variables are called a *block*. Blocks can overlap if they share some variables. A classical problem of size n, of epistasie level k with overlapping is the *NK-landscape* (Kauffman, 1989; Kauffman, 1993). The idea of the NK-landscape, or of its extensions the *NKp-landscape* (Barnett, 1998) and the *NKq-landscape* (Newman & Engelhardt, 1998), is to allow the easy building of problems with scalable difficulty and epistasie level. It has been demonstrated that the problem is NP-complete[2] as soon as k is equal to two or more and when the problem is not decomposable into independent sub-problems (Thompson & Wright, 1996).
Deceptive (or trap) functions are functions that have been defined to be difficult for hill-climber algorithms. Ackley has suggested one of these functions and has shown that it produces an exponential number of local maxima in the landscape (with a Hamming neighborhood) (Ackley, 1987). Deceptive functions have been intensively studied and are often used as benchmark functions to validate exploration algorithms (Goldberg, 2002; Gras et al., 2004; Gras, 2004; Martin et al., 2003; Pelikan, 2002; Sastry et al., 2004; van Nimwegen et al., 1997). They can be viewed as a special case of the problem of the local maxima number. Knowing that local maxima are, by definition, linked to the chosen neighborhood, the notion of deceptive function is also linked to the neighborhood. It is possible to give an informal definition of deceptive function. An entirely ordered landscape can be obtained considering the set of all the possible values of $F(X)$ for all $X \in C$ sorted by growing value. If all the points of M, that is all global maxima, are execluded from this set and assuming C' is the new set, a deceptive function can be informally defined by : a function for which the instantiation of variables x_i of the points of the sub-set of C' points with the higher values[3] is the most different from the instantiation of the variables x_i of M points. In case of a binary function, the notion of "different" corresponds to the Hamming distance. This definition is linked to the Hamming neighborhood but it does not involve the notion of local maximum and is therefore almost independent of the chosen landscape. Then, it is possible to define intrinsically complex functions since this definition of complexity does not directly refer to a

---

[1] The onemax problem, in which one searches the maximum of $F(X)$, where $F(X)$ is the sum of the value of variables X, is a classical problem with zero epistasie.

[2] Indeed, the problem can be transformed into MAX-2-SAT which is NP-complete.

[3] The size of this sub-set is not specified but the higher it is, the more deceptive the function is.

specific landscape. Among classical deceptive function, we can cite the Ackley $trap_5$ function (Ackley, 1987) or the Mitchell, Forrest and Holland *royal road* function (Mitchell et al., 1992).

2. Genetic algorithms

The complexity of combinatorial optimization problems is hard to define and to measure since numerous properties are involved and that these properties need a large amount of computation to be evaluated. The neighborhood, which produces a specific landscape for a function, is a major component of the complexity. It means that there is a great correlation between the exploration algorithm that is used (and then several neighborhoods) and the function to optimize: a given algorithm is efficient for a given class of function and vice versa a given function has a low complexity if an algorithm using its intrinsic properties is discovered. In this section, we are interested in the study of this link while uniquely considering evolutionary explorative methods (Michalewicz & Fogel, 2000; Baluja, 1996). For a wider study, including all the major exploration methods see (Gras, 2004).

2.1 The cannonical approach

The initiation step of a standard genetic algorithm is the random generation of a population, of a given size *Tp* of vectors *X* (the chromosomes). Each vector corresponds to a point of the search space and therefore to a given instantiation of all the variables. The algorithm consists in a repetition of three successive steps: (1) a fitness value equal to *F(X)* is associated to each vector *X*; (2) *Tp* vectors are randomly selected in the population with a probability depending on the fitness value of each vectors; (3) a series of genetic operators is applied stochastically to these vectors and the transformed vectors are then inserted in a new population. The three steps (called generations) are re-applied to this new population of size *Tp*.

There are a large number of selection operators. The most frequent ones are the fitness proportionate selection, the elitist selection and the tournament selection. They allow the modulation of the selection pressure that is put on the population, that is the importance of the statistical bias towards the best solutions. Genetic operators of step (2) are also very varied. The most classical are the punctual mutation of a gene (the change of the instantiation of a variable) and the uniform one or two points crossovers (the instantiations of a series of variables are exchanged between two vectors). These operators allow the exploration of the search space by transforming one point into another.

Numerous operators are necessary for genetic algorithms, for example the size of the population, the probabilities that are associated with the genetic operators, the selection pressure, etc. A lot of experimental studies have been carried out to evaluate the influence of each parameter. The conclusions show that the influences vary considerably depending on the class of problem that is considered. Other studies focus on the comparison of exploration capacities of genetic algorithms and more specifically of crossover operators with those of multi-start strict hill-climbers (Jones, 1995; Baluja, 1996; Goldberg & Segrest, 1987; Sharpe, 2000). Results show that in most cases, and more specifically in deceptive problems, standard genetic algorithms do not have better and even sometimes worse results results than hill-climber algorithms. However, we present more complete results in section 3, showing in which circumstances genetic algorithms are efficient.

Several theoretical studies have been carried out to understand the behavior of genetic algorithms during the exploration process. They are based on either a modelization by a

Markovian process (Goldberg & Segrest, 1987; Moey C.J., Rowe, 2004), or on the study of the cumulants (average, standard deviation…) of the fitness value of the population of chromosomes during the successive generations (Prugel-Bennett & Rogers, 2001). These works are still limited to simple problems and it hardly seems realistic to apply them to more complex non-zero epistasie problems. The first attempt to analyze the convergence behavior of classical genetic algorithms involving the epistasie concept is linked to the notion of schemes (Holland, 1968). Goldberg (Goldberg, 1989) uses this notion to explain the behavior of classical genetic algorithms[4]. The idea is that the function to be optimized is composed of sub-functions, each of them based on a sub-set of variables that are represented by a scheme. The genetic algorithm selects and combines the best schemes to discover a good solution faster. Goldberg shows that a genetic algorithm handles Tp^3 schemes in parallel and that is why it is efficient to solve such problems.
Thierens et Goldberg have published several works on the evaluation of the capacities of genetic algorithms to solve deceptive problems (Thierens & Goldberg, 1993; Thierens & Goldberg, 1994; Sastry & Goldberg, 2002; Thierens, 1999). When functions that are composed of a juxtaposition of deceptive sub-functions of size k are considered, they have evaluated the time t (number of generations) that is needed for the schemes corresponding to variables of sub-functions to mix correctly and to build the complete solution. They deduce from these evaluations the size of the population that is needed to assure the convergence of the exploration process towards the global maximum. These calculations show that the time of convergence and the size of the population of the genetic algorithm with one or two points crossovers is exponential with the number of dependences and the number of sub-functions. They conclude from these results that classical genetic algorithms are not able to solve these difficult problems. These studies have initiated the development of a new evolutionary approach aiming at discovering dependences between variables and solving the corresponding problem. We present this approach in the next section.

2.2 The statisticall approach

In parallel with the continuous developments of the canonical approach, a new kind of genetic algorithm appeared: probabilistic model-building genetic algorithms (*PMBGA*) (Muhlenbein & Mahnig, 2001; Larranaga & Lozano, 2002). On principle the population of chromosomes is considered as a sample of the search space, and the algorithm builds a probabilistic model of this sample and uses the model to generate a new population. The general algorithm is:

1. $t = 0$
   Generate the initial population *P(t)*
2. Select *S(t)* a set of promising solutions (chromosomes)
3. Construct *M* a statistical model of this set
4. Generate *O(t)* a new set of solutions from this model
5. Create a new population *P(t+1)* by replacing some solutions from *P(t)* by solutions from *O(t)*
   $t = t + 1$
6. If the stop criterion is not reached then go to (2)

---

[4] In this case the used genetic algorithm consists in a fitness proportionate selection, a punctual mutation and a one point crossover.

The first works in this domain are the Bit Based Simulated Crossover (BSC) (Syswerda, 1993), the Population Based Incremental Learning (PBIL) (Baluja, 1994) and the Univariate Marginal Distribution Algorithm (UMDA) (Muhlenbein & Voigt, 1996). The idea of the last one was to replace the recombination step by a global recombination over the complete population. All these algorithms extract some statistics from the population for each variable independently. As a consequence, their performances are very poor (in particular less than the performances of a strict hill-climber) when the epistasis level of the problem is above zero. To get around this difficulty, others PMBGA have been proposed taking into account the probability distribution of more than two variables simultaneously. The factorized distribution algorithm (FDA) (Muhlenbein et al., 1999) for example, is based on the construction of a model M of the dependences between variables using a Bayesian network (Frez, 1998). It turns out that this algorithm is very efficient if it is fed with a sample of adequate size (function of k as we present later) and if the problem decomposition is already known (the network structure is an input of the algorithm). This efficiency is not surprising since when a problem is decomposable in independent sub-problems its complexity is considerably lowered. The main difficulty lies precisely in the discovery of these dependences for further exploitation.

The approach called linkage learning has been devised to treat this difficulty (Harik, 1997). We focus on a sub-class called *probabilistic linkage learning* (Pelikan, 2002) or *learning a Bayesian network* (LFDA) (Muhlenbein & Mahnig, 2001). The principle is to learn a bayesian network representing the dependences between the problem variables during the exploration of the search space by the genetic algorithm. It is the approach chosen for the *Bayesian Optimization Algorithm* (BOA) (Pelikan et al., 1999). Learning a Bayesian network implies two things: to discover the network structure, that is, to discover the dependences, and to determine the conditional probabilities associated to the edges. The conditional probabilities are easily estimated from the observed frequencies in the sample (the population) of the simultaneous occurrences of each instance of each variable. Learning the network is much more complex since it involves determining which one of 2^{n^2} possible networks best represents the data (the sample). It is a NP-complete problem (Chickering et al., 1997) and a non-exact heuristic method must be used to build the network. Therefore it is not possible to guarantee the quality of the network obtained. BOA uses a greedy strategy to build the network by adding edges successively, beginning with the empty network. The algorithm needs a metric to measure the quality of the network (how good the network to model the data is) at each step of the construction. Then the algorithm is: (1) Initialize the network without any edge; (2) Between the basic operations (add, remove or inverse) for all the possible edges, choose the operation which best increases the quality of the network; (3) If the stop criterion is not reached, go to (2). The metric used in BOA is the *Bayesian Information Criterion* (BIC) (Schwarz, 1978). There is no perfect measure of network quality. The BIC measure is sensitive to noisy data and can overestimate the number of dependences. The Bayesian network learning process is a non-exact heuristic based on a measure likely to produce errors, therefore it is not possible to guarantee that the final network is composed of all and only all the real dependences of the problem.

The global complexity is $O(k \cdot 2^k \cdot n^2 \cdot Tp + k \cdot n^3)$ (Sastry et al., 2004). It implies that the choice of the edge to add at each step is not made through computing the gain in measure for the global network for each possible edge but is only made through the value of gain from the empty network to the network with one edge (the values are pre-calculated in $O(n^2 \cdot Tp)$). In this case, the choices are made only according to dependences between couples of variables and are therefore likely to be biased by deceptive problems in which dependences can be discovered only when *k* variables are observed simultaneously. Then, the Bayesian network is used to generate the new population. The total complexity of the generation of a new population is in $O(k \cdot n \cdot Tp)$.

Pelikan and Goldberg (Goldberg , 2002; Pelikan, 2002) propose a convergence proof for BOA based on the calculation of the size of the population. The size *Tp* of the population can be deduced: $O(2^k \cdot n^{1.05})$. However, these calculations are performed with several approximations. The value of $F_i(X)$[5] is supposed to have a normal distribution in the population. The probabilistic model is supposed to be exact, that is being a perfect model of the population statistics, but it is built with a drastic heuristic (greedy) algorithm. The quality measure is the BIC measure, but the BD measure is used in the complexity calculation. Finally, and this is also true for the calculation done on the canonical genetic algorithm, the mutation operator is never taken into account[6]. However, from these calculations, they give the convergence proof of BOA in $O(\sqrt{n})$ generations. Associated with the values reported about the building of the Bayesian network, the global complexity of BOA can be deduced: $O(k \cdot n^{7/2} \cdot (2^{2k}+1))$. Pelikan and Goldberg have proposed an extension of BOA called hierarchical bayesian optimization algorithm (hBOA) (Pelikan et al., 2001). Its goal is to solve multi-level deceptive problems in which there are blocks of blocks, each level having its own fitness sub-function. hBOA principle is similar to that of BOA except that hBOA uses decision graphs to store the frequency table of the dependent variables and uses ecological niches system within its populations.

Recent works bring several improvements to hBOA and others PMBGA (Sastry et al.., 2004a). A first one bears on the *mutation Building-Block-Wise* concept (Sastry et al.., 2004b; Sastry & Goldberg., 2004a; Sastry & Goldberg., 2004b). Its principle consists in the discovery of blocks from the probabilistic model of the population. Then, it uses a mutation operator acting as a strict hill-climber on the sub-space of all the possible instantiations of each block. Therefore, a total of $m \cdot 2^k$ evaluations are needed if the problem is composed of *m* blocks of size *k*. They have extend recently this approach to the BOA method (Lima et al., 2006). This approach is in fact strictly equivalent to the principle of dividing a problem into independent sub-problems and to solve each of them independently. This is, of course, much faster than solving directly the global problem. For that purpose, there is still a need for a population that should be large enough to discover the right model and a guarantee that the problem is decomposable into independent sub-problems. Another work is about the notion of *fitness inheritance* (Pelikan & Sastry, 2004). Here, the idea is to avoid explicit computing of the fitness of each new explored point of the search space using estimation. This estimation is done by inheritance of information from the previous populations. The probabilistic model is used to determine what the schemes are, then, for each of them, their contribution to the total fitness is estimated. This estimation is realized by studying the

---

[5] Which is the value of the sub-function corresponding to the block of *i*.

[6] The mutation operator does not explicitly exist in BOA but it has its equivalent. The process of generation of solution from the model is able to generate block instantiations that are not present in the initial population.

fitness distribution, in the previous population, of the solutions containing these schemes. The estimated values are used to calculate the fitness for a fraction of the new population. In spite of the loss in precision due to the estimation, the global improvement in total computing time can be significant.

3. Efficiency of genetic algorithms

3.1 Definition of the Problem

We have carried out a study on the effects of the different properties presented in section 1.2 on the efficiency of several evolutionary algorithms. We focus on the epistasie level, the relative position of variables in the representation of the problem and deceptive functions. We have studied the classical genetic algorithm behavior on these problems, of hBOA and of several simple PMBGAs using different probabilistic models. The functions that we have used in our study are all built according to a simple model: the sum of independent sub-functions deceptive or not. Thus, the fitness function F is defined by :

$$F(X) = \sum_{i=1}^{m} F_i(X_i) \tag{1}$$

with m the number of sub-functions F_i of size $k = n \,/\, m$ and X_i the k variables of X involved in the sub-function F_i. Therefore, k corresponds to the epistasie level of F. There are two kinds of F_i sub-functions:

$$F_i(X_i) = \sum_{x_i \in X_i} x_i \tag{2}$$

if F_i is not deceptive and :

$$\begin{cases} F_i^t(X_i) = 1 - \dfrac{\left(\sum_{x_i \in X_i} x_i\right) + 1}{k} & \text{if } \sum_{x_i \in X_i} x_i < k \\ F_i^t(X_i) = 1 \quad \text{if } \sum_{x_i \in X_i} x_i = k \end{cases} \tag{3}$$

if F_i^t is deceptive.

The position of variables of each sub-function in the complete representation of a solution (chromosome) can be in two different configurations: adjacent and non-adjacent. In the first configuration the numbering of variables of *Fi* is as follows:

$$X_i = \left\{x_{(i-1)\cdot k+1}, x_{(i-1)\cdot k+2}, \ldots, x_{(i-1)\cdot k+k}\right\} \quad with\ i \in \{1, \ldots, m\} \tag{4}$$

In the non-adjacent configuration, the numbering of variables of F_i is as follows:

$$X_i = \left\{x_i, x_{i+m}, \ldots, x_{i+(k-1)\cdot m}\right\} \quad with\ i \in \{1, \ldots, m\} \tag{5}$$

All tests have been realized with Athlon 1.5 Ghz processors.

3.2 The canonical genetic algorithm

The genetic algorithm we have used contains a punctual mutation with a probability of occurrence of 0.05, a one point crossover with a probability of occurrence of 0.45 and a two points crossover with a probability of occurrence of 0.5. One operator at most is applied to a given chromosome. It uses also a tournament selection of size 10. The value of these parameters has few consequences on the results. The first test function is composed of 120 variables ($|X|$ =120) and of $m = 120/k$ deceptive sub-functions F_i^t of size k. The values of k vary from 4 to 12. We use the adjacent configuration. The size of the population is calculated with the formula proposed by Pelikan and Goldberg, $Tp = 2^k \cdot n^{1.05}$, in order to compare the performances of each algorithm in the same condition. For each k value, the presented results correspond to the number of run, over 60 performed each time, for which the global maximum has been reached in less than 100 generations. Table 1 gives the number of failures over 60 runs.

k	4	6	8	10	12
Nb failures	58	7	0	0	0

Table. 1. Number of failures of the classical genetic algorithm among 60 runs for each k value and for the adjacent deceptive function.

The results that are obtained in term of computation time and number of generations are given in figure 1. Because of the huge memory that is needed to store the population for the higher k value (Tp = 622 592 for k = 12), we limited the size of the population to Tp = 480 000. We observe that the classical genetic algorithm can easily discover the right solution even in problems that are considered to be very difficult ones (n = 120, $k \geq 10$) if the population is large enough. It seems also that for high epistasie level the size of the population that is necessary to find the maximum is smaller than the size that is required by hBOA. However the population size of 2400 that is used for k = 4 is too small to discover the maximum in most cases.

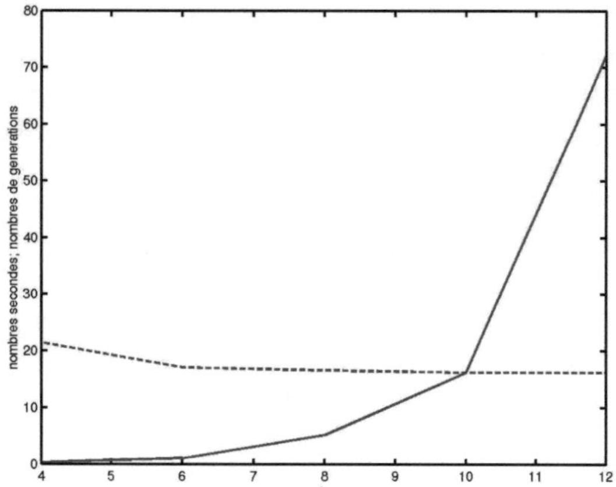

Fig. 1. Average time in seconds (plain line) and average number of generations (dot line) to discover the global maximum depending on the size k of the sub-functions (epistasie level).

The second test function is the same as the first one but with a non-adjacent configuration. The results that are obtained are very different from those of the first function. Indeed, the classical genetic algorithm is unable to discover the solution (100% fails) for *k* values, even if the population size is much more important than the necessary size for hBOA. For example, when $k = 4$ the population size should be 2432 and we have used a size of 480 000! It can be deduced that the operators that are used to explore the search space (mutation and crossover) are unsuited to the structure of the problem. They produce a neighborhood that makes the landscape particularly hard to explore. Crossovers destroy every block, or parts of blocks, that were previously built since the operator inevitably separates the variables of a given block. Thus, two neighboring points of the landscape, that is distant of one operator application, are totally different considering the function to optimize. On the other hand, in the adjacent configuration, crossovers are optimal neighborhood operators since they preserve and mix most of the blocks. That explains why classical genetic algorithm performances are extremely good for this problem. In general, it can be concluded that, if the problem has unknown dependences, the configurations used are very likely to be non-adjacent and therefore the problem is unsolvable for classical genetic algorithm. Solvable problems for classical genetic algorithm are those that have no or few dependences, or those for which a deep knowledge about the problem structure can be used to design specifically adapted and efficient operators. (a) The manuscript must be written in English, (b) use common technical terms, (c) avoid abbreviations, don't try to create new English words, (d) spelling: Follow Merriam Webster´s Collegiate Dictionary, Longman or Oxford Dictionaries.

3.2 The hBOA algorithm

The population size is computed with $Tp = 2^k \cdot n^{1.05}$ and the maximum number of generations is 100. All the other parameters are hBOA default parameters. The first test function is composed of 100 or 96 variables and of $m = 100/k$ or $m = 96/k$ (in order that *m* is an integer) deceptive sub-functions F_i^t of size *k*. The *k* value varies from 4 to 12 and the variables are in an adjacent configuration. The running time of hBOA is much higher than the one of the classical genetic algorithm, so only 12 runs have been performed for each problem. The results vary much more, so each result is detailed independently.

1. $n = 100$, $k = 4$, $Tp = 2\,016$. The global maximum (25) has been reached for each run with an average number of generations of 25 and an average running time of 20 seconds.
2. $n = 96$, $k = 6$, $Tp = 7\,720$. The global maximum (16) has never been reached during the 12 runs. The average value is 15.7, which is much higher than the "trap" value (14.4) and close to the global maximum. It is reasonable to suppose that the maximum should have been reached with a few more generations. The average running time was 13 minutes.
3. $n = 96$, $k = 8$, $Tp = 30\,720$. The global maximum (12) has never been reached during the 12 runs. The value that has been reached was 10.8 for each run, which is the "trap" value. It is reasonable to suppose that the exploration process was trapped for a long time in a local maximum and was not able to reach the global maximum. The average running time was 1 hour and 53 minutes. A second experimentation (12 runs) has been done with the same function but with a double size population ($Tp = 61\,440$). The

average running time was 4 hour and 50 minutes. The global maximum has never been reached during the 12 runs and the "trap" value has been slightly overtopped with a value of 10.9 each time.

4. n = 100, k = 10, Tp = 129 000. The global maximum (10) has never been reached during the 12 runs. The value that has been reached was 9.1 for each run, which is the "trap" value. It is reasonable to suppose that the exploration process was trapped for a long time in a local maximum and was not able to reach the global maximum. The average running time was 12 hours 40 minutes.
5. n = 96, k = 12, Tp = 491 520. The average running time was 61 hours, so we have only done 6 runs. The global maximum (8) has never been reached during the 6 runs. The value that has been reached was 7.4, which is slightly above the "trap" value (7.2). It reasonable to suppose that the process was not definitively trapped in a local maximum and that the result should have been slightly improved with more generations.

One can already observe that, contrary to what has been published, in each situation in which it is supposed to be efficient, hBOA cannot discover the global maximum using the parameters established in the convergence proofs. hBOA results, presented in the literature, have always been obtained with function containing few dependences (maximum 6 or 8). The running time became prohibitive when the level of epistasie increased and there is no guarantee that the global maximum is discovered or that local maximum traps can be escaped. Heuristics that are used during the construction of the Bayesian network and not evaluated in the convergence proofs possibly have dramatic consequences on the efficiency of the exploration process.

During our tests, we have observed a particular sensitiveness of hBOA to the structure of the fitness function. To our knowledge, this phenomenon is not described in the literature and does not appear in the convergence calculation of Pelikan and Goldberg. We have therefore carried out another series of tests (12 in each case) in order to have a better understanding of this phenomenon. In the previous tests, the function F_i^t for n=96, k=8 and Tp=30 720 was the function presented in figure 2. We have done several tests in which we change this function by those which are presented in figure 3 to 5. These new functions correspond to change in the value of the difference between the global maximum value and the "trap" value of the function. Once we have changed this function but with the same n=96, k=8 and Tp=30 720, very different results are obtained. For the function of the figure 3, the same results were obtained, that is the global maximum was never reached and the process was trapped in a local maximum corresponding to the "trap" value 10.8. For the function, of the figure 4, five global maxima were obtained for twelve runs with an average 56 generations. For the seven failed runs the average score was 11.8, which is close to the global maximum. For the function, of the figure 5, the global maximum was obtained for the twelve runs with an average 15 generations.

During our tests, we have observed a particular sensitiveness of hBOA to the structure of the fitness function. To our knowledge, this phenomenon is not described in the literature and does not appear in the convergence calculation of Pelikan and Goldberg. We have therefore carried out another series of tests in order to have a better understanding of this phenomenon. In the previous tests, the function F_i^t for n = 96, k = 8 and Tp = 30 720 was the following the one of figure 2.

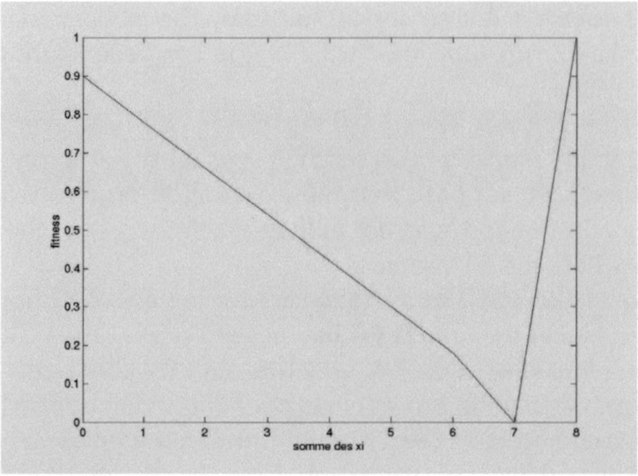

Fig. 2. The initial trap function

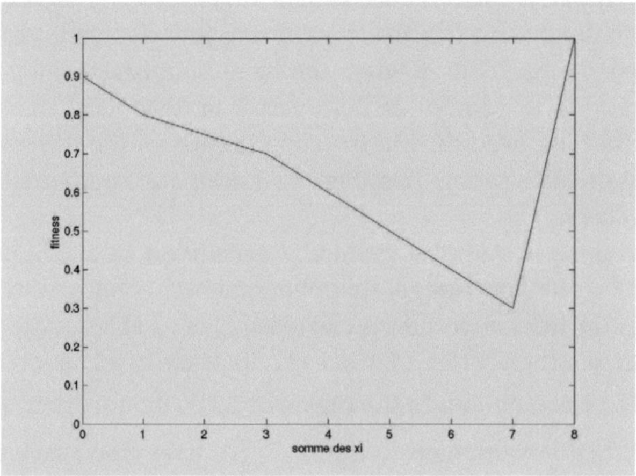

Fig. 3. The second trap function

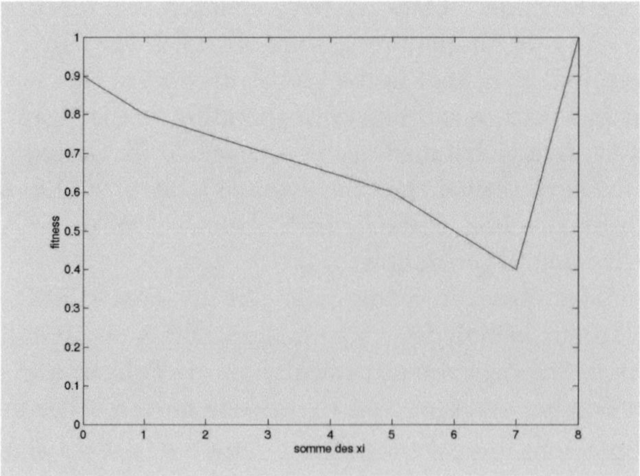

Fig. 4. The third trap function

Even though these results need to be confirmed with more of experiments, the phenomenon seems to be relatively clear. It seems that a too large difference value between the global maximum and the solutions the most similar to the global maximum (in Hamming distance) makes the probabilistic model harder to construct and disables the discovery of the right dependences. Even though the heuristic for the bayesian network of hBOA construction has not been described in detail, results that are obtained tend to show that it rests in, at least in part, univariate frequencies. Indeed, the previous series of functions increasingly favor the selection of vectors that are composed of a majority of '1'. The global maximum is the vector entirely composed of '1'. Since the functions that favor the selection of '1' also favor the construction of a model that predicts '1' at each position, these functions are logically easier to solve. Another possible explanation for this phenomenon can be linked to the system that is used in hBOA to generate the population from the model. As it is emphasized in section 2.2, Pelikan and Goldberg's algorithm that generates the new population is not clear as it does not give any clue about the initialization process. It is therefore possible that this initialization is done from uni or bivariate frequencies and consequently introduces a bias in the population in favor of the values that are instantiated in the previous generation.

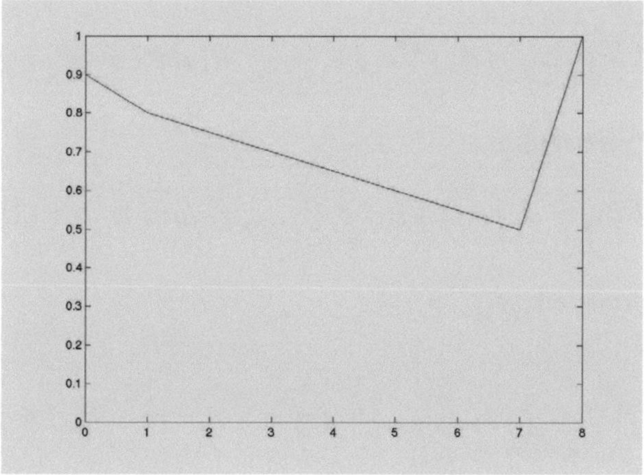

Fig. 5. The fourth trap function.

All these experimentations have been realized with the adjacent configuration. We have done the same experimentations with the non-adjacent configuration and the results are practically identical. That means that hBOA is not disrupted by the relative position of variables that are involved in a same block. It is to be expected because the position of variable in the chromosome/vector in the hBOA concept is not taken into account. It is an important result, which has not been published, because, as we have seen in the previous section, the classical genetic algorithm is totally unable to escape from the local maximum traps. The result demonstrates that hBOA is able to discover and exploit the problem dependences in a complex situation if the epistasie level is reasonable and if the structure of the function does not prevent the heuristics of the probabilistic model building and that of population generation from guiding the exploration towards the global maximum.

4. Tables and figures

We have tried to understand what is possible to discover if only one piece of information about the problem is exploited. We have studied other probabilistic models to discover the dependences and designed new operators based on these models. We have limited our model to the representation of dependences of maximum size two and we have designed an algorithm, a variant of a classical genetic algorithm with a tournament selection, using specific operators based on our model. Then, we have tested our approach on problems with epistasie level above two (the problems presented in section 3.1 and 3.2). The principle of our algorithm is as follows. The frequencies of occurrence of all the couples of variables instantiations that are encountered in the population are computed at each generation. Then, we use these statistics to measure correlations between instantiations of variables. Operators that are based on these measurements are used to generate new solutions for the new population.

We have compared different measures to study their capacities to discover the couples of dependent variables among the blocks of size above two (in our test problems, the sizes of the blocks range from 4 to 12). We have used the following measures:

- The conjoint frequencies of two variables instantiations:

$$f(x_i = \phi_1, x_j = \phi_2)\ \forall i,j \in \{1,\cdots,n\}\ and\ \phi_1,\phi_2 \in \{0,1\} \tag{6}$$

- The conditional probability:

$$P(x_i = \phi_1 \mid x_j)\ \forall i,j \in \{1,\ldots,n\}\ and\ \phi_1 \in \{0,1\} \tag{7}$$

- The mutual information $M(x_i, x_j)$:

$$M(x_i,x_j) = \sum_{x_i=\phi_1,x_j=\phi_2} f_{x=\phi_i x_j=\phi_2} \cdot \log \frac{f_{x_i=\phi x_j=\phi_2}}{f_{x_i=\phi_1} \cdot f_{x_j=\phi_2}} \quad \forall i,j \in \{1,\cdots,n\} \\ and\ \phi_1,\phi_2 \in \{0,1\} \tag{8}$$

- The statistical implication (Blanchard et al., 2003; Kuntz et al., 2002)

$$q(x_i = \phi_1, x_j = \overline{\phi_2}) = \frac{n_{x_i=\phi_1 \cap x_j=\overline{\phi_2}} - \dfrac{n_{x_i=\phi_1} \times n_{x_j=\overline{\phi_2}}}{Tp}}{\sqrt{\dfrac{n_{x_i=\phi_1} \times n_{x_j=\overline{\phi_2}}}{Tp}}} \quad \forall i,j \in \{1,\cdots,n\} \tag{9}$$

with $n_{x_i=\phi_1}$ et $n_{x_j=\overline{\phi_2}}$ the number of times where x_i is instantiated to ϕ_1 and x_j is instantiated to non ϕ_2 respectively in the whole sample of size Tp and:

$$\varphi\left(x_i=\phi_1,x_j=\phi_2\right)=\frac{1}{\sqrt{2\pi}}\int_{q(x_i=\phi_1,x_j=\overline{\phi_2})}^{\infty}e^{-\frac{t^2}{2}}dt \tag{10}$$

This last measure is a value of the degree of implication between two variable instantiations. It has been shown as being much more sensitive than the conditional probability.

These tests have shown that none of these four measures is able to detect the instantiations of two variables corresponding to their instantiation in their own block in the global maximum. For example, in the case of blocks of size 8, if the variables x_1 to x_8 belong to the same block and have an instantiation of '1' in the global maximum and an instantiation of '0' in the local deceptive maximum, the four measures detect the strongest dependences for couples of variables instantiated to '00' and the weakest for those instantiated to '11'. Thus, we confirm that it seems to be impossible to discover the right dependences when all the variables of a same block are not considered together (in the example, it would be necessary to measure dependences between the 8 variables simultaneously). When dependences of a problem are not known, it is therefore necessary to discover them completely to find the global maximum. The number of combination corresponding to the total number of possible dependences is the number of partitions of *n* variables and is therefore exponential with *n*. Consequently, either a heuristic is needed, for example the one that is used in hBOA for the construction of the bayesian network, or some information known about the problem structure has to be used to determine the dependences and then solve the problem (for example, sort variables so that they are in adjacent configuration).

In this perspective, we have chosen to use an information about the problem structure, i.e. the fact that the sub-functions are deceptive, to try to build an efficient algorithm for theses problems. We use a PMBGA based on the four previously defined measures. We have designed an extremely simple operator to generate the new population. Knowing that the sub-functions to be optimized are deceptive, we have chosen to favour the less frequent instantiations in the population after a tournament selection. Indeed, with deceptive sub-functions, instantiations corresponding to or similar to those of the deceptive local maxima are present in the population and selected with higher probabilities. Consequently, instantiations corresponding to or similar to those of the global maxima are largely under represented in the sample population. Therefore, our operator consists in the random selection of two variables x_i and x_j, then in choosing among the four possible instantiations of these two variables the one, $\phi_i\phi_j$, with the lowest value for the measure (that is the one with the lowest correlation). Finally, for the instantiation ϕ_i of the variable x_i, the instantiation of all other variables x_k are chosen in the following way:

$$choice(x_k)=\arg\min_{\phi_k} measure(x_i=\phi_i,x_k=\phi_k) \qquad \forall k\neq i \tag{11}$$

with $measure(x_i=\phi_i,x_k=\phi_k)$ one of the four measures previously defined. A new solution is then built from these instantiations. We have used this algorithm for all the problems that are presented in section 3.1. We have observed that, using the same population size than the one that is calculated for hBOA[7], the global maximum is found in only one generation (that is, the computation of the first random population and its fitness evaluation, the tournament selection, the computation of the value of one of the four measures and the construction of one new solution) for all the tested problems, even those of size 120 with blocks of size 12 ! The optimal solution is therefore discovered in few minutes (few seconds for the smallest problem and 5 minutes for the largest ones, the global complexity is in $O(n^2)$) for problems for which hBOA does not find the solution in several days of computation! Thus, with no information about the dependences and their number, but uniquely using the information that the function is deceptive, we have designed a strategy that discovers the solution in 100% of the cases in few minutes even for very complex problems.

To establish the limits of our approach, we have constructed a problem composed of half deceptive sub-functions and half non-deceptive sub-functions. In this case, our approach is totally unable to discover the solution. We have modified our method to handle such mixed problems. We have used several operators: classical mutation and crossover, our previously defined operator, and several operators doing mixed instantiation choices between high and low value of the measures (that is choosing very highly or very lowly correlated instantiations). Even with these new operators our method fails to discover the optimal solution. It can be easily understood because the discovery of the variables that participate to deceptive sub-functions and those that participate to non-deceptive sub-functions is it-self an NP-complete problem. We have verified that those kinds of mixed problem do not perturb hBOA. Indeed, hBOA reaches the same performances with this kind of function as with complete deceptive function in section 3.2.

5. Conclusion

A large number of properties are involved in the intrinsic complexity of a global combinatorial optimization problem. We have focused our studies on two particularly important properties: epistasis and deceptiveness. We first show that the canonical genetic algorithm is unable to solve problems (even simple ones) with epistasie when no information is available on the nature of the dependencies. We then propose to distinguish two classes of strategies: (1) those based on an algorithm that is dedicated to a unique problem using expert knowledge on the structure of this problem - we call it the expert strategy - and (2) those based on the discovery, through modeling a bias sample of the search space, of the structure of the function to be optimized to determine a pertinent neighborhood for exploration - we call it the automated strategy. We study the capability of these two strategies using one representative of each class: hBOA for the automated class and a very simple algorithm, exploiting the unique knowledge that the problem is deceptive, for the expert class. Depending on the nature of the problem, either one or the other of these classes can be efficient. If the first one is highly dependent to the information exploited and therefore to the expert's knowledge, the second one is limited if the number of

[7] We have as well noticed that these results are still true with population of size 2 or 4 times smaller.

dependences between the problem variables is high. However we have shown that hBOA can really discover dependences even in non-adjacent and mixed configurations. We have also shown how the use of partial information on the problem structure can lead to the definition of a highly efficient algorithm, solving very complex problems in a few minutes. Future work should focus on the study of new heuristic strategies building an informative probabilistic model of the problem and incorporating new probabilistic measures in this model and on how they can be coupled with an expert strategy. Such approaches should be applied to real complex problems, in particular in bioinformatics (Hernandez et al., 2008; Armañanzas et al., 2008), to assess their efficiency to solve real problems and to examine what new knowledge about the problem itself the probabilistic model is able to reveal.

6. References

Ackley, D.H. (1887). An empirical study of bit vector function optimization, In *Genetic Algorithms and Simulated Annealing*. pp 170-204, Morgan Kaufmann

Armañanzas, R.; Inza, I.; Santana, R.; Saeys, Y.; Flores, J.L.; Lozano, J.A.; Van de Peer, Y.; Blanco, R.; Robles, V.; Bielza, C. & Larrañaga P. (2008). A review of estimation of distribution algorithms in bioinformatics. *BioData Mining*, 1, 6

Baluja, S. (1994). Population-Based Incremental Learning: A Method for Integrating Genetic Search Based Function Optimization and Competitive Learning. CMU-CS-94-163, Carnegie Mellon University

Baluja, S. (1996). An Empirical Comparison of Seven Iterative and Evolutionary Function Optimization Heuristics. *Proceedings of the Eleventh International Conference on Systems Engineering*

Barnett, L. (1998). Ruggedness and neutrality - the NKp family of fitness landscapes, *Proceedings of the sixth international conference on artificial life*, pp 18-27

Blanchard, J.; Kuntz, P.; Guillet, F. & Gras, R. (2003). Implication intensity: from the basic statistical definition to the entropic version. In *Statistical data Mining and Knowledge Discovery*. Chapman H. (Ed.), Washington, pp 473-485

Chickering, D.M.; Heckerman, D. & Meek, C. (1997). Learning Bayesian Network is NP-Hard, MSR-TR-97-07. Redmond, Microsoft Research

Forrest, S. & Mitchell, M. (1993). Relative building-block fitness and building-block hypothesis, In *Foundations of Genetic Algorithms 2*, pp 109-126, Whitley L.D. (Ed.), Morgan Kaufmann

Frez, B.J. (1998). *Graphical Models for Machine Learning and Digital Communication*, MIT Press

Garey, M.R. & Johnson, D.S. (1979). *Computers and Intractability: a Guide to the Theory of NP-Completeness*. Freeman

Goldberg, D.E. & Segrest, P. (1987). Finite Markov chain analysis of genetic algorithms, *Proceedings of the Second International Conference on Genetic Algorithms*, Grefenstette, J.J. (Ed.)

Goldberg, D.E. (1989). *Genetic Algorithm in Search, Optimization and Machine Learning.*, Addison-Wesley. 1989

Goldberg, D.E. (2002). *The Design of Innovation: Lessons from and for Competent Genetic Algorithms*, Kluwer Academic Publishers

Gras, R.; Hernandez, D.; Hernandez, P.; Zangger, N.; Mescam, Y.; Frey, J.; Martin, O.; Nicolas, J. & Appel, R.D. (2004). Cooperative metaheuristics for exploring proteomic data, In *Artificial Intelligence Methods and Tools for Systems Biology*. Dubitzky, W.; Azuaje, F. (Ed.), Springer

Gras, R. (2004). Structure des espaces de recherche, complexité des algorithmes d'optimisation combinatoire stochastique et application à la bioinformatique, *Habilitation à diriger les recherches*, University of Rennes, Thesis/Dissertation

Harik, G.R. (1997). Learning gene linkage to efficiently solve problems of bounded difficulty using genetic algorithms, *PhD Thesis,* University of Michigan

Hernandez, D.; Gras, R. & Appel, R. (2008). Neighborhood Functions and Hill-Climbing Strategies dedicated to the Generalized Ungapped Local Multiple Alignment, *European Journal of Operational Research,* 185(3), pp 1276-1284

Holland, J.H. (1968). Hierarchical descriptions of universal spaces and adaptive systems, Report, University of Michigan

Jones, T. (1995). Evolutionary Algorithms, Fitness Landscapes and Search, *PhD Thesis,* University of New Mexico.

Kallel, L.; Naudts, B. & Reeves, C.R. (2001). Properties of Fitness Functions and Search Landscape. In *Theoretical Aspects of Evolutionary Computing,* pp 175-206, Kallel L., Naudts B., Rogers A. (Ed.), Springer

Kauffman, S.A. (1989). Adaptation on rugged fitness landscapes, *Lecture in Sciences of Complexity,* 1, pp 527-618

Kauffman, S.A. (1993). The Origins of Order. In *Self-Organization and selection in Evolution,* New York: Oxford University Press

Kuntz, P.; Gras, R. & Blanchard, L. (2002). Discovering Extend Rules with Implicative Hierarchies. *Proceedings of the conference on the new frontiers of statistical data mining and knowledge discovery*. Knoxville Tennesse

Larranaga, P. & Lozano, J.A. (2002). *Estimation of Distribution Algorithms: A new tool for evolutionary computation,* Kluwer Academic Publishers

Lima, C.; Pelikan, M.; Sastry, K.; Butz, M. & Goldberg, D.E. (2006). Structural neighborhoods for local search in Bayesian optimization algorithm, *proceeding of the Parallel Problem Solving from Nature,* pp 232-241

Martin, O.; Gras, R.; Hernandez, D. & Appel, R.D. (2003). Optimizing Genetic Algorithms Using Self-Adaptation And Explored Space Modelization, pp 291-294, *proceedings of 5th International Workshop on Frontiers in Evolutionary Algorithms,* North Carolina

Michalewicz, Z. & Fogel, D. (2000). *How to Solve It: Modern Heuristics*. Springer-Verlag

Mitchell, M.; Forrest, S. & Holland J.H. (1992). The royal road for genetic algorithms: Fitness landscapes and GA performance. *Proceedings of the First European Conference on Artificial Life,* pp 245-254, Varela, F.J. & Bourgine P. (Ed.), MIT Press

Moey, C.J. & Rowe, J.E. (2004). Population aggregation based on fitness. *Natural Computing,* 3, pp 5-19

Muhlenbein, H. & Voigt, H.M. (1996). Gene pool recombination in genetic algorithms, In *Metaheuritics: Theory and Applications,* pp 53-62, Kelly, J.P. & Osman, I.H. (Ed.), Kluwer Academic

Muhlenbein, H.; Mahnig, T. & Rodriguez. A.O. (1999). Schemata, distributions and graphical models in evolutionary optimization, *Journal of Heuristics*, 5, pp 215-47

Muhlenbein, H. & Mahnig, T. (2001). Evolutionary Algoritms: From Recombination to Search Distributions, In *Theoretical Aspects of Evolutionary Computing*, pp 135-173, Kallel, L.; Naudts, B. & Rogers, A. (Ed.), Springer

Newman, M. & Engelhardt R. (1998). Effect of neutral selection on the evolution of molecular species, *Proc. R. Soc. London*, 256, pp 1333-1338

Papadimitriou, C.H. & Steiglitz, K. (1998). *Combinatorial Optimization: Algorithms and Complexity*, Dover

Pelikan, M.; Goldberg, D.E. & Cantu-Paz, E. (1999). The Bayesian Optimization Algorithm, *Proceedings of the Genetic and Evolutionary Computation Conference I*, pp 525-532, San Francisco, CA, Morgan Kaufmann

Pelikan, M.; Goldberg, D.E. & Cantu-Paz, E. (2000). Linkage Problem, Distribution Estimation, and Bayesian Networks, *Evolutionary Computation*, 8, pp 311-340

Pelikan, M. (2002). Bayesian Optimization Algorithm: From Single Level to Hierarchy, *PhD thesis*, University of Illinois

Pelikan, M. & Sastry, K. (2004). Fitness Inheritance in the Baysian Optimization Algorithm, *Proceedings of the Genetic and Evolutionary Computation Conference*, pp 48-59

Prugel-Bennett, A. & Rogers, A. (2001). Modelling Genetic Algorithm Dynamics. In *Theoretical Aspects of Evolutionary Computing*, pp 59-85

Sastry, K. & Goldberg, D.E. (2002). Analysis of Mixing in Genetic Algorithms: A survey, 2002017 IlliGAL report

Sastry, K.; Goldberg, D.E. & Pelikan, M. (2004a). Efficiency Enhancement of Probabilistic Model Building Genetic Algorithms, *proceeding of Genetic and Evolutionary Computation Conference*

Sastry, K.; Pelikan, M. & Goldberg, D.E. (2004b). Efficiency Enhancement of Genetic Algorithms via building-block-wise fitness estimation, *proceeding of IEEE Conference on Evolutionary Computation*, pp 720 -727

Sastry, K. & Goldberg, D.E. (2004a). Designing Competent Mutation Operators via Probabilistic Model Building of Neighborhoods, *Proceedings of the Genetic and Evolutionary Computation Conference*

Sastry, K. & Goldberg, D.E. (2004b). Let's Get Ready to Rumble: Crossover Versus Mutation Head to Head, *Proceedings of the Genetic and Evolutionary Computation Conference*

Schwarz, G. (1978). Estimating the dimension of a model, *The Annals of Stat*istics, 6, pp 461-464

Sharpe, O.J. (2000). Towards a Rational Methodology for Using Evolutionary Search Algorithms, *PhD Thesis*, University of Sussex

Syswerda, G. (1993). Simulated Crossover in genetic algorithms, In *Foundations of Genetic Algorithms 2*, pp 239-255, Whitley, L.D. (Ed.), Morgan Kaufmann

Thierens, D. & Goldberg, D.E. (1993). Mixing in genetic algorithms, *Proceedings of the International Conference on Genetic Algorithms*, pp 38-45

Thierens, D. & Goldberg, D.E. (1994). Convergence models of genetic algorithm selection schemes. *Proceedings of Parallel Problem Solving from Nature*, pp 116-121

Thierens, D. (1999). Scalability Problems of Simple Genetic Algorithms. *Evolutionary Computation*, 7, pp 331-352

Thompson, R.K. & Wright, A.H. (1996). Additively decomposable fitness functions, University of Montana, Computer Science department, Report

van Nimwegen, E.; Crutchfield, J.P. & Mitchell M. (1997). Finite populations induce metastability in evolutionary search, *Physics Letters A*, 229, pp 144-150

Interactive Genetic Algorithms with Individual's Uncertain Fitness

Dun-wei Gong, Xiao-yan Sun and Jie Yuan
China University of Mining & Technology
China

1. Introduction

Interactive genetic algorithms (IGAs), proposed in mid 1980s, are effective methods to solve an optimization problem with implicit or fuzzy indices (Dawkins, 1986). These algorithms combine traditional evolution mechanism with a user's intelligent evaluation, and the user assigns an individual's fitness rather than a function that is difficult or even impossible to explicitly express. Up to now, they have been successfully applied in many fields, e.g. face identification (Caldwell & Johnston, 1991), fashion design (Kim & Cho, 2000), music composition (Tokui & Iba, 2000), hearing aid fitting (Takagi & Ohsaki, 2007).

The obvious character of IGAs, compared with traditional genetic algorithms (TGAs), is that the user assigns an individual's fitness. The user compares different individuals in the same generation and assigns fitness based on their phenotypes through a human-computer interface. The frequent interaction results in user fatigue. Therefore, IGAs often have small population size and a small number of evolutionary generations (Takagi, 2001), which influences these algorithms' performance to some degree and restricts their applications in complicated optimization problems. Accordingly, how to evaluate an individual and express its fitness becomes one of the key problems in IGAs.

Since user fatigue results from the user's evaluation on an individual and expression of its fitness, in order to alleviate user fatigue, a possible alternative is to change the approach to express an individual's fitness. The goal of this chapter is to alleviate user fatigue by adopting some appropriate approaches to express an individual's fitness.

An accurate number is a commonly used approach to express an individual's fitness. As is well known, the user's cognitive is uncertain and gradual, therefore the evaluation of an individual by the user and the expression of its fitness should also be uncertain and gradual. It is difficult to reflect the above character if we adopt an accurate number to express an individual's fitness.

We will present two kinds of uncertain numbers to express an individual's fitness in this chapter, one is an interval described with the lower limit and the upper limit, the other is a fuzzy number described with a Gaussian membership function. These expressions of an individual's uncertain fitness well accord with the user's fuzzy cognitive on the evaluated object.

In addition, we will propose some effective strategies to compare different individuals in the same generation on condition of an individual's uncertain fitness. We will obtain the probability of an individual dominance by use of the probability of interval dominance, and translate a fuzzy number into an interval based on α-cut set. We will determine the dominant individual in tournament selection with size being two based on the probability of an individual dominance.

We will apply these proposed algorithms to a fashion evolutionary design system, a typical optimization problem with an implicit index, and compare them with a traditional interactive genetic algorithm (TIGA), i.e. an interactive genetic algorithm with an individual's accurate fitness (Gong et al., 2007), to show their advantages in alleviating user fatigue and looking for user's satisfactory individuals.

In the next section, we will review some related work on methods to alleviate user fatigue, and some basic knowledge on interval analysis as well as fuzzy numbers. The emphasis of this chapter is section 3 and 4 where we will present an IGA with an individual's interval fitness and an IGA with an individual's fuzzy fitness. Their applications in a fashion evolutionary design system and some experimental results are given in section 5. Finally, we will draw some conclusions and provide possible opportunities for future researches in section 6.

2. Related work

2.1 Approaches to evaluate individuals

Generally speaking, there are two approaches to evaluate an individual. One is that the user directly evaluates an individual based on his/her preference, e.g. Takagi proposed a fitness assignment method which combines a continuous fitness with a discrete one (Takagi & Ohya, 1996). The other is that surrogate-assisted models evaluate a part of or even all individuals in some generations, e.g. Sugimoto et al. presented a method to estimate an individual's fitness using fuzzy logic based on the distance and the angle between the evaluated individual and the optima being found (Sugimoto & Yoneyama, 2001). Biles and Zhou et al. adopted neural networks (NNs) to learn the user's intelligent evaluation, and the number of individuals being evaluated by the user decreases by use of NNs evaluating an individual in an appropriate time (Biles et al., 1996)(Zhou et al., 2005). In order to improve learning precision and reduce network complexity, we ever adopted multiple surrogate-assisted models (Gong et al., 2008), in which a single surrogate-assisted model only learns the user's evaluation in a part of the search space. Wang et al. transformed the user's evaluation into an absolute rating fitness and adopted it to train a support vector machine (SVM) to evaluate an individual (Wang et al., 2006). Hao et al. did it based on "the fitness" of a gene sense unit (Hao et al., 2006). The common character of the above methods is that an accurate number expresses an individual's fitness.

In order to conveniently understand the proposed algorithms, we will introduce some basic knowledge on interval analysis and fuzzy numbers.

2.2 Interval analysis

Interval analysis is the mathematic foundation of this chapter. Therefore, we introduce some definitions of interval analysis in this subsection.

Interval (Liu, 2005) For any $\underline{x},\overline{x}\in R$ and $\underline{x}\leq\overline{x}$, a set X satisfying $X\triangleq[\underline{x},\overline{x}]=\{x|\underline{x}\leq x\leq\overline{x},x\in R\}$ is called a limited and closed interval, where $\underline{x}$ and $\overline{x}$ are called the lower limit and the upper limit of the interval, respectively. In case that $\underline{x}=\overline{x}$, X is called a point interval. The midpoint and the width of X are defined as follows.

$$m(X)=\frac{\underline{x}+\overline{x}}{2}$$
$$w(X)=\overline{x}-\underline{x}$$

Interval dominance (Limbourg & Aponte, 2005) For any two intervals $X_i=[\underline{x}_i,\overline{x}_i]$ and $X_j=[\underline{x}_j,\overline{x}_j]$, there are 2 cases of their dominance relations,shown as follows.

If $\overline{x}_i \geq \overline{x}_j$ and $\underline{x}_i \geq \underline{x}_j$, then we call that X_i dominates over X_j in interval, and denote $X_i \succ_{in} X_j$, which is shown as Fig. 1.

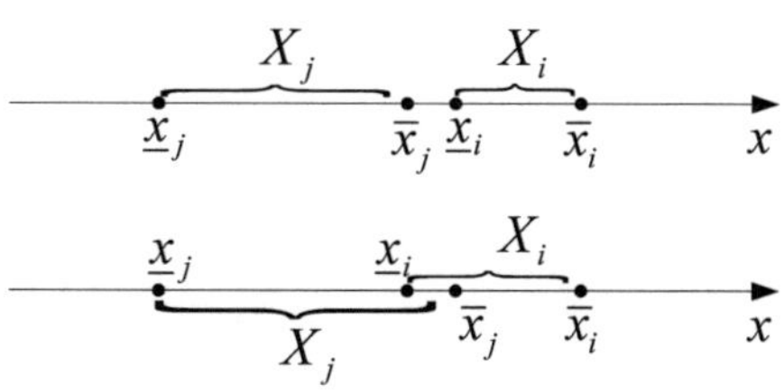

Fig. 1. X_i dominates over X_j in interval

If $\exists x'' \in X_j, \ni: x'' \in X_i$, and $\exists x' \in X_i, \ni: x' \in X_j$, then we call that X_i and X_j is incomparable in interval, and denote $X_i \| X_j$, which is shown as Fig. 2.

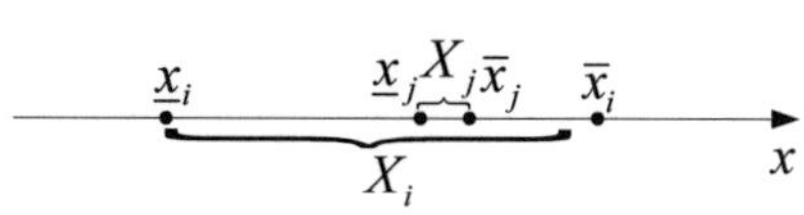

Fig. 2. X_i and X_j is incomparable in interval

2.3 Fuzzy numbers

A fuzzy number is a number with fuzzy meaning. There are many fuzzy numbers in real world, e.g. "about 10", "close to 48", "around 95". It is easy to observe that a fuzzy number is usually composed of a fuzzy operator and an accurate (or a precise) number. The fuzzy operator is to "fuzzify" a word with crisp meaning or to make a word with fuzzy meaning fuzzier. Some commonly used fuzzy operators are "about", "near", "close to", "around", etc. Some modal operators, e.g. "very", "quite", "greatly" can also match with these fuzzy operators. In fuzzy mathematics, we often define a fuzzy number with a fuzzy set as follows.

Fuzzy number (Wei, 2004) A fuzzy number $\tilde{f}$ is a normalized, convex fuzzy set in domain U.

We call a fuzzy set $\tilde{f}$ normalized if there exists at least an element u belonging to U whose membership degree $\mu_{\tilde{f}}(u)$ is equal to 1, i.e. $\max_{u\in U} \mu_{\tilde{f}}(u)=1$.

We call a fuzzy set $\tilde{f}$ convex if its membership function satisfies that $\forall u \in [u_i,u_j] \subseteq U, \ni: \mu_{\tilde{f}}(u) \geq \min\{\mu_{\tilde{f}}(u_i), \mu_{\tilde{f}}(u_j)\}$.

Therefore, we can also define a fuzzy set $\tilde{f}$ as follows:

$$\mu_{\tilde{f}}: \quad U \rightarrow [0,1],$$
$$\max_{u\in U} \mu_{\tilde{f}}(u) = 1,$$
$$\forall u \in [u_i, u_j] \subseteq U, \ni: \mu_{\tilde{f}}(u) \geq \min\{\mu_{\tilde{f}}(u_i), \mu_{\tilde{f}}(u_j)\}.$$

There are many kinds of membership functions, and some typical ones are Gaussian, triangular, and trapezoidal. If describing $\tilde{f}$ with a Gaussian membership function, we have:

$$\mu_{\tilde{f}}(u) = e^{-\frac{1}{2}(\frac{u-c}{\sigma})^2}.$$

where c and σ are the center and the width of $\tilde{f}$, respectively.
A single-point fuzzy number $\tilde{f}$ is special in that except one element u_0 belonging to U with $\mu_{\tilde{f}}(u_0) = 1$, the membership degree of other elements is 0, i.e.

$$\mu_{\tilde{f}}(u) = \begin{cases} 1 & u = u_0 \\ 0 & u \neq u_0 \end{cases}.$$

α-cut set For $\forall \alpha \in (0,1)$, the α-cut set of $\tilde{f}$, denoted as $\tilde{f}_\alpha$, is a subset of U satisfying that the membership degree of its element u is larger than or equal to α, i.e.

$$\tilde{f}_\alpha = \left\{u \middle| \mu_{\tilde{f}}(u) \geq \alpha, u \in U\right\}$$

It is easy to observe from the definition of α-cut set that $\tilde{f}_\alpha$, obtained from a line $\mu_{\tilde{f}}(u) = \alpha$ intercepting $\tilde{f}$, is a crisp set, and the degree of its element belonging to $\tilde{f}$ is not less than α.
It is easy to understand that if the membership function of $\tilde{f}$ is Gaussian, $\tilde{f}_\alpha$ is a closed interval, i.e.

$$\tilde{f}_\alpha = \left\{u \middle| \mu_{\tilde{f}}(u) \geq \alpha, u \in U\right\} = [\underline{\tilde{f}_\alpha}, \overline{\tilde{f}_\alpha}].$$

where $\underline{\tilde{f}_\alpha}$ and $\overline{\tilde{f}_\alpha}$ are the lower limit and the upper limit of $\tilde{f}_\alpha$, respectively. In particular, if $\tilde{f}$ is a single-point fuzzy number, we have $\underline{\tilde{f}_\alpha} = \overline{\tilde{f}_\alpha}$, and therefore $\tilde{f}_\alpha$ is a point interval, a special interval.
We consider the following general optimization problem in this chapter:

$$\begin{aligned} &\max \quad f(x) \\ &\text{s.t.} \quad x \in S \subseteq R^D \end{aligned} \tag{1}$$

where $f(x)$ is a performance index to be optimized, and cannot be expressed with an explicit function, x is a decision variable belonging to a domain S. On condition of not causing confusion, we also denote x and S as corresponding individual and the search space, respectively.

3. IGA with individual's interval fitness

3.1 Methodology of algorithms

By applying interval analysis to evaluate an individual in IGAs, an interactive genetic algorithm with an individual's interval fitness (IGA-IIF) is presented in this section. An individual's fitness is an interval in this algorithm, and the width of the interval decreases gradually along with the evolution which embodies that the user's cognitive on the evaluated object is fuzzy and gradual. In addition, the dominance among different individuals is based on interval dominance and probability dominance, which makes the comparison among different individuals more objective.

3.2 Individual's interval fitness

Let the *i*-th individual of a population in some generation be x_i, $i = 1, 2, \cdots, N$, and the population size be *N*. Because of the user's fuzzy cognitive on x_i, he/she hardly assigns x_i's exact fitness, but easily assigns its range which is expressed with an interval. Therefore x_i's fitness can be described as $f(x_i) = [\underline{f}(x_i), \overline{f}(x_i)]$, where $\underline{f}(x_i)$ and $\overline{f}(x_i)$ are the lower limit and the upper limit of the user's evaluation on x_i, respectively.

It is easy to observe that the larger the lower limit of $f(x_i)$ together with the smaller of its width is, the higher and the more exact the evaluation on x_i assigned by the user is; otherwise, the smaller the upper limit of $f(x_i)$ together with the larger its width is, the lower and the rougher the evaluation on x_i assigned by the user is. In general, the user's cognitive on x_i is fuzzy at early stage of the evolution, therefore $w(f(x_i))$ is large. This cognitive will become clearer and clearer along with the evolution, and hence $w(f(x_i))$ will become narrower and narrower. Therefore, compared with the accurate fitness, it more approximates the mode of the user's thought that an interval is adopted to express an individual's fitness, which embodies the user's fuzzy and gradual cognitive on the evaluated object validly.

3.3 Comparison between two Individuals with interval fitness

Generally speaking, the user has different preferences to different individuals, hence assigning them different interval fitness. As we all know, the quality of an individual is much crucial information in TGAs, which has close relation with genetic operation, hence determining that of offspring. Then how to compare the priority of different individuals in case of interval fitness? In this subsection, we will present the strategy of comparing two individuals with interval fitness.

Considering two individuals x_i and x_j, $i, j = 1, 2, \cdots, N$, their interval fitness are $f(x_i) = [\underline{f}(x_i), \overline{f}(x_i)]$ and $f(x_j) = [\underline{f}(x_j), \overline{f}(x_j)]$, respectively. To determine which one is dominant, the following 2 cases are considered.

Case 1 $f(x_i) \succ_{in} f(x_j)$, in which case there are 2 possibilities.

(I) $\underline{f}(x_i) \geq \overline{f}(x_j)$, which indicates that the lower limit of evaluation on x_i assigned by the user is not less than the upper limit of evaluation on x_j. Therefore, it is reasonable that x_i

dominates over x_j with the probability of 1, and it is impossible for x_j to dominate over x_i. In this case x_i is the dominant individual in tournament selection.

(II) $\underline{f}(x_i) < \overline{f}(x_j)$, which indicates that $f(x_i)$ dominates over $f(x_j)$, but the lower limit of evaluation on x_i assigned by the user is less than the upper limit of evaluation on x_j, i.e. their interval fitness have superposition, and the superposition interval denotes the commonness of evaluation on these two individuals. It is easy to understand that the larger the superposition interval is, the smaller the difference of the user's preference to individuals is, and vice versa. First, we consider an interval $[\overline{f}(x_j), \overline{f}(x_i)]$, the probability of x_i's fitness falling into this interval is $\frac{\overline{f}(x_i)-\overline{f}(x_j)}{w(f(x_i))}$, where x_i dominates over x_j with the probability of 1. And then we consider an interval $[\underline{f}(x_i), \overline{f}(x_j)]$, the probability of x_i's fitness falling into this interval is $\frac{\overline{f}(x_j)-\underline{f}(x_i)}{w(f(x_i))}$, where x_i dominates over x_j with the probability of $0.5\cdot\frac{\overline{f}(x_j)-\underline{f}(x_i)}{w(f(x_j))}+\frac{\underline{f}(x_i)-\underline{f}(x_j)}{w(f(x_j))}$. Therefore x_i dominates over x_j with the probability of

$$p(x_i,x_j)=\frac{\overline{f}(x_i)-\overline{f}(x_j)}{w(f(x_i))}+\frac{\overline{f}(x_j)-\underline{f}(x_i)}{w(f(x_i))}\cdot\left(0.5\cdot\frac{\overline{f}(x_j)-\underline{f}(x_i)}{w(f(x_j))}+\frac{\underline{f}(x_i)-\underline{f}(x_j)}{w(f(x_j))}\right) \tag{2}$$

Then the probability that x_i becomes the dominant individual in tournament selection is $p(x_i,x_j)$.

Similarly, we can obtain the following probability with which x_j dominates over x_i

$$p(x_j,x_i)=0.5\cdot\frac{\overline{f}(x_j)-\underline{f}(x_i)}{w(f(x_j))}\cdot\frac{\overline{f}(x_j)-\underline{f}(x_i)}{w(f(x_i))} \tag{3}$$

That is to say, the probability that x_j becomes the dominant individual in tournament selection is $p(x_j,x_i)$.

At early stage of the evolution, the difference of different individuals' interval fitness is much obvious, which is common as case (I). Along with the evolution, the difference of different individuals decreases gradually, and so does their interval fitness. In addition, the width of these intervals decreases gradually too, resulting in the superposition intervals of different individuals increasing gradually, which is common as case (II). In this case, the probabilities that different individuals are dominant ones in tournament selection are nearer and nearer.

Case 2 $f(x_i)\|f(x_j)$, i.e. $\overline{f}(x_i)\le\overline{f}(x_j), \underline{f}(x_i)\ge\underline{f}(x_j)$ or $\overline{f}(x_j)\le\overline{f}(x_i), \underline{f}(x_j)\ge\underline{f}(x_i)$. Because of x_i's randomicity, only the former is considered in this subsection, i.e. $\overline{f}(x_i)\le\overline{f}(x_j), \underline{f}(x_i)\ge\underline{f}(x_j)$. In the case above, it is shown that the evaluation on x_i assigned by the user is incomparable with that on x_j, but the former is more exact. First, an interval $[\overline{f}(x_i), \overline{f}(x_j)]$ is considered. The probability of x_j's fitness falling into this interval is $\frac{\overline{f}(x_j)-\overline{f}(x_i)}{w(f(x_j))}$, where x_j dominates over

x_i with the probability of 1. Then we consider an interval $[\underline{f}(x_i), \overline{f}(x_i)]$, the probability of x_j's fitness falling into this interval is $\frac{\overline{f}(x_i)-\underline{f}(x_i)}{w(f(x_j))}$, where x_j dominates over x_i with the probability of 0.5. Therefore, x_j dominates over x_i with the following probability

$$p(x_j, x_i) = \frac{\overline{f}(x_j)-\overline{f}(x_i)}{w(f(x_j))} + 0.5 \cdot \frac{w(f(x_i))}{w(f(x_j))} \tag{4}$$

Hence the probability that x_j becomes the dominant individual in tournament selection is $p(x_j, x_i)$.
Similarly, we can obtain the following probability with which x_i dominates over x_j

$$p(x_i, x_j) = 0.5 \cdot \frac{w(f(x_i))}{w(f(x_j))} + \frac{\underline{f}(x_i)-\underline{f}(x_j)}{w(f(x_j))}. \tag{5}$$

That is to say, the probability that x_i becomes the dominant individual in tournament selection is $p(x_i, x_j)$.
It is easy to obtain through simple deduction that $p(x_i, x_j) + p(x_j, x_i) = 1$ in the 2 cases above.
The results above are obtained on condition that the fitness of these 2 individuals are both ordinary intervals. If their fitness are both point intervals, then the method to compare their quality degenerates as the traditional one. If only $f(x_i)$ is a point interval and dominates over $f(x_j)$, we have $p(x_i, x_j)=1, p(x_j, x_i)=0$. If only $f(x_i)$ is a point interval and incomparable with $f(x_j)$, we have $p(x_j, x_i) = \frac{\overline{f}(x_j)-f(x_i)}{w(f(x_j))}$ and $p(x_i, x_j) = \frac{f(x_i)-\underline{f}(x_j)}{w(f(x_j))}$. Similarly, if only $f(x_j)$ is a point interval and dominated by $f(x_i)$, we have $p(x_i, x_j)=1, p(x_j, x_i)=0$. If only $f(x_j)$ is a point interval and incomparable with $f(x_i)$, we have $p(x_i, x_j) = \frac{\overline{f}(x_i)-f(x_j)}{w(f(x_i))}$ and $p(x_j, x_i) = \frac{f(x_j)-\underline{f}(x_i)}{w(f(x_i))}$.
Here x_i and x_j are dominant individuals in tournament selection with the probability of $p(x_i, x_j)$ and $p(x_j, x_i)$, respectively. The method to perform tournament selection above is as follows. First, calculate the accumulative probabilities of x_i and x_j, i.e. $c_i = p(x_i, x_j), c_j = c_i + p(x_j, x_i) = 1$. And then generate a random number r in [0, 1]. At last, compare r with c_i. If $r \le c_i$, then x_i is the dominant individual in tournament selection; otherwise, x_j is the dominant one.

3.4 Steps of algorithm

The steps of the proposed algorithms in this section can be described as follows.

Step 1. Set the values of control parameters in the algorithms. Let t=0, and initialize a population.

Step 2. Decode and assign an individual's interval fitness based on the user's evaluation.
Step 3. Determine whether the algorithm stops or not, if yes, go to Step 6.
Step 4. Select two candidates $x_i(t)$ and $x_j(t)$, $i,j=1,2,\cdots,N$ for tournament selection, calculate $p(x_i(t),x_j(t))$ and $p(x_j(t),x_i(t))$ according to formula (2) to (5), and generate the dominant individual in tournament selection.
Step 5. Perform genetic operation and generate offspring. Let $t=t+1$, go to Step 2.
Step 6. Output the optima and stop the algorithm.

3.5 Further explanations

Compared with TIGAs, an obvious character of the proposed algorithm in this section is that an individual's fitness is an interval not an accurate value, resulting in the comparison of different individuals not being based on their fitness. What to be obtained is a probability with which an individual is the dominant one in tournament selection based on interval dominance. It is remarkable that an individual is the dominant one in tournament selection with some probability, but not the absolutely dominant one.
An individual's interval fitness proposed in this section reflects the user's cognitive law on the evaluated object. On the one hand, it embodies that the user's cognitive on the evaluated object is fuzzy. The user's fuzzy cognitive process makes the evaluation on an individual is also fuzzy, which cannot be appropriately described by an accurate value, but by an interval. An individual's interval fitness expresses that an individual's fitness falls into an interval, not exact evaluation on the individual by the user, which reflects that the user's cognitive is fuzzy. On the other hand, it embodies that the user's cognitive on the evaluated object is gradual. It is a gradual process from fuzzy to clear to evaluate an object by the user. Along with deep cognitive on the evaluated object during the evolution, the user evaluates individuals clearer and clearer, and the width of an individual's interval fitness is narrower and narrower, which is a gradual process, reflecting the development of the user's cognitive.

4. IGA with individual's fuzzy fitness

An IGA with an individual's fuzzy fitness (IGA-IFF) is an IGA which expresses the result of the user's evaluation on an individual with a fuzzy number, and adopts traditional genetic operation. Some new problems will result from the fuzzy expression of an individual's fitness, in which the primary one is how to compare different individuals in the same generation. It will directly influence selection operation adopted in the algorithm. In addition, it will also influence the human-computer interface.

4.1 Methodology of algorithms

The methodology of the proposed algorithm is as follows. First, we adopt a fuzzy number to express the result of the user's evaluation on an individual, which is different from all existing IGAs. Then, in order to compare two individuals in the same generation, we generate two crisp sets of individuals' fitness based on α-cut sets, and obtain the dominance probability of an individual on the basis of the composition of these crisp sets. Finally, considering tournament selection with size being two, we generate the superior individual based on these dominance probabilities, and then perform the subsequent genetic operation after generating all parents.

Our contributions in this section mainly embody the following two aspects. First, we adopt a novel expression of an individual's fitness, which much accords with the user's fuzzy cognitive on the evaluated object. Second, we present an effective method to compare different individuals when an individual's fitness is expressed with a fuzzy number, which is necessary for a population to evolve. These contributions can improve the performance of existing IGAs in alleviating user fatigue and looking for the optimal solutions of an optimization problem, therefore it is beneficial to solve complicated problems with implicit or fuzzy indices.

4.2 Individual's fuzzy fitness

In the initial phase of the evolution, the user's preference is fuzzy and his/her cognitive degree to the evaluated object is low. Along with the evolution, the number of individuals being evaluated by the user increases, hence he/she is gradually familiar with the evaluated object. Therefore, the user's cognitive on the evaluated object is fuzzy and gradual. In addition, the evaluation process is influenced by an individual's phenotype and user fatigue. So it is difficult for an individual's accurate fitness to accurately reflect the process and the user's cognitive result, while an individual's fuzzy fitness can.

We consider an individual x, and express its fitness as $\tilde{f}(x)$. We define a function in $[f_{\min}, f_{\max}]$ as follows

$$\mu_{\tilde{f}(x)}: \ [f_{\min}, f_{\max}] \rightarrow [0,1].$$

to express the degree of a $f \in [f_{\min}, f_{\max}]$ belonging to $\tilde{f}(x)$, where $f_{\min}$ and $f_{\max}$ are the smallest and the largest fitness of an individual. It is easy to observe that an individual's fitness should lie in the range of $[f_{\min}, f_{\max}]$, i.e. there exists at least one number in $[f_{\min}, f_{\max}]$ which is x's real fitness, i.e. its membership degree w.r.t. $\tilde{f}(x)$ is 1. Therefore, $\tilde{f}(x)$ is normalized. In addition, the further a number in $[f_{\min}, f_{\max}]$ from x's real fitness is, the smaller its membership degree w.r.t. $\tilde{f}(x)$ should be. Therefore, $\tilde{f}(x)$ is convex. According to the definition of fuzzy number, $\tilde{f}(x)$ is a fuzzy number.

For not losing generality, we adopt a Gaussian membership function to express an individual's fuzzy fitness, and define the membership function of $\tilde{f}(x)$ as follows:

$$\mu_{\tilde{f}(x)}(f) = e^{-\frac{1}{2}\left(\frac{f-c(x)}{\sigma(x)}\right)^2}. \tag{6}$$

where $c(x)$ is $\tilde{f}(x)$'s center, it is the fitness whose membership degree w.r.t. $\tilde{f}(x)$ is 1. $\sigma(x)$ is $\tilde{f}(x)$'s width satisfying that the membership degree of fitness within $[c(x)-\sigma(x), c(x)+\sigma(x)]$ w.r.t. $\tilde{f}(x)$ is not less than $1/\sqrt{e} \approx 0.6$.

We now further explain the above x's fuzzy fitness as follows.

In general, for different individuals, the membership functions of their fitness have different centers and width, i.e. for $x_i, x_j \in S, x_i \neq x_j$, we have $c(x_i) \neq c(x_j), \sigma(x_i) \neq \sigma(x_j)$.

The user's cognitive on the evaluated object is influenced by an individual's phenotype and user fatigue, therefore for the same individual in different generations, the center and the width of its membership function may be different, i.e. the center and the width of a membership function are also relative to generation t, i.e. for $0 \le t_i, t_j \le T, t_i \ne t_j$, we may have $c(x,t_i) \ne c(x,t_j)$, $\sigma(x,t_i) \ne \sigma(x,t_j)$, where T is the maximum generation. Whereas in TGAs, an individual's fitness is uniquely determined by its phenotype, and does not change along with the evolution. Therefore, we think it an essential difference between IGAs and TGAs.

Generally speaking, along with the evolution, the user is gradually familiar with the evaluated object, and assigns an individual's fitness with high confidence. Therefore, the sum of all width of the membership functions of these individuals' fitness in the same generation will be narrower and narrower, at the same time, the sum of all their centers will be larger and larger as a result of more superior individuals being reserved as well as more inferior ones being eliminated, i.e. for $0 \le t_i < t_j \le T$, we have $\sum_x \sigma(x,t_i) \ge \sum_x \sigma(x,t_j)$, $\sum_x c(x,t_i) \le \sum_x c(x,t_j)$.

If $f = c(x)$, we have $\mu_{\tilde{f}(x)}(f) = e^{-\frac{1}{2}(\frac{f-c(x)}{\sigma(x)})^2} = 1$, whereas if $f \ne c(x)$ and $\sigma(x) \to 0$, we have $\mu_{\tilde{f}(x)}(f) = e^{-\frac{1}{2}(\frac{f-c(x)}{\sigma(x)})^2} = 0$, which indicates that the fuzzy number degenerates as an accurate one. Therefore, it is rational to regard an individual's fuzzy fitness as the extension of an accurate one, whereas an individual's accurate fitness as a special case of a fuzzy one.

When we adopt an accurate number to express an individual's fitness, it often takes the user very much time to assign an individual's appropriate fitness, and the user bears considerable mental pressure during evaluation. Whereas when we adopt a fuzzy number, described with a Gaussian membership function, to express an individual's fitness, it seems that we require two parameters, i.e. $c(x)$ and $\sigma(x)$, but $c(x)$ need not be very precise, and we can determine $\sigma(x)$ beforehand or change it with selected fuzzy modal words. Therefore, the user only assigns an individual's approximate fitness, which greatly decreases his/her pressure during evaluation.

It is easy to understand that the proposed algorithm requires a new human-computer interface when adopting a fuzzy number to express an individual's fitness. In comparison with TIGAs whose individual's fitness is expressed with an accurate number, the obvious difference lies in the approach to input an individual's fitness. In addition to input $c(x)$'s value through a text box or a scroll bar, the user also selects a fuzzy modal word, e.g. "about", "close to", "very close to", etc., in order to determine $\sigma(x)$. Besides, the proposed algorithm calculates $\sum_x \sigma(x,t), \sum_x c(x,t)$, and displays their change curves through the interface to reflect the progress of the evolution.

4.3 Comparison between two Individuals with fuzzy fitness

It is very easy to compare individuals when we adopt an accurate number to express an individual's fitness. We only determine the relationship of their fitness, therefore, it is a case of comparing some accurate numbers. When we adopt a fuzzy number to express an individual's fitness, the comparison of individuals will become a case of comparing some fuzzy sets. It will be a case of comparing some sets. Therefore, it is very difficult to compare individuals in this case.

In this subsection, we consider the comparison of two individuals based on α-cut set whose idea is as follows. First, we choose a fuzzy level α, and obtain two α-cut sets of these individuals' fuzzy fitness. They are crisp sets and often intervals. Then, we determine two dominance probabilities by use of the relationship of two intervals. Finally, considering tournament selection with size being two, we determine the dominant individual by use of the roulette wheel method based on these dominance probabilities.
We will expound the proposed strategy in detail as follows.
Let two fuzzy fitness of individuals x_i and x_j be $\tilde{f}(x_i)$ and $\tilde{f}(x_j)$, and their membership functions be $\mu_{\tilde{f}(x_i)}(f)=e^{-\frac{1}{2}(\frac{f-c(x_i)}{\sigma(x_i)})^2}$ and $\mu_{\tilde{f}(x_j)}(f)=e^{-\frac{1}{2}(\frac{f-c(x_j)}{\sigma(x_j)})^2}$, respectively. The α-cut sets of $\tilde{f}(x_i)$ and $\tilde{f}(x_j)$ are

$$\tilde{f}_\alpha(x_i)=\left\{f\,|\,\mu_{\tilde{f}(x_i)}(f)\geq\alpha, f\in[f_{\min}, f_{\max}]\right\}\triangleq[\underline{\tilde{f}_\alpha}(x_i),\overline{\tilde{f}_\alpha}(x_i)],$$
$$\tilde{f}_\alpha(x_j)=\left\{f\,|\,\mu_{\tilde{f}(x_j)}(f)\geq\alpha, f\in[f_{\min}, f_{\max}]\right\}\triangleq[\underline{\tilde{f}_\alpha}(x_j),\overline{\tilde{f}_\alpha}(x_j)],$$

respectively, where both $\tilde{f}_\alpha(x_i)$ and $\tilde{f}_\alpha(x_j)$ are crisp sets, and reflect that the fitness lying in which belongs to $\tilde{f}(x_i)$ and $\tilde{f}(x_j)$ respectively with the membership degree being not less than α, or the value lying in $\tilde{f}_\alpha(x_i)$ and $\tilde{f}_\alpha(x_j)$ is the fitness of x_i and x_j respectively with the confidence degree being not less than α.
According to the positions of $\mu_{\tilde{f}(x_i)}$ and $\mu_{\tilde{f}(x_j)}$, there are two cases when x_i compares with x_j.
Case 1 $c(x_i)=c(x_j)$, in which case there are two possibilities.
The first one is $c(x_i)=c(x_j)$ and $\sigma(x_i)=\sigma(x_j)$, which indicates that $\tilde{f}(x_i)=\tilde{f}(x_j)$, i.e. the fitness of x_i is the same as that of x_j. Therefore, x_i dominates x_j with the probability of 0.5, and so does x_j.

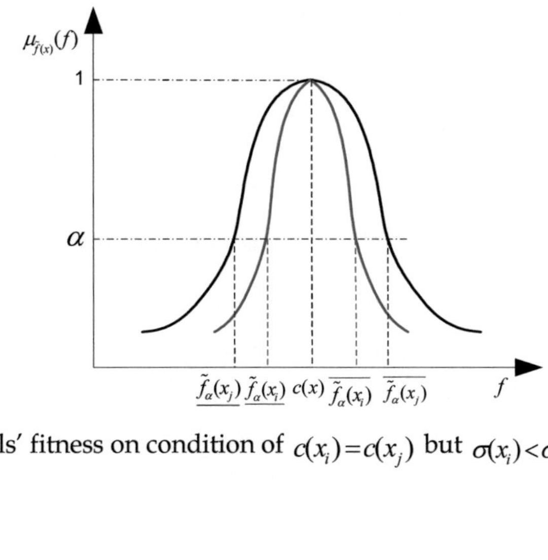

Fig. 3. Two individuals' fitness on condition of $c(x_i)=c(x_j)$ but $\sigma(x_i)<\sigma(x_j)$.

The second one is $c(x_i)=c(x_j)$ but $\sigma(x_i)\neq\sigma(x_j)$. For not losing generality, we only consider the case that $c(x_i)=c(x_j)$ but $\sigma(x_i)<\sigma(x_j)$, shown as Fig. 3. The comparison between x_i and x_j at α level is equal to the comparison between $\tilde{f}_\alpha(x_i)$ and $\tilde{f}_\alpha(x_j)$.

Similar to the deduction in subsection 3.3, we can easily obtain that x_j dominates over x_i with the probability of

$$p(x_j,x_i)=\frac{\overline{\tilde{f}_\alpha(x_j)}-\overline{\tilde{f}_\alpha(x_i)}+0.5\cdot w(\tilde{f}_\alpha(x_i))}{w(\tilde{f}_\alpha(x_j))}=0.5\cdot \tag{7}$$

And x_i dominates over x_j with the following probability

$$p(x_i,x_j)=\frac{0.5\cdot w(\tilde{f}_\alpha(x_i))+\underline{\tilde{f}_\alpha(x_i)}-\underline{\tilde{f}_\alpha(x_j)}}{w(\tilde{f}_\alpha(x_j))}=0.5\cdot \tag{8}$$

Case 2 $c(x_i)\neq c(x_j)$. For not losing generality, we only consider the case that $c(x_i)<c(x_j)$. Let $\alpha_0=\max\limits_{f\in[f_{\min},f_{\max}]}\mu_{\tilde{f}(x_i)\cap\tilde{f}(x_j)}(f)$. We will discuss the following two cases based on the relationship between α and α_0.

If $\alpha>\alpha_0$, shown as Fig. 4, we have $\underline{\tilde{f}_\alpha(x_j)}>\overline{\tilde{f}_\alpha(x_i)}$, which indicates that at α level the lower limit of evaluation on x_j is larger than the upper limit of evaluation on x_i. Therefore it is reasonable that x_j dominates over x_i with the probability of 1, and it is impossible that x_i dominates over x_j.

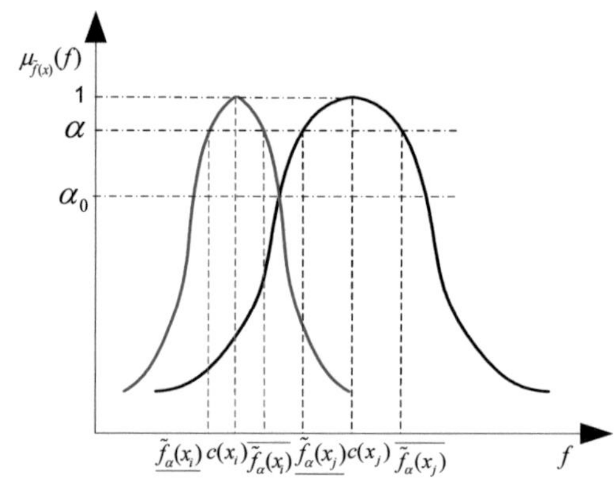

Fig. 4. Two individuals' fitness on condition of $c(x_i)<c(x_j)$ and $\alpha>\alpha_0$.

If $\alpha\leq\alpha_0$, shown as Fig. 5, we have $\underline{\tilde{f}_\alpha(x_j)}\leq\overline{\tilde{f}_\alpha(x_i)}$, which indicates that though $\tilde{f}_\alpha(x_j)$ dominates over $\tilde{f}_\alpha(x_i)$, at α level the lower limit of evaluation on x_j is less than or equal to the upper limit of evaluation on x_i. Adopting the same method as that in subsection 3.3, we can easily obtain that x_j dominates over x_i with the probability of

$$p(x_j,x_i)=\frac{\overline{\tilde{f}_\alpha(x_j)}-\overline{\tilde{f}_\alpha(x_i)}}{w(\tilde{f}_\alpha(x_j))}+\frac{\overline{\tilde{f}_\alpha(x_i)}-\underline{\tilde{f}_\alpha(x_j)}}{w(\tilde{f}_\alpha(x_j))}\cdot\left(1-0.5\cdot\frac{\overline{\tilde{f}_\alpha(x_i)}-\underline{\tilde{f}_\alpha(x_j)}}{w(\tilde{f}_\alpha(x_i))}\right). \tag{9}$$

And x_i dominates over x_j with the following probability

$$p(x_i,x_j)=\frac{0.5\cdot(\overline{\tilde{f}_\alpha(x_i)}-\underline{\tilde{f}_\alpha(x_j)})^2}{w(\tilde{f}_\alpha(x_i))\cdot w(\tilde{f}_\alpha(x_j))}. \tag{10}$$

The above results are obtained based on both individuals' fitness being ordinary fuzzy numbers. If their fitness are both single-point fuzzy numbers, the approach to compare these two individuals degenerates to the traditional one. If only one individual's fitness is a single-point fuzzy number, for not losing generality, we assume that $\tilde{f}(x_i)$ is a single-point fuzzy number, i.e. $\overline{\tilde{f}_\alpha(x_i)}=\underline{\tilde{f}_\alpha(x_i)}$. If $\overline{\tilde{f}_\alpha(x_i)}=\underline{\tilde{f}_\alpha(x_i)}\geq\overline{\tilde{f}_\alpha(x_j)}$, we have $p(x_i,x_j)=1, p(x_j,x_i)=0$; If $\underline{\tilde{f}_\alpha(x_j)}\leq\overline{\tilde{f}_\alpha(x_i)}=\underline{\tilde{f}_\alpha(x_i)}\leq\overline{\tilde{f}_\alpha(x_j)}$, we have $p(x_j,x_i)=\frac{\overline{\tilde{f}_\alpha(x_j)}-\overline{\tilde{f}_\alpha(x_i)}}{w(\tilde{f}_\alpha(x_j))}, p(x_i,x_j)=\frac{\underline{\tilde{f}_\alpha(x_i)}-\underline{\tilde{f}_\alpha(x_j)}}{w(\tilde{f}_\alpha(x_j))}$; If $\overline{\tilde{f}_\alpha(x_i)}=\underline{\tilde{f}_\alpha(x_i)}\leq\underline{\tilde{f}_\alpha(x_j)}$, we have $p(x_i,x_j)=0, p(x_j,x_i)=1$.

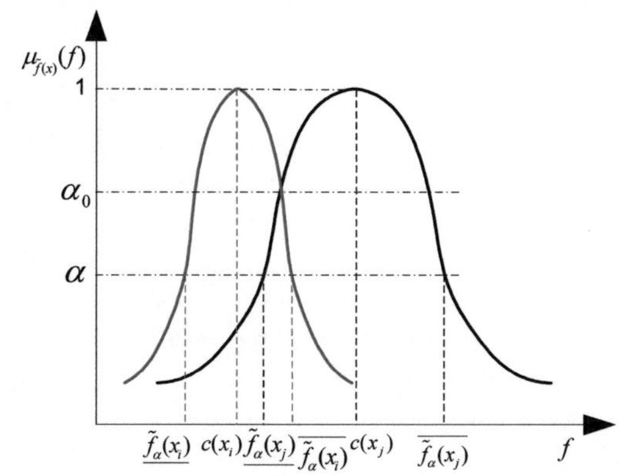

Fig. 5. Two individuals' fitness on condition of $c(x_i)<c(x_j)$ and $\alpha\leq\alpha_0$.

Also, we adopt the same method as that in subsection 3.3 to select the dominant individual in tournament selection.

It is easy to observe from the process of comparison between x_i and x_j that what determines an individual to be the dominant one in tournament selection is $p(x_i,x_j)$ and $p(x_i,x_j)$. For case 2 both dominance probabilities have close relation with α-cut set. Even if we have the same fuzzy set, different α will lead to different α-cut sets. That is, α directly influences the comparison result.

Generally speaking, at the initial phase of the evolution, we expect a population with good diversity so as to search in exploration. It requires an inferior individual having some opportunities as the parent one. We can achieve it by choosing a small value of α; on the contrary, at the later phase of the evolution, we expect a population with good convergence in order to converge in a timely manner. It requires a superior individual having more opportunities as the parent one. We can do it by choosing a large value of α.

In addition, it can be seen from the user's fuzzy and gradual cognitive that at the initial phase of the evolution, we usually require a small value of α so as to make up the deviation of the user's evaluation by reserving some potential individuals. Whereas at the later phase of the evolution, the user has been familiar with the evaluated object, we often require a large value of α to select the superior individual with large confidence.

Based on these, an approach to change α is as follows:

$$\alpha(t) = \min\{\alpha_{\min} + \frac{t}{T}, 1\} \quad t \le T \tag{11}$$

where $\alpha_{\min}$ is the minimum of $\alpha(t)$ set by the user in prior.

4.4 Steps of algorithms

Similar to that of IGA with an individual's interval fitness, the steps of the proposed algorithm in this section can be described as follows.

Step 1. Set the values of control parameters in the algorithm. Let t=0, and initialize a population.

Step 2. Decode and assign an individual's fuzzy fitness based on the user's evaluation.

Step 3. Determine whether the algorithm stops or not, if yes, go to Step 6.

Step 4. Select two candidates $x_i(t)$ and $x_j(t)$, $i, j = 1, 2, \cdots, N$ for tournament selection, calculate $p(x_i(t), x_j(t))$ and $p(x_j(t), x_i(t))$ according to formula (7) to (10), and generate the dominant individual in tournament selection.

Step 5. Perform genetic operation and generate offspring. Let t=t+1, go to Step 2.

Step 6. Output the optima and stop the algorithm.

It can be observed from the above steps that except for Step 2 and Step 4, the rest have no difference with those of TIGAs. For Step 2, different from TIGAs in which we adopt an accurate number to express an individual's fitness, in IGA-IFF we adopt a fuzzy number, described with a center and width, to express an individual's fitness. In Step 4, the core of IGA-IFF, we give the process of generating the dominant individual in tournament selection based on an individual's fuzzy fitness. Comparing with TIGAs, the above process is obviously complicated as a result of the fuzzy fitness, but can be automatically achieved through the computer. Therefore in contrast with time taken to evaluate an individual, we can ignore time taken during the above process, which implies that it does not take the proposed algorithm much additional time to select the dominant individual; on the contrary, as a result of alleviating the user's pressure in evaluating an individual, time to evaluate an individual will sharply decrease, and so will the whole running time.

4.5 Fuzzy fitness and interval fitness

Both Fuzzy fitness (FF) and interval fitness (IF) are uncertain fitness, and reflect the user's fuzzy and gradual cognitive on the evaluated object, which are their common character.

But there are some differences between them. The first one is that they emphasize different aspects. IF emphasizes the range that an individual's fitness lies in, reflecting the uncertainty of an individual's fitness; while FF emphasizes the fuzziness degree, reflecting the diversity of the fuzziness degree of an individual's fitness. The second one is that different kinds of uncertain fitness require different parameters. IF requires the lower limit and the upper limit; while FF described with a Gaussian membership function requires the center and the width.

Besides, the comparison of two FF is based on the comparison of two IF. Therefore, we say from this point that IF is the base and a special case of FF; while FF is the extension and a generalization of IF.

Which kind of uncertain fitness should be adopted in an IGA is determined by the acquired knowledge in prior. When having acquired the fuzzy knowledge on an individual's fitness, we should choose FF; otherwise, when having acquired the range in which an individual's fitness lies, it would be better to choose IF.

5. Applications in fashion evolutionary design system

5.1 Backgrounds

Fashion design is a very popular vocation, for everyone likes to wear satisfactory fashions but few can design a satisfactory one. In fact, fashion design is a very complicated process and often completed by designers who have been systematically trained. Although there is some software available for fashion design, they are often too professional for an ordinary person to use. With the development of society pursuing personality becomes a fad. That is to say, people often like to wear fashions with some personalities. It is much necessary for a fashion design system available for an ordinary person to design his/her satisfactory fashions.

We aim to establish a fashion design system for an ordinary person to generate a suit by combining all parts from different databases. That is to say, all parts of a suit are stored in databases in advance. What a person does is to combine different parts into his/her most satisfactory suit by using the system. In fact, the above is a typical combinational optimization problem and solved by evolutionary optimization methods.

But what is "the most satisfactory suit"? Different persons may have different opinions on it because of different personalities, and these opinions are often fuzzy and implicit. Therefore it is impossible to get a uniform and explicit index to be optimized. It is infeasible for TGAs to deal with it, whereas suitable for IGAs to do.

We develop two fashion evolutionary design systems based on IGA-IIF and IGA-IFF, respectively by using Visual Basic 6.0. We also develop a fashion evolutionary design systems based on TIGA by using the same development tool, and conduct some experiments to compare their performances.

5.2 Individual codes

The same individual code is adopted in these systems. For simplification, the phenotype of an individual is a suit composed of coat and skirt, and its genotype is a binary string of 18 bits, where the first 5 bits expresses the style of coat, the 6th to 10th bits expresses the style of skirt, the 11th to 14th bits expresses the color of coat, and the last 4 bits expresses the color of skirt. There are 32 styles of coats and skirts respectively, and their names correspond to the integers from 0 to 31, which are also their decimals of these binary codes. The colors and their codes are listed as Table 1. They are all stored in different databases. According to the user's preference, these systems look for "the most satisfactory suit" in the design space with $2^5 \times 2^5 \times 2^4 \times 2^4 = 262144$ suits during evolutionary optimization.

color	code	color	code
black	0000	gray	1000
blue	0001	bright blue	1001
green	0010	bright green	1010
cyan	0011	bright cyan	1011
red	0100	bright red	1100
carmine	0101	bright carmine	1101
yellow	0110	bright yellow	1110
white	0111	bright white	1111

Table 1. Colors and their codes

5.3 Parameter settings

In order to compare the performances of these three algorithms, the same genetic operation and parameters but different approaches to evaluate an individual during running are adopted. The population size N is equal to 8. In order to express an individual's fuzzy fitness, a scroll bar is adopted to set $c(x)$, and its range is restricted between 0 and 1000, i.e. $f_{\min}$ and $f_{\max}$ are 0 and 1000, respectively. Besides, tournament selection with size being two, one-point crossover and one-point mutation operators are adopted, and their probabilities p_c and p_m are 0.6 and 0.02, respectively. In addition, $\alpha_{\min}$ and T are 0.5 and 20, respectively. That is to say, if the evolution does not converge after 20 generations, the system will automatically stop it. When the evolution converges, i.e. there are at least 6 individuals with the same phenotype in some generation, the system will also automatically stop it. Also, when the user is satisfied with the optimal results, he/she can manually stop the evolution.

5.4 Human-computer interface and individual evaluation

The human-computer interface of IGA-IIF, shown as Fig. 6, includes 3 parts. The first one is individuals' phenotypes and their evaluations. In order to assign a suit's fitness, the user drags two scroll bars under it. Of the two scroll bars, the upper one stands for the lower limit of the fitness, and the lower one stands for its upper limit. The values of the lower limit and the upper limit are also displayed under these scroll bars. The second one is some command buttons for a population evolving, e.g. "Initialize", "Next Generation", "End" and "Exit". And the third one is some statistic information of the evolution, including the number of individuals being evaluated (distinct ones), the current generation and time-consuming. Having evaluated all suits, if the user clicks "Next Generation", the system will perform genetic operation described as subsection 5.3 to generate offspring, and then display them to the user. The system will cycle the above procedure until automatically or manually stops the evolution.

The human-computer interface of IGA-IFF, shown as Fig. 7, includes 3 parts. The first one is individuals' phenotypes and their fitness. The user evaluates a suit through selecting one of these modal words in the list box, i.e. "about", "close to" or "very close to" with their corresponding values of $\sigma(x)$ being 60, 40 and 20, respectively, and dragging the scroll bar. The second one is the same as that of IGA-IIF. And the third one is also some statistic information of the evolution, including $\sum_x \sigma(x,t), \sum_x c(x,t)$, the number of individuals being evaluated, the current generation and time-consuming.

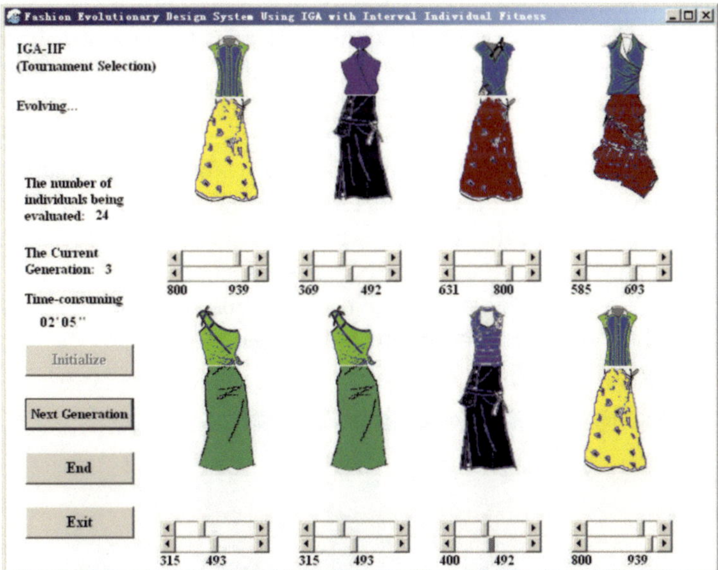

Fig. 6. Human-computer interface of IGA-IIF.

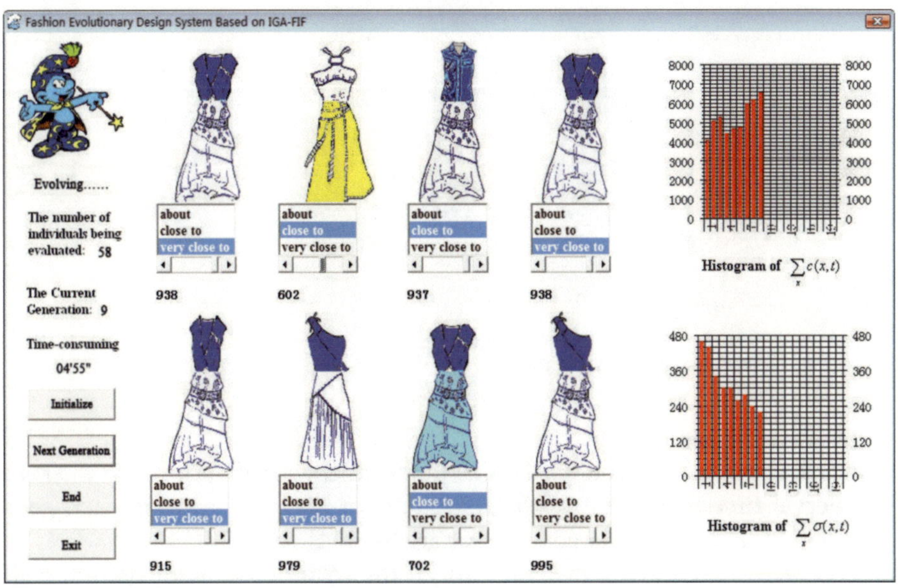

Fig. 7. Human-computer interface of IGA-IFF.

During the evolution, the user evaluates a suit through dragging the scroll bar under it to provide the membership function's center of its fitness, and clicking the corresponding modal word in the list box to provide the membership function's width. For example, the user drags the scroll bar to "938" and clicks "very close to" to obtain the fuzzy fitness "very close to 938" of the first individual, shown as Fig. 7. Having evaluated all individuals, if the user clicks "Next Generation", the system will look for the dominant individual in tournament selection based on the proposed method in subsection 4.3. After that, the system will perform genetic operation described as subsection 5.3 to generate offspring, and then display them to the user. The system will cycle the above procedure until automatically or manually stops the evolution.

Similarly, the human-computer interface of TIGA, shown as Fig. 8, also includes 3 parts. The first one is individuals' phenotypes and their evaluations. In order to assign a suit's fitness, the user drags the scroll bar under it only once. The second and the third parts are the same as those of IGA-IIF. Having evaluated all suits, if the user clicks "Next Generation", the system will perform genetic operators described as subsection 5.3 to generate offspring, and then display them to the user. The system will cycle the above procedure until automatically or manually stops the evolution. The interested reader can refer to our newly published book for detail (Gong et al., 2007).

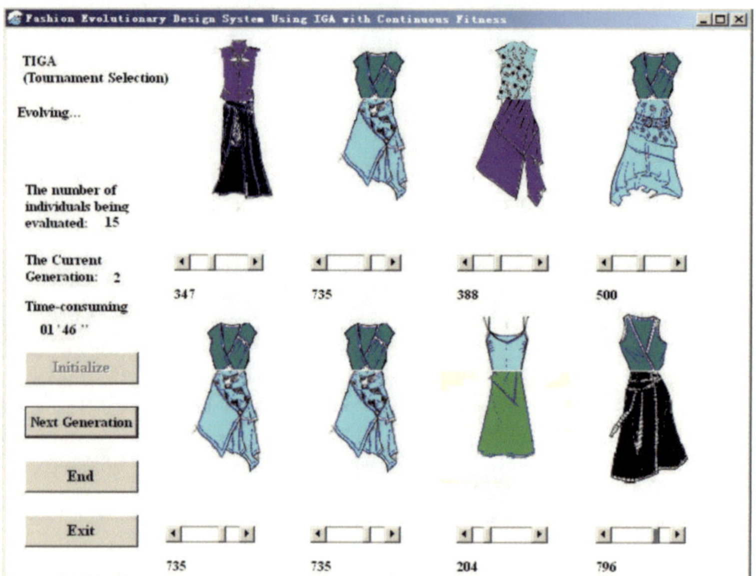

Fig. 8. Human-computer interface of TIGA.

5.5 Results and analysis

First, we run the system based on IGA-IIF 20 times independently, calculate the sum of the width of interval fitness and that of the midpoints of interval fitness in each generation. Their averages of the 20 runs in 15 generations are listed as Table 2.

It can be observed from Table 2 that the sum of the width of individuals' interval fitness gradually decreases along with the evolution, which reflects that the user's cognitive on the evaluated object is from fuzzy to clear, i.e. the user's cognitive is gradual. In addition, the sum of the midpoints of individuals' interval fitness increases along with the evolution, which indicates that the quality of optimal solutions gradually improves.

We then run the system based on IGA-IFF 8 times independently, and calculate $\sum_x \sigma(x,t)$ and $\sum_x c(x,t)$ in each generation. Their averages of the 8 runs are shown as Fig. 9.

generations	sum of width of interval fitness	sum of midpoints of interval fitness
1	5012	4100
2	4970	4404
3	4075	4437
4	3791	4265
5	3854	4870
6	3067	5167
7	2997	5411
8	2373	5268
9	2647	5031
10	2707	5923
11	2071	5966
12	1925	6148
13	1797	6264
14	1577	6629
15	1173	6611

Table 2. Sum of width and midpoints of interval fitness

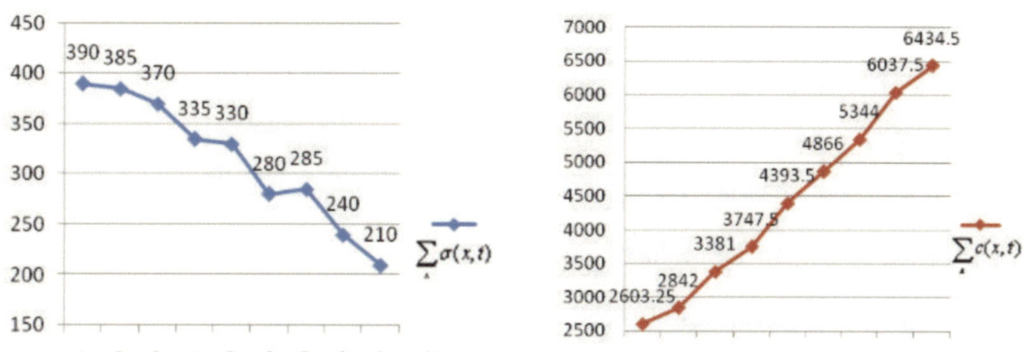

Fig. 9. Trends of $\sum_x \sigma(x,t)$ and $\sum_x c(x,t)$.

It is obvious from Fig. 9 that the trends of $\sum_x \sigma(x,t)$ and $\sum_x c(x,t)$ change with t. $\sum_x \sigma(x,t)$ changes from 390 in the 1st generation to 210 in the 9th generation. In general, it gradually decreases along with the evolution, reflecting that the user's cognitive is from fuzzy to clear, i.e. the user's cognitive is gradual. On the other hand, $\sum_x c(x,t)$ changes from 2603.25 in the 1st generation to 6434.5 in the 9th generation, and increases along with the evolution,

indicating that individuals' quality gradually improves, which is the result of more and more superior individuals being reserved and inferior individuals being eliminated. Therefore, an individual's fuzzy fitness described with a Gaussian membership function can correctly and clearly reflect the user's cognitive.
Now we compare the performance of three systems based on IGA-IIF, IGA-IFF and TIGA respectively. To achieve this, we run three systems 8 times independently, record time-consuming for evaluating individuals, the number of distinct individuals being evaluated in each run, and calculate their sums. The results are listed as Table 3 and Table 4.
It can be observed from Table 3 that for IGA-IIF, IGA-IFF and TIGA, the longest time-consuming for evaluating individuals in each run is 5'11", 8'33" and 7'44" ,respectively. They are all less than 10 minutes, which is acceptable because the user often does not feel fatigue within 10 minutes. This means that it often takes the user less time to design a satisfactory suit by using these systems.
It is easy to observe from Table 4 that for IGA-IFF, the largest number of individuals being evaluated is 93, which is equivalent to the population evolving about 12 generations. That is to say, the user finds "the most satisfactory suit" in small generations by using IGA-IFF. For IGA-IIF, all runs find "the most satisfactory suit" in also about 12 generations. For TIGA, all runs find "the most satisfactory suit" in about 11 generations. In the three algorithms, the number of generations required by the user is less than the given maximum generations, i.e. 20, which indicates the three algorithms are feasible to deal with fashion design.

No. of run	IGA-IIF	IGA-IFF	TIGA
1	7'48"	3'42"	5'40"
2	3'00"	4'15"	4'02"
3	6'10"	3'34"	6'58"
4	**8'33"**	**5'11"**	**7'44"**
5	3'44"	3'53"	3'10"
6	3'41"	4'50"	5'02"
7	3'53"	3'02"	5'49"
8	5'17"	3'47"	6'15"
sum	42'06"	32'14"	44'40"

Table 3. Time-consuming for evaluating individuals

No. of run	IGA-IIF	IGA-IFF	TIGA
1	81	45	59
2	28	59	42
3	65	46	63
4	**96**	**93**	**86**
5	35	65	39
6	38	68	45
7	39	41	56
8	62	62	69
sum	444	479	459

Table 4. Number of individuals being evaluated

It is obvious from Table 4 that the number of individuals being evaluated in IGA-IFF is the largest, i.e. 479, whereas combined with the Table 3, its time-consuming for evaluating individuals is the shortest, which implies that its number of generations may not be the largest. This is because the fuzzy fitness and the approach to compare different individuals increase the diversity of a population, therefore IGA-IFF can prevent the evolution from premature convergence to some extent, and increase the opportunities to find satisfactory solutions.

In order to compare the performance of different algorithms in alleviating user fatigue, we calculate the average time-consuming for evaluating individuals in each run and the average time-consuming for evaluating an individual, listed as Table 5. The items in Table 5 are calculated from the data in Table 3 and Table 4. We obtained the 2nd column of Table 5 through dividing the last row of Table 3 by 8, and the 3rd column of Table 5 through dividing the last row of Table 3 by that of Table 4.

algorithm	for evaluating individuals in each run	for evaluating an individual
IGA-IIF	5′16″	5.7″
IGA-IFF	4′02″	4.0″
TIGA	5′35″	5.8″

Table 5. Average time-consuming for evaluating individuals

It is obvious from Table 5 that the average time-consuming for evaluating individuals in each run of IGA-IFF is 4′02″, which is less than that of IGA-IIF (5′16″) and TIGA (5′35″). In addition, the average time-consuming for evaluating an individual of IGA-IFF is 4.0″, which is also less than that of IGA-IIF (5.7″) and TIGA (5.8″). Different time-consuming for evaluating an individual is due to different approaches of evaluation. For TIGA, the user needs to assign an accurate fitness to an individual, therefore it takes him/her much time to consider what the fitness should be. For IGA-IIF, the user does not need to assign an accurate fitness to an individual. In order to obtain an individual's fitness, the user needs to assign its upper limit and lower limit. Different from TIGA, in IGA-IFF, the user evaluates an individual without spending much time in providing an accurate fitness, leading to small time-consuming. Comparing IGA-IFF with IGA-IIF, the user spends shorter time in IGA-IFF as the result of convenient assignment through human-computer interface. In IGA-IFF, the user evaluates a suit through dragging the scroll bar once, and clicking the corresponding modal word in the list box. While in IGA-IIF, the user evaluates a suit through dragging the scroll bar twice. Therefore an individual's fuzzy fitness can alleviate user fatigue to some degree.

The success rate to find "the most satisfactory suit" within limited time is another index to compare the performance of these algorithms. We calculated the success rate to find "the most satisfactory suit" within 5 minutes, 7 minutes and 9 minutes respectively. Considering the 8 independent runs, we recorded the times to find "the most satisfactory suit" within 5 minutes, 7 minutes and 9 minutes respectively, and then divided these numbers by 8. For example, there are 4 times for IGA-IIF to find "the most satisfactory suit" within 5 minutes, therefore the success rate of IGA-IIF within 5 minutes is $(4/8)\times 100\% = 50\%$. The success rate of different algorithms within different time is listed as Table 6.

algorithm	within 5′	within 7′	within 9′
IGA-IIF	50	75	100
IGA-IFF	87.5	100	100
TIGA	25	87.5	100

Table 6. Success rate(%)

It is easy to observe from Table 6 that when the user spends 5 minutes in evaluating individuals, 7 runs of IGA-IFF find "the most satisfactory suit", only 4 runs of IGA-IIF find it, and 2 runs of TIGA find it. When time increases to 9 minutes, they all find "the most satisfactory suit". This indicates that IGA-IFF has more opportunities to find "the most satisfactory suit" in short time than the other two algorithms.

To sum up, compared with TIGA, the proposed algorithms in this chapter have good performances in alleviating user fatigue and looking for "the most satisfactory suit".

6. Conclusion

User fatigue problem, resulted from evaluation on an individual and expression of its fitness by the user, is very important and hard to solve in IGAs. It is key for IGAs to improve performance in case of successfully solving user fatigue problem.

It is easy to understand that user fatigue can alleviate to some degree if we adopt some appropriate approaches to express an individual's fitness. Based on this, we propose two novel interactive genetic algorithms, i.e. IGA-IIF and IGA-IFF in this chapter. We adopt an interval described with the lower limit and the upper limit as well as a fuzzy number described with a Gaussian membership function to express an individual's fitness. These expressions well accord with the user's fuzzy and gradual cognitive on the evaluated object. In order to compare different individuals in the same generation, we obtain the probability of an individual dominance by use of the probability of interval dominance, translate a fuzzy number into an interval based on α -cut set, and determine the dominant individual in tournament selection with size being two based on the probability of an individual dominance. We develop fashion evolutionary design systems based on these proposed algorithms, and compare them with TIGA. The experimental results show their advantages in alleviating user fatigue and looking for user's satisfactory individuals.

An individual's uncertain fitness is a novel research direction. How to extract some information on a population evolving on condition of an individual's uncertain fitness to guide the subsequent evolution so as to improve the performance of IGAs is a significant research topic. In addition, another way to alleviate user fatigue is to adopt surrogate-assisted models. How to build and apply surrogate-assisted models on condition of an individual's uncertain fitness is also a very meaningful research issue.

7. Acknowledgements

This work was completed when Dun-wei Gong was visiting CERCIA, School of Computer Science, the University of Birmingham. It was jointly supported by NSFC with granted No. 60775044 and Program for New Century Excellent Talents in University with granted No. NCET-07-0802.

8. References

Biles, J.A.; Anderson, P.G. & Loggi, L.W. (1996). Neural network fitness functions for a musical IGA, *Proceedings of International Symposium on Intelligent Industrial Automation and Soft Computing*, pp. 39-44

Caldwell, C. & Johnston, V.S. (1991). Tracking a criminal suspect through 'face-space' with a genetic algorithm, *Proceedings of 4th International Conference on Genetic Algorithms*, pp. 416-421, Morgan Kaufmann

Dawkins, R. (1986). *The Blind Watchmaker*, Longman, Essex, U.K.

Gong, D.W.; Hao G.S.; Zhou Y.; et al. (2007). *Theory and Applications of Interactive Genetic Algorithms*, Defense Industry Press, Beijing, China

Gong, D.W.; Zhou, Y. & Guo, Y.N. (2008). Interactive genetic algorithms with multiple approximate models. *Control Theory and Applications*, 25, 434-438

Hao, G.S.; Gong, D.W.; Shi, Y.Q.; et al. (2006). Method of replacing the user with machine in interactive genetic algorithm. *Pattern Recognition and Artificial Intelligence*, 19, 111-115

Kim, H.S. & Cho, S. B. (2000). Application of interactive genetic algorithm to fashion design. *Engineering Applications of Artificial Intelligence*, 13, 635-644

Limbourg, P. & Aponte, D.E. (2005). An optimization algorithm for imprecise multi-objective problem functions, *Proceedings of IEEE Congress on Evolutionary Computation*, pp. 459-466, IEEE Press

Liu, B.K. (2005). NN global optimization based on interval optimization. *Computer Engineering and Applications*, 23, 90-92

Sugimoto, F. & Yoneyama, M. (2001). An evaluation of hybrid fitness assignment strategy in interactive genetic algorithm, *Proceedings of 5th Australasia-Japan Joint Workshop on Intelligent and Evolutionary Systems*, pp. 62-69

Takagi, H. & Ohya, K. (1996). Discrete fitness values for improving the human interface in an interactive GA, *Proceedings of IEEE Conference on Evolutionary Computation*, pp. 109-112, IEEE Press

Takagi, H. (2001). Interactive evolutionary computation: fusion of the capabilities of EC optimization and human evaluation. *Proceedings of the IEEE*, 89, 1275-1296

Takagi, H. & Ohsaki, M. (2007). Interactive evolutionary computation-based hearing aid fitting. *IEEE Transactions on Evolutionary Computation*, 11, 414-427

Tokui, N. & Iba, H. (2000). Music composition with interactive evolutionary computation, *Proceedings of 3rd International Conference on Generative Art*, pp. 215-226

Wang, S.F.; Wang, X.F. & Takagi, H. (2006). User fatigue reduction by an absolute rating data-trained predictor in IEC, *Proceedings of IEEE Congress on Evolutionary Computation*, pp. 2195-2200, IEEE Press

Wei, W. (2004). *Intelligent Control Technology*, Machine industrial Press, Beijing,China
Zhou, Y.; Gong, D.W.; Hao, G.S.; et al. (2005). Phase estimations of individual's fitness based on NN in interactive genetic algorithms. *Control and Decision*, 20, 234-236

3

A Genetic Algorithm for Optimizing Hierarchical Menus

Shouichi Matsui and Seiji Yamada
Central Research Institute of Electric Power Industry & National Institute of Informatics
Japan

1. Introduction

Hierarchical menus are one of the primary controls for issuing commands in GUIs. These menus have submenus as menu items and display submenus off to the side when they are selected. Cellular phones that have only small displays show submenus as new menus, as shown in Fig. 1. The performance of the menu, i.e., the average selection time of menu items, depends on many factors, including its structure, layout, and colours.
There have been many studies on novel menus (e.g., Ahlström, 2005; Beck et al., 2006; Findlater & McGrenere, 2004), but there has been little work improving the performance of a menu by changing its structure (Amant et al., 2004; Francis, 2000; Francis & Rash, 2002; Liu et al., 2002; Quiroz et al., 2007). A very simple search method gave a fairly good improvement (Amant et al., 2004); therefore, we can expect further performance improvements by optimizing the structure.

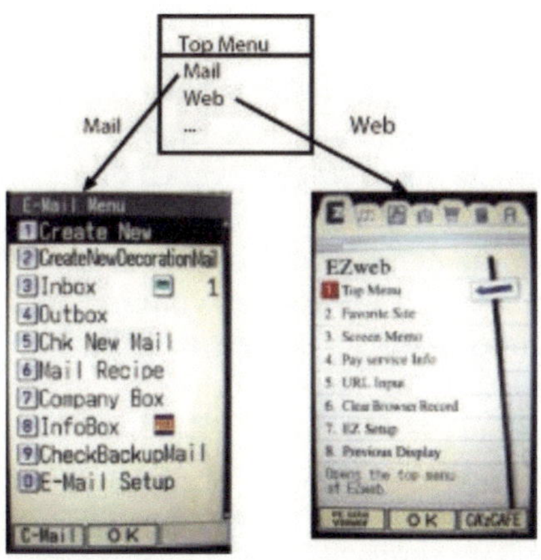

Fig. 1. Example of hierarchical menu for a cellular phone

There have been many studies on menu design, menu layout from the standpoint of the user interface. Francis et al. were the first to optimize a multi-function display that was essentially the same as a hierarchical menu by using Simulated Annealing (SA) (Francis, 2000; Francis & Rash, 2002). Quiroz et al. proposed an interactive evolution of a non-hierarchical menu using an interactive evolutionary computation (IEC) approach (Quiroz et al., 2007).

Liu et al. applied a visual search model of to menu design (Liu et al., 2002). They used the Guided Search (GS) model to develop menu designs. They defined a GS simulation model for a menu search task, and estimated the model parameters that would provide the best fit between model predictions and experimental data. Then they used an optimization algorithm to identify the menu design that minimized the predicted search times according to predefined search frequencies of different menu items, and they tested the design. Their results indicate that the GS model has the potential to be part of a system for predicting or automating the design of menus.

Amant et al. showed the concepts to support the analysis of cellular phone menu hierarchies (Amant et al., 2004). They proposed a model-based evaluation of cellular phone menu interaction, gathered data and evaluated three models: Fitts' law model, GOMS, and ACT-R. They concluded that the prediction by GOMS was the best among the three models. They also tried to improve menu selection time by using a simple best-first search algorithm and got over 30% savings in selection time.

This chapter shows an algorithm based on the genetic algorithm (GA) for optimizing the performance of menus. The algorithm aims to minimize the average selection time of menu items by considering the user's pointer movement and search/decision time (Matsui & Yamada, 2008a; Matsui & Yamada, 2008b). We will show results on a static hierarchical menu of a cellular phone as an example for a device with a small screen and limited input capability.

2. Formulation of the problem

2.1 Overview

The optimization problem of hierarchical menus can be considered as one dealing with placing menu items on the nodes of a tree. Let us assume a tree where the maximum depth is D, the maximum number of children that a node has is W, the root is the initial state, and menu items are on nodes. An example of a hierarchical menu in tree structure is shown in Fig. 2. As shown in the figure, some menu items have children; i.e. some menu items have submenus. The time to select the target item is the time to traverse from the root to the target node. The problem is to minimize the average traversal time with respect to the given search frequencies of menu items.

We cannot arbitrarily arrange the menu purely for efficiency. We must respect the semantic relationships between the items. That is, "Ringer Volume" is under the "Settings" category rather than vice versa for good reason. To cope with the difficulties of representing and reasoning about menu item semantics, we introduce two metrics, *functional similarity* and *menu granularity*.

Functional similarity is a metric that represents the similarity of two menu items in terms of their functions. We assume that the functional similarity takes a value between 0 and 1; 0 means that the two items have no similarity, and 1 means that the two items have very high similarity. For example, it is very natural to assume that "Create New Mail" and "Favorite Web Site" have low similarity and that "Create New Mail" and "Inbox of Mail" have high similarity. We use this metric to avoid placing items with low similarity on the same submenu of a node. If items with low similarity are put on the same submenu, it becomes difficult for a user to remember the menu layout. The formal definition will be given later.

Menu granularity is a metric that reflects the number of submenus a node has as its descendants. We introduce this metric to avoid placing an item that has many children and an item that has no child as children of the same node. The formal definition will be given later.

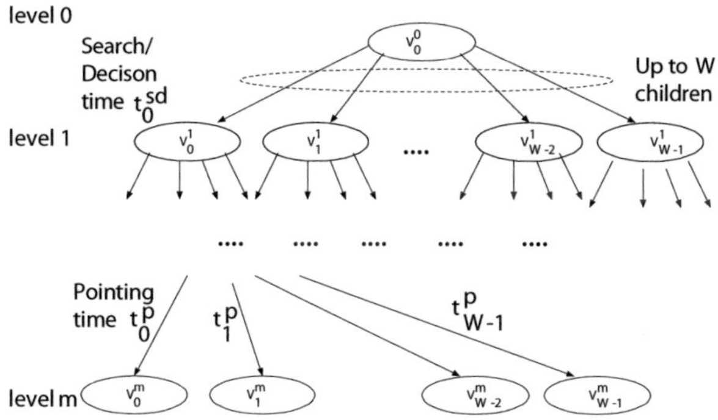

Fig. 2. Tree structure of a hierarchical menu

The problem of minimizing the average traversal time is a very difficult one because of the following constraints;

- The traversal time from a node to its children is not constant; it varies depending on the starting and ending nodes.
- Menu items usually belong to groups, and they have hierarchical constraints.
- We should consider the functional similarity and the menu granularity of each item from the standpoint of usability.

2.2 Formulation

2.2.1 Notation

Let l be the level number, i be the ordering number in siblings, and v_i^l be a node of a tree (Fig. 2). Moreover, let $M=(V,E)$ be a tree where $V=\{v_i^l\}$ denotes the nodes and $E=\{e_{ij}\}$ denotes the edges. We call the leaf nodes that correspond to generic functions "terminal nodes."

There are two kinds of menu item or node in *M*. One type is terminal nodes that correspond to generic functions, and the other is intermediate nodes. The terminal nodes cannot have children.

Let I_i represent a menu item and the total number of items be N; i.e., there are $I_i(i=1,\cdots,N)$ menu items. Items that correspond to generic functions are less than N and some items/nodes are intermediate items/nodes that have submenu(s) as a child or children. We assume that a menu item I_i is assigned to a node v_i^l; therefore, we use I_i and v_i^l interchangeably. We also assume that the selection probability of the terminal node/generic function is represented by Pr_i.

2.2.2 Selection time

The selection time t_i^l of a menu item/node v_i^l on the hierarchical level l can be expressed using the search/decision time t_i^{sd} and the pointing time t_i^p as follows (Cockburn et al. 2007):

$$t_i^l = t_i^{sd} + t_i^p. \tag{1}$$

We also consider the time to reach level l; therefore, the whole selection time T_i of a node v_i^l on level l can be expressed as follows:

$$T_i = \sum_{j=0}^{l-1} t_{i_j}^j + t_i^l. \tag{2}$$

Thus, the average selection time T_{avg} is defined as follows:

$$T_{avg} = \sum_{i=1}^{N} Pr_i T_i. \tag{3}$$

2.2.3 Pointing time

As Silfverberg et al. (Silfverberg et al., 2000) and Cockburn (Cockburn et al., 2007) reported, the pointing time t_i^p can be expressed by using the Fitts' law as follows:

$$t_i^p = a + b \log_2(A_i / W_i + 1), \tag{4}$$

where the coefficients a and b are determined empirically by regressing the observed pointing time, A_i is the distance moved, and W_i is the width of the target.
Fitts' law describes the time taken to acquire, or point to, a visual target. It is based on the amount of information that a person must transmit through his/her motor system to move to an item - small, distant targets demand more information than large close ones, and consequently they take longer to acquire. Therefore the term $\log_2(A_i / W_i + 1)$ is called the *index of difficulty (ID)*,

2.2.4 Search/decision time

We assume that the search/decision time t_i^{sd} can be expressed as follows (Cockburn et al., 2007).

- For an inexperienced user, the time required for a linear search is as follows:

$$t_i^{sd} = b^{sd} n^l + a^{sd}, \tag{5}$$

where n^l is the number of items that a level l node has, and the coefficients a^{sd} and b^{sd} are determined empirically by regressing the observed search time.

- For an expert, we can assume that the time t_i^{sd} obeys Hick-Hyman's law.

$$t_i^{sd} = b^{sd} H_i + a^{sd}, \tag{6}$$

$$H_i = \log_2(1 / Pr_i^l), \tag{7}$$

where the coefficients a^{sd} and b^{sd} are determined empirically by regressing the observed search time. If we can assume that all items are equally probable, the following equation holds.

$$H = \log_2(n^l) \text{ iff } \forall Pr_i^l = 1 / n^l. \tag{8}$$

2.2.5 Functional similarity

Toms et al. reported the result of generating a menu hierarchy from functional descriptions using cluster analysis (Toms et al., 2001). However, this approach is time consuming; therefore, we choose to use another one.

We represent the functional similarity of item I_x and I_y by using a function $s(I_x, I_y)$ which takes a value between 0 and 1. Let us assume that generic function of each item I_i can be specified by some words $wl_i = \{w_0, w_1, \cdots\}$, and let $\mathbf{WL} = \bigcup_i wl_i$ be the whole words. Let us also assume that an intermediate node can be characterized by the words by which the children are specified. Let $\mathbf{x}$ be a vector in which element x_i represents the frequency of the i-th word in its specification, and let $\mathbf{y}$ be a vector of node y. Then, the functional similarity $s(I_x, I_y)$ is defined as follows:

$$s(I_x, I_y) = \frac{\mathbf{x} \cdot \mathbf{y}}{|\mathbf{x}||\mathbf{y}|} \tag{9}$$

Let us consider a node v_i^l that has m children. The penalty of functional similarity $P_{v_i^l}^s$ of node v_i^l is defined as follows:

$$P_{v_i^l}^s = \sum_{i=0}^{m-1} \sum_{j=0}^{m-1} (1 - s(I_i, I_j)). \tag{10}$$

And the total penalty P^s is defined as follows:

$$P^s = \sum_{v_i^l \in \{V \setminus v_0^0\}} P_{v_i^l}^s. \tag{11}$$

2.2.6 Menu granularity

The menu granularity $g_{v_i^l}$ of a node v_i^l is defined as the total number of descendants. If node v_i^l is a terminal node, then $g_{v_i^l} = 0$. Moreover, if node v_i^l has m children $(v_j^{l+1}, j = 0, \cdots, m-1)$ whose menu granularities are $g_{v_j^{l+1}}, (j = 0, \cdots, m-1)$, then $g_{v_i^l}$ is defined as follows:

$$g_{v_i^l} = \sum_{j=0}^{m-1} g_{v_j^{l+1}}. \tag{12}$$

The penalty of menu granularity $P_{v_i^l}^g$ of node v_i^l is defined as follows:

$$P_{v_i^l}^g = \sum_{i=0}^{m-1} \sum_{j=0}^{m-1} | g_{v_i^l} - g_{v_j^l} |. \tag{13}$$

And the total penalty P^g is defined as follows:

$$P^g = \sum_{v_i^l \in \{V \setminus v_0^0\}} P^g_{v_i^l}. \tag{14}$$

2.2.7 Objective function

The problem is to minimize the following objective function:

$$f = T_{avg} + \alpha P^s + \beta P^g, \tag{15}$$

where α and β are the constants that control the preference of functional similarity and menu granularity.

2.3 Local/partial optimization

2.3.1 Placing Items as children of a node

Let us consider a node v_i^l on level l that has $n \le W$ children $v_j^{l+1}(j = 0, \cdots, n-1)$ and represent the traversal time from v_i^l to v_j^{l+1}, i.e., the pointing time for v_j^{l+1}, by t_j^l. When we want to place $I_j, (j = 0, \cdots, n-1)$ menu items whose selection probabilities are represented by Pr_j as the children of the v_i^l, the average pointing time $T_{v_i^l}$,

$$T_{v_i^l} = \sum_{j=0}^{n-1} Pr_j t_j^l, \tag{16}$$

is minimized as follows:

1. Sort I_i using Pr_i as the sort key in descending order, and let the result be $I'_i(i = 0, \cdots, n-1)$,
2. Sort v_i^{l+1} using t_i^l as the sort key in ascending order, and let the results be $v_i^{'(l+1)}(i = 0, \cdots, n-1)$
3. Placing I'_i on the node $v_i^{'(l+1)}$ gives the minimum average pointing time from node v_i^l.

2.3.2 Optimization problem

When menu items that are placed as the children of a node V are given, the placement that minimizes the average pointing time is straightforward. Therefore, the problem is to find the best assignment of menu items to nodes of a tree that minimizes Equation (15), where nodes have a fixed capacity of W items. There should be at least $L = \lceil N / W \rceil$ nodes in the tree, and N items placed on some node. The first node has W items chosen from N items, and the second node has W items chosen from $N - W$ items, and so on, so the search space of the problem is roughly ${}_N C_W \times {}_{N-W} C_W \times \cdots \times {}_{N-LW} C_W = N! / (W!)^L$; therefore, the problem is a difficult combinatorial optimization problem. For instance, consider the case of $N = 200$, $W = 10$. The search space is roughly $200! / ((10!)^{20}) \sim 10^{243}$.

3. Genetic algorithm

3.1 Basic strategy

Previous studies showed that breadth was preferable to depth (Kiger, 1984; Larson & Czerwinski, 1998; Schultz & Curran, 1986; Zaphiris, 2000; Zaphiris et al. 2003). Schultz and Curran reported that menu breadth was preferable to depth (Schultz & Curran, 1986). Larson and Czerwinski reported the results of depth and breadth tradeoff issues in the design of GUIs (Larson & Czerwinski, 1998). Their results showed that, while increased depth did harm search performance on the web, a medium condition of depth and breadth outperformed the broadest shallow web structure overall.

Zaphiris studied the effect of depth and breadth in the arrangement of web link hierarchies on user preference, response time, and errors (Zaphiris, 2000). He showed that previous menu depth/breath tradeoff procedures applied to the web link domain. He also showed that task completion time increased as the depth of the web site structure increased. Zaphiris et al. also showed the results of the study investigating age-related differences as they relate to the depth versus breadth tradeoff in hierarchical online information systems (Zaphiris et al. 2003). They showed that shallow hierarchies were preferred to deep hierarchies, and seniors were slower but did not make more errors than their younger counterparts when browsing web pages.

Because the previous studies showed that breadth was preferable to depth, we use a kind of breadth-first search algorithm (shown later), as the core of the proposed GA.

3.2 Chromosome and mapping from genotype to phenotype

A simple way to represent a solution of the problem is a tree. But there is a problem that genetic operators such as crossover or mutation may generate an infeasible solution; i.e., the tree does not contain all the generic functions. There are two ways to cope with this problem. The first way is to convert an infeasible solution into a feasible one and modify the chromosome. The other way is to use a chromosome representation that does not generate infeasible solutions. We base the proposed algorithm on the latter approach.

Since breadth is preferable to depth, an algorithm that places menu items I_i one by one on a usable node that has the smallest node number can find a good solution. We number each node from root to bottom and from left to right. We use an algorithm that assigns I_i to a node as follows:

1. A chromosome of the GA is a sequence of I_i; i.e., a chromosome can be represented as a permutation of numbers.
2. According to the permutation, assign menu items I_i one by one to vacant positions of the node that has the smallest node number.
3. If a generic function is assigned to a node, then the number of children that the node can have is decreased by 1.

If we have a sufficient number of intermediate nodes, we can search enough space to find the optimal solution.

Two examples of assignment according to permutation are depicted in Fig.3, where W is 4. In the figure, numbers with underline ($\underline{1}$, $\underline{2}$, $\underline{3}$) represent the intermediate nodes. Let us consider "Permutation 1". In this case, we can assign "10", "5", and "11" to the root node. But we cannot assign "7" to the root node, because the root node cannot have any children if we did. Therefore, we should assign "7" to the next level node, and the remaining position of the root node should be an intermediate node. Because there is an intermediate node in the root node, we can assign "1" to the root node.

In the case of "Permutation 2", the mapping is straightforward. The first number "1" is an intermediate node, so we assign it to the root node, and the number of vacant positions in the tree is incremented by 4. The next number "10" can be assigned to the root node, and "3" and "5" can be assigned to the root node. The remaining numbers are assigned to the children of the root nodes.

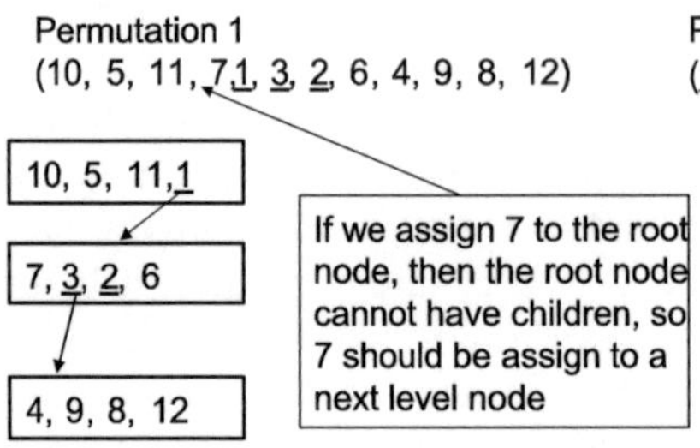

Fig. 3. Mapping a permutation to a tree structure

3.3 Local search

We use a local search method to improve the performance of GA. The method finds an unused node v_i^l, i.e., finds an intermediate node that has no child, and swaps v_i^l with a node that is the sibling's child v_j^{l+1}. Figure 4 shows an example of this procedure. In the left tree, the intermediate node "int2" has no child, so it is swapped with "func3", and the result is the right part.

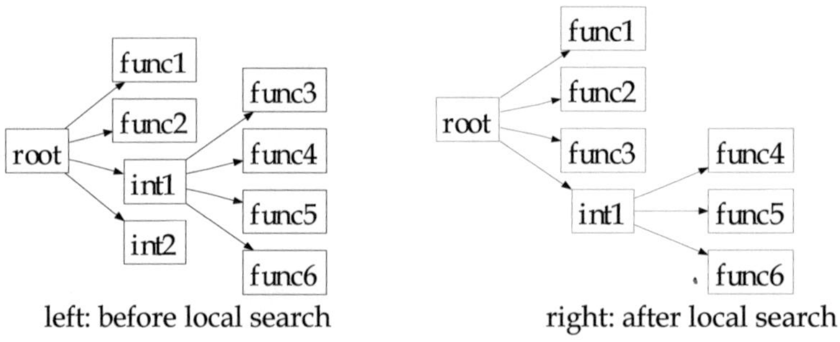

Fig. 4. Local search

3.4 Crossover and mutation

We use a crossover operator that does not generate an invalid chromosome. As described above, a chromosome is a permutation of numbers; therefore, we use crossover operators that are developed for the representation. Based on the results of preliminary experiments, we chose CX (Cycle Crossover) for the crossover operator.

We use the swap mutation as the mutation operator. Randomly chosen genes at position p and q are swapped.

The crossover and mutation operators do not generate invalid chromosomes; i.e., offspring are always valid permutations.

3.5 Other GA parameters

The selection of the GA is tournament selection of size 2. The initial population is generated by random initialization, i.e., a chromosome is a random permutation of numbers. We use a steady state GA, for which the population size is 100, and the mutation rate is one swap per chromosome.

4. Numerical experiments

We conducted numerical experiments to confirm the effectiveness of the proposed algorithm. The target was a cellular phone that is used by one of the authors. The phone (KDDI, 2006) has 24 keys as shown in Fig. 5.

The target phone has hardware keys for "E-mail", "EZweb", "Phone book", and "Application". And there is a "Shortcut"key (cursor down). The root menu thus has the four submenus corresponding to the hardware keys.

Fig. 5. Key Layout of the Target Cellular Phone.

4.1 Experimental data

4.1.1 Pointing time and decision time

The index of difficulty for 24×24 key pairs was calculated as follows. We measured the relative coordinates of the center (x,y) of each key and measured the width and height of each key. We calculated the index of difficulty to an accuracy of one digit after the decimal point. This gave us 28 groups of indexes of difficulty as shown in Table 1. We named each key, from top to bottom and left to right, as follows: "App", "Up", "Phone book", "Left", "Center", "Right", "Mail", "Down", "Web", "Call", "Clear", "Power", "1", thru "9", "*", "0", and "#".

We measured the pointing time of one-handed thumb users for the above 28 groups by recording the tone produced by each key press (Amant et al., 2004). There are two ways to measure the pointing time. Silfverberg et al. measured the time by counting the number of characters generated by key presses in 10 seconds (Silfverberg et al., 2000). Amant et al. measured the time by recording the tone produced by each key press (Amant et al., 2004). Because the target has keys that do not generate any character, such as cursor keys, we measured the time by recording the tone.

Unpaid volunteers participated in the experiment. We prepared 28 tasks corresponding to the 28 groups. The "Read Email Message" function of the phone was used during the tasks, except for the one task (ID=1.4, "2" to "Clear"). For the exceptional case, the "write memo" function (with number mode selected) was used. The participants repeated the task of pressing the "From" key and the "To" key 10 times for each task. The pointing time was calculated by subtracting the starting time of the tone of "From" from the starting time of tone of "To."

We got the following equation for predicting the pointing time, and the equation is very similar to the one reported by Silfverberg et al.(Silfverberg et al., 2000)[1]

$$t_i^p = 192 + 63\log_2(A_i / W_i + 1)(\text{ms}). \quad (17)$$

Although the target phone has the ability to select a menu item by pressing a key that is prefixed to item title, we assumed that all selections were done by cursor movements.

The target of this experiment was an expert; therefore, we used the following equation for the search/decision time (Cockburn et al. 2007)[2]:

$$t_i^{sd} = 80\log_2(n^l) + 240(\text{ms}). \quad (18)$$

group #	ID	Example of pairs		# of pairs	group #	ID	Example of pairs		# of pairs
		from	to				from	to	
1	3.7	*	Up	2	15	2.3	1	3	33
2	3.6	0	Up	3	16	2.2	2	Center	20
3	3.5	9	Up	6	17	2.1	1	8	25
4	3.4	8	Up	8	18	2.0	2	Call	17
5	3.3	8	Right	17	19	1.9	1	7	21
6	3.2	9	Down	22	20	1.8	Mail	Call	7
7	3.1	8	Down	25	21	1.7	1	5	50
8	3.0	6	Right	28	22	1.6	1	2	16
9	2.9	1	Up	29	23	1.4	2	Clear	9
10	2.8	8	Center	29	24	1.3	Right	Up	12
11	2.7	1	*	33	25	1.2	1	4	21
12	2.6	2	Right	29	26	1.1	Center	Down	4
13	2.5	1	9	29	27	0.8	Right	Center	4
14	2.4	1	0	53	28	0.0	1	1	24

Table 1. Index of Difficulty for the Target Phone (24 keys)

---

[1] $t_i^p = 176 + 64\log_2(A_i / W_i + 1)$ (ms).

[2]The equation is derived from experiments conducted for a computer display, and is not for a cellular phone.

4.1.2 Usage frequency data

We gathered usage frequency data as follows. The first author recorded the daily usage of each function for two months, and we generated the usage frequency data from the record. There were 129 terminal nodes in the data.

4.1.3 Similarity

We assigned three to five words to each generic function according to the users' manual of the target phone (KDDI, 2006).

4.2 Results

We conducted the following experiments.

- **Case 1: Typical Usage**: This experiment was conducted to assess the typical improvement by the GA. The maximum width W was 16.
- **Case 2: Limited Breadth**: Although breadth is preferable to depth, pressing a far key or pressing a "Down" key many times is sometimes tedious. This experiment was conducted to see the effects of limiting the breadth. In this case, we set W to 12, 9, and 6.

Because GA is a stochastic algorithm, we conducted 50 runs for every test case, and the results shown in Table 2 and Table 3 are averages over 50 runs. The two parameters for weights were set to $\alpha = 10.0$ and $\beta = 1.0$. The maximum number of fitness evaluations was 100,000.

Case	T_{ave} (ms)	(%)	P^s	P^g
Original	3331	0.0	454	793
Local Move	2812	15.5	454	793
Case 1 (W =16)	2036	38.9	727	1259
Case 2 (W =12)	1998	40.0	541	856
Case 2 (W =9)	1959	41.2	402	291
Case 2 (W =6)	2237	32.8	279	173

Table 2. Improvement in average selection time

In Table 2, "Local Move" shows the results of a local modification that places menu items according to their frequency, i.e., the most frequently used item is placed as the top item, and so on. As the table shows, the proposed algorithm can generate menu with shorter average selection time. Moreover, limiting the breadth gives better menus. This is partly because the search/decision time is proportional to $\log_2(n)$, where n is the number of items. As the number of items increases, the search/decision time increases; therefore, the average selection time increases. Limiting the breadth to 6 gave a longer selection time and smaller penalties.

The original menu (T_{ave}=3331 (ms)) and the best menu of Case 2 (9 keys) (T_{ave} =1913 (ms)) are shown in Fig. 7. In the two figures, items and intermediate nodes are shown in boxes and the vertical ordering shows the placement in a single level menu. The box is omitted for low usage frequency items/intermediate nodes for the sake of saving space.

In Fig. 7, items with high usage frequency are placed on a smaller level and on an upper position. For example, the most frequently used "Inbox folder 2" which is placed under the "Inbox" menu in the original menu, is placed as a child of "E-Mail" in the optimized menu. Note also that "Shortcut" is not used in the original menu, but it is fully utilized in the optimized menu; frequently used URLs are placed in "Shortcut".

4.3 Effects of weights

We introduced two weights for the penalties of functional similarity and of menu granularity. Table 3 shows the results of different weights settings for the case $W = 9$. The average selection time increased as we increased α. The table also shows that the difference in average selection time was larger than that of the penalty factor of P^s. Setting them to zero gave a shorter selection time, but the penalties were larger.
There is a tradeoff among the average selection time, functional similarity, and menu granularity; therefore, a multi-objective approach might be a more natural formulation.

α	β	T_{ave} (ms)	(%)	P^s	P^g
0.0	0.0	1837	44.9	584	448
5.0	1.0	1935	41.9	405	278
10.0	1.0	1959	41.2	402	291
20.0	1.0	1990	40.3	396	300
40.0	1.0	2066	38.0	395	309
20.0	5.0	2011	39.6	397	274
20.0	10.0	2028	39.1	405	260

Table 3. Effect of weights

4.4 Convergence speed

Figure 6 shows fitness, average selection time, and two penalty terms in the best case ($W = 9$). GA found a fairly good solution within 50,000 fitness evaluations. The penalty term of "Functional Similarity" decreased almost monotonically, but the term of "Menu Granularity" oscillated in the early stage. The average selection time initially decreased rapidly, but sometimes increased in the middle of iteration because of the penalty terms.

5. Discussion and future work

The experiments show that the proposed algorithm can generate better menu hierarchies for the target phone. Because our targets of are not limited to cellular phones, and the preliminary results are promising, we will apply the algorithm to wider varieties of targets such as Web browser bookmarks.
In this paper, we focused on a static menu as the target; adaptive/dynamic menu (e.g., Ahlström, 2005; Beck et al. 2006; Findlater & McGrenere, 2004) that changes menu contents depending on usage will be a future target.
The data used in the experiments, especially selection frequency data, were limited. Therefore, we should gather a wider variety of usage data and use that to confirm the effectiveness of the proposed method.

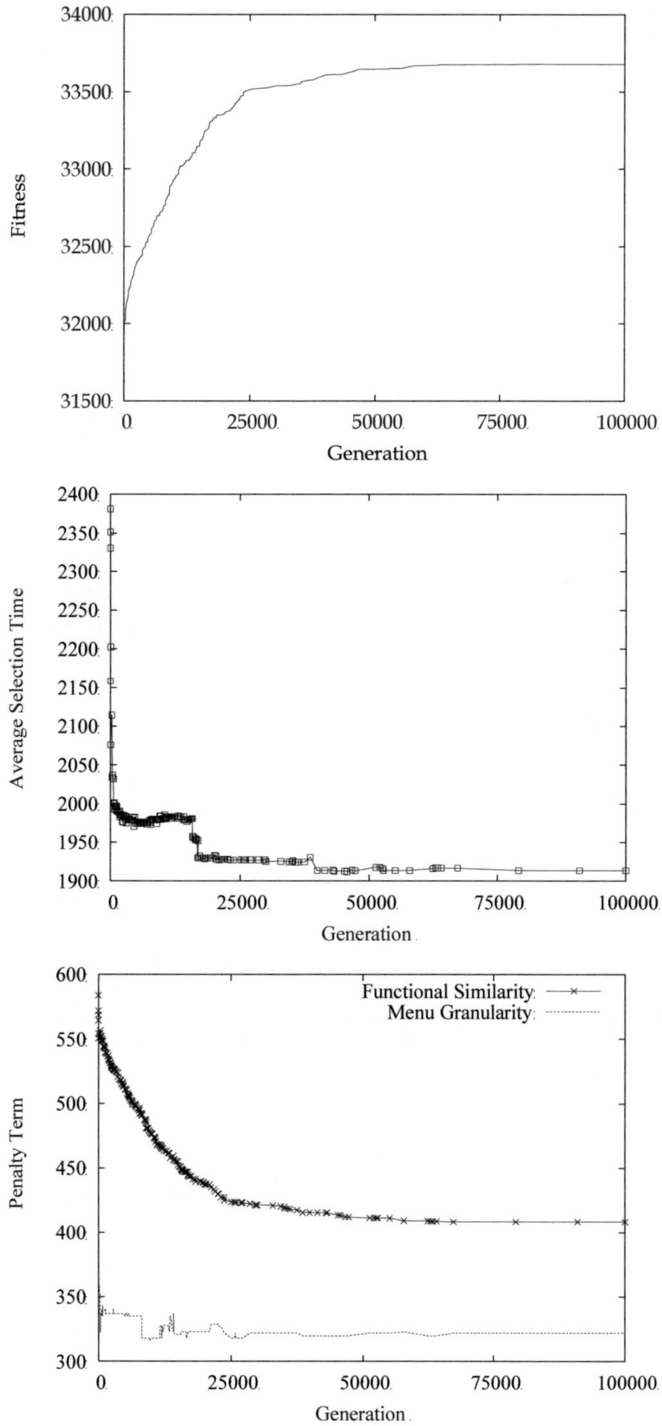

Fig. 6. Fitness, Average selection time, Penalty terms

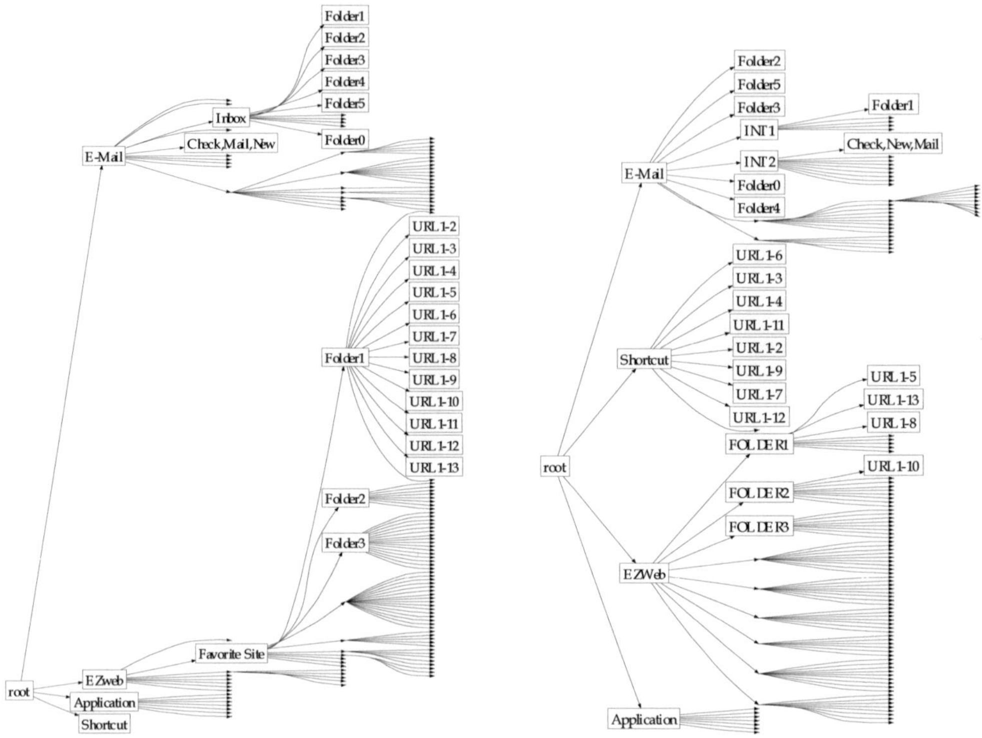

Left: Original menu Right: Generated Menu

Fig. 7. Original menu and best menu (W=9)

6. Conclusion

We proposed a GA-based algorithm for minimizing the average selection time of menu items that considers the user's pointer movement time and the decision time. The preliminary results showed that the algorithm can generate a better menu structure. The target of the proposed algorithm is not limited to cellular phones.

7. References

Amant, St.; Horton, T.E. & Ritter, F.E. (2004). Model-based evaluation of cell phone menu interaction, *Proceedings of CHI 2004*, pp.343–350, 1-58113-702-8, Vienna, Austria, ACM Press, New York

Ahlström, D. (2005). Modeling and improving selection in cascading pull-down menus using Fitts' law, the steering law and force fields, *Proceedings of CHI 2005*, pp.61–70, 1-58113-998-5, Portland, Oregon, USA, ACM Press, New York

Beck, J.; Han, S.H. & Park, J. (2006). Presenting a submenu window for menu search on a cellular phone, *Int. J. of Human-Computer Interaction*, vol.20, no.3, pp.233–245

Cockburn, A.; Gutwin, G. & Greenberg, S. (2007). A predictive model of menu performance, *Proceedings of CHI 2007*, pp.627–636, 978-1-59593-593-9, San Jose, California, USA, ACM Press, New York

Francis, G. (2000). Designing multifunction displays: an optimization approach, *International Journal of Cognitive Ergonomics*, vol.4, no.2, pp.107–124

Francis, G. & Rash, C. (2002). MFDTool (version 1.3): a software tool for optimizing hierarchical information on multifunction displays, USAARL Report No.2002-22

Findlater, L. & McGrenere, J. (2004) A comparison of static, adaptive, and adaptable menus, *Proceedings of CHI 2004*, pp.89–96, 1-58113-702-8, Vienna, Austria, ACM Press, New York

KDDI (2006). Manual for CASIO W43CA http://www.au.kddi.com/torisetsu/pdf/w43ca/w43ca_torisetsu.pdf,

Kiger, J.I. (1984). The depth/breadth trade-off in the design of menu-driven user interfaces, *International Journal of Man-Machine Studies*, vol.20, no.2, pp.201–213

Larson, K. & Czerwinski, M. (1998). Web page design: implication of memory, structure and scent for information retrieval, *Proceedings of CHI 1998*, pp.25–32, 0-201-30987-4, Los Angeles, California, USA, ACM Press/Addison-Wesley Publishing Co., New York

Liu, B.; Francis, G. & Salvendy, G. (2002). Applying models of visual search to menu design, *Int. J. Human-Computer Studies*, no.56, pp.307–330

Matsui, S. & Yamada, S. (2008a). Genetic algorithm can optimize hierarchical menus, *Proceedings of CHI 2008*, pp.1385–1388, 978-1-60558-011-1, Florence, Italy ACM Press, New York

Matsui, S. & Yamada, S. (2008b). A genetic algorithm for optimizing hierarchical menus, *Proceedings of Evolutionary Computation, 2008, CEC 2008. (IEEE World Congress on Computational Intelligence 2008).*, pp.2851–2858, 978-1-4244-1822-0, Hong Kong, IEEE, New York

Quiroz, J.C.; Louis, S.J. & Dascalu, S.M. (2007). Interactive evolution of XUL user interfaces, *Proceedings of GECCO 2007*, pp.2151–2158, 978-1-59593-697-4, London, England, ACM Press, New York

Silfverberg, M.; MacKenzie, I.S. & Kauppinen, T. (2000). Predicting text entry speed on mobile phones, *Proceedings of CHI 2000*, pp.9–16, 1-58113-216-6, The Hague, The Netherlands, ACM Press, New York

Schultz, E.E. Jr. & Curran, P.S. (1986). Menu structure and ordering of menu selection: independent or interactive effects?, *SIGCHI Bull.*,vol.18, no.2, pp.69–71

Toms, M.L.; Cummings-Hill, M.A.; Curry, D.G. & Cone, S.M. (2001). Using cluster analysis for deriving menu structures for automotive mobile multimedia applications, SAE Technical Paper Series 2001-01-0359, SAE

Zaphiris, P. (2000). Depth vs breadth in the arrangement of web links, *Proceedings of 44th Annual Meeting of the Human Factors and Ergonomics Society*, pp.139–144, San Diego, California, USA, Human Factors and Ergonomics Society, Santa Monica

Zaphiris, P.; Kurniawan, S.H.& Ellis, R.D. (2003). Age related difference and the depth vs. breadth tradeoffs in hierarchical online information systems, *Proceedings of User Interfaces for All*, LNCS 2615, pp. 23–42, 978-3-540-00855-2, Paris, France, Springer, Berlin/Heidelberg

Ziefle, M. & Bay, S. (2004). Mental models of a cellular phone menu. Comparing older and younger novice users, *Proceedings of MobileHCI 2004, LNCS 3160*, pp.25–37, 978-3-540-23086-1, Glasgow, UK, Springer, Berlin/Heidelberg.

4

Scheduling of Berthing Resources at a Marine Container Terminal via the use of Genetic Algorithms: Current and Future Research

Maria Boile, Mihalis Golias and Sotirios Theofanis
Rutgers, The State University of New Jersey
USA

1. Introduction

The tremendous increase of containerized trade over the last several years, the resulting congestion in container terminals worldwide, the remarkable increase in containership size and capacity, the increased operating cost of container vessels and the adoption by liner shipping companies of yield management techniques strain the relationships between ocean carriers and container terminal operators. Shipping lines want their vessels to be served upon arrival or according to a favorable priority pattern and complete their loading/unloading operations within a prearranged time window, irrespective of the problems and shortage of resources terminal operators are facing. Therefore, allocating scarce seaside resources is considered to be a problem deserving both practical and theoretical attention. Scientific research has focused on scheduling problems dealing primarily with two of the most important seaside resources: berth space and quay cranes. Comprehensive reviews of applications and optimization models in the field of marine container terminal operations are given by Meersmans and Dekker (2001), Vis and de Koster (2003), Steenken et al. (2004), Vacca et al. (2007), and Stahlbock and Voß (2008).

Scheduling of berth space, also called the berth scheduling problem (BSP), can be simply described as the problem of allocating space to vessels at the quay in a container terminal. The quay crane scheduling problem (QSP) can be described as the problem of allocating quay cranes to each vessel and vessel section. Vessels arrive at a container terminal over time and the terminal operator assigns them to berths to be served. To unload/load the containers from/onboard the vessel a number of quay cranes are assigned to each vessel. Ocean carriers, and therefore vessels, compete over the available berths and quay cranes, and different factors affect the berthing position, the start time of service, and the number of quay cranes assigned to each vessel. Several formulations have been presented for the BSP, the QSP, and recently for the combination of the BSP and QSP, the berth and quay crane scheduling problem (BQSP). Most of the model formulations have been single objective and it was not until recently that researchers recognized the multi-objective and multi-level character of these problems and introduced formulations that capture berth scheduling policies using the latter two formulations. The formulations that have appeared in the literature, in most cases, lead to NP-hard problems that require a heuristic or meta-heuristic algorithm to be developed in order to obtain a solution within computationally acceptable

times. Evolutionary algorithms, and more specifically Genetic Algorithms, have been used in some of these studies and are increasingly gaining popularity as main resolution approaches for these problems due to their flexibility and robustness as global search methods.
The topic of this Chapter is the application of Genetic Algorithms (GAs) based heuristics as resolution approaches to problems relating to the seaside operations at marine container terminals; namely the BSP, the QSP, and the BQSP. The first part of this Chapter presents a critical, up-to-date, review of the existing research efforts relating to the application of GAs based heuristics to these three classes of problems. Strengths and limitations of the existing algorithms to address the resolution of these problems are discussed in a systemic and coherent manner. The second part of the chapter summarizes and groups the different chromosome representations, genetic operations, and fitness function selection techniques presented in the published scientific research. It provides generic guidelines of how these components can be implemented as resolution approaches to different formulation types (i.e. single objective, single level multi-objective, and multi-level multi-objective) and the berth and quay crane scheduling policies the latter represent (e.g. minimum service time, minimum vessel delay, minimum quay crane idle time etc). In addition, the second part provides an in-depth analysis and proposed improvements on how these components may address two main "weak spots" of GAs based heuristics: a) the lack of optimality criteria of the final solution, and b) how to exploit the special characteristics of the physical problem and construct improved approximations of the feasible search space. The Chapter concludes with a critical review of the issues that need to be addressed to make GAs more relevant, applicable and efficient to berth scheduling real world applications, and provides some insights for future research directions.

2. Literature review

In this section we present a critical, up-to-date review of the existing research efforts relating to the application of GAs based heuristics to problems relating to the seaside operations at marine container terminals (namely the berth scheduling problem, the quay crane scheduling problem, and the combination of the two problems). For a more comprehensive literature review on the berth scheduling and quay crane scheduling problem and the different terminal operator policies we refer to Bierwirth and Miesel (2009a) and Theofanis et al. (2009). Strengths and limitations of the existing algorithms to address the resolution of these problems are discussed in a systemic and coherent manner.

2.1 Berth scheduling

As we mentioned earlier, the berth scheduling problem (BSP) can be simply described as the problem of allocating berth space to vessels in a container terminal. Vessels usually arrive over time and the terminal operator needs to assign them to berths to be served (unload and load containers) in a timely manner. Ocean carriers and therefore vessels compete over the available berths and different factors, discussed in detail later, affect the berth and time assignment. The BSP has three planning/control levels: the strategic, the tactical, and the operational. At the strategic level, the number and length of berths/quays that should be available at the port are determined. This is done either at the initial development of the port or when an expansion is considered. At the tactical level, usually midterm decisions are taken, e.g. the exclusive allocation of a group of berths to a certain ocean carrier. At the operational level, the allocation of berthing space to a set of vessels scheduled to call at the port within a few days time horizon has to be decided upon. Normally, this planning horizon does not exceed seven to ten days. Since ocean carrier vessels follow a regular schedule, in most cases the assignment of a berth to the vessel has to be decided upon on a regular and usually periodical basis. At the operational level the BSP is typically formulated as combinatorial optimization problem. After the BSP has been solved, the resulting Berth Scheduling Plan is usually presented using a time-space diagram.

The BSP has been formulated according to the following variations: a) Discrete versus Continuous Berthing Space, b) Static versus Dynamic Vessel Arrivals, and c) Static versus Dynamic Service Time, involving different assumptions on the utilization of the space of the quay, the estimation of the handling time of the vessels and the arrival time of the vessels as compared to the beginning of the planning horizon. Time-space representations of BSP variations are shown in Figure 1. The BSP can be modeled as a discrete problem if the quay is viewed as a finite set of berths, where each berth is described by fixed-length segments or as points. Typically, however, vessels are of different length and dividing the quay into a set of predefined segments is difficult, mainly due to the dynamic change of the length requirements for each vessel. One solution to this problem is to use longer segments (a solution resulting in poor space utilization), or short segments (an approach leading in infeasible solutions). To overcome these drawbacks continuous models have appeared in the literature, where vessels can berth anywhere along the quay. In the former case, the BSP can be, and in the majority of the cases has been, modeled as an unrelated parallel machine-scheduling problem (Pinedo, 2008) whereas in the latter case as a packaging problem. The BSP can also be modeled as a static problem (SBSP), if all the vessels to be served are already at the port when scheduling begins or as a dynamic problem (DBSP), if all vessels to be scheduled for berthing have not yet arrived but arrival times are known in advance. Service time at each berth depends on several factors; with the two most important being the number of cranes operating on each vessel and the distance from the preferred berthing position, i.e. from the berth with the minimum distance from the storage yard blocks, where containers to be (un)loaded from/onboard the vessel are stored. If the model does not take under consideration the number of cranes operating at each vessel, then the problem can be considered as static in terms of the handling time. On the other hand, if this number is decided upon from the model, the formulation can be considered as dynamic in terms of the vessel service time. Finally, technical restrictions such as berthing draft, inter-vessel and end-berth clearance distance are further assumptions that have been considered. The model formulations that have appeared in the literature combine two or more of these assumptions and, in most cases, lead to NP-hard problems that require heuristic algorithms to be developed for computationally acceptable solution times.

The first paper to appear in the literature that applied Genetic Algorithms as a resolution approach to the berth scheduling problem was by Go and Lim (2000). In their paper the authors represent the continuous space and dynamic vessel arrival time berth scheduling problem (CDBSP) using a directed acyclic graph and investigate the efficiency of several variants of the Randomized Local Search, Tabu Search and Genetic Algorithms. The authors based their representation of the problem on the work by Brown et al. (1997) and their objective was to determine the minimum length of the wharf to serve all the vessels. The authors observed that a combination of the different methods (i.e. Tabu Search and GAs) can have improved results as compared to each method being applied individually. In the next section we will expand on this observation and critically discuss why this phenomenon is to be expected.

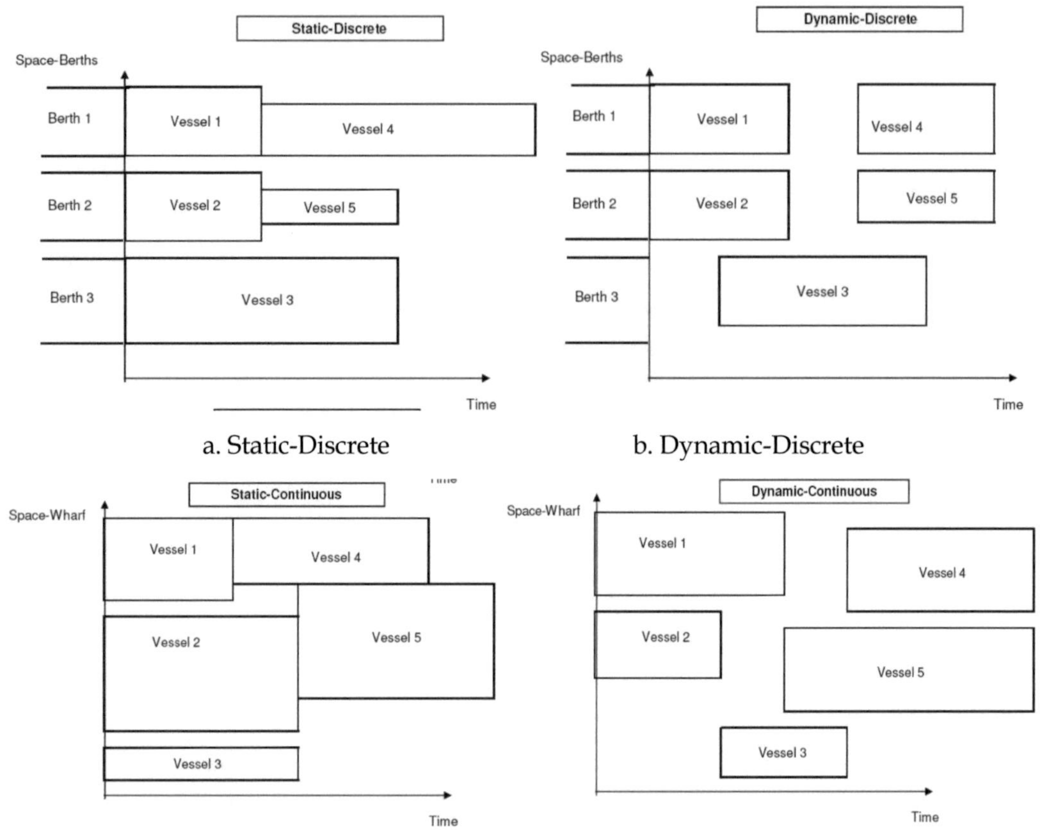

a. Static-Discrete b. Dynamic-Discrete

c. Static-Continuous d. Dynamic-Continuous

Fig. 1. Berth Scheduling Problem (BSP) Variations

In 2001, Nishimura et al. (2001) extended the work by Imai et al. (1997) and Imai et al. (2001) and presented a GAs heuristic for a discrete space and dynamic vessel arrival time BSP (DDBSP) at a public berth system. The objective was to minimize the total service time of all the vessels served. A one-dimensional representation with genetic operations of reproduction, crossover and mutation and a fitness function defined by the reciprocal of the actual objective function were implemented. No justification was provided for the use of the selected genetic operations or fitness function. The proposed GAs heuristic was compared against results from a Lagrangian relaxation heuristic, with the latter performing better but without significant differences. Following this work, Imai et al. (2003) presented a formulation for the DDBSP, based on the unrelated machine scheduling problem, where vessel service was differentiated based on weights assigned to each vessel. The authors initially proposed a Lagrangian relaxation based approach, which then was replaced by the GAs based heuristic proposed by Nishimura et al. (2001), due to the difficulty of applying the sub-gradient method to the relaxed problem. The authors commented only on the berth scheduling policy and not on the efficiency or consistency of the proposed GAs heuristic, which cannot be assumed to have the same behavior as the one observed for the policy presented in Nishimura et al. (2001). Imai et al. (2006) presented a formulation for the DDBAP at a terminal with indented berths. The authors used the GAs based heuristic presented by Nishimura et al. (2001) with the addition of a procedure to obtain feasible solutions. In a similar fashion to the previous research by the authors (Imai et al. 2003) the experimental results focused on the evaluation of the proposed policy and terminal design, as compared to a conventional terminal without indented berths, and no results were provided as to the efficiency of the GAs based heuristic.

Han et al. (2006) studied the DDBSP with the objective of minimizing the total service time of all the vessels (similar to Imai et al., 2001; and Nishimura et al., 2001) and presented a hybrid optimization strategy of a combination of a GAs and a Simulated Annealing (SA) based heuristic. This is the first time that GAs were combined explicitly with another heuristic (which is part of the new area of research called Memetic Algorithms, see Goh et al., 2009) for the berth scheduling problem. The authors used the same GAs characteristics (i.e. representation and fitness function) as in Nishimura et al. (2001) and applied a Metropolis based stochastic process based on parameters given by the SA approach to select the individuals of the next generation. The proposed heuristic was compared to results obtained from the GAs heuristic without the stochastic component and, as expected, it performs better.

For the first time in 2006 the DDBSP was formulated as a stochastic machine scheduling problem by Zhou et al. (2006), with the objective of minimizing the expected values of the vessels waiting times. The authors assumed that the vessel arrival and handling times at the berths are stochastic parameters, resulting in a binary problem with stochastic parameters in the objective function as well as in the constraints. A GAs based heuristic was proposed as a resolution algorithm using the representation introduced by Nishimura et al. (2001), two simple crossover and mutation operations, and a fitness function based on the actual value of the objective function and a penalty for violating the waiting time constraint. Experimental results focused on the CPU time and convergence patterns of the proposed algorithm and to a brief comparison with a first come first served (FCFS) policy The next year, Golias et al. (2007) studied the DDBSP where vessel arrival and handling times were considered as stochastic variables. They presented and conceptually compared three different heuristic solution approaches: a) a Markov Chain Monte Carlo simulation based heuristic b) an Online Stochastic Optimization based heuristic, and c) a deterministic solution based heuristic. A generic Genetic Algorithms based heuristic that can be used within the former two heuristics was also proposed. Computational results were not provided.

Imai et al. (2007a) studied the DDBSP and presented a bi-objective formulation to minimize the total service time and delayed vessel departures. The GAs proposed in Nishmiura et al. (2001) and the Subgradient Optimization procedure proposed in Imai et al. (2001) were used as resolution approaches. The two procedures were compared and it was shown that the former outperformed the latter. We should note that the proposed GAs heuristic can only solve single objective problems and cannot be compared to GAs that are used in multi-objective optimization problems, which will be presented later on in this Chapter. In the same year Theofanis et al. (2007) were the first to present an optimization based GAs heuristic for the DDBSP. The proposed resolution algorithm could be applied to any linear formulation of the BSP (i.e. different berth scheduling policies). The authors applied the GAs based heuristic proposed by Golias (2007) and followed the same representation to Nishimura et al. (2001), but differentiated the genetic operations using four different types of mutation (presented by Eiben and Smith, 2003) without applying crossover. This approach was justified by the large number of infeasible solutions that crossover operations produce and the increase in CPU time that would be required to deal with this issue. The authors also used the objective function value as the fitness function and the roulette wheel selection algorithms (Goldberg, 1989). Similar to the research presented so far, the proposed heuristic was only compared to the GAs heuristic without the optimization component, and results showed that the former outperformed the later in terms of variance and minimum values of the objective function, especially as the problem size increased. The increase in computational time due to the optimization component was negligible.

Imai et al. (2008) extended their previous work and presented a formulation for the DDBSP where ships which would normally be served at a terminal but their expected wait time exceeds a time limit are assigned to an external terminal. Similar to their previous work, the GAs based heuristic proposed as a resolution approach used the fitness function proposed by Kim and Kim (1996), a two-point crossover and a tournament process proposed by Ahuja et al. (2000). The proposed heuristic was not evaluated in terms of obtaining optimality, as it was the case with their previous published work. In the same year, Boile et al. (2008) proposed a 2-opt based heuristic for the DDBSP where the GAs heuristic proposed in Golias (2007) was used to reduce the computational time required. Finally, in 2008, Hansen et al. (2008) presented a new berth scheduling policy for the DDBSP and proposed a variable neighborhood search heuristic as the resolution approach. The proposed heuristic was compared to the GAs heuristic by Nishimura et al. (2001), Multi-Start Algorthm, and a Memetic Search algorithm. The latter was an extension of the GAs heuristic with local Variable Neighborhood Descent search instead of mutation. Results showed that their proposed heuristic outperformed the latter three.

In 2009, Golias et al. (2009a) were the first to formulate and solve the DDBSP as a multi-objective combinatorial optimization problem. A GAs based heuristic was developed to solve the resulting problem. Results showed that the proposed resolution algorithm outperformed a state of the art metaheuristic and provided improved results when compared to the weighted approach. The authors used the same chromosomal representation, reproduction, and selection as in Golias (2007) but used a different fitness function equal to the difference of the maximum objective function among all the chromosomes and the objective function value of the chromosome. Similar to Boile et al. (2008), Golias et al. (2009b) used the GAs heuristic in Golias (2007) as an internal heuristic to an adaptive time window partitioning based algorithm for the DDBSP. In the same year Golias et al. (2009c) presented a new formulation for the DDBSP where vessel arrival times are optimized in order to accommodate an environmentally friendly berth scheduling policy and increase the opportunities for vessel berthing upon arrival. The problem was formulated as a bi-level optimization model and a stochastic GAs based heuristic was proposed as the resolution algorithm. The same year Theofanis et al. (2009b), solved the same problem but as a multi-objective optimization problem using a variant of the GAs heuristic presented in Golias et al. (2009c). Finally, Saharidis et al. (2009) presented a concrete methodology on the bi-level multi-objective DDBSP and proposed an innovative GAs based heuristic that followed the example of the k-best algorithm (Bialas and Karwan, 1978, 1984).

2.2 Berth and Quay Crane scheduling

The goal of studying the QC scheduling problem is to determine the sequence of discharging and loading operations that quay cranes will perform so that the completion time of a vessel operation is minimized. This problem assumes that a berth schedule has already been provided. In practice though, the BSP is mainly affected by the vessel handling times which are dependent on three key parameters: a) the distance between the berthing position of the vessel and the storage area allocated to the containers to be unloaded from/ loaded onboard the vessel, b) the number of QCs assigned to the vessel, and c) the number of internal transport vehicles (ITVs) assigned to the vessels' quay cranes. For example, the further away a vessel is berthed from its assigned storage yard area, the largest the distance that the ITVs will travel between the QCs serving the vessel and the storage yard, increasing the ITVs turnaround time. If the number of ITVs assigned is not adequate this may result in QC idle time. Proximity of the vessel's berth location to its assigned yard area would potentially reduce the number of ITVs required. In another instance, when the number of ITVs assigned to a vessel is fairly large, a different case may occur, in which ITVs may remain idle waiting to be served by a QC. These simple examples indicate that there is a need to simultaneously optimize vessel berthing with QC and ITV assignments to achieve better seaside operation efficiencies. We refer to Steenken et al. (2004) and Mastrogiannidou et al. (2008) for more details. To our knowledge, the complex relationship between the vessel handling time and these parameters (i.e. number of QCs and ITVs assigned to a vessel, and the vessels' preferred storage yard location and berth allocation) has not been addressed in the literature.

Some researchers have attempted to formulate and solve the combination of the quay crane and berth scheduling problem. There is no unique objective for optimization when dealing with the QSP or the BQSP. Minimization of the sum of the delays of all vessels; maximization of one vessel's performance; or a well-balanced or economic utilization of the cranes, are some indicative objectives. The most general case of the QSP or the BQSP is the case in which ships arrive at different times at the port and wait for berthing space if all berths are occupied. The objective in this case is to serve all the ships while minimizing their total delay. Crane to ship allocation has to reflect several constraints like technical limitations and the accessibility of cranes at various berths. Crane split allocates a respective number of cranes to a ship and its bays/sections (on hold and deck) and decides on which schedule the bays have to be operated. The QSP or the BQSP problem can be considered as a machine-scheduling or project-scheduling problem (Peterkofsky & Daganzo, 1990), usually formulated as a MIP, either studied independent from the other processes or as part of the berth planning, container allocation to the yard and vehicle dispatching. One of the decisions that have to be made is the exact number of QCs that work simultaneously on one ship to minimize vessel delays. Decisions at the operational level (which crane loads which container onboard the vessel and which container should be taken out of the hold first) are in practice determined by the vessel loading and unloading plan and are typically followed by the crane operator. Figure 2 shows graphical representations of BQSP and QSP problems.

Very few papers applied GAs based heuristics as resolution approaches to the QSP or the BQSP. Interest in using this type of heuristics began in 2006 and based on the number of publications, is increasing ever since. In 2006, Lee et al. (2006) presented a bi-level formulation of the BQSP where the upper level schedules the vessels and the lower level schedules the quay cranes. In the upper level the total service time for all the vessels is minimized, while the lower level minimizes the total makespan of all the vessels and the

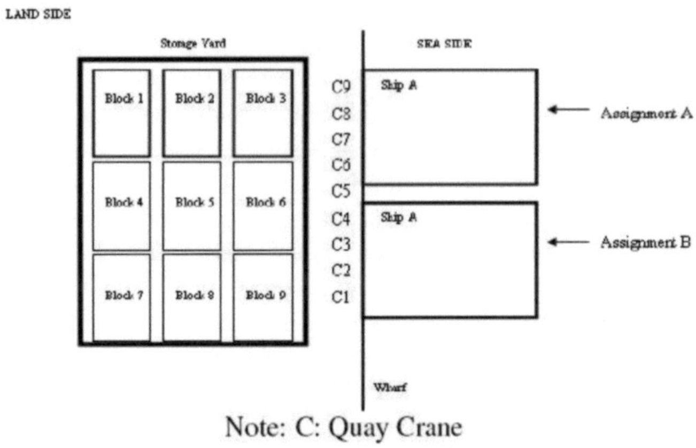

Source: Golias et al. (2007)
Fig. 2a. Berth and Quay Crane Scheduling Problem (BQSP)

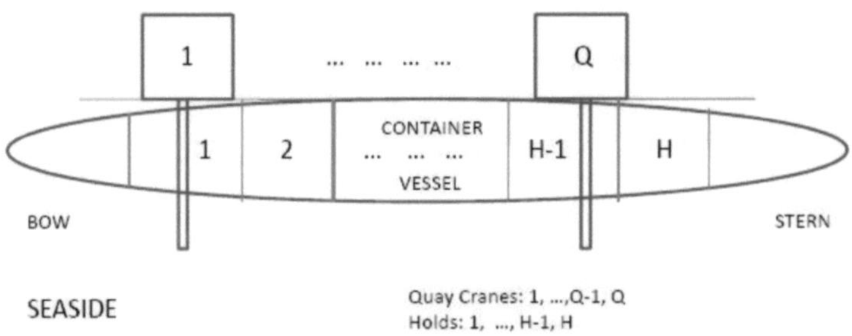

Source: Adapted from Lee et al. (2008)
Fig. 2b. Quay Crane Scheduling Problem (QSP)

Fig. 2. BQSP and QSP Illustrative Examples

completion time of all the QCs. A GAs based heuristic with a similar representation to the one by Nishimura et al. (2001) is used to solve the upper level problem, while LINDO is used to solve the lower level problem. The authors adopt order-based crossover and mutation for the genetic operations, a fitness function equal to the objective function of the upper level problem, while the selection process is confined in the 100 best chromosomes. Computational examples where very limited and no conclusion could be drawn for the efficiency of the heuristic. The following year, Theofanis et al. (2007) and Golias et al. (2007) formulated the BQSP as an integer programming model with the objective to minimize costs resulting from the vessels delayed departures and inadequate berth productivity service levels. These models simultaneously assign quay cranes and dynamically allocate vessels along a wharf, assuming that the handling time of each vessel is a function of the number of cranes assigned and the location along the wharf, and include wharf length constraints. Rectangular chromosome GA based heuristic and tabu mutation based heuristic procedures were developed to solve the resulting problem. The fitness function was set equal to the objective function of each chromosome, while no crossover was performed. The roulette wheel selection routine was used to select the new generations. As in Lee et al. (2006), the computational examples performed to evaluate the proposed heuristic were not substantial to produce robust conclusions on the efficiency of the GAs heuristic.

Imai et al. (2008) introduced a formulation for the simultaneous berth and crane allocation problem with the objective to minimize the total vessel service time. A GAs based heuristic was employed to find an approximate solution to the berth scheduling problem without consideration of the QCs. The QC assignment was performed by a maximum flow problem-based algorithm. The proposed GAs heuristic was very interesting as the chromosomes only produced the vessel-to-berth service order and before reproduction, crane scheduling was performed. A two-point crossover was used for reproduction, and selection was based on the fitness function presented in Nishimura et al. (2001). Based on trend analysis of the results of numerical experiments, the authors concluded that the proposed heuristic is applicable to solve the problem.

Lee et al. (2008a) and Lee et al. (2008b) studied the QSP with and without vesssel priority in order to determine a handling sequence of holds for quay cranes assigned to a container vessel considering interference between quay cranes with the objective of minimizing the vessel completion time. The GAs based heuristic proposed in both papers as the resolution algorithm had very similar chromosome representation to the one presented in the berth scheduling problem by several researchers. The fitness value was set equal to the reciprocal of the objective function value and the roulette wheel selection routine was applied as the selection algorithm. Order crossover and swap mutation were adopted for reproduction of new chromosomes. CPLEX was used to obtain lower bounds of an exact solution to a relaxed formulation of the same problem and computational examples showed that the proposed heuristic produces near-optimal results. Liang et al. (2009) studied the BQSP with the objective to minimize service time and delays for all the vessels. A GAs based heuristic was proposed with a three layer chromosome. The first layer provided vessel priority, the second the berth to vessel assignment and the third the assignment of QCs to the vessels. One-cut point crossover and swap mutation where applied to reproduce future generations of chromosomes.

Finally, Tavakkoli-Moghaddam et al. (2009) presented possibly the most interesting QSP formulation capturing a very practical container terminal operators policy (also described in Golias 2007) of maximizing premiums from early departures and minimizing costs from late departures and variable vessel handling cost. In the proposed GA, a chromosome consisted of a rectangular matrix, different from the one in Theofanis et al. (2007). The authors proposed a heuristic approach to initial the chromosome, while arithmetic and extended patch crossover were used as reproduction operations. The authors use swap mutation to retain diversity in the solutions as the GAs heuristic proceeds and similar to other research they use the roullete wheel selection technique to sample future generations, based on a semi-greedy strategy. The fitness value is derived directly from the values of the objective function of each chromosome. Computational results showed that the proposed resolution algorithm produces results with reasonable gaps as compared to the optimal solutions found using an exact resolution algorithm within reasonable computational time.

3. Resolution algorithms details

This section of the Chapter attempts to summarize the different chromosome representations, genetic operations, and fitness function selection techniques presented in the published scientific research. From the presented literature it is obvious that the papers by Go and Lim (2000) and Nishimura et al. (2001) initiated the use of GAs based heuristics as resolution algorithms for seaside related operational problems at marine container terminals. In general GAs based heuristics consist mainly of four parts: a) the chromosomal representation, b) the reproduction operations, c) the fitness function evaluation and d) the selection process. In the following subsections we discuss in depth f each one of the four components.

3.1 Representation

For scheduling problems (like the BSP, the QSP, and the BQSP) integer chromosomal representation is more efficient, since the classical binary representation can obscure the nature of the search. Most of the papers presented to date dealing with the BSP and the QSP used an integer chromosomal representation to exploit the characteristics of the problem. An illustration of the typical chromosome structure for the BSP and QSP is given in figure 3 for a small instance of the problem with 6 vessels and 2 berths. As seen in figure 3a the chromosome has twelve cells. The first 6 cells represent the 6 possible service orders at berth1 and the last 6 cells the 6 possible service orders at berth 2. In the assignment illustrated in figure 3a vessels 2, 4, and 5 are served at berth 1 as the first, second and third vessel respectively, while vessels 1, 3, and 6 are served at berth 2 as the first, second, and third vessel respectively. Fig. 3b shows a somewhat typical chromosomal representation for the QSP where there are two QCs. The first QC will work on holds 1, 3, 6, and 7 (in this order) and the second QC will work on holds 8, 9, 12, and 10 (in this order). This representation has the advantage of including QC interference constraints in a natural way.

Berth	1						2					
Vessel	2	4	5	0	0	0	1	3	6	0	0	0

Source: Golias et al. (2009a)

Fig. 3a. Chromosome Representation for the BSP

Quay Crane	QC 1				QC 2			
Hold	1	3	6	7	8	9	12	10
Sequence	1	2	3	4	1	2	3	4

Fig. 3b. Chromosome Representation for the QSP

Fig. 3. Illustration of Chromosomal Representations for the BSP and the QSP

For the BQSP we cannot claim that there is a typical chromosome representation, as the number of publications that have appeared is rather small (as compared to the BSP). Some authors used a variation of the chromosome representation shown in figure 3. In figure 4 we show the two representations found in the literature that deviate from the one string representation shown in figure 3. The chromosome on the left of figure 4 consist of a rectangular matrix with (V x (A + 1)) genes, where V and A represent number of vessels and the greatest number of jobs on the vessels, respectively. In each column for each vessel, the first gene represents the number of QCs assigned to that vessel. The rows in the chromosome represent the number of QCs assigned to vessels. The chromosome on the right of figure 4 also consists of a rectangular matrix with (QxT) cells where Q and T represent the total number of Quay Cranes and T is the total planning period. In this chromosome vessel 1 is serviced by quay cranes 1 through 3, starts service at the beginning of the planning horizon, finishing service 3 hours later. Cells with zero value indicate that no vessel is serviced at that time.

V_1	V_2	V_3
2	3	1
2	4	3
1	2	1
7	1	2
4	5	4
6	6	5
3	3	0
5	0	0
0	0	0
0	0	0

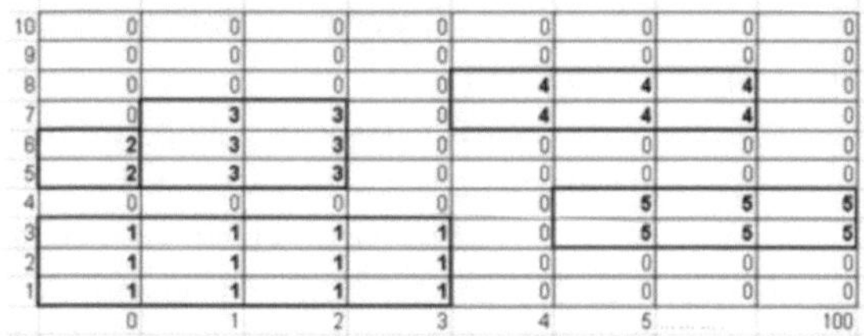

Source: Tavakkoli-Moghaddam et al. (2009) Source: Golias et al. (2007)

Fig. 4. Illustration of Chromosomal Represenations for BQSP

3.2 Reproduction

GAs reproduction operations can be distinguished into two broad categories: a) crossover, and b) mutation. Crossover is explorative; it makes a big jump to an area somewhere "in between" two parent areas. On the other hand, mutation is exploitative; it creates random diversions of a single parent. There is a debate on the use of crossover and mutation and which approach is the best to use. In fact, the performance of either mutation or crossover is highly affected by the problems' domain. In the reviewed literature most of the researchers applied both differernt types of crossover and mutation with the exception of a few papers that claimed that at each generation the crossover operation will generate a large number of infeasible children. The latter chose to apply more complex mutation and did not include crossover operations. Unfortunately, no experimental results have been presented to direct research to the use of either one approach. It is worthnoting though that crossover operations, where applied, usually implemented simple crossover techniques and where dominated by the one or two point crossover reproduction technique (fig. 5).

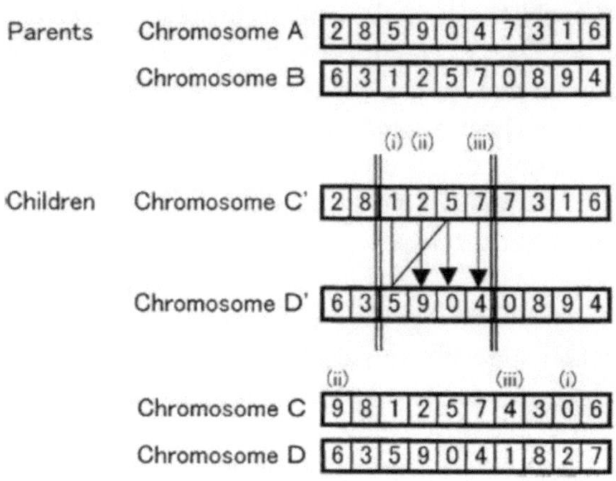

Source: Nishimura et al. (2001)

Fig. 5. Schematic Representation of the Crossover Operations

Figure 6 shows the main four different types of mutation that were identified during the literature review. Each of the four types of mutations has its own characteristics, in terms of preserving the order and adjacency information. Insert mutation picks two cells at random and moves the second one to follow the first, thus preserving most of the order and adjacency information. Inverse mutation picks two cells at random and then inverts the substring between them preserving most adjacency information (only breaks two links), but disrupting the order information. Swap mutation picks two cells from a chromosome and swaps their positions preserving most of the adjacency information but disrupting the order. Finally, scramble mutation scrambles the position of a subset of cells of the chromosome. Each of the four types of mutations has its own characteristics in terms of preserving the order and adjacency information (Eiden and Smith, 2003).

INSERT Mutation

	Berth	1						2					
Before	Vessel	2	4	5	0	0	0	1	3	6	0	0	0
After	Vessel	2	3	4	5	0	0	1	6	0	0	0	0

SCRAMBLE Mutation

	Berth	1						2					
Before	Vessel	2	4	5	0	0	0	1	3	6	0	0	0
After	Vessel	4	3	1	0	0	0	6	5	2	0	0	0

Swap Mutation

	Berth	1						2					
Before	Vessel	2	4	5	0	0	0	1	3	6	0	0	0
After	Vessel	3	4	5	0	0	0	1	2	6	0	0	0

INVERT Mutation

	Berth	1						2					
Before	Vessel	2	4	5	0	0	0	1	3	6	0	0	0
After	Vessel	5	4	2	0	0	0	6	3	1	0	0	0

Source: Boile et al. (2008)

Fig. 6. Schematic Representation of the Mutation Operations

3.3 Fitness function and evaluation

Fitness evaluation and selection refers to the evaluation of the strength of each chromosome and the selection of the next generation based on the fitness. Usually, the BSP, the QSP, and BQSP are minimization problems; thus the smaller the objective function value is, the higher the fitness value must be. The best solutions are likely to have an extremely good fitness value among solutions obtained, where there is no significant difference between them in the objective function value. The most common fitness functions found in the literature were the reciprocal of the actual objective function (Nishimura et al., 2001), or the actual value of the objective function. Unfortunately, no experimental results exist to justify or suggest the use of one fitness function over the other.

3.4 Selection

Although several selection algorithms exist in the literature (Taboada, 2007), the most common one found to be implemented in almost all the literature reviewed is the so-called roulette wheel selection (Goldberg, 1989). This selection approach has the benefit of combining elitism (by selecting the best chromosome from each generation) and a semi-greedy strategy (when solutions of lower fitness are included), which has shown to reduce the computational time of the genetic algorithms performance (Tavakkoli-Moghaddam et al., 2009).

3.5 General guidelines of GAs implementation

From the literature presented in the second section of this Chapter it becomes apparent that GAs have been shown to be very efficient and effective in scheduling problems that arise at the seaside operations of a container terminal. As most of these problems are NP-hard or NP-complete, GAs have the advantage of flexibility over other more traditional search techniques as they impose no requirement for a problem to be formulated in a particular way, and there is no needfor the objective function to be differentiable, continuous, linear, separable, or of any particular data-type. They can be applied to any problem (e.g. single or multi-objective, single or multi-level, linear or non-linear etc) for which there is a way to encode and compute the quality of a solution to the problem. This flexibility provides GAs with an important advantage over traditional optimization techniques. Using the latter techniques, the problem at hand is usually simplified to fit the requirements of the chosen search method, whereas GAs do not make any simplification of the problems' original form and produce solutions that describe the system as is. To that extend we can observe that the reproduction and evaluation techniques, as well as the fitness functions, presented to date are very simplistic, and can be easily tranferable to different objectives for the same problem, i.e. the GAs heuristic presented in Nishimura et al. (2001) has been used as a resolution algorithm to accomodate a large number of different berth scheduling policies (Imai et al., 2003; Imai et al., 2007 etc).

To this end we would like to emphasize that as the need to tackle real world applications increases, multi-objective problem formulations tend to be more suitable. GAs have been the main a posteriori methods adopted for solving multi-objective optimization problems and generating the set of Pareto optimal solutions from which a decision maker will decide upon the best solution. Although, very few papers have been presented in the literature with multi-objective formulations of seaside operations policies, the trend towards adoption of this modeling approach seems more likely in the near future, which will lead to an increasing use of GAs based heuristics as resolution approaches.

An additional advantage, that will increase the popularity of GAs as resolution algorithms in container terminal operations, is the recent focus of researchers to the use of hybrid GAs combining exact resolution algorithms (e.g. branch and bound), local search (i.e. Memetic Algorithms), and/or other (meta)heuristics (e.g. tabu search) to guarantee at least local optimality of the solution (single or Pareto set) or improve the convergence patterns.

Despite these advantages the GAs based heuristics presented to date suffer from two main weaknesses: a) optimality guarantees of the final solution, and b) the selection of a direction during the search to avoid trapping the algorithm at local optimal/feasible locations of the solution space. Very few researchers tried so far to combine local search heuristics or other (meta)heuristics to guide the search of the feasible space and even fewer applied exact resolution algorithms, within the GAs to provide guarantees of optimality of the final solution. It is the authors' opinion that this is an area that will attract more attention in the future, as we will move from ad-hoc search of the feasible space to a more guided search.

In addition, most of the GAs presented for the seaside operations take full advantage of the special characteristics of the problem in the representation phase of the GA only in the case of the BSP, and lack in the representation phase of the QSP and the BQSP. Furthermore, for all three problems the GAs presetned to date lack in the design of sophisticated reproduction techniques, as they rely on existing methodologies (e.g. simple swap and instert techniques). Several methods that can be used and enhance the search procedure in the reproduction phase including optimization or problem based heuristic techniques, such as valid inequalities or tabu mutation, have yet to be presented. The same remark applies to the limited fitness functions and evaluation techniques presented to date,where a very interesting research direction would be the use of Game Theoretical Equilibrium techniques, especially in the cases of multi-objective problems.

As a final comment, we would like to note that to date there are rather few research groups focusing on using GAs to solve container terminal seaside operational problems and consequently there are rather limited research results published (i.e. Boile et al. 2008; Imai et al., 2001, 2003, 2007, 2008; Golias et al., 2007, 2009a, 2009b, 2009c; Lee et al. 2006, 2008a, 2008b; Theofanis et al. 2007, 2009a, 2009b), a fact which might explain the limited variety of chromosomal represenations, reproduction operations and fitness functions. As more researchers are becoming interested in marine container terminal operations and as we look into the near future, we see that there is potential for more investigation as to the effects of new reproduction and fitness selection schemes as well as into the application of multi-dimensional chromosomal representations for the BQSP that will better capture and represent the problem at hand.

4. Conclusions

In this Chapter we presented a critical, up-to-date, literature review of existing research efforts relating to the application of GAs based heuristics as resolution algorithms to three operational problems of seaside operations at marine container terminals: the BSP, the QSP, and the BQSP. We presented the different chromosome representations, genetic operations, and fitness function selection techniques in the published scientific research and provided an analysis of how these components can be improved to address two main "weak spots" of GAs based heuristics: a) the lack of optimality criteria of the final solution, and b) the relatively poor exploitation of the special characteristics of the physical problem and how to construct improved approximations of the feasible search space. From the existing literature it became apparent that the future of GAs based heuristic as resolution algorithms to marine container terminal seaside operational problems is quite promising, especially if the GAs will be combined with exact resolution, heuristic or local search algorithms. Although we have yet to see how these research directions will be tackled, even in problems outside this research area, the future looks certainly very exciting and it is expected that more researchers will dwell into this field of research.

5. References

Boile. M.; Theofanis S. & Golias M.M. (2008) A 2-opt based heuristic for the minimum service and minimum weighted service time berth allocation problem. *Proceedings of 10th International Conference on Applications of Advanced Technologies in Transportation*. Greece, May 2008, NTUA, Athens.

Brown, G.G.; Cormican, K.J.; Lawphongpanich, S. & Widdis, D.B. (1997) Optimizing submarine berthing with a persistence incentive. *Naval Research Logistics*. Vol. 44; pp. 301–318.

Ahuja, R.K.; Orlin, J.B. & Tiwari, A. (2000). A greedy genetic algorithm for the quadratic assignment problem. *Computers and Operations Research* Vol. 27; pp. 917–934.

Bialas, F.W. & Karwan H.M. (1978) *Multilevel linear programming*. Technical Report 78-1, State University of New York at Buffalo. Operations Research Program.

Bialas, F.W. & Karwan H.M. (1984) Two-level linear programming. *Management Science*. Vol. 30; No. 8; pp. 1004-1020.

Bierwirth C. & Meisel F. (2009a) A survey of berth allocation and quay crane scheduling problems in container terminals. *European Journal of Operational Research*. DOI:10.1016/j.ejor.2009.05.031

Eiben A.E. & Smith, J.E. (2003). *Introduction to Evolutionary Computing*. Springer-Verlag, Berlin, Germany.

Go, K-S. & Lim, A. (2000) Combining various algorithms to solve the ship berthing problem. *Proceedings of 12th IEEE International Conference on Tools with Artificial Intelligence*, November 2000, ISBN 0-7695-0909-6, Vancouver, British Columbia, IEEE Computer Society

Goh, C-K.; Ong, Y-S. & Tan, K.C. (2009) *Multi-Objective Memetic Algorithms*. Studies in Computational Intelligence. Springer, ISBN: 978-3-540-88050-9, USA.

Goldberg, D.E. (1989). *Genetic algorithms in search, optimization, and machine-learning*. Reading, MA: Addison-Wesley.

Golias, M.M. (2007) T*he Discrete and Continuous Berth Allocation Problem: Models and Algorithms*. Ph.D. Dissertation. Rutgers University, New Jersey, 2007.

Golias, M.M.; Theofanis, S. & Boile, M. (2007) Berth and quay crane scheduling a formulation reflecting start and finish of service deadlines and productivity agreements. Proceedings *of 2nd Annual National Urban Freight Conference*, CA, December 2007, METRANS, Long Beach.

Golias M.M.; Boile M. & Theofanis S. (2009a) Service time based customer differentiation berth scheduling. *Transportation Research Part E*. DOI: 10.1016/j.tre.2009.05.006

Golias, M.M.; Boile, M. & Theofanis, S. (2009b) An adaptive time window partitioning based algorithm for the discrete and dynamic berth scheduling problem. *Transportation Research Record* (Forthcoming)

Golias, M.M.; Theofanis, S. & Boile, M. (2009c) A bi-level formulation for the berth scheduling problem with variable vessel release dates to reduce port emissions. *Proceedings of 2009 International Conference on Shipping, Port, Logistics Management*, Inha University, Korea, April 2009, ISLC, Incheon.

Han, M.; Ping, L. & Sun, J. The algorithm for berth scheduling problem by the Hybrid Optimization Strategy GASA. *Proceedings of the 9th International Conference on Control, Automation, Robotics and Vision*, Singapore, December 2006, IEEE, Singapore.

Imai, A.; Chen, H.C.; Nishimura, E. & Papadimitriou S. (2008) The simultaneous berth and quay crane allocation problem. *Transportation Research Part E*, Vol. 44; No 5; pp. 900-920.

Imai, A.; Nishimura, E. & Papadimitriou, S. (2003) Berth allocation with service priority. *Transportation Research Part B*, Vol. 37; pp. 437-457.

Imai, A.; Nishimura, E. & Papadimitriou, S. (2001) The dynamic berth allocation problem for a container port. *Transportation Research Part B*, Vol. 35; pp. 401-417

Imai, A.; Zhang, J-T.; Nishimura, E. & Papadimitriou, S. (2007) The Berth Allocation Problem with Service Time and Delay Time Objectives, Maritime Economics & Logistics, Vol. 9; pp. 269–290.

Imai, A.; Nagaiwa, K. & Tat, C-W. (2001) Efficient Planning of Berth Allocation for Container Terminals in Asia. *Journal of Advanced Transportation*, Vol. 31; 1997, pp. 75–94.

Kim, J.-U. & Kim, Y.-D.; (1996). Simulated annealing and genetic algorithms for scheduling products with multi-level product structure. *Computers and Operations Research*, Vol. 23; pp. 857–868.

Lee, D-H.; Song, L. & Wang, H. (2006) A Genetic Algorithm for a Bi-level Programming Model of Berth Allocation and Quay Crane Scheduling. *Proceedings of the 85th Annual Meeting of the Transportation Research Board*, Washington, D.C., January 2006, TRB, Washington D.C.

Lee, D-H.; Wang, H.Q. & Miao L. (2008a) Quay crane scheduling with handling priority in port container terminals. Engineering *Optimization*, Vol. 40; No. 2; pp. 179-189.

Lee, D-H.; Wang, H.Q. & Miao L. (2008b) Quay crane scheduling with non-interference constraints in port container terminals. *Transportation Research Part E*, Vol. 44; pp. 124-135.

Liang C.; Huang Y. & Yang Y. (2009) A quay crane dynamic scheduling problem by hybrid evolutionary algorithm for berth allocation planning. Computers and Industrial Engineering, Vol. 56, pp. 1021-1028

Mastrogiannidou, C.; Theofanis, S.; Ziliaskopoulos, A. & Boile, M. (2008) Intraterminal transport problem: system description, literature review, and research recommendations. *Proceedings of the 87th Annual Meeting of the Transportation Research Board*, Washington, D.C., January 2008, TRB, Washington D.C.

Meersmans, P.J.M. & Dekker, R. (2001). Operations research supports container handling. *Econometric Institute Report 234*, Erasmus University Rotterdam.

Peterkofsky, R.I; & Daganzo, C.F. (1990) A branch and bound solution method for the crane scheduling problem, *Transportation Research Part B*, Vol. 24; pp.159–172.

Pinedo, M. *Scheduling: Theory, Algorithms, and Systems*. Third Edition, Springer, New York, 2008

Saharidis G.K.D.; Golias M.M.; Boile M.; Theofanis S. & Ierapetritou M. (2009) The berth scheduling problem with customer differentiation: A new methodological approach based on hierarchical optimization. *International Journal of Advanced Manufacturing Technology*. (Forthcoming)

Stahlbock, R. & Voß, S. (2008). Operations research at container terminals: a literature update. *OR Spectrum*, Vol. 30; No. 1, pp. 1–52.

Tavakkoli-Moghaddam , R.; Makui, A.; Salahi, S.; Bazzazi, M. & Taheri F. (2009) An efficient algorithm for solving a new mathematical model for a quay crane scheduling problem in container ports. *Computers and Industrial Engineering*, Vol. 56; pp. 241-248.

Theofanis, S.; Boile, M. & Golias, M.M. (2007) An optimization based genetic algorithm heuristic for the berth allocation problem. *Proceedings of the IEEE Conference on Evolutionary Computation*, Singapore, September 2007, IEEE, Singapore.

Theofanis S.; Boile M. & Golias M.M (2009a) Container terminal berth planning: critical review of research approaches and practical challenges. *Transportation Research Record* (Forthcoming)

Theofanis S.; Golias, M.M. & Boile M. (2009b) A multi-objective berth scheduling policy to optimize vessel fuel consumption and schedule integrity. *Proceedings of International Transport Economics Conference*, Minnesota, June 2009, ITEC, Minneapolis.

Vacca, I.; Bierlaire, M. & Salani, M. (2007). Optimization at container terminals: Status, trends and perspectives. *Proceedings of the Swiss Transport Research Conference*, Ascona, September 2007, STRC, Switzerland.

Vis, I.F.A. & de Koster, R. (2003). Transshipment of containers at a container terminal: an overview. *European Journal of Operational Research*, Vol. 147, No. 1, pp. 1–16.

Zhou, P.; Kang, H. & Lin L. (2006). A dynamic berth allocation model based on stochastic consideration. *Proceedings of the 6th World Congress on Intelligent Control and Automation*, Dalian, June 2006, IEEE, China.

5

Optimization of Oscillation Parameters in Continuous Casting Process of Steel Manufacturing: Genetic Algorithms versus Differential Evolution

Arya K. Bhattacharya and Debjani Sambasivam
Automation Division, Tata Steel
India

1. Introduction

Continuous casting is a critical step in the steel manufacturing process where molten metal is solidified in the form of slabs of rectangular cross-section. Minor variations in this step can impact the production process widely – from excellent product quality to breakdown in the production chain.

In continuous casting the liquid steel from a ladle is first poured into a buffer vessel called a *tundish*, from where it flows continuously through a bifurcated submerged entry nozzle into a water-cooled copper mould. This mould is about a meter in length; with sectional width about one-and-half meters and thickness about two hundred millimeters. Water is circulated through pipes embedded in the mould walls to extract heat from the liquid steel. Consequently, a thin solidified steel shell develops next to the mould inner walls while inside this shell the steel remains liquid. The shell grows in thickness internally even as it is continuously withdrawn from the mould on rollers and further cooled using water sprays. Finally, the completely solidified slab of required length is cut from the continuously cast 'strand'. The schematic representation of continuous casting is shown in fig 1, see also (World Steel University, 2009).

The continuous casting process itself is facilitated by two interlinked sub-processes, namely, mold oscillation and lubricant addition. These essentially seek to neutralize two major and intrinsic problems associated with continuous casting – sticking of the formative steel shell to the internal walls of the mould, and non-uniform development of shell across the strand perimeter due to uneven heat transfer.

The mold is made to oscillate along its longitudinal axis with an amplitude less than 10 mm and frequency between 50 and 250 cycles per minute (cpm). The oscillation directly helps in detaching the solidified shell from the mould wall (like a mild AC current 'disengages' a human finger coming in touch with a live wire), and indirectly enables the lubricant placed at the meniscus of the strand to penetrate uniformly further down into the small gap between the shell and mould.

Lubricant in the form of solid powder is poured from the top onto the meniscus where it melts in contact with the hot material. The liquid 'lubricant' then penetrates into the gap between strand and mould. Both upward and downward movements in the oscillation cycle enable this penetration. Since the strand inside the mould is always moving downwards with a certain speed (the 'casting speed'), in relative terms the mold moves downward only when its downward speed is greater than strand speed. This part of the oscillation cycle is referred to as "negative strip" while its supplement is "positive strip". While negative strip aids in deeper penetration of lubricant, the positive strip pulls the lubricant from meniscus top towards the sides and also enables uniformity of spread within this gap. Since the lubricant is the intervening medium through which the heat flows from the shell to the mould, its uniform penetration in this gap is vital to the consistency of heat transfer across the shell perimeter, the absence of which create irregularities in the shell that persist all the way down to the rolled sheet.

Neutralization of the prime problems of continuous casting using mould oscillations leaves certain side effects. These are, firstly, the formation of 'oscillation marks' on the slab surface during negative strip (Thomas, 2002) that look like cracks. Apart from being a quality issue in itself, these marks also tend to degenerate into fault lines for the formation of transverse cracks. Secondly, during the positive strip the relative speed between strand and mould maximizes leading to a 'peak friction' which is higher than what would have been under non-oscillating conditions. This peak friction can potentially cause tearing of the formative shell near the meniscus, leading to sticking. Thus it is apparent that the designer of oscillation strategies has to plan for maximizing the desirable effects, while minimizing the undesirable ones.

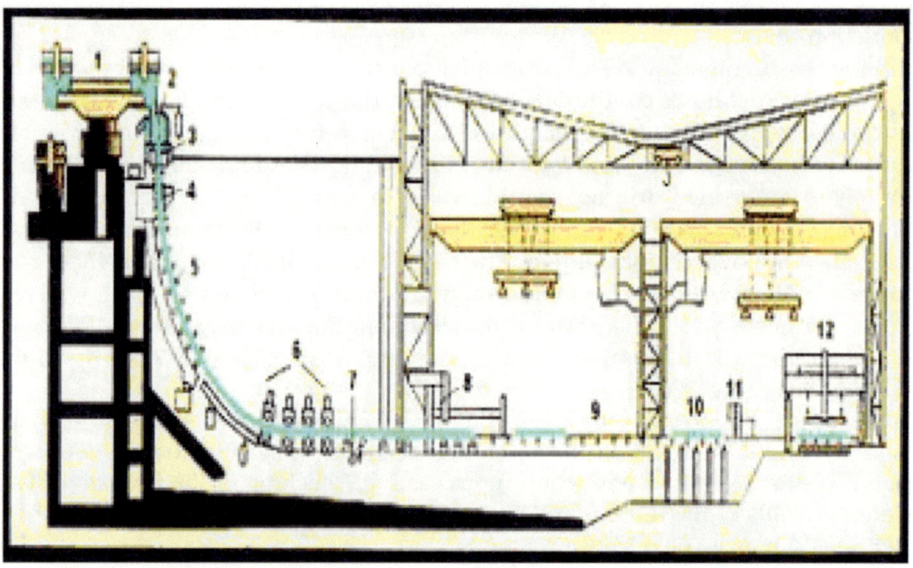

Fig. 1. Slab caster machine configuration: (1) Ladle Turret, (2) Tundish/Tundish Car, (3) Mould, (4) First Zone (Secondary Cooling), (5) Strand Guide (plus Secondary Cooling), (6) Straightener Withdrawal Units, (7) Dummy bar disconnect roll, (8) Torch cut-off unit - to generate discrete slabs from continuous strand.

The oscillation designer does not have too many degrees of freedom with him for effecting an optimization as above. Only the oscillation frequency f and amplitude a or s (stroke; $s = 2a$) are available. Suzuki and others (Suzuki et al., 1991) showed that the waveform could also be varied from the sinusoidal towards the saw-tooth form with gainful effects. Slower speed and longer time for upward movement, accompanied by faster and shorter downward plunge, as shown in fig. 2., will result in smaller negative strip time (time spent in negative strip within one cycle) as well as lower peak friction. The depth and transverse spread of oscillation marks vary directly with negative strip time. Reduction in negative strip time is illustrated in fig. 3, while the reduction in peak friction with lower upward maximum speed follows simply from the reduction of peak relative speed between strand and mold in the oscillation cycle. Using τ (=0.5 for sinusoidal and $0.5 < \tau < 1$ for gainful nonsinusoidal) to indicate degree of variation from sinusoid, the designer now has s, f and τ as free parameters. He has to select an optimum schedule of these parameters across the range of casting speed v to achieve maximum lubrication with minimum peak friction and oscillation mark depth. The quality and productivity of steel making depends significantly on this choice.

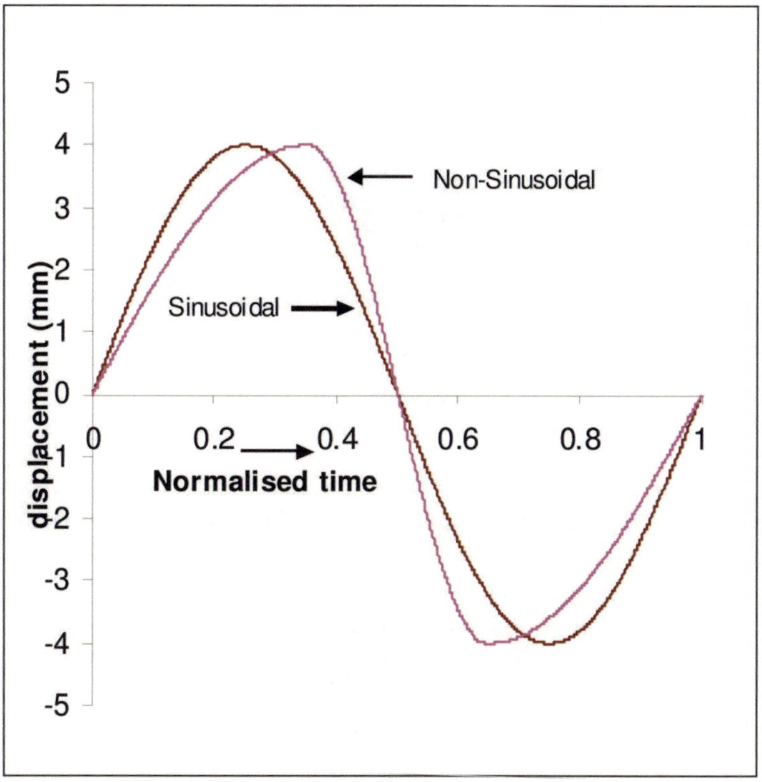

Fig. 2. Variation of mold displacement in an oscillation cycle – sinusoidal versus non-sinusoidal wave pattern

Designing an oscillation parameter schedule to maximize the beneficial effects and minimize the undesirable ones relates to the designer's interpretation of the relationship between the free parameters and their consequential effects. This interpretation is largely heuristic, particularly in the case of the dependency of lubrication on parameters s, f and τ. This may be seen in the internal reports of supplier organizations of continuous casting equipment, who also provide optimum oscillation schedules for their casters. In this chapter an attempt is made to express the relationship between oscillation free parameters and their consequential effects within an explicit mathematical framework. This framework is used to generate cost functions that drive evolutionary algorithms towards optimal values of s, f and τ that maximize lubrication and minimize depth of oscillation marks and peak friction, for every single discrete value of casting speed within operating range.

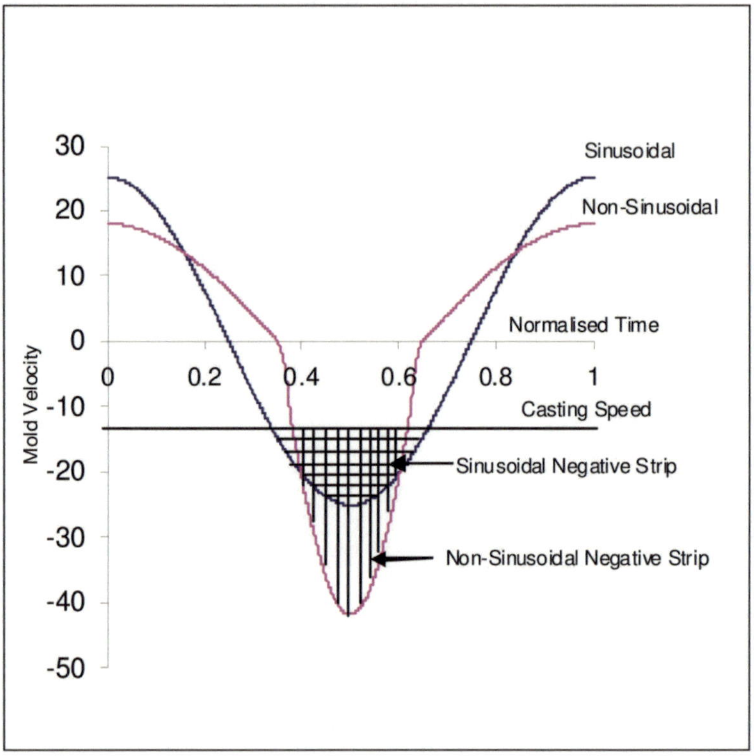

Fig. 3. Mold velocity and negative strip time in an oscillation cycle, under sinusoidal and non-sinusoidal waveforms.

Evolutionary Algorithms offer a choice of approaches, and in this study two different approaches are followed and mutually compared. These are Genetic Algorithms (Goldberg, 1989) and the Differential Evolution approach (Storn & Price, 1995). The object of investigation is twofold - to see if they both yield exactly the same solution across the range of casting speeds, and to compare their efficiencies in terms of computation times and convergence characteristics.

In principle this problem lies within the domain of multi-objective evolutionary optimization, for which different solution approaches such as (Horn et al., 1994; Deb et al., 2002) lead to a pareto-optimal surface of non-dominated solutions for every discrete casting speed. The utility of such a sequence of surfaces could be to provide the domain practitioner (in this case the continuous casting expert) with a wide choice of trajectories of points (in three dimensions - s, f and τ; points on trajectory selected from successive speed-dependant surfaces) to select from using judgment based on domain heuristics, without worrying about the basic optimality of points on that trajectory. However, that would amount to offloading too much on the domain practitioner. A more systematic and practical approach is to convert the surface of non-dominated solutions for a given speed into a single optimum

point by transforming the multiple objectives through weighted combination into a single one, where the choice of weights itself varies across the speed range based on domain heuristics. This is the approach followed here.
The section below describes the oscillation performance metrics. The next section outlines the optimization approach, with fitness functions, constraints and alternate evolutionary techniques. Finally results are discussed and conclusions drawn.

2. Oscillation performance metrics

The primary function of oscillation is to maximize lubrication between the strand and mould. As explained in the last section, this is effected in two ways, first, by creating a detachment between the strand and mould, and second, by facilitating entry and spread of lubricant into the thin gap between the two. Using LI to denote Lubrication Index, it follows that one of the tasks of optimization is to maximize LI.
Likewise one may denote Peak Friction and depth of Oscillation Marks as PF and OM respectively. As discussed, these are the two undesirable side effects of oscillation and obviously they are sought to be minimized.
From the above considerations one may define a performance metric PM1 for maximization as

$$PM1 = w_1 \times (LI)^2 - w_2 \times (PF)^2 - w_3 \times (OM)^2 \quad (1)$$

For the purpose of optimization a fitness function needs to be defined that can be expressed in terms of the free parameters v, s, f and τ denoting casting speed, stroke, frequency and deviation from sinusoid, respectively. This function would provide the performance 'fitness' of any selected parameter set $\{v, s, f, \tau\}$. It is shown in the next section that the effect LI can be explicitly defined in terms of these parameters. However, PF and OM are dependent on many lateral conditions and a reliable mapping between the parameter set and these effects cannot be easily extracted, thus ruling out direct use of metric PM1 within a fitness function for simulated optimization.
Figure 4 provides a view of the nature of physical relationship between the free parameters and the three effects. Each effect is shown as a circle, with a '+' or '-' at the top denoting desirability or otherwise. The arrows represent the four free parameters, with a '+', a '-' or a '0' next to the arrow denoting direct, inverse or no relationship with the effect shown in the corresponding circle, when other parameters are held constant. If the product of the sign shown near an arrow and the sign within the circle is a plus, the parameter is desirable from the viewpoint of that effect, else it is undesirable. Thus, if a circle is negative, and a parameter varies inversely with the effect shown in that circle, then it is desirable to increase this parameter.
The figures themselves need a physical explanation. As stated in the introduction, also (Suzuki et al, 1991), (Araki & Ikeda, 1999), increasing τ reduces peak friction as also the depth of oscillation marks. Thus τ contributes negatively to these circles. From detailed analysis of the mechanism of formation of oscillation marks, as in (Badri et al., 2005) or (Thomas, 2002), it is known that higher frequency damps oscillation mark depth while stroke increases it. The signs are shown accordingly. Considering peak friction, both frequency and stroke increase mold upward velocity and hence amplify PF. As for lubrication, it is understood that higher stroke has a beneficial effect while frequency tends to mildly damp it (Thomas, 2002; Araki & Ikeda, 1999), the figures reflect accordingly.

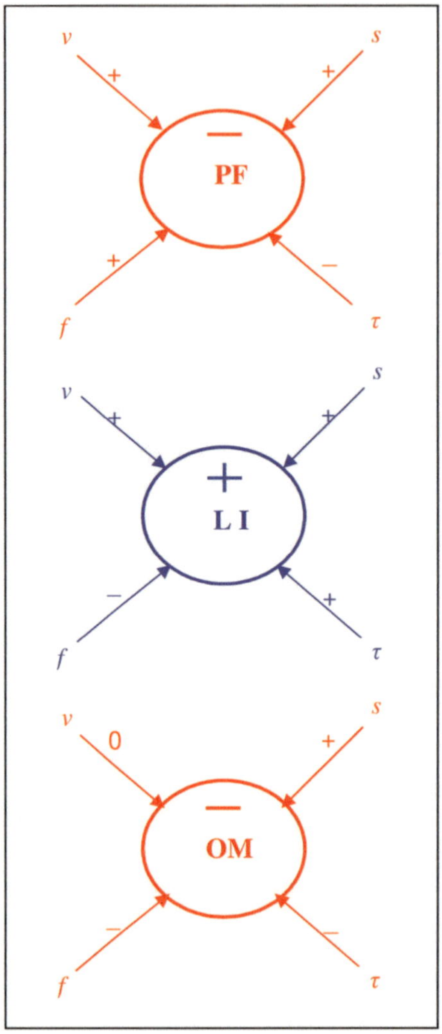

Fig. 4. Impacts of different parameters on described effects, LI-Lubrication Index, PFPeak Friction, OM-Oscillation Mark. Casting speed- *v*, Stroke- *s*, Frequency- *f*, Dev. from sinusoid- τ; a '+' or a '-' next to a directed line denotes that the impact of the parameter on the effect is direct or inverse

From an analysis of the above figures, and the physics behind these figures, one can generate a substitute for PM1 bypassing the need for explicit mathematical relationship between PF & OM, and the parameter set {v, s, f, τ}. Since LI can be expressed mathematically, the focus is on PF and OM. From fig. 4, one may see that stroke s is undesirable for both. Frequency f is undesirable from the viewpoint of PF, but desirable for OM. If one considers OM as more critical, then it is desirable to increase f but the relationship is not as explicit as in the case of stroke. Accordingly, a new performance metric PM2 may be created for maximization as

$$PM2 = w_1 \times (LI)^2 - w_2 \times (s)^2 + w_3 \times (f)^2 \quad (2)$$

where one would like to choose

$$w1 >> w2 >> w3 \tag{3}$$

Although PM2, unlike PM1, is numerically tractable in the sense that given a parameter set {v, s, f, τ} the performance metric can be numerically evaluated thus making it usable within an evolutionary optimization algorithm, it is somewhat simplistic in that it short-circuits the free design parameters directly into the metric (the last two terms). Optimization results using PM2 (i.e. eq. (2)) as a cost function have been carried out and reported in (Bhattacharya et al., 2007), steep variation in frequency with casting speeds have been observed and the benefits in LI seem to be sub-optimal, primarily because forced reduction in stroke is enforced in this metric - and stroke, as just discussed, contributes positively to lubrication. Thus a more realistic, numerically tractable representation of PM1 is sought.
In the following sections, it is shown (eq. 19) that the peak friction PF can be approximated by a term called peak-frictionfactor or PFF which can be numerically calculated from a given parameter set. Also, the depth of oscillation mark or OM can be replaced by the negative strip time or NST that is numerically deducible from the given parameter set. Accordingly, one may express PM1 as

$$PM3 = w_1 \times (LI)^2 - w_2 \times (NST)^2 - w_3 \times (PFF)^2 \tag{4}$$

where the metric PM3 is sought to be maximized. Selection of positive weights w1, w2 & w3, as a function of casting speed based on domain-heuristic considerations, in the above scalar objective function are expected to provide an optimal solution for each discrete speed using evolutionary algorithms, bypassing the need for generation of non-dominated solution surfaces using multi-objective optimization for further processing by domain experts, as explained in the introductory section.

3. Optimization using evolutionary algorithms

In this section the mathematical relationship between Lubrication Index LI and the parameter set **S** = {v, s, f, τ} is described, from which an explicit expression for fitness function can be constructed. The constraints based on machine limits are stated. Features of the two Evolutionary Algorithms, one a Genetic Algorithm (GA) and the other a Differential Evolution (DE) approach, used for optimization are then described.
Araki and Ikeda (Araki & Ikeda, 1999) have proposed a relationship between LI and other intermediate casting variables, which in turn may be described in terms of parameter set **S**. This relationship has been shown to be working well on comparing computed LI with rate of powder (lubricant) consumption, which is an indication of the effectiveness of oscillation in enhancing lubrication. The authors have independently verified this relationship by performing simulations on the IISI website (World Steel University, 2009). The relation states

$$LI = R_{NA}^{0.3} \times t_p^{0.5} \tag{5}$$

where R_{NA} is defined as

$$R_{NA}(\%) = f \frac{N_d}{V_c} \times 100 \tag{6}$$

with N_d the negative strip distance, i.e. distance covered by mold relative to strand during the negative strip in one cycle, $V_c = v$ (casting speed), and t_p the positive strip time.
Further, the negative strip distance N_d may be expressed as

$$N_d = s.\sin(\pi f t_{neg}) - V_c.t_{neg} \tag{7}$$

where t_{neg} is the negative strip time expressed as

$$t_{neg} = \frac{2(1-\tau)}{\pi f}\cos^{-1}\left(\frac{4(1-\tau).V_c}{\pi.2sf}\right) \tag{8}$$

Equations (7) and (8) for non-sinusoidal oscillations are according to Moerwald et al (Moerwald et al., 2000); under sinusoidal conditions, i.e. $\tau = 0.5$, they reduce to standard equations for negative strip time NST or t_{neg} found in open literature, i.e.

$$\text{NST} = t_{neg} = \frac{1}{\pi f}\times\cos^{-1}\frac{V_c}{\pi sf} \tag{9}$$

with positive strip time t_p defined as

$$t_p = \frac{1}{f} - t_{neg} \tag{10}$$

In the above expressions all times t are defined in seconds, frequency in cycles per sec, speeds in millimeters per sec and stroke s in millimeters.
Substituting eq. (8) in eqs. (7) and (10), eq. (7) in eq. (6), and eqs. (6) and (10) in eq. (5), one may write the expression for LI as

$$LI = \left[\frac{100fs}{V_c}\left\{\sin\left[\cos^{-1}\left(\frac{2V_c(1-\tau)}{\pi fs}\right)\right] - \frac{2V_c(1-\tau)}{\pi fs}\cos^{-1}\left(\frac{2V_c(1-\tau)}{\pi fs}\right)\right\}\right]^{0.3} \times \left\{\frac{1}{f} - \frac{2(1-\tau)}{\pi f}\cos^{-1}\left(\frac{2V_c(1-\tau)}{\pi fs}\right)\right\}^{0.5} \tag{11}$$

The fitness function is obtained by substituting eq. (11) in eq. (4) for PM3, thus providing a performance measure for any selected parameter set $\mathbf{S} = \{V_c, s, f, \tau\}$.
Constraints are defined in terms of the following

$$100 \le f \le 140 \tag{12}$$

$$2 \le s \le 10 \tag{13}$$

$$0.5 \le \tau \le 0.7 \tag{14}$$

$$\frac{s\pi f}{2(1-\tau)} \le 0.8\times V_{\max} \tag{15}$$

$$\frac{s\pi^2 f^2}{2(1-\tau)^2} \le 0.8\times a_{\max} \tag{16}$$

While relations (12-14) are generally taken as standard limits for mold oscillation and considered here accordingly, the LHS of relations (15-16) are derived from equations

describing non-sinusoidal waveforms and correspond to the maximum attainable values of mold velocity and acceleration for a selected waveform. These are derived in Appendix A. V_{max} and a_{max} in the equations represent machine limits of velocity and acceleration provided by the equipment manufacturers.
At a given value of v (=Vc), the peak friction PF may be expressed as

$$PF = \eta \frac{V_{max}^{up} - V_c}{d_t} \tag{17}$$

where V_{max}^{up} is the maximum upward speed in a cycle, η is the viscosity of lubricant and d_t the thickness of lubricant film in the gap between strand and mould. The latter two being extraneous factors to an oscillation schedule, a Peak Friction Factor PFF may be defined such that

$$PF = k.PFF \tag{18}$$

with

$$PFF = V_{max}^{up} - V_c \tag{19}$$

and $k = (\eta / d_t)$.
An Evolutionary Algorithm is used to derive that parameter set **S** which maximizes the fitness function defined by performance metric PM3. In this process the casting speed v is fixed, and s, f, and τ are evaluated as a function of v. Different values of v are fed as input, the evolutionary algorithm generates corresponding optimal sets of s, f and τ.
As stated earlier, two alternate evolutionary algorithms are used competitively in this study and their results and performances assessed. Genetic Algorithms (GA) constitute the original method to have been developed in the field of evolutionary algorithms, and represent the baseline for further advances in this field. A standard GA process is well known and not described here. The parameters to be optimized, namely s, f, and τ, are binary coded and concatenated to form bit strings (chromosomes) that constitute the population members operated upon in parallel. Each of the parameters are encoded using 10 bits, which implies that their respective ranges of variation, eqs. (12-14), are discretized into 1024 intervals, and that each chromosome is 30 bits long. In every generation the fitness of a population member is evaluated by calling the fitness function, expressed as eq. (4), the components of (4) provided by eqs. (9), (11) & (19).
Genetic Algorithms tend to slow down after nearing an optimum solution point in the n-dimensional (here n = 3) solution space, and some means are usually implemented for accelerating the GA process. The acceleration methods used here are, first, elitism (Bhandari et al., 1996) where the best solution obtained in a certain generation is preserved in succeeding generations until a better one is found thus preventing 'loss' of good solutions, second, cyclical variation of mutation rate across generations (Pal et al., 1998), and third, differential mutation of bits according to significance in good and bad schema in solution strings (Bhattacharya & Sivakumar, 2000; Bhattacharya et al., 2004).
The method of Differential Evolution (DE) was first proposed by Storn and Price (1995) and differs from GA primarily in the manner in which population members (i.e. solution parameter vectors) in a candidate solution pool are varied to create new solutions, and thus explore the solution space for the global optimum. In fact, most evolutionary optimization

techniques fundamentally differ from one another in the manner of inducing variation in candidate solutions. GA's use crossover between randomly selected solution pairs, and also mutation, to create new solutions. Differential Evolution, on the other hand, modifies a candidate solution by first creating a trial vector from three other solution vectors simply by adding the weighted vector difference of two of these to the third, and then operating a crossover between the trial vector and the original candidate solution to yield the new candidate. In the last step it follows the "greedy" approach, i.e. the newly generated solution replaces the original only if its fitness value is better.
Expressed mathematically, a trial vector $\overline{x}_{i,g}$ for a candidate i in a pool of size N at generation g is created as

$$\overline{x}_{i,g} = \overline{X}_{r1,g} + F(\overline{X}_{r2,g} - \overline{X}_{r3,g}) \tag{20}$$

where $r_1, r_2, r_3 \in [0, N\text{-}1]$; are integers and different from one another and from i, and F is a damping factor usually between 0.5 and 1.
Crossover is then executed between $\overline{x}_{i,g}$ and the original candidate $\overline{X}_{i,g}$ to yield the potential new candidate solution which is allowed to replace the original only if its fitness value is found to be better.
The actual implementation in this study is a variant of eq. (20) for generating the trial vector, on the lines of Karaboga and Ogdem (2004), and is expressed as

$$\overline{x}_{i,g} = \overline{X}_{r1,g} + R(\overline{X}_{best,g} - \overline{X}_{r1,g}) + F(\overline{X}_{r2,g} - \overline{X}_{r3,g}) \tag{21}$$

where the subscript *best* represent the vector having best fitness value in the population at generation g, and R is set at 0.5 while F varies randomly with generation g (constant across all i in a generation) within the range -2 to +2. The probability of crossover is set at 0.7, the same value as used in the GA.

4. Results and discussion

Evolutionary Algorithms as described above are used to optimize the oscillation parameters stroke, frequency and waveform (deviation from sinusoid), with the objective of maximizing lubrication and minimizing peak friction and oscillation marks. This is achieved by optimizing the fitness function according to eqs. (4), (9), (11) & (19), under the constraints expressed in relations (12-16). The results obtained from Genetic Algorithm are first described in detail. Next the results from Differential Evolution are shown in comparison to those obtained applying the GA approach.
The GA is tested with different population sizes and a size of 20 is selected for performing downstream executions. A test case with $w_1 = 0.85$, $w_2 = 0.13$ and $w_3 = 0.02$ (refer eq. 2) is taken at speed $v = 1.4$, and the variation of convergence history and final converged solution with arbitrary changes in initial population is observed. The objective function PM2 (eq. (2)) is used, and the solution is stopped after 5000 generations, a stage when it is assumed to have fully converged. Variations in convergence are seen only within the first 1000 generations; the final solution is always same with practically no variation. The convergence history is shown in figs. 5 & 6 for this test case, fig. 5 shows convergence of fitness function, and fig. 6 the evolution of stroke and frequency for first 3000 generations. In these test cases frequency is allowed to vary between 80 to 200, which is a wider range than that specified in

eq. (12). This case takes less than a minute of computation time on a Pentium D 2.6 GHz desktop.

Production runs are executed to cover the entire range of casting speed, from 0.05 meters/min to 1.95 m/min, at intervals of 0.05 m/min. The performance metric PM3 is used as cost function (weight selection details are explained below), and the constraints are exactly as specified in eqs. (12-16). The resultant values of s, f, and τ for each case were tabulated, with the objective of generating a schedule for the oscillation parameters against casting speed. In each speed case the complete GA solution to 30000 generations was executed. The net computation time is approximately 3 hours on the mentioned desktop.

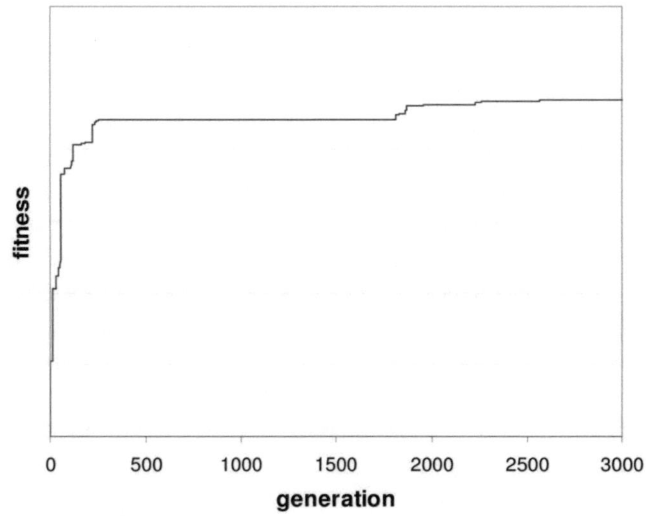

Fig. 5. Convergence history of fitness value; converged after 2500 generations, however, all optimization runs allowed to continue till 5000 generations for perfect repeatability

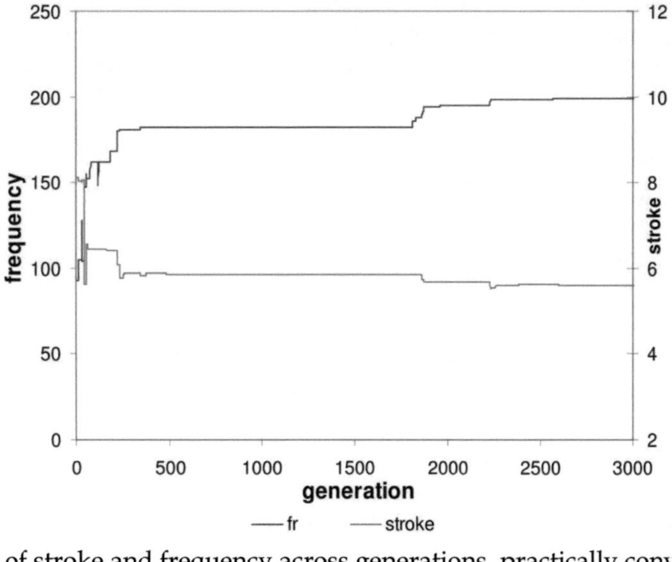

Fig. 6. Evolution of stroke and frequency across generations, practically converged after 2500 generations. Range of frequency is from 80 to 200 cpm, that of stroke from 2 to 10 mm.

Referring back to the discussion on Oscillation Performance Metric 3 (PM3, eq. (4)), the oscillation schedule designer would like to arrange the weights w1, w2 & w3 given to LI, NST and PFF in a manner consistent with his understanding /interpretation of domain heuristics. The three weights should preferably add up to one to normalize different weight allocation strategies.

Facilitating lubrication being the prime purpose of oscillations, prima-facie the major share of weight should be allocated to LI (i.e. w1). Between NST and PFF, one may say that NST is more important as it can directly affect product quality while the latter can be somewhat compensated with higher LI. Thus, one may broadly set an inequality of the form

$$w1 > w2 > w3 \tag{22}$$

Now, for a class of steels called "peritectic" primarily on the basis of their carbon concentration, oscillation marks and their consequential effects are of greater concern than in case of low or medium carbon grades. Correspondingly, the LI is of a slightly lower concern in peritectic grades. (Figures (9-10) showing variation of LI and NST with casting speed as calculated from oscillation schedules provided by an OEM (Original Equipment Manufacturer), for peritectic and low/mid-C grades, corroborate this relative prioritization of oscillation performance objectives across steel grades. These figures also show GA results on which we are not focusing right here, but will return to later for discussion). Thus, between w1 and w2 (weights of LI and NST), the designer's preference is for higher difference (w1 - w2) for low/mid Carbon steels as compared to peritectic. Also, this difference should increase with casting speeds, to offset lower LI at higher speeds and deeper oscillation marks at lower speeds.

From the above discussions the following requirements can be defined on the selection of weights w1, w2 & w3. First, $w1 > w2 > w3$ and $\sum_{i=1}^{3} wi = 1$.

Second, difference D = (w1 - w2) should be greater in the case of low/mid-C as compared to peritectic grades. Third, D should be gradually increasing with casting speeds.

Based on the above requirements, the following pattern of variation of weights was implemented:

For peritectic grades:

Case (a) w1 = 0.6, w2 = 0.3, w3 = 0.1; for cs $\leq$ 0.8 m/min.; cs denotes casting speed

Case (b) w1 = 0.7, w2 = 0.2, w3 = 0.1; for cs $\geq$ 1.4, and

Case (c) w1 and w2 vary linearly from case (a) to (b) for 0.8 < cs < 1.4.

For low- and mid- C grades:

Case (a) w1 = 0.6, w2 = 0.3, w3 = 0.1; for cs $\leq$ 0.8 m/min.

Case (b) w1 = 0.85, w2 = 0.075, w3 = 0.075; for cs $\geq$ 1.4, and

Case (c) w1, w2 and w3 vary linearly from case (a) to (b) for 0.8 < cs < 1.4.

Figures 7 and 8 show variation of stroke and frequency, respectively, with casting speed for the two GA solutions against the schedules provided by the Original Equipment Manufacturer (OEM) for the same two grade cases. The value of deviationfrom-sinusoid τ quickly converges to the maximum (0.7) and hardly moves from there across the speed range, and hence this is not plotted. Recall from fig. 4 that increased τ was desirable from the perspective of all 3 effects, and the GA solutions strongly confirm this. One needs to keep in mind that both OEM schedules are provided at sinusoidal waveform, i.e. $\tau = 0.5$.

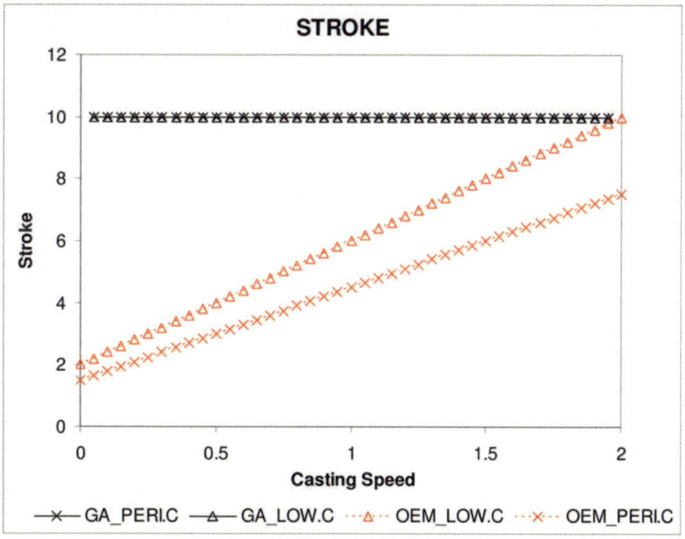

Fig. 7. Variation of stroke with casting speed. GA Synthesized solutions, low/mid-C mode and peritectic mode, versus OEM-supplied values for corresponding grade types. It is important to note that GA solutions converge at a non-sinusoidal waveform factor τ = 0.7 all through the speed range, while OEM solutions are all at sinusoidal waveform, τ = 0.5.

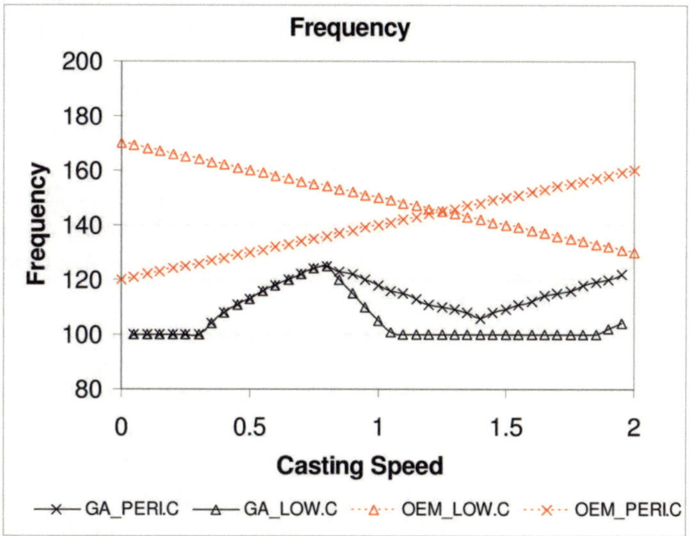

Fig. 8. Variation of frequency with casting speed. GA Synthesized solutions, low/mid-C mode and peritectic mode, versus OEM-supplied values for corresponding grade types. It is important to note that GA solutions converge at a nonsinusoidal waveform factor τ = 0.7 all through the speed range, while OEM solutions all are at sinusoidal waveform, τ = 0.5.

In the GA solutions the value of stroke remains at 10 (the maximum limit) throughout the speed range. It is seen in fig. 4. that large stroke is desirable from the viewpoint of increasing lubrication, but undesirable for NST and PFF. However, as the allocated weight to LI makes it dominant, the value of stroke is driven towards its maximum.

Increasing frequency has only a weakly detrimental effect on LI, but is desirable from the viewpoint of reducing NST. These effects also vary with casting speed, and moreover the objective function weights are also scheduled across casting speed. Relative higher weights given to LI compared to NST, as in case of low/mid-C mode, tends to keep frequency on the lower side. For peritectic mode where relative weight to NST is higher, there are conflicting pulls on frequency across the speed range, making it tend to converge to higher values.

Figures 9-11 show variation of LI, NST and PFF respectively against casting speed. Values obtained from GA optimization using weights corresponding to peritectic mode, and low/mid-C mode, are shown and compared against values provided by OEM for the same two grade-classes and currently installed in the casters of Tata Steel, Jamshedpur. The following explicit observations can be made:

1. The values of Lubrication Index LI obtained from GA are higher than those obtained from OEM all across the casting speed range. This value is about 55% higher than the higher OEM value (for low/mid-C) at a speed of 0.8 meters/min, and about 25% higher at a speed of 1.95. This is significant, since insufficient lubrication is assumed to be one reason why casting becomes difficult at high speeds. In particular, the value of LI equaling 1.78 at the highest speed of 1.95 is touched by the higher OEM curve at a low speed of 0.45, and then continues to fall thereafter.
2. Between the OEM-provided values, LI for low/mid-C is consistently higher than that for peritectic -C
3. Somewhat unexpectedly, the LI generated by GA from both the modes of weight selection are practically identical. The reason behind this is explained later
4. All through the range of production speeds, the NST and consequently the depth of oscillation marks, are lower for peritectic-C as compared to low/mid-C, both for the two OEM curves when mutually compared, as well as for the two GA curves. This is exactly as expected
5. When comparing NST between low/mid-C from OEM versus low/mid-C from GA, the GA values are lower (equaling OEM at a few points), while comparing NST for peritectic-C from OEM against that from GA shows that they are more or less similar across the range of production speeds
6. Looking at peak friction factor (Fig. 11), it is seen that throughout the operating speed range, both GA from low/mid-C mode and peritectic-C mode produce lower PFF as compared to OEM for low/mid-C grades; however, OEM values from peritectic grades, with lower PFF, are at par with GA solutions for these grades.

Figures 12 and 13 compare Negative Strip Distance or NSD (this may be defined as the distance traversed by the mold within the part of one oscillation cycle when it is moving downwards faster than the strand), and Positive Strip Time or PST, between GA from the two modes, and OEM schedules provided for the two grade types. This comparison is necessary as there is a perception that low NST leads to lower lubrication. This perception is true for a sinusoidal waveform, but wrong for non-sinusoidal waveforms. It is NSD and not NST which facilitates penetration of lubricant into the mold-strand gap. When waveform is sinusoidal, NST and NSD vary directly, while for non-sinusoidal waveform this variation gets reversed. Thus lower NST may be associated with lower lubrication for sinusoidal waveforms (as, e.g., provided by OEM schedules), but not all so for non-sinusoidal waveforms, as provided by the GA solutions.

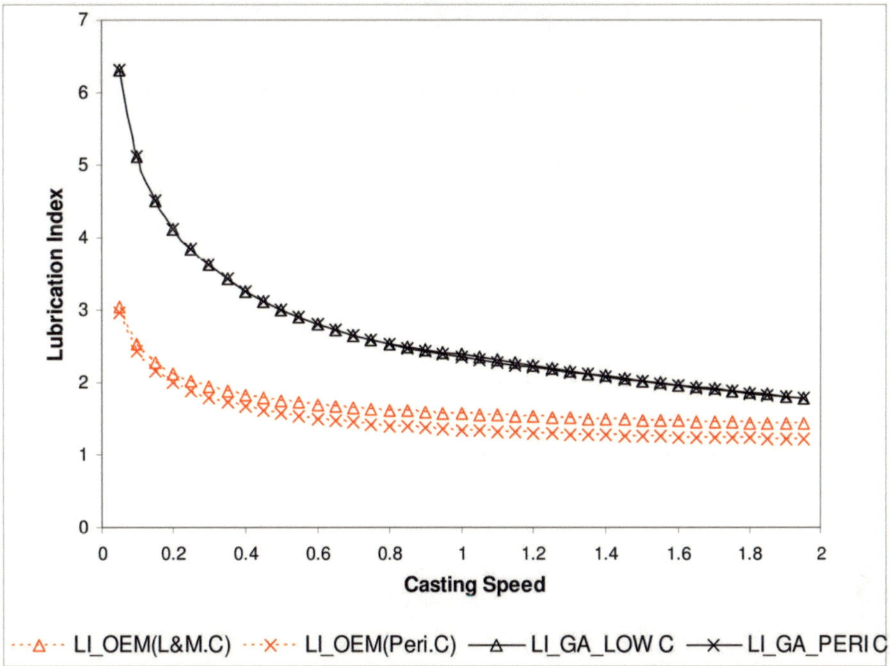

Fig. 9. Variation of Lubrication Index (LI) with casting speed. Comparing GA synthesized solution at the two grades versus OEM provided values at the same grades.

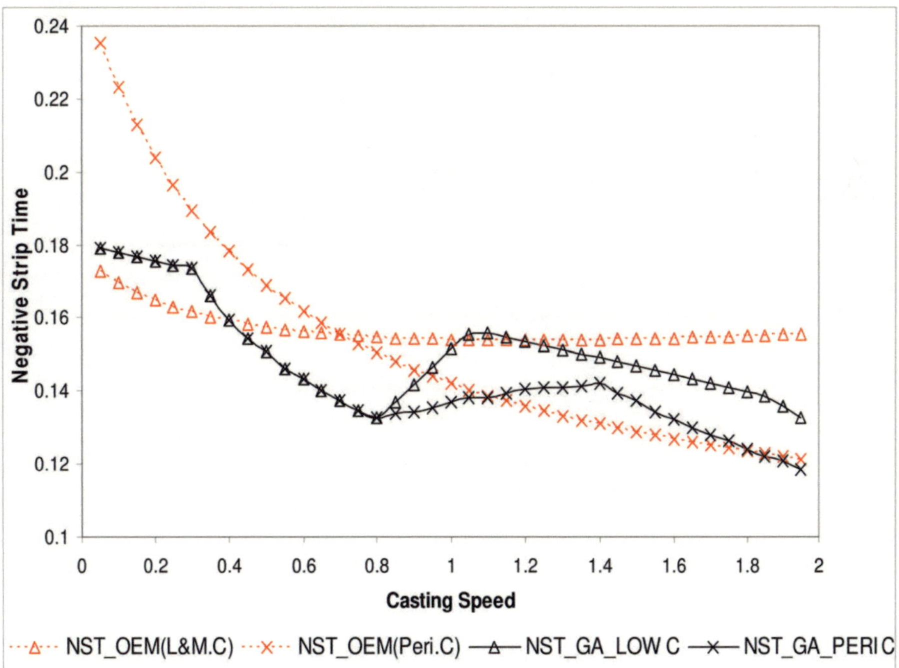

Fig. 10. Variation of Negative Strip Time (NST) with casting speed. Comparing GA synthesized solution at the two grades versus OEM provided values at the same grades.

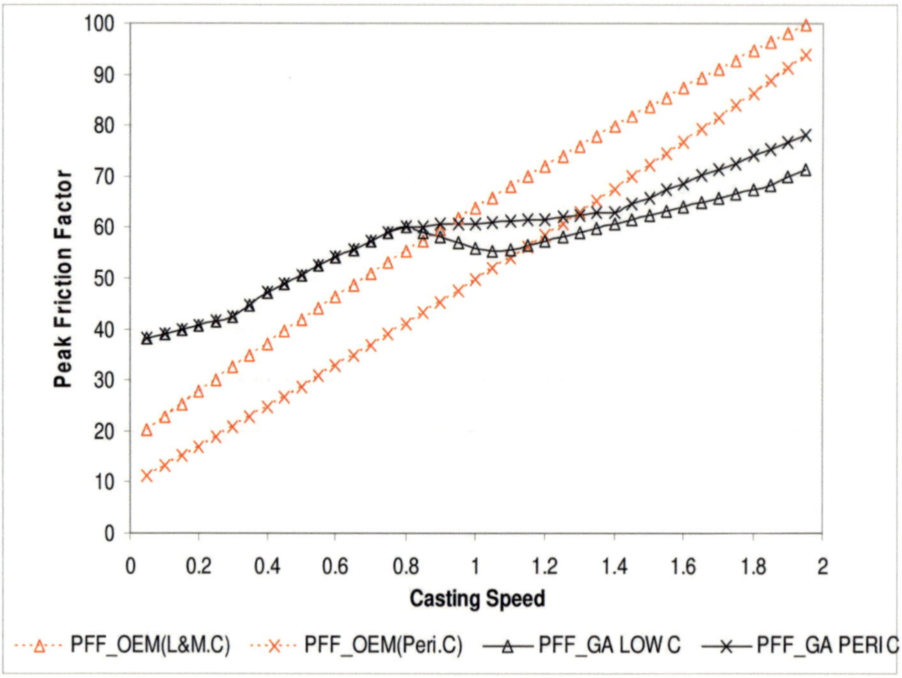

Fig. 11. Variation of Peak Friction Factor (PFF) with casting speed. Comparing GA synthesized solution at the two grades versus OEM provided values at the same grades.

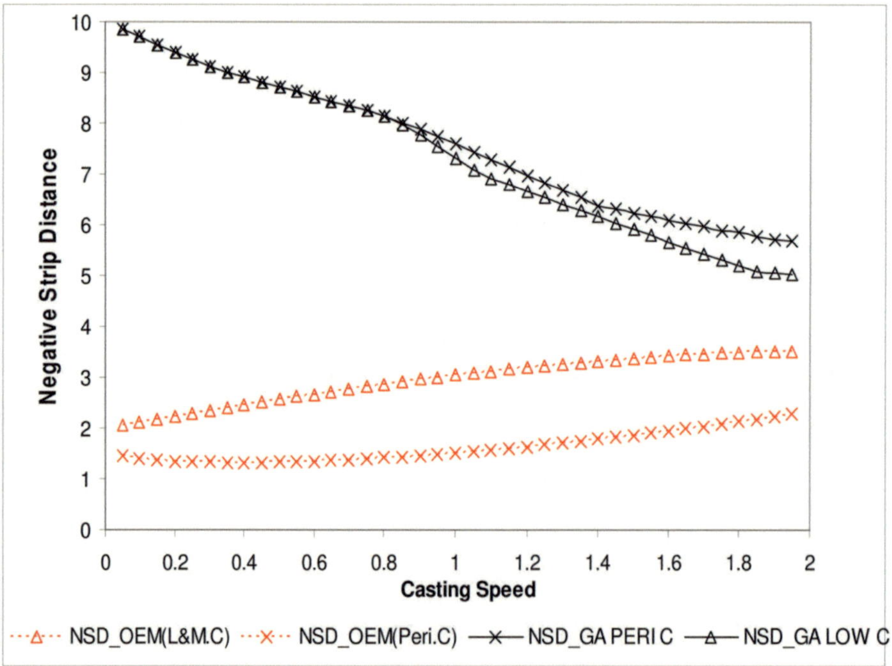

Fig. 12. Variation of Negative Strip Distance (NSD) with casting speed. Comparing GA synthesized solution at the two grades versus OEM provided values at the same grades.

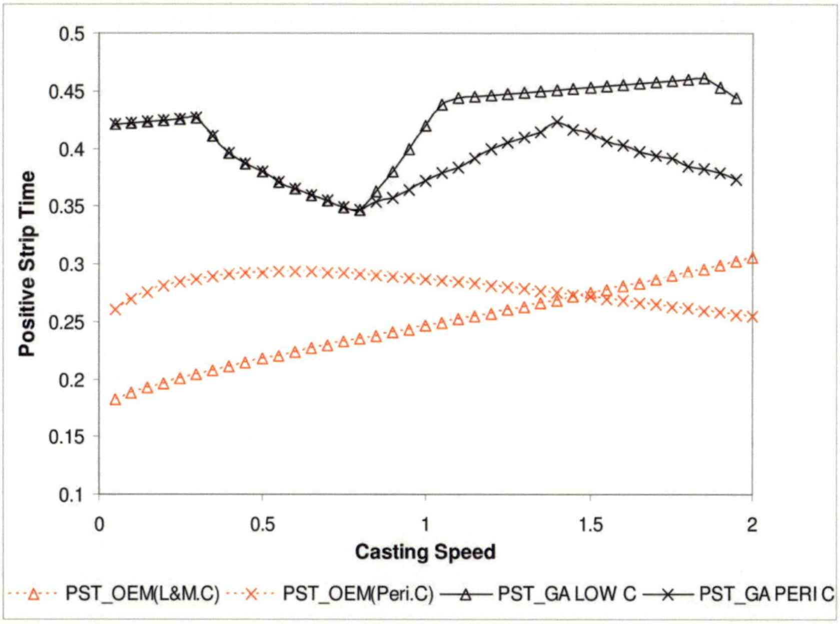

Fig. 13. Variation of Positive Strip Time (PST) with casting speed. Comparing GA synthesized solution at the two grades versus OEM provided values at the same grades.

Looking at figs. 10 and 12 together, it may be observed that between the OEM values, NST is higher for low/mid-C, while NSD is also higher for the same grades, as compared to peritectic-C. It has to be kept in mind that OEM values are on sinusoidal waveforms. This illustrates that for sinusoidal waveforms, if the designer wants to reduce NST and hence the depth of oscillation marks, he has to perforce reduce NSD and hence the lubrication. For the GA solutions, however, it is seen that peritectic-C provides lower NST as compared to low/mid-C, but it also provides higher NSD. The waveform of GA solutions converge to a τ-factor (degree of deviation from sinusoid, 0.5 corresponds to sinusoid) of 0.7. This demonstrates that lower NST is associated with higher NSD, and consequently better lubrication, for non-sinusoidal conditions. Figure 3 explains the physics behind this variation. It shows that as the deviation from sinusoidal waveform increases, the NST (represented by intercept on the x-axis) reduces, while the NSD (shaded area between mold velocity and strand velocity (i.e. casting speed)) increases.

Figure 13 shows variation of PST for the four cases. The only point of observation in these curves is that PST from peritectic-C GA solution is lower than from low/mid-C GA. It is a combination of NSD and PST that facilitate lubrication; between the two GA modes peritectic-C provides higher NSD but lower PST, which combine to provide net LI at similar levels as from low/mid-C GA solution. This explains the unexpected observed similarity in LI values between these two GA modes.

Overall, one can take the view that between the OEM values and the GA solutions, the latter is better in all the performance indicators of oscillation, namely, better Lubrication Index, lower NST (i.e. shallower oscillation marks), and lower PFF (i.e. lower friction overhead of oscillation). Further, it appears that both GA solutions, one for peritectic-C and the other for low/mid-C, have the same distribution of LI across casting speeds, while the former provides lower NST and the latter lower PFF. Since NST is a more important factor in casting than PFF, one may converge to the view that the GA solution for low/mid-C mode can be over-ridden by the GA solution for the peritectic mode, for casting all categories of steel grades.

The above results and analyses were generated using Genetic Algorithms. A similar exercise for synthesizing stroke, frequency and waveform across the speed range exactly on above lines, i.e. using eqs (4), (9), (11) & (19) for the objective function and eqs (12-16) as constraints, was performed using Differential Evolution algorithms. The synthesized parametric values were observed to be exactly the same for every single discrete value of casting speed, the degree of similarity surprising even the authors. This independently serves to validate the two methods and their corresponding codes, and also implies that a further discussion on the results from the domain perspective, on the lines of the above, is unnecessary. What is however noteworthy is the difference in speed of convergence in terms of the number of generations. Table 1 shows the results and convergence rates from five representative casting speeds. The reduction in the number of generations for convergence is easily more than an order of magnitude. Furthermore, it was evaluated that the computation time per generation from either algorithm was approximately same - which implies that the reduction in the number of generations for convergence directly translates into computation times.

The present study has shown that DE is at least one order faster than GA. To be able to frame a view as to whether the same could be true for most (or all) problems, one has to first analyze the reasons why DE is turning out to be so much faster. Figure 14 illustrates the standard DE process conceptually without getting into precision or details. As stated earlier, the basic difference between various evolutionary algorithms lies in the manner in which they extract new solutions from the current population pool. DE works on the principle of the superposition of the weighted difference between two vectors in a generation onto a third vector for obtaining a new solution. Figure 14 shows a two-dimensional space (denoted x_1 & x_2), three existing vectors, $\mathbf{x}^1$, $\mathbf{x}^2$ and $\mathbf{x}^i$ in that space, and how a new vector is extracted from among them. In the early generations when there is sufficient diversity among the candidate vectors, this method facilitates a random search of the entire space.

The "greedy" approach ensures that every solution gradually approaches the optimum point. This also implies that they come closer to one another, i.e. the difference between them reduces, and hence new vectors being created remain very near to the earlier ones. Thus the closer they come to the optimum, the search limits itself to a smaller neighborhood around it - this process intensifying continuously till that optimum is attained. This is illustrated in fig. 15, which represents the same process shown in fig. 14 but now after the evolution has advanced significantly. If we recall a standard GA process, the fundamental mechanisms for generating a new solution are crossover and mutation. It would not really matter whether the solution is near or far to the global optimum, each solution would continue hopping around the entire solution space till the optimum is attained. In other words, the solution can come quickly close to the global optimum, but then will "beat around the bush" as it does not know how to get right in.

The question is, will this apparent advantage of a DE vis-à-vis a GA continue to hold when the dimension of the solution space increases significantly? Implicit in the discussion above is an admission - that as the solution evolves the DE is losing its ability to search the total solution space, in comparison to a GA. When the population size is large relative to the

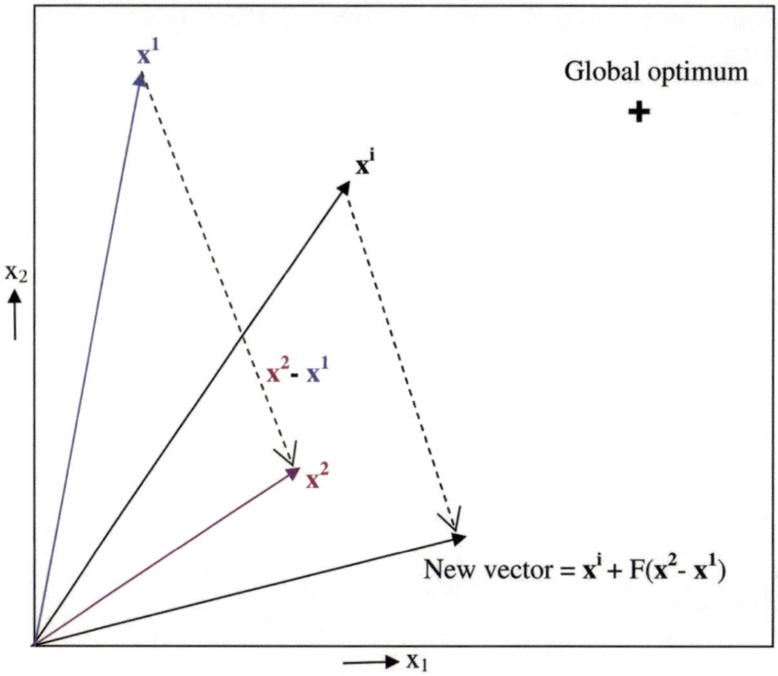

Fig. 14. Illustration of Differential Evolution Process – conditions prevailing a little after initialization.

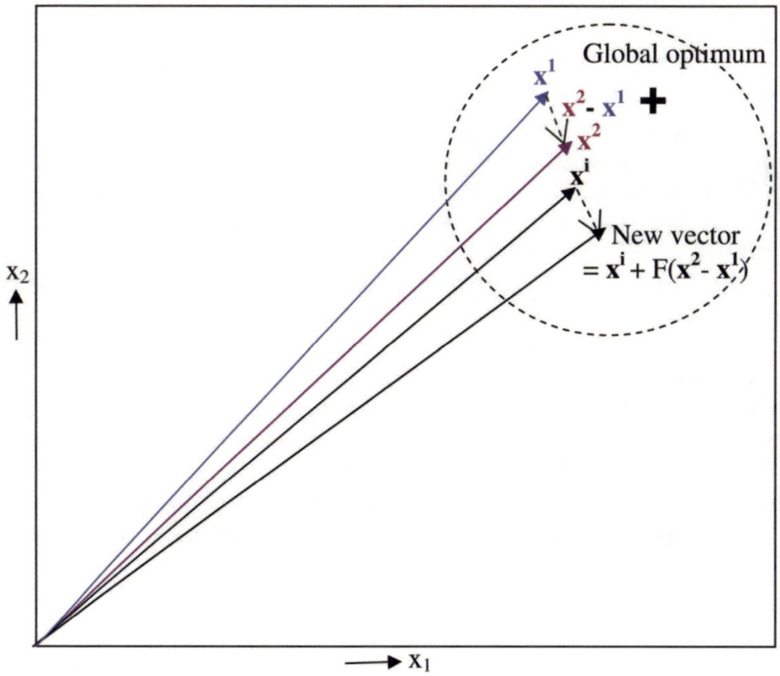

Fig. 15. Illustration of Differential Evolution Process – conditions prevailing close to convergence.

parametric degrees of freedom, and the initial choice sufficiently diverse, the possibility of quickly reaching a neighborhood of the global optimum is also high. But under the opposite conditions, i.e. large dimensionality of solution space and relatively smaller population size and initial diversity, the DE can possibly get trapped in a local minimum unless certain mechanisms for diversity retention are built in. These very mechanisms will, however, affect convergence rates in the final stages.
From the above discussion it appears that the best approach would be to use DE alone whenever it is possible to have a large population size relative to the dimension of the solution space. If this is not possible, then it is advisable to use GA in the initial stages and switch to DE later when convergence rates fall significantly.

Casting Speed (m/min)	Stroke-GA (mm)	Stroke - DE (mm)	Frequency-GA (cpm)	Frequency-DE (cpm)	Final Fitness-GA (Eq. 4)	Final Fitness - DE (Eq. 4)	**Number of Generations-GA**	**Number of Generations-DE**
0.5	10	10	113	113	0.2011	0.2011	**3835**	**46**
0.8	10	10	125	125	0.157	0.157	**1240**	**75**
1.1	10	10	115	115	0.159	0.159	**1731**	**67**
1.4	10	10	106	106	0.1651	0.1651	**2830**	**49**
1.7	10	10	115	115	0.145	0.145	**1350**	**70**

Table 1. Results from GA and DE compared; the exact similarity of synthesized parameters, and the significant speedup achieved using DE may be noted.

5. Conclusions

The relationships between oscillation performance metrics like lubrication, oscillation mark depth and peak friction and the design parameter set consisting of stroke s, frequency f and deviation from sinusoidal waveform τ, are expressed in a mathematical framework. This enables the definition of explicit objective functions and constraints that are used to drive a Genetic Algorithm towards the best-performing parameter set across the entire range of casting speed. Comparison with parameter sets provided by OEM and implemented currently, shows that the synthesized set provides much better lubrication - the prime objective of oscillating the mold - while also reducing oscillation marks and peak friction. Furthermore, this is achieved with only minor variation of the parameters across the speed range.
Substitution of a Genetic Algorithm by a Differential Evolution algorithm for the above synthesis generates exactly identical results from the engineering domain perspective, but with a convergence rate that is faster by at least one order of magnitude. The reasons for this are analyzed, leading to a conclusion that for small dimensioned problems DE is definitely a better approach, but for larger dimensioned ones it is advisable to use GA in the initial phases and switch to DE at a later stage as the approach to global optimum becomes asymptotic.

6. Acknowledgment

The authors acknowledge support provided by the management of Tata Steel for this development. They also express their gratitude to other members of the Slab Expert System development team, members of the Flat Products Technology Group and continuous casting operations personnel for their support.

7. Appendix A: derivation of constraint equations on velocity and acceleration

The maximum values that stroke s, frequency *f* and waveform deviation from sinusoid τ can attain are limited not only by their range but the maximum velocity and acceleration that the mold can acquire within its oscillation cycle under the limiting conditions imposed by the machinery. These limits need to be converted into constraining equations for combinations of s, f, and τ. These constraining equations are derived in this Appendix.
Figure 16 shows how the waveform for a single cycle of oscillation can be split into four zones – A, B, C and D – each zone represented by a different equation for displacement versus time. Under sinusoidal conditions the four zones merge into one to be represented by a single equation

$$y = a \sin (2\pi T) \tag{A.1}$$

where

$$T = f\,t \tag{A.2}$$

represents normalized time varying from 0 to 1 for a cycle, and a is the amplitude of oscillation (half of stroke).

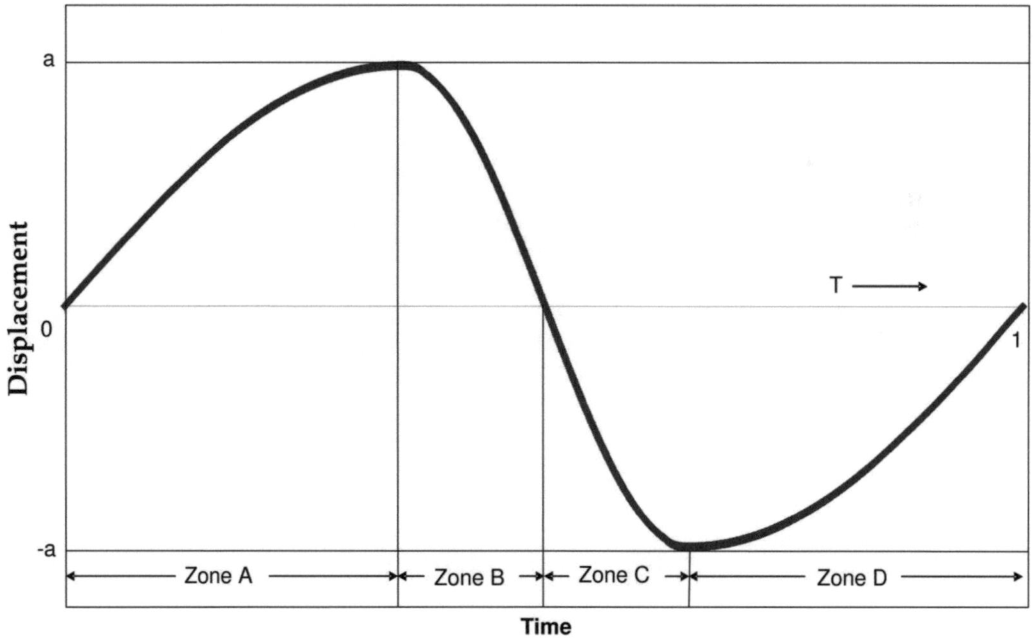

Fig. 16. Dissecting a non-sinusoidal waveform into four zones: Zone A: +(ve) velocity and –(ve) acceleration; Zone B: - (ve) vel and +(ve) accl; Zone C: -(ve) vel and +(ve) accl – in this zone the load on the oscillator is maximum; Zone D: +(ve) vel and +(ve) accl. T = tf is normalized time, and a is amplitude of oscillation.

To obtain the velocity constraint equation, first the corresponding velocities versus time equations are evaluated. The value of T at which they maximize is obtained by setting the derivatives of these equations to zero and then solving for T. The expression for T_{max} is substituted back into the equation for velocity in the relevant zone to obtain the equation for V_{max} as a function of s, f, and τ. This provides the maximum attainable value of V for a given combination of these parameters in one oscillation cycle. This expression is set to be less than 80% of the manufacturer-provided machine limit for velocity, thus generating the constraint equation (or inequation) for velocity.
A similar approach is followed to generate the constraint equation for acceleration.
The displacement equations for the four zones may be written as
Zone-A

$$y = a\sin\left(2\pi T\frac{0.5}{\tau}\right) \tag{A.3}$$

Zone-B

$$y = a\sin\left[2\pi\left(0.25 + \frac{(2T-\tau)}{(1-\tau)}\times 0.25\right)\right] \tag{A.4}$$

Zone-C

$$y = a\sin\left\{2\pi\left[0.75 - \frac{2(1-T)-\tau}{(1-\tau)}\times 0.25\right]\right\} \tag{A.5}$$

Zone-D

$$y = a\sin\left(2\pi(T-1)\frac{0.5}{\tau}\right) \tag{A.6}$$

In eqns.(A.3-6), τ is the oscillation mode and is given by,

$$\tau = \frac{\text{Maximum amplitude location (in } T\text{)}}{0.5} \tag{A.7}$$

Since the higher derivatives of y tend to become very steep around the points of transition from Zone A to B, and from Zone C to D, two new patching zones are further created around these points and termed as Zone-AB and Zone-CD. These are defined below as
Zone AB:

$$y = w_a y_{\text{zone A}} + w_b y_{\text{zone B}} \tag{A.8}$$

where w_a and w_b are given by,

$$w_b = \{T - (\tau/2 - 1/40)\}/\{1/20\} \tag{A.9}$$

and

$$w_a = 1 - w_b \tag{A.10}$$

The range of Zone-AB on the T-axis is from $T = \left(\frac{\tau}{2} - \frac{1}{40}\right)$ to $T = \left(\frac{\tau}{2} + \frac{1}{40}\right)$.

Zone CD:

$$y = w_c y_{\text{zone C}} + w_d y_{\text{zone D}} \tag{A.11}$$

In eqn. (A.11), w_c and w_d are given by,

$$w_c = -\left\{T - (1 - \frac{\tau}{2} + \frac{1}{40})\right\} \Big/ \left\{\frac{1}{20}\right\} \tag{A.12}$$

and

$$w_d = 1 - w_c \tag{A.13}$$

Zone-CD extends from $T = \left\{(1 - \frac{\tau}{2}) - \frac{1}{40}\right\}$ to $T = \left\{(1 - \frac{\tau}{2}) + \frac{1}{40}\right\}$.

Expressions for the velocity of the mould are evaluated for all six zones, but an inspection of fig. 14 shows that the maximum velocity will occur in Zone B or Zone C, due to the very nature of the non-sinusoidal waveform. Accordingly, only the velocity for Zone B is shown hereunder:

$$\frac{dy}{dT} = \frac{a\pi}{(1-\tau)} \cos\left(2\pi\left(0.25 + \frac{(2T-\tau)}{(1-\tau)} \times 0.25\right)\right) \tag{A.14}$$

which may be written in terms of time t as

$$\begin{aligned} v &= \frac{dy}{dt} = \frac{dy}{dT}\frac{dT}{dt} = f\frac{dy}{dT} \quad \text{(refer eq. (A.2))} \\ &= \frac{a\pi f}{(1-\tau)} \cos\left(2\pi\left(0.25 + \frac{(2ft-\tau)}{(1-\tau)} \times 0.25\right)\right) \end{aligned} \tag{A.15}$$

Setting the derivative of this equation to zero with the aim of obtaining t for maximum velocity, one gets

$$-\frac{a\pi^2 f^2}{(1-\tau)^2} \sin\left(2\pi(0.25 + \frac{(2ft-\tau)}{(1-\tau)} \times 0.25)\right) = 0 \tag{A.16}$$

whence

$$\sin\left(2\pi(0.25 + \frac{(2ft-\tau)}{(1-\tau)} \times 0.25)\right) = \sin(n\pi) \tag{A.17}$$

for n = 0, 1, 2, 3 …. for extremum positions, and where the maximum positions are attained at n = 1, 3, 5, …

Considering n = 1 for the maximum position in the first cycle (and all cycles being identical this corresponds to the relative maximum position from the start of a cycle), one obtains

$$t_{\max} = \frac{1}{2f} \tag{A.18}$$

Substituting the value of $t = t_{max}$ from eq. (A.18) into the equation for velocity (A.15), the expression for maximum mold velocity $v = v_{max}$ is obtained as

$$v_{max} = -\frac{s\pi f}{2(1-\tau)} \tag{A.19}$$

where the stroke s = 2a.
If V_{MLim} is the machine limit for v, then one may enforce a condition

$$v_{max} \leq 0.8 * V_{MLim} \tag{A.20}$$

from where it follows that

$$\frac{s\pi f}{2(1-\tau)} \leq 0.8 * V_{MLim} \tag{A.21}$$

which is exactly the eq. (15) in the chapter.
The treatment of acceleration is on a similar vein. The only point of distinction is that, as seen from a manual inspection of fig. 14, the maximum accelerations will be attained towards the start of zone B, where it is downwards, and the end of zone C, where it is upwards. However, since upward acceleration is executed against gravity, it is more valuable to consider that point, i.e. in zone C.
The equation for acceleration in zone C is

$$\frac{d^2y}{dt^2} = -\frac{a\pi^2 f^2}{(1-\tau)^2}\sin\left(2\pi(0.75 - \frac{(2(1-ft)-\tau)}{(1-\tau)}\times 0.25)\right) \tag{A.22}$$

Setting the derivative of this equation to zero, one obtains

$$\cos\left(2\pi(0.75 - \frac{(2(1-ft)-\tau)}{(1-\tau)}\times 0.25)\right) = \cos\left((2n+1)\frac{\pi}{2}\right) \tag{A.23}$$

where n = 0, 1, 2, 3, … provides extremum positions and 1, 3, 5 correspond to maximum positive accelerations.
Taking n = 1 for the first cycle, which will provide a relative position for t in any cycle considered from the start of that cycle, one may derive

$$t_{max} = \frac{2-\tau}{2f} \tag{A.24}$$

One may notice that this value lies next to the transition point between zones C and D, i.e. within the patch CD where the transition has been modified precisely to dampen the acceleration (and jerk). However, for the purpose of imposing a constraint, this may be considered as a conservative value. Substituting the value of $t = t_{max}$ into the eq. (A.22), one obtains the expression for maximum acceleration $A = A_{max}$ in terms of s, f and τ as

$$A_{max} = \frac{s\pi^2 f^2}{2(1-\tau)^2} \tag{A.25}$$

If A_{MLim} is the machine limit for A, then one may enforce a condition

$$A_{\max} \leq 0.8 * A_{\mathrm{MLim}} \tag{A.26}$$

whence

$$\frac{s\pi^2 f^2}{2(1-\tau)^2} \leq 0.8 * A_{\mathrm{MLim}} \tag{A.27}$$

which is exactly the eq. (16) in the chapter.

8. References

Araki, T. & Ikeda, M. (1999). Optimization Of Mould Oscillation For High Speed Casting–New Criteria For Mould Oscillation. *Canadian Metallurgical Quarterly*, Vol 38, No. 5., 1999, pp. 295-300.

Badri, A., et al. (2005). A Mold Simulator for Continuous Casting of Steel: Part II. The Formation of Oscillation Marks during the Continuous Casting of Low Carbon Steel. *Metallurgical and Materials Transactions*, Vol. 36B, June 2005, pp. 373- 383.

Bhattacharya, A.K. & Sivakumar, A.K. (2000). Design of Fuzzy Logic Controller for unstable fighter aircraft using a Genetic Algorithm for rule optimization. AIAA Guidance, Navigation and Control Conference, (Denver) August 2000, *AIAA Paper 2000-4278*.

Bhattacharya, A.K.; Kumar, J. & Jayati, P. (2004). Optimal routing of concurrent vehicles in a minefield using Genetic Algorithms. *Tata Search* Vol. 2, 2004, pp. 436-442.

Bhattacharya, A.K.; Debjani, S.; RoyChoudhury, A. & Das, J. (2007). Optimization of Continuous Casting Mould Oscillation Parameters in Steel Manufacturing Process using Genetic Algorithms. *Proceedings of 2007 IEEE Congress on Evolutionary Computation.*

Bhandari, D.; Murthy, C.A. & Pal, S.K. (1996). Genetic Algorithm with Elitist Model and its Convergence. *Int. J. PatternRecognition and Artificial Intelligence*, Vol.10, 1996, pp. 731-747.

Deb, K.; Agrawal, S.; Pratap, A. & Meyarivan, T. (2002). A fast and elitist multi-objective genetic algorithm: NSGA-II. *IEEE Transactions on Evolutionary Computation*, 6(2): 182-197, 2002.

Goldberg, D. E. (1989). *Genetic Algorithms in Search, Optimization, and Machine Learning*, Addison-Wesley Professional, ISBN 978-0201157673.

Horn, J.; Nafpliotis, N. & Goldberg, D.E. (1994). A niched Pareto Genetic Algorithm for multiobjective optimization. *Proceedings of 1st IEEE Conf. on Evolutionary Computation*, Vol 1, 1994, pp. 82-87.

Karaboga, D. & Okdem, S. (2004). A simple and global optimization algorithm for engineering problems: Differential Evolution Algorithm. Turkish J. Elec Engg. Vol. 12, No. 1, 2004, pp. 53-60.

Moerwald, K.; Steinrueck, H. & Rudischer, C. (2000). Theoretical Studies to Adjust Proper Mould Oscillation Parameters. *AIST Conference* 2000.

Pal, S.K.; Bandopadhyay, S. & Murthy, C.A. (1998). Genetic Algorithms for generation of Class Boundaries. *IEEE Trans. On Systems, Man and Cybernetics¾ Part B: Cybernetics*, Vol. 28, No. 6, December 1998, pp. 816-828.

Storn, R. & Price, K. (1995). Differential Evolution – a simple and efficient adaptive scheme for global optimization over continuous spaces. *ICSI Technical Report* TR-95-012, March 1995.

Suzuki, M. et al. (1991). Development of a New Mould Oscillation Mode for High-speed Continuous Casting of Steel Slabs. ISIJ International, Vol 31, No. 3, 1991, pp. 254-261.

Thomas, B.G. (2002). Modelling of the Continuous Casting of Steel – Past, Present and Future. Electric Furnace Conf. Proc., Vol. 59, ISS, Warrendale, PA, (Phoenix, AZ), 2001, 3-30, also *Metallurgical and Materials Transactions B*, Vol 33B, No. 6, Dec 2002, pp. 795-812.

World Steel University site. (2009). Continuous casting link:
http://www.steeluniversity.org/content/html/eng/default.asp?catid=27&pageid=2081271520

6

Genetic Programming and Boosting Technique to Improve Time Series Forecasting

Luzia Vidal de Souza, Aurora T. R. Pozo,
Anselmo C. Neto and Joel M. C. da Rosa
Federal University of Parana
Brazil

1. Introduction

An essential element for many management decisions is an accurate forecasting. There are several methods and techniques to forecast time series that include traditional forecasting techniques with theoretical foundations in statistics. These methods present some obstacles and complexities to overcome; one of the most important ones is the difficulty to select the model that can provide the best adjustment for a specific dataset, many attempts have to be usually done until the best model can be obtained. Considering this scenario, different machine learning techniques have been recently used in this problem, such as Artificial Neural Network (ANN), Evolutionary Computation (EC), in particular, Genetic Programming (GP), which is considered a promising approach to forecast noisy complex series (Kaboudan, 2000), there are many other works founded in the literature that use (GP) to Time Series Prediction. On the other hand, recently advances in the machine learning field show that the application of the Boosting algorithm is a powerful approach to increase the accuracy of forecasting methods. Boosting algorithm was proposed and developed by Freund and Schapire (1996). According to Allwein et al. (2000), Boosting is a method of finding a highly accurate hypothesis by combining many "weak" hypotheses, each of which is only moderately accurate. Paris et al. (2004) proposed GPBoost that uses the Boosting algorithm with the GP as base learner. We have proposed a new formula for the updating of the weights and for obtain the final hypothesis of the predictor. This algorithm was called of Boosting Correlation Coefficients (BCC) and it is based on the correlation coefficient instead of the loss function used by traditional Boosting algorithms. To evaluate this approach we conducted three experiments. In the first one, the BCC was used to forecast real time series, in this experiment the mean squared error (MSE) has been used to compare the accuracy of the proposed method against the results obtained by GP, GPBoost and the traditional statistical methodology (ARMA). In the second, to prove the efficiency of the proposed methodology a widespread Monte Carlo simulation was done covering the entire ARMA spectrum, in which artificial series were generated from the parametric space of the principal ARMA models, they are AR(1), AR(2), MA(1), MA(2) e ARMA(1,1). The database generated was composed by 214.000 time series with 150 observations each one. The training set was composed by 90% of date and the others 10% composes the test set. The results were compared out of sample and the BCC showed better performance than ARMA methodology, Genetic Programming and GPBoost. Finally, the BCC algorithm was also applied to multiple regressions problem and the results obtained from this method were compared with the results from Artificial Neural Network, Model Tree and Boosting. This comparison showed that the BCC supplied better results than other ones. In way compare the performance of the BCC methodology with other methods, many statistical tests were performed such as Median Square Error (MSE), Root Median Square Error (RMSE) and a non parametric test Friedman. The results were compared out of sample and the BCC methodology had been presented accurate forecasts. Future research Considering that GP is able to provide solutions of high quality, and after the success of our own experiments (Souza et al., 2007a), we are encouraged to further explore GP towards finding solutions to the problem of modeling and pattern discovery of complex time series and in additional we will investigate the procedure BCC using GP as a base learner to analyze probabilistic and stochastic processes. We will investigate new tools that can work GP to more effectively solve this problem. One of the most important applications for the time series analysis is in stock markets. The goal of this task is to choose the best stocks when making an investment, and to decide which is the best strategy at the moment. Therefore, we will investigate the appropriate means for using GP in this task, as well as other general problems in financial time series. An another application that we must investigate is in Biological Networks, for example, gene regulatory network.

2. Genetic programming

Genetic Programming (GP) is an Evolutionary Computation Technique in which the individuals are computational programs. This theory was developed by John Koza (1992) and it is based on Genetic Algorithm (GA) presented by John Holland (1975). In accordance to Banzhaf (1998) and Kaboudan (2000) GP is known as an effective research paradigm in Artificial Intelligence and Machine Learning, and have been studied in the most diverse areas of knowledge, such as: digital cirucuits, data mining, molecular biology, optimization taks and another ones. In nature, those individuals that better adapt to the environment that surrounds them, have greater chance to survive. They pass their genetic characteristics to their descendents, who will suffer modifications to better adapt to the environment. After many generations, this population reaches a natural evolution. In Genetic Programming (GP), the evolutionary algorithm operates over a population of programs that have different forms and sizes. The initial population must have enough diversity, that is, the individuals must have most of the characteristics that are necessary to solve the problem, because characteristics that do not exist in the initial population will probably not appear during the evolutionary process. The evolutionary process is guided by a fitness function that measures the individual's ability to solve the problem. Those individuals that better solve the problem will receive a better fitness value and consequently, will have a better chance to be selected for the next generation. The choice of this function depends on the domain of the problem. A good choice is essential to provide good results. Once the individuals are selected, it is time to apply the genetic operators. These are: Reproduction – an individual is replicated to the next generation, with no modification in its structure; Crossover – two programs are recombined to generate two offspring and Mutation – a new sub-tree replaces a randomly selected part of a program. This process is repeated until a satisfactory solution or a stop criterion is reached. Instead of a population of beings, GP works with a population of computer programs. The goal of the GP algorithm is to select, through recombination of "genes", the program that better solves a given problem. The main elements of GP are:

- Program Structure: a tree is the most used structure to represent programs in GP. Each node can be a function or a terminal. A function has to be evaluated considering its parameters while a terminal has its own value. The terminal (T) and function (F) datasets must be provided by the user in accordance to the current problem. For example, if the datasets are: F = {+, −, *, /} and T = {x, 2} are one simple variable arithmetic expression can be generate, such as x * x + 2 or (x^2+2). Figure 1 shows the abstract syntax tree for that expression.

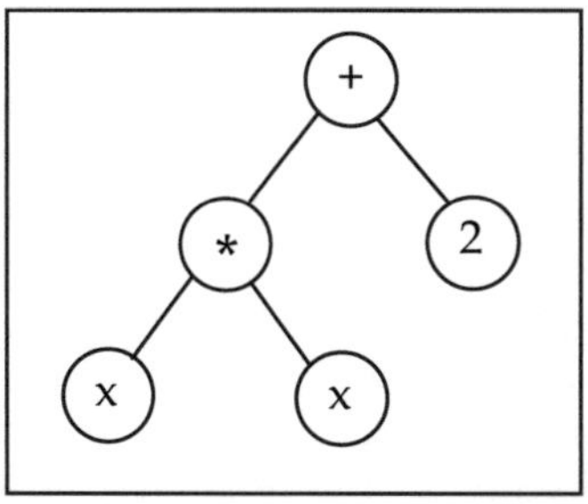

Fig. 1. Sintax tree for (x*x+2)

- Fitness Function and Selection: in nature, individuals are selected based on how well they fit to the environment. The individuals that are able to better solve the problem have better chance to be selected.
- Parameters: there are some parameters that will guide the evolutionary process, these parameters will limit and control the search performance. Some of them are: genetic operators rates (crossover rate, mutation rate), population size, selection rate (tournament size), maximum depth of the individual, etc.

In GP the population is composed by individuals that are computational programs (Koza, 1992). The first step of the algorithm is to create randomly the initial population that is the Generation 0. After that, there are two majors tasks processed in a loop with two main steps:

1. The evaluation of each program by using a fitness function: the GP algorithm receives the set that includes the values that represent the solution for the problem. For example, in a Symbolic Regression problem, it is necessary to provide the set of values of x and f (x) to the GP algorithm. These values are applied to the programs generated with the defined sets of operators and terminals. At the end, the fitness value is obtained.
2. The new population is created by selecting individuals that have better fitness value and by applying the genetic operators.

```
1. Randomly create an initial population
2. Repeat until a good solution or a stop criterion is reached.
   2.1 Evaluate of each program by means of the fitness function
   2.2 Select a subgroup of individuals onto which applies the genetic operators
   2.3 Apply the genetic operators
   2.4 Replace the current population by this new population
3. End
```

Fig. 2. Pseudo code of Genetic Programming

Each run of this loop represents a new generation of individuals, that are the new population that will substitute the previous one. This process is repeated until a solution is found or until a maximum number of generations is reached. At the end, the GP algorithm presents the best tree that is able to solve the given problem in the best way. The pseudo code of the GP algorithm is showed in the Figure 2.

3. Boosting algorithms

The Boosting algorithm was proposed and developed by Freund and Schapire (1996) for binary problems. According to Schapire and Singer (1997) Boosting is a method to find a highly accurate hypothesis by combining many weaker hypotheses, each of which is only moderately accurate. It manipulates the training examples to generate multiple hypotheses. In each iteration the learning algorithm uses different weights on the training examples and returns a hypothesis h_t. The weighted error of h_t is computed and applied to update the weights on the training examples. The result of the change in weights is to place higher weights in training examples that were misclassified by h_t, and lower weights on examples that were correctly classified. The final classifier is composed by the weighted vote of the individual classifiers. Freund and Schapire (1996) introduced the AdaBoost algorithm commonly referred to as the Discrete Boosting algorithm, Ridgeway (1999) developed for binary classification problems. Freund and Schapire (1997) extended AdaBoost to a multi-class case, which they called AdaBoost.M1 and AdaBoost.M2. In order to solve regression problems, Schapire (2002) extended the AdaBoost.M2 and called it AdaBoost.R. It solves regression problems by reducing them to classification ones. Drucker (1997) developed AdaBoost.R2 algorithm, which is an ad hoc modification of AdaBoost.R. He carried out some experiments with AdaBoost.R2 for regression problems and obtained some promising results (Solomatine and Shrestha, 2004). All these approaches follow the view of boosting as a gradient descent procedure (Breiman, 1997), or as residual-fitting, (Buhlmann and Yu, 2003), (Mason et al. 1999). Instead of being trained on a different sample of the same training set, as in previous boosting algorithms, a regressor is trained on a new training set that has different target values (e.g., the residual error of the sum of the previous regressor) (Assad and Bone, 2003). Bone et al. (2003) adapted a Boosting algorithm to time series forecasting using neural networks as base learners. Their experiments showed that Boosting actually provides improved results in regression problems. Iba (1999) proposed a version of AdaBoost for GP and regression. In his work the distribution was implemented picking up examples to generate a new learning set for each Boosting round. The probability of an example being picked up is proportional to its weight, and any example can be picked from 0,1 up to several times. According to Paris (2002), this approach makes the implementation easier, but the precision of weights is somewhat lost in the process.

3.1 GPBoost

Paris proposed a Boosting method that retains the precision of weights and operates on the whole set of examples for every round of Boosting. Their algorithm, named GPBoost, uses a weighted based fitness function in GP and the generic AdaBoost.R2 algorithm to update the weights its pseudo code is showed in the figure 3. The GP technique allows us to obtain accurate models from different datasets with diverse characteristics, and from the obtained model to estimate or predict the behavior of the system along time. On the other side, using Boosting, the results obtained with the merging hypothesis are always better than the results obtained with GP technique.

Algorithm 2 - GPBoost

1. Given a training set $S = \{(x_1, y_1), (x_2, y_2), \ldots, (x_m, y_m)\}$; $x_i \in X$, $y_i \in R$, GP is the base algorithm
2. $D_1(i)$ is the weight of the example (x_i, y_i), $D_1(i) := 1/m \; \forall (x_i, y_i) \in S$

   Repeat: $t = 1$ to T

   Run GP over Dt using the function fitness:

   $$fit = \sum_{i=1}^{m} \left(\left| f(x_i) - y_i \right| * D_t(i) \right) * m,$$

   where f is a function in GP population and f_t is the best individual in the run t.

   Calculate: the loss function $L_i = \dfrac{|f_t(x_i) - y_i|}{\max_{i=1\ldots m} |f_t(x_i) - y_i|}$

   Calculate the average loss function: $\bar{L} = \sum_{i=1}^{m} L_i D_i$

   Let $\beta_t = \dfrac{\bar{L}}{1 - \bar{L}}$ is the confidence given to the function f_t

   Update for the next round:

   distribution $D_{t+1}(i) := \dfrac{D_t(i)^{1-L_i}}{Z_t}$, Z_t is a normalization factor.

3. Output: Final Hypothesis $F(x) = \min\{y \in R : \sum_{t: f_t(x) \le y} \log\left(\frac{1}{\beta_t}\right) \ge \frac{1}{2} \sum_{t=1}^{m} \log\left(\frac{1}{\beta_t}\right)\}$

Fig. 3. Pseudo code of GPBoost Algorithm

3.2 Boosting Correlation Coefficients (BCC)

After many studies through the Boosting algorithms, it is possible to point out that these algorithms have been sufficiently explored over classification problems. Less emphasis, however, has been given to regression problems. The Boosting algorithm for regression problems is an adaptation of the concepts used in classification. The traditional form of obtaining the weights of each example is based on error or loss function. However, the loss function is one of the possible information that can be used to obtain these weights. Recently, (Souza et al., 2007; 2009) used the BCC algorithm that is Boosting using Correlation Coefficients to time series forecasting and regressions problem. The method is a new approach of the Boosting algorithm for regression and is empirically based. BCC uses the coefficients of correlation for the updating of the weights and it has been observed that this directly influences the minimization of the loss function. The same coefficients can also be used in the final combination of predictors. The correlation coefficient is a statistical measure of the interdependence of two or more random variables. Fundamentally, the value indicates how much of a change in one variable is explained by a change in another. The BCC method is based on this measure and will be described within this section, but firstly, a brief review on the definition of Correlation Coefficients is given.

Definition: The correlation between two samples X and Y, with m observations, is calculated by using the Equation 1.

$$\rho(x,y)=\frac{\sum_{i=1}^{m}(x_i-\overline{x})(y_i-\overline{y})}{\sqrt{\sum_{i=1}^{m}(x_i-\overline{x})^2\sum_{i=1}^{m}(y_i-\overline{y})^2}} \tag{1}$$

where $\overline{x}$ and $\overline{y}$ are the mean values of the samples X and Y respectively. The coefficient ranges from −1 to 1. If the coefficient has the value 1 it means that a linear equation describes the relationship perfectly and positively, with all data points lying on the same line and with Y increasing with X. A score of −1 shows that all data points lie on a single line but that Y increases as X decreases.

The Boosting Correlation Coefficient is a metric function that measures the relation degree between two variables, in this case between the real and the predicted values. The structure of the BCC algorithm is similar to the GPBoost algorithm. First of all, the weight distribution D_t is initialized in Step 1 and the boosting iterations start (Step 2) by calling each time the GP algorithm. After the GP's complete execution, the best individual ft in the run is chosen. After, the loss function is computed. To calculate the loss function different forms can be used, such as the exponential showed in Equation 2. Then, the correlation coefficients are calculated (Equation 3) and after the next weights are updated using the Equation 4. Finally, Step 3, the output must be computed as a combination of the different generated hypotheses. To calculate the final hypothesis F, T functions ft will be combined using again the correlation coefficients, see Equation 5.

$$L_t(x_i)=1-\exp\left(-\frac{|f_t(x_i)-y(x_i)|}{\max_{i=1\ldots m}|f_t(x_i)-y(x_i)|}\right) \tag{2}$$

$$\rho_t(f_t(x_i),y(x_i))=\frac{\sum_{i=1}^{m}\left(f_t(x_i)-f_t(\overline{x})\right)\left(y(x_i)-y(\overline{x})\right)}{\sqrt{\sum_{i=1}^{m}\left(f_t(x_i)-f_t(\overline{x})\right)^2\sum_{i=1}^{m}\left(y(x_i)-y(\overline{x})\right)^2}} \tag{3}$$

$$P_{t+1}(x_i)=\rho_t\left(f_t(x_i),y(x_i)\right)*P_t*L_t(x_i) \tag{4}$$

$$F(x_{i-1})=\frac{\sum_{t=1}^{T}\rho_t\left(f_t(x_i),y(x_i)\right)*f_t(x_i)}{\sum_{t=1}^{T}\rho_t\left(f_t(x_i),y(x_i)\right)},\ i=1,\ldots,m\text{-}1 \tag{5}$$

$$F(x_m)=\frac{\sum_{t=1}^{T}f_t(x_i)}{T},\ i=m$$

The intention in use the correlation coefficients is to promote a smoothness in the update of the weights, because it was observed that there is an inherent roughness on it, on the other hand the correlation coefficients were used to combine the obtained hypothesis in only one hypothesis that can be better than each one because of its goodness of estimation.

4. Time Series Forecasting

Time Series Forecasting is an important area of the knowledge and there are many applications in the real world. Accurate forecasting is an essential element for many management decisions. There are several methods and techniques to find a good model that can be used to produce accurate forecasting the traditional techniques have your foundations in statistics. The most important model statistical methodology is the Autoregressive and Moving Average (ARMA) models. These methods presents some obstacles and complexities to overcome. The major difficulty is to select the good model that can best adjustment for a specific dataset, usually many attempts must be performed until the best model must be found. Because of these difficulties, many researchers have been done several efforts to overcome these problems, such as Artificial Neural Network (ANN), Evolutionary Computation (EC) and in special Genetic Programming (GP) that have been provided good results in time series forecasting.

5. Experiments using real time series

This section will describe the experiments that have been accomplished using the BCC algorithm with GP as a base learner and the results are compared with other techniques such as Box & Jenkins; traditional GP and GPBoost. In the first experiment the algorithms were used in a group of academic series, in the second one (Section 6) we used a widespread Monte Carlo simulation covering the entire ARMA spectrum. First of all, we will describe the data sets that were used in the experiments, second the configuration of the methodology that were used and after the results are presented and the evaluate of the algorithms is done.

5.1 Academic and Benchmark Time Series

The academic series used in this experiment can be found at the website: (www.ime.usp.br/~pam/ST.html) and the Benchmark series at (www.economatica.com). A brief explanation about the series is presented at Table 1. Each data set was divided into two other data sets: training set that contains the 90% first values from the data set that were used to train the methods and the second one that contains the remaining values.

5.2 Box and Jenkins methodology- ARMA models

The Box & Jenkins methodology is one of the most important and recognized work in Time Series area. The research was made by George Box and Gwiliyn Jenkins (1970) and it is based on the Wold (1954) studies, who proved that any time series can be represented by a structure of infinity moving average . The methodology adjust Autoregressive and Moving Average Models ARMA(p, q) to the data set, where p is the parameter of the Autoregressive and q is the parameter of the Moving Average models and they represent the order of the model to be used. The Box and Jenkins methodology is composed by four steps.

Step 1. Identification of the model to be used on the dataset, the best model is selected by using Akaike (1974) Information Criterion (AIC), see Equation 6, where k is the number of parameters in the statistical model, and L is the maximized value of the likelihood function for the estimated model.

$$AIC = 2k - 2\ln(L) \qquad (6)$$

Real Time Series	
Atmosphere:	daily measurements of the temperature in degrees centigrade, at twelve o'clock from 1/1 to 12/31/1997, São Paulo, Brazil, 365 examples.
Beverages:	monthly figures of drinks industrial production, from 1/1985 to 7/2000, Brazil, 187 examples.
Consumption:	monthly figures of product sales, from 1/1984 to 10/1984, São Paulo, Brazil, 154 examples.
Fortaleza:	annual measurements of atmospheric precipitation, from 1849 to 1997, Fortaleza, Brazil, 149 examples.
ICV:	monthly figures, pricing index, from 1/1970 to 6/1980, São Paulo, Brazil, 126 examples.
IPI:	monthly observations of Food products (Industrial Production index), from 1/1985 to 7/2000,187 examples.
Lavras:	monthly measurements of atmospheric precipitation, from 1/1966 to 12/1997, Lavras, Brazil, 384 examples.
Sunspots:	annual observations of the Wolfer Sunspots, from 1749 to 1924, 176 examples.
Djiad, Nasdaq Ibovd	daily figures of the Stock returns from their respective financial markets, from 13/08/2001 to17/08/2005, 1100 examples each dataset.

Table 1. Real Time Series

Serie	Dataset (100%)	Training set (90%)	Test set (10%)
Atmosphere	365	329	36
Beverage	187	169	18
Consumption	154	139	15
Fortaleza	149	135	14
ICV	126	114	12
IPI	187	169	18
Lavras	384	346	38
Sunspots	176	159	17
Djiad	1100	990	110
Ibovespa	1100	990	110
Nasdaq	1100	990	110

Table 2. Number of examples of each data set

Step 2. Estimation of the parameters to adjust the order of the model to be used.
Step 3. Adaptability verification of the model. Trough the residual analysis is verified if the model has a good fit to the dataset.
Step 4. Forecasting is made using the chosen model.

5.3 Configuration of GP, GPBoost and BCC

To apply these algorithms, we chose the tool Lil-GP 1.0 (Zongker, 1995) which is a free and easily configurable software, implemented according to Koza's GP (1992). To solve the problems it is necessary to provide the configuration files, standard GP parameters, functions and variables used to generate the models, input and output files (training and test set), as well as to specify the fitness function. The parameters used in this work to configure GP tool are showed at Table 3. These parameters have been gotten empirically after many tests have been accomplished. The terminal set used was T = { Z_{t-1}, Z_{t-2}, Z_{t-3}, Z_{t-4}} that is, the last four observations are used to make a prediction at the time t. Beside these a constant α is also used and the functions set is F = {+, −, *, /, log, cos, sin, exp, root}. This Function set allows us to obtain non linear models that have better adjust to the complex series than linear models. The fitness function used was defined as the Weighted Root Mean Square Error (WRMSE) that is, in general, used to measure the accuracy of a forecasting method. The WRMSE is showed in Equation 7, where x_i is the real value, $\hat{x}_i$ is the estimated value, D_i is the weight of each example and n is the size of the dataset. In this experiment, individuals with WRMSE equal to 0 or near to 0 are the best.

$$Fitness = \sqrt{\frac{\sum_{i=1}^{n} (x_i - \hat{x}_i)^2 D_i m}{n}} \tag{7}$$

The Boosting algorithm with the different output hypotheses has been implemented in C computer language. For each data set, ten models of each algorithm (GP, GP-Boost and BCC) were obtained using a different random initial seed and for the GPBoost and BCC algorithm it was used ten Boosting iterations. After that, each generated model was used to forecast the values in the test set.

Parameters	Value
Population Size	4,000
Population initialization method	Full
Number of generations	250
Selection method	Best
Initial depth	2 - 10
Maximum depth limit	10
Maximum number of nodes	50
Crossover rate	0.7
Reproduction rate	0.2
Mutation rate	0.1

Table 3. Parameters of GP, GPBoost and BCC

5.4 Results

In order to evaluate the performance of these methods, we used the average of the Mean Square Error (MSE) obtained by using 10 initial seeds over the test set. This measure was used as a parameter of comparison because it is accepted by the statistical community. For the ARMA model, there is only one prediction and then the value of n is one. The results of this experiment are summarized in Table 4. The BCC algorithm presented the best performance, in almost all the data set the MSE average was the lowest.

Serie	ARMA	GP	GPBoost	BCC
Atmosphere	38.98	38.08	36.72	**7.59**
Beverage	308.25	245.65	231.76	**62.59**
Consumption	137.76	236.15	140.52	**60.86**
ICV	445,690.37	423,083.18	400,212.40	**209,855.37**
IPI	624.96	130.99	124.45	**17.05**
Lavras	5,335.99	13,788.93	8,249.27	**4,623.50**
Sunspots	902.70	320.85	**318.76**	329.10
Djiad	0.05	0.00	0.00	0.00
Ibovd	0.26	0.00	0.00	0.00
Nasdaq	0.06	0.00	0.00	0.00

Table 4. Average values of MSE from 10 run of the algorithms.

Beside the MSE, it was applied a non parametric test, Friedman Test (Siegal, 1988) and (Demsar, 2006), to estimate the BCC performance against the other methods. The null hypothesis that all the algorithms are equivalent was tested and rejected, after that the post-hoc multiple comparisons were performed. The results are summarized in Table 5. The algorithms ARMA, GP, GP-Boost and BCC and the result of the test shows that there is a significant difference between ARMA and BCC and between GPBoost and BCC all the other algorithms have no significant difference.

Algorithms	Statistical Difference
ARMA - GP	FALSE
ARMA - GPBoost	FALSE
ARMA - BCC	TRUE
GP - GPBoost	FALSE
GP - BCC	FALSE
GPBoost - BCC	FALSE

Table 5. Multiple comparisons among evaluated methods after Friedman test

6. Experiment using Monte Carlo simulation

A widespread Monte Carlo simulation has been done to exhaustively evaluate the performance of the BCC algorithm with GP as a base learner, in which we simulated artificial time series that belong to the entire spectrum of the structures AR(1), MA(1), AR(2), MA(2) and ARMA(1,1). To generate these series we used the free statistical software R). The parameters were put through variations within their respective parametric spaces and a noise component was added. The noise has normal distribution with mean 0 and standard deviation 1.

6.1 Parameters setting

In order to setting the parameters that were used in this simulation, it was considered the stationary region in the parametric space of the principal structure of the ARMA models: AR(1), AR(2), MA(1), MA(2), ARMA(1, 1). The stationary region of the AR(1) and MA(1) structure are represented by the Equation 8. Where ϕ_1 is the autoregressive parameter and θ_1 is the moving average parameter, both of them are defined from -1 to 1. This space was divided using step 0.1

$$-1 < \phi_1 < 1$$
$$-1 < \theta_1 < 1 \qquad (8)$$

The parametric space of the stationary region of the AR(2) structure is defined by the Equation 9. Where ϕ_1 and ϕ_2 are the autoregressive parameters, for the MA(2) structure there is no restriction of the stationary (Morettin and Toloi, 2004), but its invertibility region is the same of the stationary region of the AR(2) structure. This region was divided using step 0.2 on the x and y axes.

$$\phi_1 + \phi_2 < 1$$
$$\phi_2 - \phi_1 < 1 \qquad (9)$$
$$-1 < \phi_2 < 1$$

Finally, the parametric space of the stationary region of the ARMA(1, 1) structure is defined by the Equation 10. Where ϕ_1 is the autoregressive parameter and θ_1 is the moving average parameter.

$$\theta_1 + \phi_1 < 1$$
$$-1 < \theta_1 < 1 \qquad (10)$$
$$-1 < \phi_1 < 1$$

Using this criterion, the data set included 214.000 series distributed for each structure as showed in the Table 6. For each set of parameter, 500 series were created, for example, the AR(1) structure has 19 parameters, then the number of series is 500 × 19 = 9,500. Each data set was divided in training and test set in the same way that was made for the real time series. The number of the examples of each data set was 150, then the training set contain 135 examples and the test set 15.

Structures	Parameters	Series
AR(1)	19	9,500
AR(2)	90	45,000
MA(1)	19	9,500
MA(2)	200	100,000
ARMA(1, 1)	100	50,000

Table 6. Monte Carlo Simulation Series

6.2 Evaluation metrics

Despite using MSE as a comparison measure, this is not enough to guarantee that the algorithm is better than another one. To analyze more precisely the performance of the proposed algorithm against other, the Friedman test was performed. The null hypothesis that states that all the algorithms are equivalent was rejected and then, the post-hoc multiple comparisons were performed. The analysis was made for each structure considering the MSE results of each set of parameters. For example, the MA(2) structure has two hundred different sets of parameters, for each of them, one MSE result is obtained for each algorithm. In this simulation, only one seed was used to GP due to the largest of the data set. The training set contains the first 90% of the values from the data set and was used to train the methods. The testing set contains the remaining values and was used to evaluate the methods.

6.3 Computational implementation

For each series from the data set (214,000) it was run 10 Boosting algorithm (GPBoost and BCC). The data sets have been run in a computational platform that includes 42 dual processor computers. The computer language used to implement the algorithms GPBoost, BCC and GP was C++ that used the Lil-GP 1.0 to run the GP as a sub routine. The data set was divided into 428 groups each one containing 500 series. Each group ran 10 Boosting algorithms including GPBoost and BCC. The computational time to run each group was 32 hours.

6.4 Results

The results were analyzed through the MSE in the test set, the MSE was calculated in accordance with Equation 11. Where serie(x_i) are the real values, ARMA(x_i) are the predicted values from ARMA models, GPBoost(x_i) are the predicted values from GPBoost and BCC(x_i) are the predicted values from BCC algorithm.

$$\text{error}(h_i) = \begin{cases} \frac{1}{500}\sum_{i=1}^{500}\left(\text{serie}(x_i) - \text{ARMA}(x_i)\right)^2 \\ \frac{1}{500}\sum_{i=1}^{500}\left(\text{serie}(x_i) - \text{GP}(x_i)\right)^2 \\ \frac{1}{500}\sum_{i=1}^{500}\left(\text{serie}(x_i) - \text{GPBoost}(x_i)\right)^2 \\ \frac{1}{500}\sum_{i=1}^{500}\left(\text{serie}(x_i) - \text{BCC}(x_i)\right)^2 \end{cases} \tag{11}$$

In Table 7 is presented the MSE in the forecasted values for all the algorithms. Table 8 shows the results of the MSE for all the structure, due to space reasons only the sum of the MSE is presented. Table 9 shows the pos-hoc multiple comparisons results. In this Table, the symbol "FALSE" is used to denote that there is no statistical difference between the methods ARMA, GP, GP-Boost and BCC. From these Tables it is possible to conclude that:

- For AR(1) structure, the BCC is significantly better than the other algorithms; GP and GPBoost algorithms have no difference, as well as, ARMA and GP algorithms.
- For AR(2) structure, the BCC is significantly better than ARMA and GP algorithms, and equal to GPBoost; ARMA and GP have no difference.
- For MA(1) structure, the BCC is significantly better than the other algorithms; there is no difference between: ARMA and GP algorithms, ARMA and GP-Boost algorithms, and GP and GP-Boost algorithms.
- For MA(2) structure, the BCC is significantly better than the other algorithms; there is no difference between ARMA and GP algorithms; GP-Boost is better than GP and ARMA algorithms.
- For ARMA(1,1) structure, the BCC is significantly better than the other algorithms; there is no difference between ARMA and GP algorithms; GP-Boost is better than GP and ARMA algorithms.

Concluding, in almost all the cases the BCC method is the best and when the method is not the best, there is no statistical differences between the methods. GP-Boost is significantly better than GP and ARMA algorithms in many cases, but GP and ARMA algorithms have no difference.

Forecasting	MSE Average	AR(1)	AR(2)	MA(1)	MA(2)	ARMA(1, 1)
e136	ARMA	2.3702	4.3479	2.3150	3.0335	1.7917
	GP	1.0567	1.3176	5.6063	2.2456	1.8133
	GPBoost	1.0118	1.1906	1.1318	2.0985	1.1327
	BCC	**0.9282**	**1.0997**	**1.0781**	**1.9234**	**1.1087**
e137	ARMA	2.3527	4.1828	1.8223	2.7355	2.0809
	GP	1.9907	1.5090	1.6281	2.1690	1.2657
	GPBoost	1.1842	1.3537	1.1394	2.0773	1.1427
	BCC	**1.0924**	**1.2563**	**1.0260**	**1.8843**	**1.0553**
e138	ARMA	2.0450	4.0820	1.8098	2.6617	2.2494
	GP	1.0470	1.3674	1.1456	3.2616	1.3300
	GPBoost	1.0311	**1.1733**	1.0935	2.0698	1.1277
	BCC	**0.9583**	1.4734	**0.9838**	**1.9117**	**1.0897**
e139	ARMA	2.1817	4.1294	1.9132	2.6473	2.3892
	GP	1.3314	1.4605	1.2253	3.0242	1.6402
	GPBoost	1.2955	1.2963	1.1898	2.0711	1.1417
	BCC	**1.2194**	**1.5489**	**1.0972**	**1.9318**	**1.0871**
e140	ARMA	2.0486	4.2354	1.7691	2.6666	2.4768
	GP	1.5099	1.6394	1.2392	2.1816	1.3522
	GPBoost	1.3779	**1.4485**	1.1130	2.0828	1.1416
	BCC	**1.2547**	1.4844	**1.0077**	**1.8970**	**1.0806**
e141	ARMA	1.9550	4.5942	1.8326	2.6444	2.5734
	GP	1.4487	1.5345	1.1601	2.3654	1.2922
	GPBoost	**1.2907**	1.3558	1.1285	2.0613	1.1399
	BCC	1.4669	**1.3466**	**1.0123**	**1.9397**	**1.1006**
e142	ARMA	1.6495	4.5034	1.8526	2.6580	2.6567
	GP	2.2842	1.6545	1.2233	2.3011	1.6019
	GPBoost	1.1341	**1.1711**	1.1996	2.0800	**1.1467**
	BCC	**1.0966**	1.2458	**1.0695**	**1.9264**	1.2413
e143	ARMA	1.4880	4.7462	1.8323	2.6514	2.6738
	GP	2.0030	1.7681	1.2425	3.1361	1.2913
	GPBoost	0.9834	**1.3549**	1.1424	**2.0581**	1.1375
	BCC	**0.9053**	1.4738	**1.0188**	4.4017	**1.0651**
e144	ARMA	1.2274	3.6964	1.7596	2.6497	2.7013
	GP	0.8461	5.0540	1.3345	2.7877	1.3619
	GPBoost	0.8106	**1.2776**	1.1668	**2.2478**	1.1386
	BCC	**0.7475**	1.5608	**1.0914**	2.6743	**1.0664**
e145	ARMA	1.4540	3.6346	1.8127	2.6596	2.7278
	GP	1.1212	1.4859	1.4670	3.0190	1.3692
	GPBoost	**1.1029**	1.2636	1.1852	**2.0717**	**1.1365**
	BCC	1.3978	**1.2616**	**1.0703**	2.4415	1.4385
e146	ARMA	1.6769	3.3792	1.8306	2.6673	2.7513
	GP	1.4171	2.4862	1.1538	2.5006	10.2940
	GPBoost	1.3755	1.2689	1.1349	**2.0858**	1.1417
	BCC	**1.2677**	**1.2078**	**1.0377**	2.4169	**1.1677**
e147	ARMA	1.2946	3.4343	1.8601	2.6690	2.7759
	GP	1.0576	1.5164	1.2334	2.7557	1.8779
	GPBoost	1.0276	1.3071	1.1368	**2.0776**	**1.1450**
	BCC	**0.9326**	**1.2561**	**1.0224**	2.5989	1.1471
e148	ARMA	1.3387	3.3868	1.7664	2.6551	2.7658
	GP	1.1235	2.2805	1.2059	2.7182	6.5438
	GPBoost	1.0967	1.2308	1.0886	**2.0734**	1.2860
	BCC	**1.0049**	**1.1477**	**1.0428**	2.1184	**1.2057**
e149	ARMA	1.2239	3.5028	1.7232	2.6740	2.8048
	GP	1.0304	1.5118	1.1609	2.7705	1.3648
	GPBoost	1.0237	**1.2823**	1.1196	2.1262	1.1386
	BCC	**0.9286**	1.8203	**1.0069**	**1.9977**	**1.0578**
e150	ARMA	1.7268	3.4916	1.7436	2.6571	2.8316
	GP	1.7379	1.6753	1.1366	2.5503	3.4325
	GPBoost	**1.5064**	**1.4174**	1.0936	**2.0637**	1.1398
	BCC	1.5922	1.4630	**0.9879**	2.0916	**1.0977**

Table 7. MSE average in the test set

Model	ARMA	GP	GPBoost	BCC
AR(1)	29.99	25.24	20.48	15.29
AR(2)	356.08	169.57	116.35	123.88
MA(1)	35.01	29.34	21.61	19.70
MA(2)	537.74	530.49	417.93	455.41
ARMA(1,1)	255.00	252.21	114.91	113.40

Table 8. Sum of MSE average in the test set

Friedman Test Comparison						
Structure	ARMA GP	ARMA GPBoost	ARMA BCC	GP GPBoost	GP BCC	GPBoost BCC
AR(1)	FALSE	TRUE	TRUE	FALSE	TRUE	TRUE
AR(2)	FALSE	TRUE	TRUE	TRUE	TRUE	FALSE
MA(1)	FALSE	FALSE	TRUE	FALSE	TRUE	TRUE
MA(2)	FALSE	TRUE	TRUE	TRUE	TRUE	TRUE
ARMA(1, 1)	FALSE	TRUE	TRUE	TRUE	TRUE	TRUE

Table 9. Multiple comparisons among evaluated methods Friedman test

7. Regression problems

In this section we describe an experiment applying the BCC algorithm for Multivariate Regressions Problems. The goal is to evaluate the proposed method in this kind of problem. In order to compare with other techniques, we used the same datasets and evaluation measures described in Souza and Vergilio (2006). In their work, they presented the results obtained with the application of Neural Networks (multi-layer perceptron, ANN), M5 Model Tree (MT), Adaboost.R2 (R2) and Adaboost.RT (RT), here replicated for comparison purposes with our approach.

7.1 Data sets

The dataset´s features are described in Table 10, these datasets are used as a benchmark for comparing results with the previous research. The dataset was divided into training (70%) and test (30%). The subsets were obtained using a random selection without replacement strategy. The procedure was repeated for ten times with different seeds in order to obtain ten statistically different subsets of data. These ten subsets were prepared to obtain consistent results. The BCC algorithm was implemented using the software R and as base learner the Cart (Classification and Regression Tree) algorithm was used. The reason to select this learning technique is that it is simple, easy and fast to train.

Data Base	Number of Instances	Number of Atributtes
CPU	209	6
Housing	506	13
Auto-Mpg	398	7
Friedman #1	1500	5

Table 10. Multiple Regression Dataset

7.2 Results

The performances of the different algorithms are presented in the Table 11. By analyzing the results we can conclude that there is no technique that will always present the best results. For some datasets the best model was obtained by using one approach, for other datasets the best model was obtained with another one. In order to analyze more precisely the algorithm's relative performance some quantitative measurement is needed rather than just subjective comparison. For this reason, following the methodology used by Souza and Vergilio (2006), we used the so-called scoring matrix. It shows the average relative performance (in %) of one technique over another technique for all the data sets considered. Element of scoring matrix SMij should be read as the ith machine's average performance (header row in Table 12) against machine j (header column in Table 12) and is calculated for a N number of datasets as is showed in the Equation 12 (for $i \neq j$). From Table 12 it can be clearly observed that BCC scores highest.

$$SM_{ij} = \frac{1}{N}\sum_{k=1}^{N}\frac{RMSE_{k,j} - RMSE_{ki}}{\max\left(RMSE_{kj}, RMSE_{ki}\right)} \tag{12}$$

Bases	BCC	MT	Bagging	ANN	AdaBoost.R	AdaBoost.RT
CPU	**22.48**	34.65	32.64	**13.91**	24.45	26.52
Housing	**1.12**	3.62	3.24	3.54	3.23	3.23
Auto-Mpg	**0.85**	3.01	2.86	3.79	2.84	2.96
Friedman	**0.7**	2.19	2.06	1.51	1.82	1.72

Table 11. Performance comparison (RMSE) between the different algorithms in the test set

Machine	MT	Bagging	ANN	R2	RT	BCC	Total
MT	0.0	-6.8	-18.1	-11.5	-14.3	-61.0	-117.7
Bagging	6.8	0.0	-12.8	-9.4	-8.0	-58.2	-81.6
ANN	18.1	12.8	0.0	6.6	7.3	-40.4	4.4
R2	11.5	9.4	-6.6	0.0	1.6	-51.2	-35.3
RT	14.3	8.0	-7.3	-1.6	0.0	-52.8	-39.4
BCC	61.0	58.2	40.4	51.2	52.8	0.0	263.6

Table 12. Scoring matrix for different machines

8. Conclusion

In this paper we present the BCC algorithm that uses the correlation coefficients between the real and the forecasting value obtained using GP as a base learner. The correlation coefficient is used for update the weights and for the generation of the final formula. Differently from works found in the literature, in this paper we investigate the use of the correlation metrics as a factor, besides the error metric. This new approach, called Boosting using Correlation Coefficients (BCC), has been empirically obtained when trying to improve the results from the other methods. The correlation coefficient was considered because two algorithms could present the same mean error and different correlation coefficients for a dataset. This difference on behavior of the two algorithms can be measured by the correlation coefficient. A good correlation coefficient results in small errors for each example. The correlation coefficient is used in the proposed algorithm with two purposes:

the first use of the correlation coefficient is for the update of the weights, here the intent is to promote a smoothness of the update, because it has been observed that the original equation has an inherent roughness. The second use is to combine the final hypothesis, and in this case the intent is to allow that each hypothesis contributes to the final hypothesis according to its goodness of estimation. This idea was evaluated through two groups of experiments. In the first group of experiments, we explore the BCC for time series forecasting, using Genetic Programming (GP) as a base learner. Differently from works found in the literature a great number of series were used considering academic series and a widespread Monte Carlo simulation. In the Monte Carlo Simulation, series were generated
in the entire parametric space for the main ARMA structures: AR(1), AR(2), MA(1) MA(2) and ARMA(1,1). From all these experiments we can conclude that in almost all cases the BCC method is the best and when the method is not the best, there is no statistical difference between the compared methods. The goal of the second group of experiments was to evaluate the proposed method in multivariate regression problems. We have compared the BCC algorithm with the results reported by other authors, comparing a M5 model tree (MT), bagging, AdaBoost.R2, AdaBoost.RT and Artificial Neural Networks (ANN). For our work, a model tree was chosen as the base learner. We use a scoring matrix to analyze the algorithms' relative performance. It shows the average relative performance (in%) of one technique over another technique. Like in time series forecasting it can be clearly observed that BCC scores the highest. We can conclude that the proposed algorithm is very advantageous for regression problems. The BCC algorithm was evaluated using two different base learners and it always showed good results. These results encourage us to carry out future experiments to explore other base learners. We intend to better evaluate the proposed approach and to explore meta-learning to select the best algorithm according to the characteristics of the datasets. The meta-learning approach will help us to better understand the problems that better fit to one algorithm or another. Other future works are the investigation of other application domains like Software Reliability. Also, an interesting idea is to extend the work for classification problems, however, the correlation coefficient can be used only for continuous variables, and then, other metrics must be considered.

9. References

Akaike, H. (1974). A new look at the statistical model identification. *IEEE Trans Autom Control,* Vol. 11, pp. 716–723.

Allwein, E. L.; Schapire, R. E. & Y. Singer. (2000). Reducing multiclass to binary: A unifying approach for margin classifiers, *Journal of Machine Learning Research,* Vol.1, pp. 113-141.

Assad, M. and Bone, R. (2003) Improving time series prediction by recurrent neural network ensembles. *Universite de Tours, Tech. Rep.,* 2003.

Banzhaf, F.; W. Nordin, Keller, P.; and Francone, F. D. (1998). *Genetic Programming: An Introduction,* Morgan Kaufmann.

Bone, R.; Assad M. and Crucianu, M. (2003). Boosting recurrent neural networks for times series prediction. *In: Proceedings of the international conference in Roanne. Springer Computer Science,* Springer, Roanne, pp 18–22

Box, G. E. P. and Jenkins, G. M. (1976). *Time series analysis: forecasting and control,* Rev. ed. San Francisco: Holden-Day.

Breiman, L. (1997). Prediction Games and Arcing Algorithms. *Neural Computation*, Vol. 11, N· 7, pp. 1493-1518.

Buhlmann, P and Yu, B. (2003). Boosting with the loss: Regression and classification. *Journal of the American Statistical Association*, Vol. 98, no 462, pp. 324–339, June 2003.

Demsar, J. (2006). *Statistical comparisons of classifiers over multiple data sets*. J Mach Learn Res Vol. 7, pp. 1–30.

Drucker, H. (1997). Improving regression using boosting techniques. *In: Proceeding of International Conference on Machine Learning, ICML97*, Orlando, 1997.

Freund, Y. and Schapire, R. E. (1996). Experiments with a new boosting algorithm. *Proceedings of the Thirteenth Conference*, pp. 148-156, Ed. Morgan Kaufmann.

Freund, Y. and Scahpire, R. E. (1997). A decision-theoretic generalization of on-line learning and an application to boosting. *Journal of Computer and System Sciences*, Vol. 55, pp. 119–139.

Kaboudan, M. A. (2000). Genetic programming prediction on stock prices, *Journal Computational Economics*, Vol. 16, pp. 207–236.

Koza, J. (1992). *Genetic programming: on the programming of computers by means of natural selection*. MIT Press, Cambridge.

Holland, J. (1975). *Adaptation in Natural and Artificial Systems*, MIT Press.

Iba, H. (1999). Bagging, boosting, and bloating in genetic programming. *In: Proceedings of the Genetic and Evolutionary Computation conference*, pp. 1053–1060

Mason, L.; Baxter, J.; Bartlett, P. and Frean, M. (1999). *Advances in Large Margin Classifiers*. MIT Press, Functional gradient techniques for combining hypotheses, Cambridge, MA, pp. 221–247.

Moretin, P; Toloi, P. A. and Toloi, C. M. C. (2004). *Análise de séries temporais*. Ed. Edgard Blucher LTDA. São Paulo.

Paris, G.; Robiliard, D. and Fonlupt, C. (2002). Applying boosting techniques to genetic programming. *In: Selected papers from the 5th European conference on artificial evolution*. Springer, London, pp 267–280.

Ridgeway, G. (1999). The state of boosting. *Computing Science And Stastic*, vol. 31, pp. 172–181.

Schapire, R. (2002). The boosting approach to machine learning: An overview. In: *MSRI Workshop on Nonlinear Estimation and Classification*, March 2002, Berkeley, CA.

Siegal, S. and Castellan, N. (1988). *Non-parametric statistics for the behavioural sciences*. McGraw–Hill, New York

Solomatine, D. P and Shrestha, D. L. (2004). Adaboost.RT: a Boosting Algorithm for regression Problems. *IEEE*, pp. 1163-1168.

Souza, L. V.; Pozo, A. R. T; Da Rosa, J. C. M. and Chaves Neto, A. (2007). The Boosting Technique using Correlation Coefficient to Improve Time Series Forecasting Accuracy, *Proceedings of Congress on Evolutionary Computation (CEC 2007)*, pp. 1288-1295. IEEE Transactions.

Souza, L. V.; Pozo, A. R. T; Da Rosa, J. C. M. and Chaves Neto, A. (2009). Applying Correlation to enhance boosting technique using genetic programming as a base learner. *Applied Intelligence*. Vol. 30, No. 7, (Feb, 2009).

Souza GA, Vergilio SR (2006). Modeling software reliability growth with artificial neural networks. *In: Proceedings of the IEEE*. Latin American test workshop, Buenos Aires, Argentina, pp 165–170

Wold, H. (1954). *A Study in the analysis of Stationary Time Series*. Almguist & Wiksell. 1st. ed., Stocolm.

Zongker, D. and Punch, B. (1995). *Lil-gp 1.0 user's manual*. Michigan State University, East Lansing.

7

Enhancement of Capability in Probabilistic Risk Analysis by Genetic Algorithms

Napat Harnpornchai
College of Art, Media, and Technology, Chiang Mai University
Thailand

1. Introduction

Probabilistic Risk Analysis (PRA) has been widely recognized for its crucial role in various disciplines. The investigation and assessment of system failure or system malfunction is a main interest in PRA. A system is considered in a failure status when the system cannot satisfy a set of prescribed performance criteria. The prescribed performance criteria are referred to as the performance functions. The performance functions are explicitly or implicitly defined in terms of random variables that characterize the problems of interest. The performance functions also divide the high dimension space of random variables into a failure domain and a safe domain. The failure domain is the subspace of random variables that result in the failure of system. The complementary subspace is the safe domain.

The essential information that is particularly desired from PRA includes Point of Maximum Likelihood (PML) in failure domain and the failure probability. PML represents the combination of variable magnitudes that most likely contribute to the failure and to the corresponding failure probability. In practice, systems under consideration can be highly non-linear and large. It is also possible that the performance functions of systems are implicit, non-linear, non-differentiable, noisy, and can only be characterized in terms of numerical values. Computation of failure probabilities under such situations of complex systems and complicated failure domains thus generally demands considerable computational efforts and resources in order to obtain results with high confidence levels, especially in case of rare-event analysis.

The objective here is to show how Genetic Algorithms (GAs) can enhance the capability in PRA for numerous key aspects of risk-based information. Fundamental problems in PRA will be first addressed. GAs in context of PRA is next described. The demonstration of capability enhancement then follows. The demonstration starts from the application of GAs to the determination of PML. A generic problem in which it is not possible to visualize the failure domain due to its dimensionality and non-linearity characteristics is considered. The capability in PRA is significantly enhanced by GAs in such a way that the PRA can be accomplished without the requirement of a priori knowledge about the geometry of failure domain. The enhancement of the capability in PRA of rare events is subsequently illustrated. A numerical technique which utilizes the GAs-determined PML is introduced. The technique is referred to as an Importance Sampling around PML (ISPML). ISPML computes the failure probabilities of rare events with a considerably less computational effort and resource than Monte Carlo Simulation (MCS). In this regards, GAs enhance the capability in

PRA, distinctively for rare-event analysis, through the use of considerably less computational effort and resource. Another important capability enhancement by GAs is the derivation of suboptimal Importance Sampling Functions (ISFs). The confidence levels of the computed failure probabilities become evidently improved with the utilization of suboptimal ISFs. The capability in PRA from the viewpoint of analysis accuracy is, therefore, enhanced through an aid of GAs. Afterwards, it is shown that the determination of multiple failure modes with almost equal magnitudes of likelihood in PRA can be realized with GAs. This is accomplished via the population-based search characteristics of GAs. Following the demonstration of GAs role in enhancing PRA capability, the crucial aspects of the chapter will be summarized at the end.

2. Fundamental problems in Probabilistic Risk Analysis (PRA)

Consider an event D_F which is defined by

$$D_F = \{\mathbf{X} \mid (g_1(\mathbf{X}) \le 0) \text{ and } (g_2(\mathbf{X}) \le 0) \text{ and} \ldots \text{and } (g_{NC}(\mathbf{X}) \le 0)\} \quad (1)$$

More specifically, the event D_F represents a failure event of multiple and parallel minor failures. $g_k(\mathbf{X})$ is the k-th performance function and NC is the total number of performance functions. The state of a system is defined by the performance function in such a way that

$$g_k(\boldsymbol{X}) = \begin{cases} \le 0 & ;\text{fail} \\ > 0 & ;\text{safe} \end{cases} ; k = 1,\ldots, NC \quad (2)$$

in which $\boldsymbol{X} = [X_1 \ldots X_{NRV}]^T$ is the vector of NRV random variables. Geometrically, D_F is the subspace in a multidimensional space of random variables $X_1,\ldots,X_{NRV}$ and will be referred to as the failure domain.

Each realization of $\boldsymbol{X}$ in D_F in (1) represents the combination of variable magnitudes that result in the system failure. Among possible realizations of $\mathbf{X}$, the so-called Point of Maximum Likelihood (PML) in failure domain is of particular interest in PRA. PML represents the combination of variable magnitudes that most likely contribute to the system failure. Determination of PML is a fundamental problem in PRA.

Apart from the information about the PML, another relevant fundamental problem in PRA is the computation of the probability p_F of the failure event D_F. The failure probability p_F is crucial information and obtained from

$$p_F = \int_{D_F} f_X(\boldsymbol{x}) d\boldsymbol{x} \quad (3)$$

in which $f_X(x)$ is the Joint Probability Density Function (JPDF) of $X_1,\ldots, X_{NRV}$.

PML yields the highest value of the JPDF in failure domain. The region in the neighborhood of PML naturally contributes to the failure probability more than the other regions in the failure domain. Such a region is referred to as an importance region. Consequently, the information about PML is highly valuable in the computation of failure probability, in addition to the characteristics of failure event. It will be shown via the numerical examples in subsequent sections that the incorporation of PML information to the computation of failure probability will considerably improve the computational efficiency. These applications include the PRA of rare events and the derivation of suboptimal ISFs.

In the next section, the application of Genetic Algorithms (GAs) to PRA will be described. The description is aimed at using GAs for solving the fundamental problems in PRA, i.e. the determination of PML and the computation of failure probability.

3. Genetic Algorithms (GAs) in PRA

3.1 General

The fundamental and other problems in PRA can be formulated in forms of optimization problems. The optimization problems include constrained and unconstrained optimization problems. The constrained optimization problem for maximizing an objective function is expressed as

Maximize $$O_1(\boldsymbol{x}) \tag{4}$$

Subject to $$g_1(\boldsymbol{x}) \le 0 \tag{5.1}$$

$$\dots$$

$$g_k(\boldsymbol{x}) \le 0 \tag{5.k}$$

$$\dots$$

$$g_{NC}(\boldsymbol{x}) \le 0 \tag{5.NC}$$

, where $O_1(\boldsymbol{x})$ is the objective function of $\boldsymbol{x} = [x_1 \quad \dots \quad x_{NRV}]^T$. x_j is the realization of the jth random variable. The constrained maximization problem appears in the determination of PML.

The constrained minimization problem which appears in the determination of multiple design points reads

Minimize $$O_2(\boldsymbol{x}) \tag{6}$$

Subject to $$g_1(\boldsymbol{x}) \le 0 \tag{7.1}$$

$$\dots$$

$$g_k(\boldsymbol{x}) \le 0 \tag{7.k}$$

$$\dots$$

$$g_{NC}(\boldsymbol{x}) \le 0 \tag{7.NC}$$

$O_2(\boldsymbol{x})$ is the objective function.

Similarly, the unconstrained optimization for minimization an objective function is expressed as

Minimize $$O_3(\boldsymbol{x}) \tag{8}$$

, where $O_3(\boldsymbol{x})$ is the objective function. Such an unconstrained minimization problem is found in the derivation of suboptimal ISFs. Each optimization problem above will be written in a more specific form for each particular PRA problem.

The objective functions of the forms represented by expressions (4), (6), and (8) are generally nonlinear. The constraints (5) and (7) represent the performance functions (2). The performance functions in practical PRA are generally implicit functions of random variables comprising a high dimensional space. In addition, the performance functions can be non-linear, non-differentiable, noisy, and can only be characterized in terms of numerical values. There can also simultaneously be several numbers of parallel performance functions.
The operational features and solution capabilities of GAs suggest that the algorithms can effectively cope with those prescribed problem characteristics and requirements. Consequently, GAs are considered a potential tool for crucial problems in PRA. The following subsections contain the GAs elements in context of PRA application.

3.2 Chromosome representation

GAs work in two spaces alternatively. The selection process is performed in the space of original variables while the genetic operations are done in the space of coded variables. Both spaces are referred to as solution and coding space, respectively (Gen & Cheng, 1997). GAs encrypt each trial solution into a sequence of numbers or strings and denote the sequence as a chromosome. A simple binary coding for real values as proposed by (Michalewicz, 1996) is employed for representing chromosomes. According to the utilized coding scheme, each realization of the jth random variable X_j in the solution space is represented by a binary string as shown in Figure 1. The combination of these strings forms a chromosome in the coding space. The evaluation of chromosome fitness is done in the solution space of X_j while the genetic operations are performed in the coding space of chromosome.

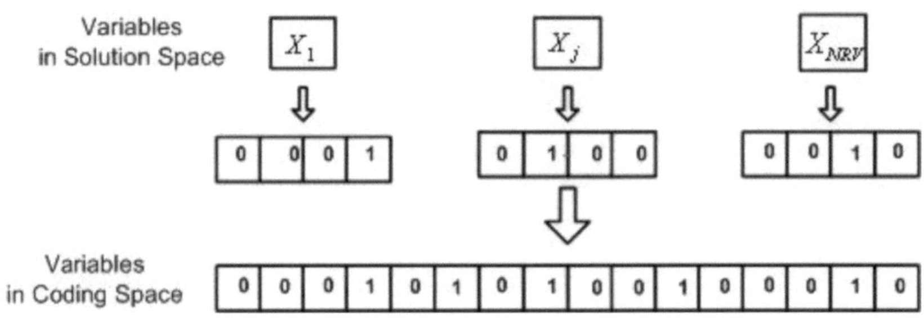

Fig. 1. Chromosome representation using binary coding for real values (Michalewicz, 1996).

3.3 Reproduction process

Reproduction in GAs is a process in which individual chromosomes are reproduced according to their fitness values. Fitness in an optimization by GAs is defined by a fitness function. Based on the optimization problem as described by Eq. (4) and the set of constraints (5), the fitness function $F(\boldsymbol{x})$ of a chromosome representing a vector $\boldsymbol{x}$ of variables in the solution space is defined as

$$F(\boldsymbol{x})=\begin{cases} O_1(\boldsymbol{x}) & ;\boldsymbol{x} \text{ is feasible} \\ O_1(\boldsymbol{x})-\sum_{j=1}^{NC} k_j v_j(\boldsymbol{x}) & ;\boldsymbol{x} \text{ is infeasible} \end{cases} \tag{9}$$

The fitness function for the constrained minimization problem defined by (6) and (7) is

$$F(x)=\begin{cases} 1/O_2(x) & ;x \text{ is feasible} \\ 1\Big/\left[O_2(x)+\sum_{j=1}^{NC} k_j v_j(x)\right] & ;x \text{ is infeasible} \end{cases} \tag{10}$$

Note that the penalty term in this minimization case is added to the objective function.
An adaptive penalty scheme which is introduced by (Barbosa & Lemonge, 2003) and improved by (Obadage & Hampornchai, 2006) will be employed to handle the constraints. The improved adaptive penalty scheme shows its excellent capability in handling a very large number of constraints (Harnpornchai et al., 2008). This adaptive scheme is given by

$$k_j=\left|\max\left(O_1^{\inf}(\mathbf{x})\right)\right|\frac{<v_j(\mathbf{x})>}{\sum_{l=1}^{NC}\left[<v_l(\mathbf{x})>\right]^2} \tag{11}$$

, where $max(O_1^{inf}(x))$ is the maximum of the objective function values at the current population in the infeasible region, $v_j(x)$ is the violation magnitude of the jth constraint. $<v_j(x)>$ is the average of $v_j(x)$ over the current population. k_j is the penalty parameter for the jth constraint defined at each generation. The violation magnitude is defined as

$$v_l(x)=\begin{cases} |g_l(x)| & ;g_l(x)>0 \\ 0 & ;\text{otherwise} \end{cases} \tag{12}$$

The reproduction operator may be implemented in a number of ways. The easiest and well-known approach is the roulette-wheel selection (see e.g. (Goldberg, 1989 and Deb, 1995)). According to the roulette-wheel scheme, the kth chromosome will be reproduced with the probability of

$$P_k=\frac{F_k}{\sum_{l=1}^{NPop}F_l} \tag{13}$$

, in which N_{Pop} is the population size. The fitness value F_k is obtained from either Eq. (9) or (10). Note that subscript k in F_k signifies that the fitness value is computed for each respective kth chromosome. It is interesting to note that GAs utilize only the numerical values of the objective function and of its associated constraints for the evaluation of the chromosome fitness, as seen from Eqs. (9) – (12). This advantageous feature makes GAs readily applicable to real-world problems where the performance functions are generally implicit with respect to random variables.

3.4 Genetic operators

In accordance with the binary representation of chromosomes, a simple binary crossover is applied (confer Figure 2).
The mutation operation also assists the exploration for potential solutions which may be overlooked by the crossover operation. According to the chromosome representation, a binary mutation is employed for the purpose (confer Figure 3).

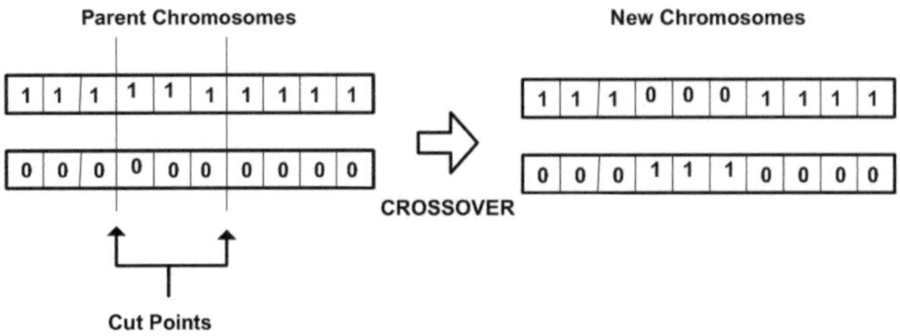

Fig. 2. Crossover of two chromosomes.

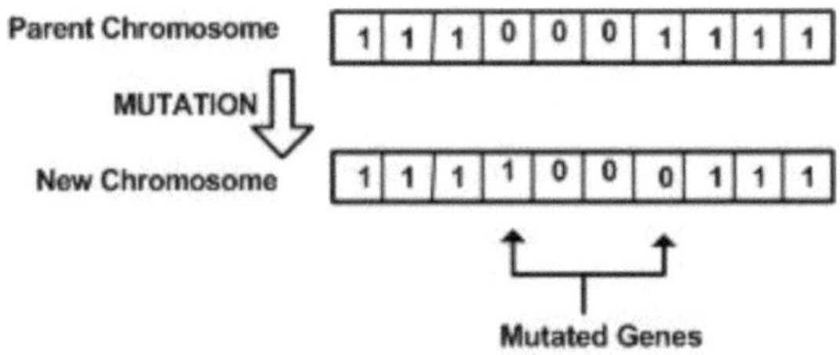

Fig. 3. Mutation on a chromosome.

3.5 Multimodal GAs

Simple GAs perform well in locating a single optimum but face difficulties when requiring multiple optima (see e.g. (De Jong, 1975; Mahfoud, 1995a; Mahfoud, 1995b and Miller & Shaw, 1995)). Niching methods can identify multiple solutions with certain extent of diversity (Miller & Shaw, 1995). Among niching methods, Deterministic Crowding Genetic Algorithms (DCGAs) (Mahfoud, 1995a and Mahfoud, 1995b) have been commonly used in multimodal functions optimization. It is noted that DCGAs is originally designed for unconstrained optimization problems. The adaptive penalty described in the previous subsection will be used in conjunction with DCGAs to handle constraints.

DCGAs work as follows. First, all members of population are grouped into *NPop/2* pairs, where *NPop* is the population size. The crossover and mutation are then applied to all pairs. Each offspring competes against one of the parents that produced it. For each pair of offspring, two sets of parent-child tournaments are possible. DCGAs hold the set of tournaments that forces the most similar elements to compete. The following provides a pseudo code of DCGAS (Brownlee, 2004).

NPop	:	Population size.
$d(x, y)$	:	Distance between individuals x and y.
$F(x)$	:	Fitness of individual population member.

1. Randomly initialize population.
2. Evaluate fitness of population.
3. Loop until stop condition:
   a. Shuffle the population.
   b. Crossover to produce $NPop/2$ pairs of offspring.
   c. Apply mutation (optional).
   d. Loop for each pair of offspring:
      i. If(d(parent1,child1)+d(parent2,child2)) ≤ (d(parent2,child1)+d(parent1,child2)).

1. If F(child1) > F(parent1), child1 replaces parent1.
2. If F(child2) > F(parent2), child2 replaces parent2.

ii. Else
1. If F(child1) > F(parent2), child1 replaces parent2.
2. If F(child2) > F(parent1), child2 replaces parent1.

In the following section, the applications of GAs to enhance the capability in PRA for numerous key aspects of risk-based information will be demonstrated.

4. Roles of GAs in enhancing PRA capability

4.1 Determination of PML

4.1.1 Problem formulation

The likelihood of each combination of variable magnitudes in contributing a failure event is an interesting issue in PRA. The focus is particular on the so-called Point of Maximum Likelihood (PML) in failure domain. PML represents the combination of variable magnitudes that most likely contribute to the failure and to the corresponding failure probability. Since PML is the point of highest JPDF in failure domain D_F, the PML $\boldsymbol{x}^*$ can be obtained from solving the following optimization problem:

Maximize $$O_4(\boldsymbol{x}) = f_X(\boldsymbol{x}) \quad (14)$$

Subject to $$g_1(\boldsymbol{x}) \le 0 \quad (15.1)$$

$$\ldots$$

$$g_k(\boldsymbol{x}) \le 0 \quad (15.k)$$

$$\ldots$$

$$g_{NC}(\boldsymbol{x}) \le 0 \quad (15.NC)$$

in which $f_X(\boldsymbol{x})$ is the JPDF of $\boldsymbol{X}$. $\boldsymbol{X} = [X_1 \ldots X_{NRV}]^T$. X_l is the lth random variable. $g_k(\boldsymbol{x})$ (k = 1, …, NC) is the kth performance function. N and NC are the total number of basic random variables and the total number of performance functions, respectively. The fitness function is defined as

$$F(\boldsymbol{x}) = \begin{cases} O_4(\boldsymbol{x}) & ;\boldsymbol{x} \text{ is feasible} \\ O_4(\boldsymbol{x}) - \sum_{j=1}^{NC} k_j v_j(\boldsymbol{x}) & ;\boldsymbol{x} \text{ is infeasible} \end{cases} \quad (16)$$

, where k_j and $v_j(\boldsymbol{x})$ are defined as in Eqs. (11) and (12), respectively.

4.1.2 Numerical example 1

Consider the following performance function (Lee et al. 2006)

$$g(\boldsymbol{Y}) = \sigma_u - \sigma_{local}^M \quad (17)$$

where $\mathbf{Y}$ is the vector of random variables constituting the performance function (17). σ_u is a random variable. σ_{local}^{M} is defined as

$$\sigma_{local}^{M} = \frac{m_{op}}{\left(M_{ref} / \sigma_y\right)} \tag{18}$$

$$M_{ref} = \frac{M_L}{1.333} \tag{19}$$

$$M_L = 4R_m^2 t\sigma_y \left[\cos\left(\frac{\pi D \Theta}{8t}\right) - \frac{D}{t}\frac{f(\Theta)}{2\Theta} \right] \tag{20}$$

$$f(\Theta) = 0.7854\Theta^2 - 0.09817\Theta^4 + 0.0040906\Theta^6 - 0.000085\Theta^8 \tag{21}$$

The description of each random variable is given in Table 1.

Variable	Distribution Type	Mean	COV
D	Normal	$4.3\text{x}10^{-3}$	0.10
L	Normal	$100\text{x}10^{-3}$	0.10
Θ / π	Normal	0.5	0.10
D_o	Normal	$114.3\text{x}10^{-3}$	0.02
Σ_y	Log-normal	$326\text{x}10^{6}$	0.07
Σ_u	Log-normal	$490\text{x}10^{6}$	0.01

Table 1. Description of random variables in Numerical Example 1 and 2.

m_{op} and t are deterministic variables. m_{op} is equal to $16\text{x}10^3$ whereas t is set to be $8.6\text{x}10^{-3}$. Rm is defined as

$$R_m = \frac{R_I + R_E}{2} \tag{22}$$

, where

$$R_I = \frac{1}{2}\left(D_o - 2t\right) \tag{23}$$

$$R_E = \frac{D_o}{2} \tag{24}$$

More specifically,

$$\mathbf{Y} = \left[D \quad L \quad \frac{\Theta}{\pi} \quad D_o \quad \Sigma_y \quad \Sigma_u \right] \tag{25}$$

GAs have been applied to determine PML. The objective function according to Eq. (14), is

$$O_5(\mathbf{Y}) = f_D(d) f_L(l) f_{\Theta/\pi}(\theta / \pi) f_{Do}(d_o) f_{\Sigma y}(\sigma_y) f_{\Sigma u}(\sigma_u) \tag{26}$$

The magnitude of the constraint violation, according to Eqs. (12) and (17), is

$$\nu(\boldsymbol{Y}) = \begin{cases} \left|\sigma_{\mathrm{u}} - \sigma_{\mathrm{local}}^{M}\right| & ; g(\boldsymbol{Y}) > 0 \\ 0 & ; \text{otherwise} \end{cases} \tag{27}$$

The corresponding fitness function is thus

$$F(\boldsymbol{Y}) = \begin{cases} O_5(\boldsymbol{Y}) & ; g(\boldsymbol{Y}) \le 0 \\ O_5(\boldsymbol{Y}) - k\nu(\boldsymbol{Y}) & ; \text{otherwise} \end{cases} \tag{28}$$

GAs search employs the population size of 100. The number of generations used in the search is 200. A two-point crossover is utilized with the crossover rate of 0.8. The mutation rate is taken as 0.002. The resulting PML is shown in Table 2.

PML	Magnitude at PML
d^*	5.28x10^{-3}
l^*	1.00x10^{-1}
θ^* / π	5.47x10^{-1}
d^*_{o}	1.07x10^{-1}
σ_{y}^*	3.24x10^{8}
σ_{u}^*	3.99x10^{8}

Table 2. PML in Numerical Example 1.

The performance function in this example is highly nonlinear and implicit function of random variables. The performance function is also defined in terms of a mixture of different types of random variable, not only a normal type. It should be noted that the operation of GAs in determining the PML does not require prior knowledge about the problem characteristics. GAs, therefore, can enhance the capability in PRA for the determination of PML in complicate situations.

4.2 PRA of rare events by Importance Sampling around PML (ISPML)

4.2.1 Background notion

The probability p_F of the failure event D_F as defined by Eq. (3) inevitably requires computational procedures for its accurate assessment in practical problems. It is widely recognized that Monte Carlo Simulation (MCS) is the only tool that is applicable to a wide range of problems in assessing failure probability. A major drawback of MCS is that the procedure requires large sample sizes in order to compute probabilities of very low orders in PRA of rare events when demanding high confidence levels. An efficient strategy for overcoming this undesirable situation is the utilization of the so-called importance sampling (Fishman, 1996). The notion behind the importance sampling is that the procedure performs more sampling in the importance region of failure domain. From the probabilistic characteristics of PML, the region in the neighborhood of PML can be regarded as the importance region because PML yields the highest value of the JPDF in failure domain. Consequently, the importance sampling should purposely concentrate around PML.

Using the importance sampling technique, Eq. (3) is modified to

$$p_F = \int I(y) \frac{f_X(y)}{h_X(y)} h_X(y) dy \tag{29.1}$$

, or

$$p_F = E_h \left[I(\mathbf{Y}) \frac{f_X(\mathbf{Y})}{h_X(\mathbf{Y})} \right] \tag{29.2}$$

in which $I(\boldsymbol{Y})$ is the indicator function and is defined as

$$I(\mathbf{Y}) = \begin{cases} 1 & ; \mathbf{Y} \in D_F \\ 0 & ; \mathbf{Y} \notin D_F \end{cases} \tag{30}$$

Note that the subscript h signifies that the expectation E is taken with respect to an importance sampling JPDF or Importance Sampling Function (ISF) $h_X(x)$. According to MCS, the failure probability is estimated as

$$P_F \cong \frac{1}{Nsim} \sum_{j=1}^{Nsim} I(\mathbf{Y}_j) \frac{f_X(\mathbf{Y}_j)}{h_X(\mathbf{Y}_j)} \tag{31}$$

in which $\mathbf{Y}_j$ is the jth realization sampled from the ISF $h_X(x)$ and N_{sim} is the sample size. The PML obtained from GAs search can enhance the efficiency of MCS. The efficiency enhancement is accomplished by employing the GAs-searched PML as the sampling center of the ISF $h_X(x)$. This sampling scheme is denoted as an Importance Sampling using PML (ISPML). For the purpose of procedure clarity, the original JPDF $f_X(x)$ will be rewritten as $f_X(x \mid \boldsymbol{\mu} = \boldsymbol{\mu}_o)$ in which $\boldsymbol{\mu}$ denotes the mean vector. $\boldsymbol{\mu}_o$ is the original mean vector. According to the ISPML, the ISF $h_X(x)$ takes the form

$$h_X(\mathbf{x}) = f_X(\mathbf{x} \mid \boldsymbol{\mu} = \mathbf{x}^*) \tag{32}$$

, where x^* is PML. That is the ISF has the same functional form as the original JPDF. The mean vector of the ISF, however, is different from that of the original JPDF and takes the PML as the mean vector. Consequently, the estimate of the failure probability is

$$P_F \cong \frac{1}{Nsim} \sum_{j=1}^{Nsim} I(\mathbf{Y}_j) \frac{f_X(\mathbf{Y}_j \mid \boldsymbol{\mu} = \boldsymbol{\mu}_o)}{f_X(\mathbf{Y}_j \mid \boldsymbol{\mu} = \mathbf{x}^*)} \tag{33}$$

4.2.2 Numerical example 2

Based on the GAs-searched PML, the ISF according to the ISPML procedure takes the form of Eq. (32), i.e.

$$\boldsymbol{\mu} = \begin{bmatrix} d^* & l^* & \theta^*/\pi & d_o & \sigma_y & \sigma_u \end{bmatrix}^T \tag{34}$$

The ISF as defined by Eqs. (32) and (34) is used to compute the failure probability according to the performance function (17). The results are compared with MCS. The estimate of the failure probability in each MCS and ISPML methodology is based on 10 independent runs. The sample size per each run of ISPML is 1,000 whereas that of MCS is 1,000,000. Table 3 compares the numerical results from both methodologies. Note that the Coefficient of Variation of the estimate of failure probability P_F (COV_{PF}) is defined as

$$COV_{PF} = \frac{S.D._{PF}}{\overline{P}_F} \tag{35}$$

$\overline{P}_F$ is the sample mean of P_F. $S.D._{PF}$ is the sample standard deviation of P_F. Lower magnitudes of COV_{PF} signify higher confidence levels of probability estimates.

Methodology	$\overline{P}_F$	COV_{PF}	$Nsim$
MCS	1.00×10^{-6}	0.94	1,000,000
ISPML	1.28×10^{-6}	0.34	1,000

Table 3. Comparison of numerical results from MCS and ISPML.

It is obvious from Table 3 that the sample size used by ISPML is much smaller than the sample size for MCS but ISPML results in smaller order of the COV_{PF}. More precisely, MCS employs the sample sizes 1,000 times larger than ISPML does. The accuracy of ISPML is, however, remarkably higher than that of MCS.

This numerical example testifies that the computation of event probability can demand considerable computation resource, though the variable space is not of high dimension, when demanding high confidence levels of analysis results. It also shows that GAs help realize the estimation of low probabilities in the situation where the sample sizes may be prohibitively provided due to constrained computational resources. From the viewpoint of computational efficiency and accuracy, the capability in PRA of rare events is thus substantially enhanced by GAs.

4.3 Derivation of suboptimal Importance Sampling Functions (ISFs)

4.3.1 Problem formulation

ISPML defines an ISF as given by Eq. (32). However, there can be other definitions of ISF. The ideal ISF is the sampling JPDF that results in a zero-variance estimate. However, it is not possible in general to obtain such an optimal ISF because the determination of the optimal ISF depends on the underlying probability being computed (Fishman, 1996). Consequently, it is most desirable to obtain other alternative ISFs that reduce the variance of probability estimate as much as possible. Such variance-minimizing ISFs will be defined herein as suboptimal ISFs. The variance of probability estimate is denoted as $VAR_h[P_F]$ or simply VAR. The subscript h informs again that the variance is taken with respect to the ISF $h_X(y)$. Since the ISF $h_X(y)$ is unknown and needs to be determined, the variance-minimization problem for determining suboptimal ISFs is necessarily taken with respect to another pre-defined JPDF $q_X(y)$. It can be shown that the variance-minimization problem (Harnpornchai, 2007) can be formulated as

$$\underset{h}{\text{Minimize}} \; E_q\left[I^2(\mathbf{Y}) \frac{f_\mathbf{X}(\mathbf{Y}) f_\mathbf{X}(\mathbf{Y})}{h_\mathbf{X}(\mathbf{Y}) q_\mathbf{X}(\mathbf{Y})} \right] \tag{36}$$

The prescribed sampling function $q_X(y)$ is referred to as a pre-sampling JPDF. The ISF $h_X(x)$ which is obtained from the variance-minimization problem is a suboptimal ISF.

If the ISF $h_X(x)$ can be completely defined by a vector of parameters $\mathbf{v} = [v_1 \quad \ldots \quad v_{NP}]^T$, in which v_j is the jth parameter characterizing the JPDF of ISF and NP is the total number of JPDF parameters, then the variance-minimization problem (36) is specifically written as:

$$\underset{\mathbf{v}}{\text{Minimize}} \quad E_q\left[I^2(\mathbf{Y})\frac{f_X(\mathbf{Y})f_X(\mathbf{Y})}{h_X(\mathbf{Y};\mathbf{v})q_X(\mathbf{Y})}\right] \tag{37}$$

The expectation in (36) is approximated by

$$E_q\left[I^2(\mathbf{Y})\frac{f_X(\mathbf{Y})f_X(\mathbf{Y})}{h_X(\mathbf{Y};\mathbf{v})q_X(\mathbf{Y})}\right] \cong \frac{1}{Npre}\sum_{k=1}^{Npre} I^2(\mathbf{Y}_k)\frac{f_X(\mathbf{Y}_k)f_X(\mathbf{Y}_k)}{h_X(\mathbf{Y}_k;\mathbf{v})q_X(\mathbf{Y}_k)} \tag{38}$$

The samples $\mathbf{Y}_k$ ($k = 1,\ldots, Npre$) are generated according to the pre-sampling JPDF $q_X(y)$. The corresponding variance-minimization problem becomes:

$$\underset{\mathbf{v}}{\text{Minimize}} \quad O_6(\mathbf{v}) \tag{39}$$

, where

$$O_6(\mathbf{v}) = \frac{1}{Npre}\sum_{k=1}^{Npre} I^2(\mathbf{Y}_k)\frac{f_X(\mathbf{Y}_k)f_X(\mathbf{Y}_k)}{h_X(\mathbf{Y}_k;\mathbf{v})q_X(\mathbf{Y}_k)} \tag{40}$$

The objective function (40) can be of highly complicate nature in practical problems, e.g., highly non-linear, non-convex, and high-dimensional. The complex nature normally arises from the collective characteristic of the JPDFs that build up the objective function (40). GAs are considered a promising tool for searching the variance-minimizing parameters $\mathbf{v}^* = [v_1^* \ \ldots \ v_{NP}^*]^T$ under the circumstance of such a complicate objective function. When using GAs for the unconstrained minimization problem (39), the fitness function is defined as

$$F(\mathbf{v}) = \frac{1}{O_6(\mathbf{v})} \tag{41}$$

The following subsection illustrates how GAs are applied for deriving a suboptimal ISF.

4.3.2 Numerical example 3

Consider two independent and identical random variables of normal type X_1 and X_2, whose JPDF is given by

$$f_X(x_1,x_2) = \prod_{j=1}^{2}(2\pi)^{-1/2} exp\left(-\frac{x_j^2}{2}\right) \tag{42}$$

The failure event D_{F3} is defined as

$$D_{F3} = \{(X_1,X_2) \mid (g_1(X_1,X_2) \le 0) \text{and} (g_2(X_1,X_2) \le 0)\} \tag{43}$$

The performance functions are

$$g_1(X_1,X_2) = 5 - X_1 \tag{44.1}$$

$$g_2(X_1, X_2) = 5 - X_2 \tag{44.2}$$

A JPDF of two identical and independent normal PDF is used as the pre-sampling PDF $q_X(\mathbf{x})$, i.e.

$$q_X(x_1, x_2) = \prod_{j=1}^{2} \left(2\pi\sigma_{Pj}\right)^{-1/2} exp\left[-\frac{\left(x_j - \mu_{Pj}\right)^2}{2\sigma_{Pj}^2}\right] \tag{45}$$

The pre-sampling is performed around the PML in failure domain. It can be shown that the PML is (5.0, 5.0) for the performance functions (44). Correspondingly, the mean vector of the pres-sampling JPDF $q_X(\mathbf{x})$ is equal to $[5.0\ 5.0]^T$, i.e., $\mu_{P1} = \mu_{P2} = 5.0$. The vector of the standard deviation is, however, set to that of the original JPDF $f_X(\mathbf{x})$, i.e., $\sigma_{P1} = \sigma_{P2} = 1.0$. The pre-sampling around PML utilizes the sample size of 100, i.e. $Npre$ = 100. Each realization $\mathbf{Y}_k = [X_1 \quad X_2]_k^T$ must be checked with the performance functions (44.1) and (44.2) in order to determine the value of $I(\mathbf{Y}_k)$, following

$$I(\mathbf{Y}_k) = \begin{cases} 1 & ; g_1(\mathbf{Y}_k) \le 0 \text{ and } g_2(\mathbf{Y}_k) \le 0 \\ 0 & ; \text{otherwise} \end{cases} \tag{46}$$

The ISF employs the same parametric JPDF as the original JPDF. Correspondingly, the ISF is

$$h_X(x_1, x_2; \mathbf{v}) = \prod_{j=1}^{2} \left(2\pi\sigma_j\right)^{-1/2} exp\left[-\frac{\left(x_j - \mu_j\right)^2}{2\sigma_j^2}\right] \tag{47}$$

in which $\mathbf{v} = [\mu_1\ \sigma_1\ \mu_2\ \sigma_2]^T$ is the vector of the ISF parameters to be optimized.

GAs are utilized to determine the variance-minimizing parameters. The search procedure employs $Npop$ = 100, the crossover rate of 0.8, and the mutation rate of 0.002. The variance-minimizing parameters $\mathbf{v}^* = [\mu_1^* \quad \sigma_1^* \quad \mu_2^* \quad \sigma_1^*]^T$ from the GAs search are $[5.1 \quad 0.3 \quad 5.1 \quad 0.3]^T$.

The suboptimal ISF with the determined variance-minimizing parameters $[5.1 \quad 0.3 \quad 5.1 \quad 0.3]^T$ is utilized for estimating the failure probability. The probability estimate is the average of 10 independent runs of the optimal ISF. The resulting VAR is also computed, based on those 10 computed values of probability. Each optimal ISF run employs a sample size of 1,000. The results are summarized in Table 4.

$\overline{P}_F$	VAR	COV_{PF}
8.33×10^{-14}	1.11×10^{-29}	0.04

Table 4. Computation of failure probability by the GAs-derived suboptimal ISF.

Although the problem considered is of low dimension, the failure probability is at extremely low order, i.e. 10^{-14}. The magnitude of the COV_{PF} from the GAs-derived suboptimal ISF is extremely low, i.e. 0.04. In other words, the confidence level of the probability estimate is considerably high. For such an order of estimate and a confidence level, MCS requires a sample sizes at least 10^{16}. The order of the sample size used by the suboptimal ISF is thus 10^{13} times less that that required by MCS for the same COV_{PF} as indicated in Table 4.

This numerical example shows that GAs facilitate the derivation of suboptimal ISFs.It should be noted that the knowledge of problem is unnecessary at all for the GAs operation. Consequently, high confidence levels in PRA of complex problems becomes possible even if there is no or little a priori knowledge of the problems.

4.4 Determination of multiple design points

4.4.1 Problem characteristics

Design point is the point on the limit state surface that is nearest to the origin in a standard normal space. In optimization context, the design point is the global minimum obtained from solving a constrained optimization problem. However, it is possible that there are other local minima whose distances to the origin are of similar magnitudes to the global minimum. The global minimum and local minima lead to the situation of multiple design points. When multiple design points exist, PRA based only on any single design point among multiple design points may result in an underestimation of failure probability. Determination of global optimum as well as local optima leads to multiple solutions, which is classified as a multimodal optimization problem.

The following subsections intend to demonstrate how GAs enhance the capability in PRA to cope with multiple failure events or modes. Such an application is important when several failure events are almost equally critical. It will be shown that the determination of multiple design points is readily accomplished using DCGAs. The adaptive penalty technique as described in the afore-mentioned subsection will be combined with DCGAs for handling constraints. This is a novelty because multimodal GAs were originally designed for unconstrained multimodal optimization.

From the definition of the design point, the design point $\boldsymbol{U}^*$ is obtained from solving the following constrained optimization problem:

Minimize
$$O_7(\boldsymbol{U}) = \|\boldsymbol{U}\| = \left(\sum_{i=1}^{NRV} U_i^2\right)^{1/2} \tag{48}$$

Subject to constraint
$$g(\boldsymbol{U}) = 0 \tag{49}$$

in which $\boldsymbol{U} = [U_1 \ldots U_{NRV}]^T$ denotes the vector of standard normal variables. $g(\boldsymbol{U})$ is the performance function. $g(\boldsymbol{U}) = 0$ denotes the limit state surface and $g(\boldsymbol{U}) \le 0$ indicates the failure state corresponding to the performance function. The equality constraint is modified to an inequality constraint

$$|g(\boldsymbol{U})| \le \varepsilon \tag{50}$$

, or

$$G(\boldsymbol{U}) \le 0 \tag{51.1}$$

, where

$$G(\boldsymbol{U}) = |g(\boldsymbol{U})| - \varepsilon \tag{51.2}$$

in which ε is the tolerance and set to a small value, e.g. 0.01.

4.4.2 Numerical example 4

Consider a parabolic performance function as introduced in (Kiureghian & Dakessian, 1998):

$$g(X_1, X_2) = b - X_2 - \kappa(X_1 - e)^2 \tag{52}$$

where b, κ, and e are deterministic parameters. X_1 and X_2 are standard normal variables. In this example, $b = 5$, $\kappa = 0.5$ and $e = 0.1$. This set of parameters leads to two design points.

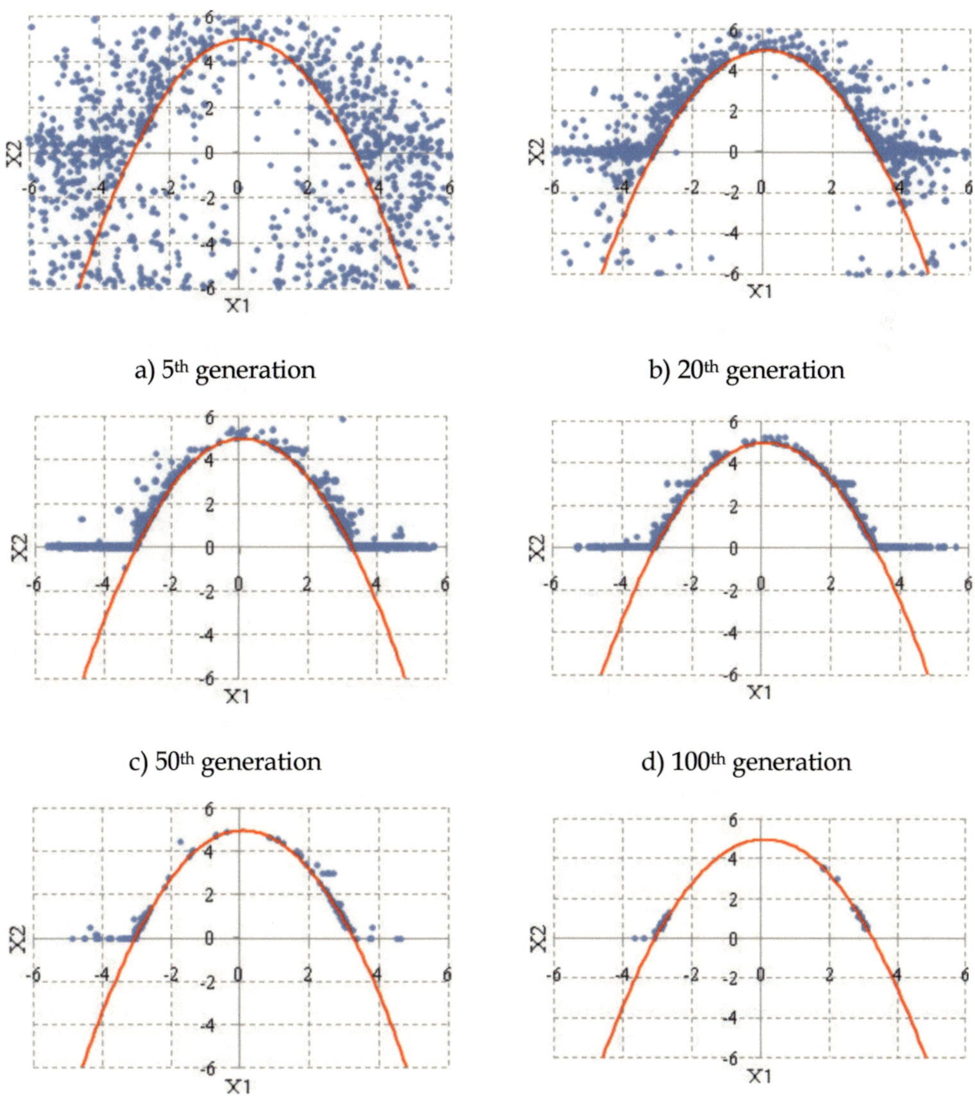

a) 5th generation b) 20th generation

c) 50th generation d) 100th generation

e) 200th generation f) 300th generation

Fig. 4. Chromosomes distribution at various generations by DCGAS for two design points problem.

DCGAs are employed to determine both design points. The tolerance parameter ε is set to 0.01. The parameters of the DCGAs are given in Table 5. The fitness function is

$$F(\boldsymbol{U}) = \begin{cases} 1/O_8(\boldsymbol{U}) & ;G(\boldsymbol{U}) \le 0 \\ 1/[O_8(\boldsymbol{U}) + k\nu(\boldsymbol{U})] & ;\text{otherwise} \end{cases} \tag{53}$$

, where

$$O_8(\boldsymbol{U}) = O_8(X_1, X_2) = \left[X_1^2 + X_2^2\right]^{1/2} \tag{54}$$

$$G(\boldsymbol{U}) = G(X_1, X_2) = \left|b - X_2 - \kappa(X_1 - e)^2\right| - \varepsilon \tag{55}$$

$$\nu(X_1, X_2) = \begin{cases} |G(X_1, X_2)| & ;G(X_1, X_2) > 0 \\ 0 & ;\text{otherwise} \end{cases} \tag{56}$$

Parameters	Value
Population Size	1000
Crossover Probability	1.0
Number of Executed Generations	300

Table 5. DCGAs parameters.

The distributions of chromosomes at consecutive generations by DCGAs are displayed in Figure 4. The solutions after the first generation are totally spread over the search area in the beginning. The solutions are then assembled in the parabolic topology during the course of optimization. After consecutive numbers of generations, the chromosomes gradually accumulate at two distinct design points. The objective function values, the optima or design points, and their corresponding distances to the origin are shown in Table 6. The numerical results are compared with the results from the literature (Kiureghian & Dakessian, 1998) in Table 6. The search method used in (Kiureghian & Dakessian, 1998) belongs to the class of gradient-based search and will be herein referred to as Gradient-based Search with Incrementally Added Constraint (GSIAC).

Optima	Method	$\boldsymbol{U}^* = (X_1^*, X_2^*)$	$g(X_1^*, X_2^*)$	$O_7(X_1^*, X_2^*)$
1	DCGAS	(-2.77, 0.88)	$1.55\text{x}10^{-3}$	2.91
	GSIAC	(-2.74,0.97)	$-2.80\text{x}10^{-3}$	2.91
2	DCGAS	(2.83, 1.27)	$3.55\text{x}10^{-3}$	3.10
	GSIAC	(2.92,1.04)	$-1.62\text{x}10^{-2}$	3.10

Table 6. Comparison of design points and their respective safety indices of two design points from DCGAS and the literature (Kiureghian & Dakessian, 1998).

It is clear that DCGAs yield the design points that are close to the results from GSIAC. It should be noted that the multimodal GAs work in a different manner from such a sequential search method as GSIAC, where the decision on the numbers of the desired design points must be made by the user. The population-based operation of GAs makes the search circumvent the problem of selecting appropriate starting search point, as appeared in the

gradient-based methods. In addition, the fundamental mechanisms of multimodal GAs are able to automatically detect and capture several design points.
The whole operation of multimodal GAs shows that a priori knowledge about the geometry of performance function is not required. This makes GAs operable to practical problems where the geometry of performance functions cannot be generally visualized. Therefore, the capability in PRA of multiple failure events with almost equal levels of likelihood can be enhanced by using GAs.

5. Conclusion

The enhancement of capability in Probabilistic Risk Analysis (PRA) by Genetic Algorithms (GAs) is described. Several key aspects of PRA that are enhanced by GAs include the determination of Point of Maximum Likelihood (PML) in failure domain, Monte Carlo Simulation (MCS)-based PRA of rare events under highly constrained computational resources, the improvement of confidence levels in PRA results by applying GAs-determined suboptimal Importance Sampling Functions (ISFs), and the automatic and simultaneous detection of multiple failure modes with almost equal likelihoods. All of these achievements are attributed to the problem knowledge-free operation of GAs. This feature of capability enhancement is testified via numerical examples where complicate and thus non-visualizable performance functions as well as mixtures of different random variables are considered. Consequently, the capability in PRA is naturally enhanced to practical problems.
The present application of GAs to PRA is limited to the uncertainty of aleatory type. Future application of GAs will be extended to the uncertainty of epistemic type or the combination of both types. Such extended application of GAs will enhance the capability in PRA to the cases where expert opinions and their corresponding degrees of belief are included in the analysis. The analysis then becomes more rationale and realistic. Since DCGAs exhibit genetic drift, it is also beneficial to develop novel multimodal GAs that reduce the genetic drift and increase the search stability in the future. The algorithms to be developed should eliminate or require least a priori knowledge about the search space so that the algorithms are efficiently and effectively applicable to practical problems.

6. References

Barbosa, H. & Lemonge, A. (2003). A new adaptive penalty scheme for genetic algorithms. *Information sciences*, 156, 215-251.

Brownlee, J. (2004). *Parallel Niching Genetic Algorithms: A Crowding Perspective*, Thesis in Master of Information Technology, Centre for Intelligent Systems and Complex Processes, School of Information Technology, Swinburne University of Technology, Australia.

Deb, K. (1995). *Optimization for Engineering Design Algorithms and Examples*, Prentice-Hall, New York.

De Jong, K.A. (1975). *An analysis of the behavior of a class of genetic adaptive systems*, Ph.D. Thesis, Department of Computer Science, University of Michigan, Ann Arbor, MI, USA.

Fishman, G. (1996). *Monte Carlo: Concepts, Algorithms, and Applications*, Springer-Verlag, New York.

Gen, M. & Cheng, R. (1997). *Genetic algorithms and engineering design*. John Wiley and Sons, ISBN : 978-0-471-12741-3, New York

Goldberg, D.E. (1989). *Genetic Algorithms in Search, Optimization and Machine Learning*, Addison-Wesley, Massachusetts.

Harnpornchai, N. (2007). Determination of Suboptimal Importance Sampling Functions by Genetic Algorithms, *Proceedings of the European Safety and Reliability Conference 2007, ESREL 2007 - Risk, Reliability and Societal Safety 2*, pp. 1169-1176, Stavanger, Norway, 25-27 June 2007.

Harnpornchai, N.; Chakpitak, N.; Chandarasupsang, T.; Tuang-Ath Chaikijkosi. & Dahal, K. (2007). Dynamic adjustment of age distribution in Human Resource Management by genetic algorithms, *Evolutionary Computation, CEC 2007, IEEE Congress* on 25-28 Sept. 2007, 1234 - 1239.

Kiureghian, A.D. & Dakessian, T. (1998). Multiple Design Points in First and Second-Order Reliability, *Structural Safety*. 20, 37-49.

Lee, S.M.; Chang, Y.S.; Choi, J.B. & Kim, Y.J. (2006). Failure probability assessment of wall-thinned nuclear pipes using probabilistic fracture mechanics, *Nuclear Engineering and Design*, 236, 350–358.

Mahfoud, S.W. (1995a). *Niching methods for genetic algorithms*, Ph.D. dissertation, Univ. of Illinois, Urbana-Champaign.

Mahfoud, S.W. (1995b). A comparison of parallel and sequential niching methods, *International Conference on Genetic Algorithms*, 136-143.

Michalewicz, A. (1996). *Genetic + Data Structures = Evolution Programs*, second ed.,Springer, ISBN : 978-3-540-60676-5, second ed. Berlin

Miller, B.L & Shaw, M.J. (1995). Genetic algorithms with dynamic niche sharing for multi-modal function optimization, *IlliGAL Report* no. 9510.

Obadage, A.S. & Hampornchai, N. (2006). Determination of point of maximum likelihood in failure domain using genetic algorithms, *Int J Press Vessels Pipe*, 83, 4, 276-82.

Tada, H. (1978). *The stress analysis of cracks handbook*, Del Research Corporation.

8

Evolutionary Computation in Coded Communications: An Implementation of Viterbi Algorithm

Jamal S. Rahhal, Dia I. Abu-Al-Nadi and Mohammed Hawa
Electrical Engineering Dept.
The University of Jordan
Amman
Jordan

1. Introduction

Quantum Computing hopefully is the future of computing systems. It still on its first steps. The development of some quantum algorithms gives the quantum computing a boost on its importance. These algorithms (such as Shor's and Grover's algorithms) proved to have superior performance over classical algorithms [1-4]. The recent findings, that quantum error correction can be used, showed that the decoherence problem can be solved and hence the quantum computers can be realized [5-7]. The quantum algorithms are based on the use of special gates applied on one, two or more qubits (quantum bits). The classical computer uses different gates (NOT, AND, NAND, OR and XOR). Quantum gates are in many aspects different from classical gates where all gates must be reversible. This makes the quantum gates act as 2^nx2^n transformation operators, where we have n input qubits and n output qubits.

To understand the quantum bits and gates we describe the group of amplitudes that describes the state of a quantum register as a vector. A qubit with state $|0\rangle$, which is guaranteed to read logic **0** when measured, is represented by the vector $\begin{pmatrix}1\\0\end{pmatrix}$, and a qubit with state $|1\rangle$ which is guaranteed to read logic **1** when measured is represented by the vector $\begin{pmatrix}0\\1\end{pmatrix}$. An arbitrary qubit state is then represented by the vector $\begin{pmatrix}\alpha\\\beta\end{pmatrix}$ as:

$$|\varphi\rangle = \alpha|0\rangle + \beta|1\rangle \tag{1}$$

where α and β are complex numbers and $|\alpha|^2 + |\beta|^2 = 1$.

One important quantum gate is the Hadamard gate given by:

$$H = \begin{pmatrix} \frac{1}{\sqrt{2}} & \frac{1}{\sqrt{2}} \\ \frac{1}{\sqrt{2}} & -\frac{1}{\sqrt{2}} \end{pmatrix} \tag{2}$$

When the input is $|0\rangle$, Hadamard gate changes the state of the qubit to:

$$|\varphi\rangle = \begin{pmatrix} \frac{1}{\sqrt{2}} & \frac{1}{\sqrt{2}} \\ \frac{1}{\sqrt{2}} & -\frac{1}{\sqrt{2}} \end{pmatrix} \begin{pmatrix} 1 \\ 0 \end{pmatrix} = \begin{pmatrix} \frac{1}{\sqrt{2}} \\ \frac{1}{\sqrt{2}} \end{pmatrix} \tag{3}$$

that is, $|\varphi\rangle = \frac{1}{\sqrt{2}}|0\rangle + \frac{1}{\sqrt{2}}|1\rangle$. So when reading the qubit at the end, we have exactly 50% chance of seeing a **0**, and an equal chance of seeing a **1**. Generalizing the above example, if an n-qubits register originally contains the value $|0^n\rangle$, it can be transformed using the Hadamard gate to the superpositional state:

$$\frac{1}{\sqrt{2^n}} \sum_{x=0}^{2^n-1} |x\rangle \tag{4}$$

where we would see each of the 2^n binary numbers x with equal probability when we observe the register. Other gates operate similar to Hadmard gate with different matrices, where Pauli gates are given by:

$$X = \begin{bmatrix} 0 & 1 \\ 1 & 0 \end{bmatrix} \quad Y = \begin{bmatrix} 0 & -j \\ j & 0 \end{bmatrix} \quad Z = \begin{bmatrix} 1 & 0 \\ 0 & -1 \end{bmatrix} \tag{5}$$

and phase gates:

$$S = \begin{bmatrix} 1 & 0 \\ 0 & \mathrm{j} \end{bmatrix} \quad U = \begin{bmatrix} 1 & 0 \\ 0 & \mathrm{e}^{\mathrm{j}\theta} \end{bmatrix} \tag{6}$$

The quantum computers use quantum gates to produce results in a faster and more efficient way than the classical computers. Implementation of quantum computers is still in its very beginning state, therefore, in this chapter, we need not to worry about the implementation issues. In addition to entanglement, the strength of quantum computing comes from the parallelism feature of the quantum computers and the fact that the quantum state is a superposition state. Using classical bits an n bit vector can represent one of 2^n symbols, but in quantum bits an n qubits vector can represent the 2^n symbols simultaneously.

Quantum Algorithms are usually organized in the following three steps:

Step 1. Initialize the quantum states.

Step 2. Apply the oracle quantum core as many times as needed.

Step 3. Measure the output states (results).

In many classical algorithms especially those used for searching mechanisms, speed and complexity are the main limiting factors in their implementation. Viterbi decoding algorithm is an important algorithm that is used to decode the received data when using Convolutional or Turbo codes at the transmitter. These codes are superior in their performance over many other types of codes. In the following we devise a quantum algorithm to implement the Viterbi algorithm (VA) [8-15].

2. Coded communication and quantum computation

Coded communication uses one type of channel coding that introduces a redundancy in the transmitted data. At the receiver different techniques are used to detect the transmitted information by correcting errors if occurred. All these techniques can be replaced by exhaustive search for the maximum likely data that is assumed to be the correct one.

Several quantum algorithms have been designed to perform classical algorithms with remarkable speedups. In adiabatic algorithms, the solution of the problem is encoded to the problem Hamiltonian. Since the mechanics of the Oracle remains unknown, the encoding process of the Hamiltonian in the adiabatic algorithm is unclear. Instead, just like Grover's algorithm did, the adiabatic search algorithm forms the Hamiltonian directly from the solution state, which means we have to know the state in prior and then perform an algorithm to show it.

Like many quantum computer algorithms, Grover's algorithm is probabilistic in the sense that it gives the correct answer with high probability. The probability of failure can be decreased by repeating the algorithm. Grover's algorithm can be used for estimating the mean and median of a set of numbers. In addition, it can be used to solve NP-complete problems by performing exhaustive searches over the set of possible solutions. This, while requiring prohibitive space for large input, would result in a considerable speed-up over classical algorithms.

3. The classical Viterbi algorithm

In classical communication systems a channel error correcting codes is used to detect and/or correct errors introduced to the data while travelling in a noisy channel. One important class of these codes is the Convolutional Code, where the data is convolved with the code generating polynomials prior to transmitting such data to the receiver. At the receiver, a decoding mechanism is used to recover the transmitted data, and detect/correct errors if they happen. An optimal decoding algorithm was used for this class of codes introduced by Viterbi [10,11]. This algorithm solves the searching problem in the trellis to obtain the maximum likelihood path that best represents the transmitted data. This search grows rapidly with the size of the tree and the length of the data frame. Faster search algorithms will speed up the overall speed of the decoding algorithm. Quantum search algorithm introduced by Grover suggested an optimal searching method that can be used in Viterbi algorithm to speed its execution.

Viterbi decoder uses a tree search procedure to optimally detect the received sequence of data. It performs maximum likelihood (ML) decoding. It calculates a measure of similarity between the received signal and all the trellis paths entering each state at time. Remove all the candidates that are not possible based on the maximum likelihood choice. When two paths enter the same state, the one with the best path metrics (the sum of the distance of all branches) along the path is chosen. This path is called the *surviving path*. This selection of surviving paths is done for all the states and makes decisions to eliminate some of the least likely paths in early calculation stages to reduce the decoding complexity.

The Viterbi algorithm (VA) calculates the branch metrics at each signalling interval and searches for the minimum branch metric. It searches for the maximum possible correct branch out of all possible branches. The total number of searches for each path (for L signalling intervals) is given by [8,9]:

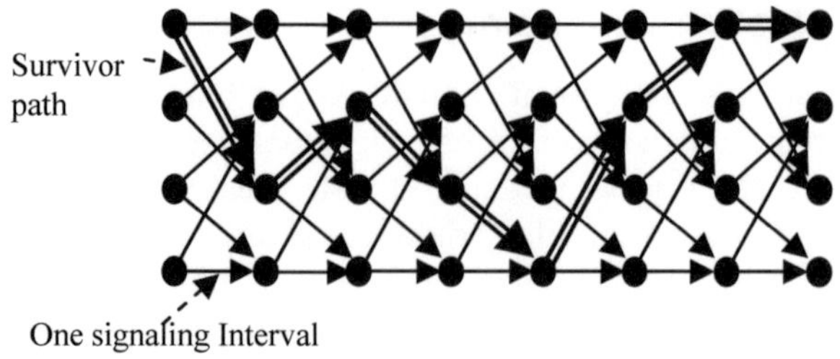

Fig. 1. Trellis Diagram Showing the Survivor Path.

$$N_T = L 2^{k+m} \tag{7}$$

where 2^k is the number of possible branches from each state and 2^m is the number of trellis states. Note that, these searchs must be conducted even in the fastest classical implementation to VA. It is worth mentioning here that the larger the number of states the better the performance of the code (i.e. less Bit Error Rate (BER)) [10, 11]. For large number of states and longer signalling intervals the processing delay become a limiting factor in the implementation of such codes, especially the Turbo-Codes where more computations and searching is required [12]. Hence the use of Quantum search algorithm might be the solution for higher dimensionality codes as it promises in the Encryption field.

We will use an example to explain the Viterbi search technique. In this example, we transmit a sequence of L data bits (say: 1011000) over a noisy channel. Some bits will be corrupted during transmission, just like when you misinterpret a few words when listening to a lousy phone connection or a noisy radio transmission. In such case, instead of receiving the above L-sequence of bits (called hidden states), the receiver might obtain a new erroneous sequence (called the observed sequence).

To overcome such a problem, the transmitter (called convolutional encoder) operates in a state machine pattern, in which it can exist in a finite number of states, and instead of transmitting the above sequence of bits, the transmitter uses that bit sequence to drive it through the state machine. The encoder tells the receiver (the decoder) about its movement through the state machine by transmitting a codeword (a new bit sequence) that is a result of the state machine transitions.

The Viterbi Algorithm at the decoder side operates on that state machine assumption, and even though the transmitted codeword (representing how the encoder went though the different states) might be corrupted, the Viterbi Algorithm examines all possible sequences of states (called paths) to find the one that is the most likely transmitted sequence. In VA terminology, this is called the *survivor path.*

Let us consider the (rate 1/2, m = 3) convolutional code, the state machine of which is shown in Figure 2. The notation (rate n/k, m) is widely used for convolutional codes, where the parameter k represents the number of input bits that control movement in the state machine, the parameter n represents the number of output bits resulting from each state machine transition, and finally the parameter $k(m - 1)$ (called the *constraint length* of the code) is related to the number of states S in the state machine, where $S = 2^m$. In our example code, we have $S = 2^3 = 8$ different states.

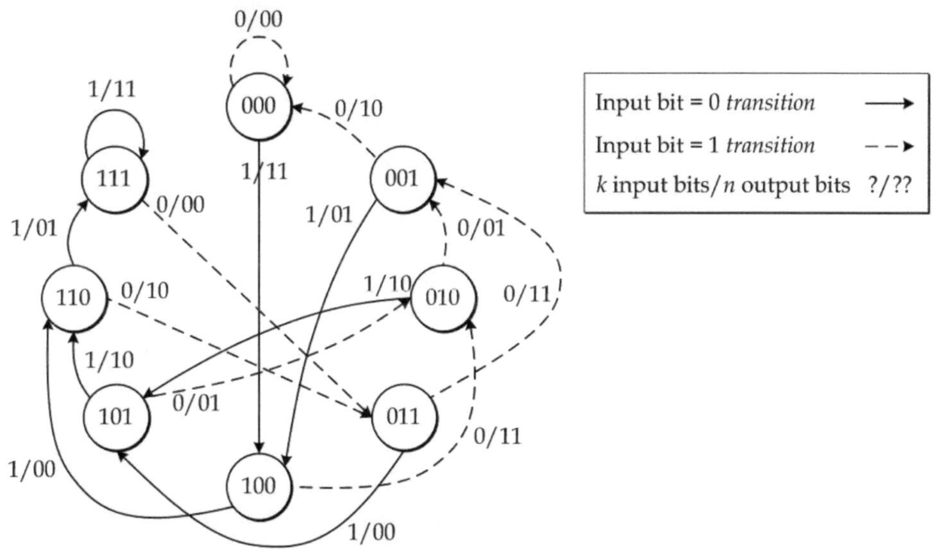

Fig. 2. The state diagram for (rate 1/2, m = 3) convolutional code.

As illustrated in Figure 2, the transmitter can exist in only one state at any given time. The transmitter always starts from state 000. To transmit one bit from the input data sequence, the transmitter looks up the *only* two possible transitions available from the current state. For example, if the transmitter is currently in state 100, and the input data bit is 1, the transmitter follows the solid-line transition to state 110 and sends the codeword 00 on the output channel. However, if the input bit is 0, the transmitter follows the dotted-line transition to state 010 and sends the codeword 11 to the decoder.

The transmitter remains in the new state until it is time to transmit the next bit in the input data sequence. The output codeword for any transition is decided by the numbers on the state diagram which are predetermined by certain generating polynomials. The ones we use in Figure 2 are G1 = [1 1 0 1] and G2 = [1 1 1 0]. Notice that one transition occurs in the state machine for each input bit (k = 1), which results in two bits being transmitted by the encoder over the channel (n = 2), resulting in the code rate of $k/n = 1/2$. If we use the input data sequence of 1011000 in the above state machine, we get the transmitted codeword of 11111010101110.

One might think that implementing the above state machine using hardware is a complex task, but it is actually very simple since it can be implemented using a shift register of size (K)(k) bits and an n group of XOR gates (to give the n output bits). The shift register and the XOR gates are connected based on the desired generating polynomials. A total of k input bits are shifted into the register each time tick to force the state machine into another state.

Since the transmitted codeword is based on a pattern (transitions in the state machine), the receiver can predict the movement in that machine even if some of the transmitted bits are corrupted by noise in the channel. To do that, the receiver uses the help of a *trellis diagram* as shown in Figure 3.

Figure 3 illustartes how the reciver decodes two incoming bits each time tick to decide which of the two possible transitions (the solid-line or the dotted-line) to be undertaken. Figure 4 shows the trasnitions that occur in the trellis for the transmitted codeword of 11111010101110, which corresponds to the input data sequcen of 1011000.

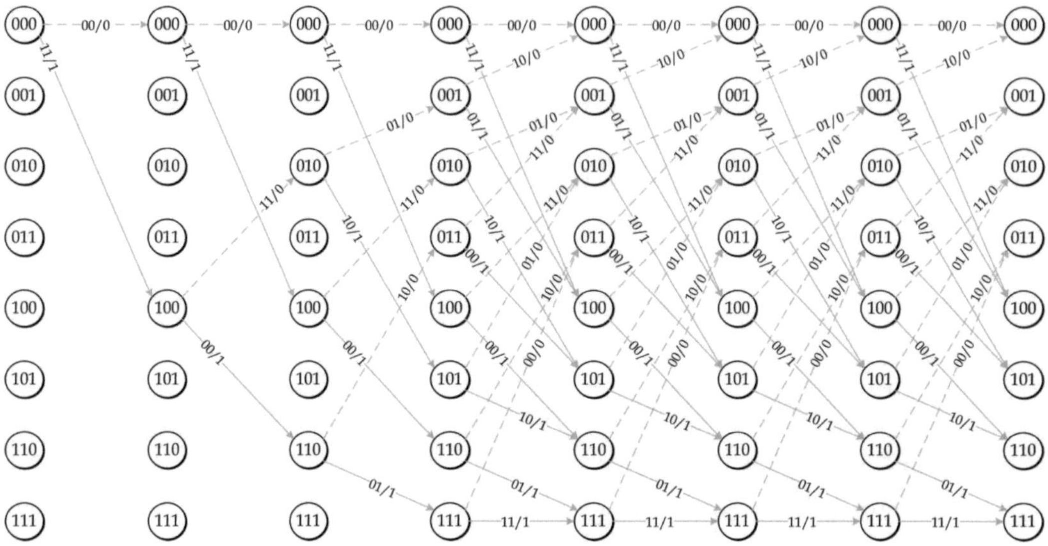

Fig. 3. Decoder trellis diagram for the convolutional code (rate 1/2, $m = 3$).

Input data sequence:	1	0	1	1	0	0	0
Transmitted codeword:	11	11	10	10	10	11	10
Received sequence:	11	11	10	10	10	11	10

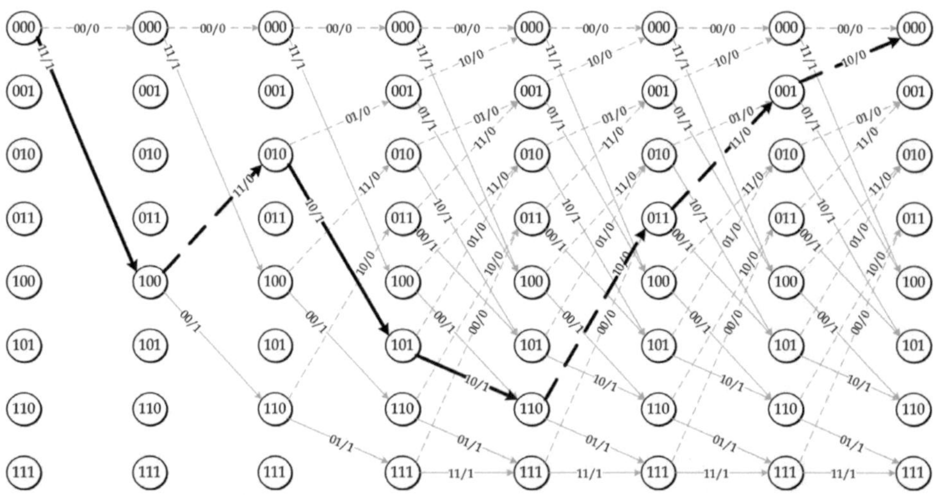

Fig. 4. Decoder trellis diagram showing the path for the input codeword of 11111010101110.

If no errors occurs while transmitting the encoder-generated codeword, the decoder will traverse the trellis without any problems and will be able to read the original data sequence of 1011000. However, due to errors in the channel, the receiver might read a different bit sequence. Since the input data sequence (1011000) is composed of 7 bits, the challenge the decoder faces is to know which of the 2^7 possibilities did the transmitter intend to send.

The idea is that because each 7 bit code will generate a unique trasnmitted codeword, the decoder will search through all the 2^7 possible codewords that can be generated by the state machine to see which one is closest to the received sequence. This is called the *brute-force* search method, which is computationally expensive. For example, imagine the case of 256-bit data bit sequence, which will force the receiver to comapre the received codeword againsts $2^{256} \approx 1.2 \times 10^{77}$ possibilities.

A more efficient method compared to the brute-force search is the Viterbi algorithm. In such method, and using the trellis shown in Figure 3, we narrow the investigated codewords (called paths) systematically each signalling interval. The algorithm goes like this: As the decoder examines an entire received codeword of a given length, the decoder computes a metric for each possible path in the trellis. The metric is cumulative across the whole path. All paths are followed until two paths converge at a trellis state. Then the path with the higher metric is kept (called the survivor path) and the one with the lower metric is discarded. Since the path with the highest metric is kept, the decoder is classified as a maximum-likelihood receiver.

There are different metrics that can be used to compare the received codeword with different valid codewords, the smiplest of which is the *Hamming distance*, which is the dot product between the received codeword and the original codeword (i.e., the bit agreements between the two bit sequences). The table below shows some exmaples of how to calculate the Hamming distance.

Data Bit Sequence	**Corresponding Codeword**	**Received Sequence (*due to errors*)**	**Bit Agreement (Hamming metric)**
0101111	00 11 11 10 10 01 11	10 11 10 10 10 11 10	10/14
0101100	00 11 11 10 10 10 11	10 11 10 10 10 11 10	10/14
1011000	11 11 10 10 10 11 10	10 11 10 10 10 11 10	13/14
1010110	11 11 10 01 10 10 10	10 11 10 10 10 11 10	10/14
1011011	11 11 10 10 10 00 10	10 11 10 10 10 11 10	11/14

To illustrate the idea of Viterbi search, we show in Figure 5 the case of decoding the codeword 11111010101110 corresponding to the data bit sequcen 1011000. An error occurs in the second bit, thus leading to the received bit sequence of **10111010101110**.

The decoder starts at state 000, just like the encoder. From this point it has two possible paths available, which should be decided by the incoming bits. Unfortunately, the two incoming bits are 01, which do not match 00 or 11. Hence, the decoder computes the path metric (Hamming distance) for both transitions and continues along both of these paths. The metric for both paths is now equal to 1, which means that *only one* of the two bits was matched with the incoming 01 sequence.

As the algorithm progresses while traversing multiple paths, we notice that certain paths start to converge at different states of the trellis (see the fourth, fifth, sixth, ... signalling intervals). The metrics are shown in Figure 5. Since maximum likelihood is employed, the decoder discards the path with the lower metric because it is least likely. This discarding of paths at each trellis state helps to reduce the number of paths that have to be examined and gives the Viterbi method its efficiency. The survivor paths are shown in darker color in Figure 5.

Once the whole codeword is traversed through the trellis, the path with the highest metric is chosen as the final path, which is 11111010101110 in our example corresponding to the input data sequence of 1011000.

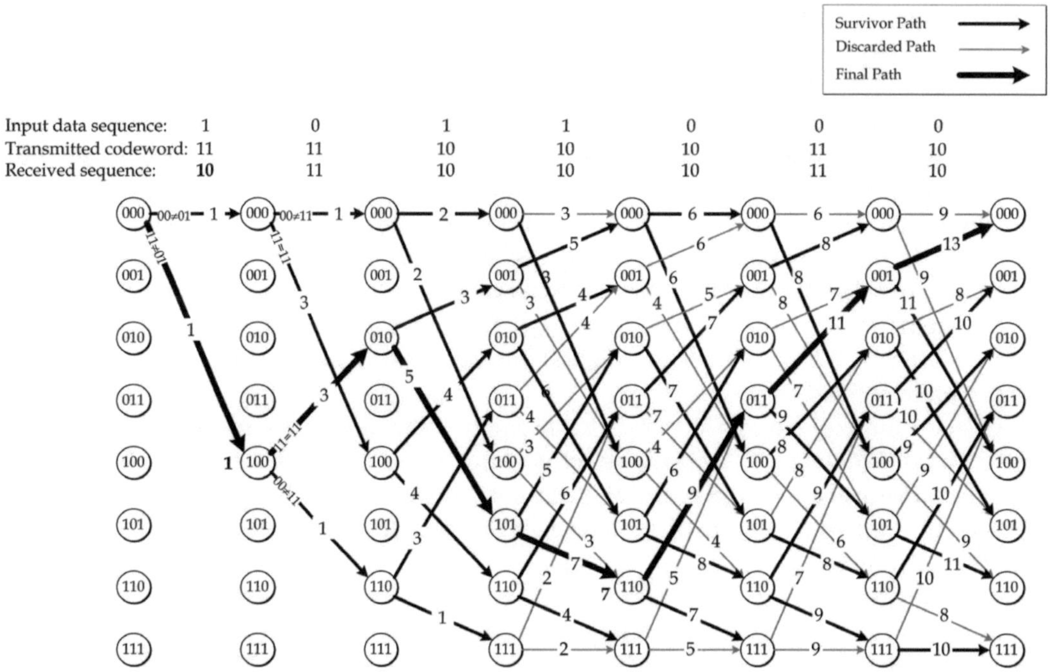

Fig. 5. Decoder trellis diagram showing the path for the input codeword of **10111010101110**.

It is worth mentioning that building the receiver hardware is much more difficult compared to the transmitter hardware. This is because we need to save path history for the algorithm to work. The length of the trellis diagram decides the memory storage requirements for the decoder, which is (in classical hardware) usually reduced by a truncation process. Truncation also reduces latency since decoding need not be delayed until the end of the transmitted codeword. Such truncation can be avoided if a parallel search is done through multiple paths at the same time.

4. The quantum Grover's algorithm

Grover's search algorithm in quantum computing gives an optimal, quadratic speedup in the search for a single object in a large unsorted database [1-4]. It can be generalized in a Hilbert-space framework for both continuous and discrete time cases. As shown in Figure 6, Grover's algorithm initializes the search space by creating an equal superposition of n qubits $|\varphi_1^n\rangle$ (the superscript denotes n qubits) by applying the Hadmard Transform **H**. Then it applies the function ***f(x)*** (The Oracle) that is equivalent to a gate operator called the **C** gate. This function is given by:

$$f(x) = \begin{cases} 0 & |\varphi_1\rangle \neq |x_r\rangle \\ 1 & |\varphi_1\rangle = |x_r\rangle \end{cases} \qquad (8)$$

where $|x_r\rangle$ is the required search result. The **C** operator will reverse the sign of the state (rotate by π) $|\varphi_1\rangle$ that most represents the required search result *(this argument will be used* *later in defining the oracle function used in our proposed implementation)* and leave all other states unchanged.

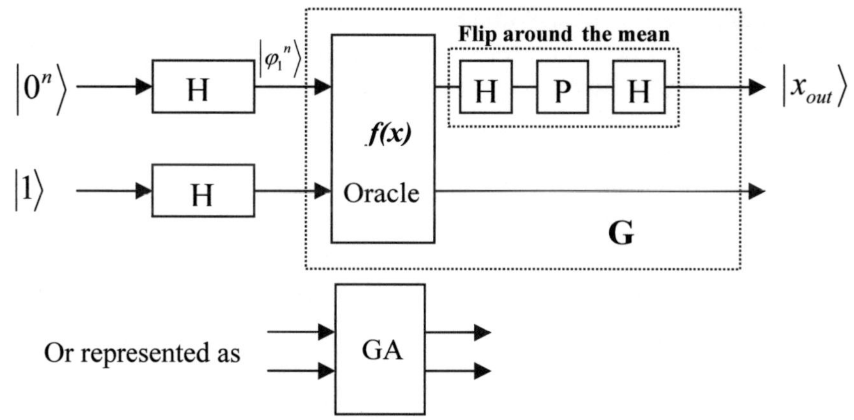

Fig. 6. Block Diagram of One Stage Basic Grover's Algorithm.

After applying **C** the result is flipped around the mean by the **H** and **P** operators. **H** is the Hadamard gate and **P** is the controlled phase shift operator gate, which for arbitrary ϕ_1 and ϕ_2 is given by:

$$P = \begin{bmatrix} e^{j\phi_1} & 0 \\ 0 & e^{j\phi_2} \end{bmatrix} \tag{9}$$

Then in matrix form we can see that:

$$|x_{out}\rangle = U^N |\varphi_1\rangle \tag{10}$$

Where:

$$U^N = H^N P^N H^N C^N \tag{11}$$

The superscript N denotes that it is an NxN operator. Applying the Grover's gate **(G)** r times to find the final search result, where:

$$r = \left\lfloor \frac{\cos^{-1}\left(\frac{1}{\sqrt{N_{paths}}}\right)}{2\sin^{-1}\left(\frac{1}{\sqrt{N_{paths}}}\right)} \right\rfloor \tag{12}$$

we see that as $N_{paths} \to \infty$ the searching order $r \to O(\sqrt{N_{paths}})$. Next we discuss the use of Grover's algorithm for implementing Viterbi algorithm.

5. Implementation of VA using Grover's Search Algorithm

Viterbi decoder searches all possible branches at each signalling interval in the code tree. This requires storage of all paths including the survivor path, computation of each branch metric and a decision making to select the survivor path. In quantum theory the components are somehow different, we have a register containing a certain number of qubits, an arbitrary transformation applied on these qubits and a measuring mechanism that measures the state of each particular qubit.
The quantum VA can be viewed as a global search in all the possible paths in the decoding trellis. This means that for a classical Convolutional Code with *(n,k,m)* parameters, *L* signalling symbols and the number of trellis states is 2^m, from equation (7) we see that the total number of possible paths is $N_T = L2^{m+k}$ when using the VA. We propose a single search quantum viterbi algorithm (*SSQVA*) and a multi search quantum viterbi algorithm *(MSQVA)*.

6. Single Search Quantum Viterbi Algorithm (SSQVA)

In this algorithm all the N_T paths are searched at once for the closest state to the received signal qubits producing a search order of $O(\sqrt{N_T})$. Then the total number of searches is given by:

$$N_{SSQVA} = \sqrt{N_T} = \sqrt{L}\,2^{\frac{m+k}{2}} \tag{13}$$

This requires large storage (especially for huge number of signalling intervals and number of trellis states). Figure 7 shows the block diagram of the *SSQVA*.

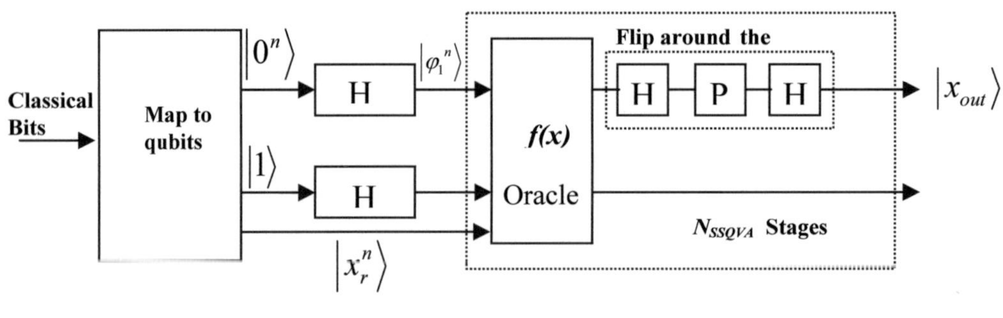

Fig. 7. Block Diagram of Single Search Quantum Viterbi Algorithm (*SSQVA*).

The *SSQVA* can be summarized as:

1. *Convert the received classical data bits into qubits* $|x_r^n\rangle$.
2. *Initialize the Grover's search engine.*
3. *Apply the search on all possible paths.*
4. *Measure the output and map it back to classical bits.*

Following the nature of the classical VA, where multi-stages are implemented, we devise the Multi Search version (MSQVA) as follows:

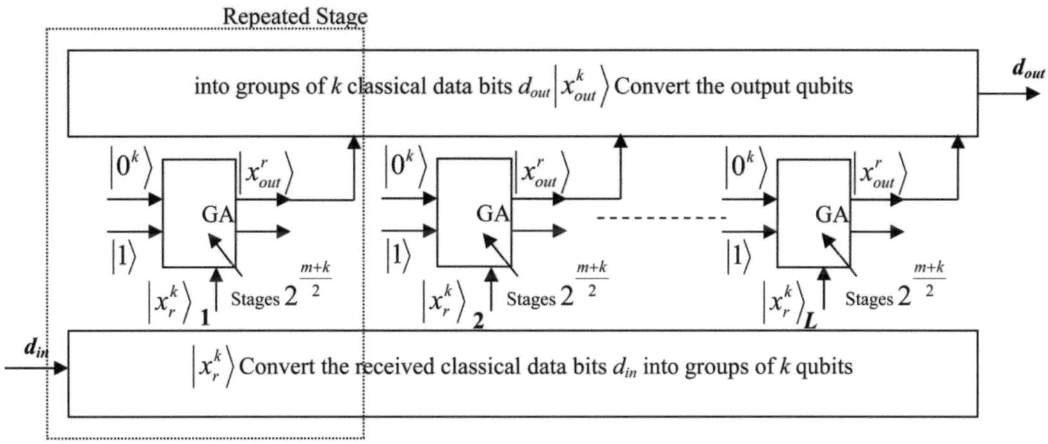

Fig. 8. Block Diagram of Multi Search Quantum Viterbi Algorithm.

7. Multi Search Quantum Viterbi Algorithm (MSQVA)

The N_T paths can be searched for the closest state to the received signal qubits in distributed fashion (Multi Search). For each stage we search only the corresponding tree branches and then combine the searches to the survivor path. This will produce a search order of $O(N_{MSQVA})$. Where the total number of searches is given by:

$$N_{MSQVA} = L\, 2^{\frac{m+k}{2}} \tag{14}$$

This requires less storage but as we can see larger number of searches. Figure 8 shows the block diagram of the *MSQVA*.

The MSQVA can also be implemented iteratively using the same one stage (the repeated stage shown in Figure 8).

The *MSQVA* can be summarized as:

1. *Convert the received classical k data bits into groups of k qubits* $|x^k_r\rangle$.
2. *Initialize the Grover's search engine.*
3. *Apply the search on all possible paths.*
4. *Measure the output and map it back to classical bits.*
5. *Go to step 1.*

The MSQVA version is implementing the VA iteratively as its classical nature; therefore, it has higher searching order. The advantage of the *MSQVA* is that the same hardware setup is used every iteration.

In both *SSQVA* and *MSQVA* the function *f(x)* is the black box of the algorithm. It differs according to the application of the VA. For example if VA is used as a Convolutional Code Decoder the function *f(x)* will decide in favour of the state that is closest to the received state. This means that the equality might not hold for all the received qubits. Then the function becomes:

$$f(x)=\begin{cases}0 & |\varphi_1\rangle \neq |x_r\rangle \\ 1 & |\varphi_1\rangle \cong |x_r\rangle\end{cases} \tag{15}$$

Then, the flipping around the mean transformation will amplify the most probable state and hence the result will be the maximum likelihood decision. Note that, *f(x)* still has the same implementation as in Grover's algorithm, since Grover's algorithm produces the most probable search result.
The implementation of quantum algorithms is in its first steps; therefore, only theoretical performance evaluation is possible. Figure 9 shows a comparison of the classical VA and the two devised algorithms at different frame lengths and number of states.

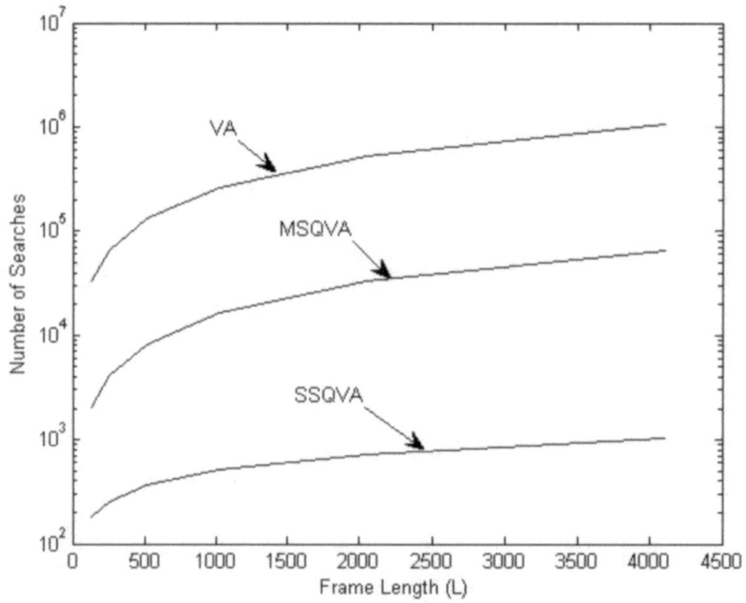

Fig. 9. Search Order as a function of Frame Length (*L*) for the Classical VA, *MSQVA* and *SSQVA* for *m*=4 and *k*=4.

8. Results and conclosions

In this chapter we discussed the use of quantum search algorithm introduced by Grover to speed the execution of Viterbi's algorithm. Two methods were discussed to implement VA using quantum search algorithm: The first is the *SSQVA* where the search domain contains all possible paths in the code tree. The number of paths depends on the signalling length (received data frame length). This domain becomes very large when long frames are used. The *SSQVA* is optimal in the global sense, because it uses all possible solutions and obtains the best one that has the minimum number of differences. The second method is the *MSQVA* where the search is divided into multiple stages just like in the classical algorithm. This method produces a sub optimal solution from speed point of view, since it uses the search algorithm partially at each signalling interval.

9. References

[1] L. K. Grover. "A fast quantum mechanical algorithm for database search." *In the Proceedings of the 28th Annual ACM Symposium on the Theory of Computing*. pp:212–219, May 1996.

[2] L. K. Grover. "Quantum mechanics helps in searching for a needle in a haystack." *Phys. Rev. Lett.* 79(2):325–328, July 1997.

[3] L. K. Grover. "Quantum computers can search rapidly by using almost any transformation." *Phys. Rev. Lett.* 80(19):4329–4332, 1998.

[4] P. W. Shor. "Quantum Computing." *Documenta Mathematica*, Extra Volume ICM 1998 I, pp. 467-480.

[5] Michael A. Nielsen and Isaac L. Chuang. *Quantum Computation and Quantum Information*. Cambridge ; New York : Cambridge University Press, 2000.

[6] J. Gruska, *Quantum Computing*. McGraw Hill, 1999.

[7] Isaac L Chuang, Neil Gershenfeld and Mark Kubinec. "Experimental Implementation of Fast Quantum Searching," *Phys. Rev. Lett.* 80(15):3408–3411, April 1998.

[8] John G. Proakis & Massoud Salehi, "Digital Communications," 5th Edition, McGraw Hill Higher Education, 2008.

[9] Bernard Sklar, "Digital Communications : Fundamentals and Applications", 2nd Edition, Prentice Hall PTR, 2001.

[10] Shu Lin and Daniel J. Costello, Jr. *Error Control Coding, Fundamentals and Applications*. Prentice Hall, 1982.

[10] A. Viterbi, "Error bounds for convolutional codes and an asymptotically optimum decoding algorithm," *IEEE Transactions on Information Theory*, vol. IT-13, pp. 260–269, April 1967.

[11] G. Forney, "The Viterbi algorithm," *Proceedings of the IEEE*, vol. 61, pp. 268–278, March 1973.

[12] L. Hanzo, T.H. Liew, B.L. Yeap, *Turbo Coding, Turbo Equalisation and Space-Time Coding*, John wiley, 2002.

[13] Elton Ballhysa, "A Generalization of the Deutsch-Jozsa Algorithm and the Development of a Quantum Programming Infrastructure." M.S. Thesis, Boğaziçi University, 2004.

[14] Andrew M. Childs, Richard Cleve, Enrico Deotto, Edward Farhi, Sam Gutmann, Daniel A. Spielman. "Exponential algorithmic speedup by a quantum walk." STOC'03, 59-68. 2003.

[15] A. Yu. Kitaev, A. H. Shen, M. N. Vyalyi. "Classical and Quantum Computation." American Mathematical Society, 2002.

Bibliography

Jamal Rahhal received the B.S. degree from the University of Jordan in 1989, the M.S. and Ph.D. from Illinois Institute of Technology, Chicago IL, in 1993, 1996 respectively. He is currently an assistant professor at the University of Jordan. His current research areas including; CDMA\OFDMA cellular communication systems, array processing, quantum computing and optimization.

D. I. Abu-Al-Nadi received BS from Yarmouk University- Jordan, MS from Oklahoma State University-USA, and PhD from the University of Bremen-Germany all in Electrical Engineering, in 1987, 1991, and 1999, respectively. He is currently an associate professor at the University of Jordan. His current research areas are array processing, quantum computing, pattern recognition, and applications of Neural Networks and Fuzzy Systems.

Mohammed Hawa received his B.S. degree from the University of Jordan in 1997, the M.S. from University College London in 1999 and Ph.D. from University of Kansas, USA in 2003. He is currently an Assistant Professor at the University of Jordan. His current research areas include: communication networks, quantum computing and Quality-of-Service.

9

Some Modeling Issues for Protein Structure Prediction using Evolutionary Algorithms

Telma Woerle de Lima, Antonio Caliri, Fernando Luís Barroso da Silva, Renato Tinós, Gonzalo Travieso, Ivan Nunes da Silva, Paulo Sergio Lopes de Souza, Eduardo Marques, Alexandre Cláudio Botazzo Delbem, Vanderlei Bonatto, Rodrigo Faccioli, Christiane Regina Soares Brasil, Paulo Henrique Ribeiro Gabriel, Vinícius Tragante do Ó and Daniel Rodrigo Ferraz Bonetti
University of Sao Paulo
Brazil

1. Introduction

Many essential functions for life are performed by proteins and the study of their structures yields the ability to elucidate these functions in terms of a molecular view. (Creighton, 1992; Devlin, 1997) The interest in discovering a methodology for protein structure prediction (PSP) is of great interesti on many fields including drug design and carriers, disease mechanisms, and the food industry. In this context, several *in vitro* methods have been applied, as X-ray crystallography and nuclear magnetic resonance. Despite their relative success, both methods have their limitations. Conversely, the knowledge of the primary sequence of the amino acids of a protein can be achieved by a relatively simpler experimental measurement. From this information, one can in principle predict the three dimensional arrangement of its atoms, which has motivated the investigation of *ab initio* methods combining such initial knowledge with effective models (force fields) in order to predict the spatial structure of a protein (Bonneau & Baker, 2001; Hardin et al., 2002).

In fact, several computational methods for PSP are *semi ab initio* methodologies in the sense that they also use *prior* knowledge from both the sequence homology and the statistics found on protein databases [see e.g. (Miyazawa & Jernigan, 1985; Poole & Ranganathan, 2006)]. However, the use of these additional information restrict the search of protein structures that could be correctly predicted from the vast universe of proteins.

This chapter focuses on the development of a *pure ab initio* approach for PSP, not using prior information. In this context, evolutionary algorithms (EAs) have been investigated as a search method due to their flexibility to solve complex optimization problems. Our researches on EAs applied to PSP are twofold: 1) the investigation of more appropriate modeling of the physical and chemical interactions of a protein for the purpose of an optimization algorithm; 2) the development of computationally efficient EAs for PSP. Two important modeling issues have been poorly investigated in the literature related to the optimization techniques for PSP: a) the combined effects of the effective Hamiltonians based on force fields and the solvation free energy contribution (Section 3), and b) the use of multiple criteria to evaluate the predicted molecules since several physical interactions drive the folding process (Section 4). We show how both modeling issues can improve protein prediction quality.

We also present recently developed computational techniques to increase the efficiency of the algorithms for PSP. Algorithms using simple lattice models can work in a relatively small search space, however, they often generate a large number of unfeasible structures (with amino acid collisions). We present in this chapter lattice models that eliminate unfeasible solutions (Section 2). To increase the capacity of an EA to overcome local minimal of the potential energy, we propose an adaptation of the Self-Organizing Random Immigrants Genetic Algorithms for the PSP problem (Section 6). To work with large proteins, we explore computational strategies to enhance the efficiency of the calculi of the more complex energy functions (Section 5). Another strategy is the use of some heuristic about the proteins or its family to create the initial population of the EA, instead of the use of random solutions (Section 7).

Finally, this chapter shows how to combine the results from the set of above described researches in order to construct an *ab initio* PSP approach able to work with large proteins independently from prior information of similar structures (Section 8).

2. Advances using lattice models

Lattice models are simplified models of proteins which represent a conformation as a set of points in a grid. The simplest topologies of lattices are the squared lattice, for two dimensions, or the cubic lattice, for three dimensions. These models were originally employed in order to reduce the computational calculi (Dill, 1985; Unger & Moult, 1993). In this research field, they have been used to quickly evaluate the effect of parameter and operator of EAs, and, thus, motivated the development of new techniques in advanced models.

One of the most studied lattice models for protein folding is the *hydrophobic-hydrophilic model* (so-called HP model), where each amino-acid is classified in two classes: hydrophobic or non-polar (H), and hydrophilic or polar (P), according to their interaction with water molecules. (Chan & Dill, 1993a, 1993b) Moreover, each pair of amino acids in a conformation can be classified as *connected* or *neighbors*. Two amino acids from positions i and j in a sequence are connected if, and only if, $j = i + 1$ or $j = i - 1$. Notice that the number of amino acids is fixed. On the other hand, two amino acids in positions i and j are neighbors if the Euclidean distance between i and j is equal to 1. There are common features and assumptions behind such model with the classical Bragg-Willians and Flory-Huggins ones (Jönsson, B. et al, 1998).

The native state of a protein is a low-energy conformation. Thus, each pair of neighbors of H type contributes with a contact free energy -1. Then, the number of HH contacts is maximized in the native state. Despite the apparent simplicity of the model, finding the globally optimal conformation under HP model is an NP-Complete problem (Berger & Leighton, 1997), justifying the use of heuristic-based techniques for solving this problem. In the following, we present EAs developed for the PSP problem.

In the HP model, a protein conformation must be represented in a particular lattice; thus, each individual of the EA represents a conformation. In general, the fold is expressed as a sequence of *movements* into lattice. The position of the first amino acid is fixed and the other positions are specified by $n - 1$ movements for a sequence of n amino acids.

Two major schemes for representing the movements can be found in the literature:

- The *absolute representation* (AR) (Unger & Moult, 1993), where each new position is defined from the previous position. However, this representation allows movements of return, i.e., movements that annul the previous movement generating amino acid collision;
- The *relative representation* (RR) (Patton et al., 1995), where a movement is generated depending on the last movement in a way to avoid amino acid collision.

Since both representation do not avoid unfeasible solutions (with collisions), a penalty function assigns lower fitness values to these solutions during the evaluation stage. However, researches on EA representations for complex problems (Rothlauf, 2006) show that populations with feasible solutions have very slow convergence, since the unfeasible solutions dominated the evolutionary process with the increasing of the problem size. This phenomenon has been also verified in the PSP problem (Krasnogor et al., 1999; Cotta, 2003; Gabriel & Delbem, 2009).

In order to solve the problem of unfeasible solutions, Gabriel & Delbem (2009) propose a new approach using AR and a conformation matrix (C_M). This representation uses a matrix to decode AR of conformations. Each position of amino acid from a RR is indexed in a position of the matrix C_M representing the lattice. If there is already an amino acid in position (x,y,z) of C_M when decoding amino acid x, a collision is identified, x is replaced for an empty position of C_M and the corresponding movement in AR is properly updated.

To guarantee the efficiency of the decoding process, an array stores permutations of a set of relative movements (that are encoded using integers numbers) from a grid position. To repair the AR due to a collision, movements from the array are probed in C_M until finding a movement that avoids collision. If all possibilities in the array have been explored, the collisions are not repairable using local movements. Then, the individual (conformation) is eliminated, i.e., the building process is is canceled out and a new individual starts to be generated. For each collision a new array of permutations is constructed.

To analyzes the effect of C_M on the reduction of unfeasible solutions, we compare the quality of initial populations generated using C_M with random initial populations produced by classical EA based on AR. The usual fitness function for

Sequences	AR			AR + C_M		
	Best	Average	Worst	Best	Average	Worst
27 amino acids	0.50	-7.44	-3.40	3.20	0.57	0.00
64 amino acids	-7.80	-23.98	-62.80	6.90	2.00	0.00

Table 1. Comparison of the fitness value of the initial population using AR alone and AR with C_M.

HP models adds -1 for each collision in the conformation and +1 for each HH interaction (Gabriel & Delbem, 2009). Table 1 compares the average value the usual fitness of initial populations generated for 20 sequences (Unger & Moult, 1993; Patton et al., 1995): 10 with 27 amino acids and 10 with 64 amino acids. The percentage of feasible conformations in the initial population generated using AR. On the other hand, all conformations are feasible when AR and C_M are employed. In some populations, there are conformations very near to the global optimum.

3. Modeling the solvent effect for protein structure prediction

An aqueous solution is the environment where almost all important (bio)chemical reactions happen. It is central to several chemical, petrochemical, pharmaceutical and food engineering processes too (Eisenberg & Kauzmann, 1969; Ben-Naim, 1994; Devlin, 1997; Loehe & Donohue, 1997; Degrève & da Silva, 1999; Guillot, 2002; Dill et al, 2005; Levy & Onuchic, 2006). Proteins are just a type of solute found in this medium whose behavior is strongly affected by liquid water due to its intrinsic properties as a hydrogen-bonding solvent (Skaf & da Silva, 1994; Dill et al, 2005; Levy & Onuchic, 2006). In physiological conditions, the picture is far more complicated, principally because the presence of electrolytes (Na^+,K^+,Cl^-, etc.) (Jönsson, Lund & da Silva, 2007).

Water is well known to be a decisive factor on the protein conformational stability and determinative in processes such as the "protein folding" via the complex interplay especially of the solvent-protein and solvent-solvent interactions (Creighton, 1992; Eisenhaber & Argos, 1996; Devlin, 1997; Dill et al, 2005; Levy & Onuchic, 2006; Chaplin, 2008). In a classic view, these intermolecular interactions are given by electronic repulsion (whose origin is the Pauli exclusion principle), multipole-multipole interactions (often used as electrostatic interactions), induction (multipole-induced multipole interaction) and instantaneous induced multipole-induced multipole interactions (the London dispersion forces) (Israelachvili, 1991; Evans & Wennerström, 1994). The induction and dispersion interactions are known as the van der Walls interactions. In addition to these enthalpic contributions, due to the thermal effect, entropy has an important participation in these processes. Combined with the high affinity that water has for water, the final result is the so-called "hydrophobic effect", (Creighton, 1992; Garde et al., 1996; Jönsson et al, 1998; Levy & Onuchic, 2006; Chaplin, 2008) which is a key driven force for the protein folding.

In a molecular modeling approach, the initial challenge is to identify the main characteristics of the real physical system (in this case, a protein in solution), and to define how the intermolecular interactions and effects above mentioned may be replaced by suitable averages. This results in a mathematical expression that describes the potential energy of the system as a function of the separation distance between the species and is called an *effective* Hamiltonian model (EHM), (Friedman, 1977, 1981; da Silva, 1999) or, more commonly, the force field (FF) definition (Levitt, 1995; Ponder & Case, 2003; Mackerell Jr, 2004; Oostenbrink et al, 2004; Guvench & Mackerell Jr, 2008; Stone, 2008). We refer to this model as "effective", because it is not identical to the reality, but it is supposed to behave as the reality. Besides an atomist description, a vast diversity of coarse-grained models has also been reported (Tozzini, 2005; Monticelli et al, 2008).

Depending on the applications and questions to be answered, water may be modeled by different ways, from explicit (or molecular) to continuum (or implicit) solvent models (Friedman, 1981; Jorgensen et al, 1983; da Silva, Jönsson & Penfold, 2001; Guillot, 2002; Chen et al., 2008) (see Fig. 1). The main difference is the variables that *explicitly* enter the EHM and the computational costs. In the explicit models, the input variables are the coordinates and momenta of the solvent (i.e., a molecular model should be used), while the solvent only enters by an averaging over of its coordinates and momenta in the implicit models (i.e., water is replaced by its bulk static dielectric constant, ε_s). The latter model has a substantial reduction on cpu time with the price of loosing details that might be relevant for some cases. In this model level, the solvent in the immediate neighborhood of any solute is assumed to behave as the bulk solvent. It is an idealization widely used in Molecular Biology (Garcia-

Moreno, 1985; Bashford & Gerwert, 1992; da Silva et al., 2001; Chen et al., 2008) that captures *part* of the water properties, neglecting its molecular structure that is responsible principally for local, short-range, interactions and might be crucial in some cases (e.g. to study the hydration phenomenon).

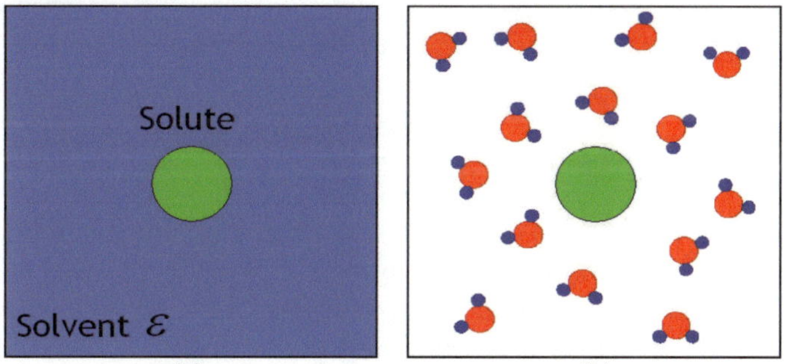

(a) (b)

Fig. 1. A representation of a solute in two different water models: (a) A solute in a structure-less continuum model (implicit solvent model). Water only enters in the calculations by means of its bulk dielectric permittivity ε; (b) A solute molecule is surrounded by an explicit solvent model.

A large number of molecular models for water with different number of interaction sites based either on empirical or quantum mechanical methods have been developed during the last forty years, including rigid [e.g., SPC/E (Berendsen et al., 1987), TIP4P (Jorgensen et al, 1983), flexible [e.g., SPCFX (Teleman, O. et al., (1987)], dissociable [e.g., DCF (Halley et al., 1993)] and polarizable [e.g., SWM4-DP (Lamoureux et al., 2003), TIP4P/FQ (Rick, Stuart & Berne, 1994) models. Most water models assume site-site pair interactions in order to facilitate their application in numerical simulations. A common characteristic of them is to define a water molecule by a set of point sites. Fractions of electric charges are attributed to these sites and used to calculate the electrostatic pair potential energy (E_{ele}) according to Coulomb's law. The van der Waals forces are normally modeled by a particular case of Mie´s interaction potential known as Lennard-Jones (E_{LJ}) pair interaction potential (Verlet, 1967; Orea et al., 2008). The combination of these two terms (E_{ele}+E_{LJ}) is applied to the system constituents and gives the total interaction energy. Often a given model shows good behavior for a few properties and fails to describe others. Several reviews and comparisons between such models are available on the literature (van der Spoel et al., 1998; Wallqvist e Mountain, 1999; Guillot, 2002).

A compromise between the model details and the simulation costs is always a challenge task. To describe the hydrophobic effect, retaining the main characteristics of a real physical system (solute-solvent) and simulate it using reasonable cpu time, we need to find an adequate way to replace the exact calculation of the intermolecular interactions and effects by suitable averages, where the use of implicit solvent models is surely appealing. There are two basic models of implicit solvent normally used for this purpose: continuum electrostatic models and approaches based on solvent accessible surface (SAS) Variations of these models and combinations of them have also been proposed. (Garcia-Moreno, 1985; Bashford & Gerwert, 1992; Street & Mayo, 1998; da Silva et al., 2001; Snow et al, 2005, Chen et al., 2008).

Biomolecular systems are surrounded by solvent particles (water molecules, cations, and anions). In this environment, ions electrically interact with the molecule, which can have an electric charge due to ionization mechanisms. (Jönsson et al., 2007) pH affects can be taken into account and give peculiar interactions. (da Silva et al, 2006; da Silva & Jönsson, 2009) The Poisson-Boltzmann equation (PBE) describes the electrostatic environment of a solute in solvent containing ions on a mean-field level of treatment. (Warwicker & Watson, 1982; da Silva, Jönsson & Penfold, 2001; Neves-Petersen & Petersen, 2003; Grochowski & Trylska, 2007; de Carvalho, Fenley e da Silva, 2008). It can be written as:

$$\nabla.\left[\varepsilon(r)\nabla\Phi(r)\right]=-4\pi\left[\rho(r)+qn_{+}\exp\left[\frac{-q\Phi(r)}{K_{B}T}-v(r)\right]-qn_{-}\exp\left[\frac{+q\Phi(r)}{K_{B}T}-v(r)\right]\right] \tag{6.1}$$

where the right term of the equation is the contribution of the fixed charges in the biomolecule, the other terms are the contribution of mobile positive and negative ions (treated here as point charges whose distribution around the central charged molecule obeys a Boltzmann distribution), $\varepsilon(r)$ is a position-dependent dielectric, $\Phi(r)$ is the electrostatic potential, $\rho(r)$ is the charge density of the solute, q is the charge of an ion, n_+ and n_- are densities of ion i at an infinite distance from the solute (bulk), K_B is the Boltzmann constant, $v(r)$ is 0 for accessible regions and infinite for unaccessible regions, and T is the temperature.
Analytical solutions of the PBE are possible only on ideal cases. One of these special situations is the infinite charged planar surface case. This example is given in details in refs. (Russel et al., 1989; Lyklema, 1991) and is usually described as the Gouy-Chapman case. (Usui, 1984) For biomolecular applications, numerical methods are necessary, and a number of different schemes have been proposed. (Lu et al, 2008) Nevertheless, despite the chosen numerical method, the PBE requires large memory resources and cpu time to be calculated without further approximations (e.g. to linearized it). (da Silva et al., 2001; de Carvalho et al., 2008) Although there are a large number of computational packages available (e.g. Melc, (Juffer, 1992) Delphi, (Sharp et al., 1998) APBS, (Holst et al., 2000) and MEAD (Bashford & Gerwert, 1992), the computational costs can still be a limitation and prohibitive when dealing with large molecules as proteins in applications that would require the systematic repetition of the same calculation for different macromolecular conformations. Critical investigations of the PBE are available elsewhere. (da Silva et al., 2001; de Carvalho et al., 2008)
The methods based on SAS arise experimentally by the linear relation between free energy and the surface area of a solute molecule (Hermann, 1972; Valvani et al., 1976; Amidon et al., 1975; Camilleri et al., 1988; Doucette e Andren, 1987; Dunn III et al., 1987; Snow et al, 2005). In this way, this method can directly provide the free energy of solvation. The continuum representation of solvent significantly reduces the cpu time. The SAS is the locus of points traced out by the inward facing part of the probe sphere, representing the solvent molecule that rotates over the van der Waals surface of the protein (see Fig. 2).
It is important to note that SAS solvent models also have limitations mainly related to:

- Viscosity: SAS and other implicit solvent models lack the viscosity, which affects the motion of solutes;
- Hydrogen-bonds with water: the directionality of the hydrogen bonds is missing in an implicit solvent. Moreover, bulk and buried water molecules are assumed to have the same behavior;
- Choice of model solvent: different atomic solvation parameters should be applied for modeling of the protein folding problem. These parameters should be derived from experimental coefficients involving organic molecules.

Nowadays, there are computational tools that calculate SAS and the free energy of solvation such as: GROMACS (Lindahl et al., 2001), POPS (Cavallo, 2003), Naccess (Hubbard e Thornton, 1993), STRIDE (Frishman e Argos, 1995), among others. In the following, we present preliminary results using SAS software based on the package STRIDE.

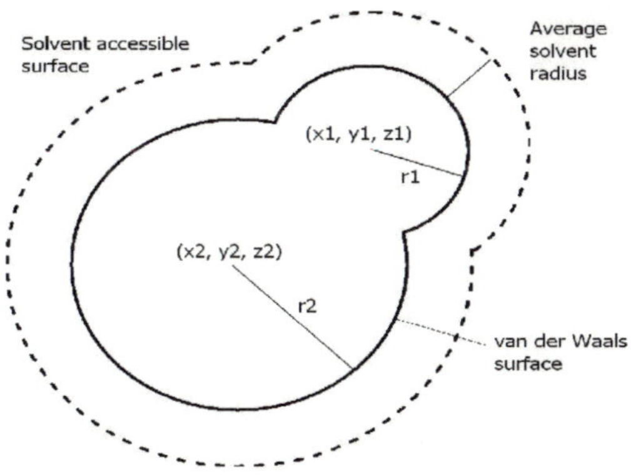

Fig. 2. A representation of van der Waals surface area and solvent accessible area surfaces (Richards, 1977).

The EA implementation for PSP, called ProtPred (Lima, 2007), was used to perform experiments to evaluate the effects of SAS and internal energies on the PSP. The potential energy functions are based on the CHARMm force fields of and solved by the Tinker package for molecular modeling (Ponder, 2001). The ProtPred uses the full-atom model (Cui et al, 1998; Cutello et al, 2005), representing the backbone and side-chain torsion angles (internal coordinates). The individuals (conformations) of the initial population are randomly generated with the angles in the constraint regions of each amino acid according to the Ramachandran map. The ProtPred code was run with 200 iterations and populations with 200 individuals were generated, using three recombination operators: i) two-point crossover, ii) uniform crossover, and iii) BLX-α (Deb et al., 2002). The algorithm uses three mutation operators: one changes all torsion angles of an amino acid by reselecting the values from the constraint regions; the others perform uniform mutation, but they differ from the use distinct step sizes.
The ProtPred minimizes a weighted objective function composed by energy functions. Fig. 3(a) shows the native protein structure of an acetylcholine receptor, obtained from PDB database (PDB id 1A11). Fig. 3(b) presents the structure obtained by ProtPred with the following weights for the objective function: 1.0 for wan der Waals, 0.5 for electrostatic, and zero for SAS. Fig. 3(c) shows the protein structure obtained changing the weights for SAS from zero to 0.001, indicating that SAS is relevant for PSP.

(a) (b) (c)

Fig. 3. Configurations of 1A11 protein.

Even though this protein is relatively small (25 aminoacids), the results encourage further works with this approach for modeling of the potential energy as a new criterion for evaluation in EAs to the PSP, considering not only the SAS, but also the internal energy.

4. Multiple criteria to evaluate predicted molecules

The PSP problem can be seen as a multi-objective problem, since it deals with several criteria involving energy functions estimating different aspects of intermolecular interactions (van der Waals, electrostatic, hydrogen-bond) and solvation free energies. A multi-criteria problem in general possesses the following characteristics:

- The determination of weights for an weighted function combining all the criteria is difficult;
- The criteria conflicts, i.e. the improvement of one objective in general involves the damage for other objective.

A protein structure with very low electrostatic energy may correspond to relatively high van der Waals energy. This kind of structure is in general inconsistent with the conformation of a real protein. Problems with conflicting objectives generally do not have a unique solution, but a solution set, called *Pareto*-optimal (Handl et al., 2006). This decade has produced relevant Multi-objective EAs, as the NSGA-II, which has been used to solve complex multi-objective problems. Unfortunately, even the NSGA-II losses performance for more than 3 objectives. For a large number of objectives, alternative solutions ought to be developed as the use of heuristics (Deb et al., 2006).

A first multiple criteria approach to PSP, called mo-ProtPred, was proposed in (Lima, 2006). This approach is based on NSGA-II (Deb, 2001), one of the main Multi-objective EA. The mo-ProtPred can work with three objectives without requiring weights for them.

The mo-ProtPred was applied to predict a transducin alpha-1 subunit (PDB id 1AQG). For this test, 500 generations with a population size equals to 400 were used. The objectives were functions corresponding to van de Waals, electrostatic, and hydrogen bond interaction energies. Fig. 4 illustrates polypeptides structures produced by the mo-ProtPred. Several of these structures are very similar to the native protein structure, displayed in Fig. 4(a). Table 2 shows the RMS values for each structure obtained.

Adequate structures for 1AQG were also achieved using a weighted function for the three objectives. Nevertheless, 27 different triples of weights were tested, 3 values (1.0, 0.5, 0.0) for each weight, and the ProtPred was executed for each triple. Thus, the ProtPred required much more running time than mo-ProtPred to achieve similar results.

	Conformations											
	a	b	c	d	e	f	g	h	i	j	k	l
RMS	0.00	3.83	4.09	3.83	3.77	4.09	4.06	3.93	3.77	4.01	4.14	3.83

Table 2. Results with 1AQG using mo-ProtPred.

5. Computation of van der Waals and electrostatic functions

The van der Waals potential energy models the induced and dispersion attraction among pairs of atoms and the electronic repulsion. It has as parameters the separation distance

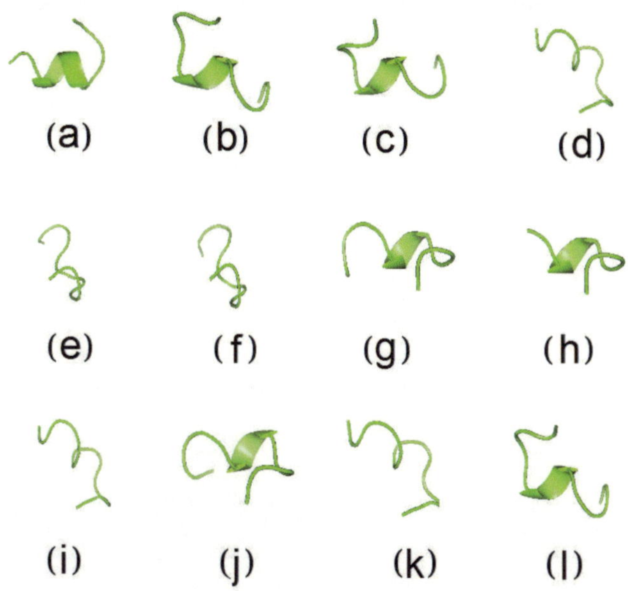

Fig. 4. Protein conformations of 1AQG obtained by mo-ProtPred.

between the atoms and van der Waals radii. At large distances, there is no attraction between pairs of atoms. However, when electron clouds of the atoms are close enough to overlap, there is a strong repulsion and its value exponentially grows. The energy is smaller when a balance point exists between the attractive and repulsive forces; this is known as van der Waals contact (Berg et al., 2002; Nelson, 2004). The Lennard-Jones 12-6 potential is frequently used to represent this interaction, because it models appropriately the attractive and repulsive forces and, from a numerical point of view, it can be efficiently implemented.

Together with the electrostatic interactions, van der Waals has considerable influence on the molecular structure. Studies have shown that the van der Waals forces contribute up to 65% of the total free energy of a protein (Becker, 2001).

In the evaluation of an individual to be used in an EA applied to PSP, there are several functions that contribute to the calculation of the minimum free energy of the protein. However, the computation of the van der Waals and electrostatic energies have time complexity $O(n^2)$, where n is the number of atoms. The interaction energy Eij is calculated for each atom pairs (i,j). The interactions in the molecule can be represented by a matrix E. Since $Eij = Eji$, E is an upper triangular matrix.

The computation time for both interaction energies corresponds to about 99% of the total EA execution time (Jain et al., 2009). It is therefore interesting to elaborate efficient algorithms and to use parallel processing wherever possible to reducing the total execution time.

There are classical methods for the parallelization of computations with upper triangular matrices. An obvious strategy is to distribute each row of the upper triangular matrix as a task for the processes. Therefore, using n processors, each one executing a task in parallel, the energy can be calculated in time $O(n)$, because the largest task would have n inter-atomic interactions to determine. On the other hand, some processors would have just some inter-atomic interactions to compute, generating a non-uniform load balancing among processors. This can be reduced by combining the first row with the last row, the second row with the last but one row, and so on. This process produces $n/2$ tasks of size n (see Fig. 5).

The new individuals created by reproduction operators of EA have atoms with different coordinates from the parents. At each new generation, those coordinates must be sent to processors that calculate the electrostatics and van der Waals energies. The parallelization of these computations produces good results for large proteins, but not for small ones, as can be seen in Fig. 6. This figure shows the speedup achieved with the use of a given number of processors. The speedup is defined as the sequential execution time divided by the parallel execution time, and is equal to the number of processors in an ideal case (shown as a straight line in this figure). For a smaller protein, the computation time is on the order of the communication time for sending the coordinates to the processors, limiting the achieved speedup. For larger proteins, the computation time grows faster than the communication one, and the speedups are better. This is typical for parallel programs, which have overhead

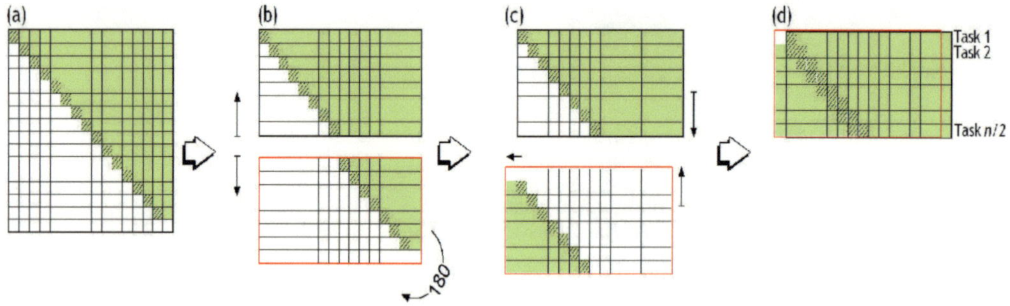

Fig. 5. (a) Upper triangular matrix of interaction. (b) Cut accomplished in the half of the matrix and the indication of the rotation of 180° of the second half. (c) Alignment of the second half to satisfy the dense matrix criterion. (d) New dense matrix of interactions with $n/2$ tasks of the same size.

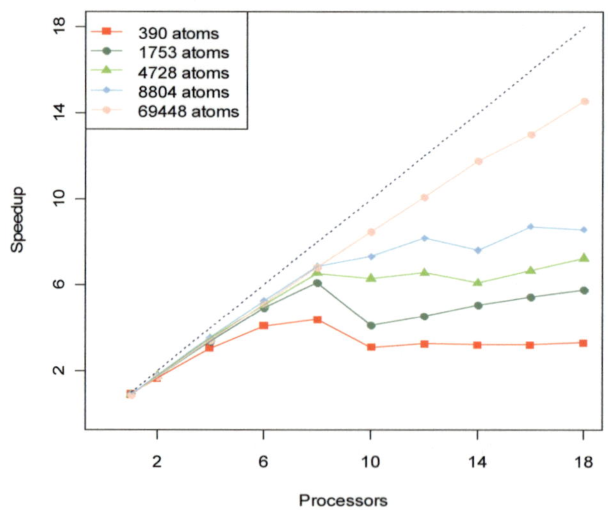

Fig. 6. The speedup reached by 5 different sizes of proteins to calculate van der Waals energy using 20 Athlon64-X2 processors.

costs that are independent of problem size (Quinn, 1994), and therefore work better for large instances. This phenomenon is also related to the Amdahl effect (Goodman & Hedetniemi, 1997). Since evaluations of different individuals are independent, rows of two or more dense matrices of interactions (Fig. 5) can be composed in larger tasks. This strategy can be especially adequate for the processing in GPUs (Graphic Processing Units) (Owens et al., 2008; Stone et al., 2007). The last generation of GPUs is capable of processing more than 3,500 matrices of 512x512 per second. This situation makes possible to compute energies of large molecules (hundreds of thousands of atoms) for several different configurations (individuals).

The computation time can also be improved using characteristics of the crossover operator used for the construction of new solutions. Since this operator preserves part of the information of each parent, the matrix of interactions of an offspring from crossover can be partly copied from that of its parents, as the energies depend only on the distances between the atoms, and those are preserved for pair of atoms that come from the same parent. Fig. 7 illustrates the areas of the upper triangular matrices that can be directly copied from the parents. The efficiency of this technique depends on the position of the crossover cut point. The worst case happens when the point is in the middle of the chromosome (see Fig. 8(a)).

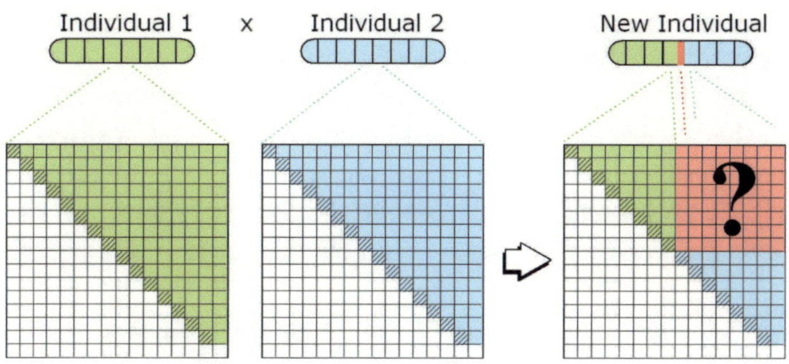

Fig. 7. Calculated values *Eij* of inter-atomic interactions for the parents are copied to the offspring. Only the pink area needs to be recalculated.

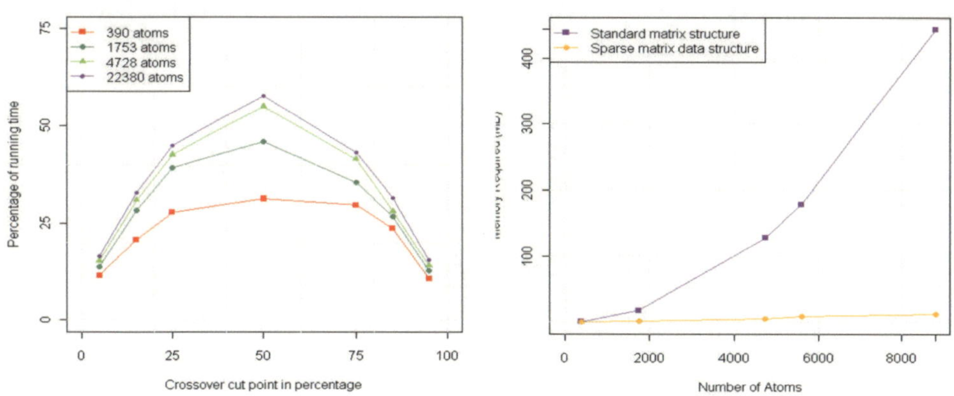

(a) (b)

Fig. 8. (a) Percentage of the required running time when *Eij's* are copied from parent. (b) Required memory to save matrix *E* of an new individual.

Because both interaction types discussed here decay with the distance, to reduce the amount of computations it is usually defined a cutoff radius of 8Å for van der Waals and 13Å for electrostatic energies (Cui et al., 1998), and the computation of these energies for larger distances is avoided.

Taking this into account, we see that the matrix of interactions is in fact a sparse matrix. This helps to overcome a possible limitation for the computation of large proteins, as the interaction matrix would otherwise grow with $O(n^2)$. The data structure used is therefore important. Fig. 8(b) shows that the memory required for saving the whole matrix E increases quadratically with the size of the molecule, while using sparse matrix data structure the size increases more slowly.

Another optimization enabled by the use of a cutoff on the calculation of van der Waals and electrostatic energies makes possible to significantly reduce the amount of calculi for large proteins. One technique is the so called "Cell Lists" (Allen & Tildesley, 1987), which splits the space into cubic cells, as Fig. 9 illustrates (for the 2D case). Each cell has edge size equals to or larger than the cutoff radius. Thus, atoms in a cell interact only with other atoms in the same cell or in one of the neighbouring cells. This technique reduces the computation complexity from $O(n^2)$ to $O(n+m)$, where m is the number of cells with atoms, because a larger number of atoms in a protein is related with increased size, and therefore increased number of cells, instead of increased number of atoms per cell.

Fig. 10(a) shows the running cpu time required by the computation of the interactions without and with the cell-list approach. These result can also be improved by using an off-line procedure that previously compute the interaction energy between each possible pair of types of atoms (C, O, H, N, and S) for inter-atomic distances in a specified range (from a minimal distance to the maximal distance given by the cutoff radius) (Lodish et. at., 2003), see Fig. 10(b).

A performance enhancement for the computation of the potential energy has also been achieved using parallel solutions base on hardware like FPGAs (Field Programming Gate Arrays) (Wolf, 2004). The development of a specific solution in hardware is in general a hard task. One of the first researches using FPGAs for protein potential energy calculi did not reach a PC performance for the same problem. (Azizi et. al., 2004) In fact, this hardware solution was four time slower than the PC-base approach. Recent researches have achieved

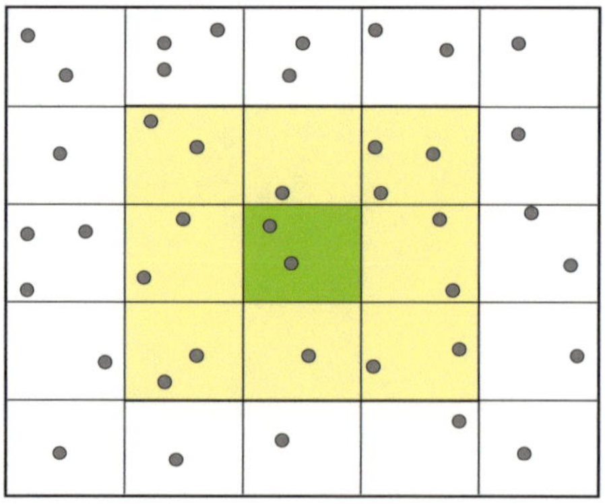

Fig. 9. 2D Cells, where the neighbour cells of the green cell are in yellow and the atoms are represented as grey balls.

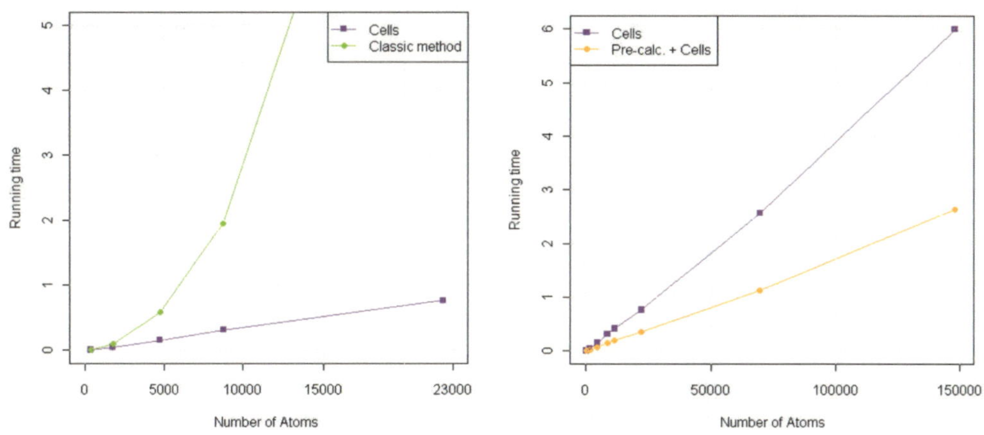

(a) (b)

Fig. 10. Running cpu time necessary to calculate van der Waals potential: (a) Enhancement produced by the cell-list approach. (b) Improvement of performance combining cell-list and off-line calculi of *Eij*.

better performances by using faster memory bus and higher clock (Kindratenko & Pointer, 2006; Jain et. al., 2009). For example, Gu (2008) using a Virtex-5 (Xilinx, 2009) reached a speedup of 16.8.

The off-line calculi of inter-atomic energies (*Eij* 's) is another aspect that can be explored in FPGA solutions. The values *Eij* can be stored in lookup tables avoiding calculi with floating-point, which in general require large number of logic gates from FPGAs. Then, the available gates can be used to implement several lookup tables in parallel. The sum of the *Eij* 's can also be implemented in a parallel way. The implementation of lookup tables and the parallel sum are relatively simple, motivating more investigation of the use of FPGAs for PSP.

6. Simplified self-organizing random immigrants genetic algorithms

A common issue related to evolutionary computation and PSP is the premature convergence of the population towards local optimal solutions. The PSP problem has extremely complex search space complicating the determination of the global optima. In this case, a fast convergence is not a desired feature, at least on the former generations. In this sense, this section presents a strategy to insert population diversity in an organized way in Genetic Algorithms (GAs) with Random Immigrants (RIs), increasing the replacement rate whenever the population is becoming uniform.

The use of RIs introduces variation in the population [Grefenstette, 1992]. Thus, a GA with RIs can be more efficient in reaching better results than the conventional GA for the PSP problem [Tragante do O & Tinos, 2009]. However, the amount of RIs to be inserted at every generation has an important role in the GA evolution. The insertion of few RIs may not produce sufficient diversity in the population. On the other side, if a large number of individuals is replaced, the number of individuals of the population that explore the current best solutions may decrease, which can result in a smaller convergence rate.

In this way, a dynamic replacement rate, i.e. the algorithm decides the number of RIs for each population, can be useful to control the population diversity of the GA for the PSP problem. This is the objective of the Simplified Self-Organizing Random Immigrants (SSORIGA), which is based on the algorithm SORIGA presented in [Tinos & Yang, 2007] for dynamic optimization problems. In the original SORIGA, the worst individual and its neighbours are replaced by randomly-generated individuals and kept in a subpopulation in order to avoid the competition of RIs with other individuals to compose the new population, since the fitness of an individual from the subpopulation is probably worse than the ones from the remaining of the population.
Instead of creating a subpopulation, the SSORIGA inserts RIs automatically in the following generation as part of the normal population. Before generating the individuals for the next generation, the individual from the current population with the worst fitness is determined. If this individual is a RI just inserted, then the amount of RIs for the next generation is increased by 2. Otherwise, the number of RIs is restarted to 2. If the number of RIs reaches 70%, it is reset to 2. Fig. 11 presents the pseudocode of SSORIGA.

```
procedure generation ()
begin
 worst=find_worst_individual(population)
 if (lower_bound<index(worst)<upper_bound)
  totalrandom=totralrandom+2
        if (totalrandom>=0.7*population)
         totalrandom=2
        end_if
       else
        totalrandom=2
       end_if
       while (total_immigrants < totalrandom)
   son=new_individual()
   new_population.add(son)
         total_immigrants++
       end_while
 for(counter=percent;counter<pop_size;counter+2)
  father1 = tournament()     //selection of father 1
  father2 = tournament()     //selection of father 2
  son=father1.crossover(father2) //crossover
  son[0].mutation(mutation_rate)
  son[1].mutation(mutation_rate)
 end_for
end.
```

Fig. 11. Pseudocode of SSORIGA.

The SSORIGA was adapted for the PSP as follows. All the Dihedral angles φ, ψ and χ_i (i the number of angles of the side chain) obtained from the protein structures found on the PDB database compose a set T of triples (φ, ψ, χ_i). Then, T is sorted according to φ generating a sequence S_T of triples. The representation of an individual (conformation of a protein of size n) is a sequence of n amino acids and pointers to (indices for) triples from T.
The mutation operator of SSORIGA only changes a pointer a little bit, automatically choosing a new triple in the neighbourhood of the pointer in S_T. The crossover operator is the usual with the one-point crossing-over. The selection operator is tournament selection, with 75% chance of the best individual being chosen to be one of the parents of the crossover.

The protein sequences *Crambin (PDB code 1CRN), Met-Enkephalin (PDB code 1PLW)* and *DNA-Ligand (PDB code 1ENH)* were used to evaluate the SSORIGA for the the PSP problem. The results indicated that SSORIGA was statistically better than the conventional GA approach and than RIGA with a fixed replacement rate of 6% or 10% depending on the protein. For other values of the replacement rate, SSORIGA was better than RIGA, indicating that SSORIGA was capable of finding the best replacement rate for RIs. It is important to note that:

- The mean number of replaced individuals in SSORIGA was between 3% and 5%;
- The small replacement rates occur in the first generations and the larger replacement rates take place periodically when the diversity is reduced.

In terms of potential energy values, the SSORIGA was able to reach much lower values than the standard GA. Comparing results with statistical tests, such as Student's T test, there is a probability of under 1.7% for all proteins of sampling error, considering as a final result the lowest energy value after the same number of evaluations of individuals for all algorithms.

In conclusion, the algorithm was suitable for reaching lower energy values than the standard GA. It can be applied to other domains, since the idea may be useful in other problems that require slight or heavy increase of diversity along time, such as Dynamic Optimization Problems.

7. Heuristics about protein to create the initial population

Although the number of sequenced proteins and their 3D structure determined experimentally grow systematically, the number of folds seems to be practically stabilized, since the year 2007, as shown by structural and topological classification of proteins databases, like SCOP and CATH. This scenario suggests that advances on computational methods, combined with the traditional techniques for theoretical prediction protein structure (Comparative modeling, Threading and *ab initio*), may improve substantially our capability for predicting protein structures. Algorithms that combine biological information from several databases with physical insights have proved to be a promising approach (Zhang, 2008). Each technique lonely has its specific strategies, advantages and limitations, as discussed in (Echenique, 2007) and illustrated in Table 3. Automated protein structure prediction is necessary because the protein folding process is not yet fully understood and experimental method (crystallographic and NMR) are relatively slow and financially expensive.

Echenique (2007) shows a schematic classification of methods for protein structure prediction, and discuss about experimental data and physical principles, emphasizing the need for more computer power and more accurate models. He concludes that, at the present stage, as more and more structural information is available, easier becomes the task for structural prediction. Indeed, in the last years we have seen increasing number and sophistication of biological databases: PDB, NCBI, Entrez, Dali Server (Holm et. al., 2008), SCOP, CATH, among others. These databases deal with experimental structural data reporting them directly (e.g. PDB), or presenting processed data information, such as in CATH.

The EA has been used for protein structure prediction as other sections discussed. The its population initialization is crucial for EA performance (Rahnamayan et al., 2007). Therefore, once considered that physical properties about protein folding, as proposed by Anfinsen (1973), in general lines, suggest that at physiological conditions the protein primary

Technique	Specific strategy
Comparative Modeling	Based on observation which proteins with similar sequences frequently share similar structure (Chotia & Lesk, 1986).
Threading	Try to identify similarities between 3D structure that aren't join by any significant sequence similarity. In other words, proteins often adopt similar folds despite no significant similarity sequence. Thus, can be to exist a limited number of protein folds in nature (Orengo et al., 2004).
Ab initio	Predict the protein native conformation from only its sequence aminoacids (Bourne & Weissig, 2003). No more information is needed.

Table 3. Technique of 3D structure prediction and their specific strategy.

sequence has all necessary information for its folding, Comparative Modeling (Table 3) may be used as a good method for generating the population initialization (Bourne & Weissig, 2003) because, beyond of being the easiest method for application, it is based in the following arguments:

- The protein structure is unique determined by its amino acid sequence (Anfinsen, 1973). Therefore, knowing the sequence it could, in principle, to obtain the corresponding native structure;
- Along the evolution process, proteins structures became resistant to changes. Therefore, similar sequences should correspond also to similar structures.

Furthermore considering the three prediction models, Comparative Modeling, has more information and accurate models than that its time computing required is lower (Echenique, 2007).

The next section will describe in more details Comparative Modeling. It is so clear that Comparative Modeling is good way for initial population for EA which will predict the 3D structure unknown. However, the difference between this initialization and the traditional approaches to Comparative Modeling is the latter choose only one and it is the solution. On the other hand, this section proposes that applying Comparative Modeling for to chose good individuals for the population instead of your random starting. The results intended are reducing the search space, number of individuals and generation.

Comparative Modeling

Greer (1981) argues that the central point to the traditional approach to Comparative Modeling is the insertion and deletion issue, which is generally treated by identifying *Structurally Conserved Regions* and doing local changes on the *Structurally Variable Regions*. This procedure may be split into eight steps (Orengo et al., 2004), namely,

- Identify one or more homologous sequences which have their structures known. These structures will be used as templates or parents;
- Align the target sequence to be modeled with the parents obtained in step 1;
- Determine the boundaries of the framework or Structurally Conserved Regions and the Structurally Variable Regions. Normally, Structurally Conserved Regions are loops;

- Inherit the *Structurally Conserved Regions* from the parents;
- Build the Structurally Variable Regions;
- Built the side-chains;
- Refine the model; and
- Evaluate errors in the model;

which are considered in more details as follows:

Step 1. The target sequence is searched through PDB database employing specific algorithms, such as Fasta and Blast to identify homologous[1] structures. Eventually, distant homologous can be identifying by PSI-Blast

Step 2. When the sequence identity is high (> 70%) the alignment is trivial. Moreover, when the identity is lower and the number of insertions and deletions is higher, it is very difficult to obtain a correct alignment which is fundamental for a good model (Orengo et al., 2004). Proteins of two (pair-wise) or more (multiple) sequence alignment may be directly compared, and this procedure is called Sequence Alignment. For pair-wise there are two types, global and local. The global alignment tries to align the entire sequences, using all their sequence characters. On other hands, local alignment tries to align sequence stretches and thus is created sub-alignments. Therefore, global alignments are used when sequences have quite similar and approximately the same length. Local alignments are employed when similar sequences have different lengths or share a conservation region or domain (Mount, 2004). Spaces may need to be inserted and there are called GAP (Pal et al., 2006). It is understood as multiple sequence alignment, that alignment of three or more sequences where each sequence columns represents the evolutionary changes in one sequence position (Mount, 2004). Simulated Annealing (Aart & Laarhoven, 1987) and Gibbs sampling (Lawrence et al., 1993), and particularly EA, have been used for multiple sequence alignment (Notredame & Higgins, 1996; Yokoyama et al. 2001; O'Sullivan et al., 2004). The difference about these EAs is their mutation operators (Pal et al., 2006)).

Step 3. *Structurally Conserved Regions* have all the same lengths are called core. The other regions, which differ structurally among parent sequences, are the *Structurally Variable Regions* (Orengo et al., 2004).

Step 4. This step can be divided into two situation:

- Single Parent - *Structurally Conserved Regions* are just copied from this parent and used as the model.
- Multiple Parents - distinct approaches may be used and choices depend on the modeler preferences, although the first step is always to fit structurally all multiple parents to one another.

Step 5. Normally, *Structurally Variable Regions* are loop regions. When the lengths of loops of the parent structures are different, they are built with lower accuracy when compared with the rest of the structure. Furthermore, even if the corresponding lengths of these regions are the same, they may adopt different structural conformations.

---

[1] *Homologous* refers to two or more sequences which have a common ancestor sequence in earlier evolutionary time. The ancestor is known after a complete alignment (Mount, 2004).

Step 6. There are various protocols to build the side chains: It can be simple like Maximum Overlap Protocol, in which side-chain torsion angles are inherited from their parent's side-chain, where possible, and additional atoms are built from a single conformation (Orengo et al., 2004). In the Minimum Perturbation Protocol Shih et. al. (1985) each substitution is guided by a rotation about the sidechain's torsion angles to relieve clashes. Another protocol, called Coupled Perturbation Protocol, developed by Mark Snow and Mario Amzel, is similar to the Minimum Perturbation Protocol, albeit the side chain torsion angles of structurally adjacent residues are also rotated.

Step 7. Model may be refined by Energy Minimization, a process in which all the atoms, governed by a previously specified force field, move until a conformation that represents a system minimum energy is reached. This issue is related to the Molecular Dynamics (MD) method (Frenkel & Smit, 1996). There are several popular software packages to run MD simulations, like Gromacs (Hess et al., 2008).

Step 8. A conventional measure of the modeling quality is done by applying the Root Mean Square Deviation (RMSD). Basically, RMSD shows how similar one structure is to another (Orengo et al., 2004). Usualy, the modeling quality may be tested first against a number of known protein structures.

Therefore, applying Comparative Model for starting the EA population may improve the efficiency of EA when compared by randomized starting population, since relevant initial information about unknown spatial structure of proteins are produced. Therefore, as argued by Zhang & Skolnick (2005), the PDB library is a systematically increasing contributor for the protein structure prediction problem. For example, such initial information can help EA get out of non-native local minimum energy; as well complementary information from specific biological databases may be used to build specific genetic operators.

8. Conclusions

It is noteworthy that the modelling, sampling and convergence properties might be a critical issue in the PSP. From a computation perspective based on EAS, different modeling issues for PSP were revised in this Chapter. Although lattice models are relatively simple, they are very appealing for EAS approaches where the computational efficiency can be highly improved, enabling the prediction of better protein structures. In fact, the data structure based on AR + C_M (Section 2) simplifies the objective function of lattice models since there is no need for an additional function penalizing amino acid collisions. As a consequence, the objective function uses only one criterion, i.e., the evaluation of the number of interactions between hydrophobic amino acids.

The hydrophobicity of protein is a measure of the interplay of the protein and solvent interactions. The objective function of the lattice models based on AR + C_M estimates this interaction. Thus, the EA using such model may also lead to a computationally efficient process in order to find protein conformations with more plausible solvent interaction.

The solvent effect on PSP is an important issue: for most cases, the solvation energy basically drives the process. Different alternatives on how to model the solvent have been pointed out on Section 3. Despite the fact that some protein structure were successfully obtained with models based on potential energy functions with no hydration free energy contributions, this is not a general rule. For a general protein case, the solvation free energy and interaction potential energy functions are recommended for the proper prediction baring on mind the computational costs and efficiency. In order to use both contributions in PSP by EAs, two main issues should be adequately considered: 1) the computational efficiency of the energy calculi, and 2) an adequate manner to combine them. Section 5 presented strategies that reduce the running time to calculate van der Waals and electrostatic interaction energies from quadratic to linear. The off-line calculi of energies for a range of inter-atomic distances and the use of interaction energies previously calculated for parent solutions by the crossover operator can also enhance the computational efficiency.

The combined effect of different potential energies terms is dependent on the folding stage, i.e., the influence of a different term of the effective Hamiltonian may dominate the initial stage of the folding and another dominates the intermediate or the final stage. The influence of such terms on folding stages also depends on the protein molecule. In this context, the EAs enable us to simulate the effects of different combinations (weight set) of the energy functions involved in the PSP (Section 3). The most adequate weight set would reveal the key contribution of a Hamiltonian on the process contributing to enlighten the quantification of each physical mechanism behind the protein folding process.

Moreover, the mo-ProtPred can consider multiple criteria without previous knowledge of weights (Section 4) producing coherent protein structures. As an interesting consequence, the effects of each intermolecular interaction together with the solvation free energy can also be considered in PSP without previous information of the relative contribution of each Hamiltonian term on the folding.

The use of heuristics about proteins to create the initial population can improve significantly the performance EAs for PSP (Section 7). However, it may drive the algorithm for local optima, which may not correspond to an adequate protein structure. The SORIGA (Section 6) can be employed when heuristics population are used, reducing significantly the premature convergence for local optima. Thus, the initial-population heuristics combined with SORIGA should produce gains on convergence or even enable to work with larger proteins maintaining the quality of the prediction.

In short, the presented research attacked fundamental questions of the numerical sampling issues of the PSP. Moreover, it brought up solutions for each of these questions showing preliminary results and directions. In the literature, the questions clustered here have been the focus of several independent studies involving different areas of Science. The present chapter proposes some suggestions on how to combine the knowledge of diverse subjects to solve the PSP problem. There are issues that can be seen as details from on point of view but they are crucial from other perspective. Some of these aspects have been neglected in the development of a global solution for PSP on previous reviews.

In fact, hard problems can be characterized by the presence of several sets of highly interacting variables (Goldberg, 2002). One strategy to deal with such problems is to determine the interactions and adequately treat them. In PSP, the variables involve different research fields. Thus, a PSP modeling based on the integration of knowledge seems a promising path to achieve relevant advances.

9. References

Grefenstette, J. J. (1992). *Genetic algorithms for changing environments*, In: *Maenner, R., Manderick, B. (eds.) Parallel Problem Solving from Nature* 2, 137–144

Tragante do Ó, V. & Tinós, R. (2009). *Diversity Control in Genetic Algorithms for Protein Structure Prediction. VII Encontro Nacional de Inteligência Artificial (ENIA'2009)*, Bento Gonçalves, RS, Brazil

Tinós, R. & Yang, S. (2007). *A self-organizing random immigrants genetic algorithm for dynamic optimization problems. Genetic Programming and Evolvable Machines*, Vol. 8 No. 3, 255-286.

Lima, T.W. and Gabriel, P.H.R. and Delbem, A.C.B. and Faccioli, R.A. and da Silva, I.N. (2007). *Evolutionary algorithm to ab initio protein structure prediction with hydrophobic interactions*, IEEE CEC.

Cock, Peter J. A. and Antao, Tiago and Chang, Jeffrey T. and Chapman, Brad A. and Cox, Cymon J. and Dalke, Andrew and Friedberg, Iddo and Hamelryck, Thomas and Kauff, Frank and Wilczynski, Bartek and de Hoon, Michiel J. L., *Biopython*, Bioinformatics, 2009

Becker et al., 2001 Becker, O. M.; Jr., A. D. M.; Roux, B. & Watanabe, M. *Computational Biochemistry and Biophysics CRC*, 2001

Berg et al., 2002 Berg, J.; Tymoczko, J. & Stryer, L. *Biochemistry 5th ed W. H. Freeman*, 2002

Cui et al., 1998 Cui, Y.; Chen, R. S. & Wong, W. H. Protein Folding Simulation With Genetic Algorithm and Supersecondary Structure Constraints *Proteins: Structure, Function, And Genetics*, 1998, *31*, 247-257

Jain et al., 2009 Jain, A.; Gambhir, P.; Jindal, P.; Balakrishnan, M. & Paul, K. FPGA Accelerator for Protein Structure Prediction Algorithms *5th Southern Conference on Programmable Logic*, 2009, 123-128

Nelson, 2009 Nelson, D. L. & Cox, M. M. *Lehninger Principles Of Biochemistry Fourth Edition w. H. Freeman*, 2004

Owens et al., 2008 Owens, J. D.; Houston, M.; Luebke, D.; Green, S.; Stone, J. E. & Phillips, J. C. GPU Computing *Proceedings of the IEEE*, 2008, *96*, 879-899

Stone et al., 2007 Stone, J. E.; Phillips, J. C.; Freddolino, P. L.; Hardy, D. J.; Trabuco, L. G. & Schulten, K. *Accelerating Molecular Modeling Applications with Graphics* Processors Journal of Computational Chemistry, 2007, *28*, 2618-2640

Cotta, C. (2003). *Protein structure prediction using evolutionary algorithms hybridized with backtraking*, International Work-conference on Artificial and Natural Neural Networks, pp. 321-328, 2003, Lecture Notes in Computer Science

Berger, B. & Leigthon, T. (1997). *Protein folding in the hydrophobic-hydrophilic model (HP) is NP-complete*, Journal of Computational Biology, 5, 1, 27-40

Dill, K.A. (1985). *Theory for the folding and stability of globular proteins. Biochemistry*, 24, 6, 1501-1509

Gabriel, P.H.R. & Delbem, A.C.B (2009). *Representations for Evolutionary Algorithms applied to Protein Structure Prediction Problem using HP Model*, Brazilian Symposium on Bioinformatics (In Press)

Krasnogor, N.; Hart, W.E.; Smith, J. & Pelta, D.A. (1999). *Protein Structure Prediction with Evolutionary Algorithms, Proceedings of the Genetic and Evolutionary Computation Conference, pp. 1596-1601, Orlando, Florida, 1999, Morgan Kaufmann*

Patton, A.L.; Punch III, W.F. & Goodman, E.D. (1995). *A standard GA approach to native protein conformation prediction*, Proceedings of the Genetic and Evolutionary Computation Conference, pp. 574-581, San Francisco, CA, 1995, Morgan Kaufmann

Rothlauf, F. (2006). *Representation for Genetic and Evolutionary Algorithms*, Springer-Verlag

Unger, R. & Moult, J. (1993). *A genetic algorithm for 3D protein structure simulations.* Proceedings of Fifth Annual International Conference on Genetic Algorithm, San Francisco, CA, 1993

Bashford, D. & Gerwert, K. (1992). *Electrostatic calculations of the pKa values of ionizable groups in bacteriorhodopsin*, J. Mol. Biol., 224, 473-486.

Ben-Naim, A. (1994). *Solvation: from small to macro molecules*, Curr. Opin. Struct. Biol., 4, 264-268.

Berendsen, H. J. C. , Grigera, J. R. & Straatsma, T. P. (1987). *The Missing Term in Effective Pair Potentials.* J. Phys. Chem., 91, 6269-6271.

Bonneau, R. & Baker, D. (2001). Ab initio protein structure prediction: progress and prospects. *Annu. Rev. Biophys. Biomol. Struct.*, 31, 173-189.

Chaplin, M. F. (2008). *Roles of Water in Biological Recognition Processes, Wiley Encyclopedia of Chemical Biology*, 2008, 1-8.

Chan, H. S. & Dill, K. A. (1993*a*). *The protein folding problem.* Physics Today, 46, 24-32.

Chan, H. S. & Dill, K. A. (1993b). *Energy landscapes and the collapse dynamics of homopolymers*, J. Chem. Phys., 99, 2116-2127.

Chen, J., Brooks III, C.L. & Khandogin, J. (2008). *Recent advances in implicit solvent-based methods for biomolecular simulations*, Current Opinion in Structural Biology, 18, 140-148.

Creighton, 1992. Creighton, T. E. *Protein Folding*, W. E. Freeman and Company, New York, 1992.

Da Silva, F.L.B., 1999. Da Silva, F.L.B. *Statistical Mechanical Studies of Aqueous solutions and Biomolecular Systems*, Lund University, SLU, Alnarp, 1999.

Da Silva, F.L.B., Jönsson, B. & Penfold, R. (2001). *A critical investigation of the Tanford-Kirkwood scheme by means of Monte Carlo simulations, Prot. Science.*, 10, 1415-1425.

Da Silva, F.L.B., Lund, M, Jönsson, B. & Åkesson, T. (2006). *On the Complexation of Proteins and Polyelectrolytes, J. Chem. Phys. B.* 110, 4459-4464.

Da Silva, F.L.B., & Jönsson, B. (2009). *Polyelectrolyte–protein complexation driven by charge regulation, Soft Matter*, no prelo.

Degrève, L. & da Silva, F.L.B. (1999). *Structure of concentrated aqueous NaCl solution: A Monte Carlo study, J. Chem. Phys.*, 110, 3070-3078.

Devlin, 1997. Devlin, T. M. *Textbook of Biochemistry with Clinical Correlations*, Wiley-Liss, New York, 1997.

Dill, K. A., Truskett, T. M., Vlachy, V. & Hribar-Lee, B. (2005). *Modeling Water, the hydrophobic effect, and ion solvation*, Annu. Rev. Biophys. Biomol. Struct., 34, 173-179.

Eisenberg & Kauzmann, 1969. Eisenberg, D. & Kauzmann, W. *The Structure and Properties of Water*, Oxford University Press, New York, 1969.

Eisenhaber, F. & Argos, P. (1996). *Hydrophobic regions on protein surfaces: definition based on hydration shell structure and a quick method for their computation*, Protein Eng., 9, 1121-1133.

Evans & Wennerström, 1994. Evans, D.F. & Wennerström, H. *The Colloidal Domain,* VCH Publishers, New York, 1994.

Friedman, H. L. (1977). *Introduction*, Faraday Discuss. of the Chem. Soc., 64, 7-15.

Friedman, H. L. (1981). *Electrolyte solutions at equilibrium, Ann. Rev. Phys. Chem.*, 32, 179-204.

Garcia-Moreno, B. (1985). *Probing Structural and Physical Basis of Protein Energetics Linked to Protons and Salt,* Methods in Enzymology, vol. 259, 512-538.

Garde, S. et al. (1996). Garde, S., Hummer, G. , Paulaitis, M. E., Garcia, A. E. & Pratt, L. R.. (1996). *Origin of entropy convergence for hydrophobic hydration and protein folding,* Phys.Rev. Letts., 77, 4966-.

Grochowski, P & Trylska, J. (2007). *Continuum Molecular Electrostatics, Salt Effects, and Counterion Binding—A Review of the Poisson–Boltzmann Theory and Its Modifications,* Biopolymers, 89, 93-113.

Guillot, B. (2002). *A reappraisal of what we have learned during three decades of computer simulations on water,* Journal of Molecular Liquids, 110/1-3, 219-260.

Guvench, O. & Mackerell Jr, A. D., 2008. *Comparison of Protein Force Fields for Molecular Dynamics*

Simulations, In: *Andreas Kukol (ed.) Methods in Molecular Biology: Molecular Modeling of Proteins,* vol. 443, 63-88, Humana Press, Totowa, NJ, 2008.

Hardin, C., Pogorelov, T.V., Luthey-Schulten, Z. (2002). *Ab initio protein structure prediction,* Current opinion in structural biology, 12, 176-181.

Halley, J. W., Rustad, J. R. & Rahman., A. (1993). *A polarizable, dissociating molecular dynamics model for liquid water, J. Chem. Phys.*, 98, 4110-4119.

Holst, M., Baker, N., Wang, F. (2000) *Adaptive multilevel finite element solution of the Poisson-Boltzmann equation I. Algorithms and examples.* J. Comput. Chem. 21, 1319-1342.

Israelachvili, J., 1991. Israelachvili, J. *Intermolecular and Surface Forces, 2nd. Ed.,* Academic Press, London, 1991.

Jönsson, B. et al, 1998. Jönsson, B., Lindman, B., Holmberg, K. & Kronberg, B. *Surfactants and Polymers in Aqueous Solution,* John Wiley, Chichester, 1998.

Jönsson, B., Lund, M. & da Silva, F.L.B., 2007. Electrostatics in Macromolecular Solution, In: *Eric Dickinson and Martin E. Leser (eds.) Food Colloids: Self-Assembly and Material Science.*, Chapter 9, 129-154, Royal Society of Chemistry, 2007.

Jorgensen, W. L., Chandrasekhar, J., Madura, J. D., Impey, R. W. & Klein, M. L. (1983). *Comparison of simple potential functions for simulating liquid water,* J. Chem. Phys., 79, 926-935.

Juffer, A. H (1992). Melc – *The Macromolecular Electrostatics Computer Program; Laboratory of Physical Chemistry,* University of Groningen: Groningen, The Netherlands, 1992.

Lamoureux, G., Mackerell Jr, A. D., & Roux, B. (2003). *A simple polarizable model of water based on classical Drude oscillators,* J. Chem. Phys., 119, 5185-5197.

Levitt, M., Hirshberg, M., Sharon, R. & Daggett, V. (1995). *Potential energy function and parameters for simulations of the molecular dynamics of proteins and nucleic acids in solution,* Computer Physics Communications, 91, 215-231.

Levy, Y. & Onuchic, J. N. (2006). *Water Mediation in Protein Folding and Molecular Recognition,* Annu. Rev. Biophys. Biomol. Struct., 35, 389-415.

Loehe, J. R. & Donohue, M. D. (1997). *Recent advances in modeling thermodynamic properties of aqueous strong electrolyte system*, AIChE J., 43, 180-195.

Lu, B. Z., Zhou, Y. C., Holst, M. J. & J.A. McCammon. (2008). *Recent Progress in Numerical Methods for the Poisson-Boltzmann Equation in Biophysical Applications, Commun. Comput. Phys.*, 3, 973-1009.

Lyklema, J (1991). *Fundamentals of Interface and Colloid Science*. Academic Press, San Diego.

Mackerell Jr, A. D. (2004). *Empirical Force Fields for Biological Macromolecules: Overview and Issues*, J. Comput. Chem., 25, 1584-1604.

Miyazawa, S. & Jernigan, R.L. (1985). *Estimation of Effective Interresidue Contact Energies from Protein Crystal Structures: Quasi-Chemical Approximation*, Macromolecules, 18, 534-552.

Monticelli, L., Kandasamy, S.K., Periole, X., Larson, R. G. , Tieleman, D. P. & Marrink, S-J. (2008). *The MARTINI Coarse-Grained Force Field: Extension to Proteins*, J. Chem. Theory and Comput., 4, 819-834.

Neves-Petersen, M.T. & Petersen, S.B. (2003). *Protein electrostatics: A review of the equations and methods used to model electrostatic equations in biomolecules - Applications in biotechnology*, Biotechnology Annual Review, 9, 315-395.

Oostenbrink, C., Villa, A, Mark, A.E. & van Gunsteren, W.F. (2004). *A Biomolecular Force Field Based on the Free Enthalpy of Hydration and Solvation: The GROMOS Force-Field Parameter Sets 53A5 and 53A6, J. Comput. Chem.*, 25, 1656-1674.

Orea, P., Reyes-Mercado, Y. & Duda, Y. (2008). *Some universal trends of the Mie(n,m) fluid thermodynamics, Phys. Letts.* A, 372, 7024–7027.

Ponder, J. W. & Case, D.A. (2003). *Force Fields for protein simulations, Adv. Prot. Chem.*, 66, 27-85.

Poole, A. M. & Ranganathan, R. (2006). *Knowledge-based potentials in protein design*, Current Opinion in Structural Biology In Membranes / Engineering and design, 16, 508-513.

Rick, S. W., Stuart, S. & Berne, B. J. (1994). *Dynamical Fluctuating Charge Force Fields: Application to Liquid Water*, J. Chem. Phys., 101, 6141−6156.

Russel, W. B. , Saville, D. A. & Schowalter, W. R. (1989). *Colloidal Dispersions*, Cambridge University Press, Cambridge.

Sharp, K. A., Nicholls, A., Sridharan, S. (1998). Delphi - *A Macromolecular Electrostatics Modeling Package*; Columbia University: New York, 1998.

Snow, C. D. D., Sorin, E. J. J., Rhee, Y. M. M. , Vijay & Pande, S. S. (2005). *How Well Can Simulation Predict Protein Folding Kinetics and Thermodynamics?*, Annu. Rev. Biophys. Biomol. Struct., 34, 43-69.

Skaf, M. S. & da Silva, F.L.B. (1994). *Explorando as propriedades moleculares de solventes*, Química Nova, 17, 507-512.

Stone, A.J. (2008). *Intermolecular Potentials*, Science, 321, 787-789.

Street, A.G. & Mayo, S. L. (1998). *Pairwise calculation of protein solvent-accessible surface areas*, Folding & Design, 3, 253-258.

Teleman, O., Jönsson, B. & Engström, S. (1987). *A molecular dynamics simulation of a water model with intramolecular degrees of freedom*, Mol. Physics, 60, 193-203.

Tozzini, V. (2005). *Coarse-grained models for proteins*, Current Opinion in Structural Biology, 15, 144-150.

Usui, S. (1984). *Electrical double layer.* In A. Kitahara and A. Watanabe, editors, *Electrical Phenomena at Interfaces : Fundamentals, Measurements, and Applications,* 15-46, New York, 1984. Marcel Dekker, Inc.

van der Spoel, D., van Maaren, P. J. & Berendsen, H. J. C. (1998). *A systematic study of water models for molecular simulation: Derivation of water models optimized for use with a reaction field,* J. Chem. Phys., 108, 10220-10230.

Warwicker, J. & Watson, H. C. (1982). *Calculation of the electric potential in the active site cleft due to α-helix dipoles,* J. Mol. Bio., 157, 671-679.

Richards, F. M. (1977). *Areas, volumes, packing and protein structure.* Annu Rev Biophys Bioeng., 6:151–176.

Aart, E. & Laarhoven, V. P. (1987). *Simulated Annealing: A Review of Theory and Applications,* Norwell, MA Kluwer, 9789027725134

Anfinsen, C. B., (1973). *Principles that Govern the Folding of Protein Chains,* Science, 181, 4096

Bourne, P. E. & Weissig, H., (2003) *Structural Bioinformatics,* Wiley-Liss, Inc, 9780471202004

Chothia, C. & Lesk, A. M., (1986). *The relation between the divergence of sequence and structure in proteins,* EMBO J. 5, 823–826

Echenique, P. (2007). *Introduction to protein folding for physicists,* Contemporary Physics, 48, 2, 81-108

Frenkel, D. & Smit, B., (1996). *Understanding Molecular Simulation,* Academic Press, INC, 9780122673511

Greer, J. (1981).*Comparative model-building of the mammalian serine proteases,* Journal of Molecular Biology, 153, 4, 1027-1042

Hess, B., Carsten, K., van der Spoel, D. & Lindahl, E. (2008). *GROMACS 4: Algorithms for Highly Efficient, Load-Balanced, and Scalable Molecular Simulation,* J. Chem. Theory Comput,. 4, 3, 435–447

Holm, L., Kääriäinen, S., Rosenström, P. & Schenkel, A. (2008) . *Searching protein structure databases with DaliLite v.3,* Bioinformatics Applications Note, 24, 23, 2780–2781

Joseph-McCarthy, D., Petsko, A.G. & Karplus, M. (1995). *Use of a minimum perturbation approach to predict TIM mutant structures,* Protein Eng. 8, 11, 1103-1115

Lawrence, C., Altschul, S., Boguski, M., Liu, J., Neuwald, A. & Wootton, J. (1993) *Detecting subtle sequence signals: A Gibbs sampling strategy for multiple alignment,* Science, 262, 208–214

Mount, D. W. (2004). *Bionformatics Sequence and Genome Analysis,* Cold Spring Harbor Laboratory Pr, 9780879697129

Moult, J., Fidelis, K., Rost, B., Hubbard, T. & Tramontano, A.(2005) *Critical Assessment of Methods of Protein Structure Prediction (CASP) – Round 6,* PROTEINS: Struct. Funct. Bioinf., 7, 3-7

Notredame, C. & Higgins, D. G., (1996). *SAGA: Sequence alignment by genetic algorithm,* Nucleic Acids Res., 24, 8, 1515–1524

Orengo, C. A., Jones, D. T. & Thornton, J. M., (2004). *Bioinformatics genes, Proteins & Computers,* Bios Scientic Publishers Limited, 9781859960547

O'Sullivan, O., Suhre, K., Abergel, C., Higgins, D. G.., & Notredame, C. (2004) *3DCoffee: Combining Protein Sequences and Structures within Multiple Sequence Alignments,* Journal of Molecular Biology, 340 2, 385-395

Pal S.K., Bandyopadhyay, S. & Ray, S.S. (2006). *Evolutionary computation in bioinformatics: a review*, Systems, Man, and Cybernetics, Part C: Applications and Reviews, IEEE Transactions on, 36, 5, 601-615

Rahnamayan S.,Tizhoosh, H. R. & Salama, M. M.A. (2007). *A novel population initialization method for accelerating evolutionary algorithms*, Computers and Mathematics with Applications, 53, 1605–1614

Shih, H. H. L., Brady, J., & Karplus, M. (1985). *Structure of proteins with single-site mutations: A minimum perturbation approach,* Proc. Nati. Acad. Sci., 82, 1697-1700

Yokoyama, T., Watanabe T., Taneda A. & Shimizu T., (2001). *A Web Server for Multiple Sequence Alignment Using Genetic Algorithm*, Genome Informatics, 12, 382–383

Zhang, C. & Wong, A. K. C., (1997). *A genetic algorithm for multiple molecular sequence alignment*, Bioinformatics, 13, 565–581

Zhang, Y. & Skolnick J. (2005). *The protein structure prediction problem could be solved using the current PDB library*, Proc Natl Acad Sci, 102, 1029-1034

Zhang, Y. (2008). *Progress and challenges in protein structure prediction*, Current Opinion in Structural Biology, 18, 342–348

Goldberg, D. E. (2002), The Design of Innovation, Lessons from and for Competent Genetic Algorithms, Kluwer Academic Publishers, Norwell, MA, USA

Deb, K. (2001), Multi-Objective Optimization using Evolutionary Algorithms, Wiley-Interscience Series in Systems and Optimization. John Wiley & Sons, Chichester.

Dill, K.A. (1995). Principles of Protein folding - A perspective form simple exact models, Protein Science, 4, :pp. 561-602

Dill, K. A. (2005). Truskett, T. M., Vlachy, V., Hribar-Lee, B. Modeling Water, the hydrophobic effect, and ion solvation, Annu. Rev. Biophys. Biomol. Struct., 34, 173-179

Verlet, L. (1967). Computer experiments on classical fluids.i. thermodynamical properties of lennard-jones molecules. Phys. Rev., v. 159, p. 98

Valvani, S. C., Yalkowsky, S. H.; Amidon , G. L. (1976). Solubility of nonelectrolytes in polar solvents: V. estimation of the solubility of aliphatic monofunctional compounds in water using the molecular surface area approach. J. Phys. Chem., p. 829

Wallqvist, A., Mountain , R. D. (1999). Molecular models of water: Derivation and description. Reviews in Computational Chemistry, v. 13, p. 183–247

Hermann, R. B. (1972). Theory of hydrophobic bonding ii. the correlation of hydrocarbon solubility in water with solvent cavity surface area. J. Phys. Cm., v. 76, p. 2754

Doucette, W. J., Andren, A. W. (1987). Correlation of octanol/water partition coefficients and total molecular surface area for highly hydrophobic aromatic compounds. Environ. Sci. Technol., v. 21, p. 821

Dunn III, W. J., Koehler, M. G., Grigoras , S. (1987). The role of solvent-accessible surface area in determining partition coefficients. J. Med. Ckem., v. 30, p. 1121

Camilleri , P., Watts , S. A., Boroaston, J. A. (1988). A surface area approach to determination ofpartition coefficients. I. C/rem. Sue. Perkin Trans., v. 11, p. 1699.

Lindahl , E., Hess , B., Spoel, D. (2001). Gromacs 3.0: a package for molecular simulation and trajectory analysis. J. Mol. Mod., p. 306–317

Hubbard , S.; Thornton , J. (1993). Naccess: computer program. Department of Biochemistry and Molecular Biology, University College London

Frishman, D., Argos, P. (1995). Knowledge-based secondary structure assignment. Proteins: structure, function and genetics, v. 23, p. 566–579

10

Surrogate-Assisted Artificial Immune Systems for Expensive Optimization Problems

Heder S. Bernardino, Leonardo G. Fonseca, and Helio J. C. Barbosa
Laboratório Nacional de Computação Científica, LNCC/MCT
Brazil

1. Introduction

When an animal is exposed to antigens an efficient immune response is developed in order to defend the organism where specific antibodies are produced to combat them. The best antibodies multiply (cloning) and are improved (hypermutation and replacement) while new antibodies, produced by the bone marrow, are generated. Thus, if the organism is again attacked by the same antigen a quicker immune response takes place. This scheme of adaptation is known as clonal selection and affinity maturation by hypermutation or, more simply, clonal selection (Garrett, 2004). Computational methods inspired by the biological immune system are called Artificial Immune Systems (AISs). Immune-inspired algorithms have found applications in many domains. One of the most important area, the optimization, is a mathematical principle largely applied to design and operational problems in all types of engineering, as well as a tool for formulating and solving inverse problems such as parameter identification in scientific and engineering situations. When applied to optimization problems, the AISs are stochastic populational search methods which do not require a continuous, differentiable, or explicit objective function, and do not get easily trapped in local optima.

However, the AISs, as well as other nature-inspired techniques, usually require a large number of objective function evaluations in order to reach a satisfactory solution. As modern problems have lead to the development of increasingly complex and computationally expensive simulation models, this becomes a serious drawback to their application in several areas such as Computational Structural Mechanics, Reservoir Simulation, Environmental Modeling, and Molecular Dynamics. Thus, a good compromise between the number of calls to the expensive simulation model and the quality of the final solutions must often be established.

A solution to this problem is to modify the search process in order to obtain either a reduction on the total computational cost or an increase in the efficiency of the optimization procedure. The solution considered here is the use of a surrogate model (or metamodel), which provides an approximation of the objective function, replacing the computationally intensive original simulator evaluation. Additionally, the surrogate model can help to smooth out the objective function landscape, and facilitate the optimization process.

The idea of reducing the computation time or improving the solutions performing less computationally expensive function evaluations can be found in the evolutionary computation literature (Bull, 1999; El-Beltagy et al., 1999; Jin, 2002; Zhou, 2004; Rasheed,

2005; Forrester, 2009). Exist many surrogate models available: some examples are polynomial models (Response Surface Methodology) (Grefenstette & Fitzpatrick, 1985), Artificial Neural Networks (Ferrari & Stengel, 2005), Kriging or Gaussian Processes (Kecman, 2001), Radial Basis Functions (Giannakoglou, 2002; Forrester, 2009), and Support Vector Machines (Emmerich et al., 2006). In addition, several surrogates may be derived from physical or numerical simplifications of the original simulation model.

In this paper we propose an artificial immune system assisted by a Similarity-Based Surrogate Model (SBSM) in which the objective is to allow the AIS to evolve for a larger number of generations, but still using a fixed number of expensive evaluations, in order to obtain improved final solutions.

This chapter is organized as follows. Section 2 gives a formulation for the optimization problems considered here. AISs are presented in Section 3. Sections 4 and 5 present the Surrogate Models and the surrogate-assisted AIS, respectively. The computational experiments and a discussion of the results obtained can be found in Section 6. The concluding remarks are given in Section 7.

2. The optimization problem

The class of optimization problems considered here can be written as

$$\begin{aligned} &\textit{Minimize} \quad f(\vec{x}) \\ &\textit{subject to} \\ &x_i^L \le x_i \le x_i^U, \quad i = 1, \cdots, n \end{aligned}$$

where $f(\vec{x})$ is the objective function to be optimized (it is easy to see that a maximization problem can also be solved by minimizing $-f(\vec{x})$), n is the number of design/decision variables, and the search space is bounded by the constraints $x_i^L \le x_i \le x_i^U, i = 1, \cdots, n$.

In practice, the value of $f(\vec{x})$ is normally computed by means of a simulator. Thus, the evaluation of a candidate solution is often computationally expensive. In the proposed algorithm, the individuals evaluated by the original function (i.e., solutions evaluated exactly) are stored in a database (memory cells). The population of memory cells is used to construct a surrogate, based on similarity, which is used along the optimization procedure to perform extra (surrogate) evaluations, resulting in a larger number of total (surrogate plus exact) evaluations. Those extra surrogate evaluations involve a simple procedure, with relatively negligible computational cost.

3. Artificial immune systems

AISs are computational techniques, inspired by the biological immune system, which can be used to solve complex real world problems. In optimization problems (Bernardino & Barbosa, 2009), the AIS algorithms evolve improved solutions by means of natural immune mechanisms, such as clonal selection, immune network theory, vaccination, or other immune system concepts.

In general, an immune optimization algorithm will have a population of antibodies (candidate solutions) and another composed by the antigens (objectives) that the antibodies attempt to reach or match (optimize). The main differences among the AIS techniques applied to optimization problems reside in which natural immune mechanism is considered to evolve the antibodies, i.e., how the candidate solutions evolve.

According to clonal selection theory - the immune mechanism used by the algorithm considered here - there is a selection process which leads to the evolution of the immune system repertoire during the lifetime of the individual (Burnet, 1959). Also, according to this theory, on binding with a suitable antigen, activation of lymphocytes occurs. The clonal expansion is the process whereby clones of the activated lymphocyte are produced expressing receptors identical to the original one that encountered the antigen. Any lymphocyte that has receptors specific to molecules of its own body must be deleted (i.e., these lymphocytes will not be cloned). Therefore, only an antigen may cause a clonal expansion. Then, the clonal selection culminates in the increase in the average affinity between the antibodies and antigens due to the somatic hypermutation and selection mechanisms of clonal expansion. It is responsible for the fact that upon a subsequent exposure to the antigen, a stronger immune response is produced (AISWeb, 2009).

The clonal selection process is directly responsible for the evolution of the candidate solutions. The affinity maturation, as it is also known, is a mutation of the individuals applied with a high rate, which is inversely proportional to the fitness of the antibody (affinity antibody-antigen), unlike the standard mutation of Evolutionary Algorithms (EAs). Thus, inferior individuals are subject to more modification than the better ones, which need a finer tuning. When applied alone, this procedure is a random search. Therefore, a selection method is necessary to keep the good solutions, eliminate the worst ones, and maintain diversity.

3.1 Clonal selection algorithm

Based on the clonal selection theory, de Castro and Von Zuben proposed an AIS algorithm that performs computational optimization and pattern recognition tasks. CLONALG, or CSA (as it was initially called), evolves the antibodies inspired by the concept of clonal selection. In this method, each antibody is cloned, hypermutated (mutation applied with high rate), and those with higher affinity are selected. The main features of this technique are (i) the mutation rate, normally inversely proportional to the affinity of the antibody with respect to the antigens and (ii) the absence of recombination operators (such as crossover in GAs). The clonal selection principle can be interpreted as a remarkable microcosm of Darwinian evolution (Cziko, 1995) and can be considered an evolutionary algorithm.

In (de Castro & Zuben, 2000) the CSA was proposed as "a powerful computational implementation of the clonal selection principle" and applied to two optimization (multimodal optimization, and a 30-city instance of the Traveling Salesman Problem) and one pattern recognition problems (binary character recognition) showing its potential as a meta-heuristic to solve multimodal and combinatorial optimization problems.

The improved CSA is known as CLONALG and was proposed in (de Castro & Zuben, 2002). Benchmark problems were considered in order to evaluate the performance of the algorithm as well as a sensitivity analysis with respect to the user-defined parameters was presented.

Figure 1 shows CLONALG's pseudo-code which is inspired in the algorithm presented in (Bernardino & Barbosa, 2009).

In the algorithm of Figure 1, *antibodies* is a population of candidate solutions, β defines the number of clones generated by each antibody (it can be the same for all antibodies or proportional to their affinities), ρ is a parameter used to define the mutation rate (de Castro

& Zuben, 2002), *nSelection* is the number of the best antibodies selected to be cloned, and *bestAffinity* is the best value found by the AIS. Also, in the same algorithm, the following functions must be considered: "calcAffinities" calculates the affinities between each antibody and all antigens (in optimization problems this value often corresponds to the value calculated by the objective function); "select" selects the *nSelection* best individuals to be cloned; "clone" clones the selected antibodies; "hypermutate" applies the somatic hypermutation in generated clones; "update" replaces some antibodies by other ones from hypermutated clones; "stopCondition" verify if the stop condition is satisfied; and "getBestAffinity" returns the best solution found.

```
begin
    affinities ⟵ calcAffinities(antibodies);
    while not stopCondition() do
        selectedAntibodies ⟵ select(antibodies, affinities, nSelection);
        clones ⟵ clone(selectedAntibodies, affinities, β);
        clones ⟵ hypermutate(clones, affinities, ρ);
        cloneAffinities ⟵ calcAffinities(clones);
        update(antibodies, affinities, clones, cloneAffinities);
    bestAffinity ⟵ getBestAffinity(antibodies);
end
```

Fig. 1. A CLONALG pseudo-code for optimization problems.

The "update" method used here selects the best candidate solutions in the union of the antibody population and the newly generated set of clones. The idea is to use a replacement method as simple as possible, considering that the focus of this work is the use of the surrogate model. A pseudo-code for the "update" procedure can be found in Figure 2.

```
begin
    for i = 0; i < λ; i ← i + 1 do
        add(antibodies[i], clones);
        add(affinities[i], cloneAffinities);
    sort(clones, affinities);
    i ⟵ 0;
    while i < λ do
        antibodies[i] ⟵ clones[i];
        affinities[i] ⟵ cloneAffinities[i];
        i ⟵ i + 1;
end
```

Fig. 2. Pseudo-code for "update" from Figure 1.

More information about artificial immune algorithms for optimization problems can be found in (Bernardino & Barbosa, 2009).

4. Surrogate models

Surrogate modeling, or meta-modeling, can be viewed as the process replacing the original evaluation function (a complex computer simulation) by a substantially less expensive approximation. The surrogate model should be simple, general, and keep the number of control parameters as small as possible (Blanning, 1974). Similarity-Based Surrogate Models (SBSMs), an example of such surrogates, will be described in the following sections.

4.1 Similarity-Based Surrogate Models (SBSMs)

In contrast to "eager" learning algorithms such as Neural Networks, Polynomial Response Surfaces, and Support Vector Machines, which generate a model and then discard the inputs, the Similarity-Based Surrogate Models (SBSMs) store their inputs and defer processing until a prediction of the fitness value of a new candidate solution is requested. Thus, SBSMs can be classified as "lazy" learners or memory-based learners (Aha, 1997) because they generate the output value by combining their stored data using a similarity measure. Any intermediate structure or result is then discarded.

Fitness Inheritance, Fitness Imitation, and the nearest neighbors method can be classified as SBSMs. The following sections present these approaches and describe in detail the nearest neighbor method, which is the surrogate model used here.

4.1.1 Fitness inheritance

First proposed in (Smith et al., 1995), the fitness inheritance surrogate model has been applied in several problems (Bui et al., 2005; Ducheyne et al., 2003; 2007; Salami & Hendtlass, 2003; Sastry et al., 2004; Zheng et al., 1997) and algorithms (Pilato et al., 2008; Reyes-Sierra & Coello, 2005). In this method, all the individuals in the initial population have their fitness value calculated by the exact objective function evaluator. Thereafter, a fraction of the individuals in the population has its affinity (or fitness) values inherited from their parents, while the remaining candidate solutions are evaluated using the original (exact) objective function.

Given a candidate solution x_h generated from the parents x_{p_i}, with $i=1,2$, the surrogate evaluation is given by:

$$\hat{f}(x_h)=\begin{cases} f(x_{p_i}) & \textit{if } s(x_h,x_{p_i})=1,\ i=1,2 \\ \dfrac{s(x_{p_1},x_h)f(x_{p_1})+s(x_{p2},x_h)f(x_{p_2})}{s(x_{p_1},x_h)+s(x_{p2},x_h)} & \textit{otherwise} \end{cases}$$

where $s(x_{pi},x_h)$ is the similarity between x_{pi} and x_h.

This kind of surrogate model assumes that the offspring are similar to their parents and thus their fitness values are determined as the weighted average of the parent's fitness. Although this approach introduces some noise in the search process and may adversely affect the final solution found (Ducheyne et al., 2007), it can be orders of magnitude less expensive than the original fitness evaluation. In the inheritance procedure an entire simulation is replaced by a technique with negligible computational cost, which may lead to large computational savings which grow with the rate of application of the inheritance technique and the cost of the fitness function evaluation (Chen et al., 2002; Sastry et al., 2001).

4.1.2 Fitness imitation

In the fitness imitation surrogate model (Jin, 2005) the individuals are clustered into groups. This task can be performed by any clustering technique (Kim & Cho, 2001). Each cluster can be represented by a candidate solution. The choice of the representative individual can be

made either deterministically or randomly (Mota & Gomide, 2006). The representative individuals are evaluated exactly while the other individuals in the same cluster will be approximated by the value of the representative solution and a similarity measure. When a new individual does not belong to any existing cluster it is evaluated by the original function. The term Fitness Imitation is used in contrast to Fitness Inheritance.
Figure 3 shows an illustration of Fitness Imitation, where the clusters are represented by dotted circles. The candidate solutions inside the same dotted circles belong to the same cluster. Black squares denote the representative individuals, i.e., those evaluated by the exact function. The remaining individuals (black circles) are evaluated by the surrogate model.

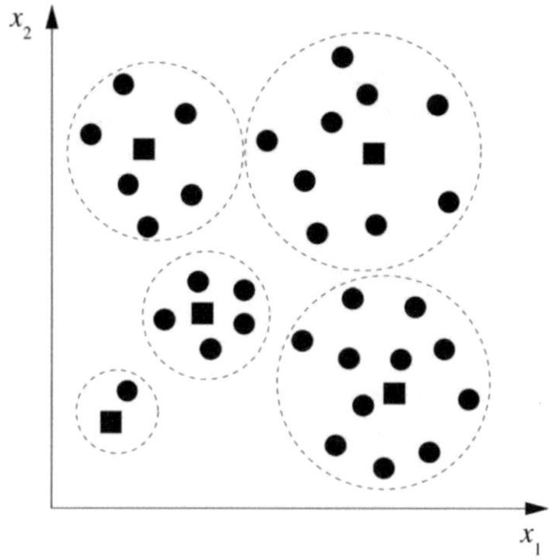

Fig. 3. Illustration of the Fitness Imitation organization.

4.1.3 Nearest neighbors

The nearest neighbors ($k\mu - NN$) is a surrogate model where the fitness values calculated are based on a set of samples μ, where $|\mu| = \eta$, evaluated exactly. Given a candidate solution x_h then we have that

$$\hat{f}(x_h) = \begin{cases} f(x_{\mu_i}) & \text{if } s(x_h, x_{\mu_i}),\ i = 1, \cdots, \eta \\ \dfrac{\sum_{i=1}^{k_\mu} s(x_h, x_{\mu_i})^u f(x_{\mu_i})}{\sum_{i=1}^{k_\mu} s(x_h, x_{\mu_i})^u} & \text{otherwise} \end{cases}$$

where $s(x_h, x_{\mu_i})$ is a similarity measure between x_h and $x_{\mu_i} \in \mu$ of the k_μ candidate solutions most similar to x_h, and u is set to 2.
For the binary-coded AIS, two similarity measures can be used. The first one, based on the Hamming distance, is given by

$$s(x_h, x_i) = 1 - \frac{d_H(x_h, x_i)}{l_c}$$

while the similarity measure based on the Euclidean distance is written as

$$s(x_h, x_i) = 1 - \frac{d_E(x_h, x_i)}{d_E(x^L, x^U)}$$

where $d_H(x_h, x_i)$ and $d_E(x_h, x_i)$ are respectively the Hamming and Euclidean distances between x_h and x_i, and l_c is the chromosome length.
The $k\mu - NN$ technique has several advantages: it is general, does not require any predefined functional form nor rely on any probability distribution, the variables can be either continuous or discrete, the databases are easy to maintain and can be updated when it is necessary to add or remove candidate solutions.
Although there is no training procedure associated, the computational cost for evaluating an individual is $O(k_\mu\ \eta)$ because of the search for the nearest neighbors.

5. Surrogate-assisted artificial immune system

Due to its simplicity, the Nearest Neighbors technique has been chosen to be used as the surrogate model. Although the Fitness Inheritance surrogate model is simpler than the Nearest Neighbor surrogate, it cannot be directly applied to the AIS algorithm. In the AIS, offspring are generated by cloning and hypermutation, and hence the fitness value of only one parent is available, while Fitness Inheritance requires at least two parents in order to build a surrogate evaluation.
Once a surrogate model has been chosen, there are many ways of introducing it into the original algorithm. Several approaches have been made in general surrogate-assisted evolutionary frameworks such as: integrating GAs with surrogate approximations (Queipo et al, 2005; Regis & Shoemaker, 2004) or landscape approximations (Knowles, 2006), the use of surrogate-guided evolutionary operators (Rasheed, 2002), surrogate-assisted local search (Lim et al, 2008; Wanner et al. 2008), accelerating the optimization process using surrogate models, pre-selection approaches (Giannakoglou, 2002; Praveen & Duvigneau, 2009), multiple surrogates (Acar & Rais-Rohani, 2008; Lim et al, 2008; Sanchez et al. 2007), and co-evolution of fitness predictors (Schmidt & Lipson, 2008). However, no Surrogate-Assisted AIS algorithm seems to have been proposed in the literature so far.
In this chapter we introduce the surrogate models into the immune inspired algorithm cycle by means of a model management procedure which, in each iteration, uses in a cooperative way both surrogate and exact models.
The first model management used here will be referred to as Random Selection (RS), i.e., a candidate solution is evaluated by the exact function, with probability $0 \le p_{sm} \le 1$. Therefore, evaluation by the surrogate model will occur with probability $1 - p_{sm}$. It is important to notice that RS applies to all clones except the ones from the best candidate solution which are evaluated exactly. This is due to the fact that the Nearest Neighbors surrogate model (Section 4.1.3) never generates a value better than the best neighbor. As a result, $\hat{\lambda} \le (\lambda - 1)\beta$ new antibodies are chosen at random to be evaluated by the surrogate model while $\lambda\beta - \hat{\lambda}$ candidate solutions are evaluated by the exact objective function, where λ is the population size. It is easy to see that $p_{sm} = 1 \Rightarrow \hat{\lambda} = 0$ and the standard CLONALG is recovered. However, $p_{sm} = 0$ does not mean that all evaluations will be performed by the surrogate model. In fact, in this case, only the clones from the best

antibody will be evaluated exactly. The modification is confined to the procedure "calcAffinities" from pseudo-code presented in Figure 1, where the decision is made as to using the surrogate model or not. A pseudo-code for the "calcAffinities" procedure can be found in Figure 4.

```
begin
    i ⟵ 0;
    foreach clone in clones do
        if random() < p_sm or i < β then
            cloneAffinities[i] ⟵ simulator(clone);
            add(clone, memoryCells);
            add(cloneAffinities[i], memoryCellAffinities);
        else
            cloneAffinities[i] ⟵ surrogateModel(memoryCells, cloneAffinities[i], clone);
        i ⟵ i + 1;
end
```

Fig. 4. Pseudo-code for "calcAffinities" from Figure 1 - Random Selection (RS) model management.

It is important to notice that the initial population of candidate solutions is evaluated exactly. Also, every individual evaluated by the exact function is stored to be used by the surrogate model. In the immunological paradigm, this database of antibodies corresponds to the memory-cells set: a sample of representative cells stored with the objective of improving the combat against the antigens in the subsequent attacks.
The Surrogate-Assisted AIS developed here will be referred to as SAAIS.

6. Computational experiments

The impact of the introduction of the surrogate model into the CLONALG algorithm is analyzed in this section. The original algorithm and the proposed one (using a surrogate model) are evaluated by means of a set of benchmark unconstrained minimization problems from the literature. The performance comparison is made varying the value of the parameter p_{sm} from 1 (original algorithm) down to 0.1 (in steps of 0.1). As p_{sm} decreases, more surrogate evaluations are introduced into the evolutionary optimization process. In both cases the genotypical (Hamming) as well as the phenotypical (Euclidean) similarity measures are analyzed. Except for the use of the surrogate model, the algorithms are compared under the same set of parameters. The algorithmic parameters of the SBSM-CLONALG are summarized in Table 1.

Table 2 shows the set of 8 benchmark unconstrained minimization problems, with the respective name, explicit representation, maximum number of exact evaluations (simulations, N_{fMax}), and lower and upper bounds ($\left[x^L; x^U\right]$). These functions were chosen because they are commonly used in the literature and have different features (such as long narrow valleys, discontinuities, noise, and a large number of significant local optima). In all cases, the dimension considered is $n = 10$ and the optimal objective function value is $f^* = 0$.

Parameters	Value
Population size (λ)	30
Representation	Binary Gray Code with 20 bits
ρ (used by hypermutation)	4
β (number of clones)	1, 2, and 3
k_μ (number of neighbors)	2 and 4
Stop criterion	Maximum number of exact evaluations (N_{fMax})
Number of independent runs	50
New individuals randomly generated	0

Table 1. Parameters used in all computation experiments

#	Name	Explicitly Function	N_{fMax}	$[x^L;x^U]$
F_{01}	Sphere	$\sum_{i=1}^{n} x_i^2$	2000	$[-5.12;5.12]$
F_{02}	Step	$\sum_{i=1}^{n}(x_i+0.5)^2$	1000	$[-100;100]$
F_{03}	Griewank	$1+\sum_{i=1}^{n}\frac{x_i^2}{4000}-\prod_{i=1}^{n}\frac{\cos(x_i)}{\sqrt{i}}$	3000	$[-600;600]$
F_{04}	Ackley	$20+e-20e^{-0.2\sqrt{\frac{\sum_{i=1}^{n}x_i^2}{n}}}-e^{\frac{\sum_{i=1}^{n}\cos(2\pi x_i)}{n}}$	3000	$[-32.768;32.768]$
F_{05}	Rosenbrock	$\sum_{i=1}^{n-1}\left[100\left(x_{i+1}-x_i^2\right)^2+(1-x_i)^2\right]$	10000	$[-5.12;5.12]$
F_{06}	Quarticnoise	$\sum_{i=1}^{n} ix_i^4+U(0,1)$	4000	$[-4.28;4.28]$
F_{07}	Rastrigin	$\sum_{i=1}^{n}\left[x_i^2-10\cos(2\pi x_i)+10\right]$	6000	$[-5.12;5.12]$
F_{08}	Schwefel	$418.982887272433n-\sum_{i=1}^{n}\left[x_i\sin\left(\sqrt{\lvert x_i\rvert}\right)\right]$	12000	$[-500;500]$

Table 2. Unconstrained minimization problems considered in the experiments

6.1 Random selection model management

In this section we analyze the impact of the parameters of the surrogate model (number of neighbors k_μ) and the algorithm (number of clones β) on the final results obtained by the SAAIS. Figures 7-14 show the contour plots of the fitness (averaged in 50 runs) obtained for functions F_{01} - F_{08} by the SAAIS, for different values of p_{sm} and number of clones. Each figure displays the results corresponding to the use of 2 and 4 neighbors to construct the surrogate model. The results for (a) Hamming similarity and (b) Euclidean similarity are shown in the figures.

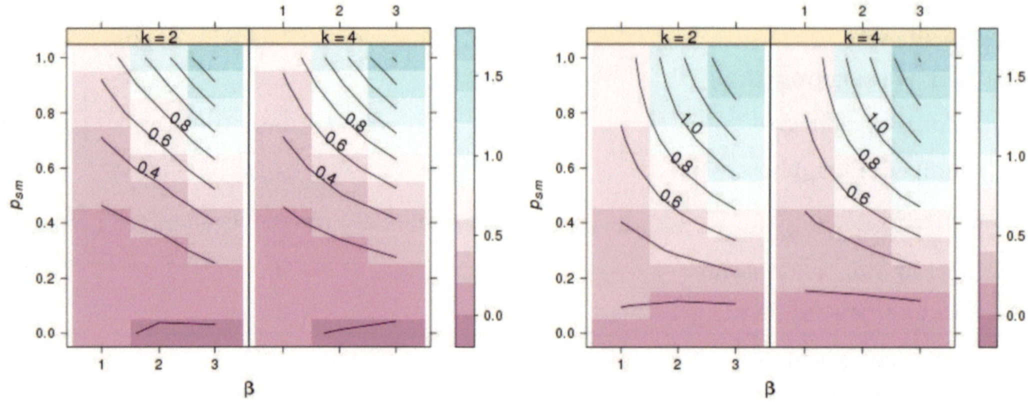

(a) (b)

Fig. 7. F_{01} - Contour plots of the fitness (averaged in 50 runs) for different number of clones (1, 2 and 3), using 2 and 4 neighbors to build the surrogate. Results for: (a) Hamming similarity, and (b) Euclidean similarity.

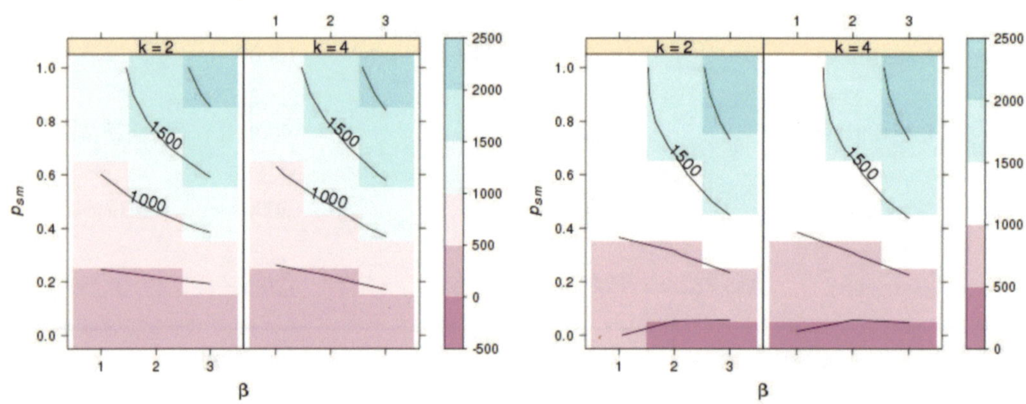

(a) (b)

Fig. 8. F_{02} - Contour plots of the fitness (averaged in 50 runs) for different number of clones (1, 2 and 3), using 2 and 4 neighbors to build the surrogate. Results for: (a) Hamming similarity, and (b) Euclidean similarity.

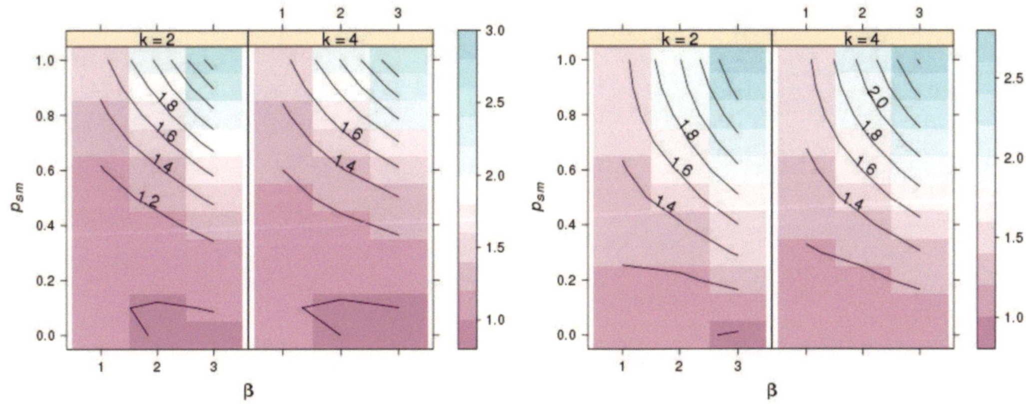

(a) (b)

Fig. 9. F_{03} - Contour plots of the fitness (averaged in 50 runs) for different number of clones (1, 2 and 3), using 2 and 4 neighbors to build the surrogate. Results for: (a) Hamming similarity, and (b) Euclidean similarity.

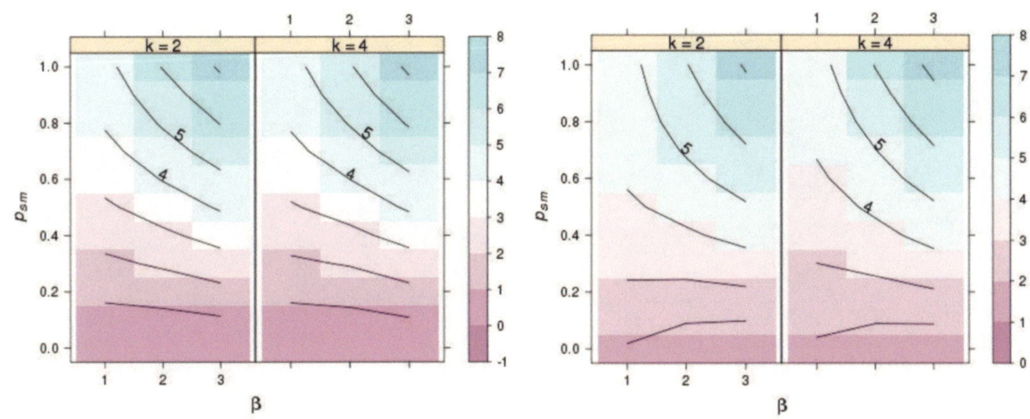

(a) (b)

Fig. 10. F_{04} - Contour plots of the fitness (averaged in 50 runs) for different number of clones (1, 2 and 3), using 2 and 4 neighbors to build the surrogate. Results for: (a) Hamming similarity, and (b) Euclidean similarity.

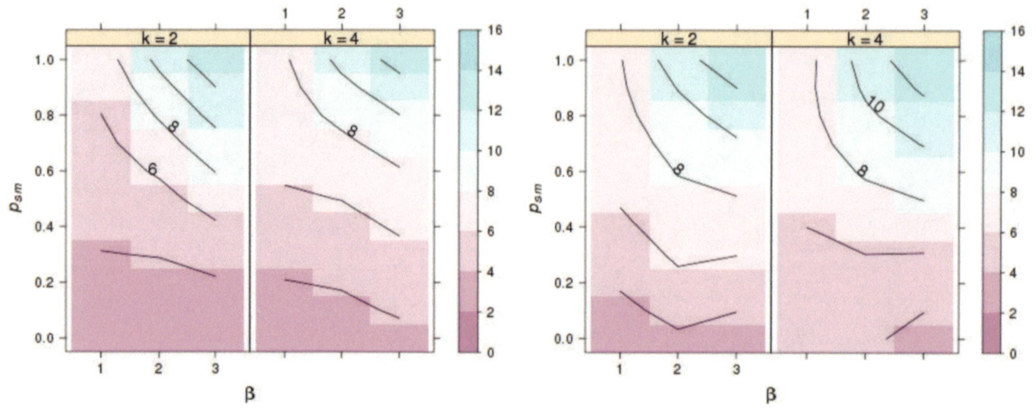

(a) (b)

Fig. 11. F_{05} - Contour plots of the fitness (averaged in 50 runs) for different number of clones (1, 2 and 3), using 2 and 4 neighbors to build the surrogate. Results for: (a) Hamming similarity, and (b) Euclidean similarity.

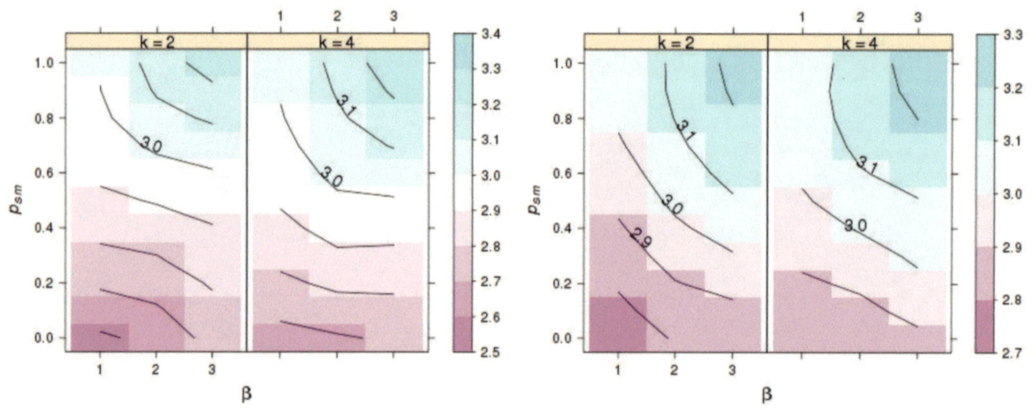

(a) (b)

Fig. 12. F_{06} - Contour plots of the fitness (averaged in 50 runs) for different number of clones (1, 2 and 3), using 2 and 4 neighbors to build the surrogate. Results for: (a) Hamming similarity, and (b) Euclidean similarity.

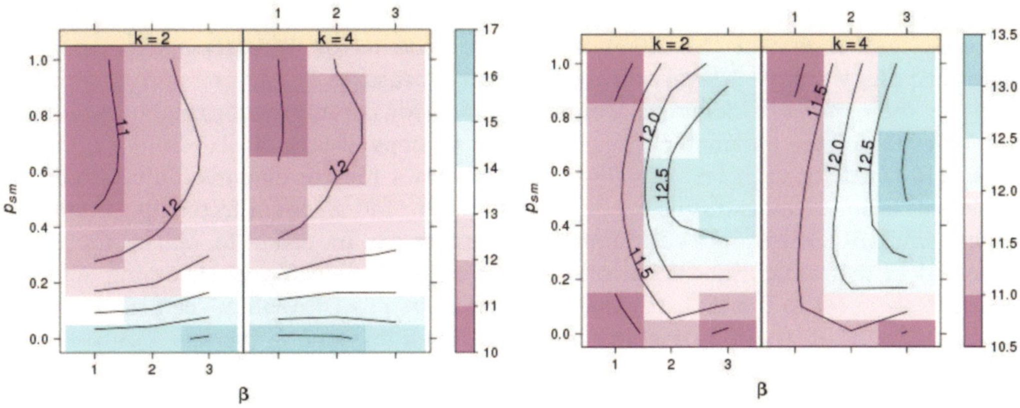

(a) (b)

Fig. 13. F_{07} - Contour plots of the fitness (averaged in 50 runs) for different number of clones (1, 2 and 3), using 2 and 4 neighbors to build the surrogate. Results for: (a) Hamming similarity, and (b) Euclidean similarity.

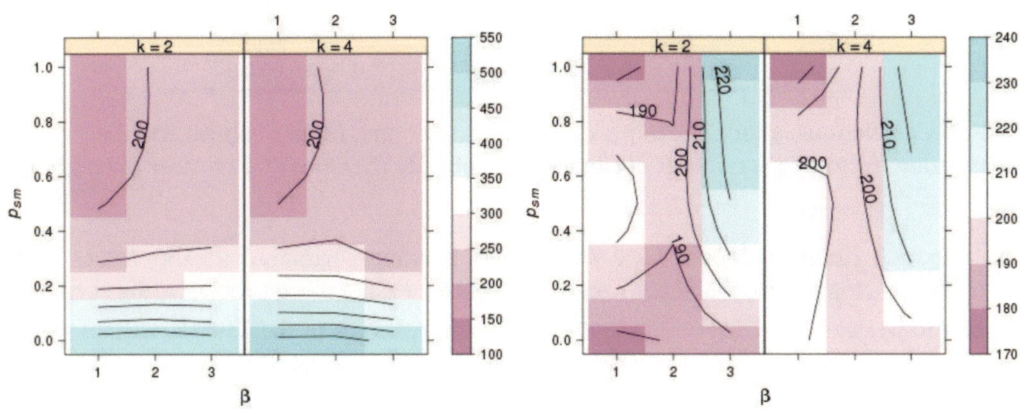

(a) (b)

Fig. 14. F_{08} - Contour plots of the fitness (averaged in 50 runs) for different number of clones (1, 2 and 3), using 2 and 4 neighbors to build the surrogate. Results for: (a) Hamming similarity, and (b) Euclidean similarity.

In order to check whether there is a linear relationship between the algorithm performance (fitness) and its parameters (p_{sm}, number of neighbors and clones, and similarity measure) an analysis of correlation was performed.

For each combination of the different levels of each factor 50 independent runs were performed. As we have 2 levels for the similarity measures (Hamming and Euclidian), 3 levels for the number of clones (1, 2, and 3), 2 levels for the number of neighbors (2 and 4) and 10 levels for the parameter p_{sm} (1-0 varying in steps of 0.1), 50x2x3x2x10 = 6000 runs were performed for each test problem. Table 3 shows the correlations found among the dependent factor (averaged fitness values) and the four independent factors (p_{sm}, number of clones, similarity measure and number of neighbors). In order to obtain the results presented in that table, the categorical values for the Euclidean and Hamming similarity measures were set to 0 and 1, respectively. The Pearson's correlation coefficient can take values between -1 (perfect negative linear correlation) and 1 (perfect positive linear correlation).

From Table 3 we can see that the number of neighbors is weakly correlated to the final fitness, and thus using 2 or 4 neighbors to build the surrogates does not affect in a significant way the fitness values in the final population of the SAAIS. Also, we can observe the same weak correlation between the similarity measure (Euclidean or Hamming) and the fitness values.

Function	Fitness	p_{sm}	Clones	Similarity	Neighbors
F_{01}	1.000	0.811	0.422	0.227	-0.004
F_{02}	1.000	0.828	0.399	0.215	0.001
F_{03}	1.000	0.786	0.436	0.195	-0.014
F_{04}	1.000	0.876	0.323	0.227	-0.011
F_{05}	1.000	0.755	0.322	0.186	0.056
F_{06}	1.000	0.787	0.349	0.268	0.119
F_{07}	1.000	-0.265	0.593	-0.114	0.112
F_{08}	1.000	-0.403	0.175	-0.410	0.079

Table 3. Correlations among the dependent factor (averaged fitness values) and the independent factors (p_{sm}, number of clones β, similarity measure and number of neighbors k_{μ})

The averaged fitness values have a strong and positive correlation to the values of the parameter p_{sm}, for all test problems, except for F_{07} and F_{08}. In these problems, the correlation appears to be negative. Observing the third and fifth columns of the Table 3, we can see that for problems F_{07} and F_{08} the fitness values tend to be worse for smaller values of p_{sm} and also when we change from Euclidean to Hamming similarity. For those problems, this behavior is observed in Figures 13(a)-(b) and 14(a)-(b). Observing the Figure 13, we can see the dependence of the fitness values with the number of clones for F_{07}. The best values of the averaged fitness are attained using a lower number of clones. Also, we note that the fitness values are not significantly altered by the number of neighbors. This behavior becomes more evident when using Hamming similarity, as shown the contour lines of Figure 13(b). A similar behavior is observed for function F_{08}. Also, as the parameter p_{sm} decreases, the fitness values become worse, and this same behavior is verified when we change from Euclidean to Hamming similarity.

Additionally, we observe that the averaged values of the fitness are positively correlated to the number of clones for all test problems, i.e., as the number of clones decreases, the values of the fitness function become smaller.

Figures 15 and 16 display a comparison between the performance the SAAIS when using Hamming and Euclidean similarities for different values of p_{sm}. When compared to the conventional AIS (red boxplot), the results obtained by the SAAIS are better for smaller values of p_{sm} for F_{01} - F_{06} . Indeed, the results obtained using the Euclidean similarity (green boxplots) are better than the ones obtained by the Hamming similarity (yellow boxplots).

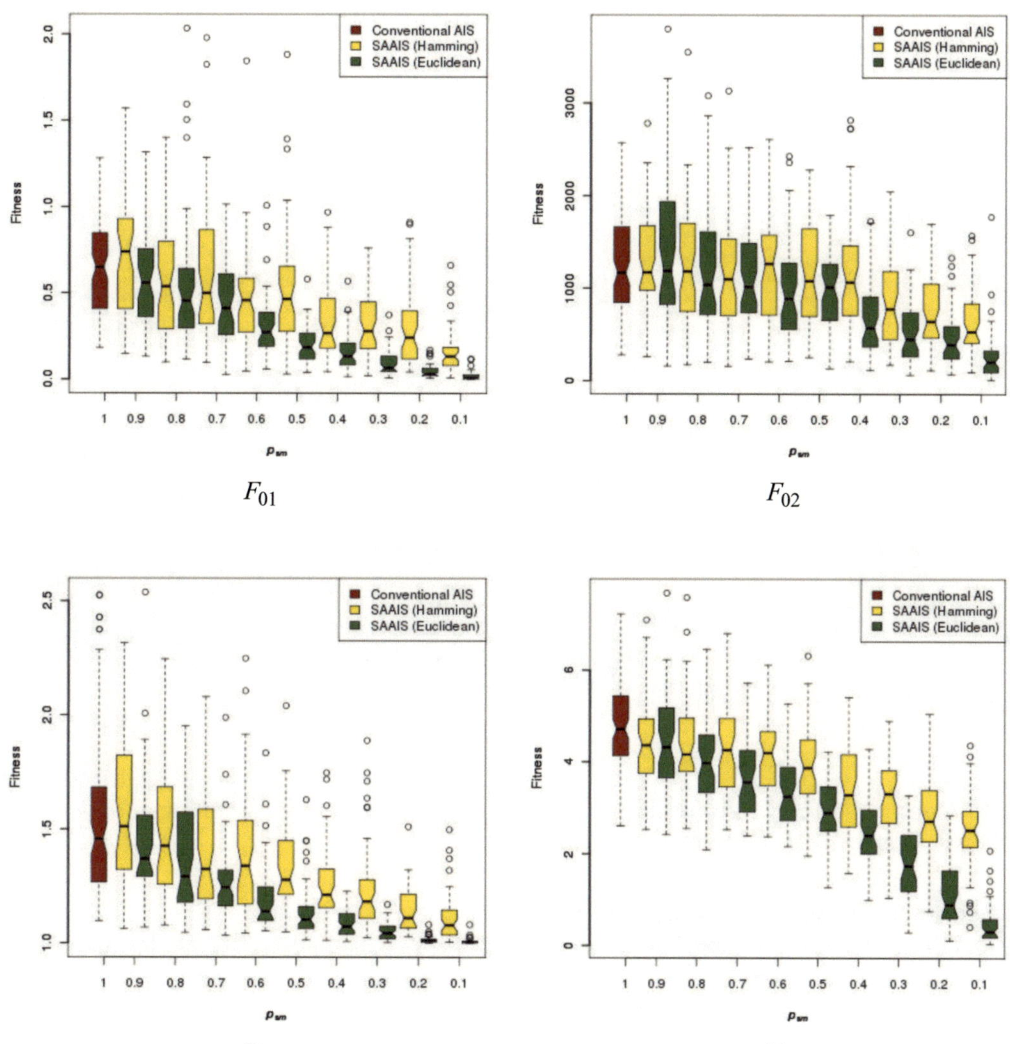

Fig. 15. Comparison of the performance of the SAAIS implementing Hamming and Euclidean similarities for different values of p_{sm}.

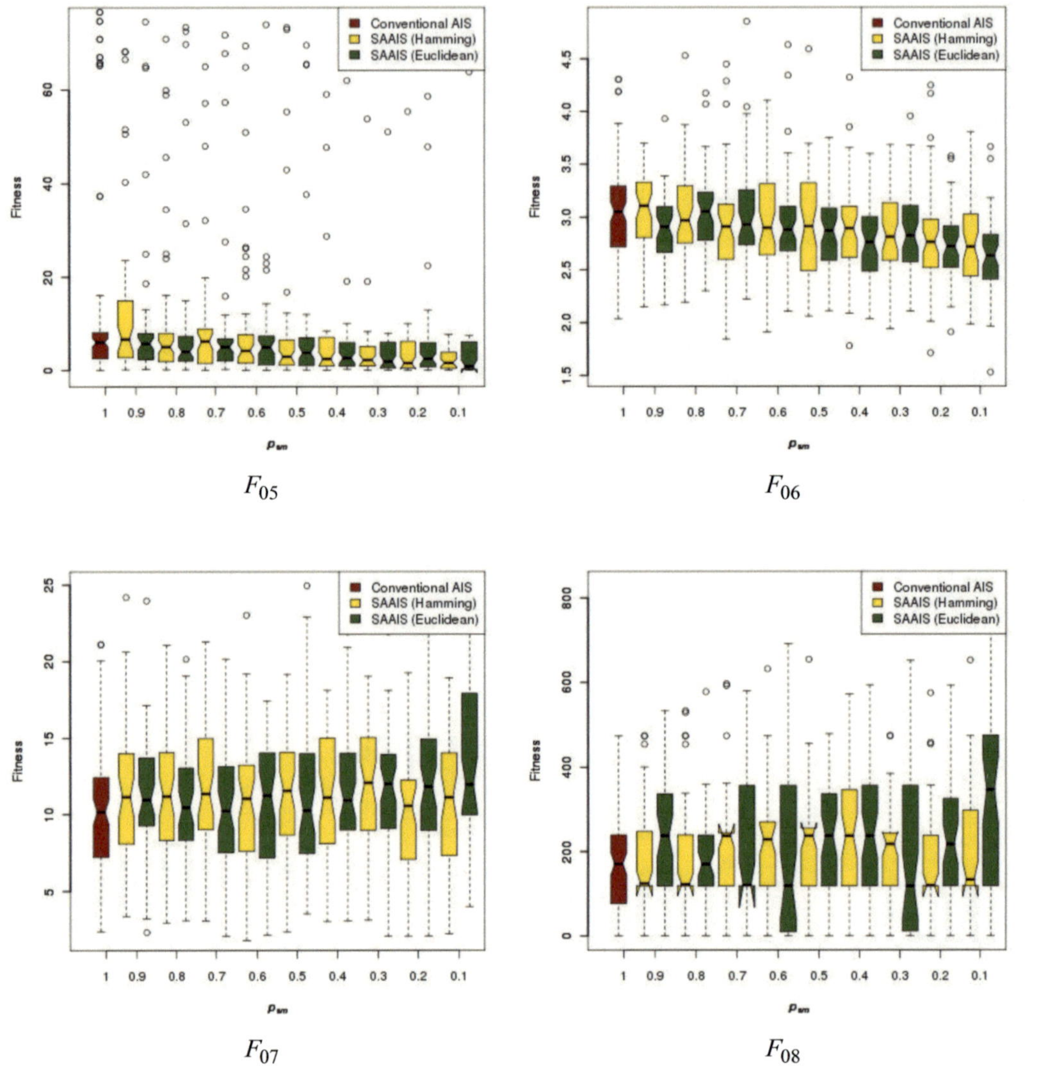

Fig. 16. Comparison of the performance of the SAAIS implementing Hamming and Euclidean similarities for different values of p_{sm}.

6.2 General comments about the experiments

The results found in the experiments show that the use of a surrogate model allows for increasing the total number of iterations of the algorithm and, for almost all problems considered, leads to solutions which are better than those provided by the baseline clonal selection algorithm (CLONALG).

In the Random Selection model management, the new candidate solutions are randomly chosen (with probability p_{sm}) to be evaluated exactly (via simulator). Also, the best antibodies from the population composed by the union of the current candidate solutions and their clones are selected to form the new population. The results found in section 6.1 show that the use of this kind of surrogate model works well for most problems considered here (except functions F_{06} and F_{07}). The authors suggest that this is due to the fact that, for those functions, the surrogate model increases the exploitation of the baseline CLONALG, inducing a faster convergence to local optima. Also, we use here a very simple surrogate model, which smoothes out the fitness landscapes and has limited capabilities to approximate complex functions.

7. Concluding remarks

In this chapter we analyze the impact of introducing a Similarity-Based Surrogate Model, the k-nearest neighbors method, in a Clonal Selection Algorithm (CLONALG). The resulting framework is referred to here as Surrogate-Assisted Artificial Immune System (SAAIS).

A surrogate model is introduced in the optimization cycle by means of a simple model management (Random Selection) in order to determine which candidate solutions will be evaluated exactly via the (expensive) simulation. Thus, we increase the total number of iterations of a baseline CLONALG algorithm providing a longer evolutionary process - which may lead to improved final solutions. The total number of exact evaluations is kept constant in order to reflect the situation of a limited budget in computationally expensive real-world problems, in which each simulation can take from minutes to hours.

The results show that the new proposed SAAIS algorithm (CLONALG+SBSM) performs better than a baseline application of the clonal selection algorithm.

The underlying idea behind the use of surrogate models with AIS algorithms is to improve the exploitation capability of the latter without increasing too much its computational cost. Obviously, other ways of combining these approaches are possible, which can potentially improve even further the performance of the resulting algorithm.

8. References

Acar, E. & Rais-Rohani, M. (2008). Ensemble of metamodels with optimized weight factors. *Structural and Multidisciplinary Optimization*, Vol. 37, No. 3, pages 279- 294

Aha, D.W. (1997). Editorial. Artificial Intelligence Review, Vol. 11, No. 1-5, pages 1–6

AISWeb (2009). The online home of artificial immune systems. URL http://www.artificial-immune-systems.org, accessed June 11, 2009

Bäck, T.; Fogel, D. & Michalewicz, Z. (2000). *Evolutionary Computation 2: Advanced Algorithms and Operations*. Taylor & Francis

Bernardino, H.S. & Barbosa H.J.C. (2009). Artificial Immune Systems for Optimization, In: *Nature-Inspired Algorithms for Optimisation*, pages 389–411. Springer Berlin / Heidelberg

Blanning, R.W. (1974). The source and uses of sensivity information. *Interfaces,* Vol. 4, No. 4, pages 32–38

Bui, L.T.; Abbass, H.A. & Essam, D. (2005). Fitness inheritance for noisy evolutionary multi-objective optimization. *Proceedings of the conference on Genetic and evolutionary computation - GECCO '05*, pages 779–785, ACM, New York, NY, USA

Bull, L. (1999). On model-based evolutionary computation. *Soft Computing,* Vol. 3, No. 2, pages 76–82.

Burnet, F.M. (1959). *The Clonal Selection Theory of Acquired Immunity*. Cambridge University Press

Chen, J.H.; Goldberg, D.E.; Ho, S.Y. & Sastry, K. (2002). Fitness inheritance in multiobjective optimization. *Proceedings of the Genetic and Evolutionary Computation Conference - GECCO'02*, pages 319–326, Morgan Kaufmann Publishers Inc., San Francisco, CA, USA

Cziko, G. (1995). The Immune System: Selection by the Enemy, In: *Without Miracles*. The MIT Press

de Castro, L.N. & Zuben, F.J.V. (2000). The clonal selection algorithm with engineering applications. *Workshop Proceedings of the Genetic and Evolutionary Computation Conference – GECCO'00*, page 37

de Castro, L.N. & Zuben, F.J.V. (2002). Learning and optimization using the clonal selection principle. *IEEE Transactions on Evolutionary Computation*, Vol. 6, No. 3, pages 239–251

Ducheyne, E.; de Baets, B. & de Wulf, R. (2003). Is fitness inheritance useful for real-world applications? *Second International Conference on Multi-criterion Optimization*, pages 31–42, Springer

Ducheyne, E.; de Baets, B.D. & Wulf, R.D. (2007). Fitness inheritance in multiple objective evolutionary algorithms: A test bench and real-world evaluation. *Applied Soft Computing*, Vol. 8, No. 1, pages 337–349

El-Beltagy, M.; Nair, P. & Keane, A. (1999). Metamodeling techniques for evolutionary optimization of computationally expensive problems: promises and limitations, *Proceedings of the Conference on Genetic and Evolutionary Computation – GECCO'99*, pages 196–203, Morgan Kaufmann, Orlando, USA

Emmerich, M.; Giannakoglou, K. & Naujoks, B. (2006). Single- and multiobjective evolutionary optimization assisted by gaussian random field metamodels. *Evolutionary Computation*, Vol. 10, No. 4, pages 421–439

Ferrari, S. & Stengel, R.F. (2005). Smooth function approximation using neural networks. *IEEE Transactions on Neural Networks*, Vol. 16, No. 1, pages 24–38

Forrester, A.I. & Keane A.J. (2009). Recent advances in surrogate-based optimization. *Progress in Aerospace Sciences*, Vol. 45, pages 50–79

Garrett, S.M. (2004). Parameter-free, adaptive clonal selection. *Congress on Evolutionary Computation – CEC'04*, Vol. 1, 1052–1058

Giannakoglou, K.C. (2002). Design of optimal aerodynamic shapes using stochastic optimization methods and computational intelligence. *Progress in Aerospace Sciences*, Vol. 38, No. 1, pages 43–76

Grefenstette, J. & Fitzpatrick, J. (1985). Genetic search with approximate fitness evaluations, *Proceedings of the International Conference on Genetic Algorithms and Their Applications*, pages 112–120

Jin, Y. (2005). A comprehensive survey of fitness approximation in evolutionary computation. *Soft Computing Journal*, Vol. 9, No. 1, 3–12

Jin, Y. ; Olhofer, M. & Sendhoff, B. (2002). A framework for evolutionary optimization with approximate fitness functions. *IEEE Transactions on Evolutionary Computation*, Vol. 6, No. 5, pages 481–494

Kecman, V. (2001). Learning and soft computing: support vector machines, neural networks, and fuzzy logic models. *Complex adaptive systems*, MIT Press, Cambridge, MA, USA

Kim, H.S. & Cho, S.B. (2001). An efficient genetic algorithm with less fitness evaluation by clustering. *Proceedings of the Congress on Evolutionary Computation*, Vol. 2, No. 2, pages 887–894

Knowles, J. (2006). Parego: A hybrid algorithm with on-line landscape approximation for expensive multiobjective optimization problems. *IEEE Transactions on Evolutionary Computation*, Vol. 10, No. 1, pages 50–66

Lim, D.; Jin, Y.; Ong, Y.S. & Sendhoff, B. (2008). Generalizing surrogate-assisted evolutionary computation. *IEEE Transactions on Evolutionary Computation*

Mota, F. & Gomide, F. (2006). Fuzzy clustering in fitness estimation models for genetic algorithms and applications. *IEEE International Conference on Fuzzy Systems*, pages 1388-1395

Pilato, C.; Tumeo, A.; Palermo, G.; Ferrandi, F.; Lanzi, P.L. & Sciuto, D. (2008). Improving evolutionary exploration to area-time optimization of FPGA designs. *Journal of Systems Architecture*, Vol. 54, No. 11, pages 1046-1057

Praveen, C. & Duvigneau, R. (2009). Low cost PSO using metamodels and inexact pre-evaluation: Application to aerodynamic shape design. *Computer Methods in Applied Mechanics and Engineering*, Vol. 198, No. 9-12, pages 1087 – 1096

Queipo, N.; Arévalo C. & Pintos, S. (2005). The integration of design of experiments, Metamodeling, and optimization for thermoscience research. *Engineering with Computers*, Vol. 20, pages 309–315

Rasheed, K. ; Ni, X. & Vattam, S. (2005). Comparison of methods for developing dynamic reduced models for design optimization. *Soft Computing Journal*, Vol. 9, pages 29–37

Rasheed, K.; Vattam, S. & Ni, X. (2002). Comparison of methods for using reduced models to speed up design optimization. *Proceedings of Genetic and Evolutionary Computation Conference*, pages 1180–1187, Morgan Kaufmann, New York

Regis, R.G. & Shoemaker, C.A. (2004). Local function approximation in evolutionary algorithms for the optimization of costly functions. *IEEE Transactions Evolutionary Computation*, Vol. 8, No. 5, pages 490–505

Reyes-Sierra, M. & Coello, C.A.C. (2005). A study of fitness inheritance and approximation techniques for multi-objective particle swarm optimization. *The IEEE Congress on Evolutionary Computation*, Vol 1, pages 65–72

Salami, M. & Hendtlass, T. (2003). A fast evaluation strategy for evolutionary algorithms. *Applied Soft Computing*, Vol. 2, pages 156–173

Sanchez, E.; Pintos, S. & Queipo, N. (2007). Toward an optimal ensemble of kernelbased approximations with engineering applications. *Structural and Multidisciplinary Optimization*, pages 1–15

Sastry, K.; Goldberg, D.E. & Pelikan, M. (2001). Don't evaluate, inherit. Proceedings of the Genetic and Evolutionary Computation Conference, pages 551-558, Morgan Kaufmann

Sastry, K.; Pelikan, M. & Goldberg, D.E. (2004). Efficiency enhancement of genetic algorithms via building-block-wise fitness estimation. *Congress on Evolutionary Computation – CEC'04*, pages 720–727

Schmidt, M. & Lipson, H. (2008). Coevolution of fitness predictors. *IEEE Transactions on Evolutionary Computation*, Vol. 12, No. 6, pages 736–749

Smith, R.E.; Dike, B.A. & Stegmann, S.A. (1995). Fitness inheritance in genetic algorithms. *Proceedings of the ACM Symposium on Applied computing – SAC'95*, pages 345–350, ACM Press, New York, NY, USA

Wanner, E.F.; Guimaraes, F.G.; Takahashi, R.H.C.; Lowther, D.A. & Ramirez, J.A. (2008). Multiobjective memetic algorithms with quadratic approximation-based local search for expensive optimization in electromagnetics. *IEEE Transactions on Magnetics*, Vol. 44, No. 6, pages 1126–1129

Zheng, X.; Julstrom, B.A. & Cheng, W. (1997) Design of vector quantization codebooks using a genetic algorithm. *Proceedings of IEEE International Conference on Evolutionary Computation*, pages 525–30, Piacataway,NJ

Zhou, Z. ; Ong, Y.S. & Nair, P.B. (2004). Hierarchical surrogate-assisted evolutionary optimization framework, *IEEE Congress on Evolutionary Computation*, pages 1586–1593.

11

Applications of the Differential Ant-Stigmergy Algorithm on Real-World Continuous Optimization Problems

Peter Korošec and Jurij Šilc
Jožef Stefan Institute, Ljubljana
Slovenia

1. Introduction

Ants have always fascinated human beings. What particularly strikes the occasional observer as well as the scientist is the high degree of societal organization that these insects can achieve in spite of very limited individual capabilities (Dorigo et al., 2000). Ants have inspired also a number of optimization algorithms. These algorithms are increasingly successful among researches in computer science and operational research (Blum, 2005; Cordón et al., 2002; Dorigo & Stützle, 2004).

A particular successful metaheuristic—Ant Colony Optimization (ACO)—as a common framework for the existing applications and algorithmic variants of a variety of ant algorithms has been proposed in the early nineties by Marco Dorigo (Dorigo, 1992). ACO takes inspiration from the foraging behavior of some ant species. These ants deposit pheromone on the ground in order to mark some favorable path that should be followed by other members of the colony. ACO exploits a similar mechanism for solving combinatorial optimization problems.

In recent years ACO algorithms have been applied to more challenging and complex problem domains. One such domain is continuous optimization. However, a direct application of the ACO for solving continuous optimization problem is difficult.

The first algorithm designed for continuous function optimization was continuous ant colony optimization (Bilchev & Parmee, 1995) which comprises two levels: global and local; it uses the ant colony framework to perform local searches, whereas global search is handled by a genetic algorithm. Up to now, there are few other adaptations of ACO algorithm to continuous optimization problems: continuous interacting ant colony (Dréo & Siarry, 2002), ACO for continuous and mixed-variable (Socha, 2004), aggregation pheromone system (Tsutsui, 2006), and multilevel ant-stigmergy algorithm (Korošec & Šilc, 2008).

In this chapter we will present so-called Differential Ant-Stigmergy Algorithm (DASA), a new approach to the continuous optimization problem (Korošec, 2006). We start with the DASA description followed by three case studies which show real-world application of the proposed optimization approach. Finally, we conclude with discussion of the obtained results.

Fig. 1. Stigmergy is an organizing principle in emergent systems in which the individual parts of the system communicate with one another indirectly by modifying their local environment. Ant colonies are a classic example. The ants communicate indirectly. Information is exchanged through modifications of the environment (local gradients of pheromone).

2. A differential ant-stigmergy approach

2.1 Continuous optimization

The general continuous optimization problem is to find a set of parameter values, $\boldsymbol{p} = (p_1, p_2, \ldots, p_D)$, that minimizes a function, $f_{\text{cost}}(\boldsymbol{p})$, of D real variables, i.e.,

$$\text{Find:} \quad \boldsymbol{p}^* \mid f_{\text{cost}}(\boldsymbol{p}^*) \leq f_{\text{cost}}(\boldsymbol{p}), \forall \boldsymbol{p} \in \Re^D. \tag{1}$$

To solve this problem, we created a fine-grained discrete form of continuous domain. With it we were able to represent this problem as a graph. This enabled us to use ant-based approach for solving numerical optimization problems.

2.2 The fine-grained discrete form of continuous domain

Let p'_i be the current value of the i-th parameter. During the searching for the optimal parameter value, the new value, p_i, is assigned to the i-th parameter as follows:

$$p_i = p'_i + \delta_i. \tag{2}$$

Here, δ_i is the so-called *parameter difference* and is chosen from the set

$$\Delta_i = \Delta_i^- \cup \mathbf{0} \cup \Delta_i^+, \tag{3}$$

where

$$\Delta_i^- = \{\delta_{i,k}^- \mid \delta_{i,k}^- = -b^{k+L_i-1}, k = 1,2,\ldots d_i\} \tag{4}$$

and

$$\Delta_i^+ = \{\delta_{i,k}^+ \mid \delta_{i,k}^+ = +b^{k+L_i-1}, k = 1,2,\ldots d_i\}. \tag{5}$$

Here

$$d_i = U_i - L_i + 1. \tag{6}$$

Therefore, for each parameter p_i, the parameter difference, δ_i, has a range from b^{L_i} to b^{U_i}, where b is the so-called *discrete base,*

$$L_i = \lfloor \lg_b(\varepsilon_i) \rfloor \tag{7}$$

and

$$U_i = \lfloor \lg_b(\max(p_i) - \min(p_i)) \rfloor \tag{8}$$

With the parameter ε_i, the maximum precision of the parameter p_i is set. The precision is limited by the computer's floating-point arithmetic. To enable a more flexible movement over the search space, the weight ω is added to Eq. 2:

$$p_i = p'_i + \omega\delta_i. \tag{9}$$

where $\omega = RandomInteger(1, b-1)$.

2.3 Graph representation

From all the sets Δ_i, $1 \le i \le D$, where D represents the number of parameters, a so-called *search graph* $G = (\boldsymbol{V}, \boldsymbol{E})$ with a set of vertices, $\boldsymbol{V}$, and a set of edges, $\boldsymbol{E}$, between the vertices is constructed (see Fig. 2). Each set Δ_i is represented by the set of vertices,

$$\boldsymbol{V}_i = \{v_{i,1}, v_{i,2}, \ldots, v_{i,2d_i+1}\}, \tag{10}$$

and

$$\boldsymbol{V} = \bigcup_{i=1}^{D} \boldsymbol{V}_i. \tag{11}$$

Then we have that

$$\Delta_i = \{\underbrace{\delta_{i,d_i}^-, \ldots, \delta_{i,d_i-j+1}^-, \ldots, \delta_{i,1}^-}_{\Delta_i^-}, 0, \underbrace{\delta_{i,1}^+, \ldots, \delta_{i,j}^+, \ldots, \delta_{i,d_i}^+}_{\Delta_i^+}\} \tag{12}$$

is equal to

$$\boldsymbol{V}_i = \{v_{i,1}, \ldots, v_{i,j}, \ldots, \underbrace{v_{i,d_i+1}}_{0}, \ldots, v_{i,d_i+1+j}, \ldots, v_{i,2d_i+1}\}, \tag{12}$$

where $j = 1,2,\ldots,d_i$.

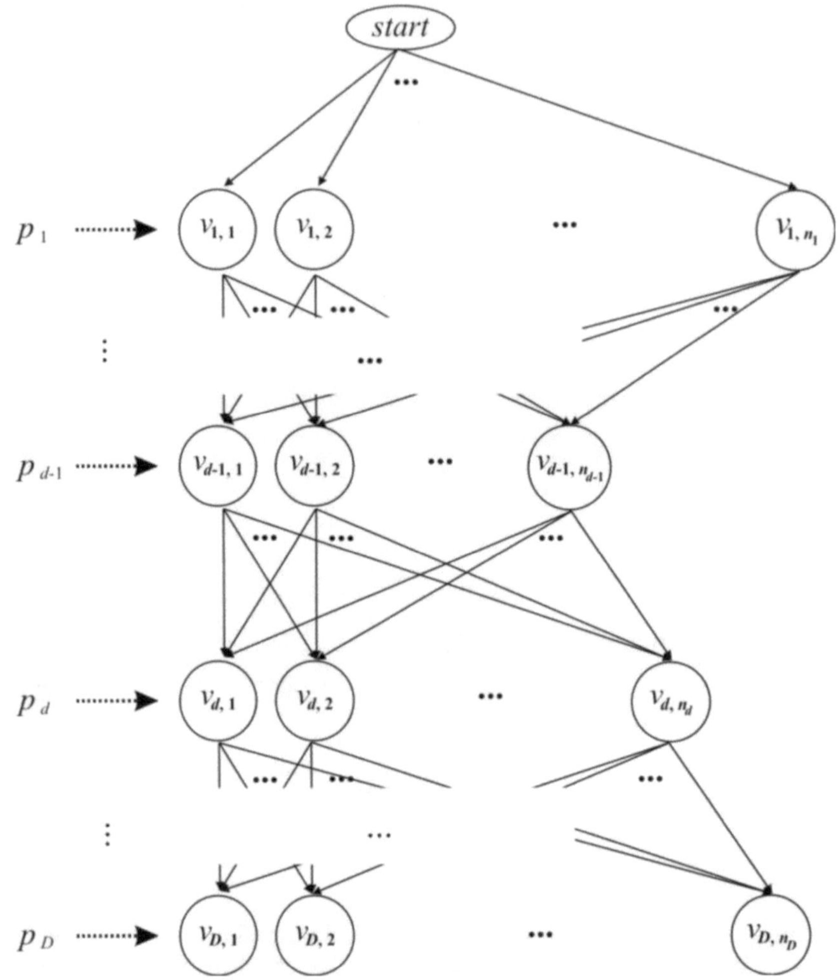

Fig. 2. Search graph representation of a discrete multi-parameter optimization problem

Each vertex of the set $\boldsymbol{V}_i$ is connected to all the vertices that belong to the set $\boldsymbol{V}_{i+1}$. Therefore, this is a directed graph, where each path $\boldsymbol{\nu}$ from start vertex to any of the ending vertices is of equal length and can be defined with v_i as:

$$\boldsymbol{\nu} = (v_1 v_2 \ldots v_D), \tag{13}$$

where $v_i \in \boldsymbol{V}_i$, $1 \le i \le D$.

The optimization task is to find a path $\boldsymbol{\nu}$, such that $f_{\text{cost}}(\boldsymbol{p}) \le f_{\text{cost}}(\boldsymbol{p}')$, where $\boldsymbol{p}'$ is currently the best solution, and $\boldsymbol{p} = \boldsymbol{p}' + \Delta(\boldsymbol{\nu})$ (using Eq. 9). Additionally, if the objective function $f_{\text{cost}}(\boldsymbol{p})$ is smaller than $f_{\text{cost}}(\boldsymbol{p}')$, then the $\boldsymbol{p}'$ values are replaced with $\boldsymbol{p}$ values.

2.4 The differential ant stigmergy algorithm

The optimization consists of an iterative improvement of the currently best solution, $\boldsymbol{p}'$, by constructing an appropriate path $\boldsymbol{\nu}$, that uses Eq. 9 and returns a new best solution. This is done as follows (see Fig. 3):

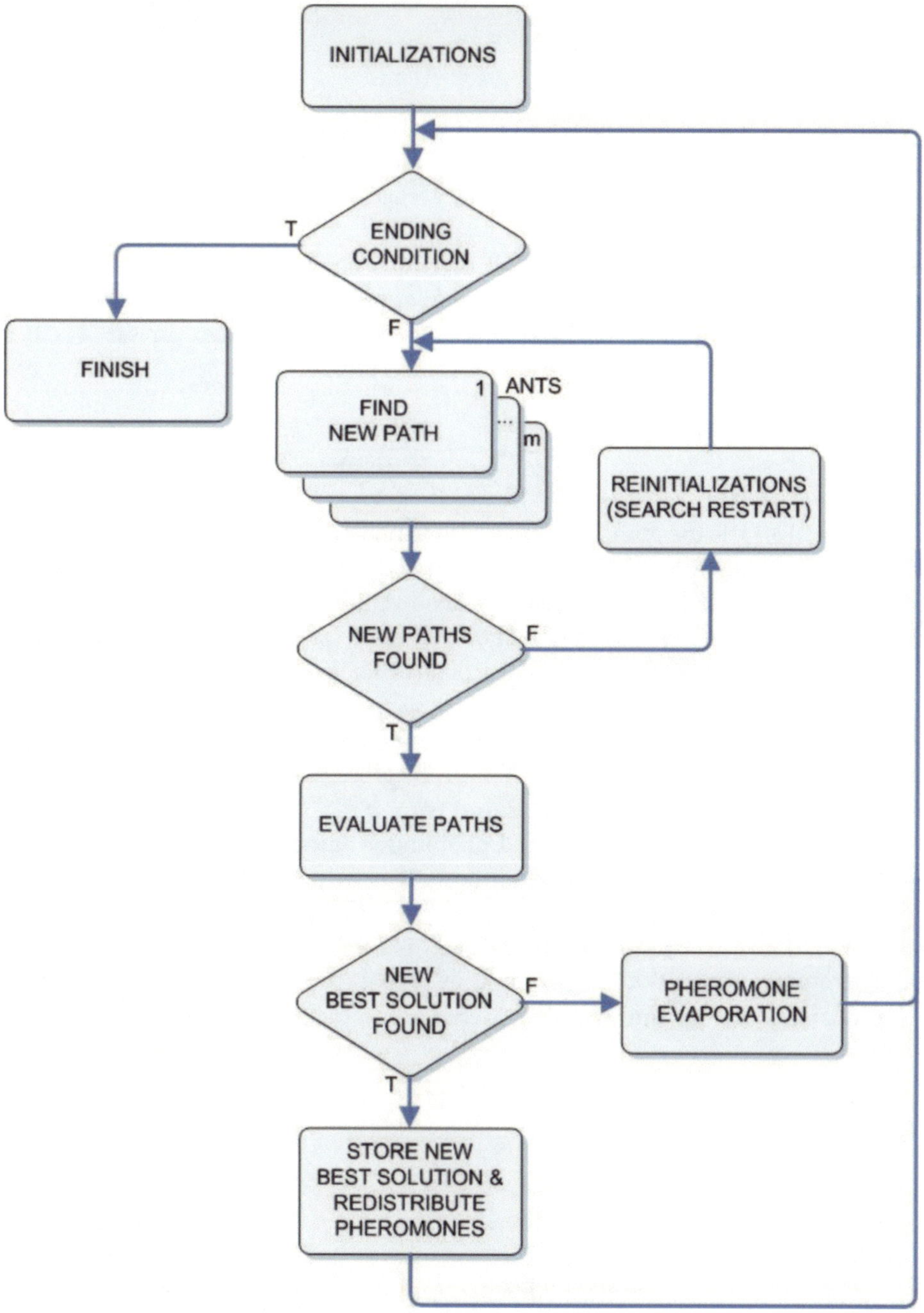

Fig. 3. The Differential Ant-Stigmergy Algorithm (DASA)

Step 1. A solution $\boldsymbol{p}'$ is manually set or randomly chosen.

Step 2. A search graph is created and an initial amount of pheromone, $\tau^0_{V_i}$, is deposited on all the vertices from the set $\boldsymbol{V}_i \subset \boldsymbol{V}$, $1 \le i \le D$, according to the Cauchy probability density function

$$C(x) = \frac{1}{s\pi + \frac{\pi}{s}(x-l)^2}, \tag{14}$$

where l is the location offset and $s = s_{\text{global}} - s_{\text{local}}$ is the scale factor. For an initial pheromone distribution the standard Cauchy distribution ($l = 0$, $s_{\text{global}} = 1$, and $s_{\text{local}} = 0$) is used and each parameter vertices are equidistantly arranged between $z = [-4, 4]$.

Step 3. There are m ants in a colony, all of which begin simultaneously from the *start* vertex. Ants use a probability rule to determine which vertex will be chosen next. More specifically, ant α in step i moves from a vertex in set V_i to vertex $v_{i,j} \in \{v_{i,1}, v_{i,2}, \ldots, v_{i,2d_i+1}\}$ with a probability, *prob*, given by:

$$prob_j(\alpha, i) = \frac{\tau(v_{i,j})}{\sum_{1 \le k \le 2d_i+1} \tau(v_{i,k})}, \tag{15}$$

where $\tau(v_{i,k})$ is the amount of pheromone on vertex $v_{i,k}$.

The ants repeat this action until they reach the ending vertex. For each ant, path $\boldsymbol{\nu}$ is constructed. If for some predetermined number of tries we get $\boldsymbol{\nu} = \boldsymbol{0}$ the search process is reset by randomly choosing new $\boldsymbol{p}^{\text{temporary\_best}}$ and pheromone re-initialization. New solution $\boldsymbol{p}$ is constructed (see Eq. 9) and evaluated with a calculation of $f_{\text{cost}}(\boldsymbol{p})$.

The current best solution, $\boldsymbol{p}^{\text{current\_best}}$, out of m solutions is compared to the temporary best solution $\boldsymbol{p}^{\text{temporary\_best}}$. If $\boldsymbol{p}^{\text{current\_best}}$ is better than $\boldsymbol{p}^{\text{temporary\_best}}$, then $\boldsymbol{p}^{\text{temporary\_best}}$ values are replaced with $\boldsymbol{p}^{\text{current\_best}}$ values. In this case s_{global} is increased (in our case for 1 %) and pheromone amount is redistributed according to the associated path $\boldsymbol{\nu}^{\text{best}}$. Furthermore, if new $\boldsymbol{p}^{\text{temporary\_best}}$ is better then $\boldsymbol{p}^{\text{best}}$, then $\boldsymbol{p}^{\text{best}}$ values are replaced with $\boldsymbol{p}^{\text{temporary\_best}}$ values. So, global best solution is stored. If no better solution is found s_{local} is decreased (in our case for 3 %).

Step 4. Pheromone dispersion is defined by some predetermined percentage χ. The probability density function $C(x)$ is changed in the following way:

$$l \leftarrow (1-\chi)l \tag{16}$$

and

$$s_{\text{local}} \leftarrow (1-\chi)s_{\text{local}}. \tag{17}$$

Pheromone dispersion has a similar effect as pheromone evaporation in classical ACO algorithm.

Step 5. The whole procedure is then repeated until some ending condition is met.

It is a well known that ant-based algorithms have problems with convergence. This happens when on each step of the walk there is a large number of possible vertices from which ant can choose from. But this is not the case with the DASA where Cauchy distribution of pheromone over each parameter was used. Namely, such distribution reduces the width of the graph to only few dominant parameter values (i.e., vertices). On the other hand, with proper selection of the discrete base, *b*, we can also improve the algorithm's convergence (larger *b* reduces the search graph size).

2.5 Software implementation and parameter settings

The DASA was implemented in the Borland® Delphi™ programming language (see Fig. 4). The computer platform used to perform the optimizations was based on AMD Opteron™ 2.6-GHz processors, 2 GB of RAM, and the Microsoft® Windows® XP 32-bit operating system.

The DASA parameters were set as follows: the number of ants, m, was set to 10, the pheromone evaporation factor, χ, was set to 0.2, and the maximum parameter precision, ε, dependent on the discrete step of each parameter.

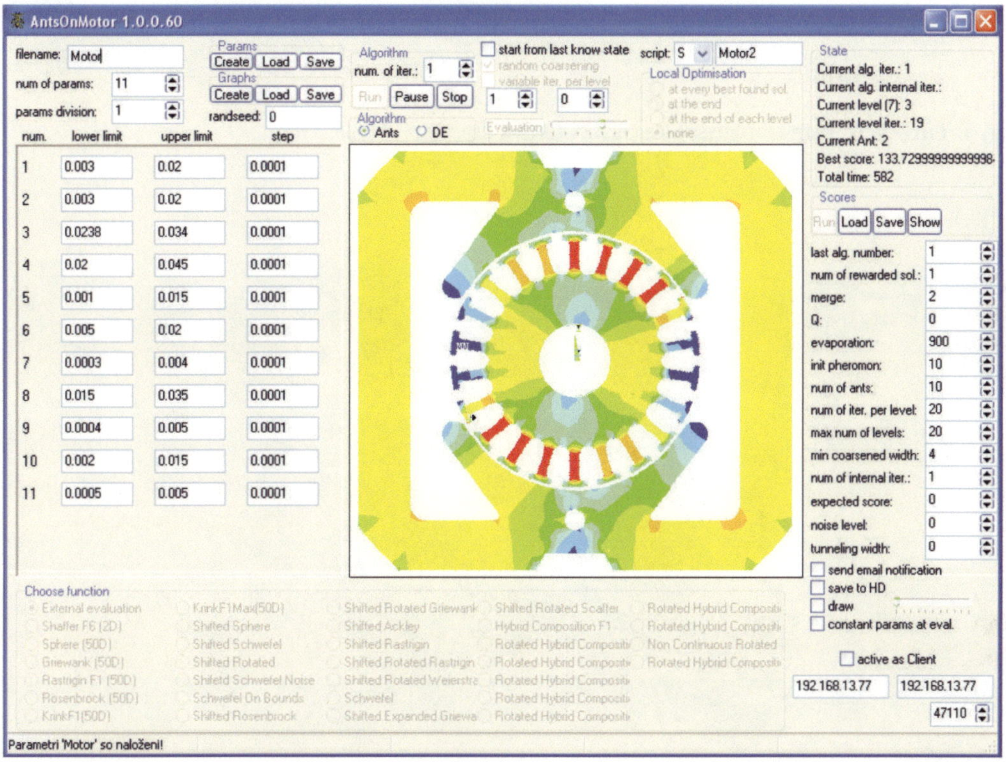

Fig. 4. GUI used for setting the DASA options

3. Case studies

Case studies presented in this section are related to the development of a new dry vacuum cleaner (Korošec et al., 2007; Tušar et al., 2007). In particular, the efficiency of the turbo-compressor unit (see Fig. 5) was improved.

3.1 An electric motor power losses minimization

Home appliances, such as vacuum cleaners and mixers, are generally powered by a universal electric motor (UM). These appliances need as low as energy consumption, that is, input power, as possible, while still satisfying the needs of the user by providing sufficient output power. The optimization task is to find the geometrical parameter values that will generate the rotor and the stator geometries resulting in the minimum power losses.

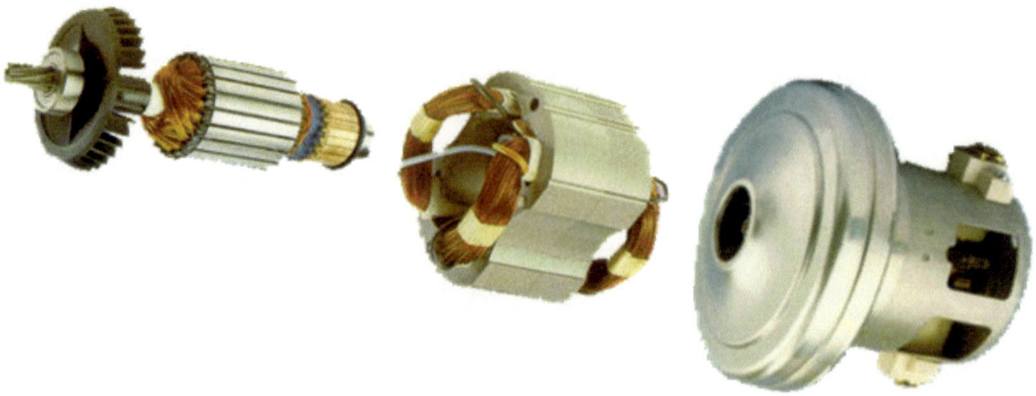

Fig. 5. Turbo-compressor unit of a dry vacuum cleaner

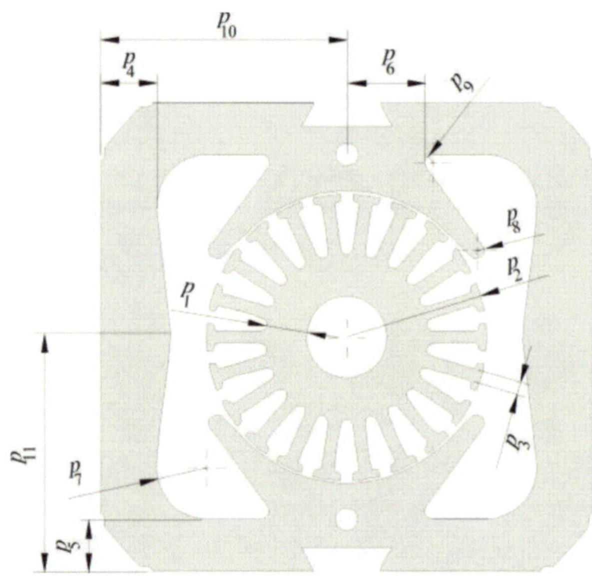

Fig. 6. Parameters that define the rotor and stator geometries

There are several invariable and variable parameters that define the rotor and stator geometries. The invariable parameters are fixed; they cannot be altered, either for technical reasons (e.g., the air gap) or because of the physical constraints on the motor (e.g., the radius of the rotor's shaft). The variable parameters do not have predefined optimum values. Some variable parameters are mutually independent and without any constraints. Others are dependent, either on some invariable parameters or on mutually independent ones.

In our case, 11 mutually independent variable parameters defining the rotor and stator geometries are subject to optimization (see Fig. 6): rotor yoke thickness, p_1, rotor external radius, p_2, rotor pole width, p_3, stator yoke horizontal thickness, p_4, stator yoke vertical thickness, p_5, stator middle-part length, p_6, stator internal edge radius, p_7, stator teeth radius, p_8, stator slot radius, p_9, stator width, p_{10}, and stator height, p_{11}. We optimized only 10 parameters (the ratio between p_{10} and p_{11} was set constant) of the UM rotor and stator geometries.

Power losses, P_{losses}, are the main factor affecting the efficiency of a UM. The efficiency of a UM, η, is defined as the ratio of the output power, P_{out}, to the input power, P_{inp} :

$$\eta = \frac{P_{\text{out}}}{P_{\text{inp}}} = \frac{P_{\text{out}}}{P_{\text{out}} + P_{\text{losses}}} \tag{18}$$

and it is very dependent on various power losses (Sen, 1997):

$$P_{\text{losses}} = P_{\text{Cu}} + P_{\text{Fe}} + P_{\text{brush}} + P_{\text{vent}} + P_{\text{frict}}. \tag{19}$$

The overall copper losses, P_{Cu}, occurring in the rotor and the stator slots are as follows:

$$P_{\text{Cu}} = \sum_i (J^2 A \rho l_{\text{turn}})_i, \tag{20}$$

where i stands for each slot, J is the current density, A is the slot area, ρ is the copper's specific resistance and l_{turn} is the length of the winding turn. The calculation of the iron losses, P_{Fe}, is less exact because iron has non-linear magnetic characteristics. The iron losses are therefore separated into two components: the hysteresis losses and the eddy-current losses. This means the motor's iron losses can be expressed with the formula

$$P_{\text{Fe}} = c_e B^2 f_r^2 m_r + c_e B^2 f_s^2 m_s + c_h B^2 f_s m_s, \tag{21}$$

where c_e is the eddy-current material constant at 50Hz, c_h is the hysteresis material constant at 50Hz, B is the maximum magnetic flux density, f_r is the frequency of the magnetic field density in the rotor, f_s is the frequency of the magnetic field density in the stator, m_r is the mass of the rotor, and m_s is the mass of the stator. Three additional types of losses occurring in the UM, i.e., the brush losses, P_{brush}; the ventilation losses, P_{vent}; and the friction losses, P_{fric}; depend mainly on the speed of the motor. When optimizing the geometries of the rotor and the stator, the motor's speed is assumed to be fixed; hence P_{brush}, P_{vent}, and P_{fric} have no impact on the motor's efficiency, and so these losses are not significantly affected by the geometries of the rotor and the stator. Therefore, in our case, the overall copper and iron losses can be used to estimate the cost function:

$$f_c(\boldsymbol{p}) = P_{\text{Cu}} + P_{\text{Fe}}. \tag{22}$$

Our goal is to find such parameter-value settings, where $f_c(\boldsymbol{p})$ is minimized.

The DASA starts its search with the existent solution. The stopping criterion was set to 1,400 calculations. The calculation of a single solution via the ANSYS Multiphysics simulation takes approximately two minutes, which means that the execution of 1,400 calculations needs about two days. The optimization method was run 20 times. The obtained results in terms of the UM power losses are presented statistically in Table 1.

Existing solution	Optimized solutions		
	Worst	Mean	Best
177.9	136.7	129.5	113.8

Table 1. Optimized UM's power losses in Watts after 1,400 calculations

Fig. 7. Laminations of the original engineering design with power losses of 177.9 W (left) and laminations of an optimized design acceptable from the production point of view with power losses of 129.1 W (right)

The engineering rotor and stator design (the existent solution) results in power losses of 177.9 W, and can be seen in Fig. 7 (left). The figure shows the magnetic flux density in the laminations (higher magnetic flux density, B, causes higher power losses). Figure 7 (right) present a typical example of a feasible rotor and stator geometry, with power losses of 129.1 W. This solution has very low iron losses in the rotor due to its small size and in spite of its high magnetic saturation. The small rotor and its saturation are compensated by large stator poles that ensure large enough a magnetic flux. This design is completely feasible from the technical and production points of view.

3.2 An electric motor casing stiffness maximization

The casing is a part of the dry vacuum cleaner motor which is built into vacuum cleaners. The casing is basically an axisymmetric shell structure which is built of steel suitable for forming. For this procedure which consists of eleven different phases it is important that the radii are growing or do not change while the height is growing. That is an important rule which must not be broken during the geometry optimization. The goal of optimization is to preserve the stiffness while using a thinner shell structure and consequently save material and reduce costs.

The computational model of the casing comprises 26 different parameters which generate the geometry variations. The classical parameters are: radius on the top, p_1, radius on the side, p_2, radius at the groove for brushes, p_3, deviation of the hole for diffuser fixation, p_4, radius of roundness at the beginning of the bearing groove, p_5, radius on the top of the bearing groove, p_6, radius on the top of air culverts, p_7, radius at the bottom of air culverts, p_8, roundness of air culverts, p_9, angle of slope, p_{22}, angle of culverts span, p_{23}, slope of bearing groove, p_{24}, height of bearing groove, p_{25}, and slope of the brushes groove, p_{26}.

Besides the above listed 14 classical parameters there are 12 more (p_{10} to p_{21}), with which the ribs on areas A, B and C are defined (Fig. 8). These are essential to improve the stiffness so we will search for those which maximize the cost function. With these parameters we can generate a lot of combinations of different rib shapes, depending on the number of given paths and accuracy of intervals for points deviations, positions and number of ribs. In our case there were several billion combinations for ribs. It is obvious that instead of a defined path at position *j*, we could define displacements for individual points but this would result in many more parameters and time consuming calculation procedure. The question still remains what would be the benefit of that. From previous designs there exist some reasonable shapes for ribs which have been defined intuitively and these then change their position, magnitude and number, which are probably sufficient for a good result, as there has been over ten different rib shapes defined earlier.

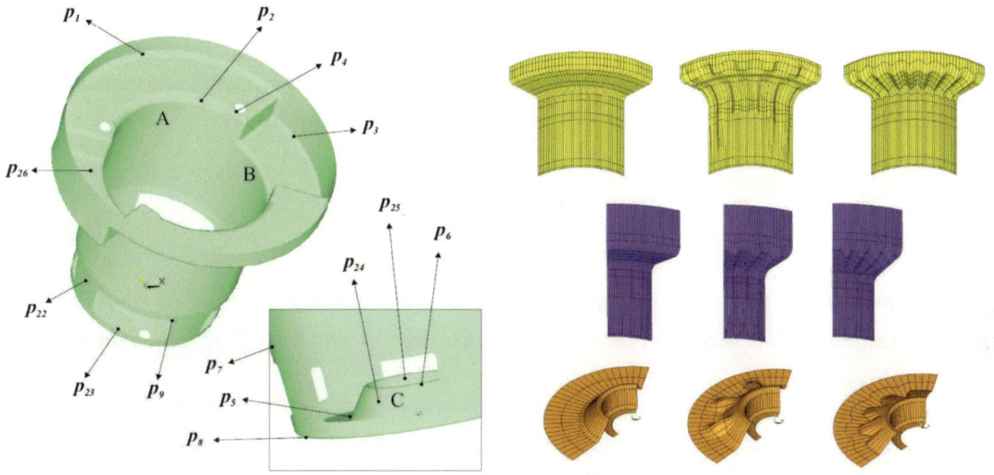

Fig. 8. Parameters of a casing and ribs. Ribs A (top), B (center), and C (bottom); basic (left) and modify forms (center and right).

Besides the parameters for the creation of ribs there are other classical parameters which also have an influence on their shape. Namely, if the radii p_1 or p_2 are varying then this is reflected in the shape of ribs of model A or if the height of bearing groove, p_{25}, and slope of groove, p_{24}, are modified then this will be reflected in the ribs of model C, etc.
The cost function is relatively simply defined when loadings are deterministic. Usually we optimize such cases with the minimization of displacements or stresses, maximization of elasticity, etc. (Dražumerič & Kosel, 2005). It is difficult to determine the cost function for a dynamically loaded assembly where the loads are stochastic. So the question is how to define the stiffness of a shell structure if we do not know the lateral loads. Let us consider a certain arbitrarily shaped plane shell. We can write its potential energy, W_p, as:

$$W_p = \frac{1}{2} \int \sigma_{ij} \varepsilon_{ij} dV. \tag{23}$$

If we consider that if the Poissons shear modulus is neglected, the stress tensor, σ_{ij}, and strain tensor, ε_{ij}, are the following:

$$\sigma_{ij} = -z \left\{ \frac{\partial^2 w(x,y)}{\partial x^2}, \frac{\partial^2 w(x,y)}{\partial y^2}, \frac{\partial^2 w(x,y)}{\partial x \partial y} \right\}^T \tag{24}$$

and

$$\varepsilon_{ij} = -zE\left\{\frac{\partial^2 w(x,y)}{\partial x^2}, \frac{\partial^2 w(x,y)}{\partial y^2}, \frac{\partial^2 w(x,y)}{\partial x \partial y}\right\}^T. \tag{25}$$

Here $w(x,y)$ is displacement in z direction and E is elasticity modulus. The potential energy can then be written as:

$$W_p = \frac{1}{2E}\int_V (\sigma_{xx}^2 + \sigma_{yy}^2 + 2\tau_{xy}^2)dV. \tag{26}$$

We can see that in this case the potential energy is an integral of squares of stresses over the volume. We define also the kinetic energy, W_k, for plate vibrations:

$$W_k = \frac{\rho\omega^2}{2}\int_V zw^2(x,y)dV, \tag{27}$$

where ρ represents the density of material. Here the second derivative of displacement is approximated with respect to time with the product of squared displacement and eigen frequency, ω.

For conservative systems the maximal potential energy is equal to maximal kinetic energy and from this follows the expression for cost function which can be in our case the stiffness itself:

$$f_c(p) = \frac{\int_V (\sigma_{xx}^2 + \sigma_{yy}^2 + 2\tau_{xy}^2)dV}{\int_V zw^2(x,y)dV}. \tag{28}$$

The DASA was run 20 times and each run consisted of 2,000 calculations. The cost function was calculated by the ANSYS Multiphysics simulation tool. The obtained results are presented statistically in Table 2.

Existing solution	Optimized solutions		
	Worst	Mean	Best
$5.87 \cdot 10^{-3}$	$6.13 \cdot 10^{-3}$	$6.81 \cdot 10^{-3}$	$7.34 \cdot 10^{-3}$

Table 2. Optimized casing's stiffness after 2,000 CFD calculations

The results of optimization were quite surprising (Fig. 9 bottom row). It was expected that the ribs would form on all the given surface but they did not. The ribs were more distinct where the vertical part of the surface was turning into the horizontal one (ribs A). There were no ribs at the surface where the stator is in a tight fit, probably because of pre-stressing of the casing through the stator. Also in the groove for brushes (ribs B) there were no distinct ribs, probably because the groove itself is a kind of rib. Instead of this there is a given slope for a groove which was not there before. The radii of roundings were in most cases bigger than before as we can clearly see at the air culverts (Fig. 9 middle bottom).

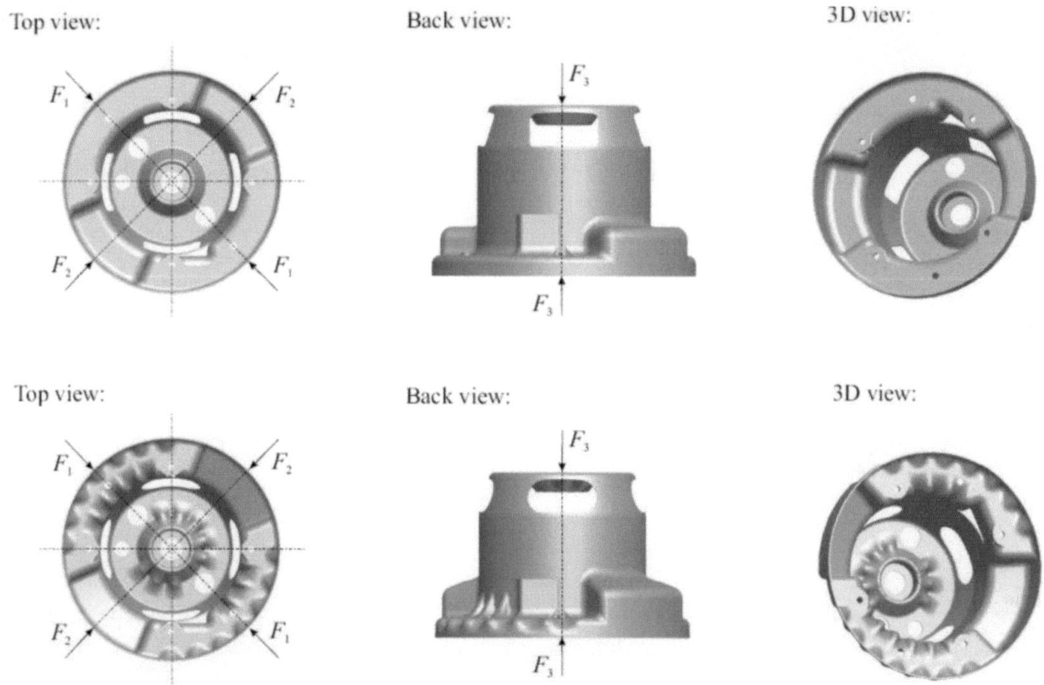

Fig. 9. Existent (up) and optimized (bottom) casing and different loading cases

3.3 A turbo-compressor aerodynamic power maximization

Radial air impellers are the basic components of many turbo-machines. In the following we will concentrate on relatively small impellers and subsonic speeds used in a dry vacuum cleaner. Our main aim was to find an impeller shape that has a higher efficiency, i.e., greater aerodynamic power, than the one currently used in production.

An impeller is constructed from blades, an upper and a lower side. The sides enclose the blades and keep them together. The blades, which are all the same, were the main part of the optimization. The geometry of a blade is shown in Fig. 10, where the gray color represents the blade. The method of modeling is as follows: we construct the points at specific locations, draw the splines through them and spread the area on the splines. Once a blade is made an air channel must be constructed in a similar way.

In Fig. 10a the point 1 has two parameters: the radius p_1 and the angle p_2. Similarly, the points 2, 5 and 6 have parameter pairs p_3 and p_4, p_5 and p_6, p_7 and p_8. The points 3 and 4 are fixed on the x axis. This is because the impeller must have a constant outer radius p_9 and the outer side of the blade must be parallel to the z axis. On the other hand, the outer angle of the blade p_{10} and the angle of the spline at points 3 and 4, can be varied. Analogously, the angles p_{11} and p_{12} are the inner-blade angles for the upper and lower edges of the blade at the input, respectively.

In Fig. 10c the points 1, 2, and 3 form the upper spline, and the points 4, 5, and 6, the lower spline. Between the points 1 and 6 is the point 7, which defines the spline of the input shape of the blade. In this figure, the points 1, 2, 5, and 6 have the parameters p_{13}, p_{14}, p_{15}, and p_{16}, respectively, describing their heights.

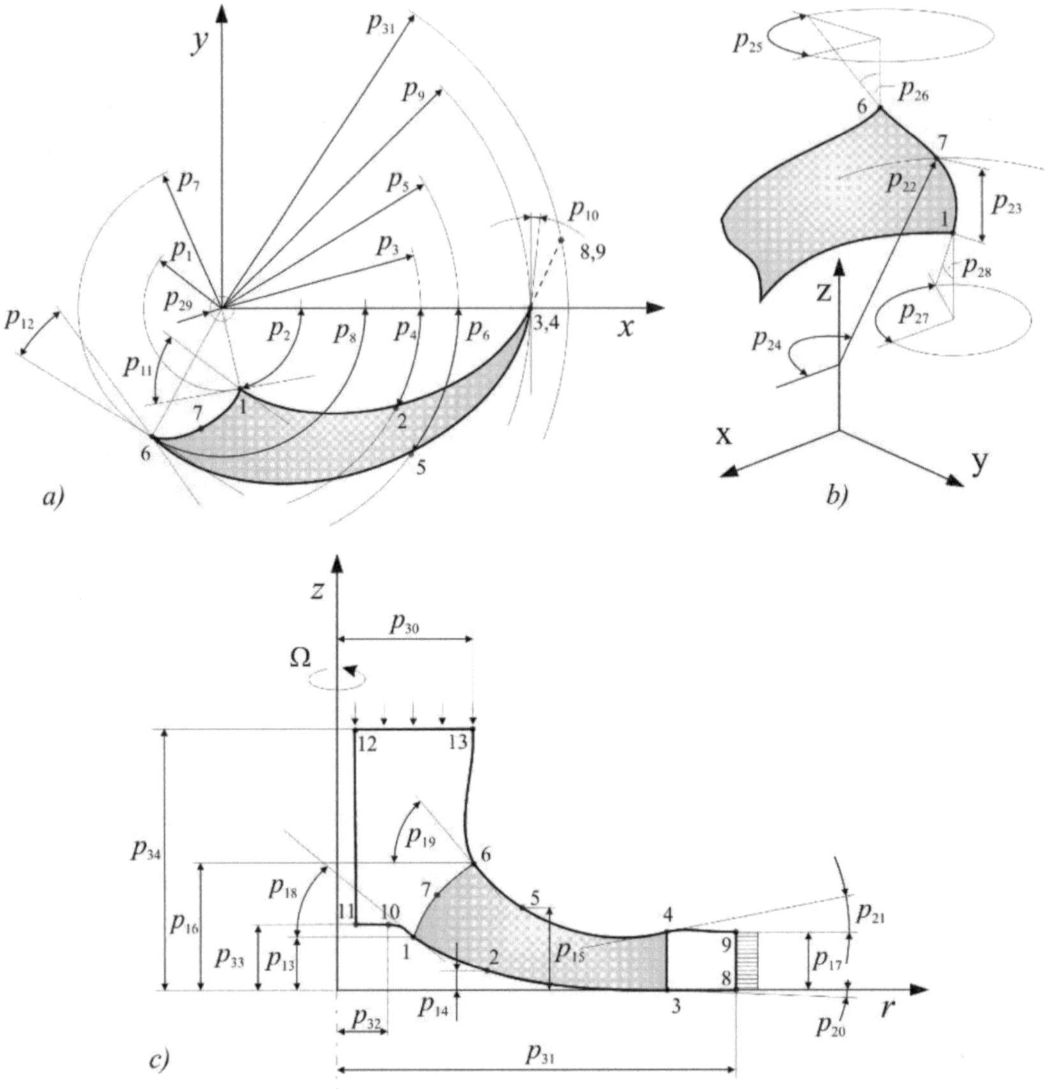

Fig. 10. Parametric modeling: a) top view; b) 3D view, c) side view

Point 3 stays on the x axis and point 4 has a constant height p_{17}. In other words, the designer of the impeller must know at least the outer diameter p_9 and the height p_{17}. The parameters p_{18} and p_{19} describe the input angles of the lower and upper parts of the blade with respect to the $r-z$ plane. Similarly, the parameters p_{20} and p_{21} describe the outer blade angle with respect to the same plane.

In Fig. 10b the meaning of point 7 is explained more precisely. The parameters p_{22}, p_{23}, and p_{24} define the radius, height, and angle, respectively. The radius and angle dictate where the point should appear with respect to the $x-y$ plane and the height with respect to the $r-z$ plane. Similarly, the angles p_{25}, p_{26}, p_{27}, and p_{28} are needed to define the starting and ending angles of the spline constructed between the points 1, 7, and 6.

If we look closely at Fig. 10c then we can see the contour surrounding the blade. This is the air channel with the following parameters: the inner radius p_{29} (see Fig. 10a), which is needed for the hexahedral mesh (explained later), the air intake radius p_{30}, the air outflow radius p_{31}, the bolt radius p_{32}, the bolt height p_{33}, and the impeller height p_{34}.

In this way we have successfully modeled the impeller geometry with 34 parameters. For each parameter we have a predefined search interval with a given discrete step. Therefore, the size of the search space can be obtained as the product of the number of possible settings over all the parameters. It turns out that there are approximately $3 \cdot 10^{34}$ possible solutions.

The mesh of the air channel between the two blades is constructed with more than 6,000 hexahedral elements. The boundary conditions are zero velocity at all the solid regions and symmetry boundary conditions at the fluid regions. At the influx and outflux the intake velocity, v_{in}, and reference pressure, p_{ref}, are defined, respectively. The intake velocity is parabolically distributed, because we expect that the intake flow is laminar and so:

$$v_{\text{in}} = v(\Phi(t))\frac{6r}{r_{\text{up}}}\left(\frac{r}{r_{\text{up}}} - 1\right). \tag{29}$$

Here, $v(\Phi(t))$ is a velocity dependent on the stream, which further depends on time, as we shall see later, r_{up} is the upper radius, defined before, and r is the radius within the limits from r_s to r_{up}. The reference pressure, p_{ref}, is set to zero.

With respect to the maximum time, $t_{\max}$, the flux is:

$$\Phi(t) = vA_{\text{in}}\frac{t}{t_{\max}}, \tag{30}$$

where A_{in} is the influx area and t is the current time.

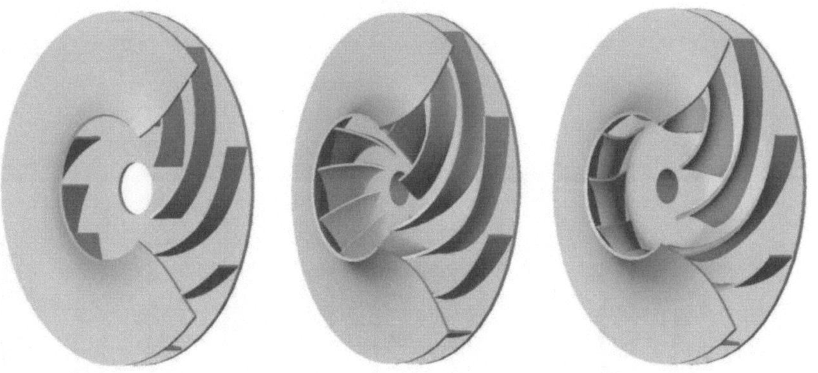

Fig. 11. The existent impeller (left), the worst optimized impeller (middle), and the best optimized impeller (right)

The distribution of the relative pressure can be used to estimate the cost function. The average pressure, p_{in}, is chosen from the air-intake area. Finally, the aerodynamic power, which represents the cost function, is as follows:

$$f_c(\boldsymbol{p}) = P_{\text{air}} = (p_{\text{out}} - p_{\text{in}})\Phi(t_{\text{opt}}), \tag{31}$$

where p_{out} is the output pressure at the radius r_{out} and $\Phi(t_{opt}) = 40\,l/s$ is the flux near the desired optimum performance of the impeller. Our goal is to find such parameter-value settings, where P_{air} is maximized.

The DASA was run 10 times and each run consisted of 2,000 CFD calculations. For the CFD calculations we used the ANSYS Multiphysics package. A single CFD calculation takes approximately seven minutes. The obtained results, in terms of aerodynamic power, are presented statistically in Table 3.

Existing solution	Optimized solutions		
	Worst	Mean	Best
411.00	432.00	472.00	483.00

Table 3 Optimized impeller's aerodynamic power in watts after 2,000 CFD calculations

Results show that we were able to increase aerodynamic power for approximately 20 %. Figure 11 shows a 3D view of the existent and two optimized impellers (best and worst of 10 runs).

4. Discussion

In this chapter the Differential Ant-Stigmergy Algorithm (DASA) was presented, where the main goal was an evaluation of the DASA on some real-world engineering applications. Case studies were selected from a R&D project where more efficient turbo-compressor for dry vacuum cleaner was developed. Here the DASA was used to improve the efficiency of an electric motor, increase casing stiffness, and increase impeller's aerodynamic power. In all these cases the improvement was evident.

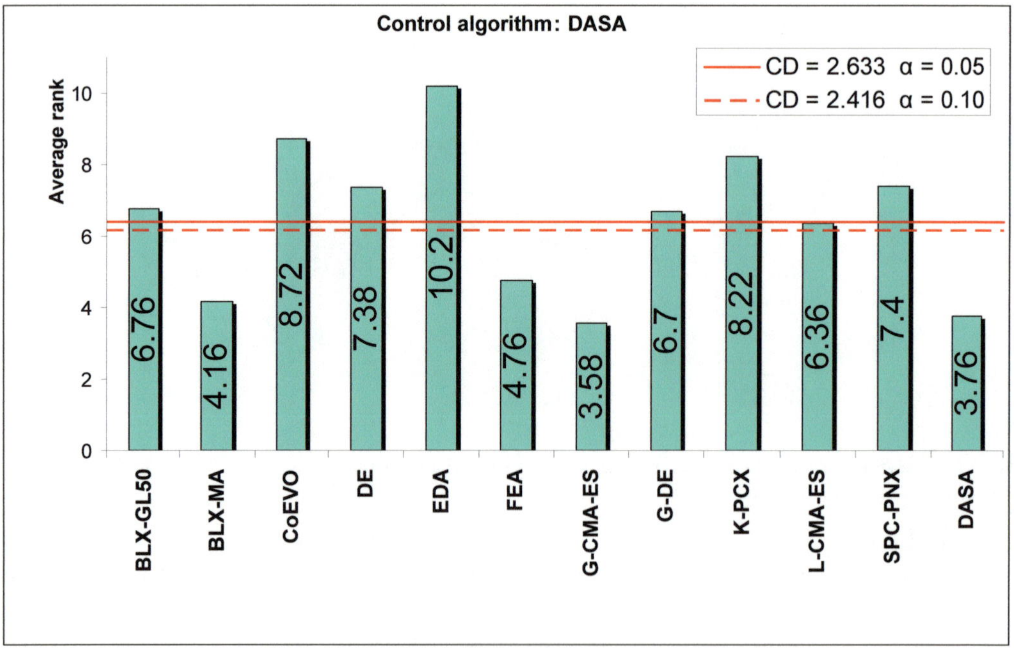

Fig. 12. The Bonferroni-Dunn post-hoc statistical test

In (Korošec & Šilc, 2009a) we also compared the DASA to the eleven state-of-the-art stochastic algorithms for continuous optimization which were presented in the CEC'2005 *Special Session on Real Parameter Optimization*. The algorithms are:

- BLX-GL50, a hybrid real-coded genetic algorithm with female and male differentiation (García-Martínez & Lozano, 2005),
- BLX-MA, a real-coded memetic algorithm with adaptive local search parameters (Molina et al., 2005),
- CoEVO, an evolutionary algorithm with mutation step co-evolution (Pošík, 2005),
- DE, a differential evolution (Rönkkönen et al., 2005),
- EDA, a continuous estimation of distribution algorithm (Yuan & Gallagher, 2005),
- FEA, a flexible evolutionary algorithm (Alonso et al., 2005),
- G-CMA-ES, a restart covariance matrix adaptation evolutionary strategy with increasing population size (Auger & Hansen, 2005a),
- G-DE, a guided differential evolution (Bui et al., 2005),
- K-PCX, a population-based steady-state procedure (Sinha et al., 2005),
- L-CMA-ES, an advanced local search evolutionary algorithm (Auger & Hansen, 2005b), and
- SPC-PNX, a steady-state real-parameter genetic algorithm (Ballester et al., 2005).

Obtained results confirmed that the DASA is comparable to above algorithms and therefore generally applicable to global optimization problems.

The experimental results have shown that the DASA ranks among the best algorithms for real-life-like applications. Its main advantage is in consistent problem solving which is indicated by 19 rankings in top third, 4 ranking in middle third and only 2 in bottom third. Statistical analysis following the Bonferroni-Dunn post-hoc test with $\alpha = 0.10$ showed that the DASA is significantly better than 8 out of 11 compared algorithms.

The algorithm was also applied to dynamic optimization problems with continuous variables proposed for CEC'2009 *Special Session on Evolutionary Computation in Dynamic and Uncertain Environments* (Korošec & Šilc, 2009b). If we compare the DASA to:

- a self-adaptive differential evolution (Brest et al., 2009),
- a dynamic artificial immune algorithm (de França & Von Zuben, 2009),
- an evolutionary programming (Yu & Suganthan, 2009), and
- a clustering particle swarm optimizer (Li & Yang, 2009),

the results show that the DASA can find reasonable solutions for all of the problems. It can be seen that the DASA performs not many worse than a self-adaptive differential evolution and much better than the other three algorithms. One obvious advantage is that was no need any changes to the original algorithm. So, it can be used as such for both cases of numerical optimization, static and dynamic. Furthermore, the algorithm is unsusceptible to different types of changes and can be used with very limited knowledge about problem, only maximal dimension and input problem parameters.

5. References

Alonso, S.; Jimenez, J.; Carmona, H.; Galvan, B. & Winter, G. (2005). Performance of a flexible evolutionary algorithm. www.ntu.edu.sg/home/EPNSugan.

Auger, A. & Hansen, N. (2005a). A restart CMA evolution strategy with increasing population size, *Proceedings of the IEEE Congress on Evolutionary Computation*, pp. 1769–1776, ISBN 0-7803-9363-5, Edinburgh, UK, September 2005, IEEE.

Auger, A. & Hansen, N. (2005a). Performance evaluation of an advanced local search evolutionary algorithm, *Proceedings of the IEEE Congress on Evolutionary Computation*, pp. 1777–1784, ISBN 0-7803-9363-5, Edinburgh, UK, September 2005, IEEE.

Ballester, P. J.; Stephenson, J.; Carter, J. N. & Gallagher, K. (2005). Real-parameter optimization performance study on the CEC-2005 benchmark with SPC-PNX, *Proceedings of the IEEE Congress on Evolutionary Computation*, pp. 498–505, ISBN 0-7803-9363-5, Edinburgh, UK, September 2005, IEEE.

Bilchev, G. & Parmee, I. C. (1995). The ant colony metaphor for searching continuous design spaces, In: *Evolutionary Computing*, L. Fogarty (Ed.), 25–39, Springer, ISSN 0302-9743, Lecture Notes in Computer Science, Vol. 993.

Blum, C. (2005). Ant colony optimization: Introduction and recent trends, *Physics of Life Reviews*, Vol. 2, No. 4, (December 2005) 35325–39373, ISSN 1571-0645.

Brest, J.; Zamuda, A.; Bosković, B.; Sepesy Maučec, M. & Žumer, V. (2009) Dynamic optimization using self-adaptive differential evolution, *Proceedings of the IEEE Congress on Evolutionary Computation*, pp. 415–422, ISBN 978-1-4244-2959-2, Trondheim, Norway, May 2009, IEEE.

Bui, L. T.; Shan, Y.; Qi, F. & Abbass, H. A. (2005). Comparing two versions of differential evolution in real parameter optimization, www.ntu.edu.sg/home/EPNSugan.

Cordón, O.; Herrera, F. & Stützle, T. (2002). A review on the ant colony optimization metaheuristic: Basis, models and new trends, *Mathware and Soft Computing*, Vol. 9, No. 3, (2002) 141–175, ISSN 1134-5632.

de França, F. O. & Von Zuben, F. J. (2009) A dynamic artificial immune algorithm applied to challenging benchmarking problems, *Proceedings of the IEEE Congress on Evolutionary Computation*, pp. 423–430, ISBN 978-1-4244-2959-2, Trondheim, Norway, May 2009, IEEE.

Dorigo, M. (1992). Optimization, learning and natural algorithms, Ph.D.Thesis, Politecnico di Milano, Italy.

Dorigo, M.; Bonabeaub, E. & Theraulaz, G. (2000). Ant algorithms and stigmergy, *Future Generation Computer Systems*, Vol. 16, No. 8, (June 2000) 851–871, ISSN 0167-739X.

Dorigo, M. & Stützle, T. (2004). *Ant Colony Optimization*, The MIT Press, ISBN 978-0-262-04219-2, Cambridge, Massachusetts.

Dražumerič, R. & Kosel, F. (2005). Optimization of geometry for lateral buckling process of a cantilever beam in the elastic region, Thin-Walled Structures, Vol. 43, No. 3, (March 2005) 515–529, ISSN 0263-8231.

Dréo, J. & Siarry, P. (2002). A new ant colony algorithm using the heterarchical concept aimed at optimization of multiminima continuous functions, In: *Ant Algorithms*, M. Dorigo et al. (Eds.), 216–227, Springer, ISSN 0302-9743, Lecture Notes in Computer Science, Vol. 2463.

García-Martínez, C. & Lozano, M. (2005). Hybrid real-coded genetic algorithm with female and male differentiation, *Proceedings of the IEEE Congress on Evolutionary*

Computation, pp. 896–903, ISBN 0-7803-9363-5, Edinburgh, UK, September 2005, IEEE.

Korošec, P. (2006). Stigmergy as an approach to metaheuristic optimization, Ph.D.Thesis, Jožef Stefan International Postgraduate School, Ljubljana, Slovenia.

Korošec, P.; Oblak, K.; Kosel, F. & Šilc, J. (2007). Multi-parameter numerical optimization of selected thin-walled machine elements using a stigmergic optimization algorithm, *Thin-Walled Structures*, Vol. 45, No. 12, (December 2007) 991–1001, ISSN 0263-8231.

Korošec, P. & Šilc, J. (2008). Using stigmergy to solve numerical optimization problems, *Computing and Informatics*, Vol. 27, No. 3, (2008) 377–402, ISSN 1335-9150.

Korošec, P. & Šilc, J. (2009a). A stigmergy-based algorithm for continuous optimization tested on real-life-like environment, In: *EvoWorkshops 2009*, M. Giacobini et. al (Eds.), 675–684, Springer, ISSN 0302-9743, Lecture Notes in Computer Science, Vol. 5484.

Korošec, P. & Šilc, J. (2009b). The differential ant-stigmergy algorithm applied to dynamic optimization problems, *Proceedings of the IEEE Congress on Evolutionary Computation*, pp. 407–414, ISBN 978-1-4244-2959-2, Trondheim, Norway, May 2009, IEEE.

Li, C & Yang, S. (2009), A clustering particle swarm optimizer for dynamic optimization, *Proceedings of the IEEE Congress on Evolutionary Computation*, pp. 439–446, ISBN 978-1-4244-2959-2, Trondheim, Norway, May 2009, IEEE.

Molina, D.; Herrera, F. & Lozano, M. (2005). Adaptive local search parameters for real-coded memetic algorithms, *Proceedings of the IEEE Congress on Evolutionary Computation*, pp. 888–895, ISBN 0-7803-9363-5, Edinburgh, UK, September 2005, IEEE.

Pošík, P. (2005). Real-parameter optimization using the mutation step co-evolution, *Proceedings of the IEEE Congress on Evolutionary Computation*, pp. 872–879, ISBN 0-7803-9363-5, Edinburgh, UK, September 2005, IEEE.

Rönkkönen, J.; Kukkonen, S. & Price, K. V. (2005). Real-parameter optimization with differential evolution, *Proceedings of the IEEE Congress on Evolutionary Computation*, pp. 506–513, ISBN 0-7803-9363-5, Edinburgh, UK, September 2005, IEEE.

Sen, P. C. (1997). *Principles of Electric Machines and Power Electronics*, 2nd edition, John Wiley & Sons, ISBN 978-0-471-02295-4, New York.

Sinha, A.; Tiwari, S. & Deb, K. (2005). A population-based, steady-state procedure for real-parameter optimization, *Proceedings of the IEEE Congress on Evolutionary Computation*, pp. 514–521, ISBN 0-7803-9363-5, Edinburgh, UK, September 2005, IEEE.

Socha, K. (2004). ACO for continuous and mixed-variable optimization, In: Ant Colony Optimization and Swarm Intelligence, M. Dorigo et al. (Eds.), 25–36, Springer, ISSN 0302-9743, Lecture Notes in Computer Science, Vol. 3172.

Tsutsui, S. (2006). An enhanced aggregation pheromone system for real-parameter optimization in the ACO metaphor, In: *Ant Colony Optimization and Swarm Intelligence*, M. Dorigo et al. (Eds.), 60–71, Springer, ISSN 0302-9743, Lecture Notes in Computer Science, Vol. 4150.

Tušar, T.; P. Korošec, P.; Papa, G.; Filipič, B. & Šilc, J. (2007). A comparative study of stochastic optimization methods in electric motor design, *Applied Intelligence*, Vol. 27, No. 2, (2007) 101–111, ISSN 0924-669X.

Yu, E. L. & Suganthan, P. (2009) Evolutionary programming with ensemble of external memories for dynamic optimization, *Proceedings of the IEEE Congress on Evolutionary Computation*, pp. 431–438, ISBN 978-1-4244-2959-2, Trondheim, Norway, May 2009, IEEE.

Yuan, B. & Gallagher, M. (2005). Experimental results for the special session on real-parameter optimization at CEC 2005: A simple, continuous EDA, *Proceedings of the IEEE Congress on Evolutionary Computation*, pp. 1792–1799, ISBN 0-7803-9363-5, Edinburgh, UK, September 2005, IEEE.

12

From Evo to EvoDevo: Mapping and Adaptation in Artificial Development

Gunnar Tufte
Norwegian University of Science and Technology
Norway

1. Introduction

Artificial development takes it's inspiration from the processes of biological development (Wolpert; 2002). The process of mapping genetic information in the genotype to a phenotype that express structure, behaviour and functions (Hall; 2003). In nature this is the processes making a zygote (fertilised egg) develop to a multicellular organism. As all living systems and their subsystems are evolved, developmental processes are also a product of evolution. In biological development, an initial unit - a cell, holds the complete building plan (DNA) for the organism. It is important to note that this plan is generative - it describes how to build the system, not what the system will look like. Units have internal state, can communicate locally, can move, spawn other units or die. Groups of units may also exhibit group-wise behaviour i.e. a group state. The developmental stages from the zygote to the multicellular organism, although interdependent and not strictly sequential, may be categorized as *pattern formation; morphogenesis; cell differentiation and growth* (Wolpert; 2002). Information carried in the ever evolving genome is the information that passes from generation to generation and the genetic information is contained within a cell that serves as both the constructor and construct of the phenotype.

An important feature of natural development is that the developing organism develops and operates within an environment. The environment is not only the arena in which the behaviour and function of the organism unfolds, it is also an important source of information for the outcome of the developmental process. As stated, the genome may be considered information exploitable by the developmental process to "build" the organism. In biology the environment also serves as a source of information for the development of the organism. As such, the developmental process can include the environmental information as an input information source enabling adaptation through the developmental process. This implies that natural organisms include developmental plasticity, i.e. phenotypic plasticity (West-Eberhard; 2003). As such, the evolved organism is a product of the information in the genome, the present environment and the cellular developmental processes that is initialised in the zygote.

Recently developmental approaches have once again come to the front in the area of bioinspired systems. The motivation for moving towards developmental system is multitudinous ranging from early work on self-reproduction (von Neumann; 1966), to more recent attempts in overcoming limitations in Evolutionary Computation (EC), e.g., scaling

and complexity (Kitano; 1990) or towards a desire to include properties inherent in living organisms that may be favourable for artificial systems, e.g. robustness (Miller; 2004) or adaptation (Tufte; 2008).
Artificial developmental mapping include various techniques and methods ranging from rewriting systems, e.g. L-Systems (Lindenmayer; 1971), to cellular approaches, where the genome is present and processed autonomously in every cell (Laing & Arbib; 1971). Further, the information available to the mapping process can be varied from systems depending only on the genotype and an axiom (Bentley & Kumar; 1999), to systems including environmental information where exploitation of this information form the phenotypic structure and behaviour together with information carried in the genome (Tufte & Haddow; 2007b).
In a system including a developmental mapping the role of the genome is radically changed from a system where the genome is considered a description, e.g. a blueprint, to a system where the genome may be viewed as information on how to build the system. That is, the genome contains information that is exploited in the generative process of development. The processing of the genome may be based on gene regulation Lantin and Fracchia (1995). Each development step, or stage in the mapping, produces a candidate phenotype which emerges during development. Gene regulation implies that different parts of the genome are expressed in different cells at different times cued in context with the environment and the emerging phenotype. As such, the genome size may not reflect the size or complexity of the phenotype and opens for systems that can generate very large scale repetitive structures (Kitano; 1998), or even structure of arbitrary size (Sekanina & Bidlo; 2005).
The generative process of development is not limited to the process of development of an adult organism, or in the artificial domain a finalized phenotype. A developmental mapping is not a process that is "turned off" when the finalized adult stage is reached. The process is working on the organism throughout it's lifetime. This ever lasting process is important to keep the organism healthy and functional. Damage, e.g. at the cellular level, can be repaired by regenerating the damage tissue and cells may be replaced if they fail to fulfil their purpose. In artificial systems an ever ongoing developmental process can, as in it's natural counterpart, obtain robustness. Such robustness is the product of a system that can regenerate itself if it is disturbed or damage (Miller; 2004). In the artificial domain, if included, the plasticity property of the artificial organisms can be exploited to target systems that based on the present environment can adapt their structure (Tufte; 2008) to obtain a target functionality despite changes in the environment in witch they operate and/or artificial organisms that can change their computational function based on the present environment (Tufte & Haddow; 2007b).
In this chapter the main topics are robustness and adaptation in evolved artificial developmental systems. The chapter includes a discussion on principles for artificial development. Possible environmental influence is described before a developmental model is covered for use in following examples. There are three examples covering robustness, plasticity and adaptation in an environmental context. Further a discussion on scalability, complexity and evolvability in developmental systems is included.

2. Artificial development

Whatever the motivation for including a developmental mapping in a system is that there exists some target purpose for the system. As we are dealing with artefacts there is no common purpose as reproduction is for living systems. Instead the purpose of the artificial evolved and developed organisms is connected to a specific problem domain. This implies that properties of artefacts are defined by the targeted problem.

In the domains of Artificial Life and Evolutionary Computation the target involves some sort of computation. Even though it is not trivial to distinguish what is computation and what is not (Toffoli; 2004), the phenotype or the developmental process itself is computational. To get a better way of defining what the purpose of a developmental system is the outcome, or developed phenotype, may be categorised in two: a structure or a structure of computational units. Constructing such categories can not be said to be an exact classification. The different classes are overlapping and for many cases there exists no clear classification category. However, to be able to clearly know, or decide, what the purpose of the artificial system is, it is crucial to know what kind of system that is targeted. That is, to be able to reach a system that fulfil its purpose we must know what function, i.e. computation, is to be the emergent result of evolution.

If systems targeting structures are considered the purpose of the system is the evolution and development of the structure itself. Here the process of development is used to create a structure from an initial condition, which may be some initial structural element(s). The structure may grow and/or reshape under some underlying developmental processes.

In Figure 1 an example taken from the work of Steiner et al. (2009) illustrates development of a structural purpose. In this figure the cellular growth can be seen as the output of the generative process growing structure by cell division. The initial structure is shown at top left and the finalized structure is shown at the two last panels at the bottom right. In the last panel a top plate is added to the developed structure. The purpose of the structure is to be a light-weight mechanical structure that can support mechanical stress from a weight placed on the added top plate.

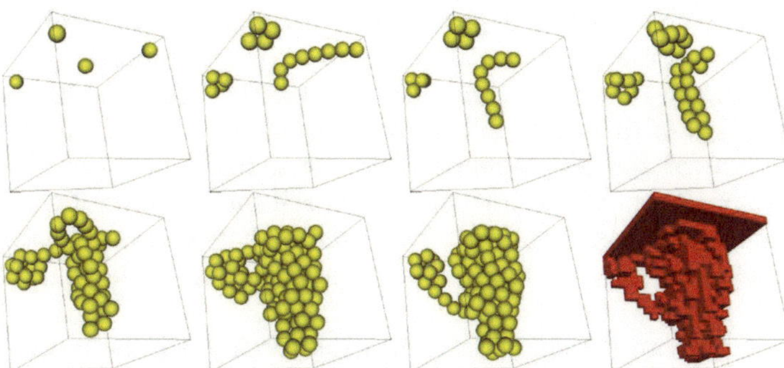

Fig. 1. Development of a mechanical structure. The developmental process starts at the top left corner. The finalized developed structure is at the bottom right corner. (Courtesy of Steiner et al. (2009))

The developmental phenotypes in Figure 2 show two developmental steps in the process of developing a structure with a computational function. Here the structure is not the target; the target is a computational function. As such, the developmental process generates structures of computational elements, here addition (+), subtraction (-) and multiplication (*). The developing structure includes input nodes, at the left, and an output node, the last block at the right. In the figure a block is marked *DUP* this is a special operator that can copy and insert parts of the current function into itself, i.e. development by self-modification.

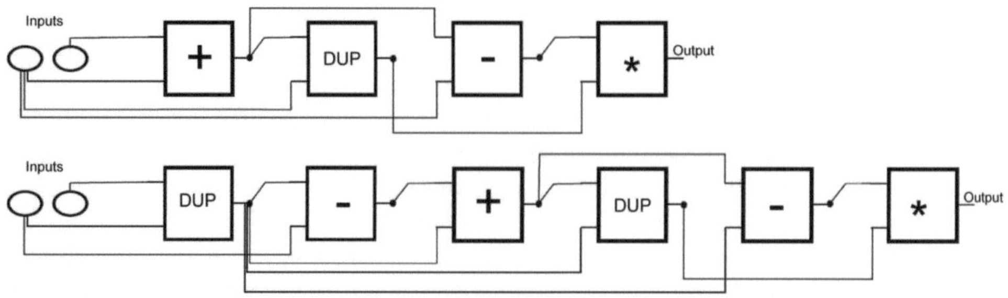

Fig. 2. Development of a structure consisting of computational and self-modification elements. Snapshot of two structures created by a developmental process. (Courtesy of Harding et al. (2007))

The two given examples of development in Figure 1 and 2 share and show key elements of developmental mappings. The evolution of a genome that carry information that is exploited by a developmental iterative process and the exploitation of information in intermediate phenotypes for the creation of the next phenotype on the developmental path toward the finalized phenotype.

In Figure 1 the genome, evolved by an Evolutionary Strategy (ES), is a short description of conditions and actions based on local cellular neighbourhood. Cell division is an action increasing the number of cells in the structure. The input information to the developmental process in a cell is local information in the cellular neighbourhood. This implies that the developmental process uses information from the emergent developing structure as information to decide the next cellular developmental action. As such, the structure emerges out of described conditions and actions in the genome regulated by information from the intermediate phenotypic structures.

The second example presented in Figure 2 also used an ES for evolving the genome. However, here the genome is an initial structure in the form of a graph consisting of connected computational nodes and some special nodes for self-modification. The iterative process can copy parts of the graph into another position or delete parts of the graph. As such, the initial size of the graph-genome can be a fraction of the developed graph-phenotype at end of development. The process of self-modification always operates on a current version of the graph generating the next intermediate graph-phenotype. This gives a system that can grow from a small graph to a large more complex graph based on self-modification.

Even though the two examples share basic principles that make them developmental they also clearly show the difference in evolutionary development of structures and computational structures. In the system of Steiner et al. (2009) the purpose was a lightweight structure that could resist mechanical stress. The structure of the phenotype itself is here directly evaluated. In the work of Harding et al. (2007) the actual structural composition is not measured. The result of an evaluation is based on the computation performed between the input nodes and the output node. As such, the developmental process works on a structure that may not reflect computational complexity of the phenotype.

This section illustrates what artificial development can be and the principles of large systems that emerges as a result of a generative process exploiting information from an evolved genome and intermediate phenotypic properties. The two examples illustrates the large diversity of developmental models and target purposes. In the following section the bio-inspired approach of artificial development will be further investigated and expanded toward a synthesis of evolution, development and environment, i.e. EvoDevo (Robert; 2004; Hall et al.; 2004).

3. Evolution, development and environment

In the previous section the mapping process itself was discussed and exemplified. However, the mapping process was taken out of context. In an evolutionary developmental system the evolutionary process include an evaluation function together with the developmental phenotype and the environment. Further, if adaptation and robustness are issues, the question of robustness and adaptation to what must be answered. The obvious answer, if looking to biology, is the environment. For an artificial system this answer may not be obvious. However, here we stick to the same answer for the artificial systems considered.

3.1 Environmental influence

Let us consider artificial developmental systems in relation to environmental information. In Figure 3 three different ways of treating an environment in artificial developmental systems are presented. Figure 3(a) shows a system that does not include an environment. In this approach an Evolutionary Algorithm (EA) is used to evolve genomes that are mapped from genotype to phenotype taking the information in the genome and possible intermediate phenotypic properties into the mapping process. The phenotype that is produced by the mapping process is evaluated by a fitness function. In the illustration the double arrow between the mapping process and the emerging organism (phenotype) shows that there is a possibility for the mapping process to exploit information from the emerging phenotype. In this system the phenotype is given by the information in the genome and the mechanisms in the mapping processes, a totally deterministic system. If the system in Figure 3(b) is considered. An environment is explicitly included. The organism develops within an environment and the fitness evaluation is based on the organism's performance in the environment present. As such, the feedback of fitness depends on the environment. In this system the fitness is connected to the organism and the environment. As such, the system depends not only on the genome and the developmental mechanisms, the environment influence on the evolutionary path of the system.

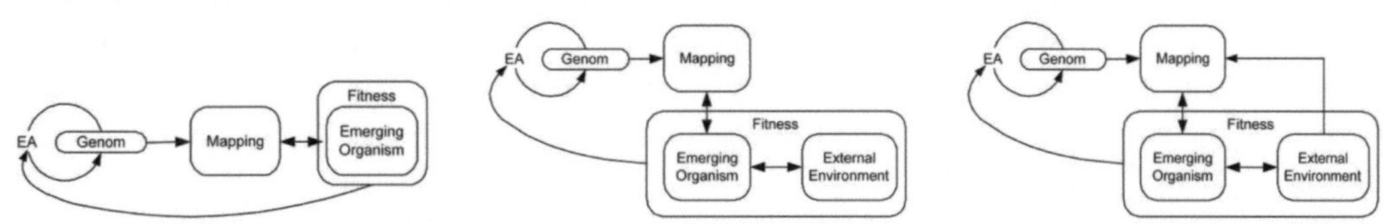

(a) No environmental influence. (b) Evolutionary environmental influence. (c) Evolutionary and developmental environmental influence.

Fig. 3. Possible environmental influence on artificial EvoDevo systems.

In the last system illustrated in Figure 3(c) the environment is, as illustrated by the extra arrow from environment to the mapping, available and can influence on the outcome of the mapping process. This implies that the emergent phenotype is a product of the genome, the emergent phenotype and the environment. This implies that the fitness feedback is based on a phenotype that depends on specific environmental conditions. As such, the phenotype

here can change structure and/or function depending on environmental conditions. Further, the double arrow between organism and environment in Figure 3(b) and 3(c) indicate that there can exist a mutual dependency between an organism and it's environment, i.e. mutual perturbatory channels (Quick et al.; 1999).
Now lets return to the question "robustness and adaptation to what"? As stated, the answer is the environment. In the presented systems the environment in all systems can be considered as information. The environment can serve as information enforced into the operating conditions of the artificial organism (Figure 3(b)). It is also possible to exploit the environmental information in the mapping process influencing on the phenotypic outcome (Figure 3(c)). Further, the environmental information is included in the evolutionary process by the possible influence of the fitness feedback to the EA. In Figure 3 the environment is termed external. External implies that environmental information is independent of the EvoDevo system and can change or fluctuate beyond the control of the EvoDevo system.

3.2 Robustness

If robustness is targeted in this context the system presented in Figure 3(b) featuring an environmental influence on the evolutionary outcome, systems with robustness to environmental fluctuations can be obtained. A system can be evolved to operate in different environmental conditions. However, this ability is based on a system operation that is robust in itself, i.e. not influenced by fluctuations in the environment. It is important to note that the view on environment as information include enforced disturbance or changes to the organism itself. As an example of this is shown by Miller (2004) where a developmental system evolved to generate a flag structure that was externally disturbed by changing parts of the structure. The system was able to regenerate itself through development.
Robustness through regeneration in developmental system is highly connected to selforganization. A system is in a state of stability and even if it is disturbed it will return to this state by regeneration.

3.3 Adaptation

Developmental adaptation is highly connected to plasticity, the ability for the individual in a species to respond to environmental conditions. Such response may materialise in form of individuals that can develop different structural and/or behaviour properties based on environmental conditions, i.e. plasticity. In an artificial developmental system plasticity gives a single genome several possible developmental paths. Witch path an organism follows is given by the specific environmental conditions present during development. Further, due to the possibility to have an active developmental process throughout the lifetime of an individual fluctuations in the environment can cue reorganisation of structur and behaviour through gene activation as to be able to operate (Tufte; 2008).
Adaptation by plasticity may also be viewed in a context of self-organizing systems. In contrast to robustness making a system capable of returning to the same state after perturbations plasticity in a system allow the system to leave it's state and there after move to a different state whilst maintaining it's operation.
Robustness and adaptation on the evolutionary and developmental level is further explained and investigated in Section 5.

3.4 Levels of environmental information

In this section environment has been seen as an external information source that can be exploited by evolution and possible environmental sensitive mechanisms in the developmental mapping. However, environment is present in developmental systems at different levels. At the cellular level environment exists as an intra-cell environment that the artificial DNA resides in, also referred to as the *cell's metabolism* (Federici; 2004; Gordon & Bentley; 2005). The next level of environment, found in most development models, is the neighbour environment referring to the *inter-cell environment*, enabling communication between neighbouring cells (Bongard & Pfeifer; 2003; Tufte & Haddow; 2003; Miller; 2004; Federici; 2004). Further, the external environment influence discussed affecting the phenotype may be part of the available information for a development process.

4. Example: a cellular approach

In this section a developmental model is presented for later use in examples and to relate the topics in the previous sections to developmental mechanisms and features. The system as a whole is close to an Evolutionary Developmental (EvoDevo) approach. This implies a developmental system with a possibility to include information from the environment, intermediate structures and behaviour in addition to the genetic information carried in the genome. The artificial organisms the model target are developing structures capable of computation. The computational architecture is based on Cellular Automata (CA) originating from von Neumann (1966). von Neumann's Self-Reproducing Automata is in itself close to artificial development (Sipper et al.; 1998), cells with a finite number of states that can selfreplicate, i.e. an expanding cellular structure. The developmental phenotypes are based on the cellular computational machine paradigm (Sipper; 1997). A non-uniform CA is developed, i.e. the structure/form, emerges out of the set of developmental rules capable of cellular growth, differentiation and cell death. The details of the system are only discussed in brief. For a complete description of the system - see Tufte (2008) (developmental model) and Tufte (2006) (evolutionary algorithm).

4.1 Developmental model

The development model is based on cellular development. This implies that the genome is present and processed autonomously in every cell. In the model, the cell also contains the functional building blocks. For the experiments herein the application sought is that of a digital circuit (phenotype). Figure 4(a) illustrates the developmental system - the cell. The cell is divided into three parts: the genome (the building plan); the development process (mechanisms for cell growth and differentiation) and the functional component of the cell. The information in the functional components represents the type of the cell and the cell's state is described by the outputs of the functional components.

The genome consists of a set of rules. Rules are restricted to expressions consisting of the type and state of the target cell and the types and state of the cells in its von Neumann neighbourhood. There are two types of rules i.e. change and growth rules. Cell growth is a mechanism to expand the organism. A growth rule result provides the direction of growth: grow from north **Gn**; east **Ge**; south **Gs** or west **Gw**. It is important to note that these rules are expressed in terms of where the source of the cell growing into the target cell is. Describing where a cell is growing from enables a fully parallel implementation of the system to be created whilst retaining the possibility that cells in effect may grow in all four

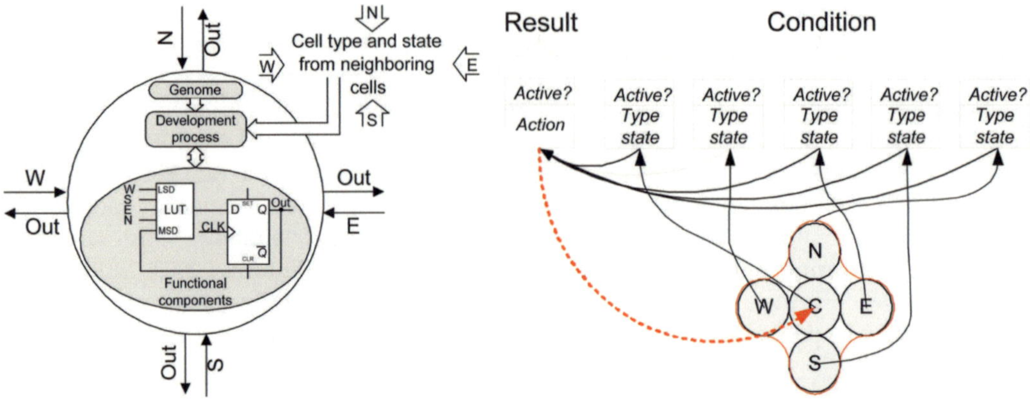

(a) Components of the cell. (b) Gene regulation shown for a single rule

Fig. 4. The basic cell and a rule showing the gene regulation in the cellular development model.

directions simultaneously. Growth rules have two restrictions. First, the target cell must be empty - this is to prevent growing over an existing cell and thus specialising the cell with a new cell type. Secondly, the cell to be copied into the target can not be empty.

Differentiation changes a cell's type i.e. its functionality. The result part of a change rule states the type of cell the target is going to be changed into. Cells have the following types: valid cell types, don't care (DC) or empty. However, the empty cell is not a valid target cell type.

Each rule consists of a result and a condition. The conditional part provides information about the cell itself and each of the neighbouring cells. In the development model presented in (Tufte & Haddow; 2005), the type of the cell was applied to describe these cells. However, to introduce external environment, state information is also needed. State information provides a way to include information relating to the functionality of the organism at a given point in time as well as information about the external environment - the empty cells in the environment also have state information. As such, a cell is represented in the condition of a rule by two genes representing its type and its state. However, a target cell is only represented by one gene: it's type for change rules or growth direction for growth rules. The state of cell may be 0, 1 or DC. DC is introduced to provide the possibility to turn on or off this environmental influence. The development model is applied with and without the information from the external environment and functional organism.

Firing of a rule can cause the target cell to change type, die (implemented as a change of type) or cause another cell to grow into it. Figure 4(b) illustrates the process of evaluating a rule. For each cell condition, the cell type and state are compared and if the conditions are true then that part of the rule is active. If all conditions are active then the result will become active and the rule will fire. Activation of the result gene is expressed in the emerging phenotype according to the action specified.

In a development genome multiple rules are present. Multiple rules imply that more than one rule of a given cell may be activated at the same time if their conditions hold. To ensure unambiguous rule firing, rule regulation is part of the development process. If the first rule is activated, the second rule can not be activated. Activation of the second rule prevents activation of the third rule, etc.

The functional components of the cell is an Sblock (Haddow & Tufte; 2000). The content of the look-up table (LUT) defines functionality and is, herein, also used to define the cell type. The LUT is the combinatorial component and the flip-flop is the memory element - capable of storing the cell state. The output value of an Sblock is synchronously updated and sent to all its four neighbours and as a feedback to itself. The LUT definition for the cell types used herein can be seen in Table 1.

Cell type	LUT hex	Function name	Graphical representation
0	$0xFFFF0000$	*no change Emty*	
1	$0x66666666$	$XOR_d\ W \oplus S$	
2	$0x3D3D3D3D$	$XOR_c\ E \oplus S$	
3	$0x0FF00FF0$	$XOR_b\ N \oplus E$	
4	$0x55AA55AA$	$XOR_a\ W \oplus N$	
5	$0x55FF55FF$	$NAND\ \overline{W \bullet N}$	
6	$0xFF00FF00$	$\downarrow$ *SouthPropagation*	
7	$0xCCCCCCCC$	$\uparrow$ *NorthPropagation*	
8	$0xF0F0F0F0$	$\leftarrow$ *EastPropagation*	
9	$0xAAAAAAAA$	$\rightarrow$ *WestPropagation*	
10	$0xE8808000$	$T \geq 4$	
11	$0xFEE8E880$	$T \geq 3$	
12	$0xFFFEFEE8$	$T \geq 2$	

Table 1. Definition of cell types and their functionality

One update of the cell's type under the execution of the development process is termed a development step (DS). A development step is thus a synchronous update of all cells in the cellular array. The update of the cell's functional components i.e. one clock pulse on the flip-flop, is termed a state step (SS). A development step is thus made up of a number of state steps.

The initial condition is applied before development starts. This means that all empty cells are set or reset depending on the given initial condition. To avoid empty cells updating their output values from their von Neumann neighbourhood, all cells of type Empty are set to update their outputs based on only their own output value at the previous clock pulse. A empty cell will retain its initial state - environmental information, until the emerging organism grows into it.

4.2 Development of cellular computation machines

Figure 5 show an example of development of a cellular machine and its behaviour. The phenotype is an emerging non-uniform Cellular Automata (CA) (top). Development of the structure goes through steps, Development Steps, where the structure is formed by growth (expanding the number of cells) and differentiation (changing the rule of a given cell). The different colours in the emerging phenotype represent what CA rule the cell contains. White cells are considered empty. The dashed lines indicate that there exists events that are not shown in the figure, e.g. the phenotypic structure between *DS 8* and *DS 98* are not shown. The behaviour of the system in Figure 5 (bottom) is the state space produced from an initial state executed by the developing non-uniform CA. The space time plots for the behaviour consists of 100 State Steps for each development step. This implies that there exist 10 000 space time plots describing the behaviour of the system. It is important to note that in this system behaviour exists from the first cell throughout the life-time of the organism.

5. Examples: plasticity, robustness and adaptation

In order to highlight the working and gain an increased understanding of developmental mappings the developmental model presented in Section 4 is applied to some examples. The examples are all targeting robustness and adaptivity. The model presented targets organisms that structurally can be seen as a non-uniform cellular automaton that emerges as a product of development. Similar, the functionality can also be seen as the result of running the developing cellular machine. As such, the developing organism is the phenotypic cellular structure, shown at the top of Figure 5, and the functionality of the system is the dynamic behaviour of the organism, shown at the bottom of Figure 5.

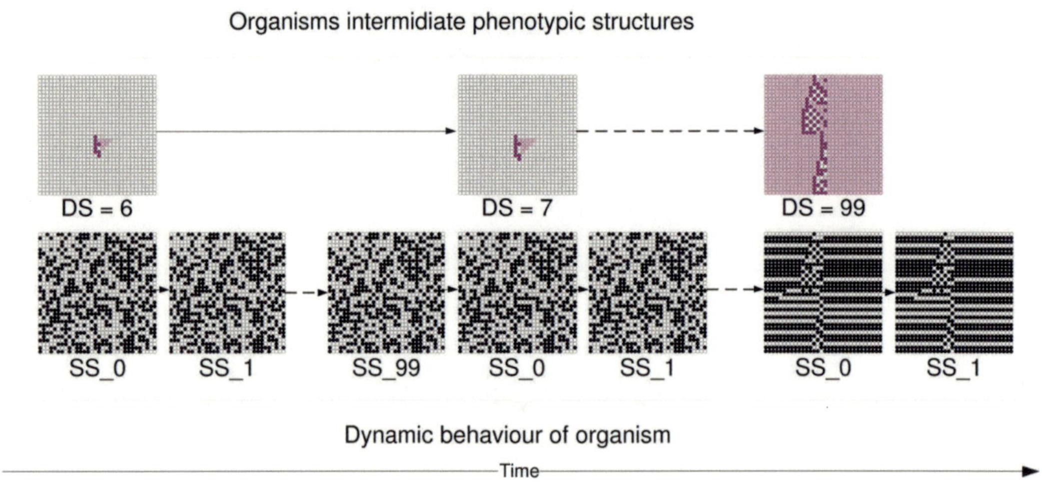

Fig. 5. Snapshot of the development of phenotypic structure (top) and the corresponding emergent behaviour (bottom) shown as space-time pattern.

The application chosen in these examples is a sequential counter where counting is based on the state information of the entire cellular space and the sequential operation of the functional components of the cells. The application thus places a requirement on the tuning of the development genome (by evolution) and the emerging phenotype (by development) for such sequential digital circuit behaviour. A counting sequence is defined in the cellular array as the number of logical "1"s in the cellular array increasing by one for each state step. As such, the functionality only concern the global count of cells outputting a logical "1", i.e. an emergent global property out of local interactions of the functional components of the cells.

The fitness function for achieving this counter behaviour is based on the best counter sequence obtained at each developmental step, i.e. a lifetime evaluation. As such, the total fitness is the sum of the longest counter sequence found on each developmental step. As the main topic here is robustness and adaptation the main common property is development in fluctuating environments.

In all the examples presented the developmental process is allocated 100 development steps. At each development step 100 state steps is executed. As such the counter sequence is a product of the dynamic behaviour caused by the state steps at each development step. The size of the genotype in all examples was set to 32 rules. Here the specific example results are selected from larger collections of experimental results. For all details on the results and setups see (Tufte & Haddow; 2007a,b; Tufte; 2008).

5.1 Robust phenotypes

As a first example the evolution of phenotypes that is robust to environmental fluctuations is presented. However to emphasis the principle of robust phenotypes an example with no evolved robustness is also presented together with a setup targeting evolved robustness. In these examples the environmental regulation, i.e. cell state information, is set to don't care in the developmental model. That is, evolutionary robustness, as illustrated previously in Figure 3(b).

The functional requirement in the two examples is the counter behaviour described. In Figure 6 the setup for showing the influence of a fluctuating environment is presented. A setup that is not exposed to environmental fluctuation during evolution is shown in Figure 6(a). In this experiment a single environment is used throughout evolutionary time (phylogeny axis). All organisms develop in this common environment (ontogeny axis). The evolved result is genomes that are specialized to cope by producing a functional phenotype in this environment. The setup in Figure 6(b) is changed to targeting genomes that can develop to functional phenotypes in a set of different environments. Here each genome is developed in ten different random generated environments. As such, the EvoDevo system targets organisms that can cope with different environments. The difference in fitness evaluation is that the system in Figure 6(a) only bases its evaluation on the functionality in a single environment while the setup in Figure 6(b) gets its fitness measurement by the average functionality in a set of ten different environments.

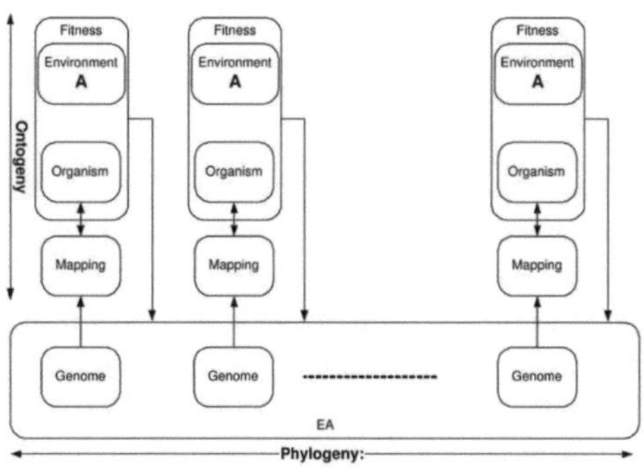

(a) A single defined environment used for all evaluations.

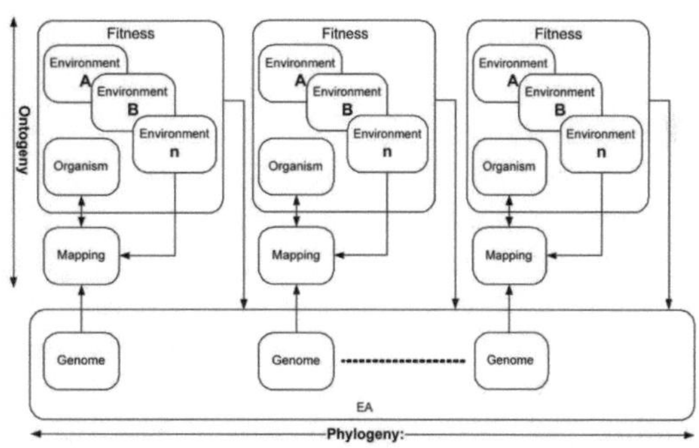

(b) Evaluation based on a set of possible relevant environments.

Fig. 6. Evolution and developmental setup including environment for the different experimental examples presented.

To actually test and expose the difference between the two approaches shown, the genomes evolved was exposed and re-developed in ten new random generated environments. The result of this exposure is shown in Figure 7. In the figure the fitness obtained from the evolutionary process is given by the black bar termed 0 on the X-axis. The resulting fitness value is given by the Y-axis in the plot. The measured fitness value for the re-evaluated and

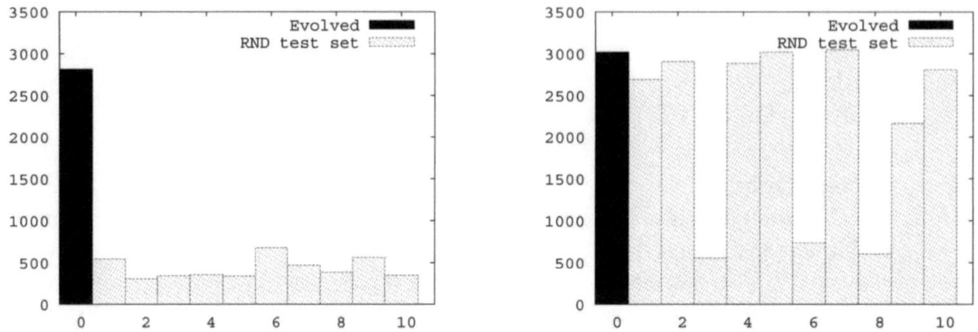

(a) Genome evolved in a single environment exposed to and re-developed in ten new random environments.

(b) Genome evolved in a set of ten random environment exposed to and re-developed in ten new random environments.

Fig. 7. Result of evolutionary robustness to fluctuating environments.

re-developed organisms in the ten new random generated environments is given by the grey bars, numbered 1 to 10. The plot in Figure 7(a) show how the evolved genome was tuned to obtain a high fitness score in the presence of a known environment. However when exposed to other environments the organism totally fails to achieve its goal functionality. This is caused by the strong evolved adaptation to the environment present during evolution. The strong evolved dependency on a single environment to achieve functionality is decreased if the result from the EvoDevo setup in Figure 6(b) is re-developed and re-evaluated. In Figure 7(b) the result of a similar re-development and re-evaluation to ten new random environments is shown. The result show how the same genome can develop and achieve the targeted functionality despite environmental fluctuations. However, the result show that some environments, i.e. 3, 6 and 8, do not provide an environment that the evolved genome can develop within whilst retaining functionality.

5.2 Plasticity

In this example the main goal is to demonstrate plasticity. Plasticity can be seen as the property of phenotypic plasticity in biological organisms. To achieve such plasticity the evolutionary algorithm is set up to target genotypes that can develop to different structural organism in two different environments, whilst the functional requirement of counting is maintained. To enable environmental influence, hence phenotypic plasticity, inclusion of a possibility to exploit cell state information in the genotype is put under evolutionary control. This move can be seen as moving from the EvoDevo system in Figure 3(b) to the system presented in Figure 3(c).

Figure 8 illustrates the setup for an EvoDevo system that can show the present of phenotypic plasticity in artificial organisms. The EvoDevo system used to evolve organisms with the preferred functionality is shown in Figure 8(a). The evolutionary algorithm presents candidate solutions to the developmental mapping process. Each genome is developed in two different environments, A and B shown in Figure 8(b) and 8(c), the initial cell (zygote) is set to be a cell of type 5 (NAND)The initial zygote is shown in Figure 8(d). This example implies that each genome is developed and evaluated twice in two different environments. As such, the difference in environmental information can be exploited to develop different structural organism by influencing on the rule regulation.

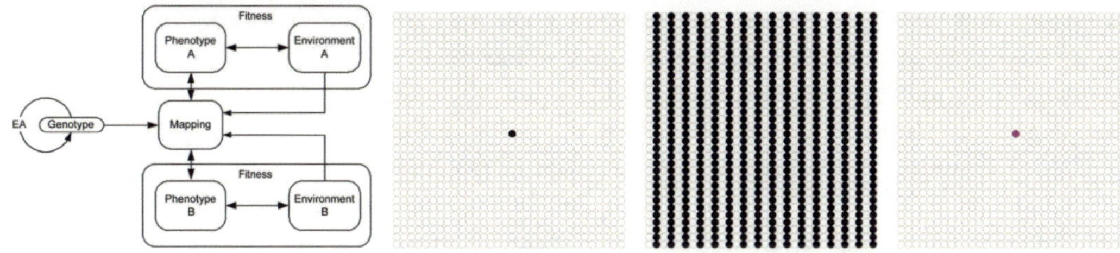

(a) Experimental setup. (b) Environment A. (c) Environment B. (d) Initial Cell.

Fig. 8. Experimental setup for the achievement of demonstrating phenotypic plasticity cued by different environments.

The result of evolving genomes that can exploit information in the environment is presented in Figure 9. The difference in structural composition of the phenotypes resulting from the two different environment can clearly be seen in Figure 9(a) and 9(d). The environmental information has, as stated, in Section 4 influence on the regulation of the rules, hence a possibility to control what rules that are expressed and eventually the timing of expressing rules. Figure 9(b) and 9(e) show the activation pattern for rules in the given genome. The plotted star (*) indicating that that specific rule was expressed at that given developmental step. The plotted line indicates the total number of cells in the organism expressing an active rule. As such, the cause of the achieved structural difference can be traced to the difference in expressing rules over the developmental time. By examining the plots it can be seen that there exist common rules expressed at different times, further there are rules that are only expressed for one of the two environments. Note also that only parts of the genome are actually expressed during development. There exist parts of the genome that is not

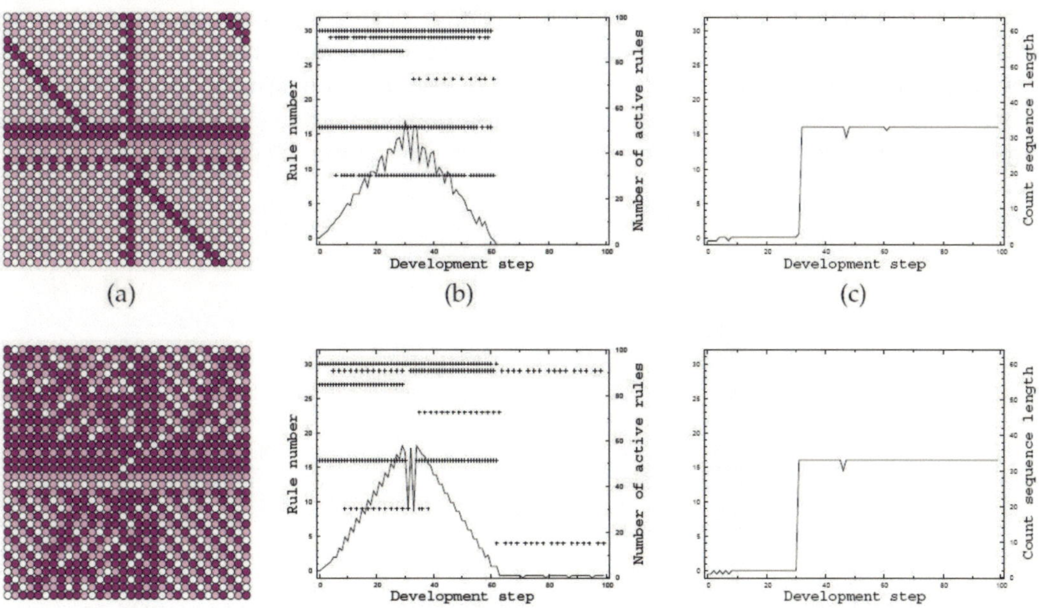

(a) (b) (c)

(d) (e) (f)

Fig. 9. Environmental influence exploited to retain functionality. Result of a genome developed in the two different environments.

expressed but may be genetic information that previously in evolutionary time was exploited. It may also be parts of the genome that has never been expressed and as such may be neutral information (Shipman et al.; 2000).
The purpose of the evolved organisms was not actually the structural composition but the functional counting behaviour of the developing organism. In Figure 9(c) and 9(f) the measured functionality, i.e. counter length, for the two developed organisms is plotted for each development step. Here the preservation of functionality despite the different environmental conditions can be observed. The two results show how the two different structural phenotypes are able to retain a common functional property by phenotypic plasticity.

5.3 Adaptive phenotypes

Toward organisms that are truly adaptive the EvoDevo example in Figure 7(b) is executed within a setting that opens for phenotypic plasticity. That is, the EvoDevo setup of Figure 3(c) is applied to the evolutionary example of evolving robust phenotypes in Figure 7(b). Now the organisms are not only robust to fluctuations in the environment, the organisms can adapt their structural composition to the environment present during development. As such, there is a possibility for evolution to exploit specific combinations of environmental trails to achieve organisms that can develop to phenotypic structures that depends on the environment which it develops within whilst retaining the functional goal.
The result of the approach can be seen in Figure 10. Here a single genome is capable of developing to functional phenotypes in all but one of the new random environments it is exposed to. If the phenotypic structure is examined, the presented result is obtained by a process that develops different phenotypic structures depending on environmental traits. However, even here the EvoDevo system does not achieve a result that is equally fit in all environments. This is caused by an evolved dependency on specific combinations of environmental traits. Such dependency can cause poor performing phenotype structures, e.g. by competing counters structures in a single organism cancelling each other out.

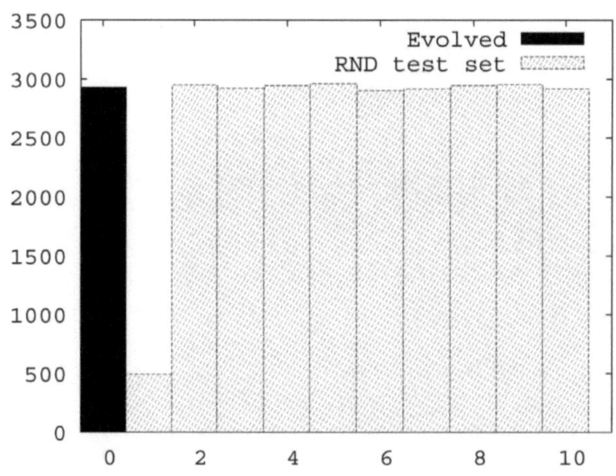

Fig. 10. Genome evolved in a set of ten random environment exposed to and re-developed in ten new random environments. Phenotypic plasticity exploitable.

5.4 Discussion

In this section robustness and adaptation was seen and presented as two different properties. However, the view on what robustness and adaptation is and imply, may be seen at different levels. If the examples given are viewed at a higher level of abstraction or in a more biological relation, the way an ability to obtain a given function in fluctuating environments is achieved only serves as two different approaches to reach the purpose of the system. Here the purpose is organisms that can produce a counting function despite fluctuations in the environment. Even though the two presented systems here serve an identical purpose the inclusion of possible phenotypic plasticity by environmental influence give two quite different systems. The difference in system attributes is the amount of information available to the developmental mapping.

In Figure 11 the examples of Section 5.1 and 5.3 is presented as trajectories (Tufte; 2009) showing the emergence of the phenotypic structures for the two examples. Figure 11(a) show the developmental paths, i.e. trajectories, from the ten environments (top) to the final stable phenotype structure (bottom). In this representation of the developmental history it is clear that this system will always develop to the same final phenotype structure, i.e. the structure of the phenotype is not influenced by external information in the environment. The trajectory for the system opening for phenotypic plasticity in Figure 11(b) on the other hand clearly show influence by external information. The ten initial conditions (in the middle) can take different paths to different phenotypic structures. In addition the developmental trajectory contain loops at several point indicating that the structure is unchanged for more then one developmental step. Such loops are broken if the state information, i.e. behaviour, changes to express a change in the phenotype by development.

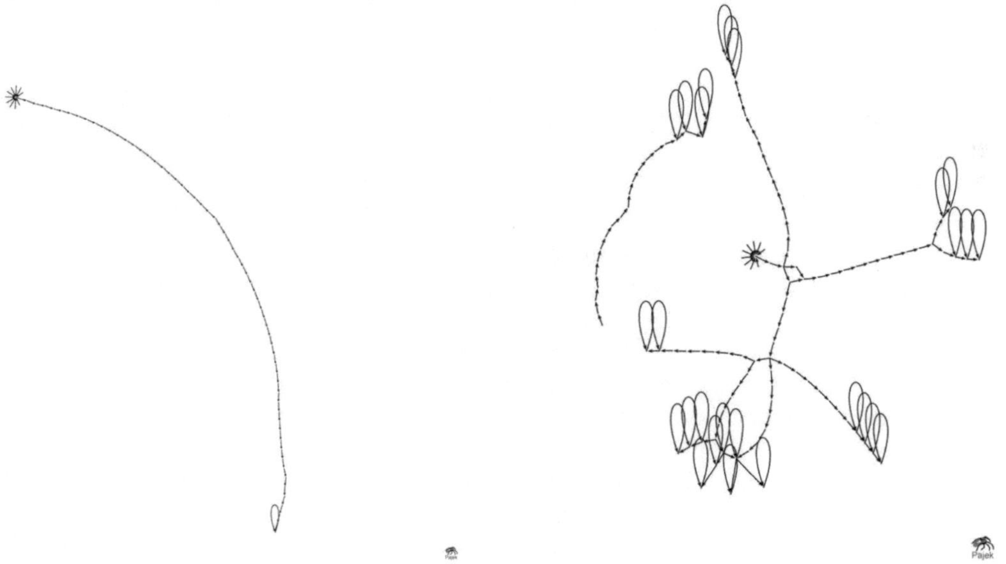

(a) Developmental trajectory for a system without inclusion of external information in the mapping process.

(b) Developmental trajectory for a system including external information in the mapping process.

Fig. 11. The developmental trajectories for the emergent phenotype structures in a fluctuating environment. The plots are generated by PAJEK (Batagelj & Mrvar; 1991).

The highlighted difference between the two examples show the importance on how information is actually incorporated in artificial developmental models. Information amount and the included mechanisms for intercommunication between cells are the factors leading to what forms that can emerge out of a given developmental mapping (Laing; 1972). As such, the construction of developmental model should be based on an awareness on what information amount and exchange that is required for the process of developmental self-organising for the sought form, function and bio-inspired properties.

6. Notes on scalability, complexity and evolvability

The main topic here is developmental mappings in the context of robustness and adaptation. However, artificial development show promising features in other domain of EC.

The issue of scalability is one of the main topics of interest in introducing mapping processes inspired by development. Bentley and Kumar (1999) addressed the scalability by investigating the performance of direct encoding versus developmental encodings to generate phenotypes of different structural size, e.g. number of cells in the final phenotype. Other similar approaches dealing with phenotypic size as the scaling factor have looked into the affect on performance of the development process regarding scaling of phenotypic size and genome size (Tufte & Thomassen; 2006). Another way of considering scaling is to look at the functional property of the developed phenotype (Kitano; 1998). In such approaches work have been done on keeping-up functional performance when the size, i.e. number of neurons, of the phenotype increases (Gauci & Stanley; 2007). Examples of general solutions to scaling in developmental systems have been found. Sekanina and Bidlo (2005) demonstrated development of arbitrarily large sorting networks. Harding et al. (2007) attacked the problem of finding a general solution that generates sequences of squares Spector and Stoffel (1996). However, these examples show scaling within a specific problem, i.e. not systems that scales toward more complex problems. The diverse approaches and views described on scaling in developmental systems calls for an understanding of what the goal of scaling is, what changes to be made to scale, e.g. change in resources, and what results of scaling that can be expected for the problem at hand.

Complexity, or rather being able to evolve and possibly develop complex machines that are capable of complex computation, or evolutionary growth of complexity (McMullin; 2001) in such systems are areas of much interest. The motivation range from an urge to create complex artificial organisms (Eggenberger; 1997; Kitano; 1998) to a more theoretical interest (McMullin; 2001; Lehre & Haddow; 2003; Kowaliw; 2008) in the working of mapping processes and artificial organisms emerged from such processes. As such, understanding of the emergence of complexity in artificial systems is important to be able to exploit artificial development toward the creation of evolved large systems capable of complex computation.

The difference in the way information in the genome is treated in developmental mappings compared to direct mapping approaches influence on the evolvability (Kirschner & Gerhart; 1998) of such systems. The fact that the information in the genome is relativly small and the information content in the phenotype is large implies that the genotype space is much smaller then the phenotype space. Even though, as shown in Section 5, a genome can be the origin of several phenotypes along the development path and that external information can be included in the gene regulation, the phenotypic space that a given genome size and mapping model can explore is usually given to larger then the genotype space. Further the intermediate phenotypes along the developmental path together with the property of having a system with an ever working developmental process influence on how and when evaluation is to be carried out, i.e. influence on the fitness landscape. The process of regulation, e.g. herein gene regulation, imply neutrality. Parts of the genome is not expressed in the phenotype hence there exists more then one genotype describing a given phenotype. As such, introducing artificial developmental mappings strongly influence the evolvability of the system (Harding & Banzhaf; 2008) by changing the focus of evolution from the content of the genotype to an interplay between genome, environment and the emerging phenotype (Taylor; 1999).

7. Conclusion

Despite the fact that ideas of artificial development have been around for almost half a century (von Neumann; 1966; Codd; 1968; Laing & Arbib; 1971) the field is still young, as shown by the renewed interest. However as most youngsters it struggle whit what to make of itself. There are promising works in areas as robustness and adaptation, as described in this chapter. Furthermore the areas of complexity and scalability toward large complex systems have shown to be areas where artificial development is a most prominent player. Further there is an increased interest often motivated by an urge toward new mediums changing today's view on a machine's components, architecture and computation (Miller & Downing; 2002). As such new machines may require a drastic reconsideration of how we as human designers can design and construct such machines. A change toward design by EvoDevo systems seems a promising direction. It is ironic that von Neumann, one of the pioneers for computers as we know them today, worked on ideas close to artificial development and at the same time showed an interest for machines made up of unreliable parts that should be capable of reliable computation (von Neumann; 1956), a scenario of high interest toward e.g. nanoscale and biochemical machines.

8. References

Batagelj, V. and Mrvar, A. (1991). Pajek program for large network analysis., http://vlado.fmf.uni-lj.si/pub/networks/pajek/.

Bentley, P. J. and Kumar, S. (1999). Three ways to grow designs: A comparison of embryogenies for an evolutionary design problem, *Genetic and Evolutionary Computation Conference (GECCO '99)*, pp. 35-43.

Bongard, J. C. and Pfeifer, R. (2003). *Morpho-functional Machines: The New Species (Designing Embodied Intelligence)*, Springer-Verlag, chapter Evolving complete agents using artificial ontogeny, pp. 237-258.

Codd, E. F. (1968). *Cellular Automata*, Association for computing machinery, Inc. Monograph series, Academic Press, New York.

Eggenberger, P. (1997). Evolving morphologies of simulated 3d organisms based on differential gene expression, *Fourth European Conference on Artificial Life*, MIT press.

Federici, D. (2004). Evolving a neurocontroller through a process of embryogeny, *Simulation of Adaptive Behavior (SAB 2004)*, LNCS, Springer, pp. 373-384.

Gauci, J. and Stanley, K. (2007). Generating large-scale neural networks through discovering geometric regularities, *GECCO '07: Proceedings of the 9th annual conference on Genetic and evolutionary computation*, ACM, New York, NY, USA, pp. 997-1004.

Gordon, T. G. W. and Bentley, P. J. (2005). Development brings scalability to hardware evolution, *the 2005 NASA/DOD Conference on Evolvable Hardware (EH05)*, IEEE, pp. 272 -279.

Haddow, P. C. and Tufte, G. (2000). An evolvable hardware FPGA for adaptive hardware, *Congress on Evolutionary Computation(CEC00)*, IEEE, pp. 553-560.

Hall, B. K. (2003). Unlocking the black box between genotype and phenotype: Cell condensations as morphogenetic (modular) units, *Biology and Philosophy* 18(2): 219-247.

Hall, B. K., Pearson, R. D. and Müller, G. B. (2004). *Environment, development, and Evolution Toward a Synthesis*, The Vienna Series in Theoretical Biology, MIT-Press.

Harding, S. and Banzhaf, W. (2008). *Organic Computing*, Springer Verlag, chapter Artificial Development, pp. 201 - 220.

Harding, S. L., Miller, J. F. and Banzhaf, W. (2007). Self-modifying cartesian genetic programming, *GECCO '07: Proceedings of the 9th annual conference on Genetic and evolutionary computation*, ACM, New York, NY, USA, pp. 1021-1028.

Kirschner, M. and Gerhart, J. (1998). Evolvability, Proceedings of the National Academy of Sciences of the United States of America 95(15): 8420-8427.

Kitano, H. (1990). Designing neural networks using genetic algorithms with graph generation systems, *Complex Systems* 4(4): 461-476.

Kitano, H. (1998). Building complex systems using development process: An engineering approach, *Evolvable Systems: from Biology to Hardware, ICES*, Lecture Notes in Computer Science, Springer, pp. 218-229.

Kowaliw, T. (2008). Measures of complexity for artificial embryogeny, GECCO '08: Proceedings of the 10th annual conference on Genetic and Evolutionary Computation, ACM.

Laing, R. (1972). Artificial organisms and autonomous-cell rules, *Technical report*, The University of Michigan.

Laing, R. and Arbib, M. (1971). Automata theory and development ii, *Engineering, college of - technical reports*, The University of Michigan.

Lantin, M. and Fracchia, F. (1995). Generalized context-sensative cell systems, *Proceedings of Information Processing in Cells and Tissues, University of Liverpool*, pp. 42-54.

Lehre, P. K. and Haddow, P. C. (2003). Developmental mappings and phenotypic complexity, *Congress on Evolutionary Computation(CEC2003)*, IEEE, pp. 62-68.

Lindenmayer, A. (1971). Developmental Systems without Cellular Interactions, their Languages and Grammars, *Journal of Theoretical Biology* .

McMullin, B. (2001). John von neumann and the evolutionary growth of complexity: Looking backward, looking forward..., *Artificial Life* 6(4): 347-361.

Miller, J. and Downing, K. (2002). Evolution in materio: Looking beyond the silicon box, *2002 NASA/DOD Conference on Evolvable Hardware*, IEEE Computer Society Press, pp. 167- 176.

Miller, J. F. (2004). Evolving a self-repairing, self-regulating, french flag organism, *Genetic and Evolutionary Computation (GECCO 2004)*, Lecture Notes in Computer Science, Springer, pp. 129-139.

Quick, T., Dautenhahn, K., Nehaniv, C. L. and Roberts, G. (1999). On bots and bacteria: Ontology independent embodiment, *ECAL '99: Proceedings of the 5th European Conference on Advances in Artificial Life*, Springer-Verlag, London, UK, pp. 339-343.

Robert, J. S. (2004). *Embryology, Epigenesis and Evolution: Taking Development Seriously*, Cambridge Studies in Philosophy and Biology, Cambridge University Press.

Sekanina, L. and Bidlo, M. (2005). Evolutionary design of arbitrarily large sorting networks using development, *Genetic Programming and Evolvable Machines* 6(3): 319-347.

Shipman, R., Shackleton, M., Ebner, M. and Watson, R. (2000). Neutral search spaces for artificial evolution: a lesson from life, *Artificial Life VII, 2000.* URL: *citeseer.ist.psu.edu/shipman00neutral.html*

Sipper, M. (1997). Evolution of Parallel Cellular Machines The Cellular Programming Approach, Springer-Verlag.

Sipper, M., Tempesti, G., Mange, D. and Sanchez, E. (1998). Von neumann's legacy: Special issue on self-replication, *Artificial Life* 4(3).

Spector, L. and Stoffel, K. (1996). Ontogenetic programming, *in* J. R. Koza, D. E. Goldberg,

D. B. Fogel and R. L. Riolo (eds), Genetic Programming 1996: Proceedings of the First Annual Conference, MIT Press, Stanford University, CA, USA, pp. 394-399. URL: citeseer.ist.psu.edu/spector96ontogenetic.html

Steiner, T., Trommler, J., Brenn, M., Jin, Y. and Sendhoff, B. (2009). Global shape with morphogen gradients and motile polarized cells, *Congress on Evolutionary Computation(CEC2009)*, IEEE, pp. 2225-2232.

Taylor, T. (1999). On self-reproduction and evolvability, *European Conference on Artificial Life*, Springer-Verlag, Berlin, pp. 94-103.

Toffoli, T. (2004). Nothing makes sense in computing except in the light of evolution, *Int. Journ. of Unconventional Computing* 1(1): 3-29.

Tufte, G. (2006). Cellular development: A search for functionality, *Congress on Evolutionary Computation(CEC2006)*, IEEE, pp. 2669-2676.

Tufte, G. (2008). Evolution, development and environment toward adaptation through phenotypic plasticity and exploitation of external information, *in* S. Bullock, J. Noble, R. Watson and M. A. Bedau (eds), *Artificial Life XI: Proceedings of the Eleventh International Conference on the Simulation and Synthesis of Living Systems*, MIT Press, Cambridge, MA, pp. 624-631.

Tufte, G. (2009). The discrete dynamics of developmental systems, *Proc. of 2009 International Conference on Evolutionary Computation (CEC 2009)*, IEEE, pp. 2716-2723.

Tufte, G. and Haddow, P. C. (2003). Identification of functionality during development on a virtual sblock fpga, *Congress on Evolutionary Computation(CEC2003)*, IEEE, pp. 731-738.

Tufte, G. and Haddow, P. C. (2005). Towards development on a silicon-based cellular computation machine, *Natural Computation* 4(4): 387-416.

Tufte, G. and Haddow, P. C. (2007a). Achieving environmental tolerance through the initiation and exploitation of external information, *Congress on Evolutionary Computation(CEC2007)*, IEEE.

Tufte, G. and Haddow, P. C. (2007b). Extending artificial development: Exploiting environmental information for the achievement of phenotypic plasticity, *7th International Conference on Evolvable Systems (ICES07)*, Lecture Notes in Computer Science, Springer, pp. 297-308.

Tufte, G. and Thomassen, J. (2006). Size matters: Scaling of organism and genomes for development of emergent structurs, *CODESOAR at Genetic and Evolutionary Computation (GECCO 2006)*, ACM.

von Neumann, J. (1956). Probabilistic logics and the synthesis of reliable organisms from unreliable components, *in* C. Shannon (ed.), *Automata Studies*, pp. 43-98.
von Neumann, J. (1966). *Theory of Self-Reproducing Automata,* University of Illinois Press, Urbana, IL, USA, 1966.
West-Eberhard, M. J. (2003). *Developmental Plasticity and Evolution,* Oxford University Press.
Wolpert, L. (2002). *Principles of Development, Second edition,* Oxford University Press.

13

Evolutionary Based Controller Design

Ivan Sekaj
*Slovak University of Technology,
Faculty of Electrical Engineering and Information Technology,
Bratislava,
Slovak Republic*

1. Introduction

Control design methods have to respect various requirements imposed on the performance of controlled systems. Controllers often include many design parameters and their various constraints. The search/optimisation process may be complicated, discontinuous or non-convex, and often some analytical methods are not able to yield satisfactory results. Opposite to this, evolution-based search techniques are able to generate new control laws and non-intuitive solutions as well. Without loss of generality, let us consider the use of genetic algorithm (GA), which is one of the most frequently used evolutionary techniques. Recently, genetic algorithms have been applied in process control to solve a wide range of optimisation and design problems. This chapter is focused on the design of controllers for continuous-time systems.

Let us classify the known approaches, which are using evolutionary algorithms (EA) in two groups. In the first group the EA's are used as a powerful optimisation/search tool in analytically formulated control design methods. The parameters of controllers (or any dynamic system) are designed analytically, based on the stability or required system performance (Kawabe et al., 1996; Krohling & Rey, 2001; Man, 2001; Sekaj & Veselý, 2005). The second group of methods applies simulation-based closed-loop time response evaluation of the model (Herrero et al., 2002; Khatib, 1999; Lewin, 2005; Mitsukura et all, 1999; Sweriduk et al., 1999; Yang, 2005). A multi-objective approach that comprises 7 different objectives including both analytically formulated and time-response performance based ones is presented in (Molina-Cristóbal, 2005).

If the design task includes not just searching for parameters of a prespecified control structure but also searches for the internal structure itself, an extension to this approach is possible using the Genetic programming (Koza, 1992; Banzhaf et al., 1999; Koza et al., 2000; Sekaj et al., 2005; Sekaj & Perkacz, 2007). To optimise controller structure also a hierarchical GA can be used (Man at al., 2001). In (Grosman & Lewin, 2005) Genetic programming has been used to generate the Lyapunov functions. Survey of evolutionary-based control system designs is e.g. in (Fleming & Purshouse; Lewin, 2005).

In this chapter a straightforward incorporating of the simulation-based closed-loop time response evaluation in the evolutionary algorithm is presented. The proposed approach deals with a direct Evolutionary-based search/optimisation in the controller parameter space combined with extensive computer simulations of the designed closed-loop system

(Sekaj, 1999; Sekaj et al., 2002; Sekaj, 2003; Sekaj et al., 2005; Sekaj & Perkacz, 2007; Sekaj 2005). Thus, the simulation is an essential part of the minimised objective function. It will be shown that according to this approach, the design of optimal parameters for a dynamic system is transformed into a "conventional" n-dimensional optimisation problem. In section 2, the design principle is described and the use of various performance indices is discussed. In the section 3 robust controller design methods are proposed. A multi-objective design approach is discussed in section 4, where multiple objectives are considered in the controller design procedure. Finally, controller internal structure design and its parameters using genetic programming is proposed in section 5.

2. Controller design

2.1 The design principle

As already mentioned, the control design objective is to provide required static and dynamic behaviour of the controlled process, usually represented in terms of the well-known performance measures: maximum overshoot, settling time, decay rate, steady state error or various integral performance indices (Dorf, 1990; Kuo, 1991; and others).
Without loss of generality let us consider a simple feedback loop (Fig. 1) where y is the controlled variable, u is the control, r is the reference and e is the control error ($e=r-y$). Let an appropriate simulation model of the controlled object be available. The closed-loop performance will be assessed using the simple integral performance index "integral of absolute control error" defined as

$$I_{AE} = \int_0^T |e(t)| dt \tag{1}$$

where T is the simulation time. The discrete form of this performance index is

$$I_{AE} = \sum_{k=1}^{N} T_{s,k} |e_k| \tag{2}$$

where $T_{s,k}$ is the simulation step size and N is the number of simulation steps.

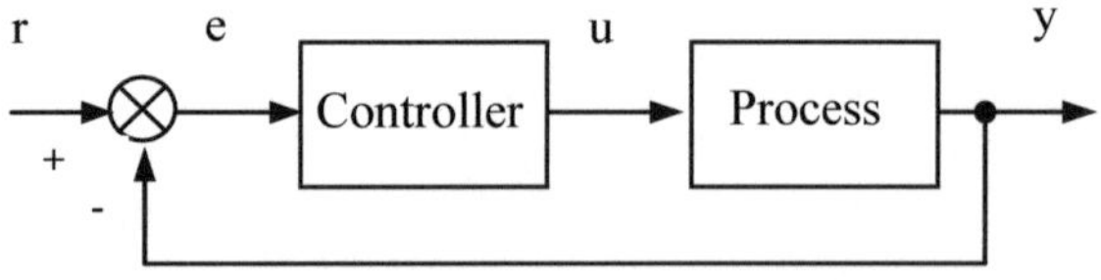

Fig. 1. Simple feedback control loop

The controller design is actually an optimisation task - search for such controller parameters from the defined parameter space that minimise the performance index (1) or (2). The cost function (fitness) is a mapping $R^n \rightarrow R$, where n is the number of designed controller parameters. The cost function evaluation consists of two steps. The first step is the closed-loop time response simulation, the second one is the performance index evaluation. Note, that when designing complex, multi-input multi-output (MIMO) control structures or the

other controller types (fuzzy controllers, neuro-controllers, etc.) the dimension n of the search space may be quite large (more than tens or even hundreds).
Graphical representation of a simple cost function corresponding to a simple PI controller design is in Fig. 2. Each point of the surface $G_{IAE}=f(P,I)$ is a result of a simulation and the performance index (1) evaluation. The optimal PI controller parameters are represented by the co-ordinates of the surface global minimum. This simple 2-D search problem can also be solved using conventional (deterministic) enumerative search/optimisation techniques. However, in case of more complex control structures comprising many parameters, the dimension of the search space is growing and the use of such methods may be no more feasible due to high computational requirements. Here, the evolutionary-based techniques, in our case the genetic algorithms can successfully be used.

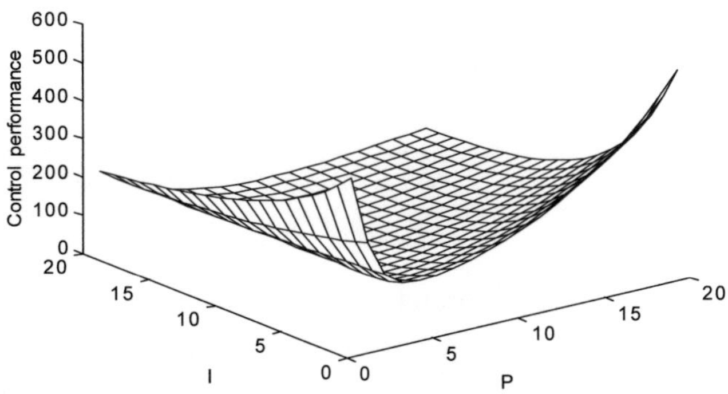

Fig. 2. Graphical representation of a cost function with the I_{AE} performance index (1) for a particular closed-loop under a PI controller

2.2 Genetic algorithm

Genetic algorithms (Goldberg, 1989; Michalewicz, 1996; Eiben & Smith, 2003; Man et al., 2001) deals with a population consisting of a set of chromosomes. Each chromosome represents a potential solution and has the form of a linear string of numbers; in our case, items of a chromosome (genes) correspond to the designed controller parameters. As the controller parameters are real-number variables and the number of the searched parameters can be large, real-coded chromosomes have been considered.
Without loss of generality consider a PID controller, which control law in time domain description is as follows

$$u(t) = Pe(t) + I\int e(t)dt + D\frac{de(t)}{dt} \tag{3}$$

where $P\in R$, $I\in R$, $D\in R$ are the proportional, integral and derivative gains, respectively. In this case a chromosome can be represented in the form $ch=\{P,I,D\}$. For any other controller type with parameters $c_1, c_2, \dots, c_q$ the corresponding chromosome would be a string

$$ch=\{c_1, c_2, \dots, c_q\}.$$

A general scheme of a GA can be described as follows:

1. Initialisation of the population of chromosomes (generating a set of random chromosomes).
2. Evaluation of the cost function (fitness) for all chromosomes.
3. Selection of parent chromosomes.
4. Crossover and mutation of parents → children.
5. Creation of a new population consisting of new children and selected members of the old population including the best individual from the current population.
6. Testing terminating conditions, jump to the Step 2 or End.

The block scheme describing the controller design principle is shown in Fig. 3.

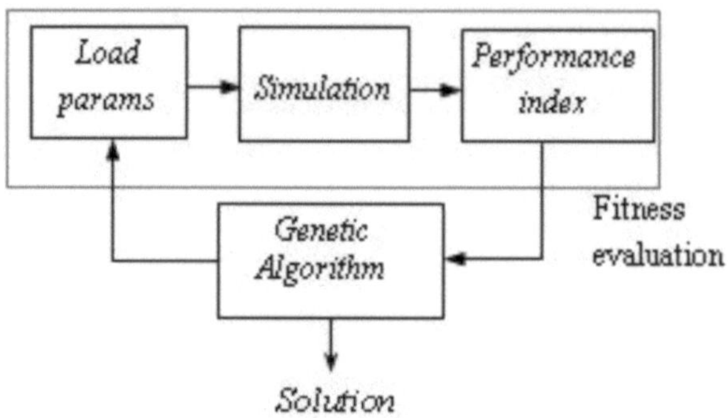

Fig. 3. Block scheme of the GA-based controller design

Example in Fig. 4 shows evolution of a PID via minimisation of the criterion (1). After a certain number of generations the best solution from the current population (its closed-loop step response) has been plotted. As after 100 generations the solution has not changed considerably, the GA run could have been terminated. The cost function convergence during three independent GA-runs (cost function of the currently best individual of the population vs. generation number) is depicted in Fig. 5.

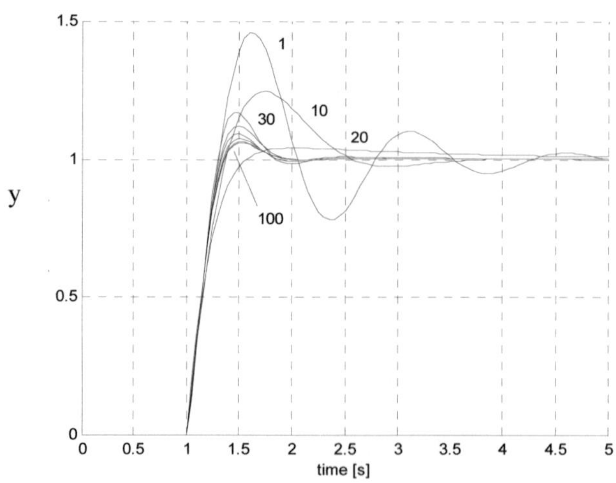

Fig. 4. Evolution of the PID controller parameters after 1, 10, 20, 30 and 100 generations

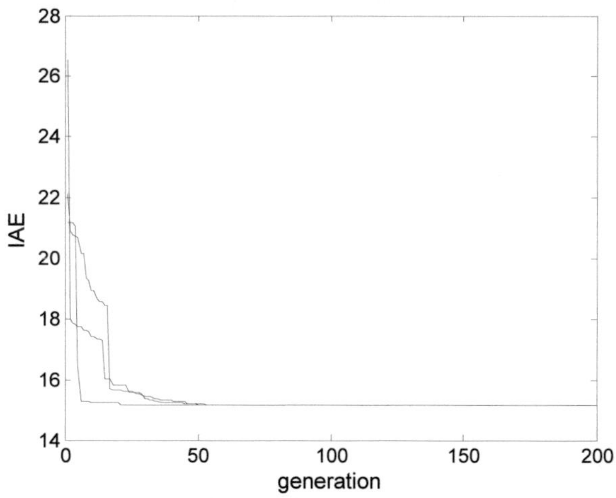

Fig. 5. Cost function convergence of the PID controller design procedure for three independent GA-runs for population size 30 individuals.

Note, that the controller design for a complex system can become a multi-modal and a time-consuming problem, where often a good sub-optimal solution is sufficient. The answer to the question about the convergence rate of the controller design procedure is similar as in case of other numerical GA-based search/optimisation problems. It depends on the search space size and dimension and on the GA performance.

2.3 Choice of the performance index

Consider that a GA has found the optimal (sub-optimal) solution in the user-defined search space of controller parameters. The choice of the performance index has a fundamental influence on the closed-loop dynamics. Normally, using (1) or (2) brings about fast control responses with small overshoots between 2-5% (Fig. 4). For various objectives different performance indices can be used (Sekaj, 1999; Sekaj, 2005).

If it is necessary to reduce overshoot or to damp oscillations, it is recommended to insert in the integral additional terms, which include absolute values of the first or also the second derivatives of the control error

$$J = \int_0^T \left(\alpha|e(t)| + \beta|e'(t)| + \gamma|e''(t)|\right)dt \tag{4}$$

and to increase β and γ with respect to α, where α, β, γ are weight coefficients. Note, that the control error derivatives can be replaced with the absolute values of output derivatives ($|y'(t)|$, $|y''(t)|$). In the discrete case the integral is replaced by the sum and the derivatives by the differences. Good results can be obtained also using the performance index in the form

$$J = \alpha\eta + (1-\alpha)t_s \tag{5}$$

where η is the overshoot, t_s is the settling time and $0 < \alpha < 1$ is the weight coefficient. Tracking the reference step response $y_r(t)$ is achieved via minimising

$$J = \int (y_r(t) - y(t))^2 dt \tag{6}$$

Control energy minimisation can be achieved using performance indices of the type

$$J = \int (\alpha e^2(t) + (1-\alpha)u^2(t))dt \tag{7}$$

where u is the control variable. A universal performance index, which combines some above criterions is as follows

$$J = \int_0^T \left(|e(t)| + a|e'(t)| + b|u(t)| + c|u'(t)| \right) dt \tag{8}$$

where e' is the control error derivative, u is the control variable and u' is its derivative. This performance index includes oscillation damping (increasing a), minimisation of the absolute value of the control signal u (increasing b) and minimisation of control signal change u' (increasing c). In Fig. 6 to Fig. 13 various configurations of parameters a, b, and c in (8) and their influence of the closed-loop time response y and control value u are depicted.
In case of designing multi-input multi-output systems the design procedure is analogical, but for each output a particular (i-th) part of the cost function with some weight is considered (9).

$$J = \sum_{i=1}^{N} w_i J_i \tag{9}$$

Remark about the closed-loop stability: Due to the applied performance index minimisation, closed-loop stability is an implicit attribute of the controller design process. Unstable chromosomes are eliminated during the evolution because of high values of performance index and thus the solution is directed into the region of stable parameters. However if necessary, it is possible to include some stability test in each fitness evaluation. Cost function values of unstable individuals can additionally obtain high penalty values.

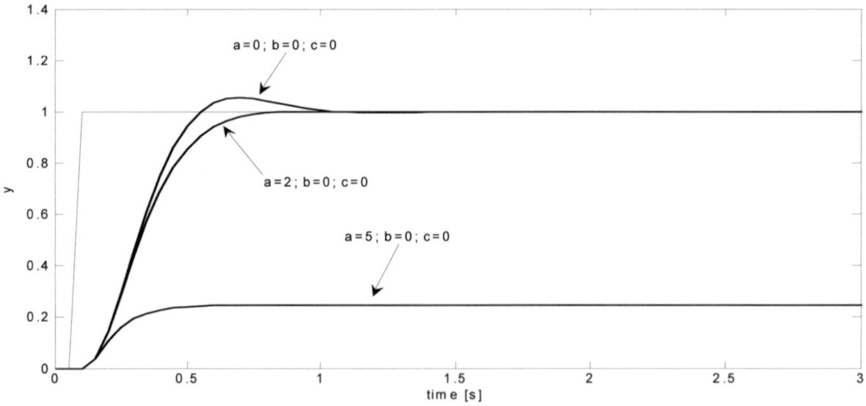

Fig. 6. Closed-loop time responses for various values of the parameter a in (8)

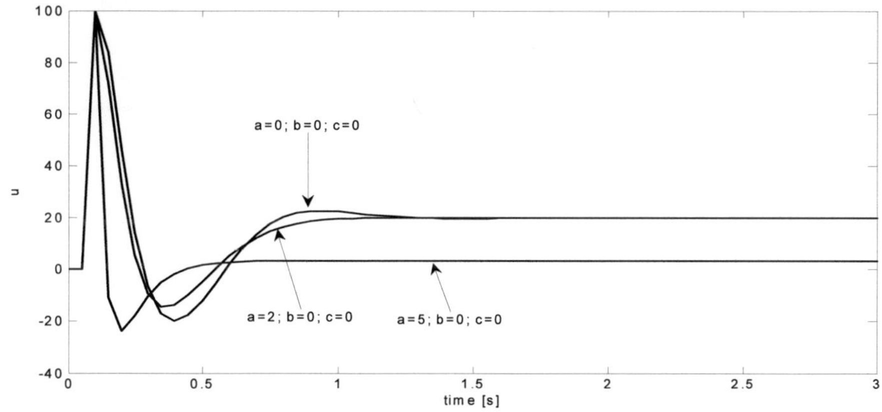

Fig. 7. Time responses of control value for various values of the parameter *a* in (8)

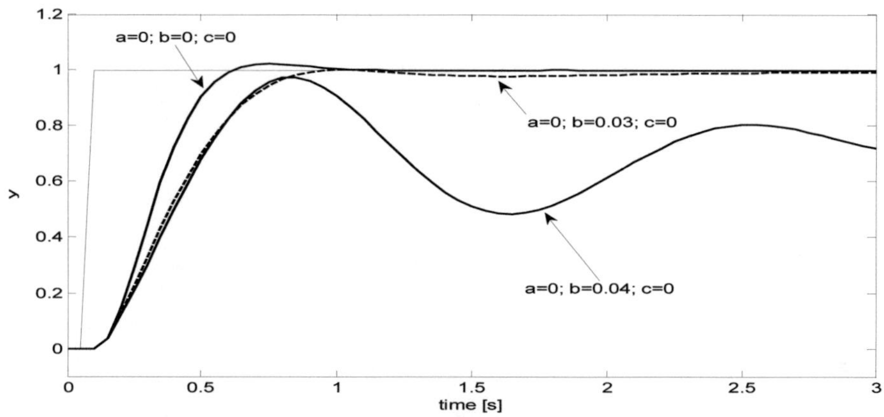

Fig. 8. Closed-loop time responses for various values of the parameter *b* in (8)

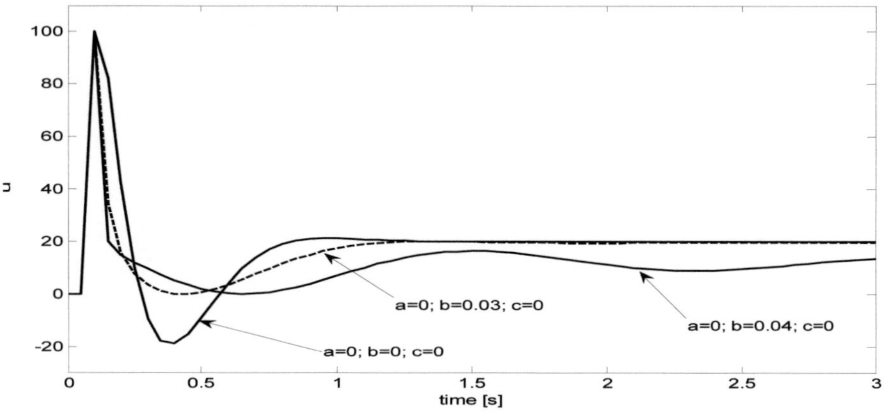

Fig. 9. Time responses of control value for various values of the parameter *b* in (8)

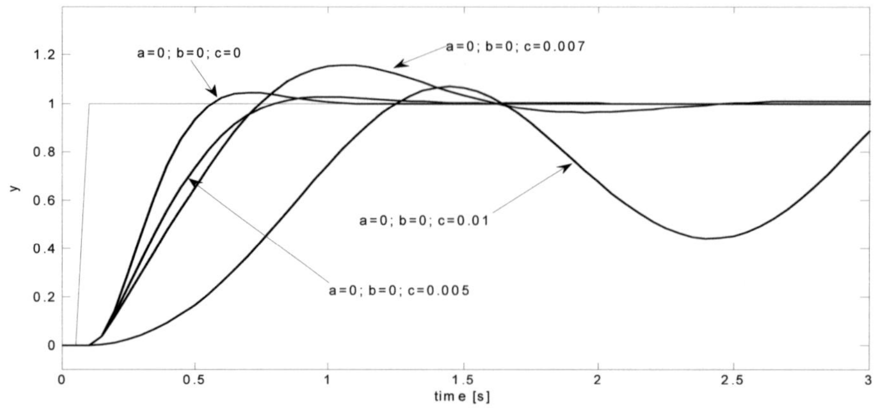

Fig. 10. Closed-loop time responses for various values of the parameter *c* in (8)

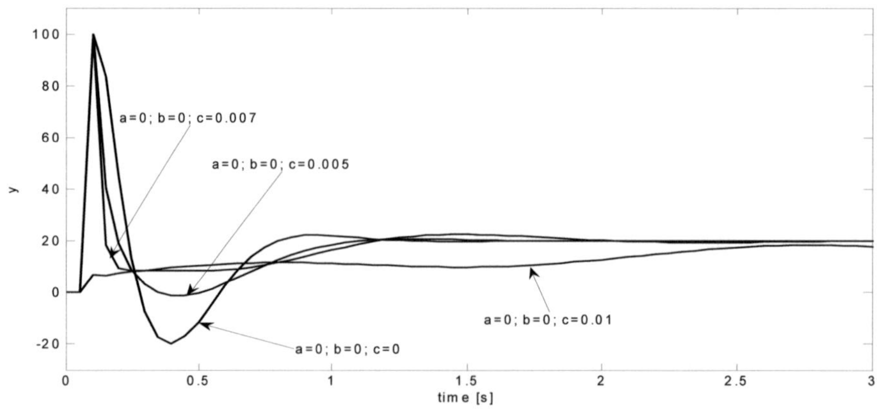

Fig. 11. Time responses of control value for various values of the parameter *c* in (8)

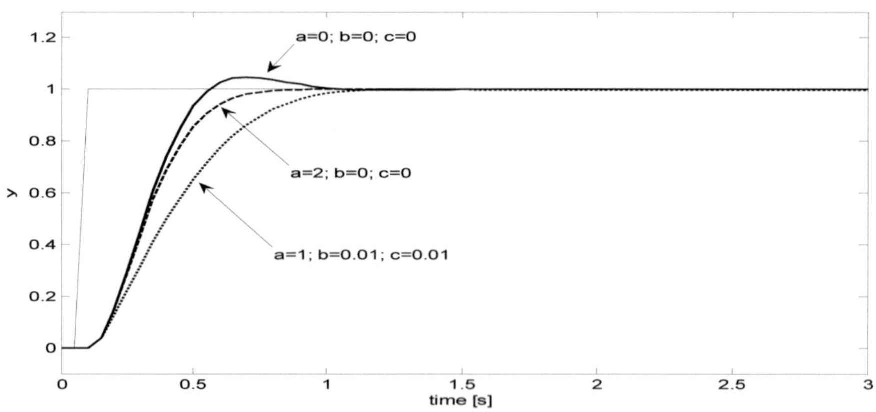

Fig. 12. Closed-loop time responses for various values of the parameters *a,b,c* in (8)

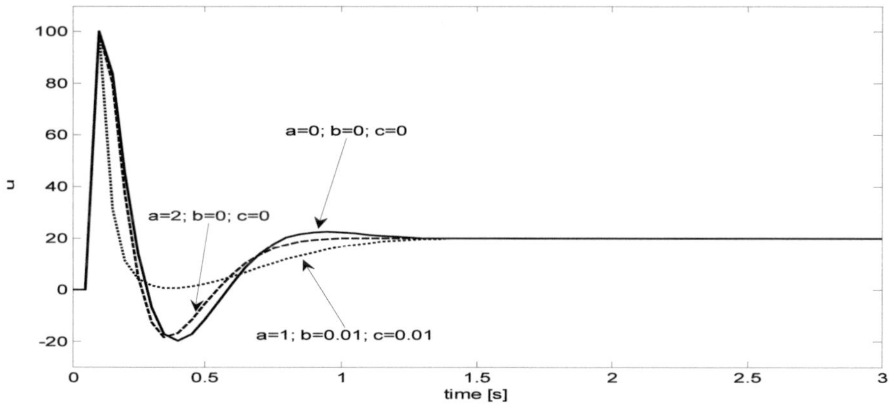

Fig. 13. Time responses of control value for various values of the parameter *a,b,c* in (8)

3. Robust controller design

3.1 Design in fixed defined working points

Consider $c = \{c_1, c_2, \dots, c_q\}$ to be the set of designed controller parameters and let the $s = \{s_1, s_2, \dots, s_r\}$ is the set of parameters of the controlled system. During the operation of the plant, the parameters s_i can move within some uncertainty space

$$S: \quad s_{i,\min} \leq s_i \leq s_{i,\max}\,; \quad i = 1,2,\dots,r \tag{10}$$

where $s_{i,min}$ and $s_{i,max}$ are the minimum and maximum possible values of the *i*-th system parameter, respectively. Consider *W* different (physical) working points of the controlled process, defined by different vectors *s*, which are to be controlled by the robust controller. For that case consider the cost function in the additive form

$$J = \sum_{i=1}^{W} J_i \tag{11}$$

comprising performance evaluation (for instance (1)) in all *W* working points. It is also recommended to include the measured noise from the real system or other possible disturbances or expected situations in the simulation model. Note, that alternatively to the set of *W* defined physical working points we can use a set of 2^r system parameter vectors located in the vertices of a polytope representing bounds of the parameter space *S*.

3.2 Random generating of working points

Alternative to the previous method, for the working point selection the following method can be considered (Sekaj & Šrámek, 2005). In each generation of the GA, *n* random working points (for all chromosomes of the population the same ones) are generated i.e. *n* vectors (say *n=100*) of system parameters *s* become random values from the space *S*. For each individual of the population the fitness function is calculated using the performance index (11). In the next generation other *n* random parameter vectors are generated. In each generation the cost function evaluation is as follows:

1. random generation of n system parameter vectors s (working points),
2. closed-loop simulation and evaluation of the performance index for each individual and each working point,
3. evaluation of the cost function (11) for each individual.

3.3 Experimental comparison of robust design methods

To demonstrate the proposed controller design methods, consider the controlled system, which is described by the non-linear differential equation

$$y'' + a_2 y' + a_1 y + a_0 y^3 = b_0 u \tag{12}$$

The gain of this system is not constant and depends on the system output value y. Let the system parameters move within the uncertainty intervals

$$b_0 \in (1;5), a_0 \in (0.02;5), a_1 \in (0.02;0.2), a_2 \in (0.01;20) \tag{13}$$

Consider a PID controller described by the transfer function

$$G_{PID}(s)=P+I/s+Ds \tag{14}$$

with the control variable limited within the range $-10 \le u \le 10$. The parameters P, I and D have been designed using the following 4 methods:

Method 1: Robust approach according to section 3.2 with 100 randomly generated working points from the space S in each generation.

Method 2: Simple PID design using GA according to section 2, eq. (1) in the nominal working point (WP_3 in next method).

Method 3: Robust approach according to the IMC+PID method (Rivera et al., 1986) designed in 3 fixed working points:

WP_1: $a_0=0.02$; $a_1=0.02$; $a_2=0.01$; $b_0=1$ - lower limits of intervals (13)

WP_2: $a_0=5$; $a_1=0.2$; $a_2=20$; $b_0=5$ - upper limits of (13)

WP_3: $a_0=2.51$; $a_1=0.11$; $a_2=10.005$; $b_0=3$ - mean values of (13), nominal working point.

Method 4: Conventional "Optimal Module" PID design method (Oldenburg & Sartorius, 1956) using a linearised system in the nominal working point.

The design results are summarised in Table 1.

Method	P	I	D	SRM
1	100	12.62	4.41	0.2898
2	98.03	8.66	8.45	0.3521
3	89.10	15.41	2.92	0.3058
4	20.56	0.98	0.36	1.0124

Table 1. Results of the Robust PID design methods

The proposed *Statistical robustness measure* (SRM) quantifies statistical evaluation of a set of closed-loop simulation experiments (in our case 1200) with randomly generated working points from the uncertainty space S. The SRM can be expressed by a scalar value calculated as follows

$$SRM = \frac{1}{N}\sum_{i=1}^{N} J_i \tag{15}$$

where N is the number of closed-loop simulation experiments and J is a selected performance index. In our case (1) has been used.

All obtained results from Tab.1 have been tested on 25 randomly selected working points from the parameter space S (all 25 are identical for all 4 design methods). Time-responses for all design methods are depicted in Fig. 14-Fig. 17.

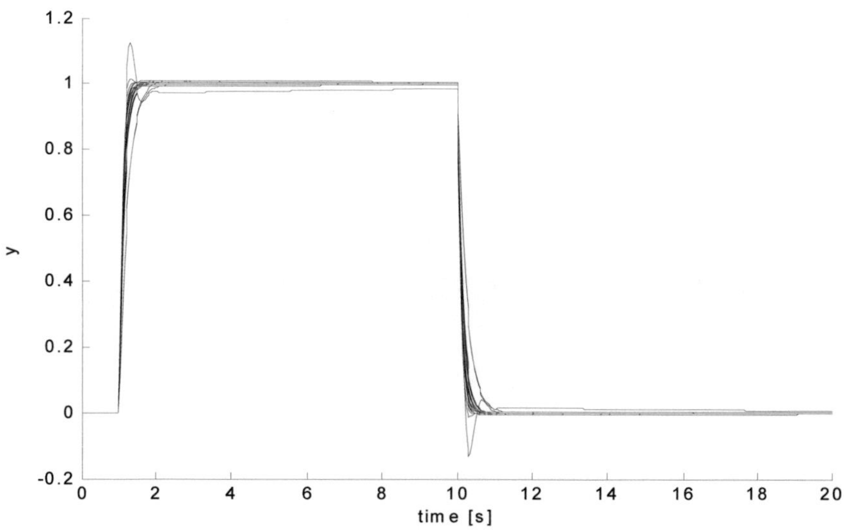

Fig. 14. Closed-loop time responses of 25 test systems for Method 1

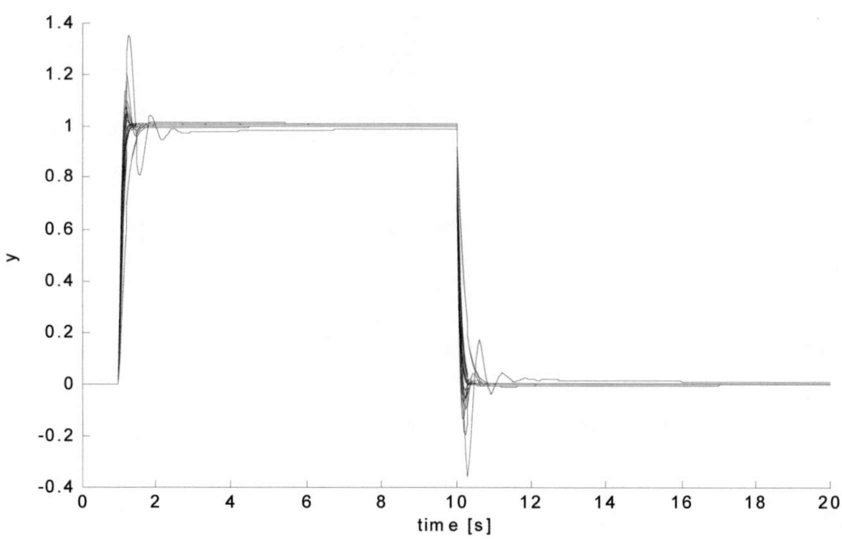

Fig. 15. Closed-loop time responses of 25 test systems for Method 2

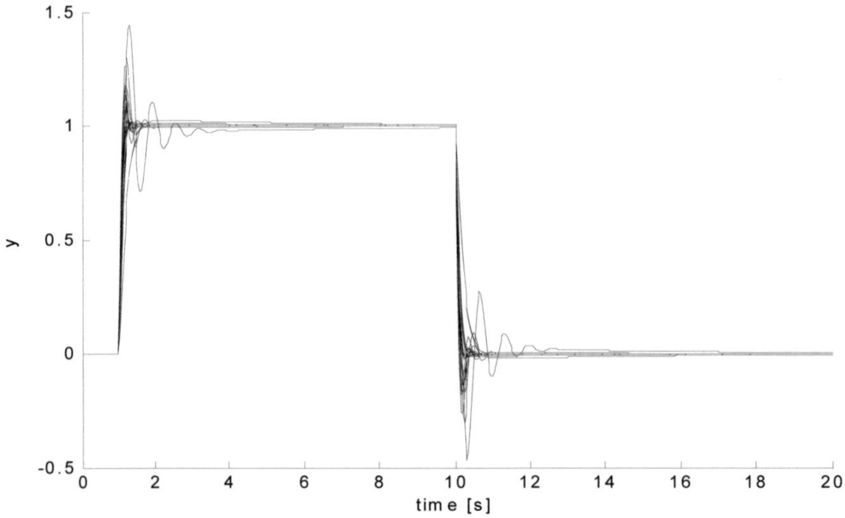

Fig. 16. Closed-loop time responses of 25 test systems for Method 3

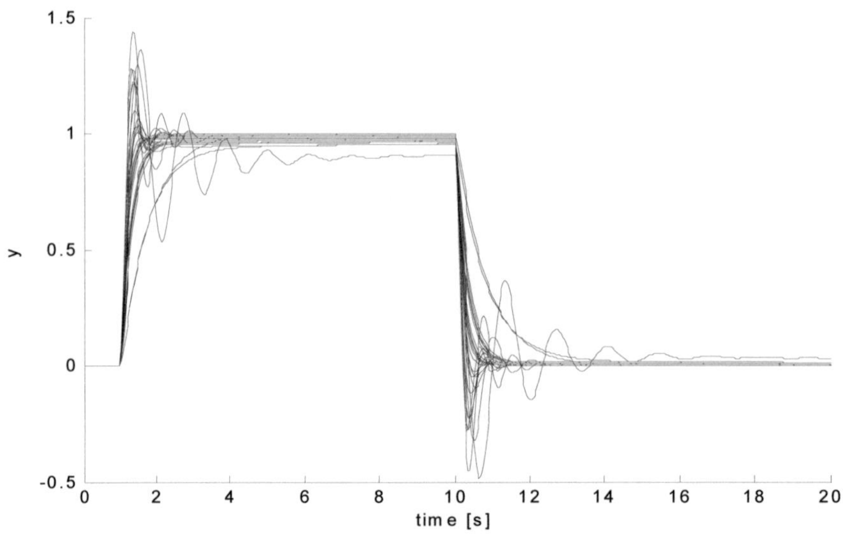

Fig. 17. Closed-loop time responses of 25 test systems for Method 4

4. Multi-objective controller design

4.1 Design principle

In solving many practical design problems not just a single optimisation objective is considered. Moreover, the particular objectives are in contradiction (e.g. performance vs. energy consumption, etc.). A common way of solving multi-objective tasks is using a single cost function consisting of multiple parts

$$J = w_1 f_1 + w_2 f_2 + \ldots + w_n f_n \tag{16}$$

where each part f_i, $i = 1, ..., n$ represents an objective with some weight w_i. The main disadvantage of this method is the high sensitivity of the solution to the weight coefficients. This can lead to solutions, which do not correspond to our primary requirements.

Another way for solving multi-objective problems is the use of the Dominance principle, which is the search for the Pareto-optimal set of solutions. This is an effective way to overcome the above mentioned problem. Several authors have used this approach in solving various multi-objective problems e.g. (Corne et al., 2000; Fleming & Purshouse; Zitzler & Thiele, 1998). Consider minimisation problem. According to the Dominance principle the individual x dominates the individual y (or the individual y is dominated by the individual x) if

$$\begin{aligned} &\forall i = 1,2,...,n\,;\; f_i(x) \le f_i(y) \text{ and} \\ &\exists j; j \in \{1,2,...,n\}\,;\; f_j(x) < f_j(y) \end{aligned} \tag{17}$$

where n is the number of objectives and f_i, $i=1,2,...,n$ is the cost function corresponding to the i-th objective. In case of maximisation tasks the formulation is analogical. A set of individuals, which are non-dominated by another individual are members of the Pareto-optimal set of solutions.

Now, the objective is not to find a single solution, but as much as possible non-dominated solutions, for which it is not possible to decide, which one is better. Each user will select the individual, which is the best with respect to his requirements. Based on the above approach the search algorithm is as follows:

1. Generating of the initial population.
2. Calculation of all objective functions for each individual of the population.
3. Domination calculation: each individual of the population will obtain such a number of "penalty points", which corresponds to the number of individuals by which it is dominated. The number of penalty points represents the final minimised cost function.
4. Individuals with zero penalty points are stored in the current group of non-dominated individuals.
5. Calculation of the new population (selection, crossover, mutation).
6. Adding the current non-dominated group to the new population.
7. Testing of terminating conditions, jump to Step 2 or end.

In case of controller design applications various objectives can be considered: integral performance indices (as in section 2), settling time, maximum overshoot, oscillation damping, various stability measures, gain/phase margin, energy consumption, other economic aspects, minimisation of negative environmental impacts of the controlled process operation, etc.

4.2 Case study

Consider the design of a DC motor speed controller. The objectives are short settling time and, on the other hand, low control energy consumption. To fulfil the first objective let us minimise the simple integral criterion (1).

The second objective can be represented by minimisation of the integral of the input motor voltage square, which is proportional to the input energy consumption

$$J_2 = \int_0^T u^2(t)dt \tag{18}$$

The results obtained using the algorithm described in the section 4 are depicted in Fig.18 (J_2 versus J_1). Individuals, which have occurred during the GA run are marked by "x". The non-dominated solutions from the last generation are in the left bottom part of the area marked with "o". Detail of the non-dominated set is also depicted in Fig.19. The individual marked "*Min(J1)*" represents the solution with the best performance with respect to the objective J_1 and the individual marked "*Min(J2)*" represents the best solution with respect to the objective J_2. The individual marked "*Compromise*" is a selected trade off between the both previous extremes. Step responses for all three mentioned solutions are depicted in Fig.20 and Fig.21.

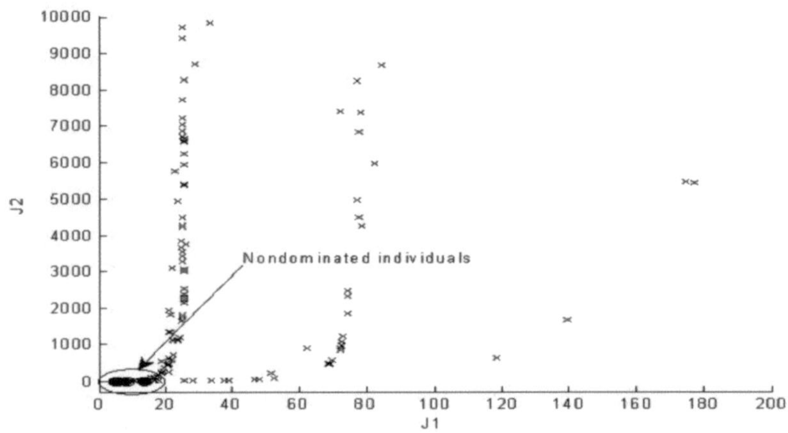

Fig. 18. Individuals occurred during the multi-objective evolution

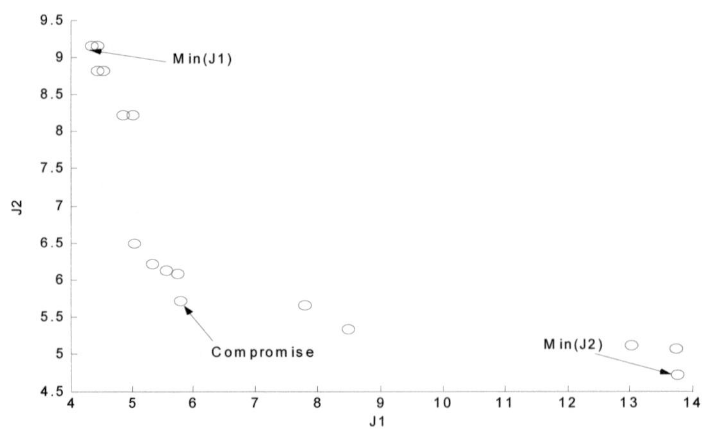

Fig. 19. Set of non-dominated individuals (Pareto-optimal set) - detail of Fig.18

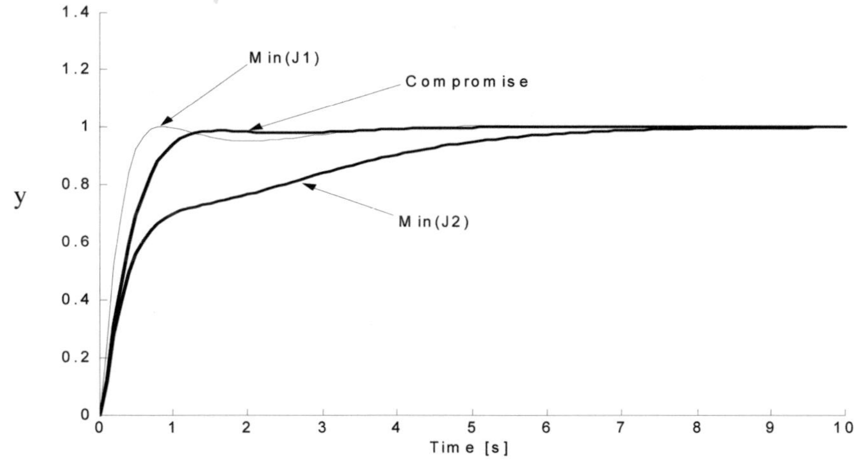

Fig. 20. Time-responses of three selected individuals

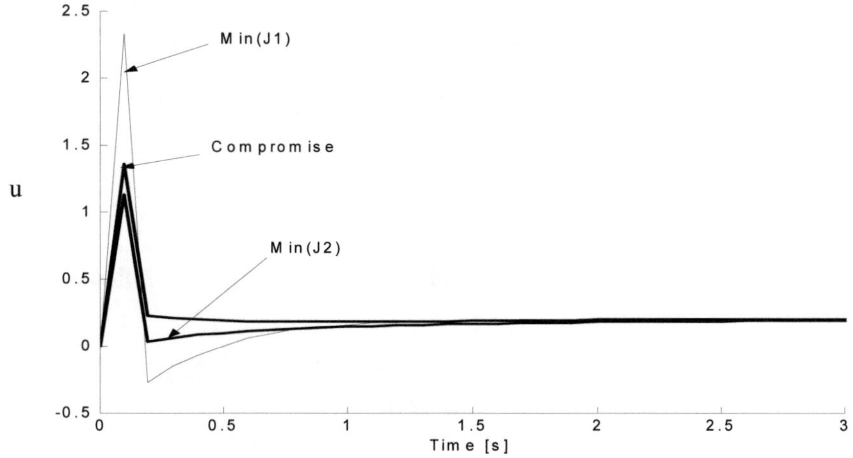

Fig. 21. Control variable time-responses of the three selected individuals

5. Controller internal structure design

In the previous parts the design goal was the optimisation of defined controller parameters. In this section also the internal structure of the controller is designed/optimised. Because the structure of the controller is unknown, also the number of its parameters is not defined. From that reason, the length of the chromosome is changing. For such a task the Genetic Programming has been used (Koza, 1992; Banzhaf et al., 1999). Next two various approaches are proposed (Sekaj et al., 2005; Sekaj & Perkacz, 2007) . In the first approach a discrete-time recurrent control algorithm is considered. In the second an interconnected network of elementary dynamic and static building blocks are used for a controller design.

5.1 Discrete-time controller algorithm design

In this proposed approach a discrete-time recurrent control algorithm has been designed as function of defined time-delayed input variables (Sekaj et al., 2005). The following variables have been considered: *e(k), e(k-1), ..., e(k-m), y(k), y(k-1), ..., y(k-n), u(k-1), u(k-2), ..., u(k-p), r(k),* where *e* is the control error, *y* is the controlled output, *u* is control value and *k* is the control step. The aim is to find the optimal form of the controller function

$$F(\theta)=? \qquad \theta=\{e(k),\ldots,\ e(k-m),\ y(k),\ldots,\ y(k-n),\ u(k-1),\ldots,\ u(k-p),r(k),c\} \tag{19}$$

such that the cost function (2) is minimised, where *c* are real constants. For the representation of the function *F* the in GP commonly used tree representation has been used. The functional nodes contain operations +, -, * and the terminating nodes include operation arguments from the vector θ. An example of such a tree is in Fig. 22.

Following genetic operations have been applied to modify the tree-represented individuals. The first one is the crossover, which is the exchange of randomly selected sub-trees in two parent trees (see Fig. 23a). From the mutation operators (unary operations) the following have been used: replacement of a randomly selected sub-tree by another randomly generated sub-tree, removal of a randomly selected sub-tree or addition of a randomly generated sub-tree (see Fig. 23b). The last mutation type is the mutation of a terminating node, which is a random change of a constant (or a variable) to another value or another variable.

Let us demonstrate the design approach on a controller design for a simple oscillatory linear system with the transfer function

$$G(s)=\frac{1}{s^2+0.001s+1} \tag{20}$$

The cost function in form (2) has been used. After 3000 generations the following recurrent control algorithm has been obtained

$$u(k) = 6.74([y(k) - y(k-2) - e(k)][e(k-2) -10.88]\ [23.25+ y(k-1) + y(k-2)]) - -87.82e(k-2)\ [9.33 + y(k-2)]+ y(k) + e(k) - e(k-1) \tag{21}$$

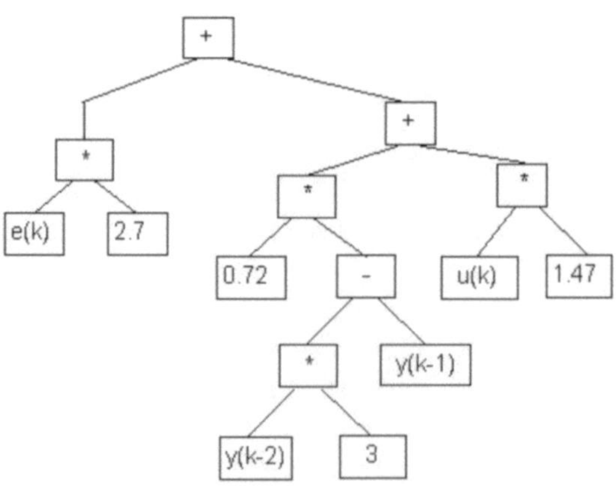

Fig. 22. Example of a controller function tree representation

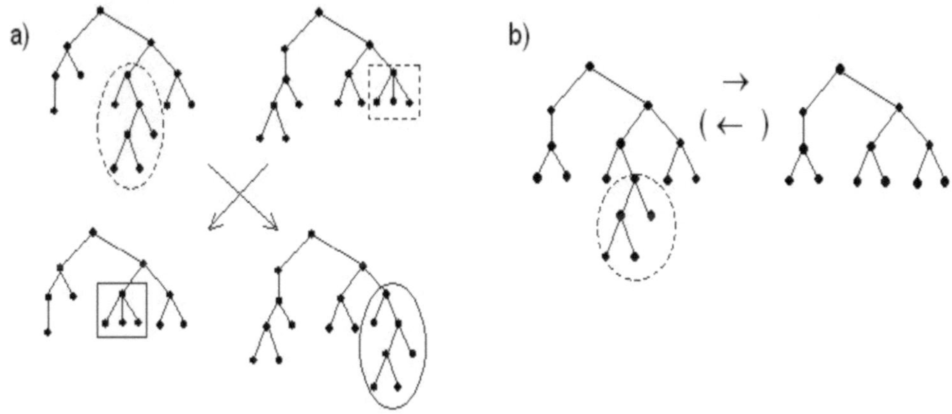

Fig. 23. a) crossover of two trees, b) mutation by removing (adding) of a sub-tree

In Fig. 24 the closed-loop response under the obtained solution after a reference signal step and an external disturbance is compared with a time response under a PID designed using GA with the same cost function.

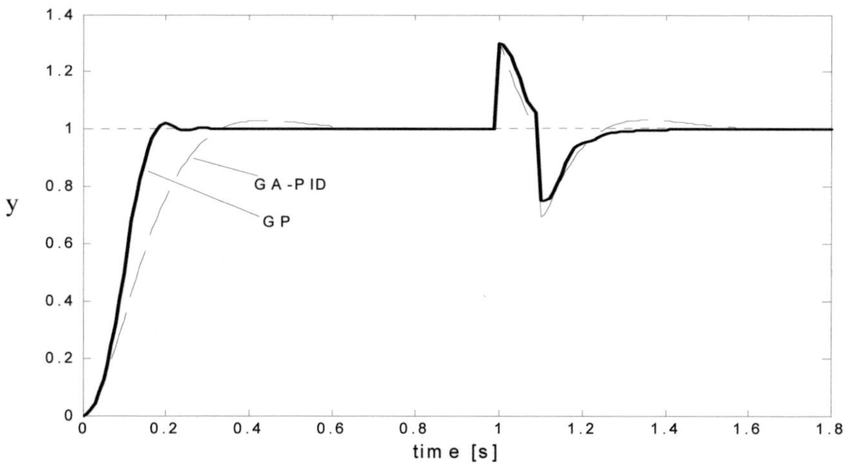

Fig. 24. Time responses with GP and GA designed controllers

5.2 Interconnected controller network

This controller representation is based on an interconnected network, which consists of the following elementary continuous-time dynamic/static function blocks: integrator, derivative unit, amplifier (multiplication by a constant) and a summation/multiplication unit (see Fig. 25) where *A*, *B* and *D* are real constants (Sekaj & Perkacz, 2007). The objective is to find the optimal control network consisting of such elementary function blocks and their interconnections, which minimises the cost function (1) or (2).

To represent each potential solution the following table or matrix format of a chromosome has been used (see example in Table 2). Each column represents one of the above-mentioned blocks. The second row includes the type of each block (Mul-multiplication, Sum-

summation, Der-derivative, Int-integral). The third row contains the number of the next block connected to its output. The number *0* indicates the controller output. The fourth row indicates the number of the previous block or signal connected to the block input. Negative numbers indicate the controller input signals, positive numbers are function blocks. It is possible to reduce the coding algorithm in such a way, that for each block it is sufficient to use only one input and one output. The last row contains a multiplicative constant of each block. Summation blocks need not be present in the table. For demonstration of the coding mechanism, the genotype in Table 2 corresponds to the controller in Fig. 26. In our case *-1* represents the control error signal *e*.

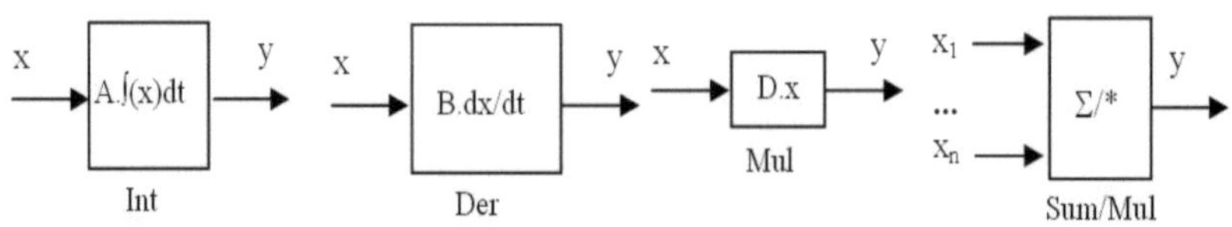

Fig. 25. Library of the used elementary function blocks

block	1	2	3	4	5
attribute	Mul	Mul	Der	Mul	Mul
	0	0	2	0	0
	-1	3	-1	-1	4
	36.92	3.57	31.96	36.08	21.54

Table 2. Chromosome representation

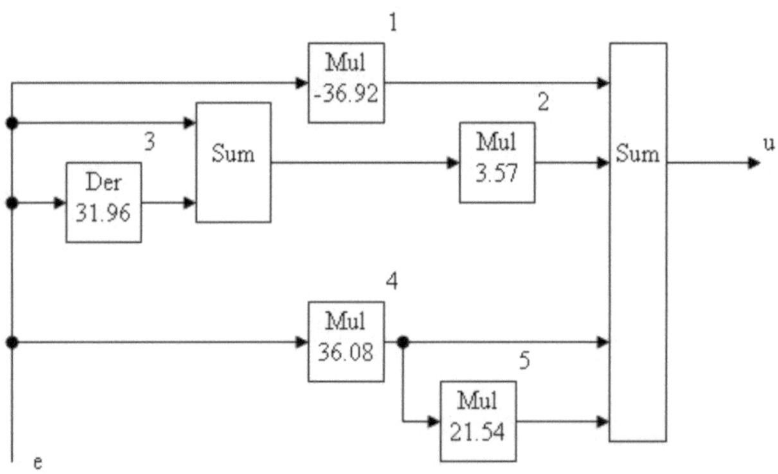

Fig. 26. Controller network example

Specialised crossover and mutation operators have been programmed to modify chromosomes. In case of crossover, two selected parent chromosomes are divided, both in random positions between two columns of the table, and then their appropriate parts are exchanged. For mutation the following operations have been used: the first is the random change of the block type, i.e. a block (for example integrator) is modified to another block type (e.g. a derivative unit). A next mutation type is the random deletion or addition of a block in the scheme. The last used mutation type is the random change of a constant, which

is a part of each block type. After each modification some connections may be missing or excessive. Therefore, the unnecessary ones are removed or the new ones are randomly added and connected to randomly selected points.
The design approach has been verified on the controller design for the linear dynamic system

$$G(s) = \frac{s^2 + 3s + 1}{4s^5 + 8s^4 + 10s^3 + 6s^2 + 3s + 1} \tag{22}$$

The objective was to minimise the performance index (2). The designed controller structure which was obtained after 3000 generations with the population size 80 individuals, mutation rate 0.3 and the crossover rate 0.3 is in Fig. 27. The closed-loop response of the obtained controller (GP) to the reference signal is in Fig. 28 compared with PID controller, which was optimised using GA (GA-PID, according section 2).

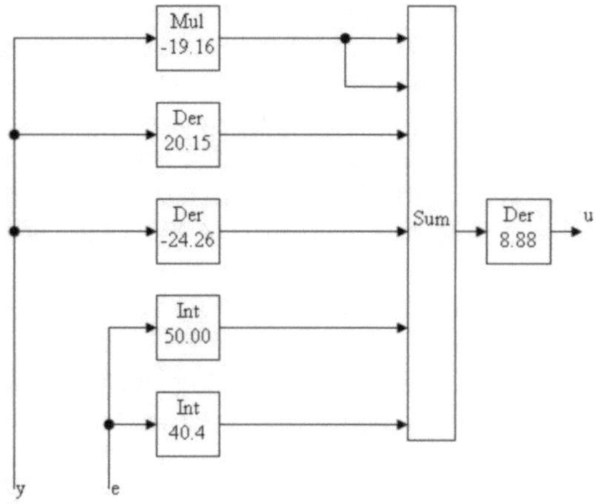

Fig. 27. Controller structure

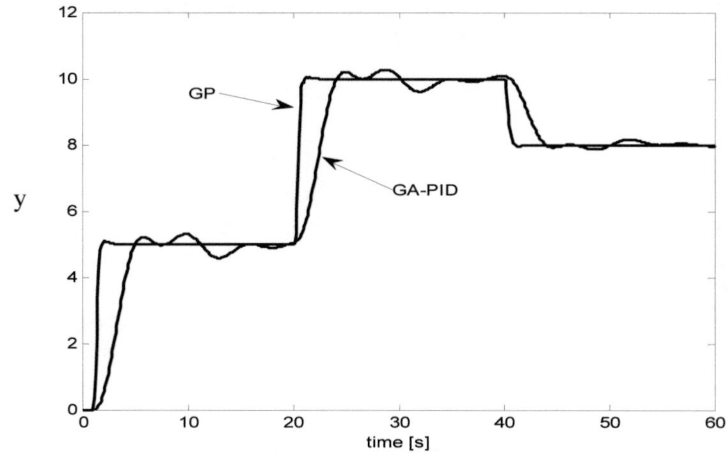

Fig. 28. Time response of the designed controller for reference signal steps from the value 0 to 5, 10 and 8

6. Conclusion

In this chapter evolutionary based design/optimisation approaches has been proposed for controller design of continuous-time process control. Parameters of controllers with fixed defined internal structure are designed as well as controllers with a-priori unknown internal structure and its parameters. The presented approaches minimise a cost function, which comprises closed-loop system simulation and performance index evaluation. In this way the controller design is transformed into a search problem in the n-dimensional parameter space.

The design/optimisation can be carried out for complex systems and control structures of various types. The main and practically the only limitation of the approach is the time-consuming computation (compared with conventional approaches) due to thousands up to ten thousands closed-loop simulations needed by each design procedure. From the point of view the user, on the other hand, the design method is simple to use. It transfers the design effort from the experienced human designer to the computer.

The design approach is simple to extend to robust controller design, for which two different methods have been proposed. In addition statistical robustness measure has been introduced, which can be considered as an objective tool for robust controller performance comparison. Next, the design idea has been extended also to a multi-objective design task, where the objective is the search for the Pareto-optimal set of solutions. From these solutions the designer can choose the representative, which is the most appropriate in the particular case.

Finally the design goal was extended from a fix defined controller structure with unknown controller parameters to the search/optimisation of the unknown internal structure of the controller. From that reason, the Genetic Programming has been used.

The proposed evolutionary-based methods can be used for design of various types of controllers for various system types (linear, non-linear, stable, unstable, SISO and MIMO, fuzzy, neural, etc.). The only condition of this approach is that there exists a simulation model of the designed closed-loop.

In the future, this design approach will be extended for solving very complex design tasks in the process control area like complex MIMO control systems for non-linear continuous-time systems and for robotic applications using parallel evolutionary algorithms.

7. References

Banzhaf, W.; Nordin, P.; Keller, R. E.; Francone, F. D. (1999). *Genetic Programming: An introduction,* Morgan Kaufmann, San Francisco

Corne, D.W.; Knowles, J.D.; Oates, M.J. (2000). Pareto Enveloped-based Selection Algorithm, In: *Proceedings of the Conference Parallel Problem Solving from Nature VI,* Springer, pp. 839-848

Dorf, R. C. (1990). *Modern Control Systems,* Addison-Wesley publishing Company, 5th edition

Eiben, A. E.; Smith, J. E. (2003). *Introduction to Evolutionary Computing,* Springer

Fleming, P. J.; Purshouse, R. C. Evolutionary Algorithms in Control System Engineering: A Survey, In: *Control Engineering Practice,* 10(11), 1223

Fonseca, C.M.; Fleming, P. J. (1993). Genetic Algorithms for Multiobjective Optimisation: Formulation, Discussion and Generalisation, In: *Proceedings of the Conference on Genetic Algorithms,* San Mateo, CA, Morgan Kaufmann

Goldberg, D. E. (1989). *Genetic Algorithms in Search, Optimisation and Machine Learning*, Addisson-Wesley

Grosman, B.; Lewin, D.R. (2005). Automatic Generation of Lyapunow Functions Using Genetic Programming, In: *16th World Congress of IFAC*, Prague, July 3-8

Herrero, J.M.; Blasco, X.; Martínez, M.; Salcedo, J.V. (2002). Optimal PID Tuning with Genetic Algorithms for Non Linear Process Models, In: *Proceedings on the 15th World Congress of IFAC*, Barcelona, July 21-26

Kawabe, T.; Tagami, T.; Katayama, T. (1996). A Genetic Algorithm based Minimax Optimal Design of Robust I-PD Controller, In: *UKACC Int. Conference on Control '96*, Conf. Publication No. 427, IEE, pp.436-441

Khatib, W.; Silva, V.; Chipperfield, A.; Fleming, P. (1999). Multidisciplinary Optimisation With Evolutionary Computing for Control Design, In: *Proceedings on the 14th World Congress of IFAC*, Beijing, July 5-9

Koza, J.R. (1992). *Genetic Programming*, Cambridge, MA, MIT Press

Koza, J.R.; Yu, J.; Keane, M.A.; Mydlowec, W. (2000). Evolution of a controller with a free variable using genetic programming. In: *Proceedings on the European Conference EuroGP 2000*, Edinburgh, Scotland, UK, Lecture Notes in Computer Science, Volume 1802. Berlin, Germany: Springer-Verlag, pp. 91–105, ISBN 3-540-67339-3, April 2000

Krohling, R.A.; Rey, J.P. (2001). Design of Optimal Disturbance Rejection PID Controllers Using Genetic Algorithms, In: *IEEE Trans. On Evolutionary Computation*, Vol.5, No.1

Kuo, B.C. (1991). *Automatic Control Systems*, Prentice-Hall International Editions

Lewin, D.R. (2005). Evolutionary Algorithms in Control System Engineering, In: *Proceedings on the 16th World Congress of IFAC*, July 3-8, Prague

Man, K.F.; Tang, K.S.; Kwong , S. (2001). *Genetic Algorithms, Concepts and Deign*, Springer

Michalewicz, Z. (1996). *Genetic Algorithms + Data Structures = Evolutionary Programs*, Springer

Mitsukura, Y.; Yamamoto, T.; Kaneda, M.; Fujii, K. (1999). Evolutionary Computation in Designing a PID Control System, In: *Proceedings on the 14th IFAC World Congress*, Beijing, 5-9 july, P.R.China, pp. 497-502

Molina-Cristóbal, A.; Griffin, I.A.; Fleming, P.J.; Owens, D.H. (2005). Multiobjective Controller Design: Optimising Controller Structure with GA, In: *Proceedings on the 16th World Congress of IFAC*, July 3-8, Prague

Oldenburg, L.C.; Sartorius, H. (1956). A uniform approach to the optimum adjustments of control loops, *Frequency response*, The MacMillan Co., N.Y.

Rivera, D.E.; Morari, M.; Skogestad, S. (1986). Internal model control for PID controller design, In: *Ind. Eng. Chem. Res. 25* (1), pp. 252–265

Sekaj, I. (1999). Genetic Algorithm-based Control System Design and System Identification, In: *Proceedings on the Int. Conference Mendel'99*, June 9-12, Brno, Czech Republic, pp.139-144

Sekaj, I.; Foltin, M.; Gonos, M. (2002). Genetic Algorithm Based Adaptive Control of an Electromechanical MIMO System, In: *Proceedings of the GECCO Conference*, July 9-13, New York, pp. 696

Sekaj, I.; Veselý, V. (2005). Robust output feedback controller design: genetic algorithm approach, In: *IMA Journal of Mathematical Control and Information*, 22, pp. 257-263

Sekaj, I. (2003). Genetic Algorithm Based Controller Design, In: *2nd IFAC conference Control System Design'03*, Bratislava, Slovak Republic, September 7-10

Sekaj, I.; Perkácz, J.; Nídel, M. (2005). Controller design based on genetic programming, In: *Proceedings of the Int. conference Mendel'05*, Brno, Czech Republic, June 15-17

Sekaj, I.; Šrámek, M. (2005). Robust Controller Design Based on Genetic Algorithms and System Simulation, In: *Proceedings on the conference CDC-ECC'05*, Seville, Spain, December 12-15

Sekaj, I.; Perkácz, J. (2007). Genetic Programming Based Controller Design, In: *Proceedings of the IEEE Congress on Evolutionary Computation'07*, Singapore, September 25-28Sweriduk, G.D.; Menon, P.K.; Steinberg, M.L. (1999). Design of a pilot-activated recovery system using genetic search methods, In: *Optimal Synthesis*

Yang, Z.Y.; Chan, C.W.; Xue, M.S.; Luo, G.J. (2005). On-line Temperature Control of an Oven Based on Genetic Algorithms, In: *Proceedings on the 16th World Congress of IFAC*, Prague, July 3-8

Zitzler, E.; Thiele, L. (1998). Strength Pareto Evolutionary Algorithm, In: *Technical Report 43, Computer Engineering and Communication Networks Lab (TIK)*, Swiss Federal Institute of Technology (ETH), Zurich, Switzerland, May 1998

14

Backbone Guided Local Search for the Weighted Maximum Satisfiability Problem

He Jiang and Jifeng Xuan
School of Software, Dalian University of Technology
P.R. China

1. Introduction

The Satisfiability problem (SAT) is a famous NP-Complete problem, which consists of an assignment of Boolean variables (true or false) and some clauses formed of these variables. A clause is a disjunction of some Boolean literals and can be true if and only if any of them is true. A SAT instance is satisfied if and only if all the clauses are simultaneously true. As a generalization of SAT, the Maximum Satisfiability problem (MAX-SAT) aims to maximize the number of satisfied clauses. When every clause is associated with some weight, the MAX-SAT turns to the weighted Maximum Satisfiability problem (weighted MAX-SAT) with numerous applications arising in artificial intelligence, such as scheduling, data mining, pattern recognition, and automatic reasoning. According to the computational complexity theory, there's no polynomial time algorithm for solving weighted MAX-SAT unless $P = NP$. Hence, many heuristic algorithms capable of finding near optimal solutions in reasonable time have been proposed for weighted MAX-SAT, including GSAT, GLS, Taboo Scatter Search, ACO, and GRASP/GRASP with path-relinking.

As an efficient tool for heuristic design, the backbone has attracted great attention from the society of artificial intelligence in recent years. The backbone is defined as the common parts of all optimal solutions for an instance. Since it's usually intractable to obtain the exact backbone, many approximate backbone guided heuristics have been developed for NP-Complete problems, including 3-SAT, TSP, QAP, et al. For SAT or MAX-SAT, some character and algorithms of backbone are in research. And a BGWalksat (backbone guided local search algorithm with Walksat operator) has been developed for MAX-SAT and achieves better performance than existing heuristics. However, as to our knowledge, there is no theoretical result or backbone guided heuristics reported in the literature for weighted MAX-SAT.

In this chapter we investigated the computational complexity of the backbone for weighted MAX-SAT and developed a backbone guided local search (BGLS) algorithm. Firstly, we proved that there's no polynomial time algorithm to retrieve the full backbone under the assumption that $P \neq NP$. In the proof, we mapped any weighted MAX-SAT instance to a biased weighted MAX-SAT instance with a unique optimal solution by slightly perturbing, which is also optimal to the original instance. Based on this proof, we indicated that it's also intractable to retrieve a fixed fraction of the backbone, by reducing any weighted MAX-SAT instance to a series of weighted MAX-SAT instances with smaller scale. Secondly, we developed a backbone guided local search algorithm with pseudo-backbone frequencies. It consists of two phases: the sampling phase records local optima to compute pseudo-backbone frequencies and the backbone phase uses such information to guide the following local search. Experimental results demonstrated that BGLS obtained better solutions than GRASP/ GRASP with path-relinking in far less time.

2. Preliminaries

In this section, we shall give some definitions and related properties.

Definition 1. Given a set of Boolean variables $V=\{x_1,x_2,\cdots,x_n\}$, a propositional formula ϕ is a conjunction on a set of m clauses $C=\{C_1,C_2,\cdots,C_m\}$. Each clause C_i is a disjunction of $|C_i|$ literals, where each literal l_{ij} is either a variable or its negation. A clause is satisfied if at least one of its literals evaluates to true, and the propositional formula ϕ is said to be satisfied if all of its clauses are satisfied. The satisfiability problem (SAT) aims to find an assignment of values to the variables such that a given propositional formula ϕ is satisfied. Formally, a SAT instance on the set of Boolean variables V and the set of clauses C can be denoted as $SAT(V,C)$.

Definition 2. Given a set of Boolean variables $V=\{x_1,x_2,\cdots,x_n\}$, a propositional weighted formula ϕ is a conjunction on a set of m weighted clauses $C=\{C_1,C_2,\cdots,C_m\}$. Each weighted clause is associated with a positive weight $w(\tilde{C}_i)$. The weighted maximum satisfiability problem (weighted MAX-SAT) consists of finding an assignment of values to the variables such that the sum of the weights of the satisfied clauses is maximized. Similar to the SAT, a weighted MAX-SAT instance can be denoted as $wMAX-SAT(V,C)$ and a solution (assignment) can be denoted as

$$s=\{x_i\,|\,x_i \text{ is assigned true}\}\cup\{\neg x_i\,|\,x_i \text{ is assigned false}\}$$

with cost function $w(V,\tilde{C},s)=\sum_{\tilde{C}_i\in\tilde{C}} w(\tilde{C}_i)[\tilde{C}_i \text{ is satified by s}]$, where $[\bullet]=1$ (0) for $\bullet$ being true (false).

Without loss of generality, we shall assume in the following part of this paper, that the weight $w(\tilde{C}_i)$ is a positive integer for each clause $\tilde{C}_i$.

Definition 3. Given a weighted MAX-SAT instance $wMAX-SAT(V,C)$, let $\Pi^*=\{s_1^*,s_2^*,...,s_q^*\}$ be the set of all optimal solutions to it, where $q=|\Pi^*|$ represents the number of optimal solutions. Backbone in weighted MAX-SAT instance $wMAX-SAT(V,C)$ is defined as $bone(V,\tilde{C})=s_1^*\cap s_2^*\cap\cdots\cap s_q^*$.

The backbone $bone(V,\tilde{C})$ is essential for heuristic algorithms design, since a heuristic cannot obtain an optimal solution to a weighted MAX-SAT instance unless it retrieves the full backbone. In contrast, if the backbone $bone(V,\tilde{C})$ is retrieved, the search space could then be effectively reduced by assigning literals in the backbone to true.

In Definition 4, we shall introduce the definition of the biased weighted MAX-SAT instance, which will be used in the following proof.

Definition 4. Given a weighted MAX-SAT instance $wMAX-SAT(V,\tilde{C})$, the biased weighted MAX-SAT instance is defined as $wMAX-SAT(V,C)$, where $\bar{C}=\tilde{C}\cup\{x_i,\neg x_i\,|\,x_i\in V\}$ and the weight associated with every clause $\bar{C}_i\in\bar{C}$ is defined as follows.

1. $\overline{w}(\overline{C}_i) = w(\overline{C}_i)$, if $\overline{C}_i \in \tilde{C}$ and $\overline{C}_i \notin \{x_j, \neg x_j | x_j \in V\}$;
2. $\overline{w}(\overline{C}_i) = w(\overline{C}_i) + 1/2^{2j}$, if $\overline{C}_i = x_j \in \tilde{C}, x_j \in V$;
3. $\overline{w}(\overline{C}_i) = w(\overline{C}_i) + 1/2^{2j+1}$, if $\overline{C}_i = \neg x_j \in \tilde{C}, x_j \in V$;
4. $\overline{w}(\overline{C}_i) = 1/2^{2j}$, if $\overline{C}_i = x_j \notin \tilde{C}, x_j \in V$;
5. $\overline{w}(\overline{C}_i) = 1/2^{2j+1}$, if $\overline{C}_i = \neg x_j \notin \tilde{C}, x_j \in V$.

Given a weighted MAX-SAT instance, it is easy to verify that the following property holds: $\sum_{\overline{C}_i \in \overline{C}} \overline{w}(\overline{C}_i) = \sum_{\tilde{C}_i \in \tilde{C}} w(\tilde{C}_i) + 1/2^2 + 1/2^3 + \cdots + 1/2^{2n+1} = \sum_{\tilde{C}_i \in \tilde{C}} w(\tilde{C}_i) + 1/2 - 1/2^{2n+1}$.

3. Computational complexity for backbone

3.1 Weighted MAX-SAT and biased weighted MAX-SAT

In this section, we shall investigate the relationship between the solution of a weighted MAX-SAT instance and that of the biased weighted MAX-SAT instance in Lemma 1 and Lemma 2.

Lemma 1. Given the set of Boolean variables V and the set of weighted clauses $\tilde{C}$, there exists a unique optimal solution to the biased weighted MAX-SAT instance $wMAX-SAT(V,C)$.

Proof. Given any two distinct solutions s_1, s_2 to the biased weighted MAX-SAT instance $wMAX-SAT(V,\overline{C})$, we will show that $w(V,\overline{C},s_1) \neq w(V,\overline{C},s_2)$.

Firstly, we construct a weighted MAX-SAT instance $wMAX-SAT(V,\{x_i,\neg x_i | x_i \in V\})$ where $w(x_i) = 1/2^{2i}, w(\neg x_i) = 1/2^{2i+1}$ for $x_i \in V$. We have that

$$w(V,\overline{C},s_1) = w(V,\tilde{C},s_1) + w(V,\{x_i,\neg x_i | x_i \in V\},s_1).$$

Since the weight $w(\tilde{C}_i)$ is a positive integer for each clause $\tilde{C}_i \in \tilde{C}$, thus $w(V,\tilde{C},s_1)$ must be the integer part of $w(V,\overline{C},s_1)$ and $w(V,\{x_i,\neg x_i | x_i \in V\},s_1)$ must be the fractional part of $w(V,\overline{C},s_1)$. Similarly, $w(V,\{x_i,\neg x_i | x_i \in V\},s_2)$ must be also the fractional part of $w(V,\overline{C},s_2)$. By assumption that $s_1 \neq s_2$, there must exist a variable $x_j \in V$ such that $x_j \in s_1 \cup s_2$ and $x_j \notin s_1 \cap s_2$. In the following proof, we only consider the case that $x_j \in s_1$, $\neg x_j \in s_2$. For the case that $\neg x_j \in s_1$ and $x_j \in s_2$, it can be proved in a similar way.

Obviously, the clause x_j can be satisfied by s_1, while it cannot be satisfied by s_2. When viewed as binary encoded strings, the $2j$ th bit of the fractional part of $w(V,\overline{C},s_1)$ will be 1, however the same bit of $w(V,\overline{C},s_2)$ will be 0. Hence, we have that $w(V,\overline{C},s_1) \neq w(V,\overline{C},s_2)$. Thus, this lemma is proved. □

Lemma 2. Given the set of Boolean variables V and the set of weighted clauses $\tilde{C}$, if s^* is the unique optimal solution to the biased weighted MAX-SAT instance $wMAX-SAT(V,C)$, then s^* is also optimal to weighted MAX-SAT instance $wMAX-SAT(V,C)$.

Proof. Otherwise, there must exist a solution s to the $wMAX-SAT(V,\tilde{C})$ such that $w(V,\tilde{C},s) > w(V,\tilde{C},s^*)$. By assumption that the weight $w(\tilde{C}_i)$ is a positive integer for each clause $\tilde{C}_i \in \tilde{C}$, thus we have $w(V,\tilde{C},s) \geq w(V,\tilde{C},s^*) + 1$. Since $w(V,\overline{C},s) = w(V,\tilde{C},s) + w(V,\{x_i,\neg x_i | x_i \in V\},s)$, we have that $w(V,\overline{C},s) < w(V,\tilde{C},s) + 1/2 - 1/2^{2n+1}$. Similarly, $w(V,\overline{C},s^*) < w(V,\tilde{C},s^*) + 1/2 - 1/2^{2n+1}$. It implies that

$w(V,\bar{C},s) > w(V,\tilde{C},s) \geq w(V,\tilde{C},s^*)+1 > w(V,\bar{C},s^*)$, which contradicts with the assumption that s^* is the unique optimal solution to the $wMAX-SAT(V,\bar{C})$. Thus, this lemma is proved. □

3.2 Computational complexity for retrieving backbone

In Theorem 1, we shall show the intractability for retrieving the full backbone in weighted MAX-SAT. In addition, we shall present a stronger analytical result in Theorem 2 that it's NP-hard to retrieve a fixed fraction of the backbone.

Theorem 1. There exists no polynomial time algorithm to retrieve the backbone in weighted MAX-SAT unless $P = NP$.

Proof. Otherwise, there must exist an algorithm denoted by Λ which is able to retrieve the backbone in weighted MAX-SAT in polynomial time.

Given any arbitrary weighted MAX-SAT instance $wMAX-SAT(V,C)$, the biased weighted MAX-SAT instance $wMAX-SAT(V,\bar{C})$ can be constructed by an algorithm denoted by Γ in $O(n)$ time.

Since the $wMAX-SAT(V,C)$ is also a weighted MAX-SAT instance, its backbone $bone(V,\bar{C})$ can be computed by Λ in polynomial time (denoted by $O(\bullet)$). By Lemma 1, the backbone is the unique optimal solution to the $wMAX-SAT(V,\bar{C})$. By Lemm2, the $bone(V,\bar{C})$ is an optimal solution to the $wMAX-SAT(V,\tilde{C})$ as well.

Hence, any weighted MAX-SAT instance can be exactly solved in $O(n)+O(\bullet)$ time by Γ and Λ. Obviously, such conclusion contradicts with the result that weighted MAX-SAT is NP-hard. Thus, this theorem is proved. □

Theorem 2. There exists no polynomial time algorithm to retrieve a fixed fraction of the backbone in weighted MAX-SAT unless $P = NP$.

Proof. Otherwise, given any weighted MAX-SAT instance $wMAX-SAT(V,\tilde{C})$, we can always construct a biased weighted MAX-SAT instance $wMAX-SAT(V,\bar{C})$ according to Definition 4. As proven in Theorem 1, the backbone $bone(V,\bar{C})$ is an optimal solution to the $wMAX-SAT(V,\tilde{C})$.

If there exists a polynomial time algorithm Λ to retrieve a fixed fraction of the backbone, we can acquire at least one literal ℓ in the $bone(V,\bar{C})$. In the following proof, we only consider the case that $\ell = x_j$ ($x_j \in V$). For the case that $\ell = \neg x_j$ ($x_j \in V$), it can be proved in a similar way.

Let $\hat{C}$ be the set of those clauses containing $\neg x_j$, let $\hat{C}'$ be the set of the remaining parts of the clauses from $\hat{C}$ after deleting $\neg x_j$. Since $\ell = x_j$, we can construct a new smaller weighted MAX-SAT instance $wMAX-SAT(V \setminus \{x_j\},\tilde{C}')$, where $\tilde{C}' = \{\tilde{C}_i | \tilde{C}_i \in \tilde{C}, \tilde{C}_i \text{ contains no } x_j \text{ or } \neg x_j\} \cup \hat{C}'$.

By repeating such procedures, an optimal solution to $wMAX-SAT(V,\tilde{C})$ can be finally obtained literal by literal in polynomial time, a contradiction. Hence, this theorem is proven. □

4. Backbone guided local search

4.1 Framework of backbone guided local search

In this section, we shall present the framework of backbone guided local search (BGLS) for weighted MAX-SAT. In BGSL, the local search process is guided by the backbone frequency, a group of probabilities representing the times of solution elements appearing in global optima. Since it's NP-hard to retrieve the exact backbone, we shall use the pseudo-backbone frequency instead, which can be computed by the approximate backbone (the common parts of local optima).

The framework of BGLS consists of two phases. The first phase (sampling phase) collects the pseudo-backbone frequencies with traditional local search and the second one (backbone phase) obtains a solution with a backbone guided local search. Every run of local search is called a try. Each of two phases uses an input parameter to control the maximum tries of local search (see Algorithm 1).

```
Algorithm 1: BGLS for weighted MAX-SAT
Input: weighted MAX-SAT instance wMAX-SAT(V,C̃), n1, n2, a
        local search algorithm H
Output: solution s*
Begin
 //sampling phase
  1. w* = -∞
  2. for i=1 to n1 do
       2.1 obtain a solution si with H;
       2.2 sample backbone from si;
       2.3 if w(V,C̃,si) > w* then w* = w(V,C̃,si), s* = si;
  //backbone phase
  3. for i=1 to n2 do
    3.1 obtain a solution si with backbone guided H;
    3.2 if w(V,C̃,si) > w* then w* = w(V,C̃,si), s* = si;
  4. return s*;
End
```

Both of the two phases use the same local search algorithm. However, in the sampling phase, a particular step is used to sample backbone information from local optima. And the backbone phase uses this sampling to guide the following local search. Although many local search algorithms can be used as the algorithm H in Algorithm 1, we proposed an improved Walksat in practice which is originally designed for MAX-SAT. Thus, some necessary modifications should be conducted for adapting it to weighted MAX-SAT.

4.2 Walksat for weighted MAX-SAT

In Algorithm 2, we shall present the Walksat for weighted MAX-SAT. In contrast to Walksat for MAX-SAT, some greedy strategies have been added to Algorithm 2 to fit weighted MAX-SAT. A try of Walksat needs two parameters. One is maximum number of flips that change the value of variables from true to false or inversely. The process of Walksat seeks repeatedly for a variable and flips it. When a variable is flipped, its break-count is defined as the number of satisfied clauses becoming unsatisfied. Obviously, the value of break-count will be nonnegative. And a variable with a zero break-count means the solution will be no worse than that before flipping. The other parameter is the probability for noise pick, which is used for determining when to use noise pick.

The Walksat for weighted MAX-SAT works as follows. After an initial assignment is generated by random values, Walksat picks a clause (clause pick) from one of the unsatisfied clauses with maximum weight randomly. Then the algorithm flips one of variables of this clause under the following rules: if there're more than one variable of zero break-count, then flip one of them randomly, otherwise flip any of variables randomly with the probability parameter (noise pick). For the case that the probability is not satisfied, pick one variable with least break-count randomly (greedy pick). Because the diversity of solutions depends on the parameter for noise pick and the static setting of it cannot react to the solving process. So we choose a dynamic noise setting strategy (step 2.6) to set the parameter for noise pick: if the solution quality decreases, the noise parameter p will increase to $p+(1-p)\cdot\varphi$, otherwise p will decrease to $p-p\cdot\varphi/2$, where φ is a predefined constant number.

In summary, there're five random actions (in step 1, 2.1, 2.3, respectively) during the whole process of the Walksat for weighted MAX-SAT. And we'll modify them in the backbone phase of BGLS (see Section 4.4).

Algorithm 2: Walksat for weighted MAX-SAT

Input: weighted MAX-SAT instance $wMAX-SAT(V,\tilde{C})$, num, a probability for noise pick p

Output: solution s

Begin

1. let s be a random assignment of variables of V, $w'=w(V,\tilde{C},s)$;
2. for $i=1$ to $num-1$ do
    - 2.1 pick c, as one of the unsatisfied clauses with maximal weight, randomly;
    - 2.2 compute the break-count of all variables in c;
    - 2.3 if a zero break-count exists
        - then pick one variable of zero break-count in c, randomly;
        - else with a probability p, pick one of all variables in c, randomly;
            - and with a probability $1-p$, pick one variable of least break-count ones in c, randomly;
    - 2.4 flip this variable and obtain solution s';
    - 2.5 if $w(V,\tilde{C},s')>w'$ then $w'=w(V,\tilde{C},s'),s=s'$;
    - 2.6 adjust the value of p;
3. return s;

4.3 Pseudo-backbone frequencies sampling

Given a particular problem instance, the exact difference between local optima and global optima cannot be exactly predicted unless those solutions are found, due to the diversity of instances. In this subsection, we analyze some typical instances to investigate the difference. The distance between local optima and global optima is defined as the number of different value of variables. For comparison among different instances, this distance is normalized by the total number of variables.

The sampling algorithm for local optima is Walksat for weighted MAX-SAT, where maximum of flips num is set to be 200 and the noise probability p is set to be 0. For every instance, the sampling algorithm was run for 50 times and 50 local optima were generated. Fig. 1 shows the distances between local optima and global optima for four instances. The weight of solutions is plotted against the normalized distances to global optima. From Fig. 1, we can draw the conclusion that all the normalized distances between local optima and the global optimum are between 0.4 and 0.8. It implies that local optima and global optima have common values for most of variables. Thus, some approximate backbone can be retrieved to guide local search to find better solutions.

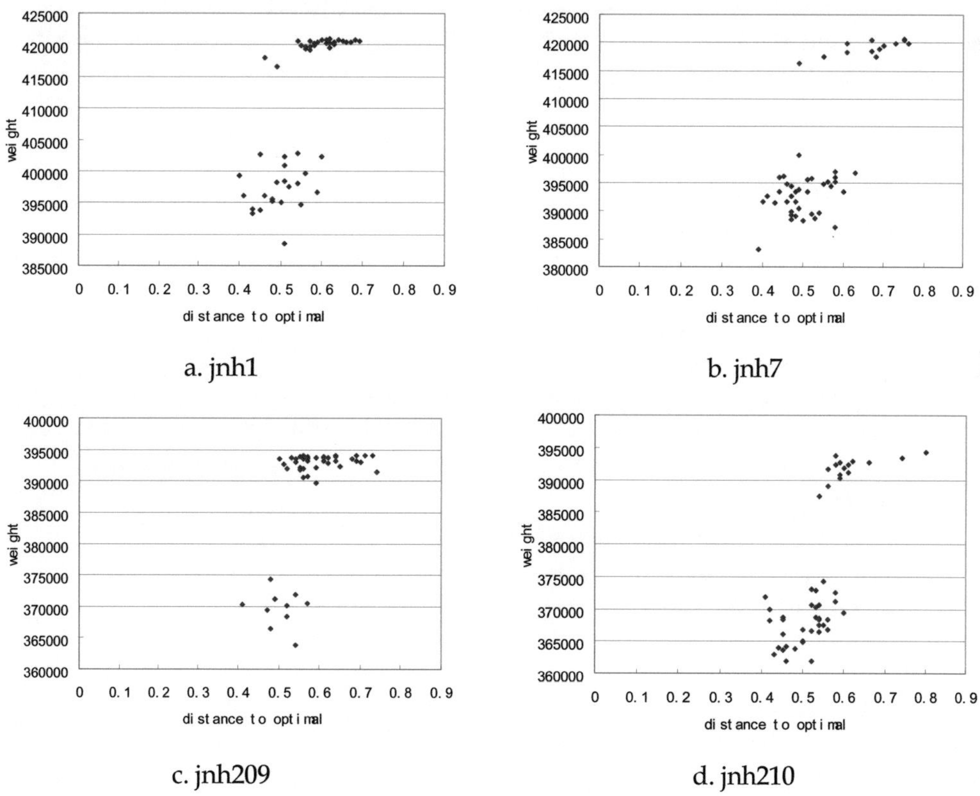

Fig. 1. Relationship between local optima and global optima for 4 typical instances

Furthermore, we recorded the number of every variable value in local optima and a probability of true or false being chosen for every variable can be computed. For every instance, we tested whether the variables in global optima tend to take the value with higher probability. And we found that more than 70% (74% for jnh1, 70% for jnh7, 73% for jnh209, and 73% for jnh210, respectively) of all variables in global optima take the values (true or false) with higher probabilities appearing in the local optima. It implies that a priority set of values can be made of those values with higher probability.

To guide the Walksat for weighted MAX-SAT, two forms of information should be recorded to construct the pseudo-backbone frequencies: the frequencies of variables and the frequencies of clauses. After obtaining any local optimum, the pseudo-backbone frequencies are updated. On one hand, the frequencies of variables record the times of the variable value appearing in local optima. On the other hand, the frequencies of clauses record the times of clauses being satisfied. The pseudo-backbone frequencies will be computed in the sampling phase (see Step 2.2 of Algorithm 1).

4.4 Backbone guided walksat for weighted MAX-SAT

As discussed in Section 3.2, there're five random actions in the Walksat. Instead of the traditional random choosing, we shall determine the variable values by the pseudo-backbone frequencies (see Algorithm 3).

Algorithm 3: Backbone guided Walksat for weighted MAX-SAT
Input: weighted MAX-SAT instance $wMAX-SAT(V,\tilde{C})$, num, a probability for noise pick p, pseudo-backbone frequencies F
Output: solution s
Begin
1. let s be a random assignment of variables of V, guided by F, $w' = w(V,\tilde{C},s)$;
2. for i=1 to $num-1$ do
    2.1 pick c from s as one of the unsatisfied clauses with maximum weight, guided by F;
    2.2 compute the break-count of all variables in c;
    2.3 if a zero break-count exists
        then pick one variable of zero break-count ones in c randomly, guided by F;
        else with a probability p, pick one of all variables in c randomly, guided by F; and with a probability $1-p$, pick one variable of least break-count ones in c, guided by F;
    2.4 flip this variable and obtain solution s';
    2.5 if $w(V,\tilde{C},s') > w'$ then $w' = w(V,\tilde{C},s'), s = s'$;
    2.6 adjust the value of p;
3. return s;
End

The first random action is an initial assignment generation in Step 1 of Algorithm 3. An initial value of a variable can be guided by the frequencies of the values. The second random is in Step 2.1. In pseudo-backbone, the frequencies of clauses satisfied in local optima have been recorded. According to this, the probability of each clause being satisfied can be computed to direct which clause should be firstly satisfied. And then Step 2.3 includes three remaining random choices. These three choices are similarly guided by the same approximate backbone as the first random and the probabilities will be computed under the same method as the second random.

5. Experimental results

In this section, we presented the experimental results for BGLS over weighted MAX-SAT benchmark. All the codes are implemented and compiled in C++ under a Pentium IV D 2.8GHz with 1GB memory. In the algorithm 1, 2 and 3, we have indicated 4 input parameters (the tries and maximum flips of two phases, respectively). In this experiment, we use identical parameters for both phases with 50 tries and 400 flips.

Since the best heuristics (GRASP/GRASP with path-relinking) for weighted MAX-SAT are tested on distinct experimental platforms, we conducted a system performance conversion according to SPEC. The system of GRASP with path-relinking is more than 15.69 times faster than ours (see Appendix) and only some of the instances' running time is available. Since there's no platform of R4400 in SPEC, we give no running time of GRASP on PD2.8G.

The problem instances of weighted MAX-SAT in the experiments include 44 instances, each of which has 100 variables and 800, 850 or 900 clauses, respectively. Tab. 1 shows the results of our experiments and the comparison with other algorithms. The column "Instance" indicates the input instances of benchmark and the column "Optima" shows the weight of global optima of instances. The following three columns "GRASP", "GRASP with path-relinking" and "BGLS" show the performance and results of the three algorithms, respectively. Each of them has sub-columns "weight" (the maximum weight obtained) and "time" (the time of running) for reporting the details. And the last column "Improvement" means the improvement of BGLS over GRASP, which is computed through dividing difference between the weight of BGLS and GRASP by the weight of global optima. A positive value means BGLS can obtain a better solution than GRASP, and vice verse.

From Tab.2, BGLS is more efficient than GRASP for nearly all the instances except instance "jnh208". The average of improvement is 0.0369%. For 19 instances out of 44, BGLS can always get global optima, however GRASP can get global optima for only 4 instances. And BGLS uses far less time than GRASP with path-relinking.

6. Conclusions

In this chapter, analytical results on the backbone in weighted MAX-SAT were presented in this paper. We showed that it is intractable to retrieve the backbone in weighted MAX-SAT with any performance guarantee under the assumption that $P \neq NP$. And a backbone guided local search algorithm was proposed for weighted MAX-SAT.

Results of this paper imply a new way to incorporate the backbone in heuristics. The approximate backbone used to guide the flipping of literals in those local search based heuristics. However, a multilevel strategy was introduced in the proof of Theorem 2. According to the proof, a new smaller weighted MAX-SAT instance could be constructed after a literal being fixed. By such a way, we can gradually reduce the original weighted MAX-SAT instance to a series of weighted MAX-SAT instances with less variables and clauses. Conversely, the solution to the original instance could be reconstructed with solutions of those reduced weighted MAX-SAT instances and fixed literals.

Instance	Optima	GRASP			GRASP with path-relinking			BGLS		Improvement
	weight	weight	time (seconds)		weight	time (seconds)		weight	time (seconds)	
			R4400	PD2.8G		Altix3700	PD2.8G		PD2.8G	
jnh1	420925	420737	192.1	-	420739	350	5491	420925	13	0.0447%
jnh4	420830	420615	467.9	-	-	-	-	420813	27	0.0470%
jnh5	420742	420488	30.9	-	-	-	-	420679	27	0.0454%
jnh6	420826	420816	504.2	-	-	-	-	420826	26	0.0024%
jnh7	420925	420925	188.1	-	-	-	-	420925	5	0.0000%
jnh8	420463	419885	546.4	-	-	-	-	420138	27	0.0602%
jnh9	420592	420078	41.2	-	-	-	-	420289	26	0.0502%
jnh10	420840	420565	591.1	-	420357	300	4707	420828	27	0.0625%
jnh11	420753	420642	757.4	-	420516	-	-	420672	26	0.0071%
jnh12	420925	420737	679.2	-	420871	-	-	420925	14	0.0447%
jnh13	420816	420533	12.9	-	-	-	-	420816	26	0.0673%
jnh14	420824	420510	197.7	-	-	-	-	420824	26	0.0746%
jnh15	420719	420360	424.6	-	-	-	-	420719	26	0.0853%
jnh16	420919	420851	392.8	-	-	-	-	420919	26	0.0162%
jnh17	420925	420807	448.0	-	-	-	-	420925	2	0.0280%
jnh18	420795	420372	142.9	-	-	-	-	420525	26	0.0364%
jnh19	420759	420323	611.3	-	-	-	-	420584	26	0.0620%
jnh201	394238	394238	604.3	-	394222	400	6276	394238	0	0.0000%
jnh202	394170	393983	348.7	-	393870	-	-	394029	25	0.0117%
jnh203	394199	393889	265.3	-	-	-	-	394135	25	0.0624%
jnh205	394238	394224	227.6	-	-	-	-	394238	4	0.0036%
jnh207	394238	394101	460.8	-	-	-	-	394238	4	0.0348%
jnh208	394159	393987	335.1	-	-	-	-	393819	25	-0.0426%
jnh209	394238	394031	170.1	-	-	-	-	394238	7	0.0525%
jnh210	394238	394238	130.7	-	-	-	-	394238	4	0.0000%
jnh211	393979	393739	270.0	-	-	-	-	393979	24	0.0609%
jnh212	394238	394043	244.1	-	394006	-	-	394227	25	0.0467%
jnh214	394163	393701	486.4	-	-	-	-	394124	24	0.1073%
jnh215	394150	393858	601.8	-	-	-	-	394066	24	0.0528%
jnh216	394226	394029	441.1	-	-	-	-	394176	25	0.0373%
jnh217	394238	394232	125.4	-	-	-	-	394238	0	0.0015%
jnh218	394238	394099	155.7	-	-	-	-	394238	1	0.0353%
jnh219	394156	393720	502.8	-	-	-	-	393993	25	0.0693%
jnh220	394238	394053	513.5	-	-	-	-	394205	24	0.0386%
jnh301	444854	444670	522.1	-	-	-	-	444842	31	0.0387%
jnh302	444459	444248	493.9	-	-	-	-	444459	28	0.0475%
jnh303	444503	444244	416.1	-	-	-	-	444296	28	0.0117%
jnh304	444533	444214	96.7	-	444125	450	7060	444318	27	0.0234%
jnh305	444112	443503	424.9	-	443815	3500	54915	443533	29	0.0068%
jnh306	444838	444658	567.8	-	444692	2000	31380	444838	28	0.0405%
jnh307	444314	444159	353.5	-	-	-	-	444314	27	0.0349%
jnh308	444724	444222	50.2	-	-	-	-	444568	28	0.0778%
jnh309	444578	444349	86.8	-	-	-	-	444488	28	0.0313%
jnh310	444391	444282	44.7	-	-	-	-	444307	28	0.0056%

Table 1. Experimental Results for Instances

Many local search operators can apply on the BGLS for adapting with different problems. For weighted MAX-SAT, we used an improved Walksat to obtain local optima. Related to the common local search, BGLS heavily depends on the backbone sampled to simplify the scale of problems and to intensify local search. The process of retrieving backbone is to collect the feature from local optima. A note to design the similar algorithm is that a backbone guided algorithm can work well if and only if the local optima and the global optimum have the certain common parts.

In the future work, some interesting things remain to be investigated. Firstly, it needs further work on computational complexity for retrieving the backbone in the SAT. Although weighted MAX-SAT is a generalization of the SAT, it is not straightforward to prove the NP-hardness of retrieving the backbone in the SAT. The difficulty lies on the fact that the SAT isn't an optimization problem like weighted MAX-SAT but a typical combinatorial problem instead. For weighted MAX-SAT, we can always construct a weighted MAX-SAT instance with a unique optimal solution (i.e., the backbone) by slightly perturbing. However, such a method could not be directly applied to the SAT. Secondly, the ways for approximating the backbone are to be further explored. The backbone was approximated by the common parts of local optimal solutions. However, we argue that there may exist better ways for approximating the backbone in weighted MAX-SAT. A good example of approximating the backbone by novel ways can be found in the traveling salesman problem (TSP). They proposed four strategies for approximating the backbone other than by the common parts of local optimal solutions: Minimum Spanning Tree, Nearest Neighbor, Lighter Than Median, and Close Pairs. By those new strategies, they claimed that very large TSP instances can be tackled with current state-of-the-art evolutionary local search heuristics. Inspired by their work, we shall approximate the backbone in weighted MAX-SAT in the future, by some similar methods which are generally exploited by exact algorithms.

Appendix

According to Tab. 2, the performance conversion from SPEC shows as follows: SGI Altix 3700: Intel 865P = 510/32.5 = 15.6923 > 15.69.

	SGI Altix 3700 Bx2 (1600 MHz 6M L3 Itaninum 2)	Intel 865P (2.8 GHz Pentium D)
CINT 2000 Rates	510	32.5

Table 2. Benchmark from SPEC

7. Acknowledgments

This work is partially supported by the Natural Science Foundation of China under Grant No. 60805024; the National Research Foundation for the Doctoral Program of Higher Education of China under Grant No. 20070141020; the Natural Science Foundation of Liaoning Province under Grant No.20051082

8. References

Garey, M. R. & Johnson, D. S. (1979). Computers and intractability: a guide to the theory of NP-completeness. San Francisco: W. H. Freeman, 1979. pp. 38

Freuder, E. C. & Wallace, R. J. (1992). Partial constraint satisfaction. *Artificial Intelligence*, 1992, 58:21-70

Hansen, P. & Jaumard, B. (1990). Algorithms for the maximum satisfiability. *Journal of Computing*, 44:279-303

Selman, B.; Levesque, H. & Mitchell, D. (1992). A new method for solving hard satisfiability instances. In: *Proceedings of the 10th National Conference on Artificial Intelligence*. 1992, 440-446.

Patrickmills, M. & Edward, T. (2000). Guided local search for solving SAT and weighted MAX-SAT problems. *Journal of Automated Reasoning*, 205-223

Dalila, B. & Habiba, D. (2004). Solving weighted MAX-SAT optimization problems using a taboo scatter search metaheuristic. In: *Proceedings of the 2004 ACM symposium on Applied Computing*

Habiba, D.; Aminc, T. & Sofianc, Z. (2003). Cooperative ant colonies for solving the maximum weighted satisfiability problem. IWANN 2003, *Lecture Notes in Computer Science 2686*, 446-453

Resende, M. G. C.; Pitsoulis, L. S. & Pardalos, P. M. (2000). Fortran subroutines for computing approximate solutions of weighted MAX-SAT problems using GRASP. *Discrete Applied Mathematics*, 100:95-113

Festa, P.; Pardalos, P. M.; Pitsoulis, L. S. & Resende, M. G. C. (2006). GRASP with path-relinking for the weighted maximum satisfiability problem. *ACM Journal of Experimental Algorithms*, 11:1-16

Dubois, O. & Dequen, G. (2001). A backbone-search heuristic for efficient solving of hard 3-SAT formula. In *Proc. IJCAI-01*, 248–253

Zhang, W. X. (2004). Phase transition and backbone of the asymmetric traveling salesman problem. *Journal of Artificial Intelligence Research*, 2004, 21(1): 471-491.

Jiang, H.; Zhang, X. C.; Chen, G. L. & Li, M. C. (2008). Backbone analysis and algorithm design for the quadratic assignment problem. *Science in China Series F-Information Science*, 51(5):476 -488

Telelis, O. & Stamatopoulos, P. (2002). Heuristic backbone sampling for maximum satisfiability. In: *Proceedings of the 2nd Hellenic Conference on Artificial Intelligence*, 129-139

Zhang, W. X.; Rangan, A. & Looks, M. (2003). Backbone guided local search for maximum satisfiability. In: *Proceedings of the 18th International Joint Conference on Artificial Intelligence*, 1179-1186

Selman, B.; Kautz, H. & Cohen, B. (1994). Noise strategies for local search. In: *Proc. AAAI-94*.

Hoos H. H. (2002). An adaptive noise mechanism for Walksat. In: Proc. AAAI-02.

Patterson, D. J. & Kautz, H. (2001). Auto-Walksat: A self-tuning implementation of Walksat. *Electronic Notes in Discrete Mathematics*, Elsevier, Amsterdam, vol.9, 2001, Presented at the LICS 2001 Workshop on Theory and Applications of Satisfiability Testing, June 14–15, Boston University, MA, 2001.

Weighted MAX-SAT Problem Lib. www.research.att.com/~mgcr/data/maxsat.tar.gz.

SPEC. http://www.spec.org/cgi-bin/osgresults?conf=cpu2000.

Fischer, T. & Merz, P. (2007). Reducing the size of traveling salesman problem instances by fixing edges. 7th European Conference on Evolutionary Computation in Combinatorial Optimization, *Lecture Notes in Computer Science* 4446, 72-83

15

Hybrid Differential Evolution – Scatter Search Algorithm for Permutative Optimization

Donald Davendra[1], Ivan Zelinka[1] and Godfrey Onwubolu[2]
[1]*Tomas Bata University in Zlin, Nad Stranemi 4511, Zlin 76001*
[2]*Knowledge Management & Mining*
[1]*Czech Republic*
[2]*Canada*

1. Introduction

Adaptive memory programming approaches have proven effective in finding high quality solutions to many real world intractable problems. Therefore, over the years, researches have attempted to combine the best features from different adaptive memory approaches to derive more powerful hybrid heuristics (Onwubolu, 2002). Combining the best features of different heuristics will give a new heuristic that is superior to the individual systems from which these features are derived.

Differential evolution (DE) algorithm (Price, 1999) is an evolutionary approach which does not inhibit any adaptive memory features. It is however a very powerful and robust heuristic for continuous optimization. Continuous optimization is a very important aspect of optimization; however a heuristics application to permutative optimization is imperative if it is to be generic. Permutative optimization encompasses many aspects of engineering. In practical settings, it is common to observe features which are discrete, such as the different discrete nut and bolt sizes, fixed number of machines in a manufacturing plant or discrete number of buses in a fixed route. All these problems are practical and challenging, which utilize discrete values. The purpose of this paper is then to introduce an enhanced different evolution algorithm for discrete optimization which is hybridized by the adaptive memory heuristic of scatter search (SS) (Glover, 1998).

SS is a highly effective heuristic which is the superset of tabu search (TS) (Glover, 1998). It has been successfully applied to many permutative optimization problems. The objective of the proposed hybrid optimization approach is then to isolate its highly effective intensification and diversification routines and embed it in the EDE structure. The result is a highly evolved hybrid enhanced differential evolution scatter search (HEDE-SS) heuristic.

The hybrid optimization scheme is applied to two difficult permutative optimization problems of quadratic assignment problem (QAP) and the flow shop scheduling problem (FSS). The results generated by the hybrid scheme are then compared with the heuristics of EDE and SS in order to show that the hybrid scheme is an improvement over the original heuristics. Additionally, the results of the hybrid scheme is compared with the optimal results from the operations research (OR) library and with the results obtained by other heuristics for the same problem instances from the literature.

This chapter is divided into the following sections; section two presents the two different discrete optimization problems, section three introduces the EDE, SS and the developed hybrid approach, section four gives the experimentation and analysis and section five concludes the research.

2. Permutative optimization

2.1 Quadratic assignment problem

The QAP is a combinatorial optimization problem stated for the first time by Koopmans and Beckman (1957) and is widely regarded as one of the most difficult problem in this class. The approach is to have two matrices of size *n* x *m* given as:

$$A = \left(a_{ij}\right) \tag{1}$$

$$B = \left(b_{ij}\right) \tag{2}$$

The objective is then to find the permutation which minimizes

$$\min_{\pi \in \prod(n)} f(\pi) = \sum_{i=1}^{n} \sum_{j=1}^{n} a_{ij}\, b_{\pi(i)\pi(j)} \tag{3}$$

where $\prod(n)$ is a set of permutations of *n* elements. QAP is considered a *NP* hard problem (Shani & Gonzalez, 1976) and problem sizes of larger than 20 are considered intractable.
Many application have been identified for QAP, which include amongst others, the allocation of plants to candidate locations; layout of plants; backboard wiring problem; design of control panels and typewriter keyboards; balancing turbine runners; ordering of interrelated data on a magnetic tape; processor-to-processor assignment in a distributed processing environment; placement problem in VLSI design; analyzing chemical reactions for organic compounds; and ranking of archaeological data. The details and references for these and additional applications can be found in Burkard (1991) and Malucelli (1993).
Two approaches have been identified to solve QAP; exact and heuristic algorithms. Exact algorithms for QAP include approaches based on dynamic programming by Christofides and Benavent (1989); cutting planes by Bazaraa and Sherali (1980); and branch and bound by Lawler (1963) and Pardalos and Crouse (1989). Among these, the branch and bound algorithms obtain the best solution, but are unable to solve problems of size larger than n = 20.
For larger sized problems, heuristic approaches have been developed. Some of the most notable are: simulated annealing by Connolly (1990), tabu searches of Taillard (1991), Battiti and Tecchiolli (1994) and Sondergeld and Voβ (1996), the hybrid genetic-tabu searches of Fleurent and Ferland (1994) and more recently the ant colony approach by Gambardella, Taillard and Dorigo (1999).

2.2 Flow shop scheduling

In many manufacturing and assembly facilities a number of operations have to be done on every job. Often, these operations have to be done on all jobs in the same order, which implies that the jobs have to follow the same route. The machines are assumed to be set up

and the environment is referred to as flow shop (Pinedo, 1995). The flow shop can be formatted generally by the sequencing on n jobs on m machines under the precedence condition. The general constraints that are assessed for a flow shop system is the time required to finish all jobs or makespan, minimizing of average flow time, and the maximizing the number of tardy jobs.
When searching for an optimal schedule for an instance of the $Fm||C_{\max}$ problem, the question can arise weather it suffices merely to determine a permutation in which the job traverses the entire system, or more logically to check the possibility for one job to bypass another while waiting in queue for a engaged machine. Changing the sequence of jobs waiting in a queue between two machines may, at times, result in a smaller makespan. Where the number of jobs is small, finding the optimal sequence of jobs which results in the minimal makespan is relatively easy. But more often the number of jobs to be processed is large, which leads to big-O order of $n!$ Consequently, some type of algorithm is essential in these large problems in order to avoid combinatorial explosion (Onwubolu, 2002).
The minimization of completion time for a flow shop schedule is equivalent to minimizing the objective function $\Im$.

$$\Im = \sum_{j=1}^{n} C_{m,j} \tag{4}$$

where $C_{m,j}$ is the completion time of job j. To calculate $C_{m,j}$ the recursive procedure is followed for any i^{th} machine j^{th} job as follows:

$$C_{i,j} = \max\left(C_{i-1,j}, C_{i,j-1}\right) + P_{i,j} \tag{5}$$

Where, $C_{1,1} = k$ (any given value) and $C_{i,j} = \sum_{k=1}^{j} C_{1,k};\ ;\ C_{i,j} = \sum_{k=1}^{i} C_{k,1}$ where i is the machine number, j is the job in sequence and $P_{i,j}$ is the processing time of job j on machine i.

3. A hybrid approach to discrete optimization

3.1 Enhanced differential evolution

Developed by Price and Storn (2001), differential evolution (DE) algorithm is a very robust and efficient approach to solve continuous optimization problems. A discrete optimization approach for DE was initially explored by Davendra (2001) and since then by many other researchers (see for details Onwubolu (2001), Onwubolu (2004) and Lampinen and Storn (2004)). The EDE approach by Davendra and Onwubolu (2009) is used as the DE approach for this hybrid system.
Onwubolu and Davendra (2004) developed the approach of a discrete DE, which utilized the highly effective approach of *Forward Transformation* and *Backward Transformation* by Onwubolu (2001) in the conversion of a discrete solution into a continuous solution and vice versa, for the operation of the DE internal mutation schema. This approach was highly effective in solving the scheduling problem of flow shop (FSS). EDE was proposed as an enhancement of the discrete DE in order to improve the quality of the solutions perturbed by DE (Davendra & Onwuolu, 2009).
The basic outline of EDE is given in Figure 1.

- **Initial Phase**
  1. *Population Generation:* An initial number of discrete trial solutions are generated for the initial population.
- **Conversion**
  2. *Forward Transformation:* This conversion scheme transforms the parent solution into the required continuous solution.
  3. *DE Strategy:* The DE strategy transforms the parent solution into the child solution using its inbuilt crossover and mutation schemas.
  4. *Backward Transformation:* This conversion schema transforms the continuous child solution into a discrete solution.
- **Mutation**
  5. *Relative Mutation Schema:* Formulates the child solution into the discrete solution of unique values.
- **Improvement Strategy**
  6. *Mutation:* Standard mutation is applied to obtain a better solution.
  7. *Insertion:* Uses a two-point cascade to obtain a better solution.
  8. *Repeat:* Execute steps 2-7 until reaching a specified cutoff limit on the total number of iterations.
- **Local Search**
  9. *Local Search:* Is initiated if stagnation occurs

Fig. 1. EDE outline

3.2 Scatter search

Scatter search (SS) and its generalized form path relinking (PR) are heuristics which are build on the principles of surrogate constraint design (Glover, 1977). In particular they are designed to capture information not contained separately in the original solutions, and take advantage of auxiliary heuristic solution methods to evaluate the combinations produced and generate new solutions.

The two principles that govern SS are;

(1) Intensification

(2) Diversification

Intensification refers to the role of isolating the best performing solutions from the populations in order to obtain a group of good solutions. Diversification in turn isolates the solutions which are the furthest from the best solutions and combined them with the best solutions. This new pool of solutions is the reference set where crossover occurs in order to create solutions from new solution regions by the combination of the intensified solutions and diversified solutions. Intensification and diversification are commonly termed as adaptive memory programming.

Many applications of discrete programming have emerged from SS. Some of these are: Vehicle Routing (Taillard, 1996), Quadratic Assignment (Cung *et al,* 1997), Job Shop Scheduling (Yamada & Nakano, 1996), Flow Shop Scheduling (Yamada & Reeves, 1997) and Linear Ordering (Laguna, *et al.*, 1997).

3.3 Hybrid approach

EDE is a highly randomized algorithm (Davendra, 2003), which utilizes a high number of randomly generated values for its operation. SS on the other hand is one of the new

optimization algorithms which have adaptive memory programming, enabling it to retain its long term memory in order to find good search space (Glover, 1998). This hybrid approach brings together the highly effective intensification and diversification aspects of SS (Glover, 1998) into the operational domain of EDE.
Figure 2 gives the outline for the hybrid structure.

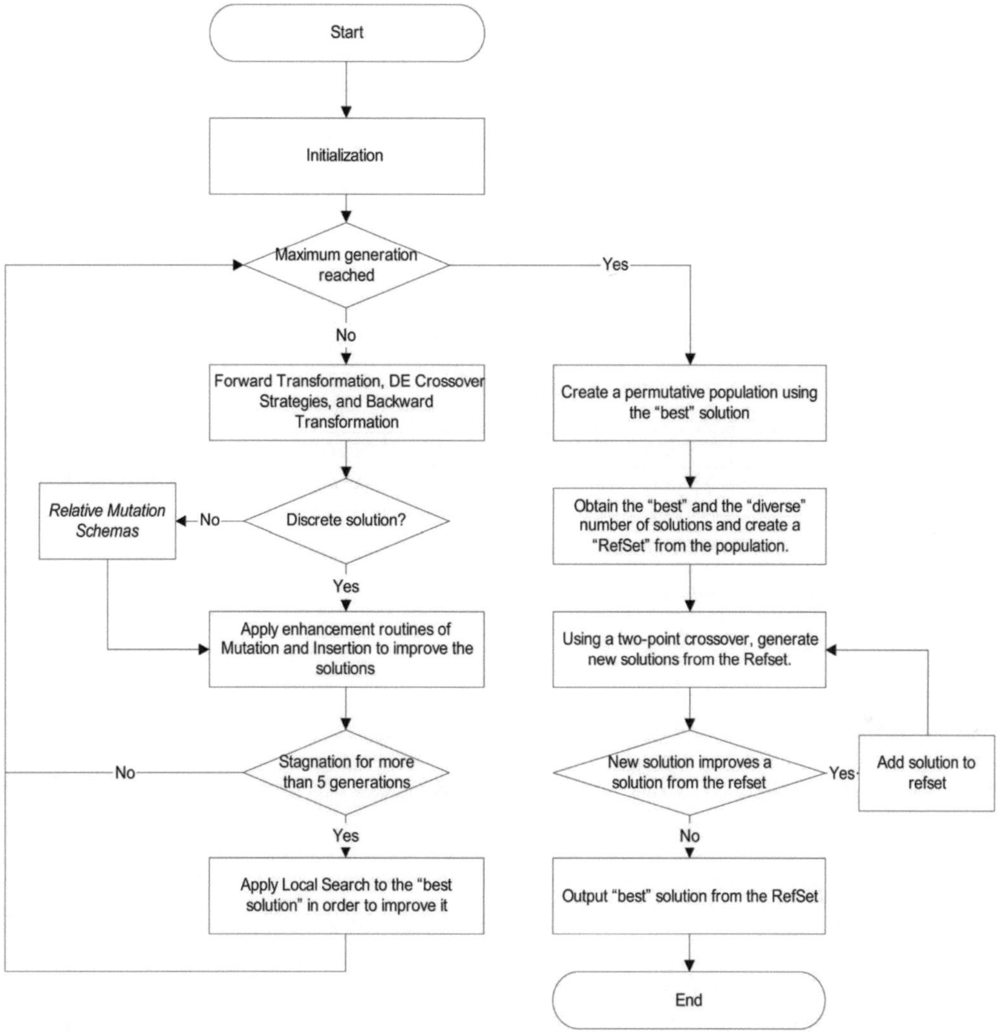

Fig. 2. Hybrid EDE/SS outline

3.3.1 Initialization

The first process in the hybrid EDE SS (HEDE-SS) is the initialization of the population and the operational parameters. HEDE-SS has several operational parameters as given in Table 1.
The lower $x_j^{(lo)}$ bound and the upper $x_j^{(hi)}$ bound specify the range of the solution. The size of the population *NP* is usually in the range of 100 to 500 solutions. The size of each solution *D* is dependent on the problem size at hand. EDE has two tuning parameters of *CR* and *F* which are also initialized; $CR \in [0,1]$ and $F \in (0,1+)$. The Strategy number refers to the type

of DE crossover employed for the problem. The Mutation refers to the type of *Relative Mutation schema* used for the discrete solution. The RefSet size is the number of solutions that are combined for the intensification and diversification.

Parameter	**Syntax**	**Range**	**Description**
Population size	NP	NP ≥ 4	The population size for HEDE-SS
Solution size	D	D ≥ 4	The size of each solution
Lower bound	$x_j^{(lo)}$	$x_j^{(lo)} \geq 1$	The lower bound of the solution
Upper bound	$x_j^{(hi)}$	$x_j^{(hi)} = D$	The upper bound of the solution
Crossover constant	CR	$CR \in [0,1]$	The crossover used for DE perturb
Scaling factor	F	$F \in (0,1+)$	Scaling factor for perturb
Strategy number	Strategy	$Str \in \{1,2,...,10\}$	The strategy to employ
Relative mutation	Mutation	$Mut \in \{1,2,3\}$	Mutation to employ
Reference Set	RefSet	RefSet ≥ 4	Size of RefSet for SS
Generations	$G_{\max}$	$G_{\max} = 500$	Number of generations of EDE

Table 1. Operational parameters for HEDE-SS

The solution created is discrete and given as:

$$x_{j,i}^{(G=0)} = \begin{cases} (\text{int})\left(rand_j[0,1] \bullet \left(x_j^{(hi)} + 1 - x_j^{(lo)}\right) + \left(x_j^{(lo)}\right)\right) \\ \text{if} \quad x_{j,i} \notin \{x_{0,i}, x_{1,i}, ..x_{j-1,i}\} \end{cases} \tag{6}$$

Each solution created is random, and multiple identical solutions can exist within an EDE population as long as it is discrete.

3.3.2 Conversion

The conversion routine is used to transform each discrete solution into a continuous solution since the canonical form of DE only operates in the continuous domain. These solutions after DE internal crossover are retransformed into a discrete solution. The two conversion schemas were developed by Onwubolu (2001). For implementation details please see Onwubolu and Davendra (2004), Onwubolu (2004), Davendra (2001) and Davendra (2003).

The forward transformation is given as:

$$x_{j,i} = x_{j,i}' \tag{7}$$

where $x_{j,i}$ represents a discrete solution and $x_{j,i}'$ represents a continuous solution.

Price and Storn (2001) described ten different working crossover schemas for DE. Each schema developed has a different approach to optimization through the crossover utilized.

The ten strategies are divided into two groups of different crossover schemas; *exponential* and *binomial*.
Exponential refers to the fact that crossover will only occur in one loop until it is within the *CR* bound. The first occurrence of a random number selected between *0* and *1*, going beyond the parameter set by *CR* stops the crossover schema and all the values remaining are left intact.
Binomial on the other hand states that crossover will occur on each of the values whenever a randomly generated number between *0* and *1*, is within the *CR* bound.
The ten different strategies are given in Table 2.

Convention (DE/x/y/z)*	Representation
DE/best/1/exp	$u_i = x_{best} + F\bullet(x_{r1} - x_{r2})$
DE/rand/1/exp	$u_i = x_{r1} + F\bullet(x_{r2} - x_{r3})$
DE/rand-to-best/1/exp	$u_i = x_i + F\bullet(x_{best} - x_i) + F\bullet(x_{r1} - x_{r2})$
DE/best/2/exp	$u_i = x_{best} + F\bullet(x_{r1} - x_{r2} - x_{r3} - x_{r4})$
DE/rand/2/exp	$u_i = x_{r5} + F\bullet(x_{r1} - x_{r2} - x_{r3} - x_{r4})$
DE/best/1/bin	$u_i = x_{best} + F\bullet(x_{r1} - x_{r2})$
DE/rand/1/bin	$u_i = x_{r1} + F\bullet(x_{r2} - x_{r3})$
DE/rand-to-best/1/bin	$u_i = x_i + F\bullet(x_{best} - x_i) + F\bullet(x_{r1} - x_{r2})$
DE/best/2/bin	$u_i = x_{best} + F\bullet(x_{r1} - x_{r2} - x_{r3} - x_{r4})$
DE/rand/2/bin	$u_i = x_{r5} + F\bullet(x_{r1} - x_{r2} - x_{r3} - x_{r4})$

Table 2. DE Crossover schemas
* x – type of solution used for crossover, y – number of solutions used, z – type of crossover used.

Each problem class has to be tuned as to what are its optimal operating parameters.
Once the DE internal crossover schemas have operated, the *backward transformation* changes the values generated into discrete values. The *backward transformation* is the reverse of the *forward transformation* and is given as:

$$x_{j,i}{}' = x_{j,i} \tag{8}$$

3.3.3 Relative mutation

The solution obtained from the *backward transformation* is not always discrete. In Onwubolu and Davendra (2004) up to 80 per cent of all solutions generated were infeasible. A new approach has been developed in order to retain discrete solutions after transformation. Two types of infeasible solution may exist:

(1) Out-of-bound values
(2) Repetitive values

Out-of-bound values are easily handled by HEDE-SS. All bound offending values are simply dragged to the bound they violate.

$$x_{j,i} = \begin{cases} x_j^{(lo)} \text{ if } x_{j,i} < x_j^{(lo)} \\ x_j^{(hi)} \text{ if } x_{j,i} > x_j^{(hi)} \end{cases} \tag{9}$$

In order to remove repetition from the solution, three relative mutation schemas have been developed; *front mutation* (FM), *back mutation* (BM) and *random mutation* (RM).

3.3.3.1 Front Mutation

Front mutation (FM) is the schema which transforms the solution into a discrete solution through the ascending order of index. The solution is firstly sorted into feasible and infeasible values starting from index one. This implies that the value which occurs first in the solution is considered feasible, whereas its next occurrence is infeasible.

$$x_{j,i} = \begin{cases} x_{j,i} & \text{if } x_{j,i} \notin \{x_{1,i},\ldots,x_{j-1,i}\} \\ \tilde{x}_{j,i} & \text{if } x_{j,i} \in \{x_{1,i},\ldots,x_{j-1,i}\} \end{cases} \tag{10}$$

In FM all infeasible values are replaced with feasible values starting from index one. A random value is generated between the lower and upper bound for each infeasible value, and checked to see whether it already exists in the solution. If repetition is detected, then another random value is generated.

$$x_{rand} = \begin{cases} x_{rand} = rnd[1,D] \\ \quad \text{where } x_{rand} \notin \{x_{1,i},\ldots,x_{D,i}\} \end{cases} \tag{11}$$

Each infeasible value within the solution is thus replaced and the solution in now discrete.
FM converts any integer solution into a discrete solution, however a forward bias is shown. FM converts from the front, starting with index one of the solutions. A reverse mutation process is also developed termed the *back mutation*.

3.3.3.2 Back Mutation

Back mutation (BM) is a mutation schema which is the complete opposite of the FM. In BM, all the values in the solutions are sorted from the back of the solution starting with the index *D*. The value occurring last within the solution is considered feasible whereas its earlier placement is considered infeasible.

$$x_{j,i} = \begin{cases} x_{j,i} & \text{if } x_{j,i} \notin \{x_{j+1,i},\ldots,x_{D,i}\} \\ \tilde{x}_{j,i} & \text{if } x_{j,i} \in \{x_{j+1,i},\ldots,x_{D,i}\} \end{cases} \tag{12}$$

As in FM, for each infeasible value, a random number between the lower and upper bounds is obtained and checked against all the values in the solution. If it is unique then it replaces the infeasible value starting from index *D*.
BM is the opposite of FM; however a reverse bias now exists. A bias is not favorable since it limits the search space of a population, and again does not represent a realizable system. The third mutation schema *random mutation* is totally random, with both its sorting and replacement.

3.3.3.3 Random Mutation

Random mutation (RM) is a total random based mutation schema. There exists no bias in this schema as it does with FM and BM. The first process in this schema is to create a random array which contains the indexes for the solution to be checked for repetition.

$$\begin{aligned} \Re_1 &= \{y_1, y_2, y_3, ..., y_D\} \\ &\text{where } \vec{x}^{(lo)} \geq y \leq \vec{x}^{(hi)} \\ &j = 1, 2, ..., D \end{aligned} \tag{13}$$

The value y_1 points to the first value to be checked, and so on until all values within the solutions are checked for repetition.

$$x_{y_j,i} = \begin{cases} x_{y_j,i} & \text{if } x_{y_j,i} \notin \{x_{y_1,i}, ..., x_{y_{j-1},i}\} \\ \tilde{x}_{y_j,i} & \text{if } x_{y_j,i} \in \{x_{y_1,i}, ..., x_{y_{j-1},i}\} \end{cases} \tag{14}$$

Repetitive values are now isolated, however their replacement is yet to be determined. Another random array is now created which will index the infeasible values in their order of replacement.

$$\begin{aligned} \Re_2 &= \{z_1, z_2, z_3, ..., z_D\} \\ &\text{where } \vec{x}^{(lo)} \geq z \leq \vec{x}^{(hi)} \\ &j = 1, 2, ..., D \end{aligned} \tag{15}$$

The value in the solution pointed by the index z_1 is checked for repetition. If repetition is indicated from the previous step, then the repetitive value in replaced by a unique random value as given in equation 13. Using the index array $\Re_2$, all the values in the solution which are infeasible are replaced with feasible values.

RM is truly random, from the point of selection of infeasible values to its replacement. The random arrays enforce random initiation of infeasible values and its replacement. All three mutation schemas; FM, BM and RM are able to convert an integer solution into a discrete solution.

3.3.4 Improvement strategies

Each discrete solution obtained is improved by the two improvement routines of *mutation* and *insertion*. Mutation is referenced from GA, where it has been highly successful in finding local optimal solutions (Goldberg, 1989). Mutation refers to the application of a single swap of values in a solution, in order to exploit better search space. In order for mutation to operate two random numbers are generated.

$$\begin{aligned} r_1, r_2 &\in rand[1, D] \\ &\text{where as } r_1 \neq r_2 \end{aligned} \tag{16}$$

These random numbers are the indexes of the positions of the two values in the solution which are to be swapped. The value in the solution $x_{r_1,i}$ indexed by r_1 is swapped by the value $x_{r_2,i}$ indexed by r_2. The new solution is evaluated with the objective function. Only if a better objective function is achieved, then the new solution is retained, else the reverse process occurs to obtain the original solution.

$$x_i = \begin{cases} x_i'' & \text{if } f(x_i'') < f(x_i) \\ x_i & otherwise \end{cases} \quad (17)$$

The inclusion of mutation introduces some probability of local improvement of a solution. Insertion also works along the same lines as mutation. Insertion is the cascade of values between two randomly generated positions in the solution. Insertion is regarded as more robust than mutation since a number of values are involved in its operation. As in mutation, two random values are generated given by equation 18. The value in the solution $x_{r_2,i}$ indexed by r_2, is removed and all the values from the value $x_{r_1,i}$ indexed by r_1 till $x_{r_2-1,i}$ are shifted one index up. The value $x_{r_2,i}$ is inserted in the place indexed by r_1. The new solution is evaluated with the objective function. Only if a better objective function is achieved, then the new solution is retained, else the reverse process occurs to obtain the original solution.

3.3.5 Local search

Stagnation is common amongst population based heuristics. The population converges to local optima and is unable to find new search regions in order to find the global optima. In order to help a heuristic just out of the local optima, a *local search* (LS) routine is embedded in the heuristic. LS is a brute force approach to find a better solution. It is also time and memory expensive. In order to minimize time, a non improving population of ten generations, is classified as stagnation. LS operates on the "best" solution in the population, since the best solution has the highest probability of being in the vicinity of a better solution. The LS employed in HEDE-SS is the 2-Opt algorithm by Onwubolu (2002).

3.3.6 Permutative population

A second population is created in order for the *intensification* and the *diversification* strategies to operate. As stipulated by Glover (1998), for a heuristic to employ memory adaptive programming, each solution in the population should be unique. The "best" solution in the population is isolated and another population is created using the best solution as the permutation base given by:

$$\mathrm{P}(\mathrm{h}) = \left(P(h:h), P(h:h-1), \ldots, P(h:1)\right) \quad (18)$$

The size of the population h is dependent on the size of the solution D and the index $h \le D$ specified. For details see Glover (1998).

3.3.7 Reference set

The reference set is generated by two aspects of the population; intensified solutions and diversified solution. The size of the reference set *refset* is defined at the beginning. It is usual to have half the solutions in the population as intensified and the rest as diversified. Intensified solutions are obtained by evaluating the population and removing the specified *refset/2* best solutions from the population into the refset.

Campos *et al.* (2001) outlined how the diverse solutions are obtained from a population. The way diverse solutions are computed is through the computation of the minimum distances of each solution in the population to the solutions in *refset*. Then the solution with the maximum of these minimum distances is selected. Population solutions are included in *refset* according to the *maxmin* criterion which maximizes the minimum distance of each candidate solution to all the solutions currently in the reference set. The method starts with *refset*= *Best* and at each step *refset* is extended with a solution P_j from the population $\Im$ to be $refset = refset \cup \{P_j\}$, and consequently $\Im$ is reduced to $\Im = \Im \setminus \{P_j\}$. Then the distance of solution *P* to every solution currently in the reference set is computed to make possible the selection of a new population solution according to the *maxmin* criterion. More formally, the selection of a population solution is given by

$$P_j = \arg\max \min_{i=1,..,|refset|} \{\zeta_{ij} : j = 1,..,|\Im|\} \tag{19}$$

where ζ is the diversity measure which is the distance between solutions P_i and P_j, which differ from each other by the number of edges which follows as:

$$\zeta_{ij} = \left|(P_i \cup P_j) \setminus (P_i \cap P_j)\right| \tag{20}$$

For details see Campos *et al.* (2001).

3.3.8 Combine solutions

The combination method is a key element in scatter search implementation (Campos *et al.*, 2001). For the combination method in HEDE-SS, the GA two-point crossover schema is used. The crossover is similar to the mutation used in EDE. Two random values are generated which are mutually exclusive and also not equal to any of the bounds.

$$r_1, r_2 \in rand[2, D-1] \quad \text{where as } r_1 \neq r_2 \tag{21}$$

Two distinct solutions P_1 and P_2 from the *refset* are selected starting from the first two solutions and using the two random values r_1 and r_2 as indexes to the solutions, the regions between the two bounds in the two solutions are swapped as follows:

$$P_1 = \{x_{11}, x_{12}, ..., x_{1n}\} \text{ Solution 1}$$

$$P_2 = \{x_{21}, x_{22}, ..., x_{2n}\} \text{ Solution 2}$$

Using the two random numbers as indexes the two solutions are now represented as:

$$P_1 = \left\{ x_{11}, x_{12}, \underset{r_1}{|}\, x_{13}, x_{14}, x_{15}, \underset{r_2}{|}\, x_{16}, ..., x_{1n} \right\}$$

$$P_2 = \left\{ x_{21}, x_{22}, \underset{r_1}{|}\, x_{23}, x_{24}, x_{25}, \underset{r_2}{|}\, x_{26}, ..., x_{2n} \right\}$$

The swap between the regions denoted by the two random numbers in now represented as:

$$P_1 = \left\{ x_{11}, x_{12}, \underset{r_1}{|}\, x_{23}, x_{24}, x_{25}, \underset{r_2}{|}\, x_{16}, \ldots, x_{1n} \right\}$$

$$P_2 = \left\{ x_{21}, x_{22}, \underset{r_1}{|}\, x_{13}, x_{14}, x_{15}, \underset{r_2}{|}\, x_{26}, \ldots, x_{2n} \right\}$$

The resulting solutions are not discrete and the RM schema is used to transform the solution into a discrete form.

The LS schema is applied to each new solution as part of the improvement routine of HEDE-SS. The new solution is evaluated and compared to the worst solution in the *refset*. If the new solution improves on the worst solution, it then replaces the worst solution in the *refset*. The whole process iterates with solutions selected from the solutions iteratively. On each iteration from the first solution to the last, the amount of addition to the *refset* of new improved solution is recorded. If no new solution is recorded in any iteration, then the *refset* has reached a point of stagnation, and the best value in the *refset* is printed as the best solution for the HEDE-SS.

3.4 Hybrid pseudo-code

A pseudo code representation of hybrid is given in order for the reader to understand how all the different routines are combined together.

/ Initial parameters are first obtained */*

GET *NP, D,* $G_{\max}$, *CR, F, Strategy Number, Mutation Type,* $x_j^{(lo)}$ $x_j^{(hi)}$ and *refset*

/ Operational parameters are initialized */*

SET $x_{\min}$, *best_sol, ObjFun, ObjDist, RefSet*

/ Create the initial population of solutions */*

FOR (i = 1 to i ≤ *NP*)

  FOR (j = 1 to j ≤ *D*)

    GET $x_{j,i}^{(G=0)} = \begin{cases} (\text{int})\left(rand_j\,[0,1]\cdot\left(x_j^{(hi)} + 1 - x_j^{(lo)}\right) + \left(x_j^{(lo)}\right)\right) \\ \text{if} \quad x_{j,i} \notin \left\{x_{0,i}, x_{1,i}, \ldots x_{j-1,i}\right\} \end{cases}$

  ENDFOR

ENDFOR

/ Find the best solution and solution cost */*

$x_{\min} = x_i$ */* The best solution is initialized as the first solution of the population */*

best_sol = 1 */* The best solution index is set to one for the initial solution. */*

FOR (i = 1 to i ≤ *NP*)

  IF ($f(x_i) < f(x_{\min})$) */* If the current solution has a less functional value*

    SET $x_{\min} = x_i$ *than* $x_{\min}$*, it replace* $x_{\min}$ *as the best and the*

    SET *best_sol* = i *index is appropriately updated. */*

  ENDIF

ENDFOR

/* *Iterate through the generations* */
FOR (k=1; k ≤ $G_{\max}$)

/* *Iterate through the solutions* */
FOR (i = 1 to i ≤ *NP*)

/* *Apply Forward Transformation to each value in the solution* */
FOR (j = 1 to j ≤ *D*)
SET $x_{j,i}{}' = -1 + (\alpha \bullet x_{j,i})$ /* α is a constant */
ENDFOR

/* *The objective function of the parent solution is calculated* */
SET Parent_ObjFun = $f(x_i)$

/* *Select two random solutions from the population other than the current one* x_i' */

GET $r_1, r_2 \begin{cases} \in rand[1, NP] \\ \text{where as } r_1 \neq r_2 \neq i \end{cases}$

/* *Perform D binomial trials, change at least one parameter of the trial solution* x_i' *and perform mutation* */
GET $t = rand[1, D]$ /* *A random starting point is obtained* */
FOR (z =1 to z ≤ *D*)

/* *If a randomly generated value is less than CR or the counter is within the specified limit* */
IF (($rand[0,1]$ < *CR*) **OR** (z = *D*-1)) **THEN**

/* *DE's internal mutation schema operates* */

$$u_i = x_i' + F \bullet (x_{best} - x_i') + F \bullet (x_{r1}' - x_{r2}')$$

/* *If condition is not correct the original solution is retained for the new generation* */
ELSE
SET $u_i = x_i'$
ENDIFELSE

/* *Increment the counter t* */
$t = z + 1$
ENDFOR

/* *Apply Backward Transformation to each value in the solution to obtain the original* */
FOR (j = 1 to j ≤ *D*)
SET $x_{j,i} = (1 + x_{j,i}{}') \bullet \beta$ /* β is a constant */
ENDFOR

/ Check if the solution is feasible or not */*

FOR (j = 1 to j ≤ *D*)

/ If infeasible solutions are found */*

$$\textbf{IF } (x_{j,i} \in \{x_{1,i}, x_{2,i}, x_{2,i}, \ldots, x_{D,i}\} / x_{j,i} \ \textbf{OR} \ x^{(hi)} > x_{j,i} < x^{(lo)})$$

/ Relative Mutation Schema first drags all out of bound values to the bound it violates */*

FOR (j = 1 to j ≤ *D*)

$$\textbf{SET } x_{j,i} = \begin{cases} x_j^{(lo)} & \text{if } x_{j,i} < x_j^{(lo)} \\ x_j^{(hi)} & \text{if } x_{j,i} > x_j^{(hi)} \end{cases}$$

ENDFOR

/ Front mutation is chosen to show how the solution is made discrete */*

FOR (j = 1 to j ≤ *D*)

/ If a value within the solution is found to be repetitive, a unique random value is created to replace it */*

$$\textbf{IF } (x_{j,i} \in \{x_{1,i}, x_{2,i}, x_{2,i}, \ldots, x_{D,i}\} / x_{j,i})$$

$$\textbf{GET } x_{rand} = \begin{cases} x_{rand} = rnd[1, D] \\ \quad \text{where } x_{rand} \notin \{x_{1,i}, \ldots, x_{D,i}\} \end{cases}$$

$$\textbf{SET } x_{j,i} = x_{rand}$$

ENDIF

ENDFOR

ENDIF

ENDFOR

/ Standard mutation is applied to the solution in the hope of getting a better solution*/*

$$\textbf{GET } r_1, r_2 \begin{cases} \in rand[1, D] \\ \quad \text{where as } r_1 \neq r_2 \end{cases}$$

$$u_i = \{x_{1,i}, \ldots, x_{r_1,i}, \ldots, x_{r_2,i}, \ldots, x_{D,i}\}$$

$$u_i'' = \{x_{1,i}, \ldots, x_{r_2,i}, \ldots, x_{r_1,i}, \ldots, x_{D,i}\}$$

/ If the objective function of the new solution is better than the original solution, the new solution is retained in the population */*

$$\textbf{IF}(f(x_i'') < f(x_i))$$

$$\textbf{SET } x_i = x_i''$$

ENDIF

/ Insertion is applied to the solution in the hope of getting a better solution*/*

$$\textbf{GET } r_1, r_2 \begin{cases} \in rand[1, D] \\ \quad \text{where } r_1 \neq r_2 \text{ and } r_1 < r_2 \end{cases}$$

$$u_i = \{x_{1,i},..,x_{r_1,i},..,x_{r_2,i},..,x_{D,i}\}$$

$$u_i'' = \{x_{1,i},..,x_{r_2,i},x_{r_1,i},x_{r_1+1,i},..,x_{r_{2-1},i},..,x_{D,i}\}$$

/ If the objective function of the new solution is better than the original solution, the new solution is retained in the population */*

IF($f(u_i'') < f(u_i)$)

SET $u_i = u_i''$

ENDIF

/ The objective function of the solution is calculated */*

SET Child_ObjFun = $f(u_i)$

/ If the child improves on the parent, then the child is included in the population */*

IF (Child_ObjFun < Parent_ObjFun)

SET $x_i = u_i$

/ The new solution is also compared against the best solution*/*

IF($f(u_i) < f(x_{min})$)

SET $x_{min} = u_i$

SET *best_sol* = i

ENDIF

ENDIF

ENDFOR

ENDFOR

/ Using the best solution x_{min}, generate a permutative population */*

SET $h = D/2$

WHILE(h >1)

SET $s = h$

SET $r \in \begin{cases} s + rh \le D \\ r > 0 \end{cases}$

WHILE(s >1)

$$\mathrm{P}(\mathrm{h{:}s}) = (s, s+h, s+2h,..., s+rh)$$

$$s = s - 1$$

ENDWHILE

/ All the sub solutions are appended together for the full solution.*

$$\mathrm{P}(\mathrm{h}) = (P(h:h), P(h:h-1),..., P(h:1))$$

$$h = h - 1$$

ENDWHILE

```
/* Evaluate the population and store the objective function. */
FOR(i=1 to i < h)
        SET ObjFun_i = f(P_i)
ENDFOR

/* Remove the best refset/2 solutions from the population and store in refset.*/
FOR(i=1 to i < refset/2)
        SET best = ObjFun_1
        FOR(j=1 to j < h)
                IF( ObjFun_j ≤best)
                        SETbest = ObjFun_j
                ENDIF
        ENDFOR

/* Remove the solution indexed from the population into the refset. */
        MOVE P_best → refset_i
        SET h = h − 1
ENDFOR

/* Remove the diverse refset/2 solutions from the population and store in refset.*/
FOR(i= refset/2 to i < refset)
        FOR(j=1 to j < i)

/* Calculate the distance from each solution in refset to the population. */
                FOR(k=1 to k < h)
                        GET evaluate (refset_j --distance--> P_k)
                ENDFOR

/* Store the maximum of the distance for a particular solution in refset. */
                ObjDist_j = max(evaluate)
        ENDFOR

/* Select the minimum of the values in ObjDist and move the corresponding solution to refset. */
                MOVE P_min(ObjDist_j) → refset_i
ENDFOR

/* Combine each of the solutions in refset with each other to obtain better solutions. */
FOR(i=1 to i < refset-1)
        FOR(j=i +1 to j < refset)
                GET r_1,r_2 ∈ rand[2, D−1]
                        where as r_1 ≠ r_2
                FOR(k= r_1 to k≤ r_1 )

/* Swap the values between the two solutions */
```

$$refset_{i,k} \overset{swap}{\leftrightarrow} refset_{j,k}$$

ENDFOR

/ A relative mutation schema is applied to the solutions to make it discrete. The pseudo code for it is described in the first section */*

/ Local search is applied to the solution to improve it. */*

$$refset_i \overset{Local\ Search}{\rightarrow} refset'_i,\ refset_j \overset{Local\ Search}{\rightarrow} refset'_j$$

/ If this solution improves on the worst solution in Refset, it then replaces that solution in refset. */*

IF($f\left(refset'\right) < f\left(refset_{refset\_size}\right)$)

MOVE $refset' \rightarrow refset_{refset\_size}$

ENDIF

ENDFOR

/ Output the best solution from the refset as the best solution in the heuristic. */*

PRINT $refset_{best}$

4. Experimentation and validation

The validation of this hybrid approach is conducted on the two demanding problems of QAP and FSS. Each experiment is conducted in two phases. The first phase is to experimentally obtain the operating parameters of HEDE-SS. The second phase is the comparison of the hybrid with other established heuristics reported in the literature.

4.1 QAP

The problem instances selected for the QAP are from the Operation Research (OR) library and reported in Gambardella *et al.* (1999). There are two separate problem modules; *regular* and *irregular*. The difference between regular and irregular problems is based on the *flow-dominance* (*fd*), which is used to differentiate among the classes of QAP instances. It is defined as a coefficient of variation of the flow matrix entries multiplied by 100. That is:

$$fd = 100\sigma/\mu \tag{22}$$

where:

$$\mu = \frac{1}{n^2} \bullet \sum_{i=1}^{n}\sum_{j=1}^{n} b_{ij} \tag{23}$$

$$\sigma = \sqrt{\frac{1}{n^2-1} \bullet \sum_{i=1}^{n}\sum_{j=1}^{n}\left(b_{ij} - \mu\right)} \tag{24}$$

4.1.1 Irregular problems

Irregular problems have a flow-dominance statistics larger than 1.2 (Taillard, 1995). Most of the problems come from practical applications or have been randomly generated with non-uniform laws, imitating the distributions observed on real world problems.

The operational parameters of EDE, found through extensive experimentation are given in Table 3 along with the size of the *refset* and the relative mutation schema selected which is RM.

Parameter	Strategy	CR	F	NP	G_{max}	RefSet	Mut
Values	1	0.9	0.3	500	500	30	3

Table 3. HEDE-SS QAP operational values.

Eighteen problem instances are evaluated of four different types; *bur, chr, els, kra* and *tai.* Comparisons were made with other heuristics of the tabu searches of Battiti and Tecchiolli (RTS), Taillard (TT) and the genetic hybrid method of Fleurent and Ferland (GH). A simulated annealing due to Connolly (SA) that is cited as a good implementation by Burkard and Celia was also included. Finally the work covered by Gambardella, Thaillard and Dorigo with Ant Colony (HAS-QAP) is compared as the best results for these instances of QAP.
Table 4 compares all the methods on long execution of G_{max} =500.

Instance	flow dom	n	Optimal	TT	RTS	SA	GH	HAS-QAP	HEDE-SS
bur26a	2.75	26	5246670	0.208	-	0.1411	0.0120	0	**0**
bur26b	2.75	26	3817852	0.441	-	0.1828	0.0219	0	**0**
bur26c	2.29	26	5426795	0.170	-	0.0742	0	0	**0**
bur26d	2.29	26	3821225	0.249	-	0.0056	0.002	0	**0**
bur26e	2.55	26	5386879	0.076	-	0.1238	0	0	**0**
bur26f	2.55	26	3782044	0.369	-	0.1579	0	0	**0**
bur26g	2.84	26	10117172	0.078	-	0.1688	0	0	**0**
bur26h	2.84	26	7098658	0.349	-	0.1268	0.0003	0	**0**
chr25a	4.15	26	3796	15.969	16.844	12.497	2.6923	3.0822	**0.023**
els19	5.16	19	17212548	21.261	6.714	18.5385	0	0	**0**
kra30a	1.46	30	88900	2.666	2.155	1.4657	0.1338	0.6299	**0**
kra30b	1.46	30	91420	0.478	1.061	1.065	0.0536	0.0711	**0**
tai20b	3.24	20	122455319	6.700	-	14.392	0	0.0905	**0**
tai25b	3.03	25	344355646	11.486	-	8.831	0	0	**0**
tai30b	3.18	30	637117113	13.284	-	13.515	0.0003	0	**0**
tai35b	3.05	35	283315445	10.165	-	6.935	0.1067	0.0256	**0**
tai40b	3.13	40	637250948	9.612	-	5.430	0.2109	0	**0**
tai50b	3.10	50	458821517	7.602	-	4.351	0.2124	0.1916	**0**

Table 4. HEDE-SS comparison with other heuristics for irregular problems.

The average quality of the solutions produced by the methods is shown, measured in per cent above the best solution value known from the OR Library. The best results obtained are indicated in boldface. From Table 4 it is shown that methods involving tabu search and simulated annealing are not well adapted for irregular problems. The well performing heuristics are able to produce solutions with at less than 1% with the same computing power and time. For the *bur...* problem instances the HAS-QAP heuristic shows optimal results, however HEDE-SS outperforms HAS-QAP by obtaining the optimal results. The most challenging problem instance is *chr25a.* All heuristics apart from HEDE-SS obtain very poor results, especially HAS-QAP getting over 3 over cent to the optimal. HEDE-SS outperforms all other heuristic by getting 0.023 per cent to the optimal. The *kra...* problem instances are also dominated by EDE, which obtains the optimal result and outperforms all other heuristics. For the *tai* problems, HEDE-SS obtains the optimal result for all problem instances while HAS-QAP fails to obtain consistent results.

4.1.2 Regular problems

Regular problems also know as unstructured problems are identified as having the flow-dominance statistics less than 1.2 (Taillard, 1995). These instances are randomly generated, and have good solutions spread over the whole solution set.
A comparison with the established algorithms from the literature is also done for the regular problems. The same heuristics as for irregular problems are retained for the comparison as shown in Table 5.

Instance	flow dom	n	Optimal	TT	RTS	SA	GH	HAS-QAP	HEDE-SS
nug20	0.99	20	2570	0	0.911	0.070	0	0	**0**
nug30	1.09	30	6124	0.032	0.872	0.121	0.007	0.098	**0**
sko42	1.06	42	15812	0.039	1.116	0.114	0.003	0.076	**0**
sko49	1.07	49	23386	0.062	0.978	0.133	0.040	0.141	**0**
sko56	1.09	56	34458	0.080	1.082	0.110	0.060	0.101	**0**
tai20a	0.61	20	703482	0.211	0.246	0.716	0.628	0.675	**0**
tai25a	0.60	25	1167256	0.510	0.345	1.002	0.629	1.189	**0**
tai30a	0.59	30	1818146	0.340	0.286	0.907	0.439	1.311	**0**
tai35a	0.58	35	2422002	0.757	0.355	1.345	0.698	1.762	**0**
tai40a	0.60	40	3139370	1.006	0.623	1.307	0.884	1.989	**0**
tai50a	0.60	50	4941410	1.145	0.834	1.539	1.049	2.800	**0**
wil50	0.64	50	48816	0.041	0.504	0.061	0.032	0.061	**0**

Table 5. HEDE-SS comparison with other heuristics for regular problems.

HEDE-SS obtains the optimal result for all instances. The performance of HAS-QAP, which was the closest heuristic in irregular problems, has decreased in regular problems. The results obtained by HAS-QAP for *nug* and *sko* are within tolerable limits, however for *tai* problem instances the results are in excess of 1 per cent to the optimal. HEDE-SS manages to obtain optimal results for the *nug, sko, tai* problem instances. The only serious competition is seen from GH, which on average outperforms HAS-QAP for the *nug* and *sko* problem instances and RTS which performs best for *tai* problem instances. The conclusion that can be drawn is that no one heuristic performs optimally for all problem instances tested apart from HEDE-SS, which outperforms all other tested heuristics for the regular problems. By the performance of the compared heuristics it can be observed that regular problems are more difficult to solve than irregular problem, yet HEDE-SS manages to perform exceptionally well for both (Davendra & Onwubolu, 2007).

4.2 FSS results

The flow shop experimentation was conducted with the Thaillard benchmark problem sets (Taillard, 1993). These sets of problems have been extensively evaluated: see Nowicki et al (1996), Reeves et al (1998). This benchmark set contains 120 particularly hard instances of 12 different sizes, selected from a large number of randomly generated problems. Of these 100 problem instances were evaluated by HEDE-SS and compared with published work. These instances are: *jobs – machines* (*n* x *m*); 20 x 5, 20 x 10, 20 x 20, 50 x 5, 50 x 10, 50 x 20, 100 x 5, 100 x 10, 100 x 20, 200 x 10, a sample of 10 instances for each set was provided in the OR Library.

A maximum of ten iterations was done for each problem instance. The population was kept at 500, and 500 generations were specified for EDE, and the RefSet was kept at 30 for the SS heuristic as shown in Table 6.

Parameter	Strategy	CR	F	NP	G_{max}	RefSet	Mut
Values	7	0.9	0.4	500	500	30	3

Table 6. HEDE-SS FSS operational values.

The results represented in Table 7 are as quality solutions with the percentage relative increase in makespan with respect to the upper bound provided by Thaillard (1993). To be specific the formulation is given as:

$$\Delta_{avg} = \frac{(H-U)\times 100}{U} \tag{25}$$

where H denotes the value of the makespan that is produced by the EDE algorithm and U is the upper bound or the lower bound as computed.

The results are compared with those produced by Particle Swarm Optimization (PSO*spv*) (Tasgetiren et al, 2004), DE (DE*spv*), DE with local search (DE*spv+exchange*) as in Tasgetiren et al (2004) and Enhansed DE (EDE) of Davendra and Onwubolu (2009).

As seen in Table 7, HEDE-SS compares very well with other algorithms. HEDE-SS outperforms PSO and DE*spv*. The only serious competition comes from the new variant of DE*spv+exchange*.. HEDE-SS outperforms DE*spv+exchange* in all but two data sets of 50x20 and 100x20.

The main indicator of the effectiveness of HEDE-SS is its comparison with EDE. The hybrid system is better performing than the canonical approach. SS enhances the application of EDE and thus the hybrid approach can be viewed a s superior heuristic.

	PSO_{spv}		DE_{spv}		$DE_{spv+exchange}$		EDE		HEDE-SS	
	Δ_{avg}	Δ_{std}	Δ_{avg}	Δ_{std}	Δ_{avg}	Δ_{std}	Δ_{avg}	Δ_{std}	Δ_{avg}	Δ_{std}
20x5	1.71	1.25	2.25	1.37	0.69	0.64	0.98	0.66	0.54	0.51
20x10	3.28	1.19	3.71	1.24	2.01	0.93	1.81	0.77	1.51	0.64
20x20	2.84	1.15	3.03	0.98	1.85	0.87	1.75	0.57	1.62	0.59
50x5	1.15	0.70	0.88	0.52	0.41	0.37	0.40	0.36	0.32	0.21
50x10	4.83	1.16	4.12	1.10	2.41	0.90	3.18	0.94	2.21	1.32
50x20	6.68	1.35	5.56	1.22	3.59	0.78	4.05	0.65	3.79	0.81
100x5	0.59	0.34	0.44	0.29	0.21	0.21	0.41	0.29	0.21	0.33
100x10	3.26	1.04	2.28	0.75	1.41	0.57	1.46	0.36	1.33	0.42
100x20	7.19	0.99	6.78	1.12	3.11	0.55	3.61	0.36	3.12	0.56
200x10	2.47	0.71	1.88	0.69	1.06	0.35	0.95	0.18	0.88	0.29

Table 7. HEDE-SS Taillard problem performance comparisons

5. Conclusion

The hybrid approach of HEDE-SS is highly effective in permutative optimization. This conclusion is reached through the experimentation that has been conducted in order to validate this new approach. Optimal results have been achieved by the HEDE-SS on all but one instance of QAP both regular and irregular problem, and on that instance of *chr25*, HEDE-SS outperforms all other listed heuristics.

In FSS problem instances, the hybrid approach is also a strong performer. It easliy improves the results of EDE and other varients of DE and PSO.

Overall, hybridization can be seen as the next evolution of meta-heuristics. With improving hardware technologies, it thus becomes viable to have multiple heuristics combined for better performace. The main concept of using two unique paradigm based systems such as DE and SS is justified as both complement each other and improve the results.

6. Acknowledgement

The author would like to acknowledge the following research grants for financial support for this research.

1. Grant Agency of the Czech Republic **GARC 102/09/1680**
2. Grant of the Czech Ministry of Education **MSM 7088352102**

7. References

Bazaraa, M.S., &. Sherali., M.D (1980), Benders' partitioning scheme applied to a new formulation of the quadratic assignment problem. *Naval Research Logistics Quarterly* 27, 29-41.

Battitti, R., & Tecchiolli, G. (1994), The reactive tabu search. *ORCA Journal on Computing*, 6, 126-140

Burkard, R. E. (1991), Location with spatial interactions: The quadratic assignment problem, In Mirchandani, P.B. and Francis, R. L. (Eds), *Discrete Location Theory*, John Wiley.

Campos, V., Glover, F., Laguna, M. & Marti´, R. (2001), An Experimental Evaluation of a Scatter Search for the Linear Ordering Problem. *Journal of Global Optimization* 21, 397-414.

Christofides, N. & Benavent E. (1989), An exact algorithm for the quadratic assignment problem. *Operations Research* 37, 760-768,

Chung, V., Mautor, T., Michelon, P. & Tavares, A. (1997), A scatter search based approach for the quadratic assignment problem, In Baeck, T., Michalewick, Z., & Yao, X. (Eds) *Proceedings of ICEC'97* 165-170, IEEE Press

Connolly, D. T. (1990), An improved annealing scheme for the QAP, *European Journal of Operation Research* 46, 93-100.

Davendra, D. (2001), Differential Evolution Algorithm for Flow Shop Scheduling, *Unpublished Bachelor of Science Degree Thesis*, University of the South Pacific.

Davendra, D. (2003), Hybrid Differential Evolution Algorithm for Discrete Domain Problems, *Unpublished Master of Science Degree Thesis*, University of the South Pacific.

Davendra, D. & Onwubolu, G (2007) Enhanced Differential Evolution hybrid Scatter Search for Discrete Optimisation. *Proceeding of the IEEE Congress on Evolutionary Computation*, Sept 25-28, Singapore. Pp. 1156–1162

Davendra, D. & Onwubolu, G. (2009) Forward Backward Transformation. In *Differential Evolution – A handbook for the combinatorial-based permutitive optimization*. Onwubolu G. and Davendra (Eds), D. Spriner, Germany.

Dorigo, M. & Gambardella, L. M. (1997), Ant Colony System: A Co-operative Learning Approach to the Traveling Salesman Problem. *IEEE Transaction on Evolutionary Computations* 1, 53-65.

Fleurent, C., & Ferland, J. A. (1994), Genetic Hybrids for the Quadratic Assignment Problem, *Operations Research Quarterly* 28, 167 – 179.

Gambardella, L. M., Thaillard, E. D., & Dorigo, M. (1999), Ant Colonies for the Quadratic Assignment Problem, *Journal of Operational Research* 50, 167-176.

Glover, F. (1998), A Template for Scatter Search and Path Relinking, In Hao, J. K., Lutton, E., Schoenauer, M. & Snyers, D. (Eds) *Lecture Notes in Computer Science* 12363, 13 – 54.

Goldberg, D.E. (1989), *Genetic Algorithms in Search, Optimization, and Machine Learning*, Addison-Wesley Publishing Company, Inc.

Koopmans, T. C. & Beckmann, M. J. (1957), Assignment problems and the location of economic activities. *Econometrica* 25, 53-76.

Laguna, M., Martí, R. & Campos, V. (1997), Tabu Search with Path Relinking for the Linear Ordering Problem. *Research Report*, University of Colorado.

Lampinen, J. & Storn, R. (2004). Differential Evolution, In Onwubolu, G. C., Babu, B. (eds.), *New Optimization Techniques in Engineering*, Springer Verlag, Germany, 123-163.

Lawler, E. L. (1963), The quadratic assignment problem. *Management Science* 9, 586-599.

Malucelli, F. (1993), Quadratic assignment Problems: Solution Methods and Applications. *Unpublished Doctoral Dissertation*, Departimento di Informatica, Universita di Pisa, Italy.

Nowicki, E. & Smutnicki, C. (1996). A fast tabu search algorithm for the permutative flow shop problem. European Journal of Operations Research, 91, 160-175

Onwubolu, G., C. (2001), Optimization using Differential Evolution Algorithm, *Technical Report TR-2001-05*, IAS, October 2001.

Onwubolu G., C. (2002), *Emerging Optimization Techniques in Production Planning and Control*, Imperial Collage Press, London.

Onwubolu, G., C., & Clerc. M. (2004), Optimal path for automated drilling operations by a new heuristic approach using particle swamp optimization. *International Journal of Production Research*, 42, 3, 473-491.

Onwubolu, G., C. & Davendra, D. (2006). Scheduling flow shops using differential evolution algorithm. *European Journal of Operations Research*, 171,674-679

Onwubolu G., C. & Davendra D. (2009) *Differential Evolution – A handbook for the combinatorial-based permutitive optimization*. Spriner, Germany.

OR Library: http://mscmga.ms.ic.ac.uk/info.html

Pardalos, P. M., & Crouse, J. (1989), A parallel algorithm for the quadratic assignment problem, *Proceedings of the Supercomputing 1989 Conference*, ACM Press, 351-360.

Ponnambalam, S. G., Aravindan, P. & Chandrasekhar, S. (2001). Constructive and improvement flow shop scheduling heuristic: an extensive evaluation, Production Planning and Control 12, 335-344.

Price, K. (1999), An introduction to differential evolution, In Corne, D., Dorigo, M., & Glover, F. (Eds.), *New Ideas in Optimization*, McGraw Hill International, UK, 79-108.

Price, K., & Storn, R. (2001), Differential Evolution homepage (Website of Price and Storn) as at 2001. http://www.ICSI.Berkeley.edu/~storn/code.html

Reeves, C. & Yamada, T. (1998). Genetic Algorithms, path relinking and flowshop sequencing problem. Evolutionary Computation 6, 45-60.

Sahni, S. & Gonzalez, T. (1976), P-complete approximation problems, *Journal of the ACM*, 23, 555-565.

Sondergeld, L., & Voβ. S. (1996), A star-shaped diversification approach in tabu search, in Osman, I., and Kelly, J. (eds) *Meta-Heuristics: Theory and Applications*, Kluwer Academic Publishers: Boston, 489-502.

Taillard, E. (1991), Robust taboo search for the quadratic assignment problem, *Parallel Computing*, 17, 443-455

Taillard, E. (1993). Benchmarks for basic scheduling problems. European Journal of Operations Research, 64, 278-285.

Taillard, E. (1995), Comparison of Iterative Searches for the Quadratic Assignment Problem. *Location Science*, 3, 87–105.

Taillard, E., D. (1996), A heuristic column generation method for the heterogeneous VRP. *CRT-96-03*, Centre de recherché sur les transports, Université de Montréal.

Tasgetiren, M. F., Sevkli, M. Liang, Y-C., & Gencyilmaz, G. (2004). Particle swamp optimization algorithm for permutative flowshops sequencing problems, *4th*

International Workshops on Ant Algorithms and Swamp Intelligence, ANTS2004, LNCS 3127, Brussel, Belgium. September 5-8, 389-390.

Tasgetiren, M. F., Liang, Y-C., Sevkli, M. & Gencyilmaz, G. (2004). Differential Evolution Algorithm for Permutative Flowshops Sequencing Problem with Makespan Criterion, *4th International Symposium on Intelligent Manufacturing Systems, IMS2004*, Sakaraya, Turkey. September 5-8, 442-452.

Yamada, T. & Nanako, R. (1996), Scheduling by Genetic Local Search with Multi-Step Crossover. *4th International Conference on Parallel Problem Solving from Nature*, 960-969.

16

Optimization with the Nature-Inspired Intelligent Water Drops Algorithm

Hamed Shah-Hosseini
Faculty of Electrical and Computer Engineering, Shahid Beheshti University, G.C. Tehran, Iran

1. Introduction

Scientists are beginning to realize more and more that nature is a great source for inspiration in order to develop intelligent systems and algorithms. In the field of Computational Intelligence, especially Evolutionary Computation and Swarm-based systems, the degree of imitation from nature is surprisingly high and we are at the edge of developing and proposing new algorithms and/or systems, which partially or fully follow nature and the actions and reactions that happen in a specific natural system or species.

Among the most recent nature-inspired swarm-based optimization algorithms is the Intelligent Water Drops (IWD) algorithm. IWD algorithms imitate some of the processes that happen in nature between the water drops of a river and the soil of the river bed. The IWD algorithm was first introduced in (Shah-Hosseini, 2007) in which the IWDs are used to solve the Travelling Salesman Problem (TSP). The IWD algorithm has also been successfully applied to the Multidimensional Knapsack Problem (MKP) (Shah-Hosseini, 2008a), *n*-queen puzzle (Shah-Hosseini, 2008b), and Robot Path Planning (Duan et al., 2008).

Here, the IWD algorithm and its versions are specified for the TSP, the *n*-queen puzzle, the MKP, and for the first time, the AMT (Automatic Multilevel Thresholding). Some theoretical findings have also been reviewed for the IWD algorithm. Next section reviews briefly the related works. Section 3 examines natural water drops. Section 4 states about Intelligent Water Drops (IWDs). Section 5 specifies the Intelligent Water Drops (IWD) algorithm. Next section, reviews the convergence properties of the IWD algorithm. Section 7 includes experiments with the IWD and its versions for the four mentioned problems. Final section includes the concluding remarks.

2. Related works

One of the famous swarm-based optimization algorithms has been invented by simulating the behaviour of social ants in a colony. Ants living in a nest are able to survive and develop their generations and reproduce in a cooperative way. Moreover, they can find the shortest path from their nest to a food source or vice versa. They can build complex nests capable of holding hundreds of thousands of ants and lots of other activities that show a high-level of intelligence in a colony of ants. Other social insects generally show such complex and intelligent behaviours such as bees and termites. Ant colony optimization (ACO) algorithm

(Dorigo & et al., 1991) and Bee Colony Optimization (BCO) algorithm (Sato & Hagiwara, 1997) are among the swarm-based algorithms imitating social insects for optimization.
Evolutionary Computation is another system, which has been inspired from observing natural selection and reproduction systems in nature. Genetic algorithms (GA) (Holland, 1975) are among the most famous algorithms in this regard. Evolution Strategy (Rechenberg, 1973; Schwefel, 1981), Evolutionary Programming (Fogel et al., 1966), and Genetic Programming (Koza, 1992) are other Evolutionary-based intelligent algorithms that are often used for optimization. Memetic Algorithms (MA) (Dawkins, 1989; Ong et al., 2006) are among the most recent area of research in the field of Evolutionary Computation. Here, a meme is the basic unit of culture that can be inherited. An individual is assumed to have both genes and memes. Therefore, not only the genes of individuals evolve, but also their memes undergo evolution.
Artificial Immune Systems (AIS) are another example of swarm-based nature inspired algorithms, which follow the processes and actions that happen in the immune systems of vertebrates. Clonal Selection Algorithms (de Castro & Von Zuben, 2002), Negative Selection Algorithms (Forrest, et al., 1994), and Immune Network Algorithms (Timmis et al., 2000) are among the most common techniques in the field of AIS.
Another swarm-based optimization algorithm is the Particle Swarm Optimization (PSO), which has been introduced by (Kennedy & Eberhart, 1995). PSO uses a swarm of particles, which each one has position and velocity vectors, and they move near together to find the optimal solution for a given problem. Infact, PSO imitates the processes that exist in the flocks of birds or a school of fish to find the optimal solution.
Another swarm-based optimization algorithm is the Electromagnetism-like mechanism (EM) (Birbil & Fang, 2003). The EM algorithm uses an attraction-repulsion mechanism based on the Coulomb's law to move some points towards the optimal positions.

3. Natural water drops

In nature, flowing water drops are observed mostly in rivers, which form huge moving swarms. The paths that a natural river follows have been created by a swarm of water drops. For a swarm of water drops, the river in which they flow is the part of the environment that has been dramatically changed by the swarm and will also be changed in the future. Moreover, the environment itself has substantial effects on the paths that the water drops follow. For example, against a swarm of water drops, those parts of the environment having hard soils resist more than the parts with soft soils. In fact, a natural river is the result of a competition between water drops in a swarm and the environment that resists the movement of water drops.
Based on our observation in nature, most rivers have paths full of twists and turns. Up until now, it is believed that water drops in a river have no eyes so that by using those eyes, they can find their destination, which is often a lake or sea. If we put ourselves in place of a water drop flowing in a river, we would feel that some force pulls us toward itself, which is the earth's gravity. This gravitational force pulls everything toward the center of the earth in a straight line. Therefore with no obstacles and barriers, the water drops should follow a straight path toward the destination, which is the shortest path from the source of water drops to the destination, which is ideally the earth's center. This gravitational force creates acceleration such that water drops gain speed as they come near to the earth's center. However, in reality, due to different kinds of obstacles and constraints in the way of this

ideal path, the real path is so different from the ideal path such that lots of twists and turns in a river path are seen, and the destination is not the earth's center but a lake, sea, or even a bigger river. It is often observed that the constructed path seems to be an optimal one in terms of the distance from the destination and the constraints of the environment.

One feature of a water drop flowing in a river is its velocity. It is assumed that each water drop of a river can also carry an amount of soil. Therefore, the water drop is able to transfer an amount of soil from one place to another place in the front. This soil is usually transferred from fast parts of the path to the slow parts. As the fast parts get deeper by being removed from soil, they can hold more volume of water and thus may attract more water. The removed soils, which are carried in the water drops, are unloaded in slower beds of the river. Assume an imaginary natural water drop is going to flow from one point of a river to the next point in the front. Three obvious changes happen during this transition:

- Velocity of the water drop is increased.
- Soil of the water drop is increased.
- Between these two points, soil of the river's bed is decreased.

In fact, an amount of soil of the river's bed is removed by the water drop and this removed soil is added to the soil of the water drop. Moreover, the speed of the water drop is increased during the transition.

It was mentioned above that a water drop has also a velocity. This velocity plays an important role in removing soil from the beds of rivers. The following property is assumed for a flowing water drop:

- A high speed water drop gathers more soil than a slower water drop.

Therefore, the water drop with bigger speed removes more soil from the river's bed than another water drop with smaller speed. The soil removal is thus related to the velocities of water drops.

It has been said earlier that when a water drop flows on a part of a river's bed, it gains speed. But this increase in velocity depends on the amount of soil of that part. This property of a water drop is expressed below:

- The velocity of a water drop increases more on a path with low soil than a path with high soil.

The velocity of the water drop is changed such that on a path with little amount of soil, the velocity of the water drop is increased more than a path with a considerable amount of soil. Therefore, a path with little soil lets the flowing water drop gather more soil and gain more speed whereas the path with large soil resists more against the flowing water drop such that it lets the flowing water drop gather less soil and gain less speed.

Another property of a natural water drop is that when it faces several paths in the front, it often chooses the easier path. Therefore, the following statement may be expressed:

- A water drop prefers a path with less soil than a path with more soil

The water drop prefers an easier path to a harder path when it has to choose between several branches that exist in the path from the source to destination. The easiness or hardness of a path is denoted by the amount of soil on that path. A path with more soil is considered a hard path whereas a path with less soil is considered an easy path.

4. Intelligent Water Drops (IWDs)

In the previous section, some prominent properties of natural water drops were mentioned. Based on the aforementioned statements, an Intelligent Water Drop (IWD) has been suggested (Shah-Hosseini, 2007), which possesses a few remarkable properties of a natural water drop. This Intelligent Water Drop, IWD for short, has two important properties:

- The soil it carries, denoted by soil(IWD).
- The velocity that it posses, denoted by velocity(IWD).

For each IWD, the values of both properties, soil(IWD) and velocity(IWD) may change as the IWD flows in its environment. From the engineering point of view, an environment represents a problem that is desired to be solved. A river of IWDs seeks an optimal path for the given problem.

Each IWD is assumed to flow in its environment from a source to a desired destination. In an environment, there are numerous paths from a given source to a desired destination. The location of the destination may be unknown. If the location of the desired destination is known, the solution to the problem is obtained by finding the best (often the shortest) path from the source to the destination. However, there are cases in which the destination is unknown. In such cases, the solution is obtained by finding the optimum destination in terms of cost or any other desired measure for the given problem.

An IWD moves in discrete finite-length steps in its environment. From its current location *i* to its next location *j*, the IWD velocity, velocity (IWD), is increased by an amount Δvelocity (IWD), which is nonlinearly proportional to the inverse of the soil between the two locations *i* an *j*, soil(*i* , *j*):

$$\Delta velocity(IWD) \propto^{NL} \frac{1}{soil(i,j)} \tag{1}$$

Here, nonlinearly proportionality is denoted by $\propto^{NL}$. One possible formula is given below in which the velocity of the IWD denoted by $vel^{IWD}(t)$ is updated by the amount of soil $soil(i,j)$ between the two locations *i* and *j*:

$$\Delta vel^{IWD}(t) = \frac{a_v}{b_v + c_v \, . \, soil^{2\alpha}(i,j)} \tag{2}$$

Here, the a_v, b_v, c_v, and α are user-selected positive parameters.

Moreover, the IWD's soil, soil(IWD), is increased by removing some soil of the path joining the two locations *i* an *j*. The amount of soil added to the IWD, Δsoil(IWD)= Δsoil(*i*,*j*), is inversely (and nonlinearly) proportional to the time needed for the IWD to pass from its current location to the next location denoted by time(*i*,*j*; *IWD*).

$$\Delta soil(IWD) = \Delta soil(i,j) \propto^{NL} \frac{1}{time(i,j;IWD)} \tag{3}$$

One suggestion for the above formula is given below in which $time(i,j;vel^{IWD})$ is the time taken for the IWD with velocity vel^{IWD} to move from location *i* to *j*. The soil added to the IWD is calculated by

$$\Delta soil(i,j) = \frac{a_s}{b_s + c_s . time^{2\theta}\left(i,j;vel^{IWD}\right)} \tag{4}$$

Where the parameters a_s, b_s, c_s, and θ are user-selected and should be chosen as positive numbers.

The duration of time for the IWD is calculated by the simple laws of physics for linear motion. Thus, the time taken for the IWD to move from location *i* to *j* is proportional to the velocity of the IWD, velocity (IWD), and inversely proportional to the distance between the two locations, d(*i,j*). More specifically:

$$time(i, j; IWD) \propto^L \frac{1}{velocity(IWD)} \tag{5}$$

Where $\propto^L$ denotes linear proportionality. One such formula is given below, which calculates the time taken for the IWD to travel from location *i* to *j* with velocity vel^{IWD}:

$$time\left(i, j; vel^{IWD}\right) = \frac{HUD(i, j)}{vel^{IWD}} \tag{6}$$

Where a local heuristic function $HUD(.,.)$ has been defined for a given problem to measure the undesirability of an IWD to move from one location to the next.

Some soil is removed from the visited path between locations *i* and *j*. The updated soil of the path denoted by soil(*i,j*) is proportional to the amount of soil removed by the IWD flowing on the path joining *i* to *j*, Δsoil(*i,j*)= Δsoil(IWD). Specifically:

$$soil(i, j) \propto^L \Delta soil(i, j) \tag{7}$$

One such formula has been used for the IWD algorithm such that $soil(i, j)$ is updated by the amount of soil removed by the IWD from the path *i* to *j*.

$$soil(i, j) = \rho_o \, . soil(i, j) - \rho_n \, . \Delta soil(i, j) \tag{8}$$

Where ρ_o and ρ_n are often positive numbers between zero and one. In the original IWD algorithm for the TSP (Shah-Hosseini, 2007), $\rho_o = 1 - \rho_n$.

The soil of the IWD denoted by $soil^{IWD}$ is added by the amount $soil(i, j)$ as shown below:

$$soil^{IWD} = soil^{IWD} + \Delta soil(i, j) \tag{9}$$

Another mechanism that exists in the behaviour of an IWD is that it prefers the paths with low soils on its beds to the paths with higher soils on its beds. To implement this behaviour of path choosing, a uniform random distribution is used among the soils of the available paths such that the probability of the IWD to move from location *i* to *j* denoted by p(i,j;IWD) is inversely proportional to the amount of soils on the available paths.

$$p(i, j; IWD) \propto^L soil(i, j) \tag{10}$$

The lower the soil of the path between locations *i* and *j*, the more chance this path has for being selected by the IWD located on *i*. One such formula based on Eq. (10) has been used in which the probability of choosing location *j* is given by:

$$p(i,j;IWD) = \frac{f(soil(i,j))}{\sum_{k \notin vc(IWD)} f(soil(i,k))} \tag{11}$$

Where $f(soil(i,j)) = \dfrac{1}{\varepsilon_s + g(soil(i,j))}$. The constant parameter ε_s is a small positive number to prevent a possible division by zero in the function $f(.)$. The set $vc(IWD)$ denotes the nodes that the IWD should not visit to keep satisfied the constraints of the problem.

The function $g(soil(i,j))$ is used to shift the $soil(i,j)$ of the path joining nodes i and j toward positive values and is computed by

$$g(soil(i,j)) = \begin{cases} soil(i,j) & if \min_{l \notin \text{vc(IWD)}} (soil(i,l)) \geq 0 \\ soil(i,j) - \min_{l \notin vc(IWD)} (soil(i,l)) & else \end{cases} \tag{12}$$

Where the function $\min(.)$ returns the minimum value of its arguments.

The IWDs work together to find the optimal solution to a given problem. The problem is encoded in the environment of the IWDs, and the solution is represented by the path that the IWDs have converged to. In the next section, the IWD algorithm is explained.

5. The Intelligent Water Drops (IWD) algorithm

The IWD algorithm employs a number of IWDs to find the optimal solutions to a given problem. The problem is represented by a graph (N, E) with the node set N and edge set E. This graph is the environment for the IWDs and the IWDs flow on the edges of the graph. Each IWD begins constructing its solution gradually by traveling between the nodes of the graph along the edges until the IWD finally completes its solution denoted by T^{IWD}. Each solution T^{IWD} is represented by the edges that the IWD has visited. One iteration of the IWD algorithm is finished when all IWDs complete their solutions. After each iteration, the iteration-best solution T^{IB} is found. The iteration-based solution T^{IB} is the best solution based on a quality function among all solutions obtained by the IWDs in the current iteration. T^{IB} is used to update the total-best solution T^{TB}. The total-best solution T^{TB} is the best solution since the beginning of the IWD algorithm, which has been found in all iterations.

For a given problem, an objective or quality function is needed to measure the fitness of solutions. Consider the quality function of a problem to be denoted by $q(.)$. Then, the quality of a solution T^{IWD} found by the IWD is given by $q(T^{IWD})$. Therefore, the iteration-best solution T^{IB} is given by:

$$T^{IB} = \arg \max_{for\ all\ IWDs} q(T^{IWD}) \tag{13}$$

Where arg(.) returns its argument.

It should be noted that at the end of each iteration of the algorithm, the total-best solution T^{TB} is updated by the current iteration-best solution T^{IB} as follows:

$$T^{TB} = \begin{cases} T^{TB} & if\ q(T^{TB}) \geq q(T^{IB}) \\ T^{IB} & otherwise \end{cases} \tag{14}$$

Moreover, at the end of each iteration of the IWD algorithm, the amount of soil on the edges of the iteration-best solution T^{IB} is reduced based on the goodness (quality) of the solution. One such mechanism (Shah-Hosseini, 2007) is used to update the $soil(i, j)$ of each edge (i, j) of the iteration-best solution T^{IB}:

$$\begin{aligned} soil(i,j) &= \rho_s \,.\, soil(i,j) \\ &- \rho_{IWD} \cdot \frac{1}{(N_{IB}-1)} \,.\, soil_{IB}^{IWD} \quad \forall (i,j) \in T^{IB} \end{aligned} \tag{15}$$

Where $soil_{IB}^{IWD}$ represents the soil of the iteration-best IWD. The iteration-best IWD is the IWD that has constructed the iteration-best solution T^{IB} at the current iteration. N_{IB} is the number of nodes in the solution T^{IB}. ρ_{IWD} is the global soil updating parameter, which should be chosen from $[0,1]$. ρ_s is often set as $(1+\rho_{IWD})$.

Then, the algorithm begins another iteration with new IWDs but with the same soils on the paths of the graph and the whole process is repeated. The IWD algorithm stops when it reaches the maximum number of iterations $iter_{max}$ or the total-best solution T^{TB} achieves the expected quality demanded for the given problem.

The IWD algorithm has two kinds of parameters:

- Static parameters
- Dynamic parameters

Static parameters are those parameters that remain constant during the lifetime of the IWD algorithm. That is why they are called "static". Dynamic parameters are those parameters, which are dynamic and they are reinitialized after each iteration of the IWD algorithm.

The IWD algorithm as expressed in (Shah-Hosseini, 2008b) is specified in the following ten steps:

1. Initialization of static parameters:

- The graph (N, E) of the problem is given to the algorithm, which contains N_c nodes.
- The quality of the total-best solution T^{TB} is initially set to the worst value: $q(T^{TB}) = -\infty$.
- The maximum number of iterations $iter_{\max}$ is specified by the user and the algorithm stops when it reaches $iter_{\max}$.
- The iteration count $iter_{count}$, which counts the number of iterations, is set to zero.
- The number of water drops N_{IWD} is set to a positive integer value. This number should at least be equal to two. However, N_{IWD} is usually set to the number of nodes N_c of the graph.
- Velocity updating parameters are a_v, b_v, and c_v. Here, $a_v = c_v = 1$ and $b_v = 0.01$
- Soil updating parameters are a_s, b_s, and c_s. Here, $a_s = c_s = 1$ and $b_s = 0.01$
- The local soil updating parameter is ρ_n. Here, $\rho_n = 0.9$ except for the AMT, which is $\rho_n = -0.9$.
- The global soil updating parameter is ρ_{IWD}. Here, $\rho_{IWD} = 0.9$.

- The initial soil on each edge of the graph is denoted by the constant $InitSoil$ such that the soil of the edge between every two nodes i and j is set by $soil(i, j) = InitSoil$. Here, $InitSoil = 10000$
- The initial velocity of each IWD is set to $InitVel$. Here, $InitVel = 200$ except for the MKP, which is $InitVel = 4$.
- Initialization of dynamic parameters:
- Every IWD has a visited node list $V_c(IWD)$, which is initially empty: $V_c(IWD) = \{\ \}$.
- Each IWD's velocity is set to $InitVel$.
- All IWDs are set to have zero amount of soil.

2. Spread the IWDs randomly on the nodes of the graph as their first visited nodes.
3. Update the visited node list of each IWD to include the nodes just visited.
4. Repeat steps 5.1 to 5.4 for those IWDs with partial solutions.

5.1. For the IWD residing in node i, choose the next node j, which doesn't violate any constraints of the problem and is not in the visited node list $vc(IWD)$ of the IWD, using the following probability $p_i^{IWD}(j)$:

$$p_i^{IWD}(j) = \frac{f(soil(i, j))}{\sum_{k \notin vc(IWD)} f(soil(i, k))} \tag{16}$$

such that

$$f(soil(i, j)) = \frac{1}{\varepsilon_s + g(soil(i, j))} \tag{17}$$

and

$$g(soil(i, j)) = \begin{cases} soil(i, j) & if \min\limits_{l \notin vc(IWD)} (soil(i, l)) \geq 0 \\ soil(i, j) - \min\limits_{l \notin vc(IWD)} (soil(i, l)) & else \end{cases} \tag{18}$$

Then, add the newly visited node j to the list $vc(IWD)$.

5.2. For each IWD moving from node i to node j, update its velocity $vel^{IWD}(t)$ by

$$vel^{IWD}(t+1) = vel^{IWD}(t) + \frac{a_v}{b_v + c_v \,.\, soil^2(i, j)} \tag{19}$$

where $vel^{IWD}(t+1)$ is the updated velocity of the IWD.

5.3. For the IWD moving on the path from node i to j, compute the soil $\Delta soil(i, j)$ that the IWD loads from the path by

$$\Delta soil(i, j) = \frac{a_s}{b_s + c_s . time^2\left(i, j; vel^{IWD}(t+1)\right)} \tag{20}$$

such that $time\left(i, j; vel^{IWD}(t+1)\right) = \frac{HUD(j)}{vel^{IWD}(t+1)}$ where the heuristic undesirability $HUD(j)$ is defined appropriately for the given problem.

5.4. Update the soil $soil(i,j)$ of the path from node i to j traversed by that IWD, and also update the soil that the IWD carries $soil^{IWD}$ by

$$\begin{aligned} soil(i,j) &= (1-\rho_n).soil(i,j) - \rho_n.\Delta soil(i,j) \\ soil^{IWD} &= soil^{IWD} + \Delta soil(i,j) \end{aligned} \quad (21)$$

6. Find the iteration-best solution T^{IB} from all the solutions T^{IWD} found by the IWDs using

$$T^{IB} = \arg\max_{\forall T^{IWD}} q(T^{IWD}) \quad (22)$$

where function $q(.)$ gives the quality of the solution.

7. Update the soils on the paths that form the current iteration-best solution T^{IB} by

$$\begin{aligned} soil(i,j) &= (1+\rho_{\mathrm{IWD}}).soil(i,j) \\ &- \rho_{IWD} \cdot \frac{1}{(N_{IB}-1)} \cdot soil_{IB}^{IWD} \quad \forall (i,j) \in T^{IB} \end{aligned} \quad (23)$$

where N_{IB} is the number of nodes in solution T^{IB}.

8. Update the total best solution T^{TB} by the current iteration-best solution T^{IB} using

$$T^{TB} = \begin{cases} T^{TB} & \text{if } q(T^{TB}) \geq q(T^{IB}) \\ T^{IB} & \text{otherwise} \end{cases} \quad (24)$$

9. Increment the iteration number by $Iter_{count} = Iter_{count} + 1$. Then, go to step 2 if $Iter_{count} < Iter_{\max}$.

10. The algorithm stops here with the total-best solution T^{TB}.

The IWD algorithm may be compared to the ant-based optimization algorithms (Bonabeau et al., 1999), which is summarized below:

- Every ant in an Ant Colony Optimization (ACO) algorithm deposits pheromones on each edge it visits. In contrast, an IWD changes the amount of soil on edges.
- In the ACO algorithm, an ant cannot remove pheromones from an edge whereas in the IWD algorithm, an IWD can both remove and add soil to an edge.
- In the IWD algorithm, the changes made on the soil of an edge are not constant and they are dependent on the velocity and soil of the IWDs visiting that edge. In contrast, in the ACO algorithm, each ant deposits a constant amount of pheromone on the edge.
- Besides, the IWDs may gain different velocities throughout an iteration of the IWD algorithm whereas in ACO algorithms the velocities of the ants are irrelevant.

6. Convergence properties of the IWD algorithm

Let the graph (N,E) represents the graph of the given problem. This graph is assumed to be a fully connected graph with N_c nodes. Let N_{IWD} represents the number of IWDs in the IWD algorithm. In the soil updating of the algorithm, two extreme cases are considered:

Case one: Only those terms of the IWD algorithm, which increase soil to an edge (arc) of (N,E), are considered.

Case two: Only those terms of the IWD algorithm, which decrease soil to an edge (arc) of (N,E), are considered.

For each case, the worst-case is followed. For case one, the highest possible value of soil that an edge can hold after m iterations, $soil(edge_{\max})$, will be (Shah-Hosseini, 2008a):

$$soil(edge_{\max}) = \left((\rho_s \rho_o)^m IS_0 \right) \tag{25}$$

Where the edge is denoted by $edge_{\max}$. IS_0 is the initial soil of an edge (i,j), which is denoted by $InitSoil$ in the IWD algorithm. ρ_0 is used in Eq. (8) and ρ_s is used in Eq. (15).

For case two, the lowest possible value of soil for an edge is computed. That edge is denoted by $edge_{\max}$. Then, after m iterations, the soil of $edge_{\max}$ is (Shah-Hosseini, 2008a):

$$soil(edge_{\min}) = \left(m\left(\rho_{IWD} - \rho_n N_{IWD}\right)\left(\frac{a_s}{b_s}\right)\right) \tag{26}$$

Where N_{IWD} is the number of IWDs. Soil updating parameters a_s and b_s are defined in Eq. (20). ρ_{IWD} is the global soil updating parameter used in Eq. (23). ρ_n is the local soil updating parameter used in Eq. (21).

Based on Eqs. (25) and (26), the following proposition is stated:

Proposition 6.1. The soil of any edge in the graph (N,E) of a given problem after m iterations of the IWD algorithm remains in the interval $[soil(edge_{\min}), soil(edge_{\max})]$.

The probability of finding any feasible solution by an IWD in iteration m is $(p_{lowest})^{(N_c-1)}$ where the probability of any IWD, going from node *i* to node *j*, is always bigger than p_{lowest}. It has been shown (Shah-Hosseini, 2008a) that p_{lowest} is always a positive value. Since there are N_{IWD} IWDs, then the probability $p(s;m)$ of finding any feasible solution s by the IWDs in iteration m is:

$$p(s;m) = N_{IWD}(p_{lowest})^{(N_c-1)} \tag{27}$$

The probability of finding any feasible solution s at the end of M iterations of the algorithm is:

$$P(s;M) = 1 - \prod_{m=1}^{M}\left(1 - p(s;m)\right) \tag{28}$$

Because $0 < p(s;m) \le 1$, then by making M large enough, it is concluded that: $\lim_{M\to\infty} \prod_{m=1}^{M}\left(1 - p(s;m)\right) = 0$. Therefore, the following proposition is true:

Proposition 6.2. If $P(s;M)$ represents the probability of finding any feasible solution s within M iterations of the IWD algorithm. As M gets larger, $P(s;M)$ approaches to one:

$$\lim_{M\to\infty} P(s;M) = 1 \tag{29}$$

Knowing the fact that the optimal solution s^* is a feasible solution of the problem, from above proposition, the following proposition is concluded.

Proposition 6.3. The IWD algorithm finds the optimal solution s^* of any given problem with probability one if the number of iterations M is sufficiently large.

It is noticed that the required M to find the optimal solution s^* should be decreased by careful tuning of parameters of the IWD algorithm for the given problem.

7. Experimental results

Every IWD in the IWD algorithm both searches and changes its environment. During this search, the IWD incrementally constructs a solution. The problem definition is presented to the IWD algorithm in the form of a graph and IWDs visit nodes of the graph by travelling on the edges of the graph. A swarm of IWDs flows in the graph often with the guidance of a local heuristic in the hope of finding optimal or near optimal solutions. In the following, the IWD algorithm is used for four different problems: the TSP, the *n*-queen puzzle, the MKP, and for the first time, the IWD algorithm is used for Automatic Multilevel Thresholding (AMT).

7.1 The Travelling Salesman Problem (TSP)

In the TSP (travelling salesman problem), a map of cities is given to the salesman and he is required to visit every city only once one after the other to complete his tour and return to its first city. The goal in the TSP is to find the tour with the minimum total length among all such possible tours for the given map.

A TSP is represented by a graph (N, E) where the node set N denotes the n cities of the TSP and the edge set E denotes the edges between cities. Here, the graph of the TSP is considered a complete graph. Thus, every city has a direct link to another city. It is also assumed that the link between each two cities is undirected. So, in summary, the graph of the TSP is a complete undirected graph. A solution of the TSP having the graph (N, E) is an ordered set of n distinct cities. For such a TSP with n cities, there are $(n-1)!/2$ feasible solutions in which the global optimum(s) is sought.

A TSP solution for an n-city problem may be represented by the tour $T = (c_1, c_2, ..., c_n)$. The salesman travels from city c_1 to c_2, then from c_2 to c_3, and he continues this way until it gets to city c_n. Then, he returns to the first city c_1, which leads to the tour length $TL(.)$, defined by:

$$TL\left(c_1, c_2, ..., c_n\right) = \sum_{i=1}^{n} d\left(c_i, c_{i+1}\right) \tag{30}$$

such that $c_{n+1} = c_1$, and $d(.,.)$ is the distance function, which is often the Euclidean distance. The goal is to find the optimum tour $T^* = (c_1^*, c_2^*, ..., c_n^*)$ such that for every other feasible tour T:

$$\forall T: \quad TL(T^*) \leq TL(T) \tag{31}$$

In order to use the IWD algorithm for the TSP, the TSP problem as mentioned above is viewed as a complete undirected graph (N, E). Each link of the edge set E has an amount of soil. An IWD visits nodes of the graph through the links. The IWD is able to change the amount of the soils on the links. Moreover, cities of the TSP are denoted by nodes of the graph, which hold the physical positions of cities. An IWD starts its tour from a random node and it visits other nodes using the links of the graph until it returns to the first node. The IWD changes the soil of each link that it flows on while completing its tour.

For the TSP, the constraint that each IWD never visits a city twice in its tour must be kept satisfied. Therefore, for the IWD, a visited city list $V_c(IWD)$ is employed. This list includes the cities visited so far by the IWD. So, the next possible cities for an IWD are selected from those cities that are not in the visited list $V_c(IWD)$ of the IWD.

One possible local heuristic for the TSP, denoted by $HUD_{TSP}(i, j)$, has been suggested (Shah-Hosseini, 2008a) as follows:

$$HUD_{TSP}(i, j) = \| \mathbf{c}(i) - \mathbf{c}(j) \| \tag{32}$$

where $\mathbf{c}(k)$ denotes the two dimensional positional vector for the city k. The function $\| . \|$ denotes the Euclidean norm. The local heuristic $HUD_{TSP}(i, j)$ measures the undesirability of an IWD to move from city i to city j. For near cities i and j, the heuristic measure $HUD(i, j)$ becomes small whereas for far cities i and j, the measure $HUD(i, j)$ becomes big. It is reminded that paths with high levels of undesirability are chosen fewer times than paths with low levels of undesirability. In the IWD algorithm, the time taken for the IWD to pass from city i to city j, is proportional to the heuristic $HUD_{TSP}(i, j)$.

A modification to the IWD-TSP has been proposed in (Shah-Hosseini, 2008b), which finds better tours and hopefully escape local optimums. After a few number of iterations, say N_I, the soils of all paths (i, j) of the graph of the given TSP are reinitialized again with the initial soil $InitSoil$ except the paths of the total-best solution T^{TB}, which are given less soil than $InitSoil$. The soil reinitialization after each N_I iterations is expressed in the following equation:

$$soil(i, j) = \begin{cases} \alpha_I \Gamma_I InitSoil & \text{for every } (i, j) \in T^{TB} \\ InitSoil & \text{otherwise} \end{cases} \tag{33}$$

where α_I is a small positive number chosen here as 0.1. Γ_I denotes a random number, which is drawn from a uniform distribution in the interval $[0, 1]$. As a result, IWDs prefer to choose paths of T^{TB} because less soil on its paths is deposited. Here, $N_I = 15$.

We may refer to the IWD algorithm for the TSP as the "IWD-TSP" algorithm. Moreover, the modified IWD algorithm for the TSP is called the "MIWD-TSP" algorithm.

The MIWD-TSP algorithm is tested with cities on a circle such that the cities are equally placed on the perimeter of the circle (Shah-Hosseini, 2008b). The number of cities is chosen from 10 to 100 cities incremented by 10. The results of this experiment are shown in Table 1 in which the average numbers of iterations to get to the global optimums are depicted. The number of IWDs is kept at the constant value 50. As the number of cities increases, the average number of iterations to find the global optimum almost monotonically increases.

No. of cities on the circle	10	20	30	40	50	60	70	80	90	100
Ave. iterations	10.4	39.6	78.6	85.5	134.5	181.9	253.1	364.7	387.4	404.5

Table 1. The average number of iterations to find the global optimum for the TSP where cities are equally spaced on the perimeter of a circle. The results are the average numbers of iterations of ten runs of the MIWD-TSP algorithm.

The IWD-TSP algorithm (Shah-Hosseini, 2007) for the TSPs of Table 1 often gets trapped into local optimums. As the number of cities of the TSP increases, the average numbers of iterations to get to the global optimums become high. For the TSPs with high numbers of cities, it is impractical to use the IWD-TSP for them, and the MIWD-TSP is recommended. In Fig. 1, such a local optimum is shown for the TSP with 10 cities along the tour obtained by the MIWD-TSP algorithm.

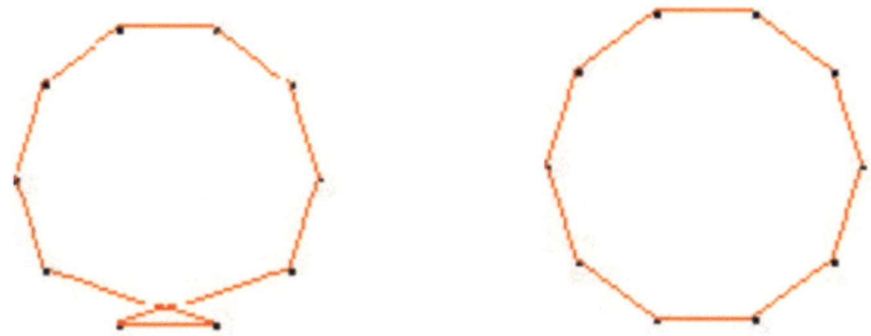

Fig. 1. The IWD-TSP converges to a good local optimum in the left image. However, it has a small self-crossing in its tour for the TSP with 10 cities. In contrast, by using the MIWD-TSP, the self-crossing is removed and it converges to the tour in the right image.

Four TSPs are taken from the TSPLIB95 (the TSP Library in the Internet) to test the performance of the MIWD-TSP algorithm (Shah-Hosseini, 2008b). The lengths of average and best tours in five runs of the MIWD-TSP algorithm are reported in Table 2. For comparison, the lengths of best tours of some other nature-inspired algorithms are also mentioned in Table 2. The table shows that the tours obtained by the MIWD-TSP algorithm are satisfactorily close to the known optimums and are comparable to the other nature-inspired algorithms.

Problem Name	Optimum length	Method					
		MMAS	BCO	EA	Improved ACO	MIWD-TSP	
						Best	Average
eil51	426	426	431.13	---	428.87	428.98	432.62
eil76	538	---	---	544.36	---	549.96	558.23
st70	675	---	678.62	677.10	677.10	677.10	684.08
kroA100	21282	21282	21441.5	21285.44	---	21407.57	21904.03

Table 2. The comparison between the Modified IWD-TSP and four other nature-inspired algorithms MMAS (Stutzle & Hoos, 1996), BCO (Teodorovic et al., 2006), EA (Yan et al., 2005), Improved ACO (Song et al., 2006) for the four TSPs mentioned below. The MIWD-TSP iterations: 3000 for eil51, 4500 for eil76, and 6000 for st70 and kroA100.

The convergence curve for the TSP "eil51" with the MIWD-TSP algorithm is shown in Fig. 2 in which the tour length of the total-best solution versus iterations is depicted. Here, the algorithm converges to the tour of length 428.98, which is shown in the figure.

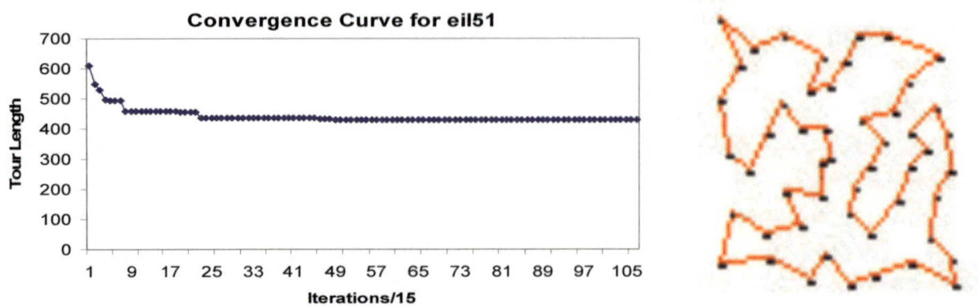

Fig. 2. The MIWD-TSP algorithm converges to the tour length 428.98 for eil51. The converged tour is shown on the right side.

7.2 The *n*-queen puzzle

The *n*-queen puzzle is the problem in which *n* chess queens must be placed on an n×n chessboard such that no two queens attack each other (Watkins, 2004). The n-queen puzzle is the generalization of the 8-queen puzzle with eight queens on an 8×8 chessboard. The 8-quuen puzzle was originally proposed by the chess player "Max Bezzel" in 1848. Many mathematicians such as "Gauss" and "Cantor" have worked on the 8-queen puzzle and its generalized n-queen puzzle. The first solutions were provided by "Franz Nauck" in 1850. He also generalized it to the n-queen puzzle on an n×n chessboard. The 8-queen puzzle has 92 distinct solutions. If the solutions that differ only by rotations and reflections of the board are counted as one, the 8-queen puzzle has 12 unique solutions. Except for n=6, as the n increases, the number of unique (or distinct) solutions increases. A solution to the 8-queen puzzle is depicted in Fig. 3.

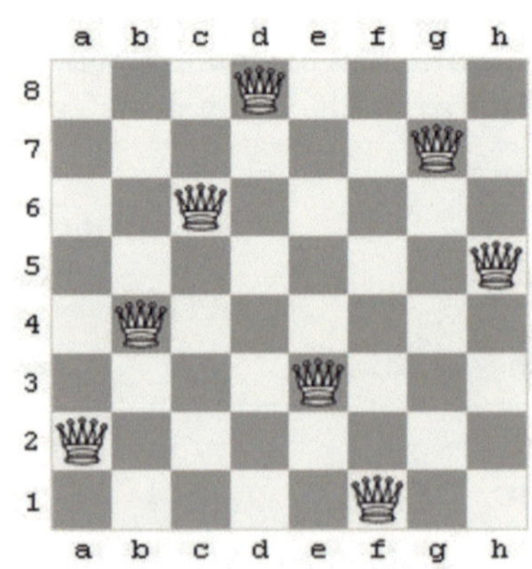

Fig. 3. A solution to the 8-queen puzzle on the chessboard.

One strategy is to put all n queens instantly on the n×n chessboard, which leads to the hug search space n^{2n} (wrongly written 64^n in (Shah-Hosseini, 2008b)). For $n = 8$, the search space contains $64^8 = 2^{48} \cong 2.8\times10^{14}$. To reduce the size of the search space of the *n*-queen problem, the n queens are placed one by one on the chessboard such that the first queen is placed on any row of the first column. Then, the second queen is placed on any row of the second column except the row of the first queen. Following this strategy, the ith queen is placed on any row of the ith column except those rows that previous queens have occupied. This incremental strategy of putting queens on the chessboard reduces the search space to $n!$ where the symbol "!" denotes the factorial.

In the incremental strategy, if every row of the chessboard is considered a city, then the n-queen problem may be considered as a TSP. The first row chosen by the first queen is considered the first city of the tour. The second row chosen by the second queen is called the second city of the tour. Continuing this way, the ith row chosen by the ith queen is considered the ith city of the tour. The constraint that no two queens are in the same row is viewed as no two cities of the TSP graph are visited by the salesman. In summary, for the n-queen problem, a complete undirected TSP graph is created.

In the n-queen puzzle, any feasible solution is also an optimal solution. Any feasible solution for an n-queen puzzle is the solution in which no two queens attack each other and that is the optimal solution. For this problem, the path to reach the final feasible (optimal) solution(s) is not wanted and in fact only the final positions of queens on the chessboard are desired.

The local heuristic undesirability $HUD_{NQ}(i, j)$, which has been proposed in (Shah-Hosseini, 2008b) to solve the n-queen puzzle, is stated as follows:

$$HUD_{NQ}(i, j) = (1+r)\left| \, | i - j | - \frac{n}{2} \right| \tag{34}$$

where $HUD_{NQ}(i, j)$ is the undesirability of an IWD to go from current row (city) i to the next row (city) j. Symbol $|.|$ denotes the absolute value. The variable r is a random number chosen uniformly from the interval $[0, 1]$. The symbol n denotes the number of cities (columns or rows) of the chessboard of size $n \times n$. In the above equation, the heuristic favours the distance between the rows of neighbouring columns to be near the length $\frac{n}{2}$.

However, it has been observed that the IWD algorithm with the mentioned local heuristic in Eq. (34) is usually trapped in the local optima in which only two queens attack each other. Sometimes, coming out of such local optima takes considerable iterations of the algorithm. For this purpose, a local search algorithm called "N-Queen Local Search" or NQLS has been proposed in (Shah-Hosseini, 2008b). This local search algorithm is activated when the current iteration-best solution T^{IB} of the IWD algorithm contains only two queens attacking each other. Specifically, the NQLS algorithm is activated when the quality of the iteration-best solution T^{IB}, $q(T^{IB})$, becomes -1. The quality of a solution T denoted by $q(T)$ is measured by

$$q(T) = -\sum_{i=1}^{n-1} \sum_{j=i+1}^{n} attack(c_i, c_j) \tag{35}$$

Where $attack(c_i, c_j) = 1$ if queens c_i and c_j attack each other. Otherwise; $attack(c_i, c_j) = 0$. It is reminded that the optimal solution T^* has the highest quality value zero: $q(T^*) = 0$. In the following, the NQLS is expressed in four steps:

1. Get the iteration-best solution T^{IB} with tour $\left(c_1^{IB}, c_2^{IB}, \ldots, c_n^{IB}\right)$ and $q(T^{IB}) = -1$.
2. initialize $T_0 = T^{IB}$.
2. For $k = 1,2,\ldots,n-1$ do the following steps (steps 2.1 to 2.3):

   2.1. Shift the cities in the tour one position to the right such that the last city becomes the first city in the tour: $T_k = shift_{Right}(T_{k-1})$.
   2.2. If $q(T_k) = 0$, then set $T_0 = T_k$ and go to step 4.
   2.3. End loop.
3. For $k = 1,2,\ldots,n-1$ do the following steps (steps 3.1 to 3.3):

   3.1. Increment each city's number (row) by one such that the highest row becomes the lowest row in the chessboard: $T_k = (T_{k-1} + k) \bmod n$, where mod is the modulus function. Moreover, the increment inside the parenthesis is applied to each city of the tour T_{k-1}.
   3.2. If $q(T_k) = 0$, then set $T_0 = T_k$ and go to step 4.
   3.3. End loop.
4. If $q(T_0) = 0$, then the total-best iteration solution T^{TB} has been obtained and is updated by $T^{TB} = T_0$; otherwise, no updating is implemented by this algorithm.

For simplicity, the IWD algorithm for the n-queen problem using the local search NQLS is called "IWD-NQ" algorithm. The IWD-NQ algorithm is tested with ten different n-queens puzzle (Shah-Hosseini, 2008b) where n is increased from 10 to 100 with step ten. The average number of iterations needed to find the optimal solution for ten runs of each n-queen puzzle is depicted in Fig. 4. It is reminded that 50 IWDs are used in the experiments. It is seen that the number of iterations to find the optimal solution(s) does not necessarily depend on the number of queens. For example, the average number of iterations for the 90-queen problem is bigger than the 100-queen problem.

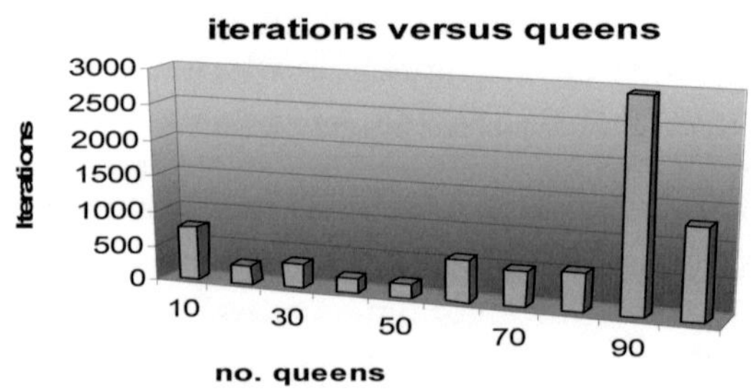

	10	20	30	40	50	60	70	80	90	100
ave. iterations	759	261	348	210	190	602	510	547	2951	1294

Fig. 4. The average number of iterations to find the global optimums versus the number of queens for the n-queen puzzle. The results are the average iterations of ten runs of the IWD-NQ algorithm. The number of queens changes from 10 to 100.

7.3 The multidimensional knapsack problem

The knapsack problem or KP is to select a subset of items i of the set I, each item i with the profit b_i and resource (capacity) requirement r_i such that they all fit in a knapsack of limited capacity and the sum of profits of the selected items is maximized.

The multidimensional knapsack problem, MKP, is a generalization of the KP. In the MKP, there exists multiple knapsacks and thus there are multiple resource constraints. The inclusion of an item i in the m knapsacks is denoted by setting the variable y_i to one, otherwise y_i is set to zero. Let the variable r_{ij} represents the resource requirement of an item i with respect to the resource constraint (knapsack) j having the capacity a_j. In other words, r_{ij} represents the amount of capacity that item i requires from knapsack j. The MKP with m constraints (knapsacks) and n items wants to maximize the total profit of including a subset of the n items in the knapsacks without surpassing the capacities of the knapsacks. For the MKP, in more specific terms:

$$\max \sum_{i=1}^{n} y_i b_i \tag{36}$$

subject to the following constraints:

$$\sum_{i=1}^{n} r_{ij} y_i \le a_j \ \ for\ j = 1,2,...,m \tag{37}$$

where $y_i \in \{ 0,1 \}$ for $i = 1,2,...,n$. Here, the profits b_i and the resources requirements r_{ij} are non-negative values.

The MKP is an NP-hard combinatorial optimization problem with applications such as cutting stock problems, processor allocation in distributed systems, cargo loading, capital budgeting, and economics.

Two general approaches maybe used for solving the MKP: the exact algorithms and the approximate algorithms. The exact algorithms are useful for solving small to moderate-size instances of the MKP such as those based on dynamic programming and those based on the branch-and-bound approach. For a more detail review on the MKP, Freville (2004) is suggested.

The approximate algorithms may use nature-inspired approaches to approximately solve difficult optimization problems. Nature-inspired algorithms include algorithms such as Simulated Annealing (Kirkpatrick et al., 1983), Evolutionary Algorithms like Genetic Algorithms, Evolution Strategies, Evolutionary Programming, Ant Colony Optimization, Particle Swarm Optimization, Electromagnetism-like optimization, and Intelligent Water Drops (IWDs).

For the MKP, the local heuristic undesirability, denoted by $HUD_{MKP}(j)$, is computed by:

$$HUD_{MKP}(j) = \frac{1}{mb_j} \sum_{k=1}^{m} r_{jk} \tag{38}$$

Where b_j denotes the profit of item j and r_{jk} is the resource requirement for item j from knapsack k. The above equation shows that $HUD_{MKP}(j)$ decreases if the profit b_j is high whereas $HUD_{MKP}(j)$ increases if the resource requirements of item j are high. As a result, the items with less resource requirements and higher profits are more desirable. $HUD_{MKP}(j)$ represents how undesirable is the action of selecting item j as the next item to be included in the knapsacks. We may refer to the IWD algorithm used for the MKP as the IWD-MKP algorithm.

Problem Name	Constraints × Variables	Quality of Optimum solution	Quality of the IWD-MKP's solution		no. of iterations of the IWD-MKP	
			Best	Average	Best	Average
WEING1	2 × 28	141278	141278	141278	59	1243.8
WEING2	2 × 28	130883	130883	130883	154	618.4
WEING3	2 × 28	95677	95677	95677	314	609.8
WEING4	2 × 28	119337	119337	119337	4	48.5
WEING5	2 × 28	98796	98796	98796	118	698.5
WEING6	2 × 28	130623	130623	130623	71	970.3
WEING7	2 × 105	1095445	1094736	1094223	100	100
WEING8	2 × 105	624319	620872	617897.9	200	200

Table 3. Eight problems of the OR-Library in file "mknap2.txt", solved by the IWD-MKP algorithm. The global optimal solutions have also been mentioned.

Constraints × Variables-Problem Number	LP optimal	L & M	Fidanova	Quality of the IWD-MKP's solutions	
		best	best	best	average
5 × 100-00	24585	24381	23984	24295	24175.4
5 × 100-01	24538	24274	24145	24158	24031.3
5 × 100-02	23895	23551	23523	23518	23404
5 × 100-03	23724	23527	22874	23218	23120.9
5 × 100-04	24223	23991	23751	23802	23737.2
5 × 100-05	24884	24613	24601	24601	24554
5 × 100-06	25793	25591	25293	25521	25435.6
5 × 100-07	23657	23410	23204	23374	23344.9
5 × 100-08	24445	24204	23762	24148	24047
5 × 100-09	24635	24411	24255	24366	24317

Table 4. The MKPs with five constraints and 100 items of the OR-Library in file "mknapcb1.txt" solved by 100 iterations of the IWD-MKP algorithm. The results are compared with the LP optimal solutions and best solutions of two ant-based algorithms: Leguizamon and Michalewicz (L & M), and Fidanova.

The IWD-MKP has been used for eight problems (Shah-Hosseini, 2008b) in file "mknap2.txt" of the OR-Library (the OR-Library in the Internet). For each MKP, the best and the average qualities of ten runs of the IWD-MKP are reported in Table 3. For comparison,

the qualities of optimal solutions are also mentioned in the table. The IWD-MKP algorithm finds the global optimums for the first six MKPs with two constraints and 28 items. However, the qualities of solutions of the problems "WEING7" and "WEING8" with two constraints and 105 items obtained by the IWD-MKP are very close to the qualities of optimal solutions. It is reminded that 50 IWDs are used in the mentioned experiments.
The first ten MKP problems in file "mknapcb1" of the OR-Library are solved by the IWD-MKP and the results of ten runs of the algorithm are shown in Table 4. For comparison, the results of the two Ant Colony Optimization-based algorithms of Leguizamon and Michalewicz (for short, L & M) (Leguizamon and Michalewicz, 1999) and Fidanova (Fidanova, 2002) are mentioned. Moreover, the results obtained by the LP relaxation method that exist in the file "mkcbres.txt" of the OR-Library are also included. The solutions of the IWD-MKP are often better than the solutions of those obtained by Fidanova.

7.4 Automatic multilevel thresholding

Image segmentation is often one of the main tasks in any Computer Vision application. Image segmentation is a process in which the whole image is segmented into several regions based on similarities and differences that exist between the pixels of the input image. Each region should contain an object of the image at hand. Therefore, by doing segmentation, the image is divided into several sub-images such that each sub-image represents an object of the scene.
There are several approaches to perform image segmentation (Sezgin & Sankur, 2004). One of the widely used techniques for image segmentation is multilevel thresholding. In doing multilevel thresholding for image segmentation, it is assumed that each object has a distinct continuous area of the image histogram. Therefore, by separating the histogram appropriately, the objects of the image are segmented correctly.
Multilevel thresholding uses a number of thresholds $\{t_1, t_2, ..., t_M\}$ in the histogram of the image $f(x, y)$ to separate the pixels of the objects in the image. By using the obtained thresholds, the original image is multithresholded and the segmented image $T(f(x, y))$ is created. Specifically:

$$T(f(x,y)) = \begin{cases} g_0 & \text{if } f(x,y) < t_1 \\ g_1 & \text{if } t_1 \le f(x,y) < t_2 \\ .... & .... \\ g_M & \text{if } f(x,y) \ge t_M \end{cases} \tag{39}$$

Such that g_i is the grey-level assigned to all pixels of the region i, which eventually represents object i. As it is seen in the above equation, the $M+1$ regions are determined by the M thresholds $\{t_1, t_2, ..., t_M\}$. The value of g_i may be chosen to be the mean value of gray-levels of the region's pixels. However, in this paper we use the maximum range of gray-levels, 255, to distribute the gray-levels of regions equally. Specifically, $g_i = i.\left[\dfrac{255}{M}\right]$ such that the function $[\,.\,]$ returns the integer value of its argument.

To multithreshold an image, the number of thresholds should be given in advance to a multilevel thresholding algorithm. However, a few algorithms have been designed to automatically determine the suitable number of thresholds based on the application at hand such as the Growing Time-Adaptive Self-Organizing Map (Shah-Hosseini & Safabakhsh, 2002). Such algorithms are called automatic multilevel thresholding. In automatic multilevel thresholding, the problem becomes harder because the search space increase hugely as the number of thresholds increases. For example, if the brightness of each image's pixel be selected from G different gray levels and the image is thresholded by M thresholds, then the search space will be of size $\dfrac{G!}{(G-M)!}$. For $G = 256$ and $M = 30$, the search space is approximately of size 3×10^{71}. It is reminded that in this paper, it is assumed that $G = 256$.

The AMT (Automatic Multilevel Thresholding) problem is converted to a TSP problem such that the number of cities is assumed to be 256. Each IWD begins its trip from city zero to city 255. There are exactly two directed links from city i to city $i+1$, which are named "Above Link" and "BelowLink". When the IWD is in city i, the next city of the IWD is city $i+1$. If AboveLink is selected by the IWD in city i, it means that $i+1$ is not the next threshold for the AMT. In contrast, if BelowLink is selected by the IWD, it means that the next threshold is the value $i+1$.

Here, a local heuristic is not suggested. As a result, the amount of soil that each IWD removes from its visiting path , $\Delta soil(i,j)$, is computed by:

$$\Delta soil(i,j) = \frac{a_s}{b_s + c_s.1000} \tag{40}$$

Where $time^2\left(i,j;vel^{IWD}(t+1)\right)$ in Eq. (20) has been replaced by the constant amount 1000.

Moreover, the local soil updating parameter ρ_n in Eq. (21) is chosen as a negative value. For the AMT, $\rho_n = -0.9$

The quality of each solution found by an IWD, denoted by $q(T^{IWD})$, is suggested to be a generalization of the Haung's method (Huang & Wang, 1995) in which a fuzziness measure is employed for bilevel thresholding. Here, the Haung's method is generalized to be used for multilevel thresholding. The first step is to define the membership function, which returns the degree of membership of any pixel to the class (object) of the image. Again, the thresholds obtained by an IWD are represented by the set $\{t_1, t_2, ..., t_M\}$. The membership function $u_f(I(x,y))$ for each pixel (x,y) of image $I(.,.)$ is defined as follows:

$$u_f(I(x,y)) = \frac{1}{1 + \left|I(x,y) - \bar{I}_{k+1}\right| / 255} \qquad if \;\; t_k < I(x,y) \le t_{k+1} \tag{41}$$

Such that $\bar{I}_{k+1}$ denotes the average gray-level in a region of the image with gray-levels $\{t_k+1, t_k+2, ..., t_{k+1}\}$. Therefore, $\bar{I}_{k+1} = \frac{\sum_{i=t_k+1}^{t_{k+1}} i\, p(i)}{\sum_{i=t_k+1}^{t_{k+1}} p(i)}$. The function $|.|$ returns the absolute value of its argument. The values of the membership function $u_f(I(x,y))$ vary within the interval $[0.5, 1]$. When M is set to one, the formula of Eq. (41) is reduced to the Haung's method for bilevel thresholding.

Given the membership function, a measure must be introduced to determine the fuzziness of the thresholded image with the original one. For this purpose, the idea introduced by Yager (Yager, 1979) is employed. The measure of fuzziness is defined as how much the fuzzy set and its complement set are indistinct. Having the membership function $u_f(I(x,y))$, the fuzziness measure is defined as:

$$D_f = \sqrt{\sum_{i=0}^{255} \left(2u_f(i) - 1\right)^2} \tag{42}$$

For a crisp set, the value of D_f is 16 whereas for the fuzziest set the value of D_f is zero. Thus, the IWD algorithm should try to maximize D_f by finding the best threshold values with the optimum number of thresholds. It is reminded that the quality of each IWD's solution T^{IWD}, denoted by $q(T^{IWD})$, is computed by D_f in Eq. (42).

We may refer to the IWD algorithm used for the AMT as the IWD-AMT algorithm.

The IWD-AMT is tested with three gray-level images, House, Eagle, and Lena shown in Fig. 5. For this purpose, 50 IWDs are used and the results are shown in Fig. 6.

Fig. 5. The three test gray-level images. From left to right: House, Eagle, and Lena.

The histogram of the original images and their thresholded images obtained by the IWD-AMT are shown in Figs. 7-8. The most important features of the images have been preserved whereas the numbers of gray-levels have been reduced dramatically. Specifically, the house image is reduced to 12 gray-levels, the eagle image is reduced to 18 gray-levels and the Lena image is reduced to eight regions. The experiments show that some regions have very small numbers of pixels. Therefore, it would be useful to remove very small regions by a simple postprocessing while keeping the qualities of the thresholded images intact.

Fig. 6. The three thresholded images obtained by the proposed IWD-AMT algorithm. From left to right: thresholded House with 12 regions, thresholded Eagle with 18 regions, and the thresholded Lena with eight regions.

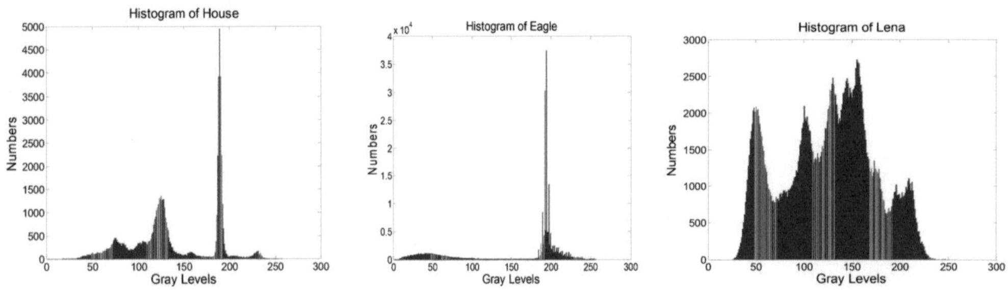

Fig. 7. The histograms of the House, the Eagle, and Lena image.

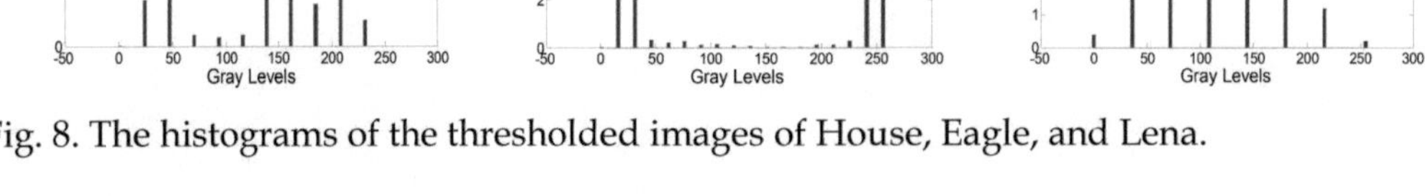

Fig. 8. The histograms of the thresholded images of House, Eagle, and Lena.

8. Conclusion

Four different problems are used to test the IWD algorithm: the TSP (Travelling Salesman Problem), the n-queen puzzle, the MKP (Multidimensional Knapsack Problem), and the AMT (Automatic Multilevel Thresholding). The experiments indicate that the IWD algorithm is capable to find optimal or near optimal solutions. However, there is an open space for modifications in the standard IWD algorithm, embedding other mechanisms that exist in natural rivers, inventing better local heuristics that fit better with the given problem, and suggesting new representations of the given problem in form of graphs. The IWD algorithm demonstrates that the nature is an excellent guide for designing and inventing new nature-inspired optimization algorithms.

9. References

Birbil, I. & Fang, S. C. (2003). An electro-magnetism-like mechanism for global optimization, *Journal of Global Optimization*, Vol. 25, pp. 263-282.

Bonabeau, E.; Dorigo, M. & Theraultz, G. (1999). *Swarm Intelligence: From Natural to Artificial Systems*, Oxford University Press.

Dawkins, R. (1989). *The Selfish Gene*, Oxford University Press.

de Castro, L. N. & Von Zuben, F. J. (2002). Learning and Optimization Using the Clonal Selection Principle, *IEEE Trans. on Evolutionary Computation*, Vol. 6, No. 3, pp. 239-251.

Dorigo, M.; Maniezzo, V. & Colorni, A. (1991). Positive feedback as a search strategy, *Technical Report 91-016*, Dipartimento di Elettronica, Politecnico di Milano, Milan.

Duan, H.; Liu S. & Lei, X. (2008). Air robot path planning based on Intelligent Water Drops optimization, *IEEE IJCNN 2008*, pp. 1397 - 1401.

Fidanova, S. (2002). Evolutionary algorithm for multidimensional knapsack problem, *PPSNVII-Workshop*.

Fogel, L.J.; Owens, A.J. & Walsh, M. J. (1966). *Artificial Intelligence through Simulated Evolution*, New York: John Wiley.

Forrest, S.; Perelson, A.S.; Allen, L. & Cherukuri, R. (1994). Self-nonself discrimination in a computer, *Proceedings of the 1994 IEEE Symposium on Research in Security and Privacy*, pp. 202-212.

Freville, A. (2004). The multidimensional 0–1 knapsack problem: An overview, *European Journal of Operational Research*, Vol. 155, pp. 1–21.

Huang, L.K. & Wang, M.J.J. (1995). Image thresholding by minimizing the measures of fuzziness, *Pattern Recognition*, Vol. 28, No. 1, pp. 41-51.

Kennedy, J. & Eberhart, R. (1995). Particle swarm optimization, *Proc. of the IEEE Int. Conf. on Neural Networks*, pp. 1942–1948, Piscataway, NJ.

Kirkpatrick, S.; Gelatt, C. D. & Vecchi, M. P. (1983). Optimization by simulated annealing, *Science*, Vol. 220, pp. 671-680.

Koza, J. R. (1992). *Genetic Programming: On the Programming of Computers by means of Natural Evolution*, MIT Press, Massachusetts.

Holland, J. H. (1975). *Adaptation in Natural and Artificial Systems*, University of Michigan Press, Ann Arbor.

Leguizamon, G. & Michalewicz, Z. (1999). A new version of ant system for subset Problem, *Congress on Evolutionary Computation*, pp. 1459-1464.

Ong, Y. S.; Lim, M. H.; Zhu, N. & Wong, K. W. (2006). Classification of Adaptive Memetic Algorithms: A Comparative Study, *IEEE Transactions on Systems Man and Cybernetics*, Part B, Vol. 36, No. 1, pp. 141-152.

OR-Library, available at http://people.brunel.ac.uk/~mastjjb/jeb/orlib/files.

Rechenberg, I. (1973). Evolutionstrategie-Optimierung Technischer Systeme nach Prinzipien der Biologischen Information, Fromman Verlag, Freiburg, Germany.

Sato, T. & Hagiwara, M. (1997). Bee System: finding solution by a concentrated search, *IEEE Int. Conf. on Computational Cybernetics and Simulation*, pp.3954-3959.

Schwefel, H.-P. (1981). *Numerical Optimization of Computer Models*, John Wiley & Sons, New-York.

Sezgin, M. & Sankur, B. (2004). Survey over image thresholding techniques and quantitative performance evaluation, *Journal of Electronic Imaging*, Vol. 13, No. 11, pp. 146–165.

Shah-Hosseini, H. & Safabakhsh, R. (2002). Automatic multilevel thresholding for image segmentation by the growing time adaptive self-organizing map, *IEEE Transactions on Pattern Analysis and Machine Intelligence*. Vol. 24, No. 10, pp. 1388-1393.

Shah-Hosseini, H. (2007). Problem solving by intelligent water drops. *Proceedings of IEEE Congress on Evolutionary Computation*, pp. 3226-3231, Swissotel The Stamford, Singapore, September.

Shah-Hosseini, H. (2008a). Intelligent water drops algorithm: a new optimization method for solving the multiple knapsack problem. *Int. Journal of Intelligent Computing and Cybernetics*, Vol. 1, No. 2, pp. 193-212.

Shah-Hosseini, H. (2008b). The Intelligent Water Drops algorithm: A nature-inspired swarm-based optimization algorithm. *Int. J. Bio-Inspired Computation*, Vol. 1, Nos. 1/2, pp. 71–79.

Song, X.; Li, B. & Yang, H. (2006). Improved ant colony algorithm and its applications in TSP, *Proc. of the Sixth Int. Conf. on Intelligent Systems Design and Applications*, pp. 1145 - 1148.

Stutzle, T. & Hoos, H. (1996). Improving the ant system: a detailed report on the MAX-MIN ant system, *Technical Report AIDA*, pp. 96-12, FG Intellektik, TU Darmstadt, Germany.

Teodorovic, D.; Lucic, P.; Markovic, G. & Orco, M. D. (2006). Bee colony optimization: principles and applications, *8th Seminar on Neural Network Applications in Electrical Engineering*, NEUREL-2006, Serbia, September 25-27.

Timmis, J.; Neal, M. & Hunt, J. (2000). An artificial immune system for data analysis, *BioSystems*, Vol. 55, No. 1, pp. 143–150.

TSP Library (TSPLIB95), Available at: http://www.informatik.uni-heidelberg.de/groups/comopt/software/TSPLIB95/STSP.html

Watkins, J. (2004). *Across the Board: The Mathematics of Chess Problems*, Princeton: Princeton University Press.

Yan, X.-S.; Li, H.; CAI, Z.-H. & Kang, L.-S. (2005). A fast evolutionary algorithm for combinatorial optimization problem, *Proc. of the Fourth Int. Conf. on Machine Learning and Cybernetics*, pp. 3288-3292, August.

Yager, R. R. (1979). On the measures of fuzziness and negation. Part 1: Membership in the unit interval, *Int. Journal of Gen. Sys.*, Vol. 5, pp. 221-229.

17

Optimization of Structures under Load Uncertainties Based on Hybrid Genetic Algorithm

Nianfeng Wang and Yaowen Yang
Nanyang Technological University
Singapore

1. Introduction

Today with the development of industry and research, reliability is more and more emphasized. However in some analysis of engineering problem, uncertainty inevitably exists. For example, wind loading on structures often varies over certain range instead of one determined value. The design of such systems should take into account the intervals of deviation of variables from their nominal values. In some uncertainty cases, the variety in the system parameters is neglected for the convenience of analysis. In certain situation it is possible to obtain the response which is valid and reasonable. However, sometimes the uncertainty analysis of system can not be neglected because the uncertainty would significantly affect the system performance.

Real structures are designed for numerous combinations of loads and load cases. In structure design it is typical that there may be several hundred important design load cases, which implies uncertainty in the loading conditions. A number of approaches have been developed to tackle such problems. According to the different types of uncertainty, several distinct methods were introduced to handle the analysis: fuzzy sets and fuzzy logic, interval analysis, and probabilistic approach. Fuzzy set theory was firstly introduced in (Zadeh 1978). The application of fuzzy sets concept into structural analysis was studied in (Ayyub 1997) systematically. In his work, a fuzzy set was utilized to describe every objective function. Some mechanical systems can be analyzed through this method (Qiu and Rao 2005). Fuzzy set theory has several advantages including the fact that the mathematics is formally defined and it can provide a potentially simple approach. The disadvantages of fuzzy set theory include validation necessary, justification of each step necessary, complexity when using many variables and the fact that the membership function may be heuristically defined. When less information is given and only range of each uncertainty quantity can be specified, interval method is widely used. Bounded uncertainty approach (Ben-Haim and Elishakoff 1990), a convex model of uncertainty was an extension to the interval analysis (Moore 1966). Some disadvantages of interval analysis are: (1) Interval arithmetic computations are slower than floating point operations, roughly by a factor of three, though there are problems that are solved faster when implemented using interval arithmetic; (2) There are no additive or multiplicative inverses for intervals; (3) There is no strict distributive law of multiplication over addition, only sub-distributivity; and (4) the number of required subproblems is much larger than that of the underestimator algorithms (Han, Manousiouthakis et al. 1997; Ju, Vasilios et al. 1997; Agoston 2005). For problems with distribution description of the variety in the system parameters, probabilistic approach is often used (Au 2005). Probabilistic approaches offer an attractive framework for designing structures in the presence of uncertainty, but they require much information about probabilistic models. When such information is inaccurate, large errors could be incurred in the calculation of failure probabilities (Elishakoff 1995).

Anti-optimization technique, on one hand, represents an alternative and complement to traditional methods, and on the other hand, it is a generalization of the mathematical theory of interval analysis (Qiu & Elishakoff 2001). When the available uncertainty data is limited, a probability distribution may not be able to be estimated accurately, but bounds for the uncertain variables may be at least estimated. The designer will generally seek for the least favorable solution for the structure within the domain defined by the bounds on the uncertain variables. This search for the worst condition for a given problem was named anti-optimization (Elishakoff 1995). The term anti-optimization was also used in a more general sense, to describe the task of finding the worst scenario for a given problem. A two species genetic algorithm (GA) was presented effectively reducing the two-level problem to a single level (Venter & Haftka 1996). The maximum strength of laminated composites was optimized under bounded uncertainty of material properties by GA (Maenghyo & Seung Yun 2004).

In recent years, hybrid genetic algorithms (GAs) have become more homogeneous and some great successes have been achieved in the optimization of a variety of classical hard optimization problems. Hybrid algorithms of GAs and those local search algorithms were proposed to improve the search ability of GAs, and their high performance was reported (Ishibuchi & Murata 1998; Deb & Goel 2001; Jaszkiewicz 2003; Wang & Tai 2007; Wang & Tai 2008). In these studies local search algorithms were suggested in order to reach a quick and closer result to the optimum solution. However, this work integrates a simple genetic local search algorithm as the anti-optimization technique with a constrained multi-objective GA proposed in (Wang & Tai 2007). A constrained tournament selection is used as a single objective function in the local search strategy. Section 2 outlines the proposed hybrid GA. And section 3 presents a morphological geometry representation scheme coupled with the GA. Formulations and numerical results of a target matching test problem in the context of structural topology optimization are presented in Section 4. Formulations and numerical results of the structural design problem are presented in Section 5. Finally, concluding remarks are given in Section 6.

2. Proposed algorithm –a hybrid GA

A general constrained multi-objective optimization problem (in the minimization sense) is formulated as:

$$\begin{aligned} \text{minimize } & \mathbf{f}(\mathbf{x}) = \left[f_1(\mathbf{x}) \quad f_2(\mathbf{x}) \quad \cdots \quad f_m(\mathbf{x}) \right] \\ \text{subject to } & g_j(\mathbf{x}) \le 0, \ j = 1, 2, \cdots, q \\ & h_k(\mathbf{x}) = 0, \ j = 1, 2, \cdots, q \\ & \mathbf{x}^L < \mathbf{x} < \mathbf{x}^U \end{aligned} \tag{1}$$

where $\mathbf{f}$ is a vector of m objectives, and $\mathbf{x} = \left[x_1 \quad x_2 \quad \cdots \quad x_n \right]$ is the vector of n design variables. g_j and h_k are the equality and inequality constraints. $\mathbf{x}^L$ and $\mathbf{x}^U$ define the lower bound and upper bound of $\mathbf{x}$, respectively.

For anti-optimization, the robustness of the objective function can be achieved by maximizing the minimum value of the objective functions. It tends to move the uncertainty parameters to the desirable range and results in higher reliability with respect to uncertainty. Therefore an anti-optimization procedure implemented in this work by local search is employed to search for the values of the worst objective functions. Consider a problem subject to u uncertain variables $\mathbf{x}_u$ and $n-u$ normal design variables $\mathbf{x}_n$. The formulation can then be written as below:

$$\begin{aligned} &\underset{\mathbf{x}}{\text{minimize}} && \mathbf{f}(\mathbf{x}) \\ &\underset{\mathbf{x}_u}{\text{maximize}} && \underset{\mathbf{x}_n \subset \mathbf{C}_N}{\mathbf{f}(\mathbf{x}_n, \mathbf{x}_u)} \\ &\text{subject to} && g_j(\mathbf{x}) \le 0, \ j = 1,2,\cdots,q \\ & && h_k(\mathbf{x}) = 0, \ j = 1,2,\cdots,q \\ & && \mathbf{x}^L < \mathbf{x} < \mathbf{x}^U \end{aligned} \tag{2}$$

where $\mathbf{C}_N$ is a particular set of solutions which are related to generation number N. The formulation considered leads to a nested optimization problem which will be solved by means of a GA for optimization and a local search for anti-optimization. Generally speaking, this is a sort of minmax search, where the "max" part is dealt with by a local search algorithm, and the "min" part is realized by a GA.

2.1 Tournament selection for local search

Since a local search strategy requires a tournament selection between an initial solution and its neighboring solution, a comparison strategy is needed. For multi-objective optimization without constraints, a single objective function converted from multiple objectives can be used. For constrained optimization, constraint handling mechanisms should be given first. In most applications, penalty functions using static (Srinivas & Deb 1994), dynamic or adaptive concepts (Michalewicz & Schoenauer 1996) have been widely used. The major problem is the need for specifying the right value for penalty parameters in advance. The method from (Ray, Tai et al. 2001) incorporates a Pareto ranking of the constraint violations, so it does not involve any aggregation of objectives or constraints and thus the problem of scaling does not arise. Note that Pareto ranking is not well suited for hybridization with local search. For an anti-optimization problem, when Pareto ranking is used, the current solution **x** is replaced with its neighboring solution **y** (i.e., the local search move from **x** to **y** is accepted) only when **x** dominates **y** (i.e., **x** is better than **y**). That is, the local search move is rejected when **x** and **y** are non-dominated with respect to each other. However, change of the rank of a given solution may require significant changes of the objective/constraint values, thus, many local moves will not degenerate the rank.

A constraint handling method (Deb 2000) was proposed which is also based on the penalty function approach but does not require the prescription of any penalty parameter. The main idea of this method is to use a tournament selection operator and to apply a set of criteria in the selection process. For an anti-optimization problem, it can be easily changed to:

i. Any infeasible solution is preferred to any feasible solution.
ii. Between two feasible solutions, the one having worse objective function value is preferred.
iii. Between two infeasible solutions, the one having bigger constraint violation is preferred.

According to these criteria, the constrained optimization can be constructed as

$$\tilde{f}(\mathbf{x}) = \begin{cases} f(\mathbf{x}) & \text{if } \mathbf{x} \in F \\ f_{\max} + vio(\mathbf{x}) & \text{otherwise} \end{cases} \tag{3}$$

where $\tilde{f}(\mathbf{x})$ is the artificial unconstrained objective function, F is the feasible region of the design domain, $f_{\max}$ is the objective function value of the worst feasible solution in the population, and $vio(\mathbf{x})$ is the summation of all the violated constraint function values. However, this approach is only suitable for single-objective constrained optimization problem if no further handling mechanisms for multiple objectives are given. And $vio(\mathbf{x})$ as summation of constraint values cannot reflect the real relative comparison between them because of different orders of magnitude among the constraints, and in this sense, it is also based on the penalty functions where all the penalty parameters are set to 1.

Extending the basic idea of Deb's method, a technique combining Pareto ranking and weighted sum is suggested in this work for the local search selection process. There are only 3 combinations for the two solutions: both feasible, both infeasible, and one feasible and the other infeasible. The main idea of the technique is to use a tournament selection operator and to apply a set of criteria in the selection process. For an anti-optimization procedure, any infeasible solution is preferred to any feasible solution. When both solutions are feasible, Pareto ranking based on objectives is calculated. The one with bigger rank value is preferred. If the situation still ties, a more sophisticated acceptance rule is used for handling the situation. The fitness function of the solution **x** is calculated by the following weighted sum of the m objectives:

$$f(\mathbf{x}) = w_1 f_1(\mathbf{x}) + w_2 f_2(\mathbf{x}) + \cdots + w_m f_m(\mathbf{x}) \tag{4}$$

where $f(\mathbf{x})$ is a combined objective, and $w_1, w_2, \cdots, w_m$ are nonnegative weights for the objectives set according to different orders of magnitude among them. Constant weight values are used in this work to fix the search direction based on user's preference. The solution with a bigger $f(\mathbf{x})$ will survive. When both solutions are infeasible, Pareto ranking based on constraints is calculated. The one with bigger rank value is preferred. If the rank is same, the one with worse fitness value survives. A tournament selection criterion can be described as below to decide whether a current solution **x** should be replaced by a neighboring solution **y**:

i. If **x** is feasible and **y** is infeasible, replace the current solution **x** with **y** (i.e., let **x** = **y**).
ii. If both **x** and **y** are feasible, then if $RankObj_{\mathbf{x}} < RankObj_{\mathbf{y}}$, then $\mathbf{x} = \mathbf{y}$, else if $RankObj_{\mathbf{x}} = RankObj_{\mathbf{y}}$ and $f(\mathbf{x}) < f(\mathbf{y})$, then $\mathbf{x} = \mathbf{y}$.
iii. If both **x** and **y** are infeasible, then if $RankCon_{\mathbf{x}} < RankCon_{\mathbf{y}}$, then $\mathbf{x} = \mathbf{y}$, else if $RankCon_{\mathbf{x}} = RankCon_{\mathbf{y}}$ and $f(\mathbf{x}) < f(\mathbf{y})$, then $\mathbf{x} = \mathbf{y}$.

2.2 Selection of initial solutions

Local search applied to all solutions in the current population in the algorithm is inefficient, as shown in (Ishibuchi, Yoshida et al. 2002). In the proposed algorithm, the computation time spent by local search can be reduced by applying local search to only selected solutions in selected generations. If n is the number of decision variables, the best n number of solutions from the current population (based on Pareto ranking) are selected. These n number of mutated solutions and elites from N-th generation after local search are then put into the next population. The generation update mechanism in the proposed algorithm is shown in Fig. 1. The implementation of the anti-optimization part is modularized.

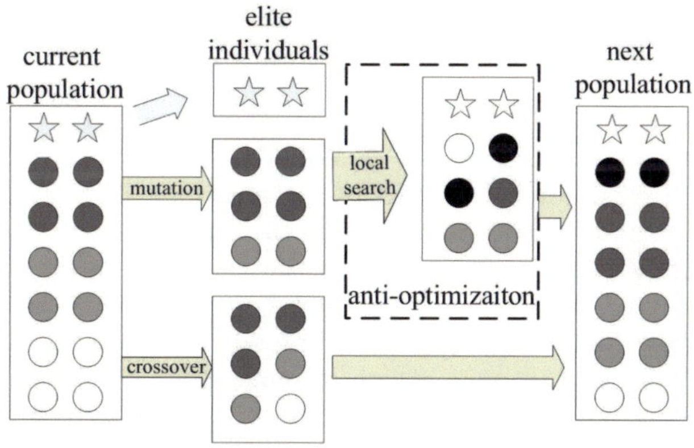

Fig. 1. Generation update mechanism.

2.3 Local search procedure

As explained in the above, a local search procedure is applied to elite individuals and new solutions generated by the mutation in selected generations. Generally, a local search procedure can be written as follows:

Step 1. Specify an initial solution and its corresponding design variable under uncertainty.

Step 2. Apply Hooke and Jeeves Method to determine the search path using the tournament selection criteria stated above as the function values.

Step 3. If the prescribed condition is satisfied, terminate the local search.

2.4 Main algorithm

The overall algorithm uses a framework which combines the method stated in (Wang & Tai 2007) and the local search proposed above. The algorithm is given below:

Step 1. Generate random initial population P of size M .

Step 2. Evaluate objective as well as constraint functions for each individual in P.

Step 3. Compute Pareto Ranking.

Step 4. Select elite individuals. Elite individuals carried from the previous generation preserve the values of their objective and constraint functions.

Step 5. Select n best individuals from P, mutate and apply local search procedure in specified generation, then put them into new population P'.

Step 6. Crossover.

Step 7. If a prescribed stopping condition is satisfied, end the algorithm. Otherwise, return to *Step 2.*

3. Enhanced geometric representation scheme for structural topology optimization

The enhanced morphological representation was first introduced in (Tai & Wang 2007), which in turn is an extension of the morphological representation scheme previously developed in (Tai & Akhtar 2005; Tai & Prasad 2007). As in any structural topology optimization procedure, the geometry of the structure has to be represented and defined by some form of design variables. The enhanced morphological representation efficiently cast structure topology as a chromosome code that makes it effective for solution via a GA. In the proposed scheme, the connectivities and the number of curves used are made variable and to be optimized in the evolutionary procedure. The process of the scheme definition is illustrated as follows.

A square design space shown in Fig. 2(a) is discretized into a 50 by 50 mesh of identical square elements. While it is initially unknown how the design space will be occupied by the structure, there must exist some segments of the structure such as the support and the loading that have functional interactions with its surroundings. The support point is some segment of the structure that is restrained (fixed, with zero displacement) while the loading point is where some specified load (input force) is applied to deform the structure. Collectively, the support and loading points represent the input points of the structure. There is also usually an output point which is some segment of the structure where the desired output behavior is attained. As shown in Fig. 2(a), the problem is defined with four I/O locations, each made up of one element in black. Six connecting curves in the illustration of Fig. 2(b), three of which are active and three of which are inactive, are used such that there is one connecting curve between any two points (i.e. every I/O point is directly connected to the other three). Before continuing, it is important to make a clear distinction between the *active* and *inactive* curves. The active curves are the curves which are in the 'on' state. The structure is generated based only on the active curves. Although the inactive curves, which are in the 'off' state, temporarily contribute nothing to the current structure, they are still very important in subsequent generations because they may be turned 'on' later through the crossover or mutation operations. In Fig. 2(b), the active curves are marked with thick lines and the inactive with thin dotted lines. The connectivity of the I/O points is based on all connecting active curves joining one point to another. Each curve is a Bezier curve defined by the position vector which can be derived from the element number of control point. The set of elements through which each active curve passes form the 'skeleton' (Fig. 2 (c)). Some of the elements surrounding the skeleton are then included to fill up the structure to its final form (Fig. 2 (d)) based on the skeleton's thickness values. Each curve is defined by three control points, and hence each curve has four thickness values. And the union of all skeleton, surrounding elements and I/O elements constitute the structure while all other elements remain as the surrounding empty space.

In order to use a GA for the optimization, the topological/shape representation variables have to be configured as a chromosome code. Hence the structural geometry in Fig. 2 (d) can be encoded as a chromosome in the form of a graph as shown in Fig. 3. Each curve is represented by a series of nodes connected by arcs in the sequence of start element number, thickness values alternating with control element number and end point. For identification purpose, the active curves are shown by solid lines and the inactive curves are represented by dotted lines. Altering the curve states can vary the connectivity of the I/O regions, and therefore the representation scheme can automatically decide the connectivity. The resulting scheme therefore increases the variability of the connectivity of the curves and hence the variability of the structure topology.

Two of the important operations in a GA are the crossover and mutation. In this implementation, the crossover operator works by randomly sectioning any single connected subgraph from a parent chromosome and swapping with a corresponding subgraph from another parent (as shown in Fig. 3.). As a result, two offsprings are produced which have a mix of the topological/shape characteristics of the two parents, and the advantages of the representation (such as no checkerboard patterns and single-node hinge connections) are maintained in the offspring. The 'on' and 'off' state of different curves which are crossed by the loop are also swapped. If the 'on' variables dominate a curve, i.e. when the number of 'on' variables is more than the number of 'off' variables, the curve of in the child chromosome will be active. Otherwise, the child curve will be inactive. As for mutation, the mutation operator works by randomly selecting any vertex of the chromosomal graph and altering its value to another randomly generated value within its allowable range. Mutation about the on-off state is simple, which is altering the state of curves. When the selected curve is active, it will be inactive after mutation, and vice verse.

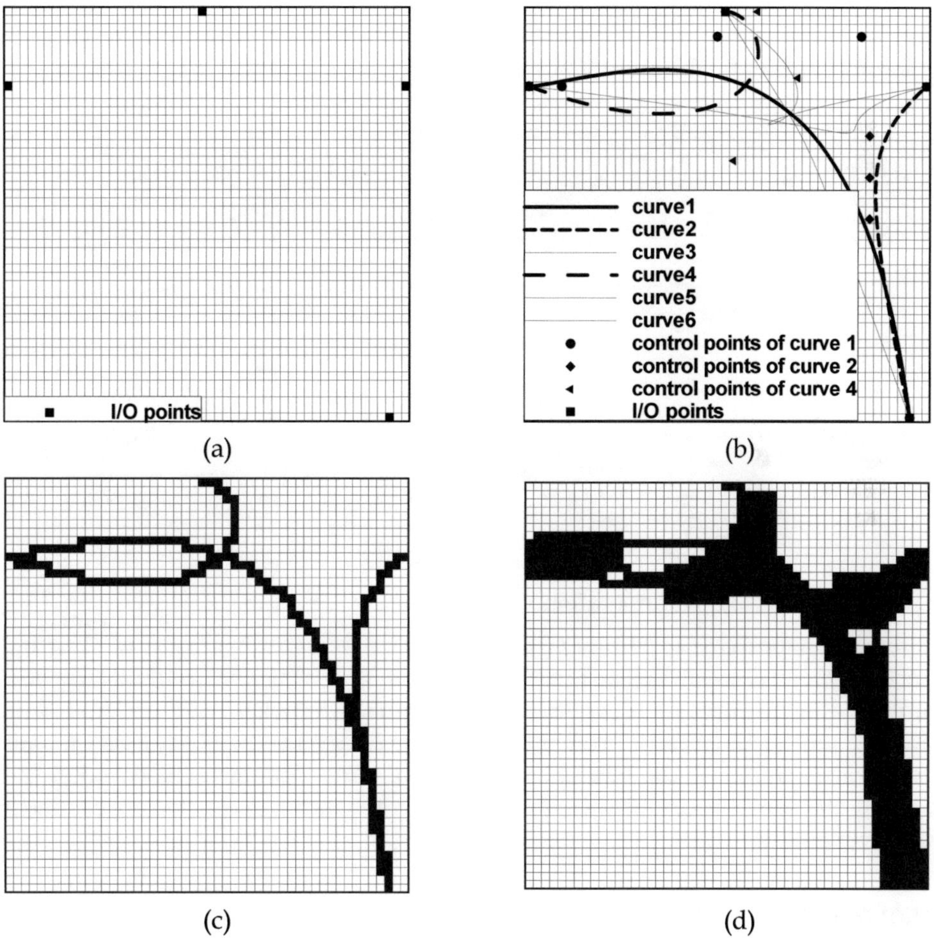

Fig. 2. Definition of structural geometry by enhanced morphological scheme (a) FE discretization of design space (I/O element marked in black) (b) Connecting I/O elements with Bezier curves (c) Skeleton made up of elements along curves (d) Surrounding elements added to skeleton to form final structure.

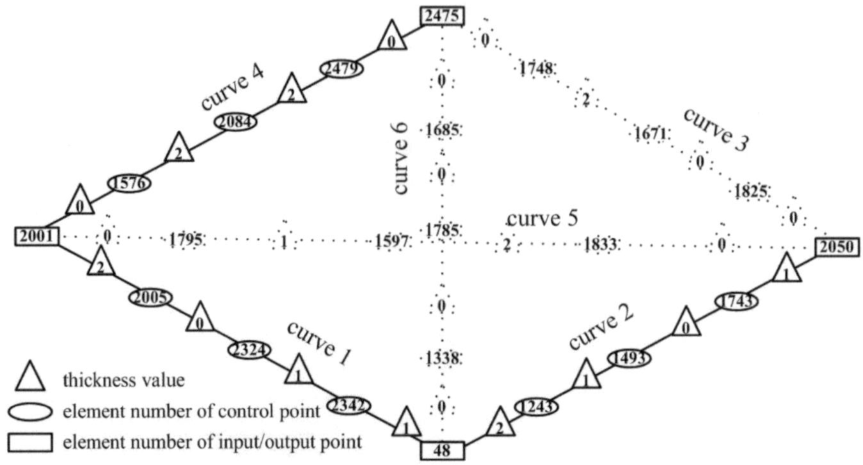

Fig. 3. Chromosome of final structure

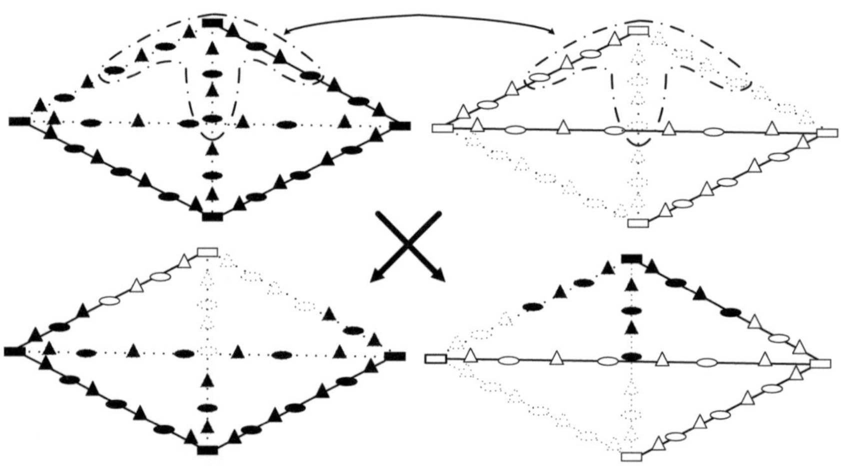

Fig. 4. Illustration of crossover operation

In summary, this morphological representation scheme uses arrangements of skeleton and surrounding material to define structural geometry in a way that will not render any undesirable design features such as disconnected segments, checkerboard patterns or single-node hinge connections because element edge connectivity of the skeleton is guaranteed, even after any crossover or mutation operation. Any chromosome-encoded design generated by the evolutionary procedure can be mapped into a finite element model of the structure accordingly.

4. Target matching problem

Before a GA is relied upon for solving a structure design problem with unknown solutions, it is important that the performance of the GA be tested and tuned by using it to solve a problem with known solutions. Various kinds of test problems (Michalewicz, Deb et al. 2000; Schmidt & Michalewicz 2000; Martin, Hassan et al. 2004) have been established for testing multi-objective GAs. They were created with different characteristics, including the dimensionality of the problem, number of local optima, number of active constraints at the optimum, topology of the feasible search space, etc. However, all of these test problems have well-defined objectives/constraints expressed as mathematical functions of decision variables and therefore may not be ideal for evaluating the performance of a GA intended to solve problems where the objectives/constraints cannot be expressed explicitly in terms of the decision variables. In essence, a GA is typically customized to tackle a certain type of problem and therefore `general-purpose' test problems may not correctly evaluate the performance of the customized GA. The test problem should, therefore, ideally suit (or be customized to) the GA being used.

In numerous real-life problems, objectives/constraints cannot be expressed mathematically in terms of decision variables. One of such real-life problems is structural topology optimization, where a procedure (structure geometry representation scheme) first transforms decision variables into the true geometry of the designed structure and then finite element analysis of the designed structure is carried out for evaluating the objectives/constraints. The GA solving such problems may have special chromosome encoding to suit the structure geometry representation used and there may also be specially devised reproduction operators to suit the chromosome encoding used. As such, the structure geometry representation scheme, the chromosome encoding and the reproduction operators introduce additional characteristics to the search space and, therefore, they are very critical to the performance of the GA. The test problem for such GAs, therefore, must use the same structure geometry representation scheme, chromosome encoding and reproduction operators. The conventional test problems found in literature cannot make use of the GA's integral procedures such as structure geometry representation scheme and therefore they are not suitable for testing such GAs.

Ideally, the test problem should emulate the main problem to be solved. The test problem should be computationally inexpensive so that it can be run many times for the GA parameters to be changed or experimented with and the effect thereof can be studied for the purpose of fine-tuning the GA. However, the main problem in the present work, being a structural topology optimization problem under uncertainty, requires structural analysis which consumes a great deal of time. Taking the running time into consideration, the test problem needs to be designed without any need for structural analysis. A test problem emulating structural topology optimization does not necessarily need structural analysis as the main aim of topology optimization is to arrive at an optimal structural geometry. Without using structural analysis, if a GA is successfully tested to be capable of converging the solutions to any arbitrary but predefined and valid `target' structural geometry, then it may be inferred that the GA would be able to converge design solutions to the optimal structural topology when solving an actual topology optimization problem. Based on this inference, a test problem can be designed such that simple geometry-based (rather than structural analysis based) objectives/constraints help design solutions converge towards the predefined target geometry. This type of test problem may be termed as ``Target Matching Problem'', which is capable of using exactly the same GA (including structural geometry representation scheme, chromosome encoding and reproduction operators) as that intended for solving the actual topology optimization problem. The present problem is similar to the Target Matching Problem solved in (Wang & Tai 2007; Tai et al. 2008; Wang & Yang 2009). The target matching problems are defined here as multiobjective optimization problems under uncertainty which are more difficult (e.g. more nonlinear problem) and computationally intensive.

4.1 Formulation

The test problem makes use of the design space shown in Fig.5, which has one support point, two loading points and one output point. The problem does not represent a structural analysis problem, but the original terms 'support', 'loading' and 'output' are still used for ease of reference. The loading point 1 is positioned anywhere along the left boundary and loading point 2 is positioned anywhere along the right boundary. The position of output point is fixed as shown in Fig.5. The support point is positioned in a specified area marked as "under uncertainty" and its position is random in the area. In this problem, the target geometry is shown in Fig. 6. The aim is therefore to evolve structures that match as closely as possible this target geometry. The problem presented here is more difficult than the original problem described in (Wang & Tai 2007), since the support point is under uncertainty that makes the geometry more complex and not easy to converge to the target.

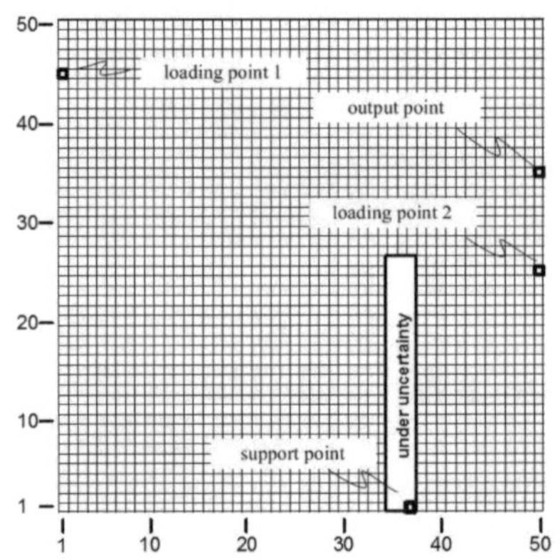

Fig. 5. Design space of Target Matching Problem.

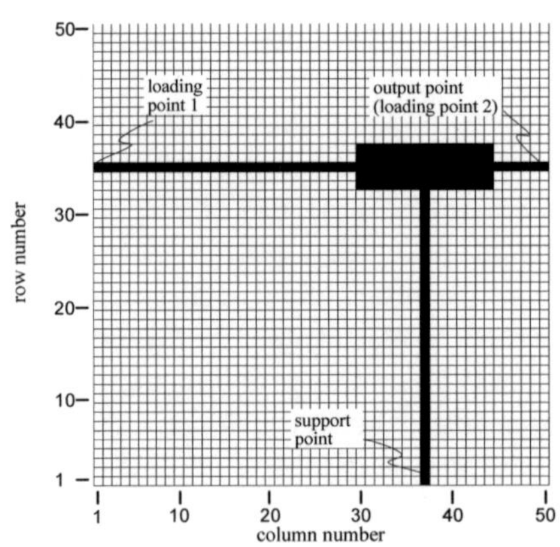

Fig. 6. Target geometry.

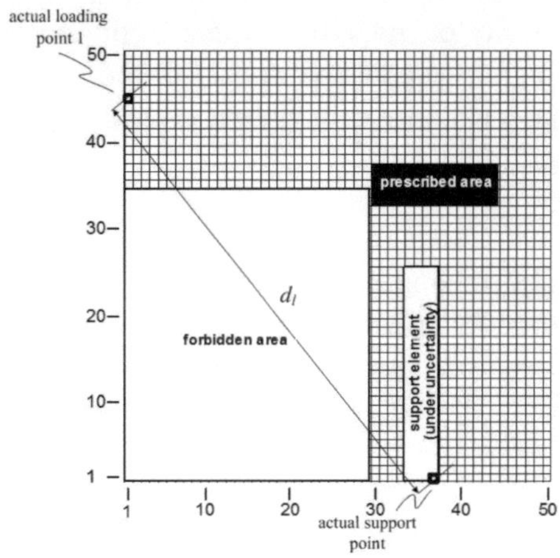

Fig. 7. Formulation of Target Matching Problem 1.

The problem is formulated with the following two objectives and two constraints: distance objective, material objective, forbidden area constraint and prescribed area constraint. Such a problem is defined with the help of Fig.7. The distance objective is given by

$$f_{distance} = d_l \tag{5}$$

where d_l is the centroid-to-centroid Euclidean distance between the actual loading point 1 and the actual support point.
The material objective is given by

$$f_{material} = \sum_{i=1}^{n} x_i \tag{6}$$

where x_i is the material density of the i-th element in the design space, with a value of either 0 or 1 to represent that the element is either void or material (solid), respectively. n is the total number of elements in the discretized design space. In other words, this objective function is defined as the summation of the material density of all elements in the current geometry.
The forbidden area constraint can be written as

$$g_{forbidden} = \sum_{i=1}^{n_f} y_i \leq 0 \tag{7}$$

where y_i is the material density of the i-th element in the forbidden area, and n_f is the total number of elements in the forbidden area. In other words, the summation of the material density of elements in the forbidden area is required to be less than or equal to zero.
The prescribed area constraint can be written as

$$g_{prescribed} = n_p - \sum_{i=1}^{n_p} z_i \leq 0 \tag{8}$$

where z_i is the material density of the i-th element in the prescribed area, and n_p is the total number of elements in the prescribed area. In other words, the summation of the material density of elements in the prescribed area is required to be more than or equal to the total number of elements in that area.

4.2 Main results

The target matching problem to be solved is defined by the design space shown in Fig. 5. The optimization was run for 1001 generations with a population size of 100 per generation. The local search procedure is triggered once every ten generations. By the end of evolutionary process 132,113 objective function evaluations have been performed. One of the solutions at the end of 1001 generations is shown in Fig. 8. It is the same as the target solution shown in Fig. 6.

As can be seen from the result, the support point is on the extreme point where the element number is 37. The following Fig. 9 illustrates how the solution shown in Fig. 8 is obtained by applying local search. Apply the Hooke and Jeeves method to determine the search path using the tournament selection criteria stated in Section 2. Each data point is labeled with its index where some indexes are coincided. At the start point, $f_{distance}$ is 37.6 and $f_{material}$ is 118. After the local search, the worst case labeled as 9 is obtained with a distance objective $f_{distance}$ value of 49.5 and a material objective $f_{material}$ value of 142. This figure demonstrates the Hooke and Jeeves direct search method for function maximization.

Fig. 10 shows a plot of the best distance objective $f_{distance}$ and the corresponding solution's $f_{material}$ versus generation number. $f_{distance}$ and $f_{material}$ values on the plot corresponding to any particular generation number belong to that generation's non-dominated feasible solution having the best distance objective. The plot starts at generation number 6, as until this generation there is no feasible solution in the population.

Fig. 11 shows plots of the best material objective $f_{material}$ and the corresponding solution's distance objective $f_{distance}$ versus generation number.

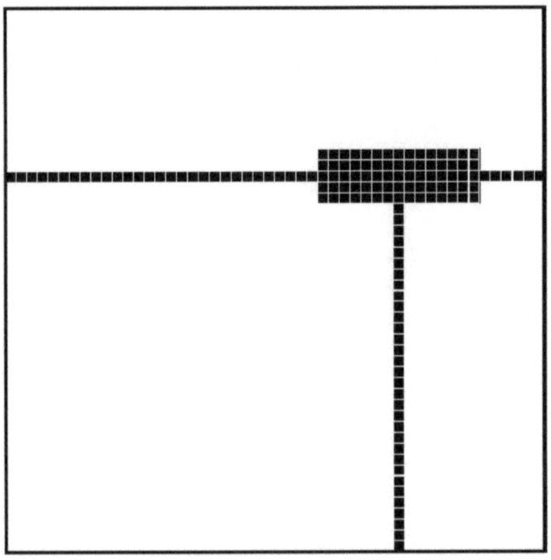

$$f_{distance} = 49.5$$
$$f_{material} = 142$$

Fig. 8. The optimal solution at 1001st generation.

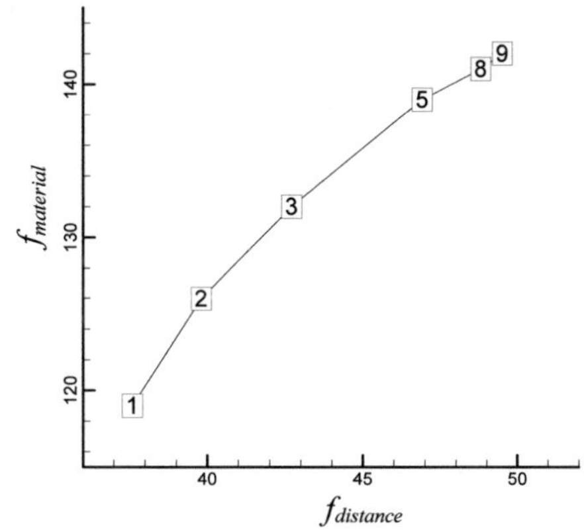

Fig. 9. Path of the local search.

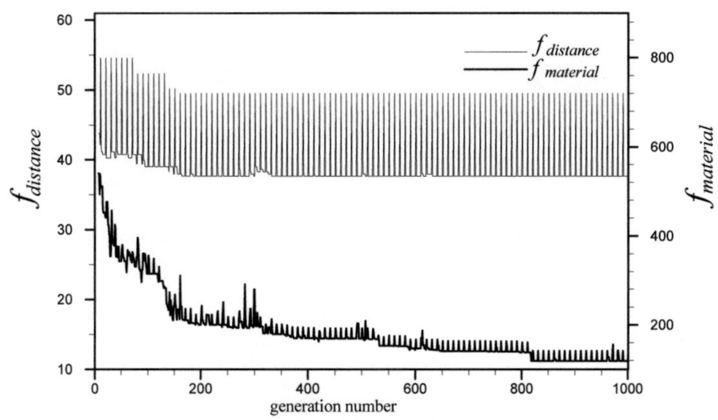

Fig. 10. History of the best distance objective ($f_{dis\tan ce}$).

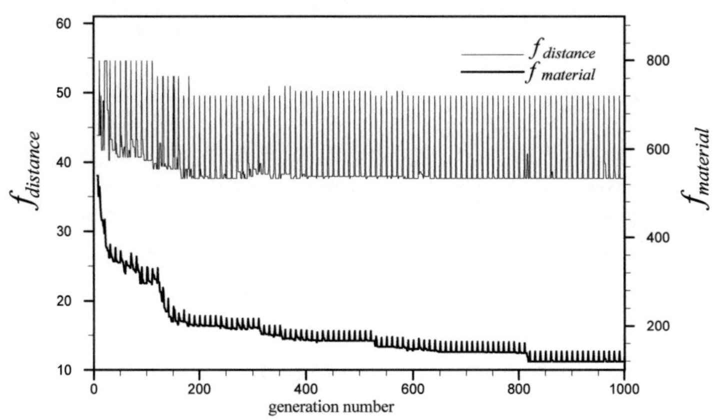

Fig. 11. History of the best distance objective ($f_{material}$).

Fig.12 shows a plot in objective space, where the solid shape markers are used to denote the feasible non-dominated solutions at any particular sample generation, viz. the 51st, 101st, 301st, 501st and 1001st generation. Although Fig.12 shows all the non-dominated solutions at any particular generation, only one or two distinct points (in the objective space) can be seen for that generation. However, a few distinct solutions in the design variable space may have the same objective function values and therefore, such solutions would coincide in the objective space. The number shown in parenthesis next to every point marker indicates the total number of such coincident solutions.

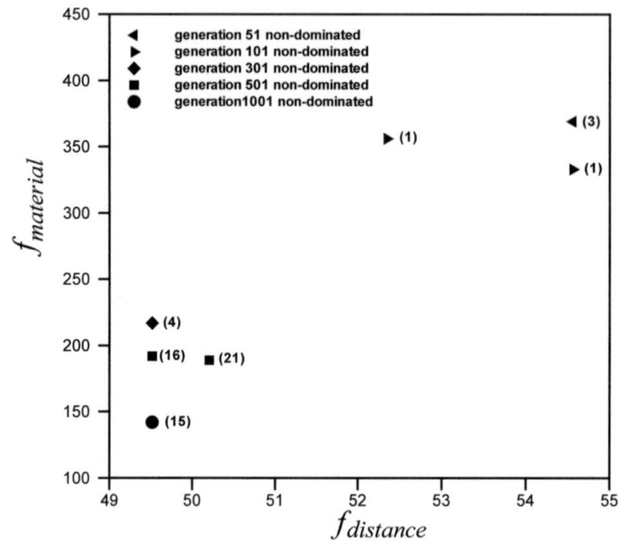

Fig. 12. History of the best distance objective ($f_{material}$).

4.3 Discussion

For the test problem, the results are summarized in Section 4.2. The hybrid GA proves its efficiency by converging the two objective function values ($f_{distance}$ and $f_{material}$) to the optimal values. The recurrent fluctuations in Fig. 10 and Fig. 11 show the effect of local search to the hybrid algorithm. Fig. 9 shows how the local search works.

5. Optimization of structures under load uncertainties

In this work, the structural optimization problem is defined in a design space shown in Fig. 13 using 4-noded quadrilateral elements. The present problem is similar to design problem solved in (Wang, Yang et al. 2008). The characteristics of the material aluminium used are as follows: the Young's Modulus E is 68948 MPa, and the mass density ρ is 2768 kg/m^3. The maximum allowable vertical displacement $d_{2,allowable}$ at loading point 2 is 0.000635m. Loading point 1 is subjected to a vertical load P_1 while loading point 2 is subjected to both a vertical load P_2 and a horizontal load P_3 as shown in Fig. 13. P_2 and P_3 are normal loads with constant values of 222N and 44.4N respectively while P_1 is an uncertain load varying between 44.4N and 55.5N.

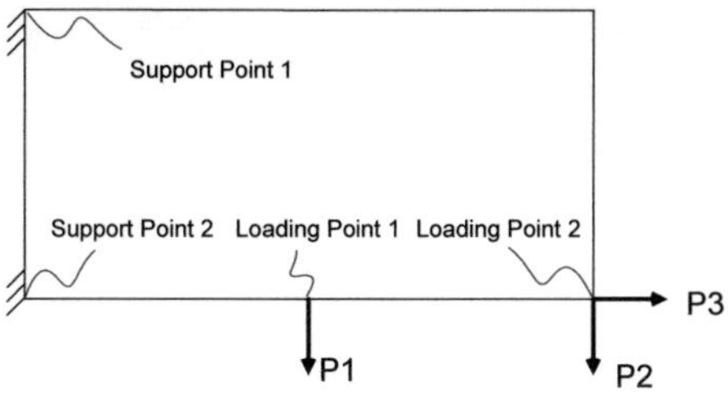

Fig. 13. Design domain.

The optimization problem can be formulated as follows:

$$\begin{aligned}&\underset{(\mathbf{x}_n,\mathbf{p})}{\text{minimize}}\ \{w(\mathbf{x}_n,\mathbf{p})\quad d(\mathbf{x}_n,\mathbf{p})\}\\&\underset{\mathbf{p}}{\text{maximize}}\ \underset{\mathbf{x}_{n_0}\subset\mathbf{C}_N}{\{w(\mathbf{x}_{n_0},\mathbf{p})\quad d(\mathbf{x}_{n_0},\mathbf{p})\}}\\&\text{subject to}\ g_d=d-0.000635\le 0\\&\qquad\qquad g_{stress}\le 0\end{aligned}\tag{9}$$

where w is the weight of the structure and d is the displacement of the loading point 2. $\mathbf{p}$ is the vector of loads under uncertainty, that is P_1 in this problem. Local search which is triggered every 10 generations in this work is only applied to selected $\mathbf{C}_N$ solutions. A constraint on the vertical displacement, g_d, is used to prevent big deformations which are supposed likely to occur. A constraint on the maximum stress in the structure (to prevent fatigue or failure) is important. A dimensionless expression for the stress constraint may be written as

$$g_{stress}=\frac{\sigma_{peak-von-Mises}-\sigma_y}{\sigma_y}\le 0\tag{10}$$

where $\sigma_{peak-von-Mises}$ is the peak von Mises stress and σ_y is the tensile yield strength of the material.

The optimization procedure and finite element analysis have been implemented through a C++ program running in the Windows environment of a PC. Values of the objective and constraint functions for every design are derived from the results of a FE analysis of the designed structure.

The optimization was run for 501 generations (with a population size of 100 per generation), by the end of which 46,415 objective function evaluations have been performed. The values of w_1 and w_2 in Equation 4 are 1 and 100 respectively. Three of the non-dominated solutions at the end of 501 generations are shown in Fig. 14. Fig. 14 (a) shows the solution with best weight objective under the worst load case where P_1 is 55.5N. Fig. 14 (c) shows the solution with the best displacement objective under the worst load case where P_1 is 55.4N. One solution with median weight and displacement objective is given in Fig. 14 (b).

Fig. 15 shows a plot of the best weight objective (w) and the corresponding solution's displacement objective (d) versus generation number. w and d values on the plot corresponding to any particular generation number belong to that generation's non-dominated feasible solution which has the best weight objective.

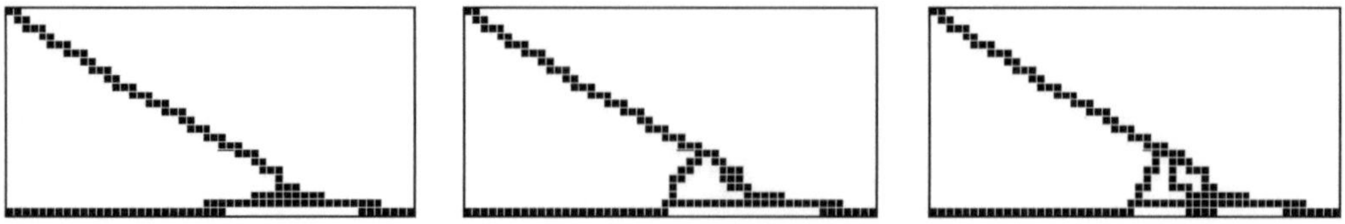

	P_1	=	55.489234		P_1	=	55.279937		P_1	=	55.394852
	w	=	0.002702		w	=	0.002790		w	=	0.003012
(a)	d	=	0.000352	(b)	d	=	0.000176	(c)	d	=	0.000140
	g_d	=	-0.055514		g_d	=	-0.016029		g_d	=	-0.088194
	g_{stress}	=	-0.000437		g_{stress}	=	-0.000613		g_{stress}	=	-0.000635

Fig. 14. Three non-dominated solutions at 501st generation.

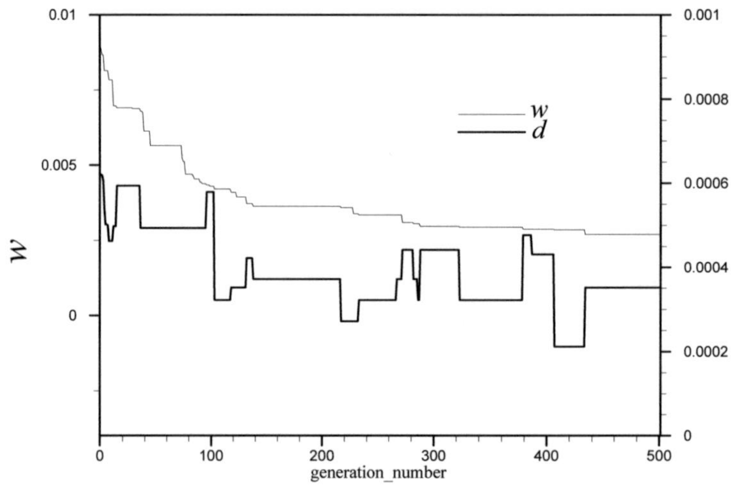

Fig. 15. History of the best weight objective (w).

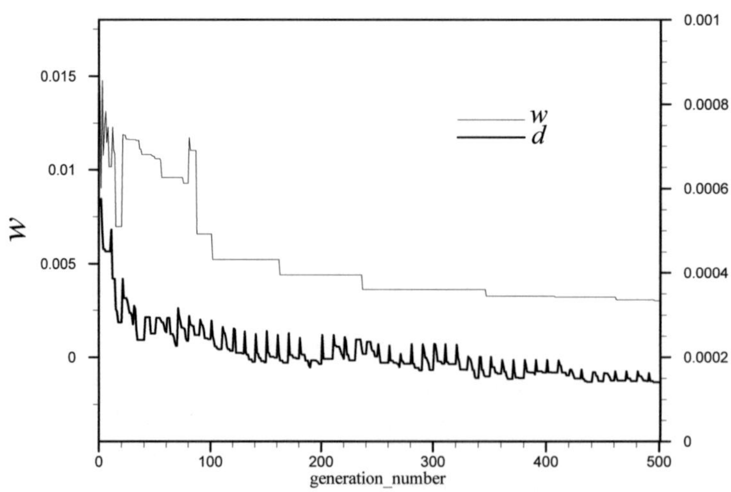

Fig. 16. History of the best displacement objective(d)

Fig. 16 shows plots of the best displacement objective (*d*) and the corresponding solution's weight objective (w) versus generation number. As can be seen from Fig. 15 and Fig. 16, there are some fluctuations because of anti-optimization.
Fig. 17 shows a plot in the objective space, where the solid shape markers denote the feasible non-dominated solutions at any particular sample generation.

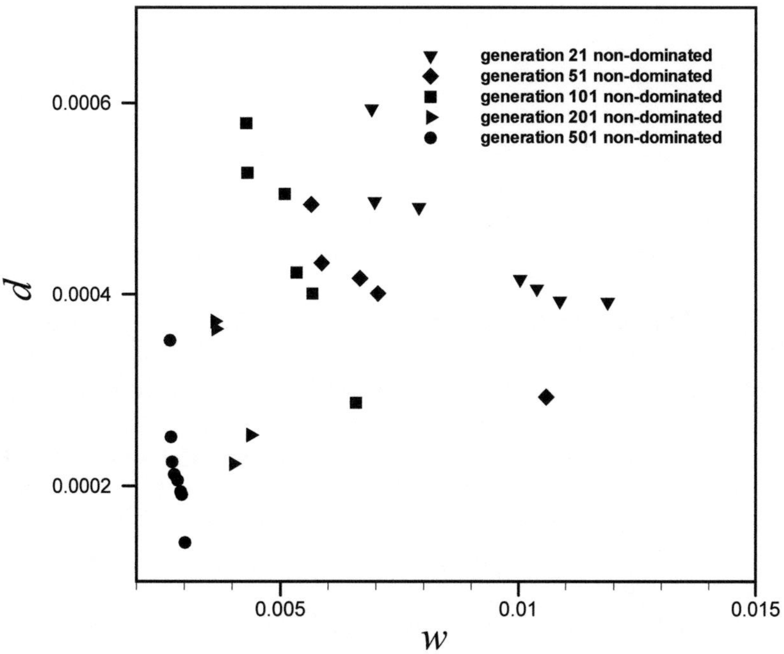

Fig. 17. Plot of non-dominated solutions and elites at some sample generations.

6. Conclusion

The versatility and effectiveness of the topology optimization methodology developed in this work rest on three key components: an efficient morphological geometry representation that defines practical and valid structural geometries, a compatible graph-theoretic chromosome encoding and reproduction system that embodies topological and shape characteristics, and a multiobjective hybrid GA with local search strategy as the worst-case-scenario technique of anti-optimization. The use of local search strategy helps to direct and focus the genetic search in uncertainty design variable space. A multiobjective target matching problem with known solutions has been formulated and solved to demonstrate the validity of presented algorithm. Simulation results of the structure optimization under load uncertainty are encouraging, which indicates that the hybrid algorithm integrates local search as anti-optimization is applicable. The proposed tournament constrained selection method works well and the computation cost is reasonable.

8. References

Agoston, M. K. (2005). *Computer Graphics and Geometric Modeling*, Springer-Verlag New York, LLC.

Au, S. K. (2005). "Reliability-based design sensitivity by efficient simulation." *Computers & Structures* **83**(14): 1048-61.

Ayyub, B. M. (1997). *Uncertainty Modeling and Analysis in Civil Engineering*, John Wiley.

Ben-Haim, Y. and I. Elishakoff (1990). *Convex models of uncertainty in applied mechanics*, Dordrecht: Elsevier Science Publishers.

Deb, K. (2000). "An efficient constraint handling method for genetic algorithms." *Computer Methods in Applied Mechanics and Engineering* 186(2-4): 311-338.

Deb, K. and T. Goel (2001). *A hybrid multi-objective evolutionary approach to engineering shape design*, Berlin, Germany, Springer-Verlag.

Elishakoff, I. (1995). "Essay on uncertainties in elastic and viscoelastic structures: from A. M. Freudenthal's criticisms to modern convex modeling." *Computers and Structures* 56(6): 871-871.

Elishakoff, I. (1995). "An idea on the uncertainty triangle." *Editors Rattle Space, The Shock and Vibration Digest* 22(10): 1.

Han, J., V. Manousiouthakis, et al. (1997). "Global optimization of chemical processes using the interval analysis." *Korean Journal of Chemical Engineering* 14(4): 270-276.

Ishibuchi, H. and T. Murata (1998). "A multi-objective genetic local search algorithm and its application to flowshop scheduling." *Systems, Man and Cybernetics, Part C, IEEE Transactions on* 28(3): 392-403.

Ishibuchi, H., T. Yoshida, et al. (2002). Balance Between Genetic Search And Local Search In Hybrid Evolutionary Multi-criterion Optimization Algorithms. *Proceedings of the Genetic and Evolutionary Computation Conference,* New York, July 9-13,2002

Jaszkiewicz, A. (2003). "Do multiple-objective metaheuristics deliver on their promises --A computational experiment on the set-covering problem." *IEEE Transactions on Evolutionary Computation* 7(2): 133-43.

Ju, H., H. Vasilios, et al. (1997). "Global optimization of chemical processes using the interval analysis." *Korean Journal of Chemical Engineering* 14(4): 270-276.

Maenghyo, C. and R. Seung Yun (2004). "Optimization of laminates with free edges under uncertainty subject to extension, bending and twisting." *International Journal of Solids and Structures* 41(1): 227-45.

Martin, E. T., R. A. Hassan, et al. (2004). "Comparing the N-branch genetic algorithm and the multi-objective genetic algorithm." *AIAA Journal* 42(7): 1495-500.

Michalewicz, Z., K. Deb, et al. (2000). "Test-case generator for nonlinear continuous parameter optimization techniques." *IEEE Transactions on Evolutionary Computation* 4(3): 197-215.

Michalewicz, Z. and M. Schoenauer (1996). "Evolutionary algorithms for constrained parameter optimization problems." *Evolutionary Computation* 4(1): 1.

Moore, R. E. (1966). Interval analysis, Prentice-Hall, Englewood Cliffs, NJ.

Qiu, Y. and S. S. Rao (2005). "A fuzzy approach for the analysis of unbalanced nonlinear rotor systems." *Journal of Sound and Vibration* 284(1-2): 299-323.

Qiu, Z. and I. Elishakoff (2001). "Anti-optimization technique - A generalization of interval analysis for nonprobabilistic treatment of uncertainty." *Chaos, Solitons and Fractals* 12(9): 1747-1759.

Ray, T., K. Tai, et al. (2001). "Multiobjective design optimization by an evolutionary algorithm." *Engineering Optimization* 33(4): 399-424.

Schmidt, M. and Z. Michalewicz (2000). Test-case generator TCG-2 for nonlinear parameter optimisation. *Proceedings of the 2000 Congress on Evolutionary Computation,* Vols 1 and 2: 728-735.

Srinivas, N. and K. Deb (1994). "Multi-objective function optimization using nondominated sorting genetic algorithms." *Evolutionary Computation* 2(3): 221-- 248.

Tai, K. and S. Akhtar (2005). "Structural topology optimization using a genetic algorithm with a morphological geometric representation scheme." *Structural and Multidisciplinary Optimization* 30(2): 113-27.

Tai, K. and J. Prasad (2007). "Target-matching test problem for multiobjective topology optimization using genetic algorithms." *Structural and Multidisciplinary Optimization* 34(4): 333-45.

Tai, K. and N. Wang (2007). An enhanced chromosome encoding and morphological representation of geometry for structural topology optimization using GA, *2007 IEEE Congress on Evolutionary Computation*, Singapore, 25-28 September 2007.

Tai, K., N. F. Wang, et al. (2008). Target geometry matching problem with conflicting objectives for multiobjective topology design optimization using GA, *2008 IEEE Congress on Evolutionary Computation*, Hong Kong, China, 1-6 June 2008.

Venter, G. and R. T. Haftka (1996). Two species genetic algorithm for designing composite laminates subjected to uncertainty, *Proceedings of the 37th AIAA/ASME/ASCE/AHS/ASC Structures, Structural Dynamics, and Materials Conference,* Salt Lake City, Utah, April, 1996

Wang, N. and K. Tai (2007). Handling objectives as adaptive constraints for multiobjective structural optimization, *2007 IEEE Congress on Evolutionary Computation*, Singapore, 25-28 September 2007.

Wang, N. and K. Tai (2007). A hybrid genetic algorithm for multiobjective structural optimization, *2007 IEEE Congress on Evolutionary Computation*, Singapore, 25-28 September 2007.

Wang, N. F. and K. Tai (2008). "Design of grip-and-move manipulators using symmetric path generating compliant mechanisms." *Journal of Mechanical Design* 130(11): 112305 (9 pp.).

Wang, N. F. and Y. W. Yang (2009). Target Geometry Matching Problem for Hybrid Genetic Algorithm Used to Design Structures Subjected to Uncertainty, *2009 IEEE Congress on Evolutionary Computation*, Trondheim, Norway, 18-21 May 2009.

Wang, N. F., Y. W. Yang, et al. (2008). Optimization of structures under load uncertainties based on hybrid genetic algorithm, *2008 IEEE Congress on Evolutionary Computation*, Hong Kong, China, 1-6 June 2008.

Zadeh, L. A. (1978). "Fuzzy sets as a basis for a theory of possibility." *Fuzzy Sets and Systems* 1(1): 3-28.

18

Optimum Design of Balanced Surface Acoustic Wave Filters using Evolutionary Computation

Kiyoharu Tagawa
School of Science and Engineering, Kinki University
Japan

1. Introduction

Surface Acoustic Wave (SAW) filters are small, rugged and cost-competitive mechanical band-pass filters with amazing frequency response characteristics. Therefore, SAW filters have played an important role as a key device in various mobile and wireless communication systems such as personal digital assistants (PDAs) and cellular phones (Campbell, 1998). Recently, the balanced SAW filter becomes widely used in the modern Radio Frequency (RF) circuits of cellular phones. That is because the balanced SAW filter can provide not only the band-pass filtering function but also some external functions, namely, the unbalance-balance signal conversion, the impedance conversion and so on. In other words, if we use balanced SAW filters in a modern RF circuit, we can reduce the number of the components of the modern RF circuit, as well as their mounted area (Meier et al., 2001). As a result, we can miniaturize the modern RF circuit of a cellular phone.

The frequency response characteristics of SAW filters including balanced one are governed primarily by their geometrical structures, namely, the configurations of Inter-Digital Transducers (IDTs) and Shorted Metal Strip Arrays (SMSAs) reflectors fabricated on piezoelectric substrates (Hashimoto, 2000). Therefore, in order to realize desirable frequency response characteristics of SAW filters, we have to decide strictly their geometrical structures, which are specified by using many design parameters such as the numbers of the fingers of respective IDTs, the length of the electrodes, and so on.

Several optimum design methods which combine the optimization algorithm with the computer simulation have been reported to decide suitable structures of SAW filters (Franz et al., 1997; Tagawa et al., 2002; Goto & Kawakatsu, 2004; Tagawa et al., 2007). In these optimum design methods of SAW filters, Evolutionary Algorithms (EAs) such as Genetic Algorithm (GA) have been also used as the optimization algorithm (Prabhu et al., 2002; Meltaus et al., 2004; Tagawa et al., 2003). However, conventional optimum design methods of SAW filters have been contrived for the unbalanced SAW filter. Therefore, conventional optimum design methods can't be applied directly to the balanced SAW filter.

The primary purpose of this chapter is to demonstrate the usage of the latest Evolutionary Computation (EC) technique in a real-world application, namely, the optimum design of balanced SAW filters. In the proposed optimum design method of balanced SAW filters, Differential Evolution (DE) is employed as the optimization algorithm. DE is one of the most recent EAs for solving real-parameter optimization problems (Storn & Price, 1997). DE exhibits an overall excellent performance for a wide range of benchmark problems. Furthermore, because of its simple but powerful searching capability, DE has got numerous real-world applications (Price et al., 2005). Actually, in our prior study about the optimum design of a balanced SAW filter, it has been shown that DE is superior to a real-coded GA in both the quality of the final solution and the computational time (Tagawa, 2008).

The computer simulation technique is very important in the optimum design method of balanced SAW filters as well as the optimization algorithm. In order to evaluate the performance of the balanced SAW filter based on the computer simulation, we have to employ a reliable model. Therefore, we explain the network model of the balanced SAW filter in detail (Tagawa, 2007). First of all, we show the equivalent circuit model of the balanced SAW filter. Then we transform the equivalent circuit model into the network model according to the balanced network theory (Bockelman & Eisenstadt, 1995).

The rest of this chapter is organized as follows. In the section 2, the basic structure and the principle of the balanced SAW filter are described briefly. The modeling and the simulation methodologies of the balanced SAW filter are also explained. In the section 3, the structural design of balanced SAW filters is formulated as an optimization problem. In the section 4, the decision variables of the optimization problem, which correspond to the various design parameters of balanced SAW filters, are embedded in the regularized continuous search space of DE. Then the procedure of a classic DE known as "DE/rand/1/bin" is described in detail. In the section 5, the structural design of a practical balanced SAW filter is formulated into two types of optimum design problems. Then the classic DE is applied to the respective optimum design problems. Furthermore, the results of computational experiments are shown and discussed. Finally, some conclusions are offered in the section 6.

2. Balanced surface acoustic wave filter

2.1 Basic structure and principle

A balanced SAW filter consists of several components, namely, Inter-Digital Transducers (IDTs) and Shorted Metal Strip Array (SMSA) reflectors fabricated on a piezoelectric substrate. Figure 1 illustrates a typical structure of the balanced SAW filter that consists of five components: one transmitter IDT (IDT-T), two receiver IDTs (IDT-R) and two SMSAs. Furthermore, port-1 is an input-port, while port-2 and port-3 are output-ports.

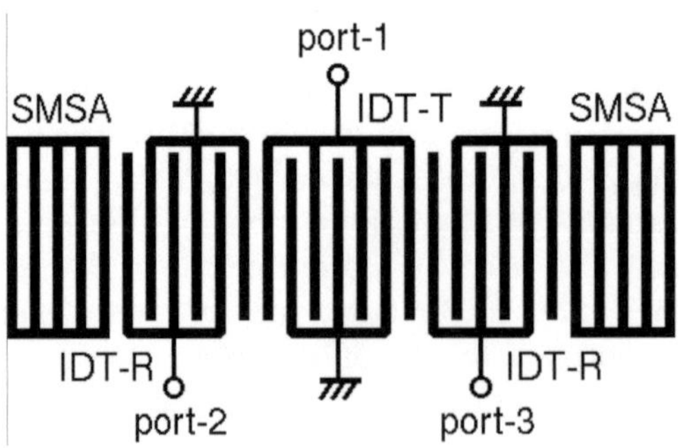

Fig. 1. Typical structure of the balanced SAW filter

Each of IDTs is composed of some pairs of electrodes called fingers and used for Surface Acoustic Wave (SAW) excitation and detection. The balanced SAW filter is a kind of the resonator-type SAW filter that has a symmetrical structure centering IDT-T. The input electric signals of port-1 are converted to acoustic signals in IDT-T. Then the acoustic signals are resonated between two SMSAs. Furthermore, the acoustic signals are reconverted to electric signals in IDT-Rs. Even though the balanced SAW filter had a symmetrical structure, the polarities of two IDT-Rs' electrodes are designed to be opposite. Therefore, a pair of port-2 and port-3 connected to respective IDT-Rs provides a balanced output-port.

2.2 Modeling and simulation

For analyzing the frequency response characteristics of SAW filters based on the computer simulation, we have to utilize their reliable models. Therefore, in order to evaluate the performance of the balanced SAW filter, we present the network model (Tagawa, 2007). The network model of the balanced SAW filter is derived from the conventional equivalent circuit model according to the balanced network theory (Bockelman & Eisenstadt, 1995).
The equivalent circuit model of a balanced SAW filter is made up from the equivalent circuit models of its components, namely, IDTs and SMSAs. First of all, Fig. 2 shows examples of the structures of IDTs with N-pair of fingers. The behavior of each IDT in Fig. 2 can be analyzed by using a three-port circuit model illustrated in Fig. 3 (Kojima & Suzuki, 1992). In the circuit model in Fig. 3, port-A and port-B are acoustic-signal ports, while port-C is an electric-signal port. Circuit elements appeared in Fig. 3, namely, transconductances A_{10} and A_{20}, impedances Z_1 and Z_2, admittance Y_m, and capacitance C_T are given as follows.

$$\begin{cases} A_{10} = \tanh\left(\frac{\gamma_s}{2}\right)\tanh(N\gamma_s) \\ A_{20} = \mp A_{10} \\ Z_1 = \frac{1}{R_0 F_s}\tanh(N\gamma_s) \\ Z_2 = \frac{1}{R_0 F_s}\left(\frac{1}{\sinh(2N\gamma_s)}\right) \\ Y_m = \frac{2F_s}{R_0}\tanh\left(\frac{\gamma_s}{2}\right)\left[2N - \tanh\left(\frac{\gamma_s}{2}\right)\tanh(N\gamma_s)\right] \\ C_T = NC_{so}\frac{K\left(\sin\left(\eta\frac{\pi}{2}\right)\right)}{K\left(\cos\left(\eta\frac{\pi}{2}\right)\right)} \end{cases} \tag{1}$$

where, the dual sign (±) means that the minus (-) is for $2N$ being an even number as shown in Fig. 2 (a), while the plus (+) is for $2N$ being an odd number as shown in Fig. 2 (b). Furthermore, R_0 denotes the characteristic impedance. F_s is the image admittance, and γ_s is the image transfer constant. $K(z)$ is the complete elliptic integral of a real number $z \in R$.
If the electric port (port-C) is shorted in Fig. 3, the equivalent circuit model of IDT becomes the equivalent circuit model of SMSA reflector (Kojima & Suzuki, 1992). Now, because all of the components of a balanced SAW filter are connected acoustically in cascade on a piezoelectric substrate, the entire equivalent circuit model of the balanced SAW filter can be composed by linking together the acoustic-ports of their equivalent circuit models.

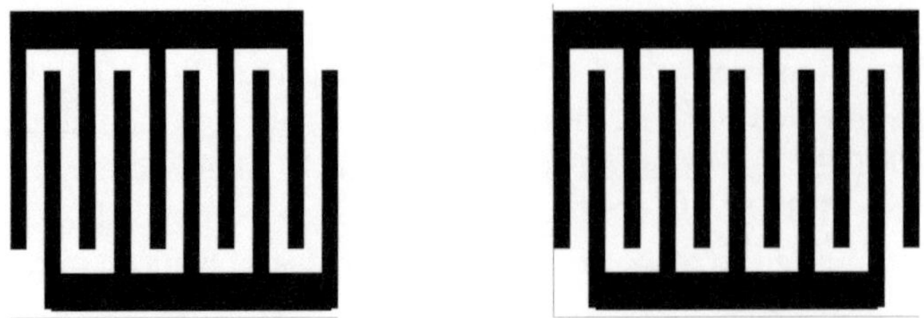

(a) N=5 (integer) (b) N=5.5 (half-integer)

Fig. 2. Structure of Inter-Digital Transducer (IDT) with N-pair of fingers

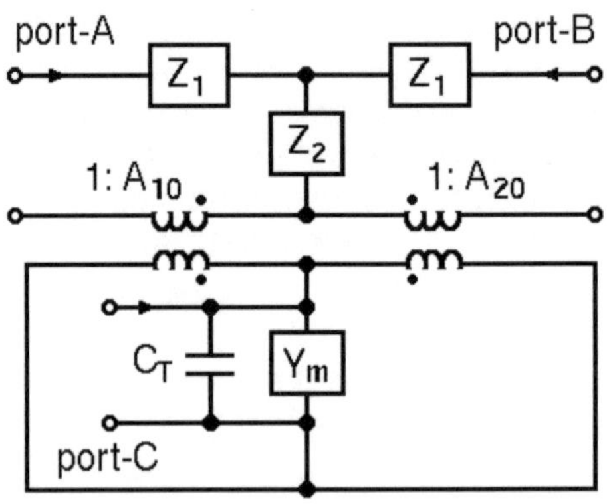

Fig. 3. Equivalent circuit model of IDT

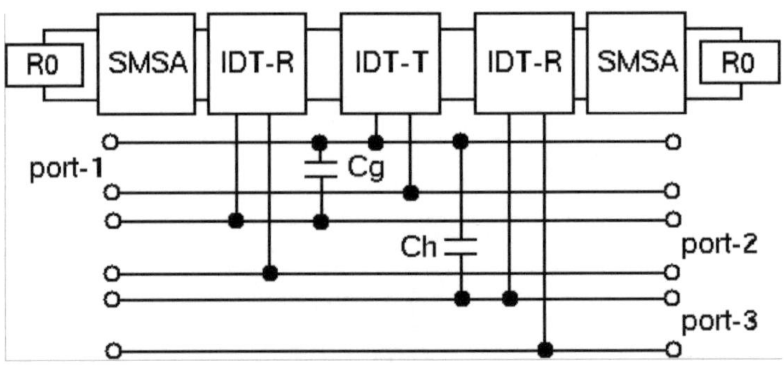

Fig. 4. Equivalent circuit model of the balanced SAW filter shown in Fig. 1

For example, the equivalent circuit model of the balanced SAW filter in Fig. 1 is given by a six-port circuit in Fig. 4, where a pair of port-2 and port-3 corresponds to the balanced output-port, while port-1 is the unbalanced input-port. Incidentally, C_h and C_g denote coupling capacitances between one IDT-T and two IDT-Rs. A serious difference between C_h and C_g causes the deterioration of the balance characteristics of the balanced SAW filter.

Terminating the three extra ports of the six-port equivalent circuit model in Fig. 4, the balanced SAW filter shown in Fig. 1 can be represented by an admittance matrix $\boldsymbol{Y}$ in (2).

$$Y = \begin{bmatrix} y_{11} & y_{12} & y_{13} \\ y_{21} & y_{22} & y_{23} \\ y_{31} & y_{32} & y_{33} \end{bmatrix} \tag{2}$$

Furthermore, considering the impedances of the input-port Z_{in} and the output-port Z_{out}, the admittance matrix $\boldsymbol{Y}$ in (2) is transformed into a scattering matrix $\boldsymbol{S}$ as shown in (3).

$$S = BA^{-1} = \begin{bmatrix} s_{11} & s_{12} & s_{13} \\ s_{21} & s_{22} & s_{23} \\ s_{31} & s_{32} & s_{33} \end{bmatrix} \tag{3}$$

where, matrixes A and B are given by using the elements of Y as follows.

$$A = \begin{bmatrix} 1+Z_{in}y_{11} & Z_{in}y_{12} & Z_{in}y_{13} \\ -Z_{out}y_{21} & 1+Z_{out}y_{22} & -Z_{out}y_{23} \\ -Z_{out}y_{31} & -Z_{out}y_{32} & 1+Z_{out}y_{33} \end{bmatrix}$$

$$B = \begin{bmatrix} 1-Z_{in}y_{11} & -Z_{in}y_{12} & -Z_{in}y_{13} \\ Z_{out}y_{21} & 1+Z_{out}y_{22} & Z_{out}y_{23} \\ Z_{out}y_{31} & Z_{out}y_{32} & 1+Z_{out}y_{33} \end{bmatrix}$$

From the scattering matrix $\boldsymbol{S}$ in (3), a three-port network model of the balanced SAW filter can be represented graphically as shown in Fig. 5 (Tagawa, 2007). In the network model in Fig. 5, nodes a_q (q=1, 2, 3) denote the input signals of the balanced SAW filter, while nodes b_p (p=1, 2, 3) denote the output signals. Scattering parameters s_{pq} on edges provide the transition characteristics from input signals a_q to output signals b_p. Furthermore, a pair of port-2 and port-3 of the network model in Fig. 5 corresponds to the balanced output-port of the balanced SAW filter in Fig. 1, while port-1 corresponds to the unbalanced input-port.

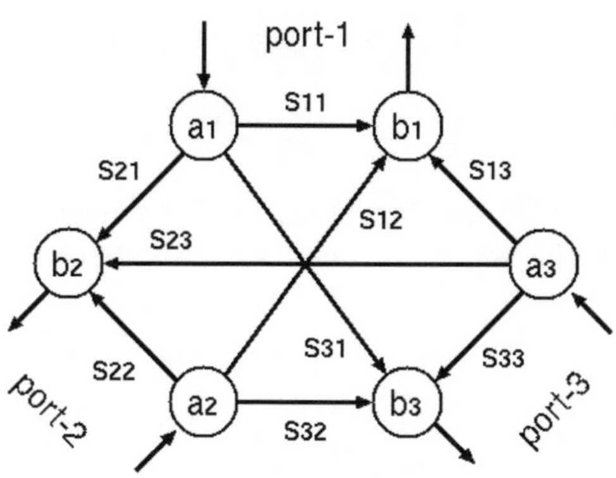

Fig. 5. Network model of the balanced SAW filter shown in Fig. 1

2.3 Balance characteristics

In the balanced SAW filter, it is desirable that the output signals b_2 and b_3 from the balanced output-port, namely, a pair of port-2 and port-3 of the three-port network model in Fig.5, have the same amplitude and 180 degrees phase difference through the pass-band. Therefore, in order to evaluate the balance characteristics of the balanced SAW filter, two criteria are usually used (Koshino et al., 2002). The amplitude balance of the balanced SAW filter is evaluated by criterion E_1 in (4). On the other hand, the phase balance of the balanced SAW filter is evaluated by criterion E_2 in (5). In an ideal condition of the balanced SAW filter, the values of both the criteria E_1 and E_2 should become zero through the pass-band.

$$E_1 = 20\log_{10}(|s_{21}|) - 20\log_{10}(|s_{31}|) \tag{4}$$

$$E_2 = \varphi(s_{21}) - \varphi(s_{31}) + 180 \tag{5}$$

where, $\varphi(s_{pq})$ denotes the phase angle of the scattering parameter s_{pq}.

2.4 Filter characteristics

The balanced SAW filter is used as a band-pass filter. In order to evaluate the band-pass filter characteristics of the balanced SAW filter strictly, we have to segregate the differential mode signal from the common mode signal in the three-port network model in Fig. 5. Therefore, according to the theory of the balanced network (Bockelman & Eisenstadt, 1995), we reorganize the entering signals a_q (q=2, 3) and the leaving signals b_p (p=2, 3) of the balanced port, or the pair of port-2 and port-3, respectively as shown in (6) and (7). Consequently, signals a_d and b_d defined in (6) correspond to differential mode signals of the balanced SAW filter, while signals a_c and b_c defined in (7) correspond to common mode signals.

$$\begin{cases} a_d = \dfrac{1}{\sqrt{2}}(a_2 - a_3) \\ b_d = \dfrac{1}{\sqrt{2}}(b_2 - b_3) \end{cases} \tag{6}$$

$$\begin{cases} a_c = \dfrac{1}{\sqrt{2}}(a_2 + a_3) \\ b_c = \dfrac{1}{\sqrt{2}}(b_2 + b_3) \end{cases} \tag{7}$$

From the definition shown in (6) and (7), the matrix $\boldsymbol{S}$ of conventional scattering parameters in (3) can be converted into the matrix $\boldsymbol{S}_{mix}$ of mix-mode scattering parameters as follows.

$$S_{mix} = TST^{-1} = \begin{bmatrix} s_{11} & s_{1d} & s_{1c} \\ s_{d1} & s_{dd} & s_{dc} \\ s_{c1} & s_{cd} & s_{cc} \end{bmatrix} \tag{8}$$

where, matrix $\boldsymbol{T}$ is given as follows.

$$T = \frac{1}{\sqrt{2}} \begin{bmatrix} \sqrt{2} & 0 & 0 \\ 0 & 1 & -1 \\ 0 & 1 & 1 \end{bmatrix}$$

In order to evaluate the band-pass filter characteristics of the balanced SAW filter as well as the unbalanced one (Tagawa et al., 2003), we use the above mix-mode scattering parameters instead of conventional scattering parameters. Therefore, the standing wave ratios of the input-port E_3 and the output-port E_4 can be defined respectively in (9) and (10). Also, the attenuation E_5 between the input-port and the output-port is defined as shown in (11).

$$E_3 = \frac{1+|s_{11}|}{1-|s_{11}|} \tag{9}$$

$$E_4 = \frac{1+|s_{dd}|}{1-|s_{dd}|} \tag{10}$$

$$E_5 = 20\log_{10}\left(|s_{d1}|\right) \tag{11}$$

3. Problem formulation

3.1 Design parameters

The frequency response characteristics of balanced SAW filters depend on their geometrical structures, or the configurations of their components fabricated on piezoelectric substrates. For example, in order to decide the structure of the balanced SAW filter in Fig. 1, we have to adjust nine design parameters (N_T, N_R, N_S, l_p, W, ξ, ξ_m, ρ_m, H) illustrated in Fig. 6. The design parameters N_T and N_R represent the numbers of the fingers of IDT-T and IDT-R respectively. Similarly, N_S is the number of the strips of SMSA. The design parameter l_p denotes the finger pitch of IDT. W denotes the overlap between facing electrodes. The metallization ratio of IDT ξ is defined as $\xi = l_m / l_p$ with the finger pitch l_p and the metal width of the finger l_m ($l_m < l_p$). The metallization ratio of SMSA ξ_m is also defined as $\xi_m = r_m / r_p$ with the strip pitch r_p and the metal width of the strip r_m ($r_m < r_p$). The pitch ratio of SMSA is defined as $\rho_m = r_p / l_p$ based on the finger pitch of IDT l_p. Besides, H denotes the metal thickness of electrode.

A set of design parameters describing the structure of a balanced SAW filter is represented by a vector of decision variables: $\boldsymbol{x}=(x_1, \ldots, x_D)$. Each decision variable $x_j \in \boldsymbol{x}$ ($j=1, \ldots, D$) is either a continuous value or a discrete value as shown in Fig. 6. Furthermore, the values of decision variables $x_j \in \boldsymbol{x}$ are bounded by their parametric limitations as follows.

$$x_j^L \le x_j \le x_j^U, \quad j = 1, \cdots, D \tag{12}$$

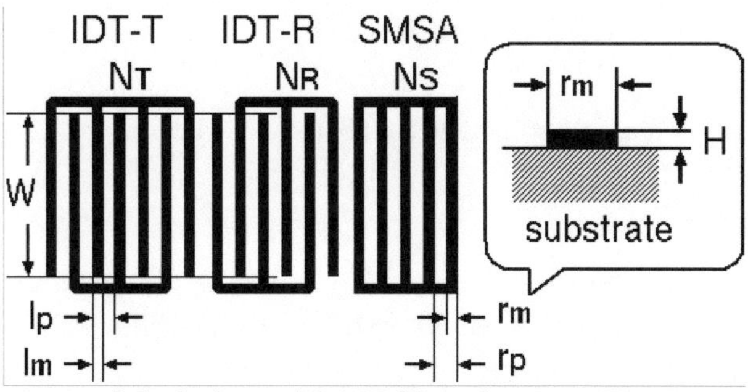

Fig. 6. Design parameters of the balanced SAW filter shown in Fig. 1

3.2 Objective function

By using the criteria E_r (r=1, ..., 5) for the balanced SAW filter described in the previous section, we define the objective function to be minimized. The values of criteria $E_r=E_r(\omega, \boldsymbol{x})$ depend on both the frequency ω and the decision variable $\boldsymbol{x}$. Therefore, let Ω_p be a set of frequency points sampled from the pass-band of the balanced SAW filter. Similarly, let Ω_s be a set of frequency points sampled from the stop-band. Then we specify the desirable band-pass filter characteristics of the balanced SAW filter $E_r(\omega, \boldsymbol{x})$ (r=3, 4, 5) by their upper $U_r(\omega)$ and lower $L_r(\omega)$ bounds at $\omega\in\Omega_p$ or $\omega\in\Omega_s$. Consequently, considering the criteria of the balance characteristics $E_r(\omega, \boldsymbol{x})$ (r=1, 2) and those of filter characteristics $E_r(\omega, \boldsymbol{x})$ (r=3, 4, 5) for the balanced SAW filter, we define the objective function $f(\boldsymbol{x})$ as follows.

$$f(x)=\sum_{r=1}^{5}\frac{\alpha_r}{|\Omega_p|}f_r(x)+\frac{\alpha_6}{|\Omega_s|}f_6(x) \tag{13}$$

where, $|\Omega_p|$ and $|\Omega_s|$ denote the number of elements included in Ω_p and Ω_s respectively. Also $\alpha_r>0$ (r=1, ..., 6) are weighting coefficients. Functions $f_r(\boldsymbol{x})$ are given as follows.

$$\begin{cases} f_1(x) &= \sum_{\omega\in\Omega_p} E_1(\omega,x)^2 \\ f_2(x) &= \sum_{\omega\in\Omega_p} E_2(\omega,x)^2 \\ f_3(x) &= \sum_{\omega\in\Omega_p} \max\{E_3(\omega,x)-U_3(\omega),0\} \\ f_4(x) &= \sum_{\omega\in\Omega_p} \max\{E_4(\omega,x)-U_4(\omega),0\} \\ f_5(x) &= \sum_{\omega\in\Omega_p} \max\{L_5(\omega)-E_5(\omega,x),0\} \\ f_6(x) &= \sum_{\omega\in\Omega_s} \max\{E_5(\omega,x)-U_5(\omega),0\} \end{cases}$$

3.3 Optimum design problem

From the boundary constraints in (12) and the objective function in (13), the structural design of the balanced SAW filter is formulated into an optimization problem as follows.

$$\min_{x\in X} f(x) \tag{14}$$

where, $\boldsymbol{X}$ denotes a set of feasible solutions that satisfy the boundary conditions in (12).

4. Differential evolution

Differential Evolution (DE) (Storn & Price, 1997) is one of the most recent EAs for solving real-parameters optimization problems. DE exhibits an overall excellent performance for a wide range of benchmark problems. Furthermore, because of its simple but powerful searching capability, DE has got numerous real-world applications (Price et al., 2005).

4.1 Representation

DE is usually used to solve the optimization problem in which the objective function to be minimized is defined on D ($D \geqq 1$) real-parameters. DE holds N_P individuals, or the candidate solutions of the optimization problem, in the population. As well as conventional real-coded GAs (Eshelman & Schaffer, 1993), every individual of DE is coded as a D-dimensional real-parameter vector. Furthermore, the i-th individual $\boldsymbol{x}_{i,g}$ ($i=1, \ldots, N_P$) included in the population of the generation g ($g \geqq 0$) is represented as follows.

$$x_{i,g} = \left(x_{1,i,g}, \cdots, x_{j,i,g}, \cdots, x_{D,i,g}\right) \tag{15}$$

As shown in the previous section 3, each decision variable $x_j \in \boldsymbol{x}$ of the optimization problem in (14) corresponds to a design parameter of the balanced SAW filter and takes either a continuous value or a discrete value. However, in order to apply DE to the optimization problem in (14), or the optimum design problem of balanced SAW filters, each of the decision variables $x_j \in \boldsymbol{x}$ ($j=1, \ldots, D$) has to be represented by a real-parameter. Therefore, we propose a new technique that converts an individual $\boldsymbol{x}_{i,g}$ into a corresponding solution $\boldsymbol{x}$.

First of all, we define the regularized continuous search space of DE as shown in (16). Each element of the individual $x_{j,i,g} \in \boldsymbol{x}_{i,g}$ is restricted within the range between 0 and 1.

$$0 \leq x_{j,i,g} \leq 1, \quad j = 1, \cdots, D \tag{16}$$

Then every decision variable of the optimization problem is embedded in the regularized continuous search space of DE defined in (16). Exactly speaking, each element $x_{j,i,g} \in \boldsymbol{x}_{i,g}$ in (16) is converted into the corresponding decision variable $x_j \in \boldsymbol{x}$ when the objective function value $f(\boldsymbol{x})$ is evaluated. If a decision variable $x_j \in \boldsymbol{x}$ takes a continuous value originally, the corresponding $x_{j,i,g} \in \boldsymbol{x}_{i,g}$ is converted into the decision variable $x_j \in \boldsymbol{x}$ as shown in (17). On the other hand, if a decision variable $x_j \in \boldsymbol{x}$ takes a discrete value with an interval e_j, the corresponding $x_{j,i,g} \in \boldsymbol{x}_{i,g}$ is converted into the decision variable $x_j \in \boldsymbol{x}$ as shown in (18).

$$x_j = \left(x_j^U - x_j^L\right) x_{j,i,g} + x_j^L \tag{17}$$

$$x_j = round\left(\frac{\left(x_j^U - x_j^L\right) x_{j,i,g}}{e_j}\right) e_j + x_j^L \tag{18}$$

where, the operator $round(z)$ rounds a real number $z \in \boldsymbol{R}$ to the nearest integer.

4.2 Procedure of differential evolution

Even though various revised DEs have been proposed (Chakraborty, 2008), we employ the classic DE named "DE/rand/1/bin" (Storn & Price, 1997). That is because the classic DE is commonly used and powerful enough for solving real-world applications (Price et al., 2005). The procedure of the classic DE is described as follows. The genetic operators used in the classic DE, namely, the generation of an initial population in Step 1, the differential mutation in Step 4 and the binomial crossover in Step 5, will be explained later. For convenience, we represent the aforementioned conversion from an individual $\boldsymbol{x}_{i,g}$ to the corresponding solution $\boldsymbol{x}$ defined in (17) and (18) by a unified operator $\boldsymbol{x}=h(\boldsymbol{x}_{i,g})$ in Step 6. Furthermore, the stopping criterion in Step 2 is usually specified by the maximum generation.

< Classic DE >

Step 1. Randomly generate N_P individuals as an initial population. Set the generation $g=0$.

Step 2. If the stopping criterion is satisfied, output the best individual and terminate.

Step 3. For each individual $\boldsymbol{x}_{i,g}$ ($i=1, \ldots, N_P$) of the population, which is called the target vector, randomly select mutually different three individuals, $\boldsymbol{x}_{r1,g}$, $\boldsymbol{x}_{r2,g}$ and $\boldsymbol{x}_{r3,g}$.

Step 4. Generate the mutated vector $\boldsymbol{v}_{i,g}$ from the above three individuals, $\boldsymbol{x}_{r1,g}$, $\boldsymbol{x}_{r2,g}$ and $\boldsymbol{x}_{r3,g}$ ($i \neq r1 \neq r2 \neq r3$) by using the differential mutation.

Step 5. Generate the trial vector $\boldsymbol{u}_{i,g}$ ($i=1, \ldots, N_P$) by using the binomial crossover between the mutated vector $\boldsymbol{v}_{i,g}$ and the target vector $\boldsymbol{x}_{i,g}$.

Step 6. If $f(h(\boldsymbol{u}_{i,g})) \leq f(h(\boldsymbol{x}_{i,g}))$ then set $\boldsymbol{x}_{i,g+1}=\boldsymbol{u}_{i,g}$, otherwise set $\boldsymbol{x}_{i,g+1}=\boldsymbol{x}_{i,g}$.

Step 7. Set $g=g+1$ and return to Step 2.

4.3 Initialization

In Step 1 of the procedure of the classic DE, individuals $\boldsymbol{x}_{i,0}$ ($i=1, \ldots, N_P$) are generated randomly as an initial population within the search space of DE defined in (16). Therefore, each element $x_{j,i,0} \in \boldsymbol{x}_{i,0}$ ($j=1, \ldots, D$) of an individual $\boldsymbol{x}_{i,0}$ can be generated as follows.

$$x_{j,i,0} = rand_j[0,1], \quad j=1,\cdots,D; \quad i=1,\cdots,N_P \tag{19}$$

where, $rand_j[0, 1]$ is the random number generator that returns a uniformly distributed random number from within the range between 0 and 1. The subscript $j \in [1, D]$ indicates that a new random value is generated for each of the elements $x_{j,i,0} \in \boldsymbol{x}_{i,0}$.

4.4 Differential mutation

Differential mutation is a unique genetic operator to DE. In order to generate the mutated vector $\boldsymbol{v}_{i,g}$ in Step 4 of the procedure the classic DE, the differential mutation amplifies difference vector between $\boldsymbol{x}_{r2,g}$ and $\boldsymbol{x}_{r3,g}$, and adds the result to $\boldsymbol{x}_{r1,g}$ as shown in (20).

$$v_{i,g} = x_{r1,g} + S_F\left(x_{r2,g} - x_{r3,g}\right) \tag{20}$$

where, the scale factor $S_F \in (0, 1+]$ is a user-defined control parameter.

Applying the above differential mutation, some elements of the mutated vector $v_{j,i,g} \in \boldsymbol{v}_{i,g}$ may go out of the search space of DE defined in (16). In such a case, these illegal elements $v_{j,i,g} \in \boldsymbol{v}_{i,g}$ are remade again within the search space of DE as shown in (21).

$$v_{j,i,g} = \begin{cases} rand_j[0,1]\,x_{j,r1,g}, & if\left(v_{j,i,g} < 0\right) \\ 1 + rand_j[0,1]\left(x_{j,r1,g} - 1\right), & if\left(v_{j,i,g} > 1\right) \end{cases} \tag{21}$$

4.5 Binomial crossover

In order to generate the trial vector $\boldsymbol{u}_{i,g}$ in Step 5 of the procedure of the classic DE, binomial crossover, which is similar to the uniform crossover of GA, is employed. The binomial crossover between the mutated vector $\boldsymbol{v}_{i,g}$ and the target vector $\boldsymbol{x}_{i,g}$ is described as follows.

$$u_{j,i,g} = \begin{cases} v_{j,i,g}, & if\left(rand_j[0,1] \le C_R \vee j = j_r\right) \\ x_{j,i,g}, & otherwise \end{cases} \tag{22}$$

In the above binomial crossover in (22), the crossover rate $C_R \in [0, 1]$ is also a user-defined control parameter that controls the fraction of decision variables copied from the mutated vector. Furthermore, $j_r \in [1, D]$ is a randomly selected subscript of the element of the mutated vector $v_{j,i,g} \in \boldsymbol{v}_{i,g}$ and it ensures that the trial vector $\boldsymbol{u}_{i,g}$ inherits at least one element from the mutated vector $\boldsymbol{v}_{i,g}$. As a result, we can expect that the trial vector $\boldsymbol{u}_{i,g}$ is different from the target vector $\boldsymbol{x}_{i,g}$, even if we choose the crossover rate as $C_R=0$.

5. Computational experiments

5.1 Problem instance

As an instance of the optimum design problem, a suitable structure of a practical balanced SAW filter illustrated in Fig. 7 is considered. In order to restrain the reflection of acoustic wave signals between IDT-T and IDT-R, the balanced SAW filter in Fig. 7 has pitch-modulated IDTs between IDT-T and IDT-R (Kawachi, 2004). Therefore, the balanced SAW filter consists of nine components, namely, seven IDTs and two SMSAs.

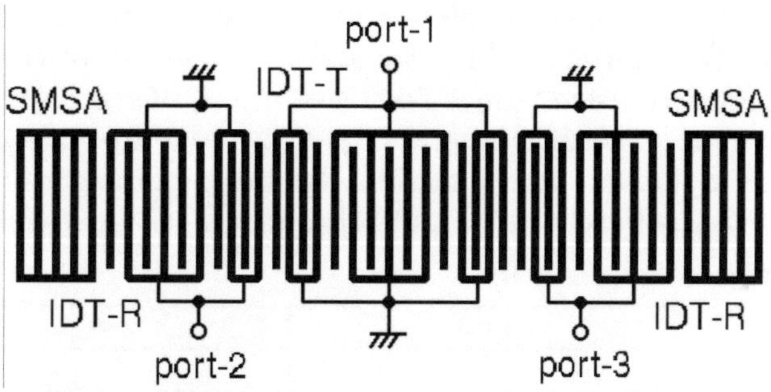

Fig. 7. Balanced SAW filter with pitch-modulated IDTs

x_j	x_j^L	x_j^U	e_j	design parameter
x_1	200	400	–	overlap between facing electrodes
x_2	10.0	20.0	0.5	number of the fingers of IDT-R
x_3	15.5	25.5	1.0	ditto of IDT-T
x_4	1.0	3.0	1.0	ditto of pitch-modulated IDT
x_5	50	150	10	number of the strips of SMSA
x_6	0.4	0.6	–	metallization ratio of IDT
x_7	0.4	0.6	–	ditto of SMSA
x_8	0.91	0.92	–	pitch ratio of pitch-modulated IDT
x_9	1.00	1.05	–	ditto of SMSA
x_{10}	1.95	2.05	–	finger pitch of IDT
x_{11}	3900	4000	–	thickness of electrode

Table 1. Design parameters of the balanced SAW filter shown in Fig. 7

In order to describe the structure of the balanced SAW filter shown in Fig. 7, eleven design parameters are chosen carefully. Table 1 shows the eleven design parameters, or the decision variables $x_j \in \boldsymbol{x}$ ($j=1, \ldots, D; D=11$) of the optimum design problem, and their upper x_j^U and lower x_j^L bounds. Furthermore, intervals e_j of design parameters x_j are also described in Table 1 if corresponding design parameters x_j have to take discrete values.
The objective function $f(x)$ in (13) is evaluated at *401* frequency points within the range between *850*[MHz] and *1080*[MHz]. The pass-band is also given by the range between *950*[MHz] and *980*[MHz]. Besides, all weighted coefficients are set as $\alpha_r=1$ $(r=1, \ldots, 6)$.

5.2 Experimental results

The program of the classic DE is realized by using MATLAB®. For evaluating the objective function values in the procedure of the classic DE, the simulator for the balanced SAW filter shown in Fig. 7 is also coded by MATLAB®. Then the classic DE is applied to the optimum design problem of the balanced SAW filter in Fig. 7. As the stopping criterion in Step 2 of the procedure of the classic DE, the maximum generation is limited to $g_{max}=100$. Also the control parameters of the classic DE are given as follows: the population size $N_P=50$, the scale factor $S_F=0.85$ and the crossover rate $C_R=0.9$. These values of the control parameters were decided through exploratory experiments in advance. Incidentally, the program of the classic DE spends about *16* minutes for one run on a personal computer.
In order to evaluate the effectiveness of the classic DE, the best solution in the final population is compared with the best solution in the initial population in Table 2. Table 2 shows the best objective function values f_{ave} averaged over *20* runs and their standard deviation σ_f. The partial function values $f_r(\boldsymbol{x}^*)$ $(r=1, \ldots, 6)$ of the objective function value $f(\boldsymbol{x}^*)$, which are related to respective criteria E_r $(r=1, \ldots, 5)$ of the balanced SAW filter, are also declared in Table 2. We can hereby confirm that the performance of the balanced SAW filter has been improved by the classic DE not only about the objective function $f(\boldsymbol{x}^*)$ but also about all the criteria E_r.

D=11	$g=0$		$g=g_{max}$	
	f_{ave}	σ_f	f_{ave}	σ_f
$f(\boldsymbol{x}^*)$	3.357	0.381	2.075	0.002
$f_1(\boldsymbol{x}^*)$	177.612	45.794	72.771	1.019
$f_2(\boldsymbol{x}^*)$	940.120	103.687	634.409	3.954
$f_3(\boldsymbol{x}^*)$	38.749	11.512	26.074	1.4793
$f_4(\boldsymbol{x}^*)$	39.061	12.229	27.018	1.4815
$f_5(\boldsymbol{x}^*)$	9.147	4.030	5.902	0.530
$f_6(\boldsymbol{x}^*)$	38.002	14.197	21.591	1.375

Table 2. Objective function values of the initial and the final best solutions $\boldsymbol{x}^*$ ($D=11$)

Figure 8 plots a representative example of the trajectory of the best objective function values achieved in the respective generations of the classic DE. From the results in Fig. 8, we can see that the classic DE has found the final best solution early in the searching procedure.

5.3 Extended optimum design problem

In order to utilize further the power of DE, we try to increase the degree of the design freedom in the above optimum design problem of the balanced SAW filter in Fig. 7.

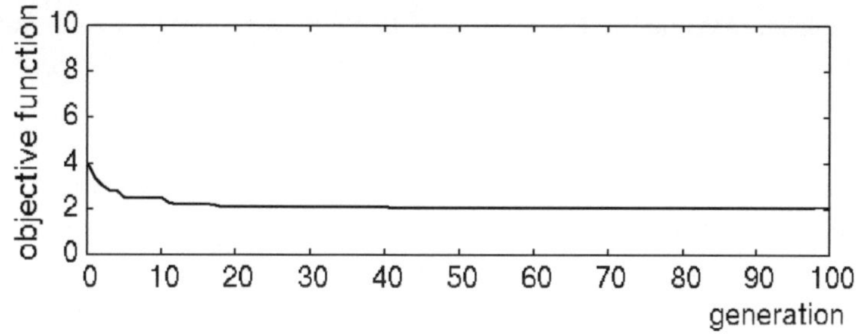

Fig. 8. Trajectory of the best objective function values ($D=11$)

The balanced SAW filter usually takes a symmetrical structure. Therefore, in the selection of the design parameters listed in Table 1, we have supposed that the balanced SAW filter in Fig. 7 takes a symmetrical structure. In other words, in the design of the balanced SAW filter, the right-side IDT-R and the left-side IDT-R have the same number of fingers. Similarly, the right-side SMSA and the left-side SMSA have the same number of stripes.

Now, in order to improve the performance of the balanced SAW filter much more, we extend the formulation of the optimum design problem. We suppose that the balanced SAW filter can take not only a symmetrical structure but also an unsymmetrical one. Then we increase the number of the design parameters $x_j \in \boldsymbol{x}$ ($j=1, \ldots, D$), which are used to describe the structure of the balanced SAW filter in Fig. 7, from $D=11$ to $D=15$.

$D=15$	$g=0$		$g=g_{max}$	
	f_{ave}	σ_f	f_{ave}	σ_f
$f(\boldsymbol{x}^*)$	9.151	7.281	0.713	0.016
$f_1(\boldsymbol{x}^*)$	263.687	323.901	55.721	4.962
$f_2(\boldsymbol{x}^*)$	2787.312	3114.794	150.003	8.113
$f_3(\boldsymbol{x}^*)$	204.174	253.710	20.120	3.817
$f_4(\boldsymbol{x}^*)$	209.172	259.212	20.273	3.845
$f_5(\boldsymbol{x}^*)$	51.108	54.495	2.831	1.145
$f_6(\boldsymbol{x}^*)$	153.565	85.198	37.010	6.951

Table 3. Objective function values of the initial and the final best solutions $\boldsymbol{x}^*$ ($D=15$)

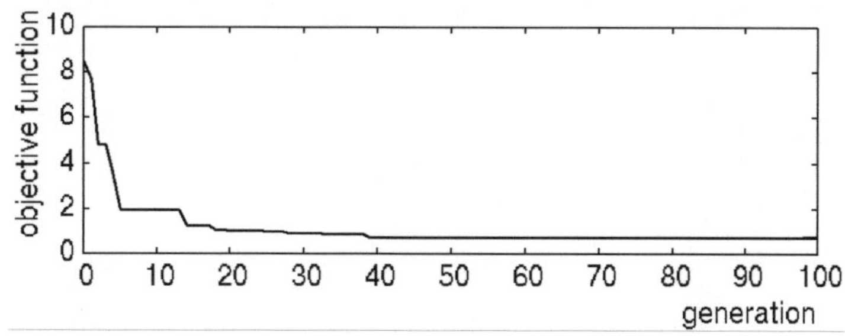

Fig. 9. Trajectory of the best objective function values ($D=15$)

By using the same values for the control parameters, the classic DE is applied to the extended optimum design problem of the balanced SAW filter. Table 3 compares the final best solution with the initial best solution in the same way with Table 2. Furthermore, Fig. 9 plots a representative example of the trajectory of the best objective function values in the same way with Fig. 8. Comparing the results in Table 2 and Table 3, in the initial generation (g=0), the best solution obtained for the extended optimum design problem (D=15) is inferior to the best solution obtained for the original optimum design problem (D=11) in every function value. However, in the final generation (g=g_{max}), the former best solution is superior to the latter best solution. We can also confirm the above-mentioned phenomenon from the comparison of the two trajectories shown in Fig. 8 and Fig. 9 respectively.

In order to verify the results in Table 2 and Table 3, we compare the final best solution of the extended optimum design problem (D=15) with the final best solution of the original optimum design problem (D=11) in the frequency response characteristics of the balanced SAW filter. Figure 10(a) compares the two best solutions in the amplitude balance $E_1(\omega, \boldsymbol{x}^*)$ defined in (4). In Fig. 10(a), solid line denotes the amplitude balance achieved by the best solution of the extended optimum design problem. On the other hand, broken line denotes the amplitude balance achieved by the best solution of the original optimum design problem. Similarly, Fig. 10(b) compares the two best solutions in the phase balance $E_2(\omega, \boldsymbol{x}^*)$

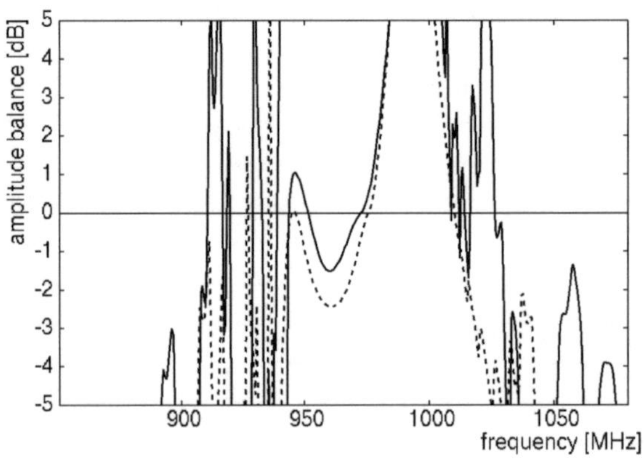

(a) Amplitude balance E_1

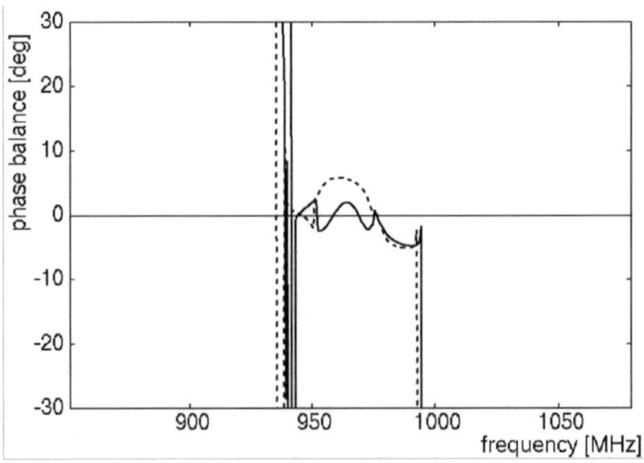

(b) Phase balance E_2

Fig. 10. Balance characteristics of the balanced SAW filter shown in Fig. 7

defined in (5). Comparing the solid lines with broken lines in Fig. 10, solid lines are closer to zero through the pass-band (*950~980*[MHz]). Therefore, from Fig. 10, we can say that the best solution of the extended optimum design problem is better than the best solution of the original optimum design in the balance characteristics of the balanced SAW filter.

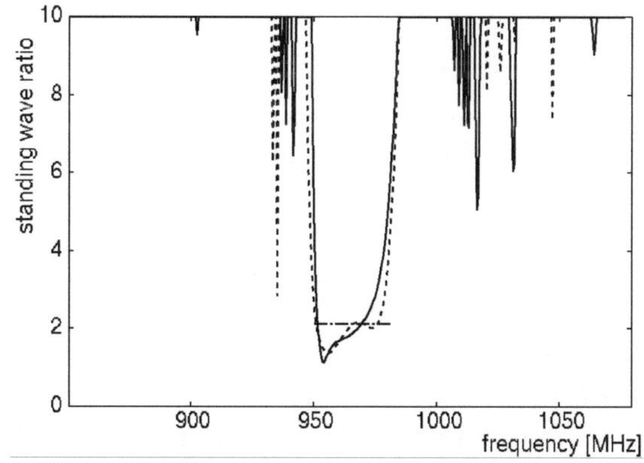

(a) Standing wave ratio of the output-port E_4

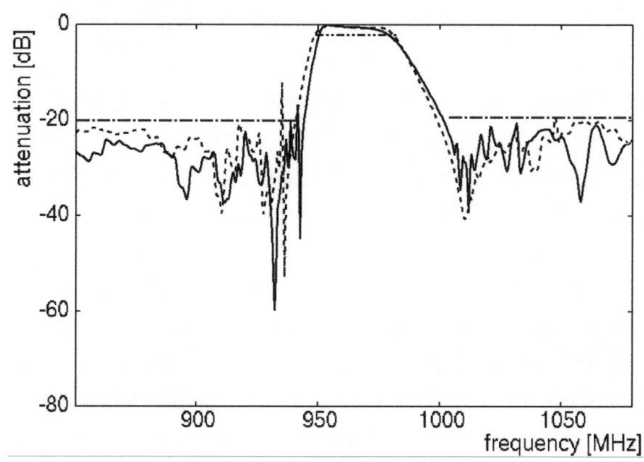

(b) Attenuation E_5

Fig. 11. Filter characteristics of the balanced SAW filter shown in Fig. 7

In the same way with Fig. 10, Fig. 11(a) compares the final best solution of the extended optimum design problem ($D=15$) with the final best solution of the original optimum design problem ($D=11$) in the standing wave ratio of the output-port $E_4(\omega, \boldsymbol{x}^*)$ defined in (10). Furthermore, Fig. 11(b) compares the two best solutions in the attenuation $E_5(\omega, \boldsymbol{x}^*)$ defined in (11). In Fig. 11, the upper bounds $U_r(\omega)$ of the respective criteria are denoted by one-broken lines. The lower bounds $L_r(\omega)$ of the respective criteria are also denoted by two-broken lines. Comparing the frequency response characteristics shown in Fig. 11, we cannot observe so much difference between the solid lines and the broken lines. In other words, as far as the band-pass filter characteristics, the performances of the balanced SAW filter achieved by the two best solutions resemble each other closely.

Consequently, from the comparison of the final best solution of the extended optimum design problem (*D=15*) with the final best solution of the original optimum design problem (*D=11*), we can say that the unsymmetrical structure of the balanced SAW filter has a capability to improve the balance characteristics of the conventional balanced SAW filter that has the symmetrical structure without losing the band-pass filter characteristics.

6. Conclusion

As an example of evolutionary computation technique in the real-world application, we presented an optimum design method for balanced SAW filters. First of all, in order to evaluate the performances of balanced SAW filters based on the computer simulation, we derived the network model of balanced SAW filters from the equivalent circuit model of them according to the balanced network theory. Then we formulated the structural design of balanced SAW filters as an optimization problem for improving their performances in both the balance characteristics and the filter characteristics. For solving the optimization problem, or the optimum design problem of balanced SAW filters, we employed DE. DE is a recent EA for solving real-parameter optimization problems. However, in the optimum design problem of balanced SAW filters, some design parameters take discrete values while others take continuous values. Therefore, in order to apply DE to the optimum design problem, we proposed a technique to insert the various design parameters of balanced SAW filters into the regularized continuous search space of DE. Finally, through the computational experiments conducted on a practical balanced SAW filter, we demonstrated the usefulness of the proposed optimum design method. Furthermore, we could obtain a new knowledge about the structural design of balanced SAW filters.

The balanced SAW filter usually takes a symmetrical structure. However, in the extended optimum design problem of the balanced SAW filter, we supposed that the balanced SAW filter could take an unsymmetrical structure. Then we compared the best solution of the extended optimum design problem with the best solution of the original optimum design problem. As a result, we found that the unsymmetrical structure of the balanced SAW filter could improve the balance characteristics without losing the filter characteristics.

If we increase the degree of the design freedom, or the number of design parameters, in the optimum design problem, the search space of DE is also expanded. As a result, the probability that DE finds the optimal solution decreases. On the other hand, the extended search space of DE may cover a new optimal solution that is better than the optimal solution in the original search space. In the optimum design of the balanced SAW filter, we could successfully increase the degree of the design freedom and utilize the power of DE.

Future work will focus on the revision of the classic DE used in this time. Since several variants of DE have been proposed (Chakraborty, 2008), we would like to compare their performances in the optimum design problems of various balanced SAW filters.

7. References

Bockelman, D. E. & Eisenstadt, W. R. (1995). Combined differential and common-mode scattering parameters: theory and simulation. *IEEE Transaction on Microwave Theory and Techniques*, Vol. 43, No. 7, pp. 1530-1539.

Campbell, C. K. (1998). *Surface Acoustic Wave Devices for Mobile and Wireless Communication,* Academic Press.

Chakraborty, U. K. (Edit) (2008). *Advances in Differential Evolution,* Springer.

Eshelman, L. J. & Schaffer, J. D. (1993). Real-coded genetic algorithms and interval-schemata, *Foundations Genetic Algorithms 2,* Morgan Kaufmann Publisher.

Franz, J.; Ruppel, C. C. W.; Seifert, F. & Weigel, R. (1997). Hybrid optimization techniques for the design of SAW filters, *Proceedings of IEEE Ultrasonics Symposium,* pp. 33-36.

Goto, S. & Kawakatsu, T. (2004). Optimization of the SAW filter design by immune algorithm, *Proceedings of IEEE International Ultrasonics Ferroelectrics, and Frequency Control Joint 50th Anniversary Conference,* pp. 600-603.

Hashimoto, K. (2000). *Surface Acoustic Wave Devices in Telecommunications - Modeling and Simulation,* Springer.

Kawachi, O.; Mitobe, S.; Tajima, M.; Yamaji, T.; Inoue, S. & Hashimoto, K. (2004). A low-pass and wide-band DMS filter using pitch-modulated IDT and reflector structures, *Proceedings of IEEE International Ultrasonics Ferroelectrics, and Frequency Control Joint 50th Anniversary Conference,* pp. 298-301.

Kojima, T. & Suzuki, T. (1992). Fundamental equations of electro-acoustic conversion for an interdigital surface-acoustic-wave transducer by using force factors. *Japanese Journal of Applied Physics Supplement,* No. 31, pp. 194-197.

Koshino, M.; Kanasaki, H.; Yamashita, T.; Mitobe, S.; Kawase, Y.; Kuroda, Y. & Ebata, Y. (2002). Simulation modeling and correction method for balance performance of RF SAW filters, *Proceedings of IEEE Ultrasonics Symposium,* pp. 301-305.

Meier, H.; Baier, T. & Riha, G. (2001). Miniaturization and advanced functionalities of SAW devices. *IEEE Transaction on Microwave Theory and Techniques,* Vol. 49, No. 2, pp. 743-748.

Meltaus, J.; Hamalainen, P.; Salomaa, M. & Plessky, V. P. (2004). Genetic optimization algorithms in the design of coupled SAW filters, *Proceedings of IEEE International Ultrasonics Ferroelectrics, and Frequency Control Joint 50th Anniversary Conference,* pp. 1901-1904.

Prabhu, V.; Panwar, B. S. & Priyanaka. (2002). Linkage learning genetic algorithm for the design of withdrawal weighted SAW filters, *Proceedings of IEEE Ultrasonics Symposium,* pp. 357-360.

Price, K. V.; Storn, R. M. & Lampinen, J. A. (2005). *Differential Evolution – A Practical Approach to Global Optimization,* Springer.

Storn, R and Price, K. (1997). Differential evolution - a simple and efficient heuristic for global optimization over continuous space, *Journal of Global Optimization,* Vol. 11, No. 4, pp. 341-359.

Tagawa, K.; Haneda, H.; Igaki, T. & Seki, S. (2002). Optimal design of three-IDT type SAW filter using local search, *Proceedings of the 28th Annual Conference of the IEEE Industrial Electronics Society,* pp. 2572-2577.

Tagawa, K.; Yamamoto, T.; Igaki, T. & Seki, S. (2003). An Imanishian genetic algorithm for the optimum design of surface acoustic wave filter, *Proceedings of the 2003 IEEE Congress on Evolutionary Computation,* pp. 2748-2755.

Tagawa, K.; Ohtani, T.; Igaki, T.; Seki, S. & Inoue, K. (2007). Robust optimum design of SAW filters by the penalty function method. *Electrical Engineering in Japan,* Vol. 158, No. 3, pp. 45-54.

Tagawa, K. (2007). Simulation modeling and optimization technique for balanced surface acoustic wave filters. *Proceedings of the 7th WSEAS International Conference on Simulation, Modelling and Optimization*, pp. 295-300.

Tagawa, K. (2008). Evolutionary computation techniques for the optimum design of balanced surface acoustic wave filters. *Proceedings of the 2008 IEEE Congress on Evolutionary Computation*, pp. 299-304.

19

Characteristics of Contract-Based Task Allocation by a Large Number of Self-Interested Agents

Toshiharu Sugawara[1], Toshio Hirotsu[2],
Satoshi Kurihara[3] and Kensuke Fukuda[4]
[1]*Waseda University,*
[2]*Toyohashi University of Technology,*
[3]*Osaka University,*
[4]*National Institute of Informatics,*
Japan

1. Introduction

Task and resource allocation is a key technology in Internet applications, such as grid computing and agent grids, for appropriately allocating tasks such as video and music downloads, scientific calculations, and language services (Cao et al., 2005; Chunlin & Layuan, 2006). In these applications, tasks should be allocated to and done in appropriate agents. Thus negotiation protocol for task allocation is one of the important issues in multi-agent systems research. In particular, the contract net protocol (CNP) and its extensions have been widely used in certain applications because of their simplicity and superior performance (Sandholm, 1993; Smith, 1980; Weyns et al., 2006). Agents in CNP play one of two roles: as *managers* that are responsible for allocating tasks and monitoring processes, or as *contractors* that are responsible for executing the allocated tasks. A manager agent announces a task to contractor agents, which bid for the task with certain promised values (such as cost, duration, and payment). The manager then awards the task to the contractor (called an *awardee*) that bid with the best tender (before the deadline) and allocates the task to it. However, the naive CNP is usually assumed to be applied to allocating tasks in small-scale, non-busy multi-agent systems (MASs).

Interference among agents is always observed in this kind of negotiation protocol. Consider many agents having to allocate tasks to other efficient contractors. In basic CNP, a contractor agent that receives task announcements bids for the tasks one by one. When many tasks are announced by many managers, however, they have to wait a long time to receive a sufficient number of bids. In the original conception of CNP (Smith, 1980), multiple bids were proposed to concurrently handle many announcements. If a contractor is awarded multiple tasks simultaneously, however, it may not be able to provide its promised quality or performance. In fact, efficient contractor agents are selected as awardees by many manager agents, leading to a concentration of tasks. In addition, when a large number of agents in a massively multi-agent systems (MMAS) interact with each other, the protocol generates an excessive number of messages, so that all agents become busy with (1) reading and analyzing many received messages (all agents), (2) deciding whether to bid for announced tasks (contractors), (3) calculating bid values (contractors), and (4) selecting awardees (managers). This phenomenon degrades the overall performance of a MAS. We believe that this kind of situation will often appear in Internet applications as mentioned before.

A simple solution to this problem is to implement manager-side control by restricting announcements to certain selected agents so as to reduce the number of messages and simplify the award process. In this article, we call this approach *restricted CNP*. We can easily expect, however, that a strong restriction may also degrade the task performance, because tasks are not announced to idle or high-ability agents. It is unclear whether the overall MAS performance will ultimately get better or worse if tasks are more widely announced, especially in an MMAS environment in which more than 1000 agents interact with each other. Restricting the audience for task announcement to improve performance, especially to avoid message congestion, has been proposed for small-scale MASs in a number of papers (Sandholm, 1993; Parunak, 1987; Schillo et al., 2002). To our knowledge, however, there has been little research on the efficiency and effectiveness of CNP (or more generally, negotiation protocols including CNP) when it is applied to a MMAS.

The goal of our research is to understand the behavior of CNP in an MMAS in order to develop efficient large-scale negotiation protocols. As a first step toward this purpose, we have investigated the performance features of CNP in an MMAS, especially the overall efficiency and the reliability of promised bid values, when tasks are allocated by CNP with a variety of manager-side controls, by using a multi-agent simulation environment that we previously developed (Sugawara et al., 2006). Manager-side controls can affect both the announcement and award phases. For this purpose, we previously reported that the relationship between overall performance and announcement control (Sugawara et al., 2007). The aim of this chapter is to discuss performance characteristics, that is, how overall performance of MMAS changes according to the manager-side control in the awarding phase.

On the other hand, we assume that all bid values from contactors reflect their states and abilities. Of course, we can also consider a number of contractor-side controls, and effective task allocation methods can be achieved through coordination of managers and contractors. The MAS performance also depends on the integrity of bid values and prior knowledge about other agents (Falcone et al., 2004). It is important, however, to clearly separate the effects of these controls; hence, this chapter is dedicated to showing that manager-side controls strongly affect the overall efficiency and the reliability of promised values.

This chapter is organized as follows. First, the restricted CNP model used in our simulation is presented. Then, we briefly discuss our experiments to investigate the performance of an MMAS when all agents use a simple version of restricted CNP, and we analyze the results to understand how the overall efficiency changes. Using these results as a baseline, we then introduce some variations of manager-side controls into restricted CNP for the award processes, and we show how the performance characteristics vary through our simulation. Finally, we discuss the meaning of our experimental results, related research, and applications.

2. Simulation of restricted CNP

2.1 Model for restricted CNP

First, we formally explain a simple version of restricted CNP in order to clarify the design of our simulation.

Let $A=\{a_1, \ldots, a_n\}$ be a set of agents, $M=\{m_j\}(\subset A)$ be a set of managers that will allocate tasks, and $C=\{c_k\}$ ($\subset A$) be a set of contractors that can execute allocated tasks if a contract is awarded. To simplify the experimental setting below, we assume that M and C are disjoint and $A=M\cup C$.

When manager m_j has task T, it will allocate T to another agent according to CNP as follows. First, m_j announces task T to all contractors in C (i.e., the announcement phase). For brevity, we assume that all contactor agents can execute T. A contractor receiving this announcement must decide whether to bid for this task. If it decides to bid, it has to send m_j a bid message with a certain value called the *bid value* (i.e., the bidding phase). Although bid values in general might include parameters such as the price for executing T, the quality of the result, and a combination of these values, timely responses are always a great concern in interactive services and real-time applications. Thus, in this chapter, we assume that all agents are rationally self-interested on the basis of efficiency, and their bid values are assumed to reflect their efficiency and workload, giving a promised time for completing T. How this time is calculated will be describe in the next section. Finally, m_j selects one awardee, which is usually the contractor that bid with the best value, and sends an award message to that contractor to allocate the announced task (i.e., the award phase).

As the basic CNP mentioned above is only adopted for a small-scale MAS in a non-busy environment, we modify it to adapt busier, MMAS environments. First, as in (Smith, 1980), we assume that contractors are allowed to submit multiple bids concurrently to handle task announcements from many managers, in order to apply this approach to busy, large-scale Internet and ubiquitous-computing applications. Second, unlike in the original CNP, two new CNP messages, *regret* and *no-bid* messages, are introduced (for example, (Sandholm, 1993; Xu & Weigand, 2001)). Regret messages are sent in the award phase to contractors that have not been awarded the contract, while no-bid messages[1] are sent to managers when contractors decide not to bid on an announced task. Using these messages avoids long waits for bid and award messages.

Next, we define restricted CNP. First, we assume that $|A|$ is large (on the order of thousands), so $|M|$ and $|C|$ are also large, and that the agents are distributed widely, like servers and customer agents on the Internet. For $m_j \in M$, let K_{m_j} be a set of contractors known to m_j; manager m_j can only announce a task to contractors in K_{m_j}. Set K_{m_j} is called *scope* in this article. Restricted CNP is thus defined as CNP where (1) multiple bids and regret and no-bid messages are allowed, and (2) any manager m_j is restricted to announcements to certain contractors in K_{m_j} according to a certain policy, called the *announcement policy*. Hereafter, the set of contractors selected according to the announcement policy is called the *audience*. We believe that an appropriate announcement policy can reduce the total number of messages and the cost of announcing bidding and awarding decisions, thus improving overall performance. In our experiments, we introduce

[1] A no-bid message might correspond to a busy response in (Smith, 1980).

various announcement policies and examine how the performance of an MMAS varied under these policies.

2.2 Simulation model

In this section, we describe the simulation settings in our experiments. First, we set $|C|=500$ and $|M|=10000$ and assume that all contractors in C are eligible to bid for any announced task[2]. The agents are randomly placed on the points of the grid space that is expressed by a 150 x 150 coordinates with a torus topology. Then, the Manhattan distance $dist(a_i, a_j)$ between agents a_i and a_j is defined on this space. According to this distance, we can set the communication cost (or delay) of messages from a_i to a_j in our simulation. This cost is denoted by $cost(a_i, a_j)$. In this simulation, the communication cost ranges over [1,14] (in *ticks*, the unit of time in the simulation), in proportion to the distance between the source and target agents. The elements of scope K_{m_j} for $\forall\ m_j \in M$ are also defined according to this distance: they consist of the nearest 50 or more contractors to m_j. More precisely, for an integer $n > 0$, let $K_{m_j}(n)=\{c\in C \mid dist(m_j, c) \leq n\}$. Then, it follows that $K_{m_j}(n) \subset K_{m_j}(n+1)$. K_{m_j} is defined as the smallest $K_{m_j}(n)$ such that $|K_{m_j}(n)| \geq 50$. K_{m_j} keeps a static value after it is initially calculated.

With every tick, *tl* tasks are generated by the simulation environment and randomly assigned to *tl* different managers, where *tl* is a positive integer. Parameter *tl* is called the *task load* and denotes *tl* tasks per tick, or simply *tl* T/t. A manager assigned a task immediately initiates restricted CNP to allocate the task to an appropriate contractor. We can naturally extend the task load for positive non-integer numbers by probabilistic task generation. For example, *tl=9.2* means that the environment generates 9 tasks (with probability 0.8) or 10 tasks (with probability 0.2) every tick.

For task T and agent a_i, we introduce two parameters: the associated cost of T, $cost(T)$, expressing the cost to complete T; and the ability of a_i, $Ab(a_i)$, expressing the processing speed of a_i. For convenience, we adjust these parameters so that contractor c_i can complete an allocated task, T, in $cost(T)/Ab(c_i)$ ticks. Since our experiments are preliminary and designed simply to understand the performance features of restricted CNP in an MMAS, we assume that all tasks have the same cost, *2500*. Instead, we assigned different abilities to individual contractors; the abilities of the contractors are initially assigned so that the values of $cost(T)/Ab(c_i)$ (where $i=1, \ldots, 500$) are *uniformly distributed* over the range [20,100]. This means that the values of $Ab(c_i)$ range from *25* to *125*.

When contractor c_i is awarded a task, it immediately executes it if it has no other tasks. If c_i is already executing another task, the new task is stored in the queue of c_i, which can hold up to 20 tasks. The tasks in the queue are then executed in turn. Tasks that cannot be stored because of a full queue are dropped. This situation is called *over-allocation*.

The bid value reflecting the state of contractor c_i is the expected response time, calculated as follows. Suppose that s tasks are queued in c_i. Then, its bid value is $s \times (2500/Ab(c_i)) + \alpha$, where α is the required time to complete the current task, so smaller bid values are better. In multiple bidding, c_i might have a number of uncertain bids whose results have not yet

[2] We assume that the agents run on the Internet, where contractor agents provide services requested by manager agents, which correspond to user-side computers.

been received. These bids are not considered, however, because it is uncertain whether they will be awarded. This means that contractors always submit bids when a task announcement arrives. Note that we can introduce a bidding strategy to all contractors in order to avoid over-allocation, by disallowing multiple bids when a contractor is busy, but we do not consider this kind of contractor-side control or strategy here. The use of other bidding strategies is discussed later.

The *completion time* of each task is the elapsed time observed by the manager from the time of sending an award message with the allocated task to the time of receiving a message indicating task completion. The completion time thus includes the communication time in both directions, and the queue time and execution time of the contractor[3]. We define the *overall efficiency of a MAS* as the average completion time observed for all managers and the *reliability* as the expected value of the differences between the completion times and the promised response times.

tl (T/t)	Condition of MAS
0.1	The task load is extremely low; multiple bids are rare.
0.5--1	The MAS is not busy.
3--6	The MAS is moderately busy; no tasks are dropped.
9--10	The task load is near the limit of the MAS performance; some tasks may be dropped.
11	The MAS is extremely busy, beyond its theoretical performance limit; many tasks are dropped.

Table 1. MAS conditions for various task load (*tl*) values.

The simulation data reported in this chapter are the mean values from three independent experiments using different random seeds. The theoretical cumulative ability of all contractors in the three MASs in the three experiments ranges from 9.7 to 10.2 T/t, with an average value of 9.9 T/t. We set parameter *tl* as 0.1, 0.5--1, 3--6, 9--10, or 11; the conditions of the MAS in each case are listed in Table 1.

3. Random selection in announcement --- overview

We introduce the announcement policy under which any manager, m_j, announces tasks to only n contractors randomly selected from K_{m_j} to reduce the number of messages in CNP. This announcement policy is called the *random selection policy* and is denoted as RSP(n), where n is a positive integer called the *announcement number* indicating the number of announcement. This policy requires neither prior knowledge nor learning about the contactors, but some tasks are not announced to highly capable contractors.

[3] Because our experiments are preliminary and our goal is to understand the effects of having many contractors and managers, the costs of processing announcement messages and selecting a bid from among bid messages are not included in the completion time. Of course, these costs should be included in our future work in order to identify their effects on performance.

We previously examined in (Sugawara et al., 2007) how overall efficiency varies with announcement number, *n*, and the task load, *tl*. The experimental data are shown in Fig. 1. The results can be summarized as follows:

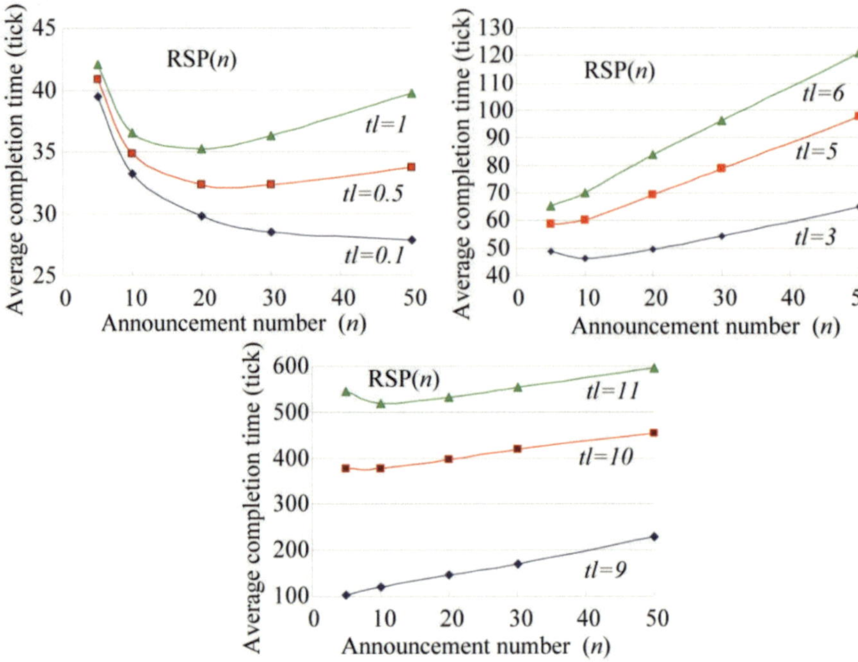

Fig. 1. Average completion time under RSP(*n*).

- Our notion that smaller *n* resulted in inefficiency in the entire MMAS because tasks were not announced to highly capable agents only applies when the task load was extremely low. Because managers send many task announcement messages under RSP(*n*) for larger *n*, we predicted task concentration in a few good contractors in busier environments, thus making the MMAS inefficient. However, our results clearly indicated that this phenomenon could be observed much earlier (i.e., even when task load was low, such as the case *tl*=0.5. See Fig. 1) than we expected.
- We conducted an experiment to find when concentration occurred. However, we found that the numbers of tasks awarded to (so executed in) individual agents in a busy case (*tl*=10) were almost equal under RSP(5) and RSP(50). This indicated that no concentration occurred in terms of the total numbers awarded against our prediction.
- We then additionally investigated the average difference between bid values (i.e., promised times) for contractor c_i and the actual queue and execution times, and the standard deviation of these differences, when *tl*=10. Note that this average difference is denoted by d_{c_i} and the standard deviation by sd_{c_i}. The results suggested that although the numbers of tasks awarded to each contractor under RSP(5) and RSP(50) eventually became almost the same, the excess tasks were only concentrated on a few contractors, and these busy contractors changed over time under RSP(50). We could observe another explicit tendency that more tasks were awarded simultaneously to contractors with less ability under RSP(50).

We also investigated what effect the learning method had by in which managers estimated which contractor was more efficient (so that completion time was expected to be shorter). We found, however, that this learning could only improve overall efficiency when task load was extremely low, which corresponds to the situation where sequential conventional CNP is used. See our previous paper (Sugawara et al., 2007) for a more detailed discussion.

4. Probabilistic fluctuation in award phase

4.1 Effect of small fluctuation

Our previous experiments showed that overall efficiency becomes worse with concentration on a few contractors caused by simultaneous and excess multiple awards. One method of avoiding such concentration is to introduce some degree of fluctuation in the award phase.
After a task announcement, manager m_j receives bids from a number of contractors, $\{c_1, \ldots, c_p\}$. We denote the bid value from contractor c_i as $b(c_i)$. Manager m_j then aselects an awardee, c_i, according to the following probabilistic distribution:

$$Pr(c_i) = \frac{1/b(c_i)^k}{\sum_{l=1}^{p} 1/b(c_i)^k} \qquad (1)$$

Note that smaller bid values are better. This award strategy is called *probabilistic award selection* and denoted as PAS_k. The larger k is, the smaller the degree of fluctuation is. To examine the effect of fluctuation as a preliminary experiment, k is set here to 2.

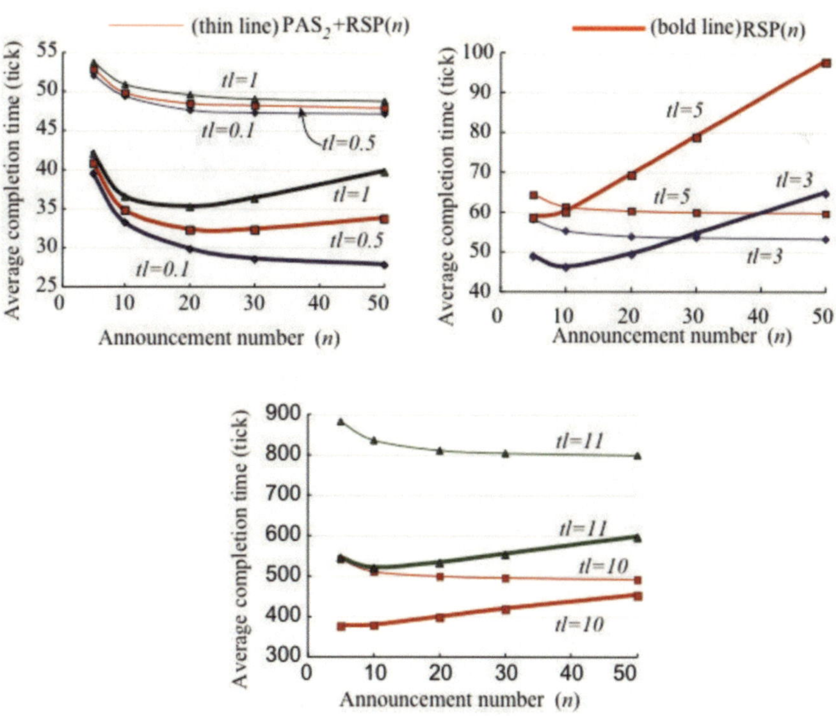

Fig. 2. Average completion times under PAS_2+RSP(n).

The graphs in Fig. 2 compare the average completion times when managers only adopt RSP(n) with these times when they adopt RSP(n) as the announcement policy and PAS_2 as the award strategy, giving a combination denoted as PAS_2+RSP(n). These graphs show that policy RSP(n) only leads to better overall efficiency (than policy PAS_2+RSP(n)) when the task load is low ($tl < 3$) or extremely high ($tl > 10$, beyond the theoretical limit of the capability of all contractors). Conversely, we can observe that the overall efficiency under PAS_2+RSP(n) is considerably improved when $3 \le tl \le 9$.

The graphs in Fig. 2 also indicate that (1) under RSP(n), if the announcement number n is larger, the overall efficiency worsens except in situations where the task load is low, (2) but under PAS_2+RSP(n), the overall efficiency slightly improves if n is larger. This suggests that a small fluctuation can ease the concentration to a few contractors, so the effect of larger announcement numbers appear as we can expected and actually PAS_2+RSP(n) outperforms RSP(n) when the system is moderately busy.

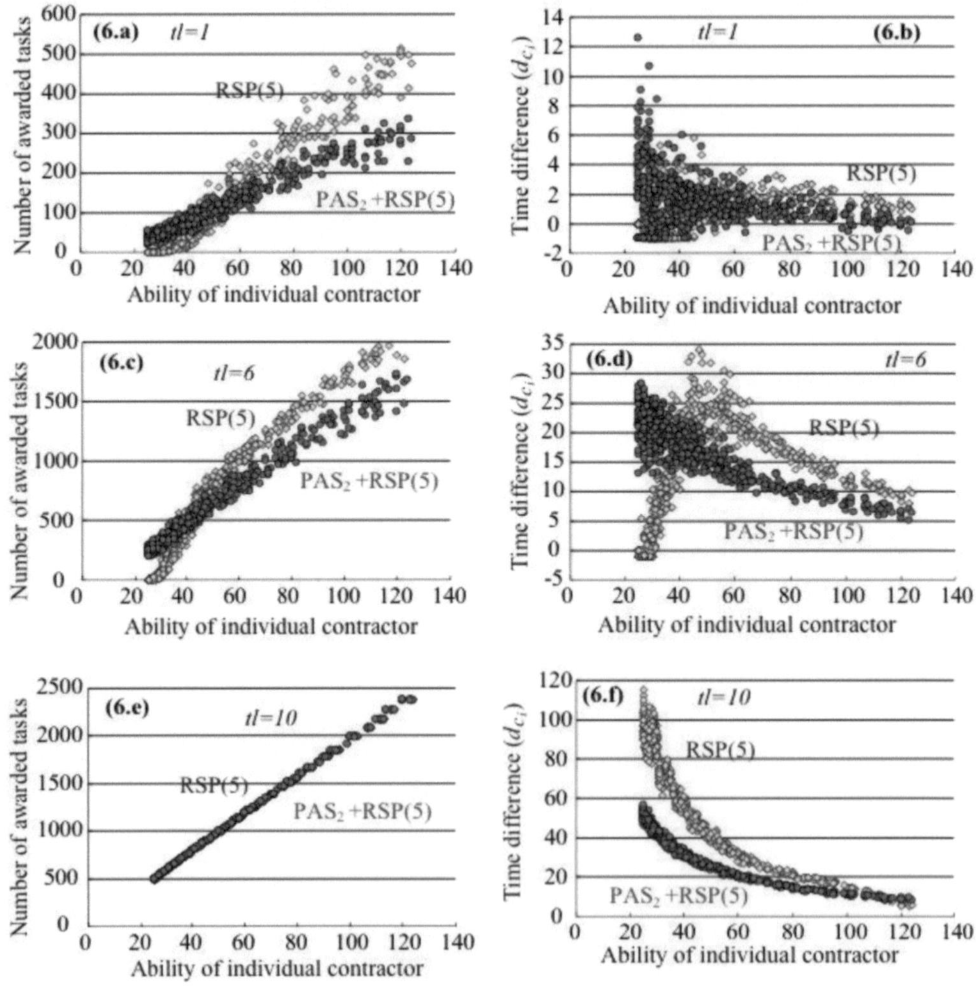

Fig. 3. Comparison of PAS_2+RSP(n) and RSP(n): Number of awarded tasks and differences between promised and actual completion times.

4.2 Distributions of awarded tasks and reliability

By comparing Fig. 2 with Fig. 1, we can observe that the overall efficiency under PAS_2+RSP(n) is considerably improved when $3 \le tl \le 9$ but considerably degraded when $tl \le 1$ or $tl \ge 10$. Figure 2 partly explains this situation. When the task load is low, awarding tasks to high-ability contractors can lead to better performance. Graphs (6.a) and (6.b) in Fig. 3 indicate that more tasks are awarded to low-ability contractors because of fluctuation, but this is unnecessary because not all contractors are busy; this results in poor efficiency. When the MAS is moderately busy, low-ability contractors are awarded few tasks under RSP(5). This does not utilize the full capability of the entire MAS. Graphs (6.c) and (6.d) in Fig. 3 show, however, that low-ability contractors are appropriately awarded as a result of fluctuation. In an extremely busy situation (graphs (6.e) and (6.f) in Fig. 3), all contractors are already very busy. The fluctuation results in some tasks being awarded to contractors whose bids are not the best values, meaning that the awardees might be occupied. In addition, graph (6.e) clearly indicates that fluctuation eventually does not affect the distribution of awarded tasks. These results suggest that applying PAS_2+RSP(5) shifted some tasks to inappropriate contractors with inadequate timing.

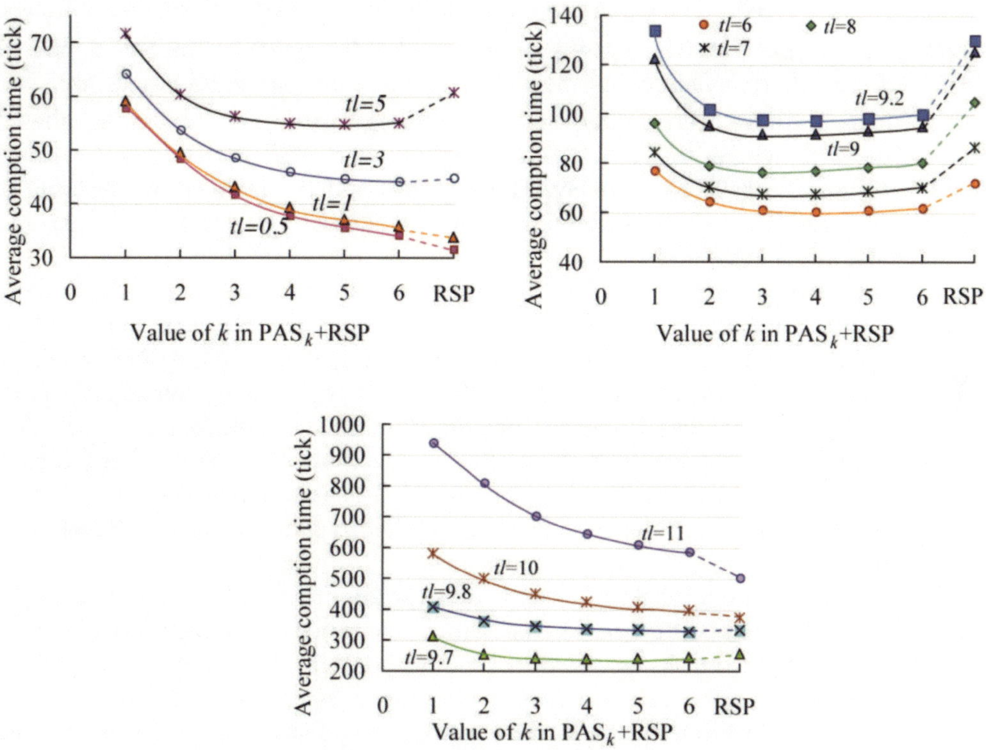

Fig. 4. Variations in completion times under PAS_k+RSP(20).

5. Effect of degree of fluctuations --- detailed analysis

5.1 Effect on overall efficiency

To understand the effect of fluctuation more clearly, we varied the value of fluctuation factor k in Eq. (1), where smaller k increases the degree of fluctuation. The results of this experiment are plotted in Figs. 4 (a) to (c), where k ranges from 1 to 6 and the announcement number, n is 20[4]. Note that "RSP" in x-axiom means the RSP policy.

These figures illustrate that policy, RSP, only results in better performance than PAS_k+RSP when task load is less than one (non-busy) or more than 10 (extremely busy, i.e., over the theoretical limits of the entire MAS). In other situations where $2 \leq tl < 10$, some degree of fluctuation can express much better performance, but a k value leading to the best performance depends on the task load. When tl is close to one, the larger k is better, when tl is greater than one, the value of k that expresses the best performance gradually approaches 3. However, after k is larger than nine, the best k value swiftly approaches 6, again. This analysis suggests that a flexible policy of selecting awards sensitive to task load is required to achieve overall efficiency in MMAS.

5.2 Effect on reliability of bids and number of dropped tasks

Another important performance measure for MMAS is the reliability of bid values; in our experiment, we define the reliability as the average difference, i.e., the expected values of $\{d_{c_i}\}_{c_i \in C}$ and the standard deviation of these differences. Of course, smaller differences indicate greater reliability. The graphs of observed differences are in Fig. 5. We also measured the standard deviation, but the shapes of the graphs are quite similar to the ones in Fig. 5. Thus, they have been omitted from this chapter. Instead, some example values are listed in Table 2, where the columns marked $k=i$ and RSP correspond to policies, PAS_i+RSP(10) and RSP(10), respectively. These graphs and the table clearly indicate that even when tl is low, the values of differences and the standard deviation are larger under RSP than those under PAS_k+RSP.

Reliability decreases when the task load increases but the graphs in Fig. 5 illustrate that introducing some fluctuation also makes the system more reliable, especially, $k=2$ or 3 generally makes it more reliable in all task loads. Conversely, policy RSP yields low reliability except when task load is extremely low. If we want to simultaneously pursue overall efficiency and reliability, PAS_2+RSP or PAS_3+RSP is reasonable for any task load.

Furthermore, if we compare graphs (a-2) and (b-2) in Fig. 5, smaller task number n results in much smaller differences. However, too few n makes the system inefficient as explained in the previous subsection. This is another trade-off between efficiency and reliability in MMASs.

To fully understand system reliability, we have to pay attention to the number of dropped tasks because of queues overflowing at contractors. The ratios of the numbers of dropped tasks to those of generated tasks are listed in Table 3 (a) and (b). Note that no dropped tasks were observed when $tl \leq 9.5$. These tables show that there is not much difference between RSP and PAS_k+RSP, in terms of the number of dropped tasks. This suggests that some appropriate degree of fluctuation can lead to properly efficient MMASs.

---

[4] We have only shown graphs when $n=20$, but other graphs when $n=10$ to 50 have almost the same shapes.

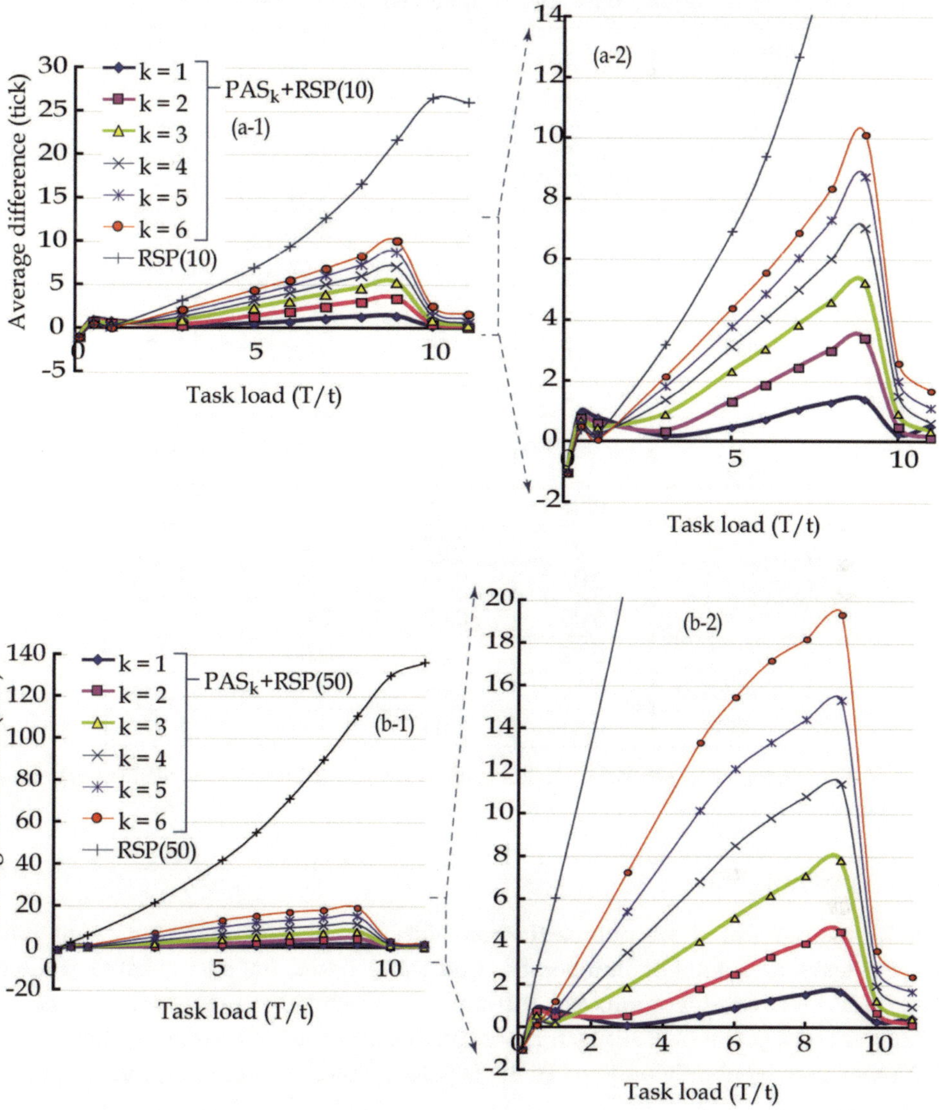

Fig. 5. Average differences between bid values and observed completion times under PAS_k+RSP(n).

Policy	$k = 1$	$k = 2$	$k = 3$	$k = 4$	$k = 5$	$k = 6$	RSP
$n = 5$	5.13	4.70	4.71	5.16	5.41	5.90	6.23
$n = 9$	20.92	22.98	25.04	27.06	28.88	30.16	39.75
$n = 10$	20.03	20.50	21.25	22.21	22.98	23.84	47.11

Table 2. Standard deviation of differences between bid values and completion times under PAS_k+RSP(10).

(a) Ratio (%) of dropped tasks when $n = 10$.

Fluctuation factor (k)	$tl = 9.7$	$tl = 9.8$	$tl = 10$	$tl = 11$
$k = 1$	0.02	0.30	2.03	11.11
$k = 2$	0.02	0.33	2.16	11.16
$k = 3$	0.04	0.48	2.34	11.17
$k = 4$	0.08	0.54	2.42	11.18
$k = 5$	0.09	0.64	2.47	11.18
$k = 6$	0.12	0.63	2.49	11.19
RSP	0.21	0.86	2.60	11.18

(b) Ratio (%) of dropped tasks when $n = 50$.

Fluctuation factor (k)	$tl = 9.7$	$tl = 9.8$	$tl = 10$	$tl = 11$
$k = 1$	0.01	0.24	1.98	11.11
$k = 2$	0.02	0.38	2.22	11.18
$k = 3$	0.06	0.52	2.38	11.18
$k = 4$	0.09	0.60	2.46	11.19
$k = 5$	0.12	0.65	2.50	11.18
$k = 6$	0.14	0.69	2.53	11.18
RSP	0.33	1.03	2.61	11.19

Table 3. Ratio of Observed Dropped Tasks in Policies RSP(n) and PAS_k+RSP(n) when task load tl is high.

6. Pursuit of reliability

It is quite natural that, if we pursue the reliability of a system, manager agents will only announce tasks to a limited number of contractors based on past reliable completions. Taking this indo consideration, we introduced an announcement policy, *more reliable contractor selection policy* (*MRSP*) as follows: manager m retains difference d_{c_i} ($c_i \in K_{m_j}$), and the manager agent only announces the task to the most reliable (i.e., the smallest d_{c_i}) n contractors.

However, MRSP cannot provide good reliability. More seriously, MRSP can neither improve the reliability nor the efficiency of the system despite many more dropped tasks. These data are listed in Table 4. More drops occur when announcement number n is larger; these are the reverse of characteristics of RSP that appeared in Table 3. More discussion is provided in Section 7.3.

Task load	$tl = 9.2$	$tl = 9.5$	$tl = 9.8$	$tl = 10$	$tl = 11$
$n = 10$	1.00	3.94	7.35	10.35	21.18
$n = 50$	0.00	0.00	1.32	2.76	12.93

Table 4. Ratio (%) of Observed Dropped Tasks under MRSP(n).

7. Discussion

7.1 Announcement restriction

Our first experiment suggests that a small announcement number *n* is better in an MMAS. We can easily expect that if the task load is high, many tasks will be awarded to high-ability contractors for a large *n*, thus lowering the performance. Our experiments also show, however, that this phenomenon appears even if the task load is not that high. From our experiments, applying RSP(*n*) with larger *n* gives better results only when *tl=0.1*. Since our simulation does not include the cost of message analysis, the overall efficiency of an actual MAS must be much worse than that obtained experimentally here. Conversely, when *tl=0.1*, using a small audience has an adverse effect.

7.2 Capriciousness -- efficiency or reliability

Our experiments expressly provide data that fluctuations in award selection will strongly affect overall efficiency and reliability; a little capriciousness in a manager's award selection will significantly improve them. This suggests that appropriate control of fluctuation is required to practically use CNP in large-scale MASs. The control of announcement number (random audience restriction) by manager agents is also required for this usage but its effect is relatively smaller.

If we carefully look at the experimental data, the required control must be slightly different depending on whether we give weight to efficiency or reliability. If reliability is more important, constant fluctuation in the award strategy with fewer announcements such as PAS_2+RSP(10) provides better results. However, if we attach a high value to efficiency, more tailored control must be investigated; i.e., (1) no fluctuation with a smaller announcement number is better when task load is extremely low or exceeds the entire processing capability of the MMAS, and (2) in the other case, the controls of fluctuation factors ranging from 2 to 6 with a relatively larger announcement number should be flexibly introduced in individual manager agents.

As described in Section 1, we have assumed that all agents are rationally self-interested on the basis of efficiency. However, the rational decisions in awarding lead to the concentrations. Our experiments suggest that sometimes selecting the second or third best contractors in awarding can provide more preferable performance to individual manager agents as well as the whole MMAS. It is, however, necessary that the degree of fluctuation should also be controlled according to the state, e.g., the task loads of the MMAS for better performance.

7.3 Effect of learning

In Section 6, we stated that MRSP leads to poor efficiency and reliability as well as more dropped tasks. This feature is quite similar to the strategy where all manager agents learn which contractors are more efficient and determine the audience for tasks based on these learning results (Sugawara et al., 2007). We believe that learning is too slow for managers to adapt to the variations in task allocations from the environment and this ironically makes the system more inflexible compared to random audience selection. Note that randomness is not uniform; although, in our experiment, tasks were generated in a constant rate and assigned to randomly but not uniformly selected managers, so slight, transient and continual variations in task assignment may always occur. However, we believe that this slight variation cannot be ignored in MMAS because local and small-scale concentrations

/biases in tasks reduce the system's efficiency and reliability. Although learning can identify high-performance contractors and other long-term variations, it cannot adapt easy-to-move concentrations derived by continual slight variations. Our experiments suggest that a small fluctuation in award selection leads to better results for this phenomenon.
Despite this, we believe that this kind of learning will be necessary for real applications from another viewpoint. For example, if there is a malicious contractor that usually bids with unreliable values, manager must exclude it from their scopes for the stable and fair task allocations.

7.4 Applications

We believe that the importance of this kind of research will become clear with the increase in large-scale interactions between agents. Consider the recent growth in the volume of e-commerce transactions on the Internet for buying goods, such as software, music, and video. These transactions usually consist of coordinated tasks including interactions with a variety of agents, which are in charge of, for example, customer authentication and management, stock management, shipping control, and payment processing. Suppose that a customer wants to download a music album from one of many music servers deployed worldwide. She (or her agent) has to determine the server to download from. Distant servers are probably inappropriate because of high latency, while nearby servers might be busy. Similar situations also occur when purchasing a good: if local sellers on the Internet are busy and the goods are transported on a FIFO basis, customers may have to wait for a long handling time and often back-ordering.
Reliability of bid values, which corresponds to the estimated completion time of required services, is also strongly required in a number of applications. Again, consider the example of downloading music. Customers do not always require immediate downloading. Suppose that a customer wants to download a music album, but the server is currently busy. She wants to listen to it tomorrow morning, so her agent only has to finish downloading it by then. Even if this album is very popular, the agent can schedule the download via a contract with an appropriate music server (i.e., a contractor in our experiment) by using the promised completion time and standard deviation. Our experiment suggests that this server should be selected probabilistically. These kinds of situations may also occur in other applications such as PC-grid computing where many tasks derived by decomposing a large computing problem should effectively be processed by distributed PC resources.

7.5 Related research

There is much existing research on improving the performance and functionality of CNP. In a city traffic scheduling system called TRACONET (Sandholm, 1993), transportation tasks are allocated by CNP, with bidding decisions based on the marginal cost. This approach to CNP has been further extended (Sandholm & Lesser, 1995) by introducing the concept of *levels of commitment*, making a commitment breakable with some penalty if a more valuable contract is announced later.
The necessity of message congestion management has also been demonstrated (Sandholm & Lesser, 1995). We believe that the first work discussing message control is (Parunak, 1987), which states that audience restriction can improve the overall efficiency. In (Parunak, 1987), this restriction is implemented by maintaining a bidding history. Because past bidding activities are known, agents lacking a specific ability cannot submit bids for tasks requiring

this ability. Another work (Gu & Ishida, 1996) analyzes how contractors' utilities change according to the ratio of contractors and managers. All this research assumes, however, that agents are not so busy that interference among agents is insignificant. Our experiments indicate that CNP in an MMAS exhibits quite different characteristics from CNP in a small-scale MAS.

More recently, (Schillo et al., 2002) discusses the issue of the eager-bidder problem occurring a large-scale MAS, where a number of tasks are announced concurrently so that CNP with levels of commitment does not work well. These authors propose another CNP extension, based on statistical risk management. The number of agents in the MAS considered in their paper is about 100, however, which is much less than in our model. More importantly, the types of resources and tasks considered are quite different: specifically, the resources are exclusive, such as airplane seats, so they should be allocated selectively, in order to gain more income. In our case, the resource is CPU or network bandwidth, which can accept a certain number of tasks simultaneously but with reduced quality. As a result, the many agents and tasks in our experiments incur floating uncertainty, which affects learning, statistical estimation, and rational decision-making.

8. Conclusion

In this chapter, we have described our experimental investigation of the performance features, especially the overall efficiency and the reliability of bid values, in an MMAS when the contract net protocol (CNP) is used with a number of manager-side controls. Our results suggest that applying a small amount of fluctuation can improve both the efficiency and the reliability. Thus, we also investigated how performance and reliability change according to the degree of probabilistic fluctuations. This experimental result indicates that there is the appropriate degree of fluctuation that can maximize the overall performance as well as that can improve the reliability of bids.

This chapter is dedicated solely to manager-side controls. It is clear that some contractor-side controls, such as strategies related to choosing to bid and calculating bid values, also affect performance. We must emphasize, however, that only manager-side controls can improve the reliability of promised values in busy situations, as well as the overall efficiency of an MMAS. For example, contractors can submit more credible bid values by taking into account the other submitted bids, whose results are uncertain. We also examined this case but found that the resulting overall efficiency was essentially the same as that obtained in the experiments described in this chapter. The effect of dynamic interference is rather strong, giving credible bids less meaning. Coordination among contractors and managers is probably required to address this issue, and this is our research direction.

9. Acknowledgement

This research was supported in part by Grant of Kayamori Foundation of Informational Science (2009-2010) and by the Ministry of Education, Science, Sports and Culture, Grant-in-Aid for Scientific Research, 20240015, 2008-2009.

10. References

Cao, J.; Spooner, D. P.; Jarvis, S. A. & Nudd, G. R. (2005). Grid load balancing using intelligent agents. *Future Gener. Comput. Syst.*, 21(1):135–149.

Chunlin, L & Layuan, L. (2006). Multieconomic agent interaction for optimizing the aggregate utility of grid users in computational grid. *Applied Intelligence*, Vol. 25, pp. 147–158.

Smith, R. G. (1980). The Contract Net Protocol: High-Level Communication and Control in a Distributed Problem Solver, *IEEE Transactions on Computers*, Vol. C-29, No. 12, pp. 1104–1113.

Sandholm, T. (1993). An Implementation of the Contract Net Protocol Based on Marginal Cost Calculations, *Proceedings of AAAI 93*, pp. 256–262.

Weyns, D.; Bouck´e, N. & Holvoet, T. (2006). Gradient Field-Based Task Assignment in an AGV Transportation System, *Proc. of 5th Int. Joint Conf. on Autonomous Agents and Multiagent Systems (AAMAS2006)*, pp. 842 – 849.

Parunak, H. V. D. (1987). Manufacturing experience with the contract net, *Distributed Artificial Intelligence*, (M. Huhns, Ed.), pp. 285–310, Pitman Publishing: London and Morgan Kaufmann: San Mateo, CA.

Schillo, M.; Kray, C. & Fischer, K. (2002). The Eager Bidder Problem: A Fundamental Problem of DAI and Selected Solutions, *Proc. of First Int. Joint Conf. on Autonomous Agents and Multiagent Systems (AAMAS2002)*, pp. 599 – 606.

Sugawara, T.; Kurihara, S.; Hirotsu, T.; Fukuda, K.; Sato, S. & Akashi, O. (2006). Total Performance by Local Agent Selection Strategies in Multi-Agent Systems, *Proc. of 5th Int. Joint Conf. on Autonomous Agents and Multiagent Systems (AAMAS2006)*, pp. 601–608.

Sugawara, T.; Hirotsu, T.; Kurihara, S. & Fukuda, K. (2007). Performance Variation Due to Interference Among a Large Number of Self-Interested Agents. *Proceedings of 2007 IEEE Congress on Evolutionary Computation*, pp. 766-773.

Falcone, R.; Pezzulo, G.; Castelfranchi, C. & Calvi, G. (2004). Why a cognitive trustier performs better: Simulating trust based Contract Nets, *Proc. of 3rd Int. Joint Conf. on Autonomous Agents and Multiagent Systems (AAMAS2004)*, pp. 1394–1395.

Xu, L. & Weigand, H. (2001). The Evolution of the Contract Net Protocol, *Proceedings of WAIM 2001*, LNCS 2118, pp. 257–264.

Sandholm, T. & Lesser, V. (1995). Issues in automated negotiation and electronic commerce: Extending the contract net framework, *Proc. of First Int. Conf. on Multi-Agent Systems (ICMAS'95)*, The MIT Press: Cambridge, MA, USA, pp. 328–335.

Gu, C. & Ishida, T. (1996). Analyzing the social behavior of contract net protocol, *Proc. of 7th European Workshop on Modeling Autonomous Agents in a Multi-Agent World (MAAMAW 96)*, LNAI 1038, Springer-Verlag, pp. 116–127.

20

The Use of Evolutionary Algorithm in Training Neural Networks for Hematocrit Estimation

Hieu Trung Huynh and Yonggwan Won
Department of Computer Engineering, Chonnam National University
Republic of Korea

1. Introduction

Evolutionary algorithms (EAs) have recently been successfully applied in optimization problems and engineering disciplines. They can solve complex optimization problems without specialized information such as gradient or smoothness of objective functions. Although pure EAs such as genetic algorithm (GA), evolutionary strategies (ES) and evolutionary programming (EP) are easy to implement and offer fair performance in many applications, experimental results have shown that a variant of evolutionary method namely Differential Evolution (DE) has good convergence properties and outperforms other well known EAs (Ilonen et al., 2003). This variation was first introduced by Storn and Price (Storn & Price, 1997) and has an increasing interest as an optimization technique in recent years due to its achievement for a global minimum. It has several important differences from the traditional genetic optimization especially in the nature of the mutation, in which instead of taking a random perturbation, DE randomly selects a pair of individuals and computes the difference between their parameter vectors. This vector of difference is then added to the individual being mutated after multiplying by a constant. Another important difference is that the DE does not require the selection of parents based on fitness. Instead, fitness determines which children are kept for the next generation. Advantages of these approaches are shown in (Storn & Price, 1997).

Using DE for training neural networks was first introduced in (Masters & Land, 1997). It was reported that the DE algorithm is particularly suitable for training general regression neural networks (GRNN), and it outperforms other training methods such as gradient and Hessian on applications which have the presence of multiple local minima in the error space. Recently, the combination of the DE and other training algorithms has also been investigated. Subudhi and Jena (Subudhi & Jena, 2008) proposed a combination of DE and Levenberg Marquardt (LM) to train neural network for nonlinear system identification. It was shown that this combination can offer better identification results than neural networks trained by ordinary LM algorithm. More comprehensive studies for using DE in the training neural networks are presented in (Ilonen et al., 2003).

Although there are many network architectures proposed for different problems and applications, it was shown that single hidden-layer feedforward neural networks (SLFNs) can form boundaries with arbitrary shape and approximate any function with arbitrarily small error if the activation functions are chosen properly (Huang et al., 2000). An efficient training algorithm namely extreme learning machine (ELM) was proposed for SLFNs. It analytically determines the output weights with random choice of input weights and hidden biases. This algorithm can obtain good performance with high learning speed in many applications. However, it often requires a large number of hidden units which takes longer time for responding to new patterns. Hybrid approaches which use DE algorithm were proposed to overcome this problem (Zhu et al., 2005; Hieu & Won, 2008). Zhu et al. (Zhu et al., 2005) introduced a method called evolutionary extreme learning machine (E-ELM) which takes advantages of both ELM and DE. In E-ELM, the input weights and hidden layer biases are determined by DE process and the output weights are determined by Moore-Penrose (MP) generalized inverse like ELM. Another improvement of ELM was shown in (Hieu & Won, 2008) which is called evolutionary least squares extreme learning machine (ELS-ELM). Unlike ELM and E-ELM, input weights and hidden layer biases in ELS-ELM are first initialized by a linear model, and then the optimization is performed by applying DE process. Experimental results showed its better performance in regression problems.

In this chapter, we have a space for introducing the use of DE process in training SLFNs for estimating hematocrit density which is an important factor for surgical procedures and hemodialysis, and is the most highly affecting factor influencing the accuracy of glucose measurements with a hand-held device that uses the whole blood. The input features of the networks are sampled from transduced current curves which are produced by the transfer of ions to an electrode. These ions are produced by the enzymatic reaction in glucose measurement using the electrochemical glucose biosensors. The networks are trained by hybrid algorithms which take advantages of DE process, linear model, and ELM to obtain good performance with compact architectures.

2. Neural Nnetworks and Extreme Learning Machine (ELM)

The artificial neural network has been vastly used in machine learning due to its ability to provide proper models for classes of problems that are difficult to handle by using classical parametric techniques. A typical neural network consists of layers with units which are also called neurons. It was shown that a single hidden layer feedforward neural network (SLFN) can approximate any function with arbitrarily small error if the activation function is chosen properly. The typical architecture of a SLFN is shown in Fig. 1. The *i*-th output corresponding to the *j*-th input pattern of a SLFN with *N* hidden units and *C* output units can be represented by

$$o_{ji}=\mathbf{h}_j \cdot \boldsymbol{\alpha}_i, \tag{1}$$

where $\boldsymbol{\alpha}_i=[a_{i1}\ a_{i2}\ \ldots\ a_{iN}]^T$ is the weight vector connecting from the hidden units to the *i*-th output unit, $\mathbf{h}_j=[f(\mathbf{w}_1\cdot\mathbf{x}_j+b_1)\ f(\mathbf{w}_2\cdot\mathbf{x}_j+b_2)\ \ldots\ f(\mathbf{w}_N\cdot\mathbf{x}_j+b_N)]^T$ is the output vector of the hidden layer corresponding to pattern $\mathbf{x}_j \in \mathbb{R}^d$, b_m is the bias of the *m*-th hidden unit, and $\mathbf{w}_m=[w_{m1}\ w_{m2}\ \ldots\ w_{md}]^T$ is the weight vector connecting from the input units to the *m*-th hidden unit. Note that $\mathbf{x}\cdot\mathbf{y}=\langle\mathbf{x},\mathbf{y}\rangle$ is the inner product of two vectors **x** and **y**.

For *n* training patterns $(\mathbf{x}_j, \mathbf{t}_j)$, $j=1,2,\ldots, n$, where $\mathbf{x}_j=[x_{j1}\ x_{j2}\ \ldots\ x_{jd}]^T$ and $\mathbf{t}_j=[t_{j1}\ t_{j2}\ \ldots\ t_{jC}]^T$ are the *j*-th input pattern and target respectively, the main goal of training process is to determine the network weights $\mathbf{w}_m$, $\boldsymbol{\alpha}_i$, and b_m so that they minimize the error function defined by

$$E=\sum_{j=1}^{n}\left(\mathbf{o}_j-\mathbf{t}_j\right)^2=\sum_{j=1}^{n}\sum_{i=1}^{C}(\mathbf{h}_j\cdot\boldsymbol{\alpha}_i-t_{ji})^2 . \tag{2}$$

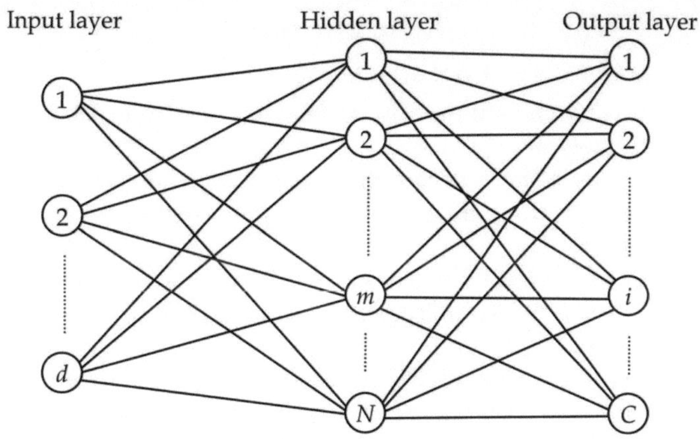

Fig. 1. Architecture of SLFN

Traditionally, this estimation of the network weights is performed based on the gradient-descent algorithms, in which the set of **G** vectors consisting of weights ($\mathbf{w}_i$, $\boldsymbol{\alpha}_i$) and biases b_i is iteratively adjusted as follows:

$$\mathbf{G}_k=\mathbf{G}_{k-1} - \eta\frac{\partial E}{\partial \mathbf{G}}, \tag{3}$$

where η is a learning rate. One of the popular methods based on the gradient descent is the back-propagation (BP) algorithm or generalized delta rule, in which gradients can be calculated and the parameter vector of the network can be determined by error propagation from the output to the input. However, the back-propagation algorithms are generally slow in learning due to improper learning parameters. They may also easily get over-fitting or be stuck in local minima. These problems have been overcome by many improvements proposed by many researchers. However, up to now, most of the training algorithms based on the gradient descent are still slow due to many learning steps which may be required in the learning processes.

Recently, a novel learning algorithm called extreme learning machine (ELM) was proposed for training SLFNs (Huang et al., 2006). The minimization process of error function in the ELM is performed by using a linear system:

$$\mathbf{HA=T}, \tag{4}$$

where **H** is called as the hidden layer output matrix of the SLFN and defined by (Huang et al., 2006) :

$$\mathbf{H} = [\mathbf{h}_1\ \mathbf{h}_2 \dots \mathbf{h}_n]^T = \begin{bmatrix} f(\mathbf{w}_1\cdot\mathbf{x}_1+b_1) & \cdots & f(\mathbf{w}_N\cdot\mathbf{x}_1+b_N) \\ \vdots & \ddots & \vdots \\ f(\mathbf{w}_1\cdot\mathbf{x}_n+b_1) & \cdots & f(\mathbf{w}_N\cdot\mathbf{x}_n+b_N) \end{bmatrix}, \tag{5}$$

$$\mathbf{T}= [\mathbf{t}_1\ \mathbf{t}_2\ \dots\ \mathbf{t}_n]^T, \tag{6}$$

and

$$\mathbf{A}=[\ \alpha_1\ \alpha_2\ \ldots\ \alpha_C]. \tag{7}$$

The ELM algorithm was based on two basic principles:

1. If the activation function is infinitely differentiable in any interval of $\mathbb{R}$ and the number of training patterns equals the number of hidden units (n=N) then the hidden layer output matrix **H** is invertible. Based on this principle, it can randomly assign the input weights and biases of hidden units and the output weights are analytically calculated by simply inverting **H**.
2. When the number of hidden units is less than the number of input patterns (N<n), the output weight matrix **A** is also determined by using pseudo inverse of **H** with a small nonzero training error.

Thus, the extreme learning machine (ELM) can be described as follows:

Assign arbitrary input weights $\mathbf{w}_m$ and biases b_m, $m=1, 2, \ldots, N$.
Determine the output matrix **H** of the hidden layer by Eq. (5).
Determine the output weight matrix **A** as follows:

$$\hat{\mathbf{A}}=\mathbf{H}^{\dagger}\mathbf{T} \tag{8}$$

This algorithm can greatly reduce learning time for finding the input weights and biases of hidden units. However, it often requires more hidden units than conventional algorithms, and therefore application of the trained network to an input pattern takes longer time. This drawback is caused by existance of redundant hidden units. Therefore, it claims that the performance of SLFNs can be improved if the input weights and biases of hidden units are chosen properly.

3. Evolutionary algorithms for training single hidden layer feedforward neural networks

This section presents evolutionary computation based approaches for reducing the number of hidden units in ELM. The first approach proposed by Q.-Y. Zhu et al. (Zhu et al., 2005) was called evolutionary extreme learning machine (E-ELM). In E-ELM, a hybrid learning algorithm was proposed, in which the input weights and biases are determined by using the differential evolutionary algorithm and the output weights are analytically determined by using Moore-Penrose (MP) generalized inverse (Serre, 2002).

3.1 Hybrid of differential evolution and extreme learning machine

Similar to other evolutionary algorithms, DE operates on a population of candidate solutions called individuals. Each individual is a set of the input weights and biases of hidden units defined by $\boldsymbol{\theta} = [w_{11}, w_{12}, \ldots, w_{1d}, w_{21}, w_{22}, \ldots, w_{2d}, \ldots, w_{N1}, w_{N2}, \ldots, w_{Nd}, b_1, b_2, \ldots, b_N]$. DE always maintains NP individuals of population. At generation G, three steps of DE being mutation, crossover and selection are applied and individuals with better fitness values are retained to the next generation. The fitness of each individual is chosen as the root-mean squared error (RMSE) on the whole training set or the validation set. The output weights corresponding to each individual are determined by using the MP generalized inverse. In addition, in order to obtain smaller weight values, the norm of output weights $\|\mathbf{A}\|$ is added to the criterion of the selection step. We can summarize the E-ELM algorithm as follows:

- Generate the initial generation composed of parameter vectors $\{ \theta_{i,0} \mid i=1, 2, \ldots, NP \}$ as the population.
- At each generation G, we do:

i. *Mutation:* the mutant vector is generated by $\mathbf{v}_{i,G+1} = \theta_{r1,G} + F(\theta_{r2,G} - \theta_{r3,G})$, where $r1$, $r2$, and $r3$ are different random indices, and F is a constant factor used to control the amplification of the differential variation.

ii. *Crossover:* the trial vector is formed so that

$$\mu_{ji,G+1} = \begin{cases} \mathbf{v}_{ji,G+1} \text{ if } rand\,b(j) \leq CR \text{ or } j = rnbr(i) \\ \theta_{ji,G+1} \text{ if } rand\,b(j) > CR \text{ and } j \neq rnbr(i) \end{cases} \tag{9}$$

where *rand b(j)* is the *j*-th evaluation of a uniform random number generator, *CR* is the crossover constant and *rnbr(i)* is an index chosen randomly which ensures at least one parameter from $\mathbf{v}_{ji,G+1}$.

iii. *Determine the output weights.*

iv. *Evaluate the fitness for each individual.*

v. *Selection:* The new generation is determined by:

$$\theta_{iG+1} = \begin{cases} \mu_{iG} \text{ if } f(\theta_{iG}) - f(\mu_{iG}) > \varepsilon f(\theta_{iG}), \\ \mu_{iG} \text{ if } \left| f(\theta_{iG}) - f(\mu_{iG}) \right| < \varepsilon f(\theta_{iG}) \\ \quad \text{and } \left\| \mathbf{A}^{\mu_{i,G}} \right\| < \left\| \mathbf{A}^{\theta_{i,G}} \right\|, \\ \theta_{iG} \quad \text{otherwise} \end{cases} \tag{10}$$

where $f(\cdot)$ is the fitness function and ϵ is a predefined tolerance rate. The DE process is repeated until the goal is met or a maximum learning epochs is reached. This algorithm can obtain a good generalization performance with compact networks. However, it does not obtain small norm of input weights and hidden layer biases. Note that a neural network can provide better generalization performance with small norm of network parameters.

3.2 Initialization of the first generation

In this section, we introduce another improvement of ELM, which is based on differential evolution and is called evolutionary least-squares extreme learning machine (ELS-ELM) (Hieu & Won, 2008). It utilizes a linear model for generating the initial population, and DE process for optimizing the parameters.

Let $\mathbf{X} = \begin{bmatrix} \mathbf{x}_1 & \mathbf{x}_2 & \cdots & \mathbf{x}_n \\ 1 & 1 & \cdots & 1 \end{bmatrix}^T$ be the input matrix, and $\mathbf{W} = \begin{bmatrix} \mathbf{w}_1 & \mathbf{w}_2 & \cdots & \mathbf{w}_N \\ b_1 & b_2 & \cdots & b_N \end{bmatrix}$ be the matrix of input weights and biases. Then, the initialization of the first generation follows a linear model defined by:

$$\mathbf{XW} = \mathbf{TP}, \tag{11}$$

where matrix $\mathbf{P} \in \mathbb{R}^{C \times N}$ should be assigned with random values.

The most commonly used method for the regularization of ill-posed problems has been Tikhonov regularization (Tikhonov & Arsenin, 1977), in which the solution for **W** of Eq. 11 can be replaced by seeking **W** that minimizes

$$\|\mathbf{WX} - \mathbf{TP}\|^2 + \lambda \|\mathbf{W}\|^2, \tag{12}$$

where $\|\bullet\|$ is the Euclidean norm and λ is a positive constant. The solution for **W** is given by

$$\hat{\mathbf{W}}=(\mathbf{X}^T\mathbf{X}+\lambda\mathbf{I})^{-1}\mathbf{X}^T\mathbf{TP}. \tag{13}$$

In the case where **W** can be expressed as linear combination of $\mathbf{x}_j$ (j=1,2, ..., n) and the number of features are large, we can obtain an indirect solution for Eq. 11 as:

$$\hat{\mathbf{W}} = \mathbf{X}^T\mathbf{Y} \tag{14}$$

where

$$\mathbf{Y} = (\mathbf{X}\mathbf{X}^T+\lambda n\mathbf{I})^{-1}\mathbf{TP}. \tag{15}$$

Thus, ELS-ELM approach for training SLFNs can be described as follows:

1. **Initialization:** *Generate the population for the initial generation composed of parameter vectors* $\{ \boldsymbol{\theta}_{i,G} \mid i=1, 2, \ldots, NP\}$, *where NP is the population size:*
   For each individual $\boldsymbol{\theta}_i$ in the population, we do:
   i. Randomly assign the values for the matrix **P**.
   ii. Estimate the input weights $\mathbf{w}_m$ and biases b_m of $\boldsymbol{\theta}_i$ by using Eq. 13 or 14.
   iii. Calculate the hidden layer output matrix **H** by using Eq. 5.
   iv. Determine the output weights **A** by using Eq. 8.
   v. Calculate the fitness value.
2. **Training process:**
   At each generation G, we do:
   i. *Mutation:* the mutant vector is generated by

   $$\mathbf{v}_{i,G+1}= \boldsymbol{\theta}_{r1,G}+F(\boldsymbol{\theta}_{r2,G} - \boldsymbol{\theta}_{r3,G}).$$

   ii. *Crossover:* the trial vector is formed using Eq. 9.
   iii. Compute the hidden layer output matrix **H** by Eq. 5.
   iv. Determine the output weights by Eq. 8.
   v. Evaluate the fitness for each individual.
   vi. *Selection:* The new generation is determined by Eq. 10.

This approach offers the improved performance for many applications, especially for regression problems.

4. Hematocrit estimation

Hematocrit is an important factor for medical procedures and hemodialysis, and is also the most highly affecting factor influencing the accuracy of glucose value measured by a hand-held device that uses the whole blood. Reports showed that the glucose measurement results are underestimated at higher hematocrit concentrations and overestimated at lower hematocrit levels (Kilpatrick et al., 1993; Louie et al., 2000; Tang et al., 2000). Consequently, estimating hematocrit concentrations plays an important role in enhancing performance of glucose measurements. Traditionally, this factor can be determined by centrifugation method performed in a small laboratory or by using automated analyzer. It can also be estimated by dielectric spectroscopy or some different techniques. However, most of the above approaches are quite complicated or require specific individual devices which are difficult to reduce the effects of hematocrit on glucose measurement by handheld devices.

With development of intelligent computional methods, simple methods for estimating hematocrit density while measuring glucose value with a biosensor-based handheld device should be investigated.

4.1 Methods

In this section, we present an approach based on DE optimation and neural networks for estimating hematocrit density. The SLFN architecture is proposed and trained by ELS-ELM algorithm. The input data are transduced current curves obtained during the process of glucose measurement by an electrochemical biosensor.

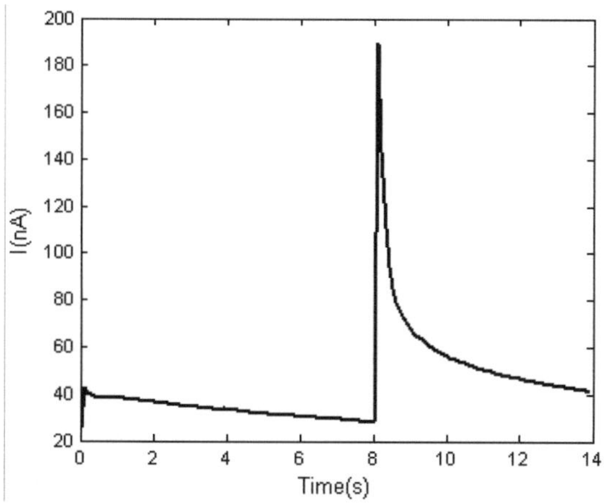

Fig. 2. Anodic Current Curve.

In the glucose measurement process by an electrochemical biosensor, the glucose oxidase(GOD) enzyme in biosensors is used to catalyze the oxidation of glucose by oxygen to produce gluconic acid and hydrogen peroxide, which is summarized as:

$$\text{Glucose}+O_2+\text{GO/FA}\rightarrow\text{Gluconic acid}+H_2O_2+\text{GO/FADH}_2$$
$$\text{GO/FADH}_2+\text{Ferricinium}^+\rightarrow\text{GO/FAD}+\text{Ferricinium}$$
$$\text{Ferrocence}\rightarrow\text{Ferrocence}^{+}+e^{-}$$

The reduced form of the enzyme ($GO/FADH_2$) is oxidized to its original state by an electron mediator (ferrocence). The resulting reduced mediator is then oxidized by the active electrode to produce the transduced anodic current. An example of the transduced anodic current curve obtained in the first 14 seconds is shown in Fig. 2. It was found that the data in the first eight seconds do not contain information for hematocrit estimation; it may be an incubation time while waiting for the enzyme reaction to be activated. Thus, in this study, we only focus on the second part of the current curve during the next six seconds. Note that this enzyme reaction characteristic may vary over biosensors from different manufacturers.

In the second period of six seconds, the anodic current curve is sampled at a frequency of 10Hz to produce the current points as shown in Fig. 3. There are 59 sampled current points used as the input features for networks. Denote $\mathbf{x}_j=[x_1, x_2, \ldots, x_{59}]^T$ as the j-th input pattern vector. Motivation of applying this anodic current curve $\mathbf{x}_j$ to SLFNs as the input vector for hematocrit estimation was introduced in (Hieu et al., 2008). It was also shown that the performance of hematocrit estimation can be improved with a new training algorithm which uses the DE process of ELS-ELM algorithm.

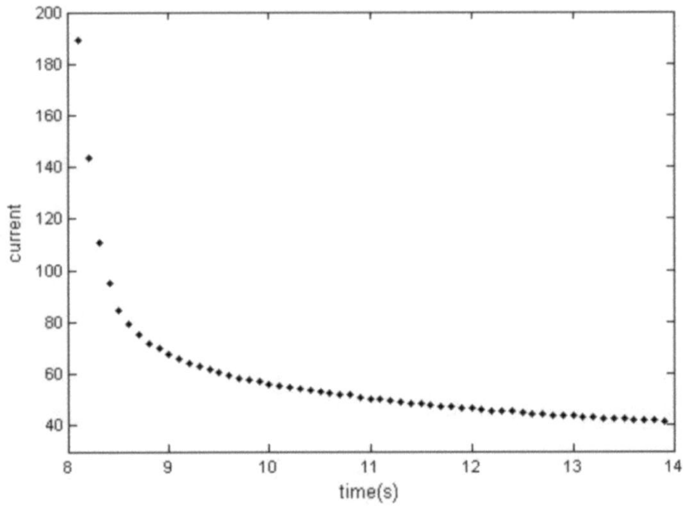

Fig. 3. The transduced current points used in hematocrit estimation.

4.2 Experimental results

In this section, performance of hematocrit estimation using SLFNs trained by ELM and DE process is presented. The data set of anodic current curves used in the experiments was obtained from 199 blood samples which were from randomly selected volunteers. For every blood sample, the accurate hematocrit density was first measured by the centrifugation method, and the anodic current curve was collected using a commercial handheld device for glucose measurement which uses an electrochemical biosensors. The distribution of reference hematocrit values collected from the blood samples used for this study by the centrifugation method is shown in Fig. 4 with mean 36.02 and deviation 6.39, which represents well the general distribution of hematocrit density values.

The data set was divided into training set (40%) and test set (60%). The input features were normalized into range [0, 1]. The algorithms were implemented on Matlab 7.0 environment.

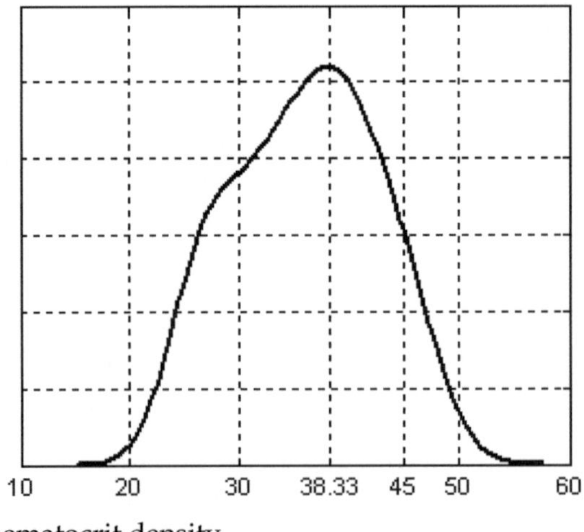

Fig. 4. Distribution of hematocrit density

Method	Training		Testing		# node
	RMSE	Mean	RMSE	Mean	
ELS-ELM	4.25	$\approx 10^{-5}$	4.63	-0.17	5
RLS-ELM	4.30	$\approx 10^{-7}$	4.91	-0.05	5
ELM	4.27	$\approx 10^{-4}$	4.90	-0.26	12

Table 1. Root mean square errors (RMSE) and the number of hidden units

The average results of fifty trials are shown in Table 1 with the root-mean-squared error(RMSE). In this table, the error was defined by the difference between the reference value measured by the centrifugation method and the output of the SLFN. From Table 1, we can see that the number of hidden units for ELS-ELM is equal to that for RLS-ELM (Hieu et al., 2008) while being much smaller than that for ELM. The errors for both training and testing are close to zero with the mean values of -0.17, -0.05 and -0.26 for ELS-ELM, RLS-ELM and ELM, respectively. The RMSE for ELS-ELM on test data set is 4.63, which empirically proves the outperformance of ELS-ELM compared to RLS-ELM (Hieu et al., 2008) and ELM. This improvement is significant to support for finding a method which can be used to reduce the effects of hematocrit density on glucose measurement by handheld devices.

5. Conclusion

Evolutionary algorithms (EAs) have been successfully applied in many complex optimization problems and engineering disciplines. Also, the single hidden-layer feedforward neural networks (SLFNs) have been widely used for machine learning due to their ability to form boundaries with arbitrary shape and to approximate any function with arbitrarily small error if the activation functions are chosen properly (Huang et al., 2000). Hematocrit density is an important factor for medical procedures and hemodialysis, and is the most highly affecting factor influencing the accuracy of glucose measurements with a hand-held device that uses the whole blood. Enzymatic reaction in glucose measurement with the electrochemical glucose biosensors is represented in the form of ion transfer to the electrode in the biosensor. Hematocrit density can be estimated while measuring the glucose value with the SLFN trained by combination of extreme learning machine (ELM) and differential evolution (DE) process.

This ionization of enzymatic reaction along time produces the anodic current curve, and is presented to SLFNs as the input vector. SLFNs trained by ELM, RLS-ELM and ELS-ELM are compared for hematocrit density estimation. It shows that they can be a good method for estimating and reducing the effect of hematocrit density on glucose measurement by handheld devices. Since this approach can provide the hematocrit density while measuring the glucose value, it can be simply implemented in the handheld devices to enhance the accuracy of glucose measurement which has to use the whole blood.

6. References

Hieu, T. H. & Won, Y. (2008). Evolutionary Algorithm for Training Single Hidden Layer Feedforward Neural Network, *The 2008 IEEE Int'l Joint Conference on Neural Networks (IJCNN2008)*, pp. 3027-3032.

Hieu, T. H.; Won, Y. & Kim, J. (2008). Neural Networks for the Estimation of Hematocrit from Transduced Current Curves, *Proc. of the 2008 IEEE Int'l Conf. on Networking, Sensing and Control*, pp.1517-1520.

Huang, G.-B.; Chen, Y.-Q. & Babri, H. A. (2000). Classification Ability of Single Hidden Layer Feedforward Neural Networks, *IEEE Trans. on Neural Networks*, Vol. 11, No. 3, pp. 799-801.

Huang, G.-B.; Zhu, Q.-Y. & Siew, C.-K. (2006). Extreme learning machine: Theory and applications, *Neurocomputing*, Vol. 70, pp. 489-501.

Ilonen, J.; Kamarainen, J. K. & Lampinen, J. (2003). Differential evolution training algorithm for feed forward neural networks, *Neural Processing Letters*, Vol. 17, pp. 145-163.

Kilpatrick, E. S.; Rumley, A. G. & Myin H. (1993). The effect of variations in hematocrit, mean cell volume and red blood count on reagent strip tests for glucose, *Ann Clin Biochem*, Vol. 30, pp. 485-487.

Louie, R. F.; Tang, Z., Sutton, D. V., Lee, J. H. & Kost, G. J. (2000). Point of Care Glucose Testing: effects of critical variables, influence of reference instruments, and a modular glucose meter design, *Arch Pathol Lab Med*, Vol. 124, pp. 257-266.

Masters, T. & Land, W. (1997). A new training algorithm for the general regression neural network, *IEEE International Conference on Systems, Man, and Cybernetics, Computational Cybernetics and Simulation*, pp. 1990-1994.

Serre, D. (2002). *Matrices: Theory and Applications*, Springer, New York.

Storn, R. & Price, K. (1997). Differential evolution – a simple and efficient heuristic for global optimization over continuous spaces, *Journal of Global Optimization*, Vol. 11, No. 4, pp. 341-359.

Subudhi, B. & Jena, D. (2008). Differential Evolution and Levenberg Marquardt Trained Neural Network Scheme for Nonlinear System Identification, *Neural Processing Letters*, Vol. 27, pp. 285-296.

Tang, Z.; Lee, J. H., Louie, R. F., Kost, G. J. & Sutton, D. V. (2000). Effects of Different Hematocrit Levels on Glucose Measurements with HandHeld Meters for Point of Care Testing", *Arch Pathol Lab Med*, Vol. 124, pp. 1135-1140.

Tikhonov, A. N. & Arsenin, A. V. (1977). *Solution of Ill-posed Problems*, Winston & Son, Washingston.

Zhu, Q.-Y.; Qin A.K., Suganthan P.N. & Huang G.-B. (2005). Evolutionary Extreme Learning Machine, *Pattern Recognition*, Vol. 38, pp. 1759-1763.

21

Applications of Neural-Based Agents in Computer Game Design

Joseph Qualls and David J. Russomanno
University of Memphis
United States

1. Introduction

Most agents in computer games are designed using classical symbolic artificial intelligence (AI) techniques. The AI techniques include production rules for very large branching and conditional statements, as well as search techniques, including branch-and-bound, heuristic search, and A* (Russel & Norvig, 2003). Planning techniques, such as STRIPS (Stanford Research Institute Problem Solver) (Fikes & Nilsson, 1971) and hierarchical task network (HTN) (Erol, 1996) planning are common. Also, situational case-based reasoning, finite-state machines, classical expert systems, Bayesian networks, and other forms of logic, including predicate calculus and its derivatives, such as description logics (Baader et al., 2003), form the foundation of many game agents that leverage AI techniques.

The game agents are typically created with *a priori* knowledge bases of game states and state transitions, including mappings of the world environment and the game agent's reactions to the environment and vice versa (Dybsand, 2000; Zaroinski, 2001; Watt & Policarpo, 2001). Fig. 1. shows an editor for the open source game *Yo Frankie!* This game uses the engine by the Blender Institute, which provides the functionality to apply AI techniques to game engine design through an interactive editor (Lioret, 2008).

There are numerous other computer games that use classical AI techniques, including Star Craft, Unreal Tournament 3, and FEAR. In general, these games use agents as tactical enemies or support characters, such as partners that interact with other agents, humans, and the environment. Since these games execute in real-time, all of the agents must have extremely fast response times. AI techniques used in games include common-sense reasoning, speech processing, plan recognition, spatial and temporal reasoning, high-level perception, counter planning, teamwork, path planning, as well as other techniques (Larid & Lent, 2000). One specific example is FEAR and its use of Goal Oriented Action Planning or GOAP (Orkin, 2004; Orkin, 2005), which is a form of STRIPS. FEAR uses GOAP to create complex behaviors while relying on classical AI techniques. This approach allows for decoupling goals and actions, layering behaviors, and dynamic problem solving. Classical symbolic AI techniques have been used with varying degrees of success, but many challenges have risen as a result of increased demand on the game agents by human opponents and increasingly complex game environments, even when games, such as FEAR, leveraged classical AI techniques to a great extent.

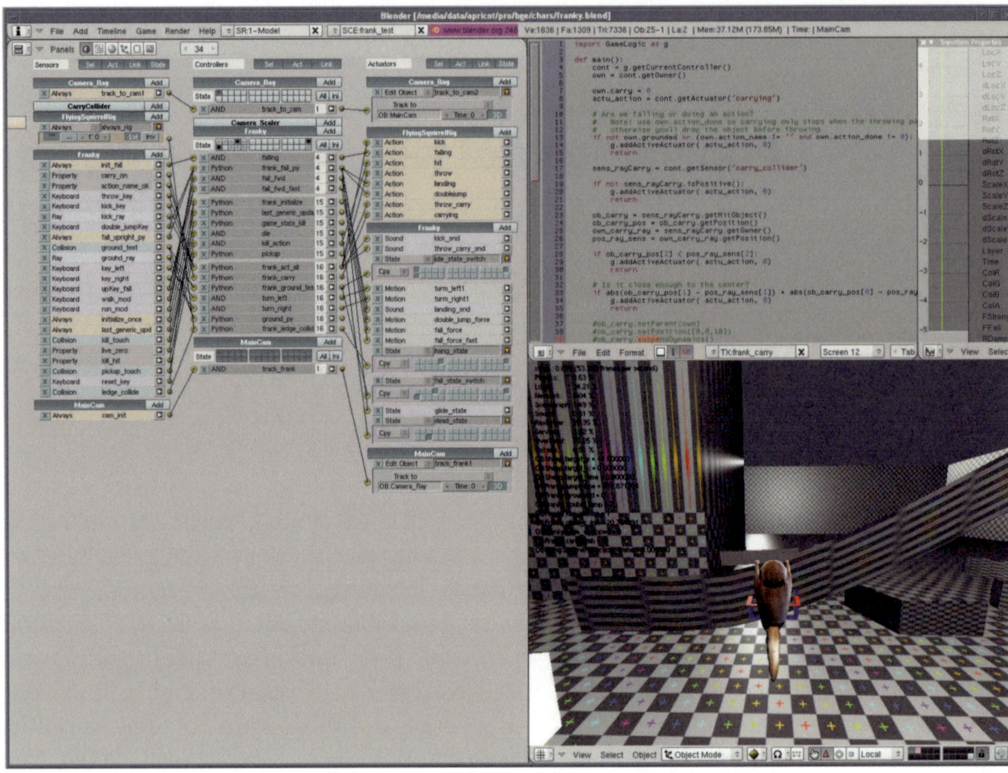

Fig. 1. Blender game engine editor from the open source game *Yo Frankie!*

Attempting to determine *a priori* every game state that the agent will face is a daunting task. Even for relatively simple games, over 20,000 possible states exist (Schaefer, 2002), which limits the applicability of some techniques. Classical AI techniques can become very complex to create, maintain, and scale as the possible game states become more complex (Larid & Lent, 2000). In many cases, since it is not feasible to plan for every event in a game, the agents have a very limited perception of the game. This limited perception of the game world creates two key problems. First, as the game environment or the human player's tactics change over time, the agents have difficulty adapting to the new environment or tactics. Without the ability to form new tactics to respond to major changes in the player's tactics or environment, the agent's performance will significantly degrade over time. Second, as the human players gain experience with the game, they can begin to predict the actions of the agents. Thus, the humans' knowledge about the game continues to improve through learning by playing, but the game agents do not learn through their experience of playing the game. These two shortcomings are common with the application of many of the classical symbolic AI techniques in game design today, which results in a game that loses challenge over time.

Neural networks have the ability to overcome some of the shortcomings associated with the application of many of the classical AI techniques in computer game agent design (Haykin, 1999). Neural networks have many advantages, including being self adaptive in that they adapt well to computer game environments that change in real-time. Neural networks can improve performance via off-line and on-line training. In other words, the game agents can be trained once before being deployed in a game or the learning algorithm can be applied in real-time for continuous improvement while the game is played. Also, for neural-based agents, the corresponding source code tends to be small and generic allowing for code reuse through libraries since the essence of most neural networks consist of a series of inputs sent across an analog weight matrix that capture states and world environments to determine their outputs. Such designs allow easy computation and incorporation of data processing techniques, such as multi-threading and parallel processing, which is a requirement for today's high-performance games. With these benefits, neural-based agents gain the capability of adapting to changing tactics by humans or other game agents and may acquire the ability to learn and generate new tactics while playing the computer game, similar to the capability of many human players. Since the neural-based agents are adapting to the game conditions and generating new tactics, the game remains challenging for a longer time than games that use only classical AI techniques.

Incorporating neural networks in game designs also has problems, such as the difficulty in obtaining training data and unexpected emergent behavior in which the computer game does not function as intended by the designer. In general, obtaining training data is very critical to neural network development. In the computer game domain, there are two common approaches that can be used. First, data can be recorded as a human plays in the role of the game agent and this data can then be used to train the neural network. Another approach is to use an evolutionary process, such as genetic algorithms, to train the neural network by seeding the network and allowing for mutations and a cost function that terminates underperforming neural networks (Miikkulainen et al., 2006). Unexpected emergent behavior can be corrected by having a performance function or a teacher that evaluates the actions and corrects the agent. If the human player begins to lose consistently, the performance function can be adjusted so that the game agent performs at the appropriate level corresponding to the human player.

The remainder of this chapter will focus on four main topics. First, the background of various methods to apply neural networks in computer games will be explained along with several examples for commercial and academic computer games. Second, a strategy will be presented that will facilitate more efficient development of neural networks in computer games. Third, the complete development of a neural network for the Defend and Gather game will be described along with the network topologies used for the neural-based agents and the evaluation process used to analyze the overall performance of the agents. Although aspects of neural networks in the Defend and Gather game were previously described by Qualls et al., 2007, that work-in-progress conference paper does not contain the context and detail of this chapter. Finally, the future for neural networks in computer games will be explored along with recommendations for subsequent work.

2. Neural gaming background

2.1 Example game applications

Neural networks can be used in a variety of different ways in computer games. They can be used to control one game agent, several game agents, or several neural networks can be used to control a single game agent. A game agent can be a non-player character or it can be used to represent the game environment. With this in mind, a neural network can be used to control and represent just about any facet of a computer game. This section will discuss

several areas in which neural networks can be applied to computer games along with several examples of neural networks being used in computer games.
Path navigation is one of the most common uses of neural networks. A neural-based agent can adapt to an ever changing environment and more importantly, learn the human player's path to make the game more challenging over time. Neural networks can also be used to control ecology for the game. This neural-based ecology may be used to just populate an environment, or it could be used to control mutations based on a player's action, such as making animals more friendly or scared of the player. Animation is another promising area for neural networks. As computer games become more powerful, game designers demand more realistic animations. As the number of complex objects increase in games, attempting to create animations for every scenario can be impossible. For example, a neural network could be used to teach a neural-based agent some task, such as teaching a dog to walk. The neural-based agent could then learn to adapt to walking over a rocky environment or over an icy lake. Finally, advanced reasoning can be used by neural networks for dialog choices and strategies for defeating humans and other agent players, as well as other tasks. One example is two neural-based game agents may need to learn to work together to complete a game, which is the focus of Section 4 of this chapter.

2.2 Example games in academic and commercial markets

Neural networks have been around for quite some time but it has only been since the 1990s that there have been attempts at integrating neural networks within computer games. One of the first available commercial games that used neural networks was Creatures. The agents in Creatures used neural networks for learning and sensory motor control in conjunction with artificial biochemistries. Together, the neural network and artificial biochemistries are genetically specified to allow for evolution through reproduction. The neural networks are made up of 1000 neurons grouped into nine lobes interconnected with 5000 synapses. The neural-based agents learn by a reinforcement signal from the human player. The human player provides feedback by stroking or slapping the agent for positive or negative learning (Grand & Cliff, 1998).
In 2001, CodeMasters created the Colin McRae Rally 2.0 (CMR) racing game for the Sony PlayStation One. The CMR game used neural-based agents to control the opponent race cars as they drove around the track. The neural-based agents learned to drive all of the tracks in the game while learning how to maneuver around other race cars on the tracks. To obtain data to train the neural networks, the developers played the game and recorded their laps around the race tracks. This recorded data consisted of drivers' reactions to other cars and the average driving line around the track. The neural networks were then trained off-line with the recorded data and the resulting neural network was integrated within the agents to control the opponent race cars (Mathews, 2000).
Other games included Black and White and Democracy 2. Black and White Versions 1 and 2 used neural networks with reinforcement learning to allow a creature (neural-based agent) to learn from a player's actions. For instance, the creature may need to learn that it needs to destroy a structure before it sends in another army to destroy the opponent. Democracy 2, which is a political simulation game, uses a highly complex neural network that simulates desires, loyalties, and motivations of game agents that make up countries on a planet (Barnes, 2002).
There are many different examples of neural networks being used in computer games in the academic domain. The NERO (Neuro-Evolving Robotic Operatives) and GAR (Galactic

Arms Race) games, which use the NEAT (Neuroevolution of Augmenting topologies) algorithm, along with NeuroInvaders and Agogino's Game are discussed in this chapter. All of these example games use genetic algorithms or some form of evolution to train their neural networks (Agogino et al., 2000; Briggs, 2004; Stanley, 2005a; Stanley, 2005b; Stanley 2006; Hastings, 2007).

First, Agogino's Game was based on Warcraft II by Blizzard Entertainment. This game contains a human-controlled player and neural-based peons. The objective of the game is for the peons to find a resource point without being killed by the human player. The peons use genetic algorithms to evolve feed-forward networks in real-time. As time progresses, the peons become more adapt at finding resource points and avoiding the human player. The peons accomplish this task by evaluating the risk of choosing between a resource point that is near a human player or a resource point that is farther away, but unguarded (Agogino et al., 2000).

Second, the game NeuroInvaders allows human opponents and neural-based agents to play against each other in a death match. The agents must seek out and shoot the human player to win and vice versa. The agents use a spiking neural network containing eight neurons. For example, if the agent's FIRE neuron activates then the agent will fire its laser or if the RIGHT neuron fires then the agent will turn right, etc. The neural network of each game agent starts with random weights and delays. When the agent dies, a mutation created by adding random Gaussians to the weights and delays is added to the original weight matrix of the dead neural-based agent and integrated within a new neural-based agent that is still alive. All of these mutations occur in real-time using genetic algorithms while the game is being played (Briggs, 2004).

The NERO and GAR games both use the rtNEAT (real-time NEAT) algorithm and the cgNEAT (content generation NEAT) algorithm developed at the University of Texas. The NEAT algorithm is similar to other evolving neural networks but it has a key difference in that it can modify and increase the neural network's complexities along with its weights. The rtNEAT game is a real-time version of NEAT that gains a computation performance boost by putting a time limit on the life span of a neural-based agent and then evaluating its performance. If the neural-based agent is performing well then it is kept in the game. If its performance does not meet certain criteria, it is then discarded and it starts over. The cgNEAT algorithm is based on the idea that neural networks can generate more interesting content for the player, which results in an overall more enjoyable player experience (Stanley, 2005a; Stanley, 2005b; Stanley, 2006; Hastings, 2007).

The game NERO is essentially a real-time strategy game in which an agent must navigate an environment and defend itself against other game agents with the same goal. In NERO there are two phases of play for the human player. In the first phase, the human player acts as a teacher and creates exercises for the neural-based agents to go through and then the player can dictate fitness-based performance parameters by examining how well the agents move around walls or hit targets. In the second phase, the player can place its trained neural-based agents against other players' trained agents to determine which agent performs the best (Stanley, 2005a).

A second game based on NEAT called GAR is very different from NERO. The NERO game has the player actively involved in the neural network development, while GAR's neural network runs primarily behind the scenes. The GAR game uses cgNEAT to generate new types of weapons for the player to use in the game. These new weapons are generated by creating variants of weapons that a player is using within the game. In short, the neural network in this case is generating interactive content for the player to use based on the player's preferences (Hastings, 2007). This last example shows that neural networks can be used in very interesting ways that may not necessarily fit the stereotypical functions of a game agent.

3. Strategies and techniques for neural networks in games

The most significant barrier to using neural networks in computer game design lies not with understanding how neural networks function but how to apply one of the various neural network techniques to a specific computer game. As seen from the previous examples, there are many different methods to develop and use neural networks in computer games. Decisions such as off-line/on-line training, neural network architecture, training algorithms, and most importantly, data acquisition, are all components of the neural network development process. This section of the chapter will discuss a simple process for incorporating a neural network inside a computer game and then follow up in Section 4 with the Defend and Gather game that uses the outlined development process in its implementation.

The first decision is to decide the scenarios in which the neural network will be used in the game. Will the neural network control a game agent, animation routine, or other function? The second decision revolves around training data. In other words, how and what data will be collected to train the neural network? This leads to questions concerning what constitutes data for the game system. Generally, the data is determined by the type of data inputted into the neural network and outputted by the neural network. The third decision that needs to be made is what type of neural network architecture is most appropriate based on the intended function of the agent. The neural network architecture can vary greatly depending on its given tasks. The fourth decision revolves around deciding between off-line/on-line training and the types of learning algorithms to be deployed. The main question is will the neural network continue to learn while the game is being played or will the neural network be trained and placed within the computer game with no further learning during game execution? There are advantages and disadvantages to both approaches. Allowing the neural network to continue to learn during game execution can provide it further refinement in playing the game but could lead to unforeseen actions that may result in the game not performing as desired. Even without further learning, anomalous game behavior can still be an issue. All of these important decisions are highly interdependent and are determined by the type of computer game being developed and the intended function of the agent.

As previously discussed, neural networks can be used to control various aspects of a computer game. For developing our simple process, we first create a hypothetical computer game in which an agent must navigate an environment to exit a simple maze. The game agent will have a sight range to allow for detection of walls and the goal of finding the exit. If the game agent gets close to a wall, it should move away from it. Fig. 2. shows a typical maze game.

For our first decision, the neural network will control all of the actions of the game agent. The neural network will determine how the agent moves around the environment. Therefore, the inputs to the agent are the directions of the walls from the perspective of the sight range of the agent and the outputs will be the direction the agent should follow. In short, we will have four inputs representing wall directions consisting of UP, DOWN, LEFT,

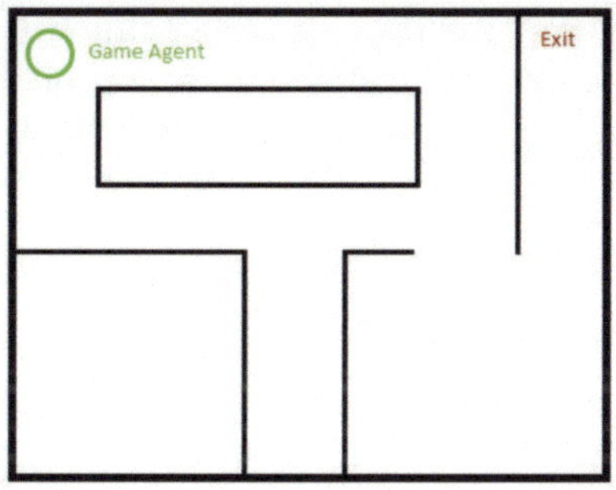

Fig. 2. Example maze game with the agent navigating the environment

and RIGHT and the outputs will be the direction the game agent travels: UP, DOWN, LEFT, and RIGHT. For the second decision, we will collect data by playing the game and recording the directions of the walls within the sight range of the game agent and the resulting direction we move the game agent. The sampling rate for data collection of the inputs and outputs was set as two samples per second. For most action games on the market today this rate will need to be increased due to the volume of information that a player may be exposed to within one second of game play. Table 1. shows an example recording of the game agent for two seconds.

Maze Game Recording Output File							
Inputs: Wall Directions				Outputs: Game Agent Direction			
UP	DOWN	LEFT	RIGHT	UP	DOWN	LEFT	RIGHT
1	0	0	0	0	1	0	0
1	0	1	0	0	1	0	1
0	1	1	0	1	0	0	1
0	0	1	0	0	0	0	1

Table 1. Agent recording for two seconds as human player moves around the maze

The third decision requires the specification of the neural network architecture. There are many types of architectures to choose from, such as recurrent, feed forward, and many more. If we look at the inputs and outputs of the game agent in this case, there are four inputs and four outputs, so we chose a feed-forward network, which is also one of the simplest architectures to implement. We also specify the number of hidden layers, as well as the number of nodes in each layer. A general rule of thumb is the number of nodes in the hidden layer should total to at least the sum of the output and input nodes to be adaptive to changing environments. Another rule of thumb is that a feed-forward network should have at least one and half times the number of input or output nodes in each hidden layer (Garzon, 2002). For the simple game in this case, there are four inputs and four outputs so there are two hidden layers with six nodes each. Fig. 3. shows the neural network architecture for our agent in the simple maze game.

The last decision involves deciding between training the neural network off-line then placing into the game or to allow the neural network to continue to learn while the game is being played. Also, the type of training algorithm must be specified. For this simple game, the neural network will be trained once off-line with back propagation. Larger and more complex games may need on-line training because the game itself may change over time, which is typical for multi-player on-line games. By answering these questions during the development of a computer game, the process for adding a neural network to a computer game can become straightforward. The following section of the chapter will go through a more complex example detailing how a neural network was added to the Defend and Gather game.

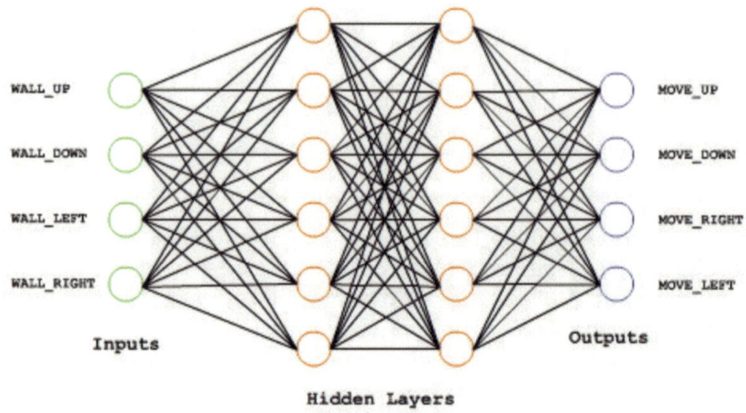

Fig. 3. Neural network architecture of the agent for the simple maze game

4. Example game with neural networks

4.1 Defend and gather

The Defend and Gather game will provide a better understanding of the benefits of neural networks in game design. In this game, neural-based agents play against classical symbolic AI agents in a contest to determine which agent will win the game. Defend and Gather was influenced by many of the games discussed in Section 2 of this chapter. One key difference is that instead of the neural-based agents facing off against human opponents they play against other game agents implemented with multiple classical AI techniques. The game agents consisting of classical AI techniques used techniques such as complex branching and conditional statements. These game agents will be referred to as BaC throughout the remainder of this chapter. Since the BaC agents use fairly simple AI techniques, it was decided that the neural-based agents would use off-line training techniques. Using off-line training also allows for better assessment of the neural-based agent's ability to cope with increasing difficulty with no additional learning while the game is being played. To facilitate the development of Defend and Gather an engine developed by Bruno Teixeira de Sousa was used (De Sousa, 2002). This game engine is a simple but robust two-dimensional open source engine that handles graphics, input/output, and simple physics computations. By choosing to use this game engine it allows other developers who may be interested in the implementation of neural-based agents to have a common platform to understand the process of developing their own neural-based agents for their respective game.

In Defend and Gather, the game agents have conflicting goals for winning the game. This was implemented to ensure that the neural-based agents will have confrontations with the BaC agents. The BaC agents have two goals to follow. First, they need to defend resource points and second they need to hunt and destroy the neural-based agents. There are two different neural-based agents in the game, each with a different goal. The first neural-based agent (Resource Collector) searches for and collects resource points while avoiding the BaC agents. The second neural-based agent (Protector) actively protects the other neural-based agents and searches for and destroys the BaC agents. An additional constraint is that the protector agent cannot destroy the BaC agents unless the resource collector agents have collected resources. This implies that the neural-based agents must work together to survive and win the game. Defend and Gather ends when one of following three conditions is met: 1) all BaC agents are killed; 2) all neural-based agents are killed; or 3) all the energy is collected and exhausted by the neural-based agents. If conditions 1 or 3 are completed then the neural-based agents win the game, or if condition 2 is completed then the BaC agents win the game. Fig. 4. shows a sample screen shot of Defend and Gather showing several environmental components, including resource points (Triangles), resource collector (Smiley Face), BaC agent patrol (Orange Plus), and several walls (Squares), all of which will be explained in further detail.

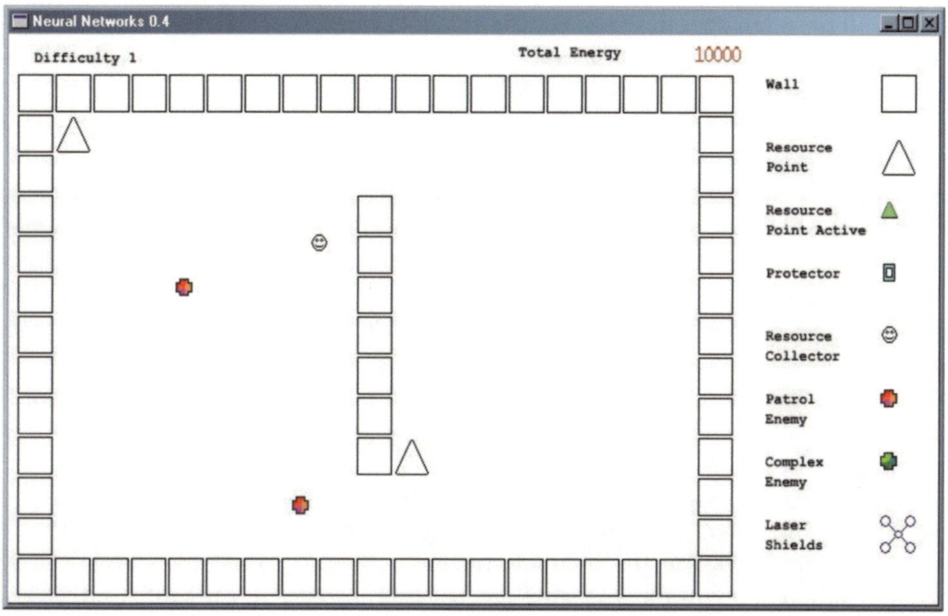

Fig. 4. Level 1 of Defend and Gather

There are four different agents in the game. The agents include two BaC agents called the patroller and the hunter and two neural-based agents called the protector and resource collector. All of these agents navigate the game environment in real-time. Mass-force vector calculations are used for movement. In other words, the agents control their thrust in four different directions for moving and slowing down. There are no limits on how fast any of the agents can move, so the agents will have to cope with not losing control. Also, if the agents run into a wall, then they will bounce off the wall based on the speed and trajectory they were traveling. So, if the agent moves too fast and hits a wall it can have the effect of bouncing around like a pin ball until control is regained. Each of the agents has a limited visibility range or field of view around them. The visibility range of each agent is a circle about three times their respective size.

The behaviors of each of the agents are dictated by their respective goals. First, the patrolling agent is a fairly simple BaC agent. It moves back and forth between two set points in the environment. If the patrolling agent detects a neural-based agent in its visibility range it will accelerate and start to fire its laser shields at the neural-based agent. Once the neural-based agent is destroyed or out of its visibility range the patrolling agent will return to its normal patrolling route and stop firing its shields. The hunter agent is a more complex BaC agent. The hunter agent moves randomly across the environment in search of the neural-based agents. If the hunter agent detects a neural-based agent in its visibility range it will start to pursue the neural based-agent by increasing its speed while also firing its laser shield. The hunter agent will continue to pursue the neural-based agent until it is destroyed or it no longer detects the neural-based agent in its visibility range. Once a neural-based agent is no longer detected, it will stop firing its laser shield and return to randomly searching for another neural-based agent. The resource collector neural-based agent simply searches for resource points while avoiding the BaC agents. The resource collectors have no laser shield for protection. The only advantage they have is that they can accelerate slightly faster than all the other agents. Once the resource collector has discovered a resource point it will hover at that location until all the resources have been collected. If a BaC agent is detected in its visibility range the resource collector will flee and try to move toward the protector agent. Once the resource collector no longer detects the BaC agent it will return to collecting resources so that the protector agent will have energy to fire its laser shield. The protector actively searches for both types of BaC agents and tries to protect the resource collector agents. The protector agent tries to stay close to the resource collectors while also searching for the BaC agents. Once a BaC agent is detected in the protector's visibility range it will start to pursue the BaC agents by accelerating if it has energy to fire its laser shield. If the protector does not have energy to fire its laser shield it will not give chase. The protector agent will continue to pursue a BaC agent until it is destroyed, no longer detected in its visibility range, has energy for its laser shields, and the resource collectors are not being attacked. If a resource collector is being attacked the protector will start to move towards that resource collector.

The Defend and Gather game consists of a closed two-dimensional environment as seen in Fig. 4. The environment contains the game agents previously mentioned along with resource points and walls for the agents to navigate around. To test the viability of all the agents, four different environments were created that increase in difficulty and pose more difficult challenges for the game agents. Fig. 5. through Fig. 8. show the four levels increasing from easy to most difficult. All levels contain one protector neural-base agent and four resource collector neural-based agents. The amount of resource points and the number and types of BaC agents varies across the levels. Fig. 5. shows the easiest level in the game. This level consists of two resource points and a single wall to navigate around. The level also contains just two patrolling BaC agents, one protector and four resource collector neural-based agents. Fig. 6. shows the next level of the game. This level consists of two resource points, two patrolling BaC agents, and one hunter BaC agent. The resource points are located in two small rooms with one of the rooms having both entrances protected by patrolling BaC agents moving in opposite directions. Fig. 7. shows the third level of the game. There are three resource points in this level each of which is in a separate room. Two of the resource points are heavily guarded while the third is not guarded. The level also contains one hunter BaC agent and three patrolling BaC agents. The concept behind this level is to see if the resource collectors will go for the unguarded resource point first and then allow the protector to try to eliminate some of the BaC agents before attempting to collect the other resource points. Fig. 8. shows the final level of the game, which is the most difficult level. This level has four resource points in separate rooms along with six patrolling BaC agents and two hunter BaC agents. All of the resource points are heavily guarded. The room itself is divided in half by a hallway that is designed as a chokepoint, which is common in many of today's games. The idea of a chokepoint is to force confrontation between players in the game.

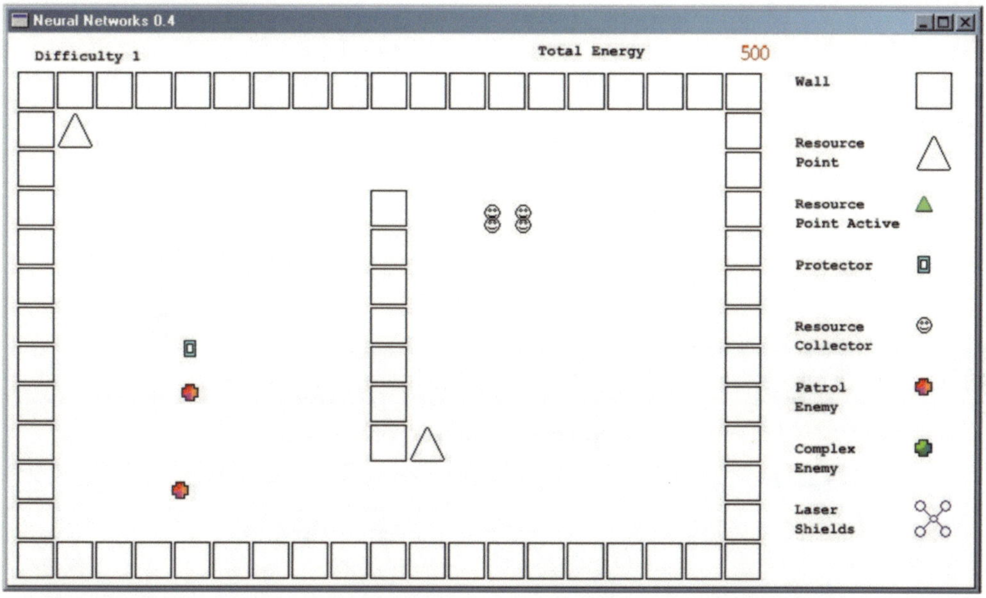

Fig. 5. Difficulty 1 – Two resource points and a single wall to navigate around

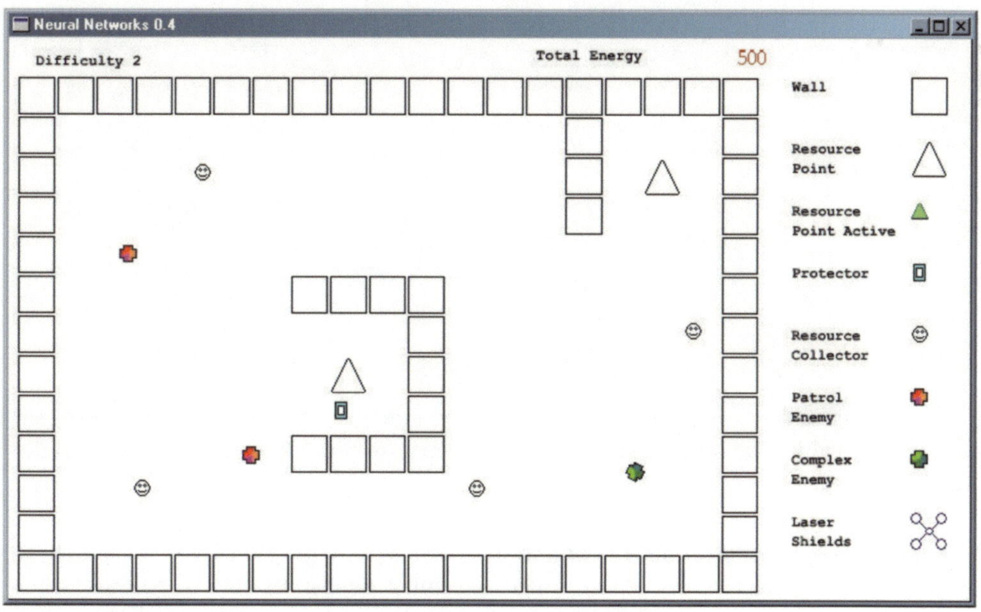

Fig. 6. Difficulty 2 – Two resource points each in a separate room

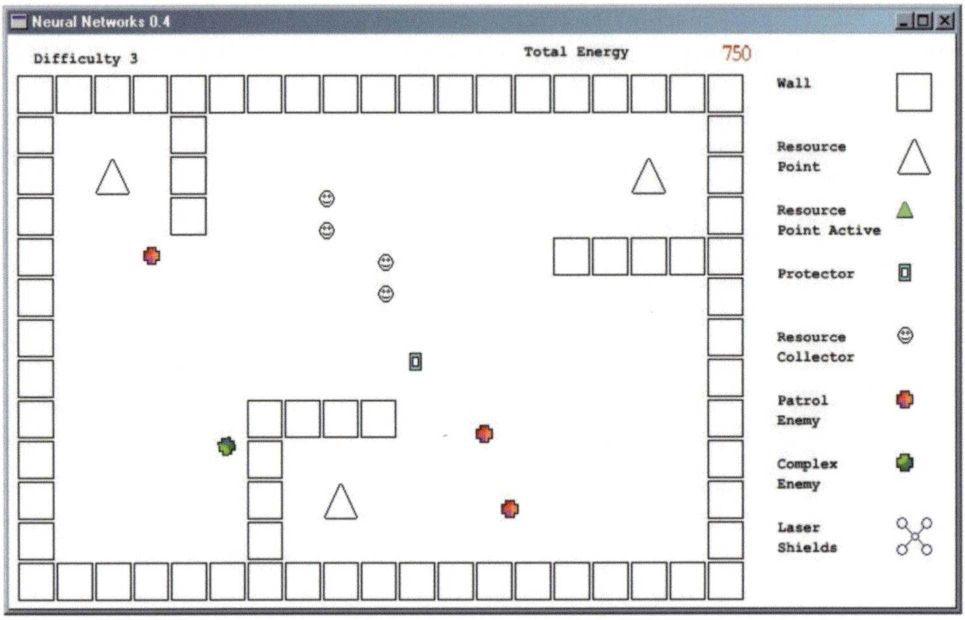

Fig. 7. Difficulty 3—Three resource points each in a separate room

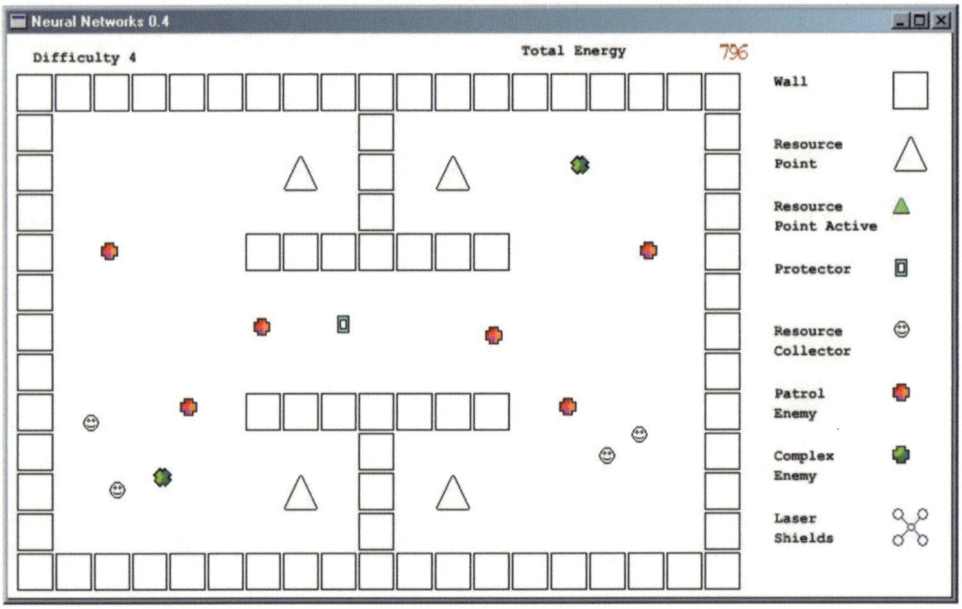

Fig. 8. Difficulty 4—Four resource points each in separate room with a choke point in the center of the level

4.2 Neural network development process

Now that the game world has been defined, we must determine how the neural network will operate in Defend and Gather. We have already defined the resource collectors and the protectors, which are the two types of agents that will use the neural networks in their design. The neural-based agents must able to move around the environment and react to the surroundings within their visibility range. Therefore, the inputs are the surroundings in its visible range and the outputs are the resulting movement. That is, the inputs of the neural network are objects in the game while the outputs control the movement of the neural-based agents. The outputs are the four directions UP, DOWN, LEFT and RIGHT. These outputs inform the agents which direction to fire their thrusters. The agents are not limited to firing their thrusters in one direction at the same speed as they can fire in several directions and at different speeds, which increases their maneuverability. The inputs of the neural network consist of directions of other game objects in different directions. The neural network has eight inputs, with the top four inputs representing the directions of walls and the bottom four inputs representing the direction of BaC agents.

4.3 Network architecture

Since each neural-based agent is a separate entity within Defend and Gather, two neural network architectures were created. Since the BaC agents use relatively simple AI techniques, the neural-based agents were designed using feed-forward networks, which is the simplest type of neural network architecture. Feed-forward networks are also straightforward to implement in gaming software. Many other topologies could have been implemented; however, it was decided to implement the simplest design first, then, try more complex networks.

One of the more difficult aspects of implementing the network architecture is determining the number of hidden nodes in the network. As stated in Section 3, we used the convention of choosing the number of hidden nodes to be approximately 1.5 to 2.0 times the number of nodes in the input/output layer. This design criterion was used for both the protector and the resource collector neural-based agents. Since the number of inputs and outputs are different, eight and four respectively, we used two hidden layers. The design criterion resulted in a network architecture that consisted of eight input units, four output units, and two hidden layers with fifteen and six nodes, respectively. Fig. 9. shows the final neural network architecture for the resource collector along with several other details. This architecture is also the same for the protector neural-based agent.

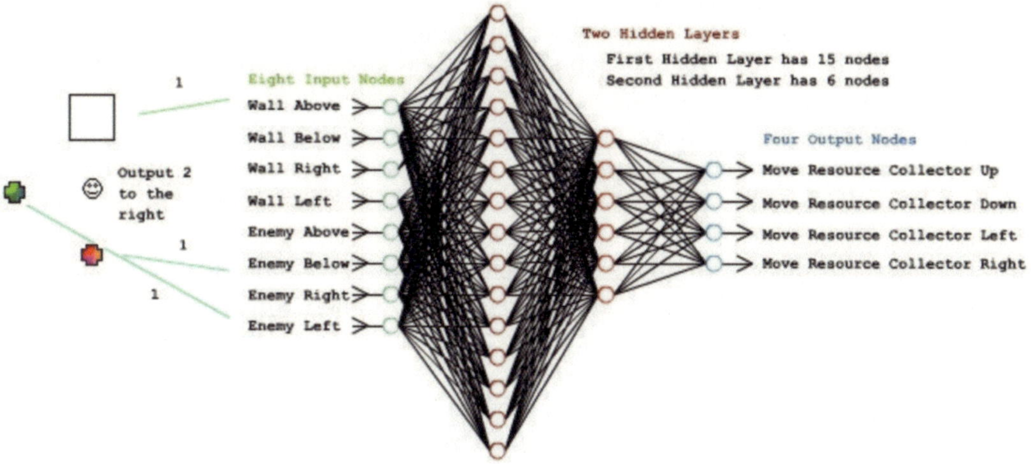

Fig. 9. Architecture of the resource collector with labeled inputs and outputs

As stated in Section 4.2, the eight inputs consist of two groups. The first four inputs in the network are used for detecting the direction of a wall and the last four inputs are used for detecting the BaC agent's direction. The four inputs for the walls and enemies operate in the same manner. These inputs remain at zero if no agent or wall is in the visible range of the neural-based agent. If detection occurs of a wall or enemy, then, the input will change to a one in the corresponding direction. For example, if there is a wall above the resource collector or protector, then, a one will be sent to the Wall_Above input in the neural network, Fig. 9.

Both the resource collector and the protector neural-based agents have the same outputs. The output determines the direction and speed of the agent with values zero, one, or two. For the resource collector, if all of the outputs are zero, then there is no detection of a wall or BaC agent in its field of view; therefore, the resource collector continues to search for resource points in the game environment. If any of the outputs are set to value one, then a wall has been detected and the resource collector will move in that direction at the same speed. If the value of any of the outputs is set to two, then a BaC agent has been detected and the resource collector will accelerate and move away from the BaC agent. Following Fig. 9., if the input value Enemy_Above for a resource collector is set to one, meaning a BaC agent has been detected above the resource collector, then the output value of Move_Down will be set to two resulting in the resource collector accelerating away from the BaC agent. If the input value Wall_Right is set to one then the output value Move_Left will be set to one to move the resource collector away from the wall. This example may appear simple but by supporting the ability for processing different multiple inputs, the resource collector can detect an enemy in different directions and detect walls. The resource collector can move in very complex directions, including arching curves. This capability is the same for the protector neural-based agent except for how it reacts to a BaC agent. If the protector detects a BaC agent, then it will accelerate toward it. For example, if the input value of Enemy_Up is set to one, then output value Move_Up will be set to two to accelerate the protector toward the BaC agent.

4.4 Training the neural networks

To obtain training data for the neural-based agents used in Defend and Gather, a similar approach that was taken in the PlayStation game Colin McRae 2.0 mentioned in Section 2 was implemented. In the game Colin McRae 2.0, human players were used to play as the opponent race car and their actions were recorded on given game states as exemplars in the training data. Based on this same approach, Defend and Gather also recorded data from humans playing the game. Training data was recorded by having humans play as the resource collector and the protector on the level two of the game Defend and Gather. Level two was chosen for play recording because both types of BaC agents, that is, hunters and patrollers, were present in this level. Essentially the inputs and outputs of the neural-based agents were recorded as the humans played the game and then the data was extracted to a file. Data was recorded at five times a second. For example, if a BaC agent or a wall was detected within the field of view of the neural-based agent while playing the game against a human, then, both the inputs of the human and agent would be recorded and logged in the output file. Table 2. shows a sample output as a human player moves down and to the left to move away from a wall to the right. The BaC agent is above the player.

Defend and Gather Sample Recording File							
Inputs: Detection of Walls and BaC agents within visibility range in game environment							
Wall Direction				BaC Direction			
ABOVE	BELOW	RIGHT	LEFT	ABOVE	BELOW	RIGHT	LEFT
0	0	1	0	1	0	0	0
Outputs: Player Movement Direction							
Acceleration Direction							
ABOVE		BELOW		RIGHT		LEFT	
0		2		1		0	

Table 2. Sample recording of player playing as the resource collector

To obtain enough training data, the humans played level two for several rounds, with each round consisting of ten games. Data was recorded for both wins and losses. Losses were included in the training set with the objective of making the neural-based agents behave in a more human-like manner and to allow them to adapt to a changing game environment. One problem with the recorded data was the large numbers of zeros in both the input and output. This was a result of the absence of a sensed percept that resulted in an action, that is, 'nothing' being detected and the player not taking any action. These large areas of zeros were parsed out of the data. After the parsing, the recorded data was then split into two parts. The first part, which consisted of seventy percent of the data, was used for training the neural networks. The remaining thirty percent was used to test the neural networks to see how well the neural-based agents learned from the training data.

There are many different ways to train a neural network but to speed the process MATLAB was used to train the two neural networks. Werbos' back-propagation algorithm was chosen to train the two neural networks (Haykin, 1999). Back-propagation was selected to train the neural networks because it is considered one of the hallmarks of training algorithms for traditional neural networks. After training the neural networks with MATLAB, the mean squared error was obtained for training the resource collectors and the protectors (7e-7 and 2e-9) as shown in Fig. 10. and Fig. 11., respectively. The two neural networks yielded an error rate of less than three percent over a training set size of 4000 separate entries. The protector converged much faster than the resource collector. This may be due to the fact that as the humans played the game in the role of the protectors, they acted more aggressively in chasing down the BaC agents, whereas in the role of the resource collectors, the human players had to act far more cautiously to avoid the BaC agents to find the resource points.

4.5 Evaluation

Evaluating the neural networks centered on the agents' abilities to play Defend and Gather well enough to cope with increasingly difficult game environments and more complex BaC agents. To determine how well the neural-based agents play Defend and Gather twenty games were completed on each of the four difficulty levels. The number of wins and losses were recorded for each of the games. The number of wins and losses for the neural-based agents are shown in Fig. 12. The last column in Fig. 12. shows the total number of wins over all four difficulty levels. Further analysis of the neural-based agents focused on how well the agents interacted with the game environments. These interactions included navigation around walls to find resource points and how well the agents found or avoided the BaC agents in the levels.

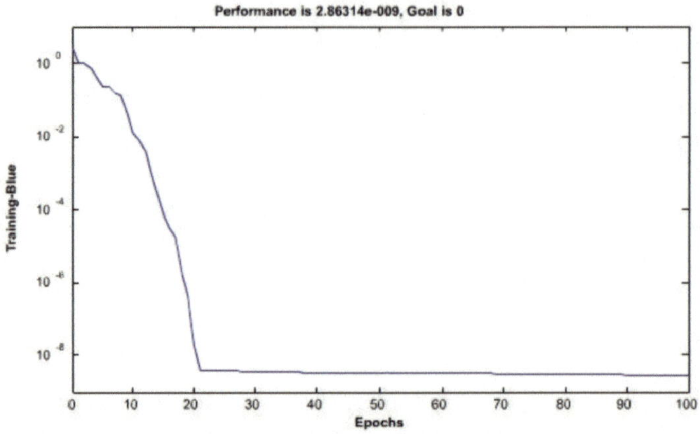

Fig. 10. Neural networks for the protector being trained in MATLAB

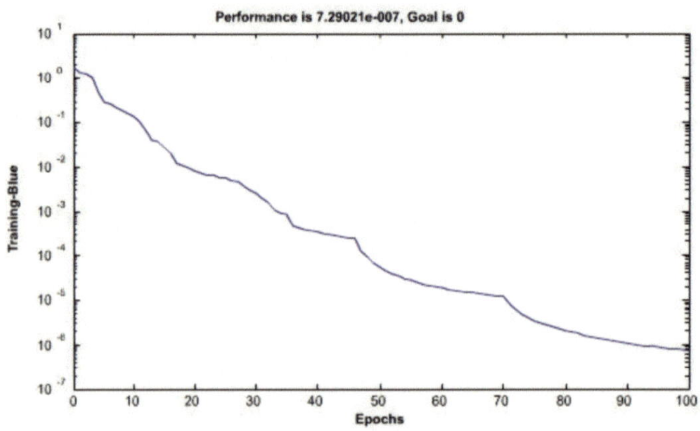

Fig. 11. Neural networks for the resource collector being trained in MATLAB

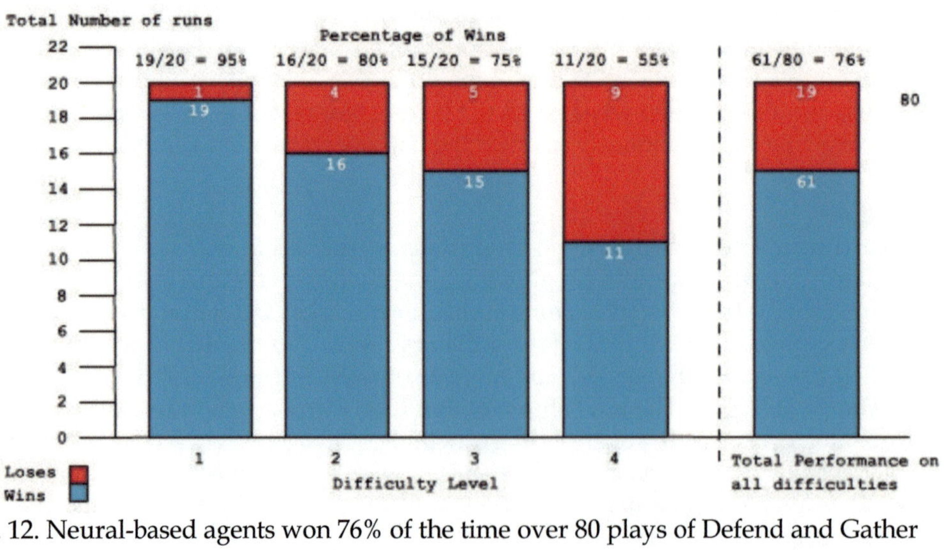

Fig. 12. Neural-based agents won 76% of the time over 80 plays of Defend and Gather

To ground the performance of the neural-based agents, a comparison is needed. While the humans played the game their resulting wins and losses were also recorded. Human players only won level two sixty percent of the time during the data recording. Human players were also asked to play other levels in the game and they won ninety five percent of the time on level one, thirty percent of the time for level three, and less than three percent for level four. The neural-based agents' performance was regarded as a success if they won more than seventy percent of the time for the total game. This benchmark was selected to ensure the agents performed better than the humans. The neural-based agents won seventy-five percent of all the games across the difficulties, thus exceeding our goal of seventy percent as shown in Fig. 12.

Next, observations were made of the neural-based agents' interactions with the game environments. In general, the neural-based agents were able to navigate the levels without too many problems. One problem scenario that consistently occurred was when a wall was placed directly between a resource point and the neural-based agent. The neural-based agents would sometimes stop at the wall and never attempt to navigate around the wall to the resource point. This scenario only happened about ten percent of the time, but it did contribute to losses incurred by the neural-based agents. The resource collectors did an excellent job of navigating around the BaC agents to find the resource points. The deaths of the resource collectors were generally the result of the agents accelerating too fast in one direction and running into the BaC agents because they could not change direction fast enough to avoid them. Other kills by the BaC agents involved trapping the resource collectors in a corner until they were destroyed. The protector also did an excellent job of hunting down the BaC agents to destroy them. Over half of the wins of the neural-based agent occurred because the protector was able to destroy all of the BaC agents in the game.

The neural-based agents were extremely effective at playing the game Defend and Gather. Their effectiveness of navigating the environment and interacting with the BaC agents led to winning over seventy percent of the games played. Even with the increasing difficulty, the neural-based agents were still able to win the game. On the most difficult level the neural-based agents were able to win half of the games, whereas the human players could only win three percent of the time.

4.6 Future work

As seen in Section 4.5, the neural-based agents designed for Defend and Gather learned to play the game quite effectively and they were able to win approximately seventy-six percent of the time. There is still opportunity for improvement in the capabilities of the neural-based agents. Various techniques could be applied to the agents to increase their performance. First, Defend and Gather used off-line learning so as the neural-based agents play the game they do not gain from their experience. The next step would be to include some form of on-line learning so that the neural-based agents can continue to learn while playing the game. Neural-based agents using on-line learning would be able to formulate better strategies during the game in real-time and over time rather than learning only once. This continuous learning may be particularly useful with dynamic obstacles and when other agents playing in the game are learning improving their performance over time through learning.

Only back-propagation was used for training in Defend and Gather. There are many other training techniques that could have also been used to increase performance. These various algorithms include genetic algorithms, dealing with mutations over time, simulated annealing, and various other methods. Different network architectures other than feed-forward networks could be implemented for future work. Architectures, such as recurrent networks, which facilitate bi-directional data flow, a self-organizing map, to remember the location of certain enemies and the topology of the game environment, stochastic networks, which introduce randomness, and finally a modular network made up of many kinds of neural networks have applicability in game design (Haykin, 1999). From these improvements alone, there are many possibilities that could be applied to Defend and Gather to improve performance of the neural-based agents.

5. Conclusions

It is clear from the implementation and analysis of the performance of the game Defend and Gather and the many other examples discussed in this chapter that neural-based agents have the ability to overcome some of the shortcomings associated with implementing classical AI techniques in computer game design. Neural networks can be used in many diverse ways in computer games ranging from agent control, environmental evolution, to content generation. As outlined in Section 3 of this chapter, by following the neural network development process, adding a neural network to a computer game can be a very rewarding process. Neural networks have proven themselves viable for agent design, but there are still many unexplored avenues that could prove to benefit from neural networks in computer games. The area of content generation has only briefly been discussed in recent research. The potential is that neural networks could generate entire worlds or even entire computer games based on human players' preferences. Neural networks have great potential for designing computer games and technology that will entertain players in terms of newly generated content and increasing challenge as the players learn the game.

6. References

Agogino, A.; Stanley, K. & Miikkulainen, R. (2000). On-line Interactive Neuro-evolution, *Neural Processing Letters*, Vol. 11, No. 1, (February 2000) (29-38), 1370-4612.

Baader, F.; Calvanese, D.; McGuinness, D.L.; Nardi, D. & Patel-Schneider, P.F. (2003). *The Description Logic Handbook: Theory, Implementation, Applications*, 0-521-78176-0, Cambridge University Press, Cambridge, UK

Barnes, J. & Hutchens, J. (2002). Testing Undefined Behavior as a Result of Learning, In: *AI Game Programming Wisdom*, Rabin, S., (Ed.), Charles River Media, 13: 978-1-58450-077-3, MA

Briggs, F. (2004). Realtime Evolution of Agent Controllers in Games, In: *Generation 5*, Accessed 2009, Available Online at: http://www.generation5.org/content/2004/realtimeevolutionagents.asp

De Sousa, B. (2002). *Game Programming All in One*, Premier Press, 13: 978-1-93184-123-8, OR

Dybsand, E. (2000). A Finite-State Machine Class, In: *Game Programming Gems*, Deloura, M., (Ed.), Charles River Media, 13: 978-1-58450-049-0, MA

Erol, K.; Hendler, J. & Nau. D. (1996). Complexity results for HTN planning. *Annals of Mathematics and Artificial Intelligence*, Vol. 19, No. 1, (1996) (pp. 69-93)

Fikes, R. & Nilsson, N. (1971). STRIPS: A new approach to the application of theorem proving to problem solving. *Artificial Intelligence*, Vol. 2, (1971) (pp. 189-208)

Garzon, M. H.; Drumwright, E. & Rajaya, K. (2002). Training a Neurocontrol for Talking Heads, *Proceedings of the International Joint Conference on Neural Networks*, pp. 2449-12453, Honolulu HI, May 2002, IEEE Press, Piscataway, NJ

Grand, S. & Cliff, D. (1998). Creatures: Entertainment Software Agents with Artificial Life, *Autononomus Agents and Multi-Agent Systems*, Vol. 1, No. 1, (1998) (pp. 39-57)

Hastings, E. J.; Gutha, R. K. & Stanley, K. O. (2007). NEAT Particles: Design, Representation, and Animation of Particle Systems Effects, *Proceedings of the IEEE Symposium on Computational Intelligence and Games*, pp. 154-160, Honolulu Hawaii, 2007, IEEE Press, Piscataway NJ

Haykin, S. (1999). *Neural Networks A Comprehensive Foundation*, 2nd ed., Prentice Hall, 13: 978-0-13273-350-2, NJ

Larid, J. & Lent, M. V. (2000). Human-Level AI's Killer Application: Interactive Computer Games, *Proceedings of the Seventeenth National Conference on Artificial Intelligence and Twelfth Conference on Innovative Applications of Artificial Intelligence*, pp. 1171-1178, 10: 0-262-51112-6, Austin Texas, August 2000, AAAI Press, Menlo Park, CA

Lioret, A. (2008). An Artifical Intelligence Nodes module inside Blender for expert modeling, texturing, animating, and rendering, *Proceedings of the Blender Conference*, Amsterdam Netherlands, October 2008.

Mathews, J. (2000). Colin McRea 2.0 (PlayStation), In: *Generation 5*, Accessed 2009, Available On-line at: http://www.generation5.org/content/2001/hannan.asp

Miikkulainen, R.; Bryant, B. D.; Cornelius, R.; Karpov, I. V.; Stanley, K. O. & Yong, C. H. (2006). Computational Intelligence in Games, In: *Computational Intelligence: Principles and Practice*, Yen, G. Y. & Fogel, D. B. (Ed.), (155-191), IEEE Computational Intelligence Society

Orkin, J. (2004). Symbolic Representation of Game World State: Toward Real-Time Planning in Games, *Proceedings of the AAAI Workshop on challenges in Game AI*, pp. 26-30, 13: 978-0-262-51183-4, San Jose, CA, July 2004, The MIT Press, Cambridge, MA

Orkin, J. (2005). Agent Architecture Considerations for Real-Time Planning in Games, *Proceedings of Artificial Intelligence and Interactive Digital Entertainment*, pp. 105-110, 13: 1-57735-235-1. Marina del Rey California, June 2005, AAI Press, Menlo Park, CA

Qualls, J.; Garzon, M. & Russomanno, D.J. (2007) "Neural-Based Agents Cooperate to Survive in the Defend and Gather Computer Game," *IEEE Congress on Evolutionary Computation*, IEEE Press, Singapore, pp. 1398-1402

Russel, S. & Norvig, P. (2003). *Artificial Intelligence a Modern Approach*, 2nd ed., Prentice Hall, 13: 978-0-13790-395-2, NJ

Schaefer, S. (2002). Tic-Tac-Toe (Naughts and Crosses, Cheese and Crackers, etc), In: *Mathematical Recreations*, Accessed 2007, Available On-line at: http://www.mathrec.org/old/2002jan/solutions.html

Stanley, K.; Bryant, B. D. & Miikkulainen, R. (2005a). Evolving Neural Network Agents in NERO Video Game, *Proceedings of the IEEE 2005 Symposium on Computational Intelligence and Games*, pp. 182-189, Essex UK, April 2005a, IEEE Press, Piscataway, NJ

Stanley, K. O.; Bryant, B. D.; Karpov. I. & Miikkulainen, R. (2005b). Real-Time Neroevolution in the NERO Video Game, *IEEE Transactions on Evolutionary Computation*, Vol. 9, No. 6, (December 2005b) (653-668), 1089-778X

Stanley, K. O.; Bryant, B. D.; Karpov. I. & Miikkulainen, R. (2006). Real-Time Evolution of Neural Networks in the NERO Video Game, *Proceedings of the Twenty-First National Conference on Artificial Intelligence*, pp. 1671-1674, Boston, MA, July 2006, AAAI Press, Menlo Park, CA

Watt, A. & Policarpo, F. (2001). *3-D Games Real-Time Rendering and Software Technology*, Addison-Wesley, 13: 978-0-20161-921-8, NY

Zarozinski, M. (2001). Imploding Combinatorial Explosion in a Fuzzy system, In: *Game Programming Gems 2*, Deloura, M., (Ed.), Charles River Media, 13: 978-1-58450-054-4, MA

22

Gravitational Singularities in Particle Swarms. Application to the Discovery of Gene Expression Patterns in DNA Microarrays.

Gerard Ramstein
Polytech'Nantes, University of Nantes
France

1. Introduction

Particle Swarm Optimization (PSO) is an evolutionary computation technique that exploits social intelligence found in bird flocking or fish schooling (Kennedy & Eberhart, 1995). The PSO algorithm generates potential solutions expressed as a particle swarm exploring the search space. Like genetic algorithms, a fitness function indicates the quality of the candidate solutions. The fitness function may have more than one optimum and some local optima may also interest the user. Many variants of PSO are capable of dealing with multimodal optimization problems. As many real world applications present several equivalent or nearby solutions, tools must be provided for the identification of multiple optima. Algorithms have been designed that either explore sequentially the search space or introduce a kind of parallelism. For instance, by analogy with bird swarms, niching strategies have been implemented.

In our model, called WPSO, particles are considered as celestial bodies, subject to the effect of gravity. A high density of particles causes the creation of a gravitational singularity called a wormhole. A particle falls into a wormhole if it crosses a boundary called the event horizon. It is then rejected into another region of space. Wormholes possess two interesting features. Firstly, a wormhole indicates a potential solution: the aggregation of particles around a particular spot reveals the existence of a local or optimal fitness value. Secondly, the presence of a wormhole avoids the premature convergence of the whole swarm since particles that are close to a previously explored region are redirected into another space region. A wormhole can then be seen as a mutation operator that dynamically preserves the diversity of the swarm.

The WPSO algorithm has been applied to the discovery of gene expression patterns in DNA microarrays. This new technology enables the simultaneous monitoring of the expression levels of thousands of genes in particular conditions (the effect of pathologies, drugs or stress, ...). Large-scale experiments can be carried out to observe the co-expression of genes in order to better understand the underlying biological processes. An expression pattern is an expression profile common to a set of genes, characterizing a cancer signature or a biological function such as immune response or programmed cell death. Since these patterns correspond generally to dense regions of the expression measurements, our method is particularly well adapted.

The rest of the paper is organized as follows. Section 2 discusses related work; Section 3 describes the principle of PSO; Section 4 is devoted to the presentation of WPSO and a study of its performances; Section 5 deals with the application of WPSO to microarray data analysis. Finally a conclusion and some perspectives are presented in Section 6.

2. Related work

Evolutionary algorithms have been successfully applied to solve multimodal optimization problems. The concept of speciation has been inspired from the observation of biological evolution. Different species are in competition with each other in territories containing finite resources. These species tend to occupy different environmental niches.

The Island model (Whitley et. al. 1998) is for instance a technique providing multiple subpopulations that helps to preserve genetic diversity. Niching methods have been incorporated in Genetic Algorithms to promote the formation and maintenance of subpopulations (Mahfoud 1995). Two kinds of approaches have been proposed: while parallel niching methods maintain several niches simultaneously, sequential niching methods apply iteratively a swarm on the search space to find multiple optima. Sequential Niching (Beasley et. al. 1993) is based on a derating function that operates on the fitness landscape at a position where a solution was found. Sharing (Goldberg 1987) is another mechanism for maintaining population diversity. The fitness of an individual is scaled by the number of similar individuals in order to penalize redundant solutions. This sharing function depends on the distance between individuals, which is a way to control the diversity of species. Deterministic Crowding (Mahfoud 1995) is a selection method that facilitates the formation of niches, these latter being maintained by an elitist scheme.

PSO algorithm can easily be extended to perform multimodal optimization. An intuitive adaptation consists in restricting the social cognition of a particle. In the SPSO algorithm (Li 2004), species are created dynamically at each iteration according to the location of the particles. A species is determined by a neighborhood, defined by a representative particle and a radius specified by the user. In the UPSO algorithm, introduced by (Parsopoulos and Vrahatis 2004), the evolution of the particle velocity is controlled by two terms related to a global and a local neighborhood. The PVPSO method proposed by (Schoeman & Engelbrecht 2005) uses vector operations to determine the particles belonging to a niche. More precisely, dot products indicate if a particle converges on the neighbourhood-best of a given niche. Another parallel niching technique has been proposed in (Brits.a et. al. 2002). The NbestPSO algorithm is based on neighborhood-best defined for each particle x_i as the center of the mass of the positions of all the particles in the topological neighborhood of x_i. Instead of a radius, the neighborhood is defined by the n closest particles of x_i. The same authors have implemented another niching algorithm, called NichePSO (Brits.b et. al. 2002). The initial swarm, called the main swarm, explores the search space using the cognition-only model (Kennedy 1997) allowing the particles to memorize their best position without exchanging any social information with their neighbors. Candidate solutions are identified by the convergence of the fitness of each particle. New sub-swarms are then created, characterized by a radius around the best particle in the sub-swarm. Sub-swarms can merge if they intersect and absorb particles from the main swarm when they cross the boundary of a sub-swarm. In (Özcan & Yılmaz 2007), the authors propose a modified version of NichePSO, called mNichePSO, that greatly improves the PSO performance by constraining the niche radius size to a predefined maximum value. The same work introduces a new algorithm called CSPSO based on a random walk and a hill climbing components. The hill climbing strategy consists in moving a particle to the position that generates a better fitness and the craziness component introduces random positions to further explore the space.

3. Particle swarm optimization

PSO is an algorithm inspired by the model of social learning that simulates the flocking behavior of birds and fish. A PSO is based on a population of interacting elements (particles). A swarm of particles explores an n-dimensional space; the location of a particle determines a potential solution. Each particle knows the most promising position (*pbest*) encountered so far, as well as the best location (*gbest*) found by its neighbors (for our needs, the neighborhood corresponds to the whole swarm). Particles adjust their flight according to their own experience but are also influenced by their peers. The displacement of a particle is defined by its current position and a velocity vector that is updated at each iteration of the algorithm.

The algorithm starts with a population composed of random particles. The location of each particle can be arbitrary defined by using a uniform random sequence but it has been shown that randomized low-discrepancy sequences better cover the search space and then improve the performances of PSO (Nguyen et. al. 2007). In our implementation, particle locations have been initialized by using Sobol quasi random sequences. In the following step of the algorithm, the fitness value is computed for each particle and *pbest* revised if necessary, as well as *gbest*. The velocity vector v_i at iteration $t + 1$ is determined as follows:

$$v_i\ (t+1) = w.\ v_i\ (t)+g_1.R_1.(pbest-x_i)+ g_2.R_2.(gbest-x_i) \tag{1}$$

where:

$$w = wmax-((wmax-wmin)/itermax).iter \tag{2}$$

In eq.1, g_1 and g_2 are weights associated to respectively the local (*pbest*) and global (*gbest*) terms, R_1 and R_2 are random values in $U(0,1)$ and x_i is the ith component of the location vector of the particle. The parameter w defined in eq.2 is a momentum coefficient that linearly decreases from $wmax$ to $wmin$. The maximal velocity of a particle must be limited. Therefore, if $v_i\ (t)$ is greater than $vmax$, it is set to this maximal value.

The next step of the algorithm consists in updating the location vector as follows:

$$x_i\ (t+1) = x_i\ (t)+ v_i\ (t+1) \tag{3}$$

The algorithm iterates until convergence is achieved or a maximal number of iterations is reached. The convergence of the swarm can be defined in different ways, a common approach being the convergence of the *gbest* particle. A common rule stipulates that its velocity must be quasi-null during a certain number of consecutive iterations.

4. Gravitational singularities and PSO

4.1 Description of the WPSO algorithm.

The WPSO algorithm proposed in this paper follows the same principles as those described previously, as long as the density of particles remains below a critical value. The convergence of many particles into a region causes the formation of a gravitational singularity, as it is the case when a massive star collapses. In our model, the agglomeration

of particles gives rise to the formation of a wormhole. An intra-universe wormhole is a hypothetical entity that connects two locations of the universe, offering a short cut through space and time. Particles approaching a wormhole are then instantaneously projected in another region (in our case a random location of the search space). This feature guarantees that a previously found solution is not reachable and it preserves the diversity of the swarm.
The algorithm works as summarized in Fig. 1. In the beginning, particles move in a uniform space as in the classical model. After a certain time, a high density of particles gives birth to a wormhole. At this stage, the wormhole is not entirely formed. The group of particles (called W) that have created the wormhole are separated from the rest of the main swarm. This group goes across the space until convergence, as if its particles are the only individuals in the search space. When W converges, the wormhole is mature and remains in a constant location, determined by the position of the best particle in W at convergence. Particles belonging to W are then released and redirected in a random location and restored to the swarm; a new cycle can then be performed.

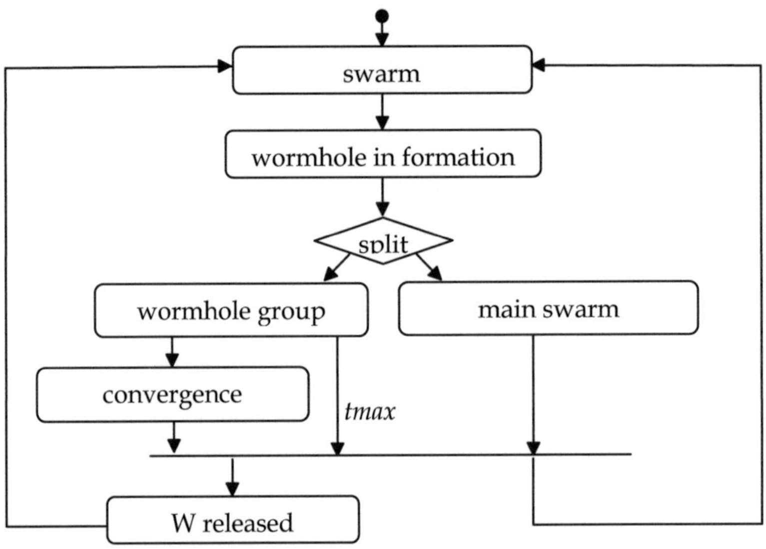

Fig. 1. Gravitational PSO algorithm

The wormhole is defined by its event horizon, that is the gravity field where the space-time is so bent that nothing can escape from it. In our case, the event horizon is the region where particles vanish. Our implementation determines this boundary by a radius around the best particle belonging to W. This radius remains constant from the birth to the mature stage of the wormhole; only the center of the wormhole moves during its formation.
We need also to specify the critical point that causes the formation of the wormhole. As already stated, the birth of a wormhole is due to a high density of particles. One could compute the density of every particle by examining its neighborhood. A less computationally expensive strategy consists in only considering the best particle at a given time. The density is then defined as the number of particles *nw* around *gbest*, its neighbourhood being defined by a constant radius. The value of the radius is the same as the one characterizing the event horizon. Our algorithm then possesses two input parameters: *r*, the radius of the event horizon; *nw*, the number of particles for the formation of a wormhole.

The formation of a gravitational singularity induces two types of particles: those at the origin of the wormhole and the rest of the swarm. The former group searches the refined location of an optimum. As one expects this group to converge in a short period of time, it is necessary to decrease the inertia of the particles. For that purpose, we consider that the particles evolve in different times; the lifetime of the group W corresponds to the maximal period of time *tmax* authorized for the maturity of a wormhole. The inertia of these particles is given by :

$$w = wmax - (wmax - wmin)*(tc/tmax) \quad (4)$$

where *tc* is the time elapsed since the formation of W ($tc \leq tmax$ by construction). This formula replaces Eq. 2 for the particles in W; the main swarm possesses a constant inertia fixed to *wmax*.

The convergence of W group is determined by the velocity of its best particle. When the velocity is less than a given threshold $\varepsilon = 10^{-5}$, we consider that the location is stable and the wormhole mature. Note that any particle can be trapped by already-formed wormholes. A group W can then be dispersed and may be eventually unable to converge after a period of *tmax* trials. In that case, the wormhole is not confirmed and a new cycle of search is performed. Another possibility has to be considered: the W group converges at the edge of a wormhole already constituted. This phenomenon can be observed when the event horizon is too small, causing particles to be repeatedly attracted by the wormhole. A solution could be to increase the radius *r* of the event horizon as long as this situation is encountered, but this has several drawbacks, it is notably time consuming and based on a false assumption: the basin of attraction is not necessary spherical. A better approach consists in merging a wormhole adjacent to a previously found wormhole. All one has to do is to keep the rejection power of the merged wormhole without considering that it corresponds to an actual optimum. A new mature wormhole is merged to a previously found wormhole if the distance between their centers is less than 1.20x*r*.

4.2 Experimental results.

Six well-known benchmark functions have been used for comparison sake. These two-dimensional functions presenting multiple global and local optima are described in Table 1.

Label	Function	Range	Global	Local
f1	$z = (x^2+y-11)^2 - (x+y^2-7)^2$	-10,+10	4	0
f2	$z = \sin(2.2\pi x+\pi/2)(2-\lvert y\rvert/2)(3-\lvert x\rvert/2) + \sin(2.2\pi y^2+\pi/2)(2-\lvert y\rvert/2)(2-\lvert x\rvert/2)$	-2,+2	4	8
f3	$z = \cos(x)^2+\sin(y)^2$	-4,+4	6	0
f4	$z = ((\cos(2x+1)+2\cos(3x+2)+3\cos(4x+3)+4\cos(5x+4)+5\cos(6x+5))(\cos(2y+1)+2\cos(3y+2)+3\cos(4y+3)+4\cos(5y+4)+5\cos(6y+5))$	-2.0,+2.5	2	38
f5	$z = (y^2-4.5y^2)xy-4.7\cos(3x-y^2(2+x))\sin(2.5\pi x) + (0.3x)^2$	-1.2,+1.2	1	9
f6	$z = 4x^2-2.1x^4+(1/3)x^6+xy-4y^2+4y^4$	-1.9,+1.9	2	4

Table 1. Bidimensional functions. The range limits the values of *x* and *y* coordinates. The two last columns respectively represent the number of global and local optima.

In (Özcan & Yılmaz 2007), these functions have been used to test the performances of the PSO algorithms presented in section 2: SPSO, NichePSO, mNichePSO, NbestPSO, UPSO, PVPSO) and CPSO. The same parameters and evaluation metrics have been taken into consideration for comparison purpose with WPSO.
The input parameters common to all the algorithms are given in Table 2. The additional parameters of WPSO are given in Table 3.

swarm size	50
number of iterations	25,000
wmin	0.6
wmax	0.8
g1	1.5
g2	1.5
vmax	range_size/20

Table 2. Input parameters. The parameter range_size is the size of the search space (e.g. for function F1, range_size = 20).

r	range_size/8
nw	15
tmax	500

Table 3. Input parameters specific to WPSO.

The measure proposed in (Özcan and Yılmaz 2007) has been retained for the estimation of performances: the overall success rate *osr* is given by:

$$osr = (gpr+gscr+lpr+lscr)/4 \tag{4}$$

where *gpr* is the global peak ratio, i.e. the ratio of the average number of global optima found to the total number of global optima. The local peak ratio lpr is a comparable measure applied to local optima. The global success consistency ratio *gscr* is the proportion of the runs in which all global optima are discovered to the total number of runs. The version dedicated to local optima is called *lscr*.
Table 4 shows the performance results observed for the functions of Table 2. CPSO and mNichePSO efficiently locate global optima in absence of local optima (functions f1 and f3). These two algorithms also respectively achieve the second and third best average performances, preceded by WPSO. Our algorithm performs well in functions presenting many local optima (functions f2, f4 and f5). It seems surprising that it is not always capable of finding all the optima of simpler functions, such as f1, but this is due to the restriction of the performance test requiring to set the same input parameters for all the functions. The experiments reveal that the most sensible parameter of WPSO is the radius denoting the event horizon. This may explain the weakness of some results, even if the merging of wormholes tends to minimize this effect.

PSO algorithm	f1	f2	f3	f4	f5	f6	avr.*osr.*	stdev.
SPSO	0.95	0.48	0.72	0.27	0.64	0.82	0.65	0.24
NichePSO	0.19	0.21	0.45	0.13	0.66	0.45	0.38	0.21
NbestPSO	0.90	0.43	0.74	0.31	0.46	0.58	0.57	0.22
CPSO	**1.00**	0.66	**1.00**	0.52	0.63	0.62	0.74	0.21
UPSO	0.88	0.54	0.55	0.48	0.45	0.54	0.57	0.16
mNichePSO	**1.00**	0.66	0.99	0.14	0.47	**0.91**	0.70	0.34
PVPSO	0.21	0.38	0.46	0.20	0.35	0.71	0.42	0.20
WPSO	0.98	**0.92**	0.99	**0.58**	**0.84**	0.62	**0.82**	0.18

Table 4. Average and standard deviation of *oscr* over 50 runs. Bold entries correspond to the best performance of the corresponding PSO algorithms.

5. Application to the analysis of DNA microarrays.

5.1 PSO for the extraction of gene expression patterns.

DNA microarrays allow to monitor the expression level of thousands of genes in a single experiment. They provide a better understanding of how cells work and respond to different stimuli. For instance, this technology is being applied to early diagnosis of cancer (Ochs & Godwin 2003) or drug discovery (Debouck & Goodfellow 1999). A common microarray data mining application consists in the analysis of the co-expression of genes. The underlying idea is that genes respecting a certain common expression pattern may be co-regulated. The identification of these patterns or signatures can help biologists to infer regulatory modules or biological functions (Yeung 2004). Generally, as microarray experiments focus on a particular disease or on the effect of a particular drug, only a low fraction of genes reveals a significant expression profile, related to the observed phenomenon. Therefore, we need to extract the most relevant signatures among many sets of poorly co-expressed genes. This task can then be seen as a multimodal optimization problem where the fitness is associated to the quality of the extracted signatures. In our application, a pattern is defined by an expression profile (i.e. a set of expression levels) and its neighborhood, that is the n closest profiles to the pattern according to the Euclidian distance. The parameter n is an input-specified value which determines the minimal number of genes constituting a signature. The fitness is defined as the mean distance of these n genes to their pattern. The signatures may be useful for further analyses; from a practical point of view, the set of genes can be easily extended to a larger neighbourhood by specifying a radius around the pattern, or to the contrary, the pattern can be discarded if its fitness is below a specified minimal value.

The WPSO algorithm described in the previous section has been adapted to the analysis of DNA microarrays. The rule leading to the merging of two wormholes has been refined. Experiments have revealed that the distance between two pattern profiles is not an optimal criterion to determinate if two signatures are similar. A more precise indicator consists in the estimation of the likelihood of this situation. The corresponding hypothesis assumes that the members of both signatures are actually issued from the same distribution. We use the Bayesian Information Criterion (BIC) to accept or reject a wormhole on this basis. The BIC (Schartz 1978) is associated to the maximization of a log likelihood function and is capable of estimating the best model. The BIC formula used in the PSO is described in (Pelleg & Moore 2000).

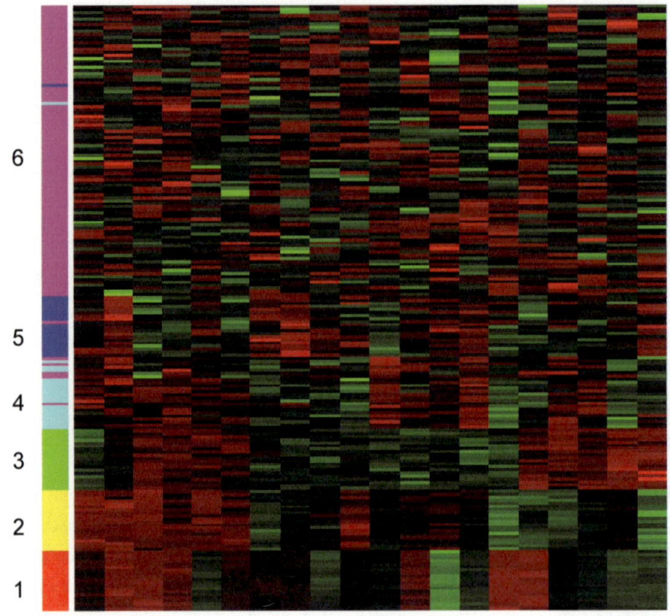

Fig. 2. Synthetic expression matrix

This figure shows a heat map graphical representation of the expression matrix. Data have been ordered in rows and columns using a hierarchical clustering, using the Euclidean distance and the ward method (dendrogram not showed). Rows correspond to genes and columns to samples (i.e. a microarray experiment). The conventional color palette shows under-expressed values in green, normal values in black and over-expressed value in red. The left bar indicates from which class each gene is issued ($\sigma(1)=0.1$, $\sigma(2)=0.2$, $\sigma(3)=0.3$, $\sigma(4)=0.4$, $\sigma(5)=0.5$, $\sigma(6)=1$). Note that the dense signatures ($\sigma=0.1$ to $\sigma=0.3$) are correctly aggregated in the figure, but the last two patterns have been aggregated with genes issued from the noise pattern.

5.2 Experiments on synthetic data.

To study the efficiency of the PSO, synthetic patterns have been generated. The creation of the expression matrix is based on the generation of five signatures. First, a pattern profile is randomly generated, using a uniform distribution in the range [-1,+1]. Second, 20 members of the pattern are generated: for each point of the profile, the gene expression value is expressed as the corresponding expression value of the pattern, perturbed by a Gaussian noise having a null mean and a standard deviation of σ. The homogeneity of the five gene sets are given by σ; the selected values are respectively (0.1, 0.2, 0.3, 0.4, 0.5). A random noise is added to the expression matrix, defined by a pattern having only null expression values and a strong standard deviation ($\sigma=1$). A fraction f of the genes belonging to this noise pattern has been added to make the extraction process more complex and realistic. For instance, a fraction f of 5% corresponds to five patterns of 20 genes and a noise pattern of 1,900 genes (that is a matrix comprising 2,000 genes). Fig. 2 shows an example of synthetic expression matrix with f=50%. One can observe that the five patterns cover a wide range of clusters, from the very homogeneous to the uncorrelated ones. For our experiments, four different fractions f of noise gene sets have been tested: 50%, 25%, 10%, 5%.

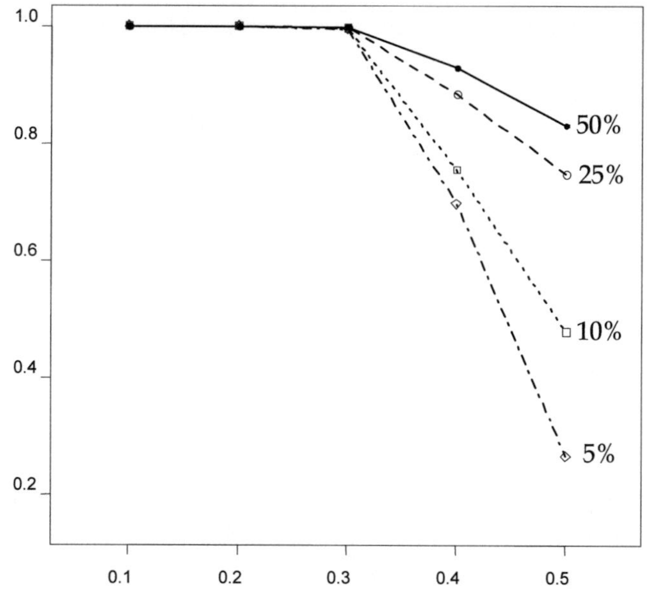

Fig. 3. Performance evaluation.

The four lines correspond to the mean value of the performance measure, expressed for five values of σ (indicated in abscise). Each line is relative to a different fraction *f*.

The same input parameters as for the previous experiments have been used, except for the event horizon radius (set to 10) and the dimension of the search space. Gene profiles have been normalized (mean set to zero and variance to one). This pre-processing reduces the variation of measurements between genes, and limits the search space to a uniform range set to [-3,+3].

The performance test identifies the patterns given by the WPSO: the 20th closest genes to each pattern of the matrix are extracted and compared to the actual list of genes generated for the creation of the matrix. The performance measure is the similarity of these two sets, expressed as the ratio of two cardinals: the intersection over the union. 50 random matrices have been produced for each of the four matrix sizes. The results are summarized in Fig. 3. One can observe that the PSO algorithm perfectly identifies strong signatures (σ=0.1 to σ=0.3), independently of the matrix size. The most heterogeneous patterns (σ=0.4 to σ=0.5) are more problematic and sensible to the matrix size. These are limit cases where the probability of finding a neighbor issued from the noise pattern is not negligible. As shown in the example of Fig. 2, the corresponding clusters are indeed not correctly discriminated by the hierarchical clustering algorithm. It is thus not surprising that the increase of the number of noisy genes decreases the performance measure.

5.2 Experiments on real data.

The WPSO algorithm has been applied to a well-known study (Ross et. al. 2000), which particularly illustrates the power of microarray analysis. This remarkable work explores the variation of expression of 8,000 genes among 60 cell lines derived from human tumors. The dataset then presents a vast potential of expression patterns, due to the variety of the observed phenotypes. In a similar manner as that proposed in the original paper, the set of genes has been filtered to remove the genes that do not show a significant variation of expression among the cell lines. After this pre-processing, a set of 1,200 genes has been retained and normalized like in the previous section. The same algorithm has also been applied.

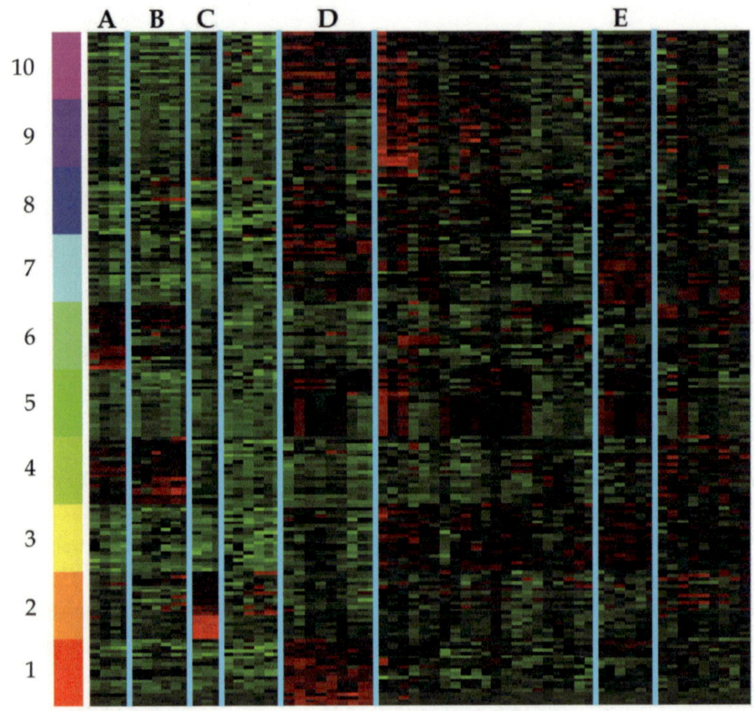

Fig. 4. Signatures obtained from the WPSO algorithm (same convention as in Fig. 2).

Fig. 4 shows the resulting expression patterns. An interesting feature of these signatures is that they are related to sub-sets of cell lines specific to certain tissue origins. The blue lines indicate the most remarkable observations: for instance, columns labeled A (resp. B, C, D, E) are notably differentially expressed in the 6th (resp. 4th, 2nd, 1st, 5th) signature and specific to samples belonging to breast (resp. colon, leukaemia, melanoma, renal) tumors.

The overall average silhouette width (*oasw*) is a measure expressing the tightness and the separation of a clustering (Rousseeuw 1987). The *oasw* of the ten extracted signatures is equal to 0.25. A positive value denotes a correct partition, the maximal theoretical value being 1. To assess the relevance of this result, different sets of ten signatures have been generated. Firstly, a clustering of the data into k clusters has been performed using the kmeans algorithm. The value of k has been issued from a uniform random value between 10 and 40. Secondly, a subset of 10 clusters has been randomly selected and for each cluster, a signature has been completed using the 20 closest data around the centroid. For 10,000 random trials, the mean score of *oasw* was 0.15 (s.d. 0.04) and the best score was *oasw* =0.24 (with k=13). This result demonstrates that WPSO discovers signature sets with remarkable high cohesion.

6. Conclusion

An original PSO algorithm called WPSO has been proposed, inspired from the concept of gravitational singularity. The convergence of particles generates a wormhole whose action is twofold: during its formation, it searches the best location of an optima; in a mature phase, it rejects particles to other regions of the search space. Experiments reveal that this algorithm provides efficient results on benchmark functions. A bioinformatics application has been implemented to extract signatures of co-expressed genes from microarray data. On a real experiment, the discovered patterns are tight, well separated and related to known phenotypes. As the size of event horizon determines the efficiency of the WPSO algorithm, a major improvement would consist in an automatic adaptation of this parameter according to the shape of the fitness function. A potential indicator for this optimization could be the frequency of particles absorbed by a wormhole.

7. References

Beasley, D.; Bull, D.R.; Martin, R.R. (1993). A Sequential Niching Technique for Multimodal Function Optimization, *Evolutionary Computation,* 1(2), p 101-125, MIT Press. ISSN 0302-9743.

Brits, R.; Engelbrecht, A.P.; van den Bergh, F. (2002). Solving Systems of Unconstrained Equations using Particle Swarm Optimization, in *Proceedings of the Int. Conf. on Sys.,Man and Cyber.*, vol. 3, p. 6, Piscataway, NJ , ISBN 0-7803-7437-1, Hammamet, Tunisia.

Brits, R.; Engelbrecht, A.P.; van den Bergh, F. (2002). A niching particle swarm optimizer, in *Proceedings of the 4th Asia-Pacific Conf. on Simulated Evolution and Learning*, vol. 2, pp. 692-696, Singapur.

Debouck, C.; Goodfellow, P. N. (1999). DNA microarrays in drug discovery and development, *Nat. Genet.*, vol. 21, pp 48—50, January.

Goldberg, D.E.; Richardson, J. (1987) Genetic Algorithm with Sharing for Multimodal Function Optimization, in *Proceedings of the Second International Conference on Genetic Algorithms*, p 41-49, Cambridge, Massachusetts, United States .

Kennedy, J.; Eberhart, R. (1995). Particle swarm optimization, in *Proceedings of the IEEE Int. Conf. on Neural Networks*, pp. 1942–1948, Piscataway, NJ.

Kennedy, J. (1997). The particle swarm: Social adaptation of knowledge, in *Proceedings of the International Conference on Evolutionary Computation*, p 303–308. IEEE Service Center, Piscataway, NJ.

Li, X. (2004). Adaptively Choosing Neighborhood Bests using Species in a Particle Swarm Optimizer for Multimodal Function Optimization, in *Proceedings of GECCO 2004*, pp. 105-116, LNCS 3102, eds. Deb, K. et al., Springer-Verlag, Seattle, USA.

Mahfoud, S. (1995). Niching Methods for Genetic Algorithms. *PhD thesis*, University of Illinois at Urbana Champaign, intern. report 95001.

Nguyen, Q. U.; Nguyen, X. H.; McKay, R. I.; Tuan, P. M. (2007). Initialising PSO with randomised low-discrepancy sequences: the comparative results, in *IEEE Congress on Evolutionary Computation*, pp 1985-1992, 25-28 September, Singapore.

Ochs, M. F.; Godwin, A. K. (2003). Microarrays in cancer: research and applications, BioTechniques,Vol. suppl., pp 4--15, March.

Özcan, E.; Yılmaz, M. (2007). Particle Swarms for Multimodal Optimization. *Proceedings of the 8th international Conference on Adaptive and Natural Computing Algorithms*, Eds. Lecture Notes In Computer Science, vol. 4431. Springer-Verlag, Berlin, Heidelberg, pp 366-375, Warsaw, Poland, April 11 - 14. ISSN 0302-9743.

Parsopoulos, K. E.; Vrahatis, M. N. (2004). UPSO: A Unified Particle Swarm Optimization Scheme, Lecture Series on Comp. and Computational Sci., Vol. 1, *Proceedings of the Int. Conf. of Computational Methods in Sci. and Eng.*, Vouliagmeni-Kavouri, Greece, pp. 868-873.

Pelleg, D. Moore, A. (2000). X-means: Extending K-means with efficient estimation of the number of clusters, in *Proceedings of the 17th International Conf. on Machine Learning*, pp 727--734. ISBN 1-55860-707-2.

Ross, D. T.; Scherf, U.; Eisen, M. B.; Perou, C. M.; Rees, C.; Spellman, P.; Iyer, V.; Jeffrey, S. S.; Van de Rijn, M.; Waltham, M.; Pergamenschikov, A.; Lee, J. C.; Lashkari, D.; Shalon, D.; Myers, T. G.; Weinstein, J. N.; Botstein, D.; Brown, P. O. (2000). Systematic variation in gene expression patterns in human cancer cell lines. Nat Genet ,march,vol. 24(3), pp 227--235, ISSN 1061-4036.

Rousseeuw, P. (1987). Silhouettes: a graphical aid to the interpretation and validation of cluster analysis. *J. Comput. Appl. Math.* No 1, vol. 20, no 1, pp, 53-65. Elsevier Science Publishers B. ISSN 0377-0427.

Schoeman, I.L.; Engelbrecht, A.P. (2005). A Parallel Vector-Based Particle Swarm Optimizer, *Proceedings of the International Conf. on Neural Networks and Genetic Algorithms*, pp. 268-271. ISBN 978-3-211-24934-5

Schwarz, G. (1978). Estimating the Dimension of a Model, *The Annals of Statistics*, vol. 6, no 2, pp 461--464, ISSN 0090-5364.

Whitley, D.; Rana, S.; Heckendorn, R.B. (1998). The Island Model Genetic Algorithm: On Separability, Population Size and Convergence, *Journal of Computing and Information Technology*, vol. 7, pp. 33—47.

Yeung, K.; Medvedovic, M.; Bumgarner, R. (2004). From co-expression to co-regulation: how many microarray experiments do we need?, *Genome Biology*, vol. 5, no 7:R48, ISSN 1465-6906.

Adaptive Formation of Pareto Front in Evolutionary Multi-objective Optimization

Özer Ciftcioglu and Michael S. Bittermann
Delft University of Technology
The Netherlands

1. Introduction

Optimization is an important concept in science and engineering. Traditionally, methods are developed for unconstrained and constrained single objective optimization tasks. However, with the increasing complexity of optimization problems in the modern technological real world problems, multi-objective optimization algorithms are needed and being developed. With the advent of evolutionary algorithms in the last decades, multi-objective evolutionary algorithms (MOEAs) are extensively being investigated for solving associated optimization problems, e.g. (Deb et al., 2000, Zitzler & Thiele, 1999, Yao et al., 1999, Eiben et al., 1999). An updated survey of Ga-based MOEAs is given by (Coello, 1999). Evolutionary algorithms are particularly suitable for this, since they evolve simultaneously a population of potential solutions. These solutions are investigated in non-dominated solution space so that the optimized solutions in a multi-objective functions space form a front which is known as Pareto surface or front. Obtaining this simultaneous solution front in a single run is an appealing property that it is the incentive for a fast growing interest on MOEAs in the last decade. Although Pareto front is an important concept, its formation is not straightforward since the strict search of non-dominated regions in the multi-objective solution space prematurely excludes some of the potential solutions that results in an aggregated solutions in this very space. This means Pareto surface is not fully developed and the diversity of the solutions on the Pareto front is not fully exercised. Conventionally, non-dominated solutions with many objectives are usually low in number making the selection pressure toward the Pareto front also low, with aggregated solutions in the Pareto dominance-based MOEA algorithms (Sato, 2007). The purpose of this research is to investigate this issue and provide effective solutions with fast convergence together with diversity of solutions is maintained on the Pareto front. This goal has already attracted attention in the literature (Laumanns et al., 2002). This work addresses this issue with a novel concept of adaptive formation of Pareto front. This is demonstrated with an application from the domain of architectural design. The method is based on relaxed dominance domains, which basically refer to a degree of relaxation of the dominance in the terminology of MOEAs. In this book-chapter contribution, the relaxed dominance concept is explicitly described and applied. The organisation of this chapter is as follows. Section two describes the relaxed dominance concept. Section three describes the adaptive formation of Pareto front in a design application. This is followed by the conclusions in section four.

2. Design computation subject to multiobjective optimization

Multi-objective optimization deals with optimization where several objectives are involved. These objectives are conflicting or in competition among themselves. For a single objective case there are traditionally many algorithms in continuous search space, where gradient-based algorithms are most suitable in many instances. In discrete search spaces, in the last decade evolutionary algorithms are ubiquitously used for optimization, where genetic algorithms (GA) are predominantly applied. However, in many real engineering or design problems, more than two objectives need to be optimized simultaneously. To deal with multi-objectivity it is not difficult to realize that evolutionary algorithms are effective in defining the search direction. Basically, in a multi-objective case the search direction is not one but may be many, so that during the search a single preferred direction cannot be identified. In this case a population of candidate solutions can easily hint about the desired directions of the search and let the candidate solutions during the search process be more probable for the ultimate goal. Next to the principles of GA optimization, in MO algorithms, in many cases the use of Pareto ranking is a fundamental selection method. Its effectiveness is clearly demonstrated for a moderate number of objectives, which are subject to optimization simultaneously (Deb, 2001). Pareto ranking refers to a solution surface in a multidimensional solution space formed by multiple criteria representing the objectives. On this surface, the solutions are diverse but they are assumed to be equivalently valid. The eventual selection of one of the solutions among those many is based on some so-called higher order preferences, which require more insight into the problem at hand. This is necessary in order to make more refined decisions before selecting any solution represented along the Pareto surface.

In solving multi-objective optimization, the effectiveness of evolutionary algorithms has been well established. For this purpose there are quite a few algorithms which are running quite well especially with low dimensionality of the multidimensional space (Coello et al., 2003). However, with the increase of the number of objective functions, i.e. with high dimensionality, the effectiveness of the evolutionary algorithms is hampered. One measure of effectiveness is the expansion of Pareto front where the solution diversity is a desired property. For this purpose, the search space is exhaustively examined with some methods, e.g. *niched Pareto ranking*, e.g. (Horn et al., 1994). However these algorithms are rather involved so that the search needs extensive computer time for a satisfactory solution in terms of a Pareto front. Because of this extensive time requirement, distributed computing of Pareto-optimal solutions is proposed (Deb et al., 2003), where multiple processors are needed. They basically share the computational task with cooperation among each other, making the task scalable (Hughes, 2005, Jaszkiewicz, 2004).

The issue of solution diversity and effective solution for multi-objective optimization problem described above is especially the due to elimination of many acceptable solutions during the evolutionary computation process, in case orthogonal standard Pareto dominance is used. This is a kind of Greedy algorithm which considers the solutions at the search area delimited by orthogonal axes of the multidimensional space. To increase the pressure pushing the Pareto surface towards to the maximally attainable solution point is the main problem and relaxation of the orthogonality with a systematic approach is needed. By such a method next to non-dominated solutions also some dominated solutions are considered at each generation. Such dominated solutions can be potentially favourable solutions in the present generation, so that they can give birth to non-dominated solution in the following generation. Although, some relaxation of the dominance is addressed in literature (Branke et al., 2000, Deb et al., 2006), in a multidimensional space, to identify the size of relaxation corresponding to a volume is not explicitly determined. In such a volume next to non-dominated solutions, dominated but potentially favourable solutions, as described above, lie. To determine this volume optimally as to the circumstantial conditions of the search process is a major and a challenging task. The solution for this task is essentially due to the mathematical treatment of the problem where the volume in question is identified adaptively during the search that it yields a measured pressure to the Pareto front toward to the desired direction, at each generation. In the adaptive process reported in this work, the volume is determined by genetic search for each member of the population. The process is adaptive, because the Pareto front is converged progressively in the course of consecutive generations, where the rate of convergence is determined with volume size, which is subject to appropriate change at each generation. In non-adaptive case, the Pareto front is also converged progressively; however the rate of convergence, in contrast to the adaptive case, is monotonically exhausted. The adaptation is explained shortly afterwards below via contour lines in the objective-functions space. Here the volume with dominated solutions is termed as *relaxed dominance region* and this novel concept is *preliminarily* introduced before (Ciftcioglu & Bittermann, 2008) for a non-adaptive case.

Some important features of the latest generation MOEAs address the selection of the potential solutions during the optimization process, and diversity-preserving strategies in objective space. Next to the principles of GA optimization, in MO algorithms, in many cases the use of Pareto ranking is a fundamental selection method. Its effectiveness is demonstrated for a moderate number of objectives, which are subject to optimization simultaneously. With respect to the conflicting objectives in a MO optimization, one has to deal with the criteria as measures of the conflicts. The increased satisfaction of one criterion implies loss with respect to satisfaction of another criterion. Regarding to this, the formation of the Pareto front is based on some newly defined objective functions of the weighted N objectives $f_1, f_2, \ldots, f_N$ which are of the form

$$F_i(\boldsymbol{x}) = f_i(\boldsymbol{x}) + \sum_{j=1, j\neq i}^{j=N} a_{ji} f_j(\boldsymbol{x}), i = 1, 2, \ldots, N \tag{1}$$

where $F_i(x)$ are the new objective functions; a_{ji} is the designated amount of gain in the j-th objective function for a loss of one unit in the i-th objective function. Therefore the sign of a_{ji} is always negative. The above set of equations requires fixing the matrix $\boldsymbol{a}$. This matrix has all ones in its diagonal elements. To find the Pareto front of a maximization problem we assume that a solution parameter vector x_1 dominates another solution x_2 if $F(x_1) \geq F(x_2)$ for all objectives. At the same time a contingent equality is not valid for at least one objective. $F_i(x)$ functions define the contour lines, which form a convex hull with the coordinate axes. This is illustrated in figure 1. In the case a_{ji} becomes zero then the contour lines are horizontal and vertical and $F_i(x)=f_i(x)$. Explicitly, figure 1 shows the contour lines corresponding to two linear functions for a two-objective MO case. In this case the objectives are in particular subject to maximization. From the figure it is important to note that the point P is ultimately

$$\begin{aligned} F_1(\boldsymbol{x}) &= f_1(\boldsymbol{x}) \\ F_2(\boldsymbol{x}) &= f_2(\boldsymbol{x}) \end{aligned} \; . \tag{2}$$

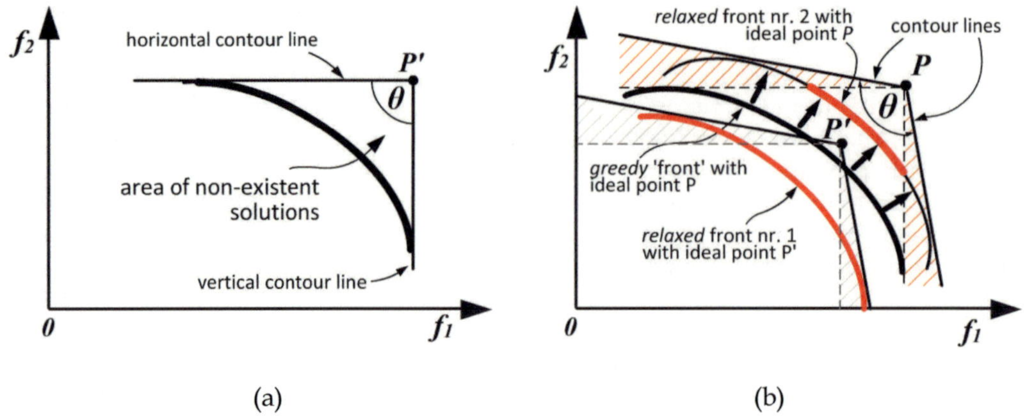

Fig. 1. Contour lines defining the dominated region via a reference point P (a); domains of relaxation that are hatched (b)

subject to identification as an ideal solution. The point P can be sought by means of appropriate methodologies one of which is the method of genetic algorithm applied in this approach. For the search process itself, different strategies can be followed. Below, two strategies are described for the sake of providing insight into the search process of the multi objective optimization approach applied in this work.

In one strategy the point P denotes the explicit ultimately attainable goal defined by the boundaries of the objective functions. The premise of the strategy is that beyond this point the solution is not acceptable or meaningless due to the limits of the objective functions.

The algorithm using the orthogonal lines is called *greedy* MO algorithm. The modification of the contour lines departing from horizontal and vertical ones defines a modified solution space. This is shown in figure 1b by hatched areas. These areas are termed as domain of relaxation in this work. Solutions found in these areas are not valid Pareto solutions, although they seemingly are solutions. For this modified solution space the area of non-existent solutions in the convex hull is diminished. This is at the expense of deviating from the strict non-dominated solution condition as shown in figure 1a. From figure 1b it should be noted that in case the strict non-domination condition is relaxed the Pareto front is smaller compared to the case of greedy search in figure 1a. However, this might be compensated by moving the Pareto surface forward more with pressure, so that the front comes closer to the point P. This strategy in the parameter space allows selection of the parameters in such a way that the relaxation domains in the objective functions space come to existence.

Figure 1b and its reference point serve as a conceptual explanation of the Pareto-optimality in order to point-out the 'trade-off' inherent to the relaxed dominance compared to the greedy dominance concept. Namely, with reference to the point P, by making the angle θ larger than 90 degrees the area of non-existent solutions is reduced compared to the greedy case. Therefore the Pareto front is allowed to establish closer to the reference point P, while at the same time the front is expected to be more diverse. In figure 1b it is seen how the greedy front comes closer to the point P through the widening of the angle θ. This is indicated by means of arrows. In the relaxed approach, the avoidance of aggregation to some extend is due to the distortion of the objective space, where the space becomes larger, and thus the density of solutions per unit length along the front is expected to become lower.

In a second strategy a hypothetical point designated as P′ denotes the explicit predefined sub-attainable goal. This goal is positioned somewhere in the convex hull defined via *P*, and is hopefully not far from the point *P*. This is shown in figure 2. It is to note that, since the point P is not explicitly known, the position assessment of the point P′ is a problematic issue. In any case P′ is a sub-optimal point implying some form of relaxation in the search process. In this case, the premise of the strategy is that the increased size of the area of non-existent solutions for orthogonal search domains is compensated with the increase of the size of the Pareto front in the relaxed case. At the same time the area of non-existent solutions is reduced for relaxed search domains. This is seen from the figure 2, where Pareto fronts having orthogonal and non-orthogonal contour lines are shown together. Domains of relaxations are also indicated in figure 2b. The latter strategy in the parameter space allows selecting the parameters in such a way that the relaxation domains in the objective functions space of figure 1b do not come to existence. However, P′ may come reasonably close to P, while this may not happen too. In the latter case still a Pareto front can be obtained. However the front remains to be poor. Due to this very reason, it is noteworthy to point out that in effective multi-objective optimization to obtain a Pareto surface is only half of the task to be accomplished. The other half is to obtain an effective front at the same time. The second strategy may not allow the parameters to explore the whole solution space due to the non-convex region defined by orthogonal and non-orthogonal axes in figure 2a. From the figure we note that as the degree of relaxation increases, the diversity of solutions along the Pareto surface increases, too. This is at the expense of reduced effectiveness of the multi objective optimization. Therefore, for effective optimization, the degree of relaxation in the search process should be kept to minimum being independent of the method of search. Although the Pareto front concept is well defined, the formation of this front is dependent on the implementation of the MO algorithm. Also it depends on the nature of the application. One interesting application is *the cone domination* approach (Branke et al., 2000), where the a_{ij} coefficients in (1) are determined in advance, so that the optimality search is carried out in the F-space in place of f-space. However, the necessity of adaptive modification of the coefficients during the search makes the approach rather impractical in the higher dimensions.

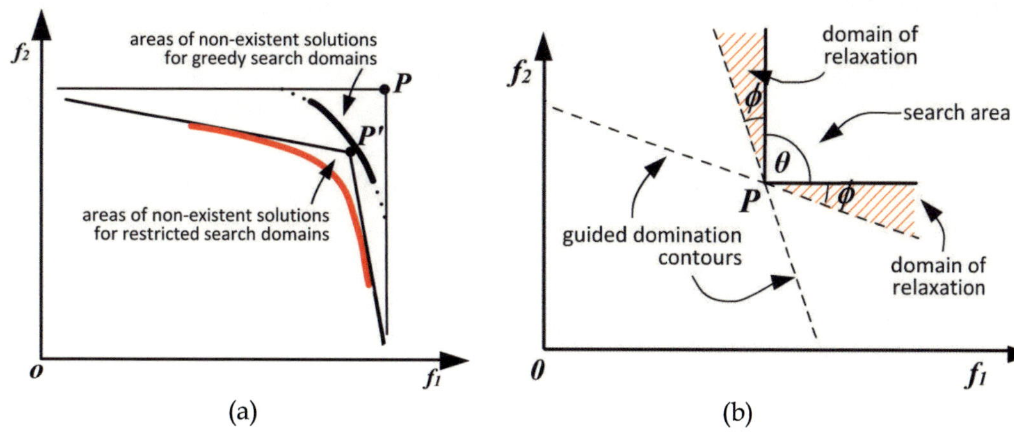

Fig. 2. Contour lines defining the dominated regions in orthogonal versus relaxed search

For the *greedy* application of the MO algorithm, one uses the orthogonal contour lines at the point P as shown in figure 2b. In this figure the point P denotes one of the individuals among the population in the context of genetic algorithm based evolutionary search. In the *greedy* search many potential favourable solutions are prematurely excluded from the search process. This is because during the search each solution of the population is represented by the point P, and the dominance is measured in relation to the number of solutions falling into the search domain within the angle $\theta=\pi/2$. This constant angle is the clear manifestation of the non-adaptivity of the conventional EMO algorithms.
Based on the strategy depicted in figure 2b the search process can be relaxed in a controlled way concerning the trade-off between solution diversity and effective multi-objective optimisation. That is the mechanism pushing the Pareto front forward is well balanced. This is a novel approach and it is explained below.

2.1 Relaxed Pareto ranking

To avoid premature elimination of potential solutions, a relaxed dominance concept is implemented, where the angle θ can be considered as the *angle of tolerance* provided $\theta>\pi/2$; the wider the angle beyond $\pi/2$, the more tolerant the search process, and vice versa. For $\theta<\pi/2$, the search becomes commensurately more greedy, and θ represents the *angle of greediness* in this case. In figure 2 the trade-offs between the *greedy* dominance and relaxed dominance methods are seen. In the earlier case the solutions are expectedly more effective due to their non-dominance, but diverse solutions are quickly exhausted due to non-adaptivity, and therefore the solutions are aggregated. In the latter case, the solutions are more diversified but preliminarily less effective. However, in the long run, the diverse solutions can develop to more effective solutions compared to those obtained from the greedy dominance approach. The implementation of the relaxed dominance approach may be simple in two-dimensional objective space as the hatched relaxation domain is easy to deal with as seen in figure 2b. However, in multi-dimensional objective space, the same domain goes even beyond a simple imagination. To be able to deal with the relaxed domain a mathematical method is developed in this work which is described below.
Let (1) be expressed by

$$\begin{aligned} F_1 &= f_1 + a_{21} f_2 + \ldots\ldots + a_{n1} f_n \\ F_2 &= a_{12} f_1 + f_2 + \ldots\ldots + a_{n2} f_n \, . \\ &\ldots\ldots\ldots\ldots\ldots\ldots \\ F_n &= a_{1n} f_1 + a_{2n} f_2 + \ldots\ldots + a_{nn} f_n \end{aligned} \tag{3}$$

In matrix equation form, (3) becomes

$$F = \begin{bmatrix} F_1 \\ F_2 \\ \ldots \\ F_n \end{bmatrix} = \begin{bmatrix} a_{11} & a_{21} & \ldots\ldots & a_{n1} \\ a_{12} & a_{22} & \ldots\ldots & a_{1n} \\ \ldots & & & \\ a_{1n} & a_{2n} & \ldots\ldots & a_{nn} \end{bmatrix} \begin{bmatrix} f_1 \\ f_2 \\ \ldots \\ f_n \end{bmatrix} = \begin{bmatrix} 1 & a_{21} & \ldots\ldots & a_{n1} \\ a_{12} & 1 & \ldots\ldots & a_{1n} \\ \ldots & & & \\ a_{1n} & a_{2n} & \ldots\ldots & 1 \end{bmatrix} \begin{bmatrix} f_1 \\ f_2 \\ \ldots \\ f_n \end{bmatrix} \tag{4}$$

where a_{11}, a_{22}, …, a_{nn} are equal to unity. For the sake of simplicity in the description below only two objectives are considered while the results are valid for any dimension. The objective functions for this case are given by

$$F_1 = f_1 + a_{21} f_2$$
$$F_2 = a_{12} f_1 + f_2 \quad (5)$$

In a two-dimensional coordinate system the contour lines in figures 1a, 1b and 2b are orthogonal and non-orthogonal respectively. The search area in the latter case includes also the domains of relaxation. These are added to the search area of the orthogonal system, as illustrated in figure 2b.

In the non-orthogonal system the search area for the favourable solutions is wider. At the same time some of the solutions are not dominating the solution at the point P seen in figure 2b. However, as a trade-off it provides more diversity at the final Pareto front, while the front is not entirely non-dominated. The solutions at the front are more probably non-dominated in the middle part of the front. This is where f_1 and f_2 are close to each other. Conversely, the solutions may be more dominated at the regions close to edges of the front (Deb et al., 2003). This is a property of the *cone dominance* approach. This situation occurs since in the cone domination approach a greedy algorithm is applied using a non-orthogonal system taking a reference point P as origin. By doing so, the search algorithm remains the same but it uses the coordinates of the new non-orthogonal system. However, this cone dominance approach does not address the problem of aggregation. This becomes especially problematic in higher multi-dimensional optimization. This means, the Pareto front is potentially wider in the F-space. However, without resolving the aggregation phenomenon the potentially wider Pareto front remains ineffective. In contrast to the cone dominance approach, in this work each member of the population is considered to be represented by point P seen in figure 2b, and the solutions falling into the relaxation domains are included to the non-dominated solutions, thereby accruing some dominated solutions to the non-dominated ones to form the next-generation solutions. This means, the orthogonal system is not replaced by the non-orthogonal system but the greedy non-dominated orthogonal search space is relaxed. The relaxed domains simply contribute to the greedy search domain with some additional, potentially lucrative solutions.

Interestingly, this situation is similar to the classical gradient-based optimization method where each iteration the step-length towards the global maxima or minima determined by a step-size parameter (Farhang-Boroujeny, 1998), also called convergence coefficient. The step-size parameter should be small enough to ensure the stability of the convergence (Bazaraa et al., 1993, Kuester, 1973). If the step-size parameter is zero, the approach to minima or maxima does not occur. If it is too big, convergence does not occur, due to instability. For similar reasons, in the evolutionary computation the angle ϕ defining the relaxation domain should be kept small. In this way the stability of the algorithm is maintained and the effectiveness is enhanced. It should be noted that, although the angle ϕ is small it plays role for each population member at each generation. This makes the net effect of the relaxation highly significant. In the adaptive Pareto front formation $\cos(\phi)$ plays the role of convergence coefficient defined in the gradient-based optimization. If $\cos(\phi)$ is maximum, i.e. $\cos(\phi)=1$, greedy search in orthogonal system occurs, leading to aggregation. This can be considered as a kind of instability in this case. From the other side, if $\cos(\phi)$ is minimal, *i.e.* $\cos(\phi)=-1$, convergence does not occur, because the evolutionary search process becomes trivial in this case. This situation already occurs for $\phi<-3\pi/4$, which corresponds to $\cos(\phi)=-.707$. This is illustrated in figure 3b.

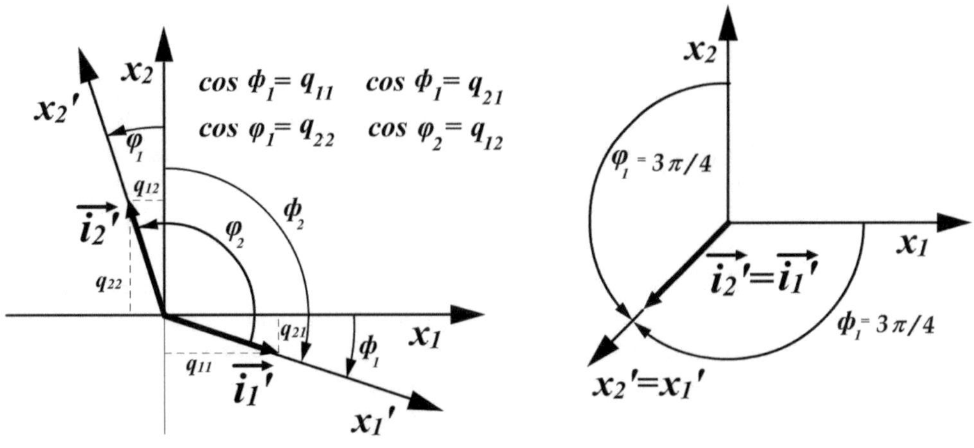

(a) (b)

Fig. 3. Direction cosines in a coordinate transformation in 2-dimensional case (a); schematic representation of relaxation domains covering the total parameter search space as an extreme situation (b)

In (4) the small-enough designation of the parameters a_{ji} is crucial for the performance of the evolutionary computation. They characterize the cosines of the angle between the respective coordinate axes. In general the angle ϕ is application dependent. The normalization of these cosines yields the directive cosines, which determine the transformation from orthogonal to the non-orthogonal, i.e., relaxed coordinate system. If we denote the direction cosines as q_{ij}, the transformation matrix becomes

$$Q = \begin{bmatrix} q_{11} \; q_{12} \; \cdots\cdots \; q_{1n} \\ q_{21} \; q_{22} \; \cdots\cdots \; q_{2n} \\ \cdots\cdots\cdots\cdots \\ q_{n1} \; q_{n2} \; \cdots\cdots \; q_{nn} \end{bmatrix}, \tag{6}$$

which transforms the non-orthogonal system to the orthogonal system and vice versa via

$$x = Q\,x' \tag{7}$$

$$x' = Q^{-1}\,x \tag{8}$$

where x′ denotes the non-orthogonal system $x' = [x_1', x_2', \ldots, x_n']^T$. The directive cosine row vectors of (4) are given by

$$d_i = \left[d_{1i}\, d_{2i} \,..d_{ni}\right] = \frac{1}{\sqrt{\sum_{j=1}^{n} a_{ji}^2}} [a_{1i} \;\, a_{2i} \;\, \ldots . \;\, a_{ni}] \tag{9}$$

which corresponds to column vectors in (6), so that

$$D = \begin{bmatrix} [d_{11}\ d_{21}\ \ .....\ d_{n1}\ ] \\ [d_{12}\ d_{22}\ \ .....\ d_{n2}] \\ .... \\ [d_{1n}\ d_{2n}\ \ .....\ d_{nn}] \end{bmatrix} = Q^T \tag{10}$$

and

$$\sqrt{\sum_{i=1}^{n} q_{ji}^2} = 1 \qquad j = 1,2,....,n \tag{11}$$

In a two-dimensional case the directive cosines are shown in figure 3a and in relation to the set of transformation equations in (3), the directive cosine row vectors are given by

$$\begin{aligned} d_1 &= [d_{11}\ d_{21}] = \left[1/\sqrt{1+a_{21}^2} \qquad a_{21}/\sqrt{1+a_{21}^2}\ \right] \\ d_2 &= [d_{12}\ \ d_{22}] = \left[\ a_{12}/\sqrt{1+a_{12}^2} \qquad 1/\sqrt{1\ +a_{12}^2}\ \right] \end{aligned} \tag{12}$$

The coordinate transformation of point P in figure 2b is given by

$$\begin{bmatrix} f_1^P \\ f_2^P \end{bmatrix} = \begin{bmatrix} q_{11} & q_{12} \\ q_{21} & q_{22} \end{bmatrix} \begin{bmatrix} F_1^P \\ F_2^P \end{bmatrix} = \begin{bmatrix} d_{11} & d_{21} \\ d_{12} & d_{22} \end{bmatrix} \begin{bmatrix} F_1^P \\ F_2^P \end{bmatrix} \tag{13}$$

and

$$\begin{bmatrix} F_1^P \\ F_2^P \end{bmatrix} = \begin{bmatrix} q_{11} & q_{12} \\ q_{21} & q_{22} \end{bmatrix}^{-1} \begin{bmatrix} f_1^P \\ f_2^P \end{bmatrix} = \begin{bmatrix} d_{11} & d_{21} \\ d_{12} & d_{22} \end{bmatrix}^{-1} \begin{bmatrix} f_1^P \\ f_2^P \end{bmatrix} \tag{14}$$

It is interesting to note that since the cosine directive q_{11} in (13) given by $q_{11}=cos(\phi_1)$ is equal to d_{11} in (12), so that

$$q_{11} = \cos(\phi_1) = 1/\sqrt{1+a_{21}^2}$$

and using the relationship

$$\cos(z) = 1/\sqrt{1+\tan(z^2)} \tag{15}$$

we obtain

$$a_{21} = \mp\tan(\phi_1) \tag{16}$$

which yields (5) in terms of the transformation angles in the form

$$F = \begin{bmatrix} F_1 \\ F_n \end{bmatrix} = \begin{bmatrix} 1 & a_{21} \\ a_{12} & 1 \end{bmatrix} \begin{bmatrix} f_1 \\ f_2 \end{bmatrix} = \begin{bmatrix} 1 & \tan(\phi_2) \\ \tan(\varphi_2) & 1 \end{bmatrix} \begin{bmatrix} f_1 \\ f_2 \end{bmatrix} \tag{17}$$

In a general form, (17) is given by

$$F = \begin{bmatrix} F_1 \\ F_2 \\ \cdots \\ F_n \end{bmatrix} = \begin{bmatrix} 1 \; a_{21} \; \ldots\ldots \; a_{n1} \\ a_{12} \; 1 \; \ldots\ldots \; a_{1n} \\ \ldots\ldots\ldots\ldots \\ a_{1n} \; a_{2n} \; \ldots\ldots \; 1 \end{bmatrix} \begin{bmatrix} f_1 \\ f_2 \\ \ldots\ldots \\ f_n \end{bmatrix} = \begin{bmatrix} 1 & \tan(\phi_2) \; \ldots\ldots \; \tan(\phi_n) \\ \tan(\varphi_2) & 1 \; \ldots\ldots \quad \tan(\varphi_n) \\ \ldots\ldots\ldots\ldots & \\ \tan(\theta_2) \; \tan(\theta_n) \; \ldots\ldots & 1 \end{bmatrix} \begin{bmatrix} f_1 \\ f_2 \\ \ldots\ldots \\ f_n \end{bmatrix} \tag{18}$$

The importance of the coordinate transformation becomes dramatic especially in higher dimensions. In such cases the spatial distribution of domains of relaxation becomes complex and thereby difficult to implement. Namely, in multidimensional space the volume of a relaxation domain is difficult to imagine. And more importantly it is difficult to identify the population in such domains. Therefore one needs a systematic approach for identification by computation and not by inspection or anything else. This systematic approach is based on the coordinate transformation as follows. Basically for each solution point, designated in general as P in figure 2b is temporarily considered to be a reference point as origin and all the other solution points in the orthogonal coordinate system are converted to the non-orthogonal system coordinate by (8). For instance for four objectives, we write

$$F = \begin{bmatrix} F_1 \\ F_2 \\ F_3 \\ F_4 \end{bmatrix} = \begin{bmatrix} 1 & a_{21} & a_{31} & a_{41} \\ a_{12} & 1 & a_{32} & a_{42} \\ a_{13} & a_{23} & 1 & a_{43} \\ a_{14} & a_{24} & a_{34} & 1 \end{bmatrix} \begin{bmatrix} f_1 \\ f_2 \\ f_3 \\ f_4 \end{bmatrix}, \tag{19}$$

where the a_{ij} parameters determine the relaxation angles and consequently the cosine directives that are computed from the relaxation angle, that is modified during the search adaptively. The relaxation of the dominance with the adaptive process guarantees the prevention of aggregation. As a numerical example, for a relaxation angle of $\phi=\varphi=\psi=\theta=7^o$ and symmetry similar to that seen in figure 3 of two-dimensional case, one obtains

$$\begin{bmatrix} F_1 \\ F_2 \\ F_3 \\ F_4 \end{bmatrix} = \begin{bmatrix} 1 & -.123 & -.123 & -.123 \\ -.123 & 1 & -.123 & -.123 \\ -.123 & -.123 & 1 & -.123 \\ -.123 & -.123 & -.123 & 1 \end{bmatrix} \begin{bmatrix} f_1 \\ f_2 \\ f_3 \\ f_4 \end{bmatrix} \tag{20}$$

so that, in view of (7) the cosine direction matrix and the corresponding weighted objectives F_1 and F_2 are given by

$$\begin{bmatrix} f_1^P \\ f_2^P \\ f_3^P \\ f_4^P \end{bmatrix} = \begin{bmatrix} .993 & -.122 & -.122 & -.122 \\ -.122 & .993 & -.122 & -.122 \\ -.122 & -.122 & .993 & -.122 \\ -.122 & -.122 & -.122 & .993 \end{bmatrix} \begin{bmatrix} F_1^P \\ F_2^P \\ F_3^P \\ F_4^P \end{bmatrix} \tag{21}$$

And in view of (8) the inverse of (21) becomes

$$\begin{bmatrix} F_1^P \\ F_2^P \\ F_3^P \\ F_4^P \end{bmatrix} = \begin{bmatrix} 1.072 & .174 & .174 & .174 \\ .174 & 1.072 & .174 & .174 \\ .174 & .174 & 1.072 & .174 \\ .174 & .174 & .174 & 1.072 \end{bmatrix} \begin{bmatrix} f_1^P \\ f_2^P \\ f_3^P \\ f_4^P \end{bmatrix} \tag{22}$$

After conversion, all points which have positive coordinates in the non-orthogonal system correspond to potential solutions contributing to the next generation in the evolutionary computation. If any point possesses a negative component in the new coordinate system, the respective solution does not dominate P and therefore is not counted. This is because otherwise such a solution may lead the search in a direction away from P. In general, the relaxation of the dominance in higher dimensions is extremely complex and therefore many different methods for effective Pareto front formation in the literature (Hughes, 2005, Jaszkiewicz, 2004) are reported. However (8) provides a decisive and easy technique revealed in this work for the same goal.

3. Adaptive formation of Pareto front in a design application

In this section adaptive formation of Pareto front with multi-objectivity is considered. The formation of Pareto front is explained by means of a design example where multi-objectivity is subjected to a Pareto front based solution. For the multi-objective optimization a genetic algorithm approach with a relaxed Pareto-ranking is used. The relaxation angle is computed adaptively for every chromosome, and at every generation. This is implemented by having the angle be a part of the chromosome of every solution. The fitness of a chromosome is obtained by considering two properties of the solution at the same time. One is the degree of dominance in terms of the amount of solutions dominating an individual, the second is the relaxation angle used to measure this amount. This is given by

$$R_{fit} = \frac{1}{N(\theta) + n} \tag{23}$$

$$N(\theta) = \frac{4}{1 + \left(\theta / \overline{\theta}\right)} \tag{24}$$

In (23) and (24) the purpose is to reward a chromosome for affording a wide relaxation angle θ, relative to the average angle of the population $\overline{\theta}$, and still having a low dominance count, denoted by n. The wide angle provides more diversity in the population for the next generation. However, when relaxation angle would be excessively big, the population for the next generation can be crowded with trivial solutions. To prevent that, in (23) the number of non-dominated solutions with respect to the particular solution considered denoted by n, is summed up with the function of the angle $N(\theta)$. This means that between two solutions with the same amount of non-dominated solutions, the one with the wider angle is preferred. This is done for every solution in the population. This implies that the average angle $\overline{\theta}$ is changing for every generation adaptively. It is noted that the $N(\theta)$ appearing in (24) is, used to adjust the relative importance of relaxation angle versus count *n*. Figure 4 shows the mean relaxation angle during the adaptive Pareto front formation by the genetic algorithm. The angle converges to a fixed angle of 7° as seen from the figure. This is a clear indication of the stochastic adaptive process.

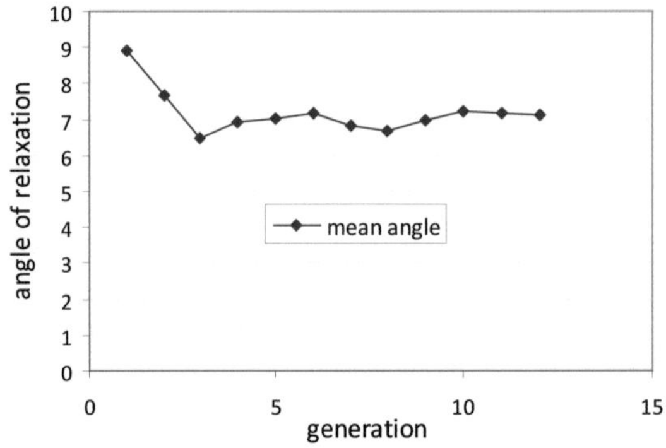

Fig. 4. Variation of mean relaxation angle during the adaptive Pareto front formation by the GA

Since design is an intelligent activity it is composed of several considerations which are soft in nature. For this reason, to invoke methods of soft computing is most appropriate. In this respect fuzzy-neural tree is considered as a knowledge model in this work as it is explained below. The application concerns the design of a building. The building consists of a number of spatial units, referred to as design objects, where every unit is designated to a particular purpose in the building. The task is to locate the objects optimally with respect to three objectives. The objects are seen from figure 5.
Object O1 is a hotel unit, O3 is a conference space, O4 and O5 are office wings, and O2 is a lobby with a restaurant. In order to let the computer generate a building from these parts, i.e. for the solution to be feasible, it is necessary to ensure that all solutions have some basic properties. These are that spaces should not overlap, and objects should be adjacent to the other objects around. This is realized in the present application by inserting the objects in a particular sequential manner into the site. This is illustrated in figure 5. One by one the objects are moved into the site starting from a point marked by a cross in the figures, then moving in west direction (lower part of the figures) until they reach an obstacle, that may be the site boundary or another object previously inserted. When they touch an object they change their movement direction from western to the northern direction, moving north until they again reach the site boundary or another object. As a third and final movement step the object will attempt to move once more in western direction, although often this is may not happen since often there is an adjacent object in the western direction blocking the way. An example of this third step is shown in figure 5c. The third step is to avoid that gaps between objects are reduced to some extend. This way of packing objects is known as *bottom-left* method in literature, and it is used mainly for packing problems. After the final object has been placed in this way the design is ready for evaluation. It is noted that the decision from which side to insert the objects, and which location to use for the insertion point is a matter of judgement, and it will strongly influence the solutions obtained. The insertion used in this application is due to the preference of the architect is to have the objects line up along the street, which is in western boundary of the site.

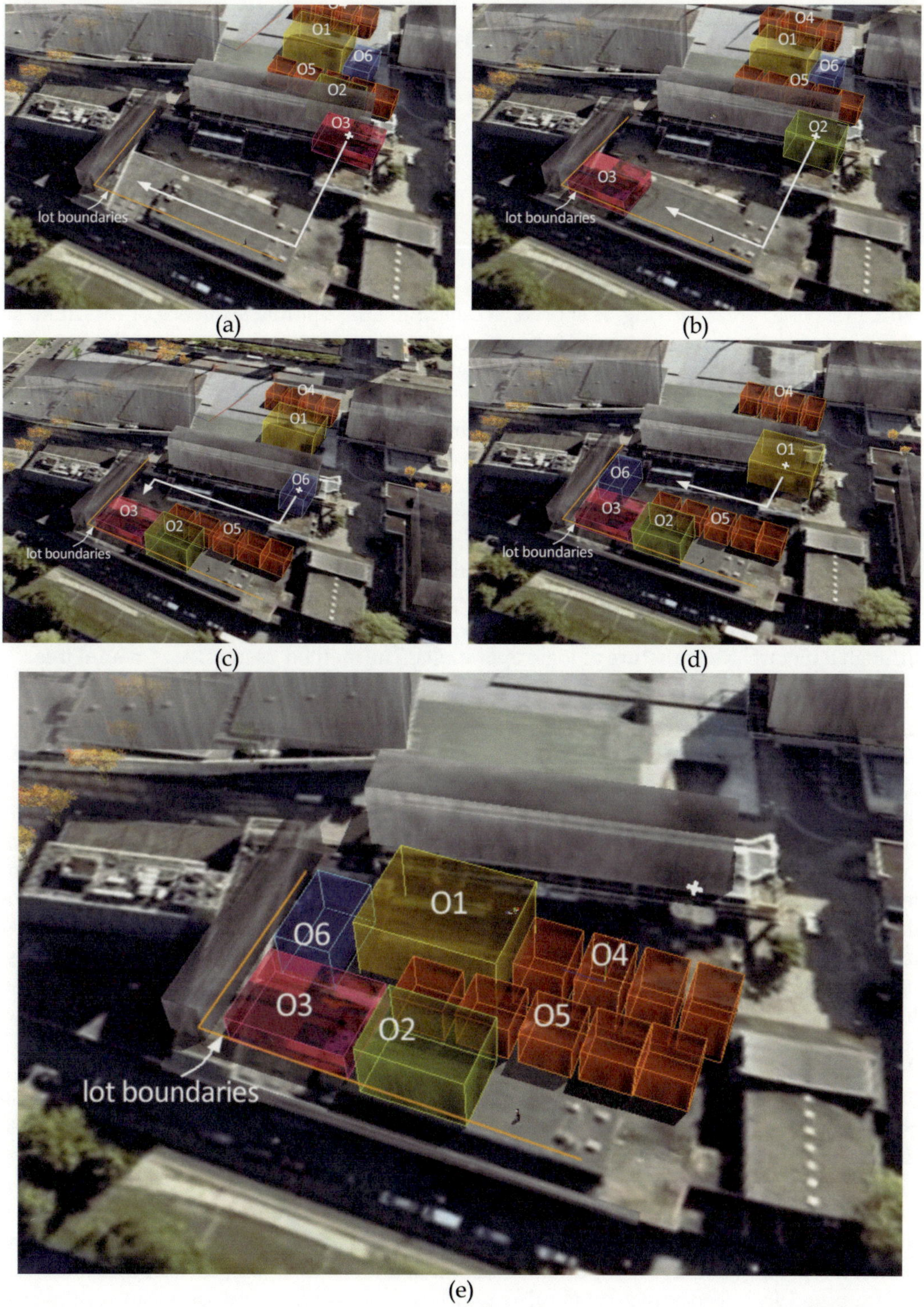

Fig. 5. Generation process of a solution through sequential insertion of the design objects

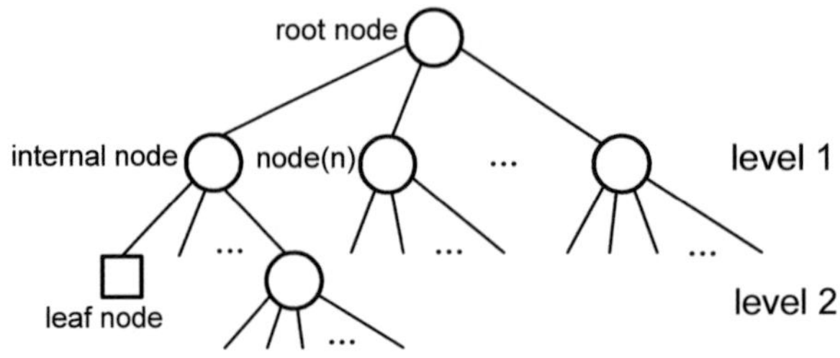

Fig. 6. The structure of a neural tree

The multi objective optimization is accomplished using a multi-objective genetic algorithm with a relaxed Pareto ranking. It is used to determine the optimal sequence of insertion, so that three objectives are maximally fulfilled. Objects are numbered, and every chromosome contains the information for every object, at which rank in the insertion sequence it is to be inserted.

The objectives are functionality of the building, certain energy performance aspects, and some form related preferences. The design performance is obtained from these three objectives. Due to the linguistic nature of these objectives a special model is formed and used to assess satisfaction of the objectives. This model is a fuzzy neural tree model. In this model the ultimate goal is to have a good design, what we term as a design with a high design performance. That is, if all three objectives are highly fulfilled then the design has a high performance. The relation of the concept of design performance with the physical properties of possible solutions, which form the model inputs, is captured in the model through a hierarchical structure of logic operations. The method used is fuzzy neural tree.

3.1 Fuzzy-neural tree modeling domain knowledge

For human-like information processing the methods of soft computing are presumably the most convenient. The salient soft computing methods are in the paradigms of neural nets and fuzzy logic (Mitra et al., 2002). In this work a neural tree is considered to assess the suitability of a solution in a human-like manner. A neural tree is composed of terminal nodes, non-terminal nodes, and weights of connection links between two nodes. The non-terminal nodes represent neural units and the neuron type is an attribute introducing a non-linearity simulating a neuronal activity. In the present case, this attribute is established by means of a Gaussian function which has several desirable features for the intended goals; namely, it is a radial basis function ensuring a solution and the smoothness. At the same time it plays the role of a fuzzy membership function in the tree structure, which is considered to be a fuzzy logic system as its outcome is based on fuzzy logic operations and thereby associated reasoning. An instance of a neural tree is shown in figure 6.

Detailed structures of a neural tree are shown in figure 7. Figure 7a shows a terminal node connected to an inner node, and figure 8b and 8c show the connections among inner nodes. Each terminal node, also called *leaf*, is labelled with an element from the terminal set $T=\{x_1, x_2, \ldots, x_n\}$, where x_i is the i-th component of the external input vector $\mathbf{x}$. Each link (i,j) represents a directed connection from node i to node j. A value w_{ij} is associated with each link as seen from figure 7. In a neural tree, the root node is an output unit and the leaf nodes, or terminal nodes, are input units. The node outputs are computed in the same way as computed in a feed-forward neural network. In this way, neural trees can represent a broad class of feed-forward networks that have irregular connectivity and non-strictly layered structures. In particular, in the present work the nodes are similar to those used in a radial basis functions network with the Gaussian basis functions.

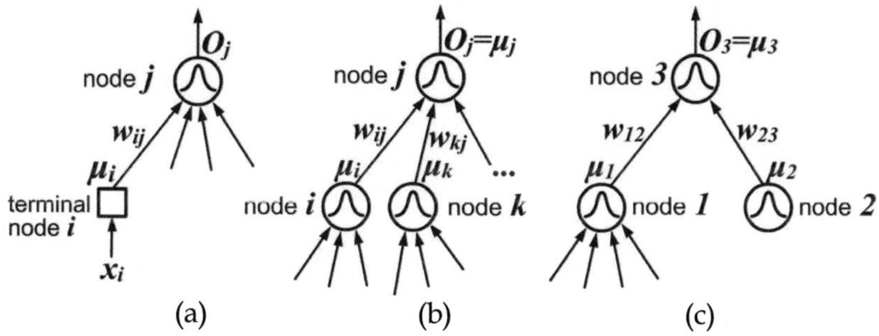

Fig. 7. Detailed structures of a neural tree with respect to different type of node connections

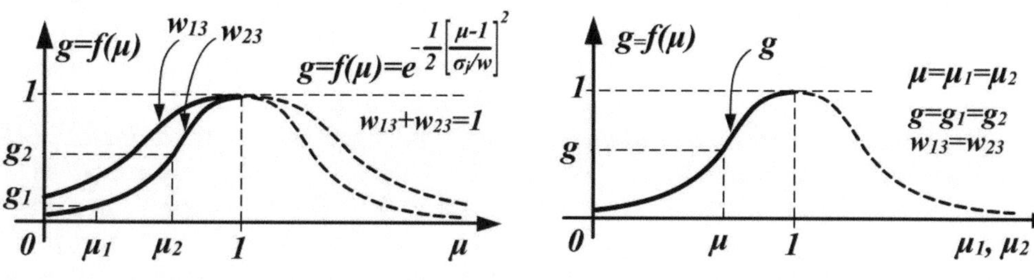

Fig. 8. Fuzzification for two inputs (a), fuzzification where $\mu = \mu_1 = \mu_2$ (b)

In the neural tree considered in this work the output of i-th node is denoted x_i and it is introduced to another node j. A non-terminal node consists of a Gaussian radial basis function.

$$f(X) = w\phi(\| X - c \|^2) \tag{25}$$

where $\phi(.)$ is the Gaussian basis function, $\boldsymbol{c}$ is the center of the basis function. The Gaussian is of particular interest and used in this research due to its relevance to fuzzy-logic. The width of the basis function σ_j at node j is used to measure the uncertainty associated with the inputs to this node, designated as external input X_j. X_j is related to the output of node i denoted as μ_i by relation

$$X_j = \mu_i w_{ij} \tag{26}$$

where w_{ij} is the weight connecting node i to node j. The centers of the basis functions are the same as the input weights of that node.
The output of node j is given by

$$O_j = \exp\left(-\frac{1}{2}\sum_i^n \left[\frac{w_{ij}\mu_i - w_{ij}}{\sigma_j}\right]^2\right) \tag{27}$$

which reduces to

$$O_j = \exp(-\frac{1}{2}\sum_i^n \left[\frac{w_{ij}(\mu_i - 1)}{\sigma_j}\right]^2) \qquad (28)$$

We can express (28) in the following form

$$O_j = \exp(-\frac{1}{2}\sum_i^n \left[\frac{(\mu_i - 1)}{\sigma_j / w_{ij}}\right]^2) \qquad (29)$$

This implies that the width of the Gaussian is scaled by the input weight w_{ij}. In other words, as to the width, the shape of Gaussian fuzzy membership function is dependent on the input weights w_{ij} determined by the domain knowledge. It should be noted that this is a novel type of computation at each node which is quite different than conventional radial basis function (RBF) type computation, where the centers are determined by other means, clustering for instance. However, a non-terminal node itself can be seen as an RBF having different width for each dimension. For such a node, there should be at least two inputs with appropriate connection weights. The connection weights of a node should be normalized, so that the sum of the weights becomes equal to 1.

In figure 8 only two inputs are considered without loss of generality. The variables w_{13} and w_{23} are input weights determining the width of the Gaussian membership functions. It is noted that in the figure $w_{13}<w_{23}$. This is clear from (29). For two inputs, two distinct standard deviations are defined. In particular, the inputs can be equal, i.e., $\mu_1 = \mu_2$. This particular case occurs when the outputs of the two nodes delivering the inputs to the node we are considering are equal. This case is illustrated in figure 9b. In figure 9a it is clear that, if w_1 and w_2 are equal then the AND operation is expressed by means of a single Gaussian denoted by g_3.

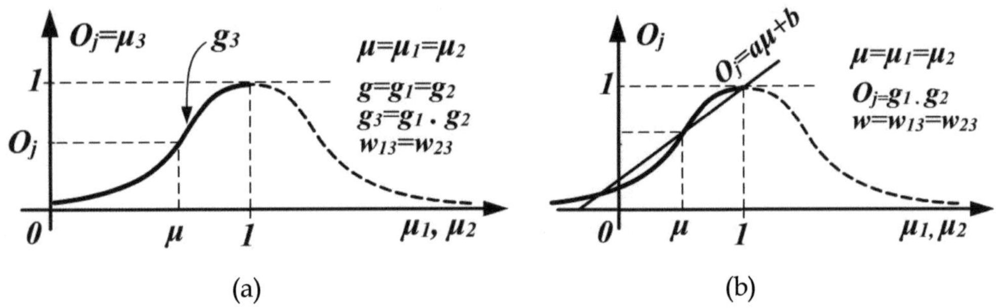

Fig. 9. And operation (a); linear approximation to Gaussian function (b)

Since σ_j is a free parameter, by giving an appropriate width via (29), the result of the AND operation is given by

$$\begin{aligned} &\mu = \mu_1 = \mu_2 \\ &f(\mu) = f(\mu_1) = f(\mu_2) = g_1 = g_2 \\ &O_j = g_1 \cdot g_2 \end{aligned} \qquad (30)$$

This is illustrated in figure 9b where the left part of the Gaussian is approximated by a straight line. In figure 9b, optimizing the σ_j parameter, we obtain

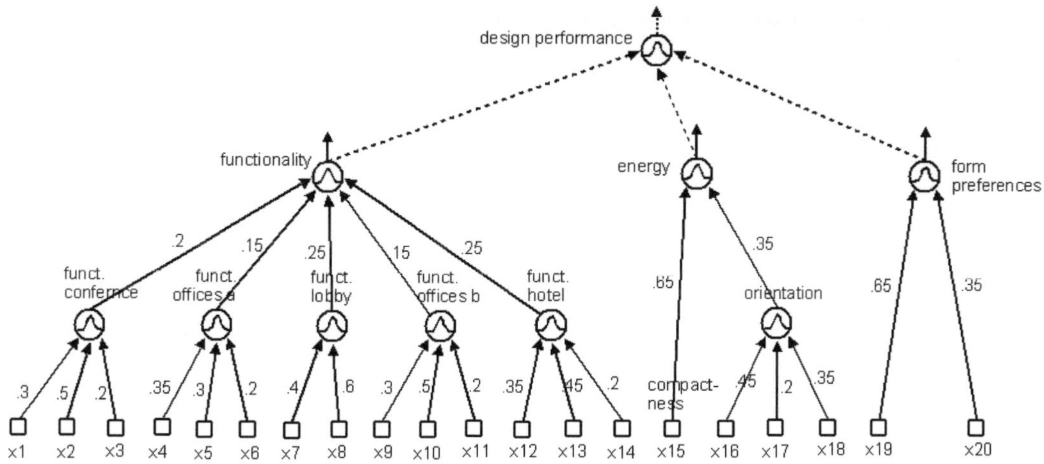

Fig. 10. Neural tree used to obtain fitness regarding three objectives

$$O_j \cong \mu \tag{31}$$

for the values μ and O_j that can take between zero and one. In any case, for a node in the neural tree, (31) is satisfied for μ=O_j=0 (approximately) and for μ=O_j=1 (exact) inherently, while g_1 and g_2 are increasing function of μ_1 and μ_2. Therefore a linear relationship between O_j and μ in the range between 0 and 1 is a first choice from the fuzzy logic viewpoint; namely, as to the AND operation at the respective node, if inputs are equal, that is $\mu=\mu_1=\mu_2$ then the output of the node of μ_1 AND μ_2 is determined by the respective *triangular membership functions* in the antecedent space. Triangular fuzzy membership functions are the most prominent type of membership functions in fuzzy logic applications. For five inputs to a neural tree node, these membership functions are represented by the data sets given by Table 1 and Table 2

.1	.2	.3	.4	.5	.6	.7	.8	.9
.1	.2	.3	.4	.5	.6	.7	.8	.9
.1	.2	.3	.4	.5	.6	.7	.8	.9
.1	.2	.3	.4	.5	.6	.7	.8	.9
.1	.2	.3	.4	.5	.6	.7	.8	.9

Table 1. Data-set at neural tree node input

.1	.2	.3	.4	.5	.6	.7	.8	.9

Table 2. Data-set at neural tree node input

In general, the data sets given in Table 1 and Table 2 are named in this work as '*consistency conditions*'. They are used to calibrate the membership function parameter σ. This is accomplished by optimization.

At this point a few observations are due, as follows. If a weight w_{ij} is zero, this means the significance of the input is zero, consequently the associated input has no effect on the node output and thus also the system output. Conversely, if a w_{ij} is close to unity, this means the significance of the input is highest among the competitive weights directed to the same node. This means the value of the associated input is extremely important and a small change about this value has big impact on the node output O_j. If a weight w_{ij} is somewhere between zero and one, then the associated input value has some possible effect on the node output determined by the respective AND operation via (29). In this way, the domain knowledge is integrated into the logic operations.

The general properties of the present neural tree structure are as follows.

If an input of a node is small (i.e., close to zero) and the weight w_{ij} is high, then, the output of the node is also small complying with the AND operation.

If a weight w_{ij} is low the associated input cannot have significant effect on the node output. This means, quite naturally, such inputs can be ignored.

If all input values coming to a node are high (i.e., close to unity), the output of the node is also high complying with the AND operation.

If a weight w_{ij} is high the associated input x_i can have significant effect on the node output.

It might be of value to point out that, the AND operation in a neural-tree node is executed in fuzzy logic terms and the associated connection weights play an important role on the effectiveness of this operation.

The neural tree employed in this work is shown in figure 10. The root node describes the ultimate goal subject to maximization, namely the design performance and the tree branches form the objectives constituting this goal. The connections among the nodes have a weight associated with them, as seen from the figure. The weight is given by a designer, as an expression of knowledge, and it specifies the relative significance a node has for the node one level closer to the root node. It is noted that in the multi-objective optimization case the weights connecting the nodes on the penultimate level of the weight tells how strongly the output of the lower node influences the output of the upper tree to the root node are not specified a-priori, but they are subject to identification after the optimization process is accomplished.

During evaluation of a design alternative the tree is provided with inputs at its leaf nodes and the fuzzification processes are carried out. The fuzzification yields the satisfaction of an elemental requirement at the terminal nodes of the neural tree. These requirements are some desirable features expressed by means of fuzzy membership functions at the terminal nodes of the tree. Three examples are shown in figure 11.

Figure 11a expresses the requirement x1 in figure 10. It demands that the conference space should be located close to the building services, which is an aspect of functionality, i.e. distance from service facilities should be low for convenient access of services. The requirement is fully satisfied, i.e. the membership degree μ becomes unity, when the distance among the objects is less than about 10m. Since distances are measured from geometric centres of both objects, this distance belongs to the case that both objects are adjacent. Distances beyond 30m mean that the conference room is not considered as being nearby services, so that this requirement is not fulfilled, i.e. μ becomes zero.

Figure 11b expresses the requirement x3. It demands that the conference space should be far from the hotel, to avoid acoustic disturbance and to keep people flows separate. From the figure we see that distances beyond 40m are considered to fully satisfy this demand. From figure 10 we note that, comparatively the requirement in figure 11a is considered 1.5 times more important than figure 11b regarding the functionality of the building.

Figure 11c expresses the requirement x19 in figure 10. It demands that the building should have an elongated shape. What is meant is that the shape of the floor plan should not be a square, but that the shape should clearly have a longer extend in north-south direction, termed length, than in east-west direction, termed width. This is an aspect of form preferences. To express this demand the input values to this membership function are the proportion length/width, being unit less. From the membership function we note that a square proportion yields a low membership degree μ, i.e. low satisfaction of this requirement. The particular proportion known as *golden section* yields approximately a satisfaction degree of μ=0.5 and proportion values beyond 2.5 are considered fully satisfying the requirement.

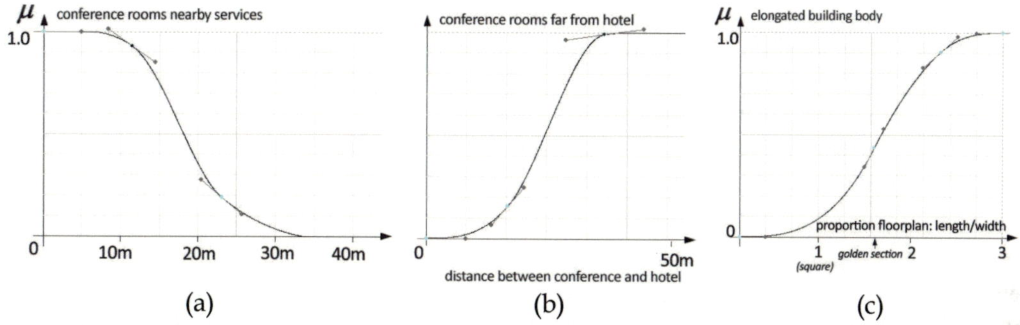

Fig. 11. Some membership functions at the terminal nodes of the neural tree in figure 10

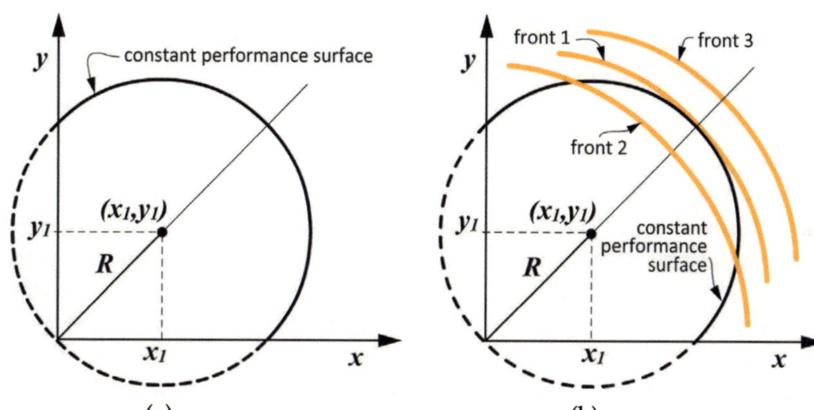

Fig. 12. Constant performance surface (a); analysis of three Pareto fronts (b)

In the same way other properties of the design are measured and converted into satisfactions using specific membership functions at the terminals. The fuzzified information is then processed by the inner nodes of the tree. These nodes perform the AND operations using Gaussian membership functions as described above. Finally this sequence of logic operations starting from the model input yield, the performance at the penultimate node outputs of the model. This means the more satisfied the elemental requirements at the terminal level are, the higher the outputs will be at the nodes above, finally increasing the design performance at the root node of the tree. Next to the evaluation of the design performance score, due to the fuzzy logic operations at the inner nodes of the tree, the performance of any sub-aspect is obtained as well. This is a desirable feature in design, which is referred to as transparency.

Having established the performance evaluation model, it is used for the evolutionary search process aiming to identify designs with maximal design performance. In the present case we are interested in a variety of alternative solutions that are equivalent in Pareto sense. The design is therefore treated as a multi-objective optimization as opposed to a single-objective optimization. In single-objective case exclusively the design performance, i.e. the output at the root node of the neural tree, would be subject to maximization. In the latter case, the solution would be the outcome of a mere convergence and any cognition aspect would not be exercised. In the multi-objective implementation the outputs of the nodes *functionality*, *energy*, and *form preferences*, which are the penultimate nodes, are subject to maximization. Their values are used in the fitness determination procedure of the genetic algorithm. Employing the fuzzy neural tree in this way the genetic search is equipped with some human-like reasoning capabilities during the search. The part of the tree beyond the penultimate nodes is for the defuzzification process, which models cognition, so that ultimately the design performance is obtained at the root node.

3.2 Design performance and the Pareto front

It is noted that generally multi-objective optimization involves no information on the relative importance among the objectives. Therefore, generally, Pareto optimal solutions cannot be distinguished without bringing into play other, i.e. higher-order criteria than the objectives used in the search. However, it is noted that the Pareto solutions may be distinguished as follows. From figure 10, at the root node, the performance score is computed by the defuzzification process given by

$$w_1 f_1 + w_2 f_2 + w_3 f_3 = p \tag{32}$$

where f_1 is the output of the node *functionality;* f_2 of node *energy;* f_3 of node *form preferences.* That is, they denote the performance values for these aspects of the design, which are subject to maximization. The variable p denotes the design performance which is also requested to be maximized. In (32) w_1 , w_2 , and w_3 denote the weights associated to the connections from *functionality*, *energy*, and *form preferences*. It is noted that $w_1+w_2+w_3=1$.
In this design exercise, the cognitive design viewpoint plays important role. This means it is initially uncertain what values $w_1,\dots w_3$ should have. Namely, the node outputs $f_1, \dots, f_3$ can be considered as the *design feature vector,* and the reflection of these features can be best performed if the weights w_1 ; …; w_3 define the same direction as that of the feature vector. Hence the components of the unit vector along the feature vector are computed as

$$u_1 = \frac{f_1}{\sqrt{f_1^2 + f_2^2 + \dots + f_n^2}}\ ; \quad u_2 = \frac{f_2}{\sqrt{f_1^2 + f_2^2 + \dots + f_n^2}}\ ; \quad \dots ; \ u_n = \frac{f_n}{\sqrt{f_1^2 + f_2^2 + \dots + f_n^2}} \tag{33}$$

Normalising the components and equating them to the weights yields

$$w_1 = \frac{f_1}{f_1 + f_2 + f_3}\ ; \quad w_2 = \frac{f_2}{f_1 + f_2 + f_3}\ ; \quad w_3 = \frac{f_3}{f_1 + f_2 + f_3} \tag{34}$$

In general, if there are n objectives at the penultimate layer of the neural tree, we can write that

$$u_1 = \frac{f_1}{\sqrt{f_1^2 + f_2^2 + ... + f_n^2}} \; ; ... ; \; u_n = \frac{f_n}{\sqrt{f_1^2 + f_2^2 + ... + f_n^2}} \tag{35}$$

Above computation implies that, the performance p for each genetic solution is given by

$$p = \frac{f_1^2 + f_2^2 + ... + f_n^2}{f_1 + f_2 + ... + f_n} \tag{36}$$

Therefore, (36) is computed for all the design solutions on the Pareto front. Then the *solution with maximal performance* is selected among the Pareto solutions. This way the particular design is identified as a solution candidate with the corresponding $w_1, w_2, ..., w_n$ weights. These weights form a priority vector w^*. In the present application (36) becomes

$$p = \frac{f_1^2 + f_2^2 + f_3^2}{f_1 + f_2 + f_3} \tag{37}$$

where f_n n-th output on the penultimate level of the neural tree. If for any reason this candidate solution is not appealing, the next candidate is searched among the available design solutions with a desired design feature vector and the relational attributes, i.e., $w_1, w_2, ..., w_n$. One should note that, although performance does not play role in the genetic optimization, Pareto front offers a number of design options with fair performance leaving the final choice dependent on other environmental preferences. Using (36), second-order preferences are identified that are most promising for the task at hand, where ultimately maximal design performance is pursued.
To this end, to make the analysis explicit we consider a two-dimensional objective space. In this case, (36) becomes

$$p = \frac{f_1^2 + f_2^2}{f_1 + f_2} \tag{38}$$

which can be put into the form

$$f_1^2 + f_2^2 - pf_1 + pf_2 = 0 \tag{39}$$

that defines a circle along which the performance is constant. To obtain the circle parameters in terms of performance, we write

$$f_1^2 + f_2^2 - pf_1 + pf_2 \equiv (x - x_1)^2 + (y - y_1)^2 - R^2 \tag{40}$$

From (40) we obtain the center coordinates x_1 ,y_1 and the radius R of the circle in terms of performance as

$$\begin{aligned} x_1 &= p/2 \\ y_1 &= p/2 \\ R &= p/\sqrt{2} \end{aligned} \tag{41}$$

The performance circle with the presence of three progressive Pareto fronts are schematically shown in figure 12. From this figure, it is seen that the maximum performance is at the locations where the either objective is maximal at the Pareto front. If both objectives are equal, the maximal performance takes its lowest value and the degree of departing from the equality means a better performance in Pareto sense. This result is very significant since it reveals that, a design can have a better performance if some measured extremity in one way or other is exercised. It is meant that, if a better performance is obtained, then most presumably extremity will be observed in this design.

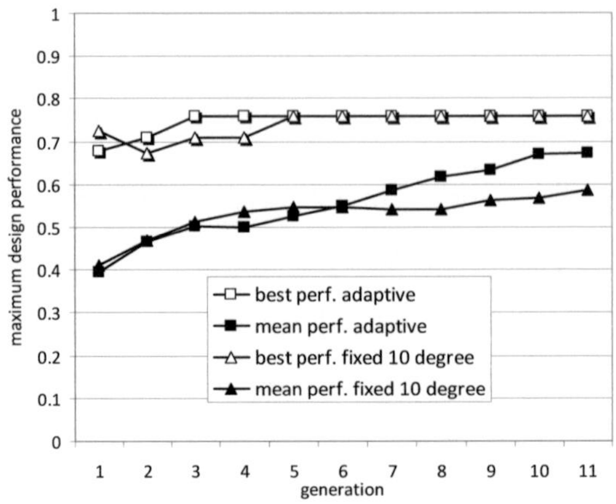

Fig. 13. Maximum design performance obtained during the multi-objective evolutionary search

3.3 Application results

The results from the design with multi-objective optimization are presented in figures 13, and 14-17. Figure 13 shows the maximum design performance p obtained using (39). From figure 13 it is seen that the average maximal performance is smoothly converging to its final value, whereas in the case a fixed angle is used, the performance is not increasing beyond a certain level after a few generations. The former result is a manifestation of the stochastic adaptive process. It indicates the superiority of the adaptive relaxation approach proposed with respect to non-adaptive relaxation.

To exemplify the solutions on the Pareto front, four resulting Pareto-optimal designs D1-D4 are shown in figures 14-17, respectively. The left part of the figure shows the instantiation of the solutions in decision space. The right part of the figure shows the same solution in objective space together with the other Pareto optimal solutions obtained. It is noted that in objective space a solution is represented by a sphere. The size of the sphere indicates the maximal performance value of the corresponding solution. That is, a large sphere indicates a high maximal design performance, and conversely a small sphere indicates a low performance.

Design D1 is the design among the Pareto solutions having the highest maximal design performance, as obtained by (37), namely p=.77. It has a high *form* and functional performance, namely .80, and .91 respectively, while its energy performance is moderate, being only .42. The high performance as to *form* is partially due to the elongated shape of the building body. The low energy performance is mainly due to the large surface of the building, and that offices O4 are exposed to the west side (lower part of the figure). These properties of the solution violate the energy requirements modelled in the fuzzy neural tree in figure 10.

Design D2 has a high energy performance (.83), while form and functionality are moderate (.54 and .41). Its maximal design performance is p=.65. The high energy performance is due to the more compact shape, and the fact that offices are not exposed in western direction, as required.

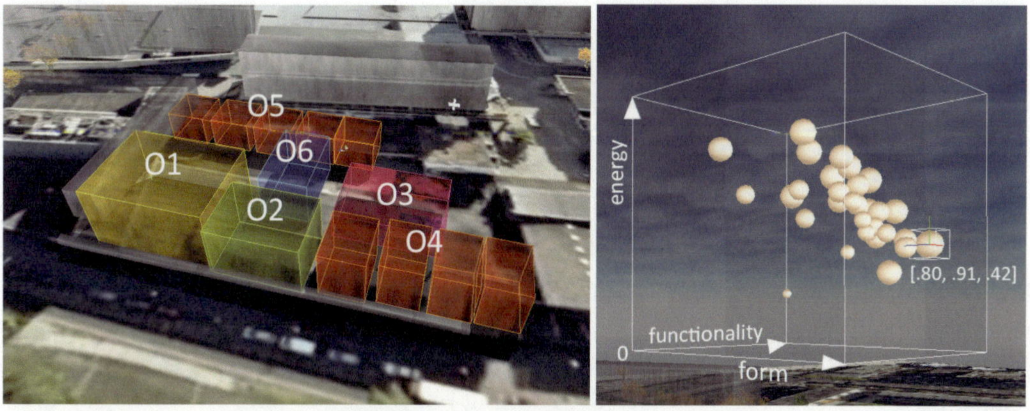

Fig. 14. Design D1 having maximal design performance

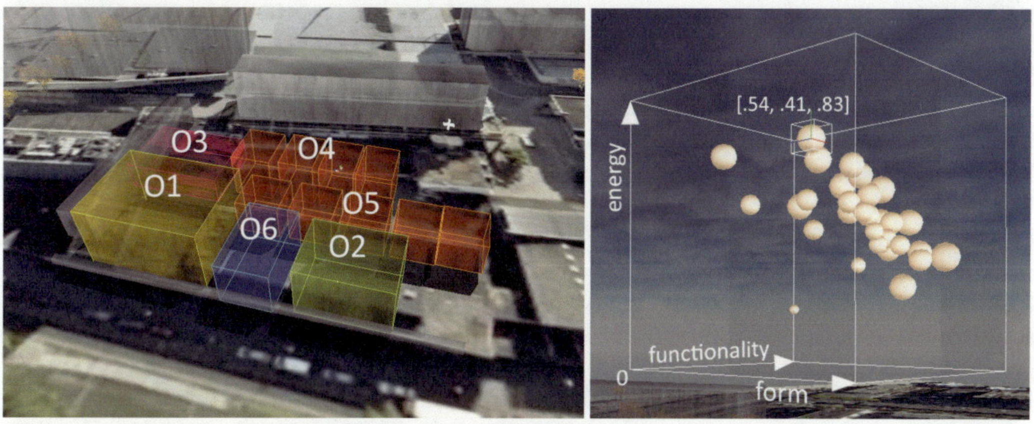

Fig. 15. Design D2 having a high energy performance

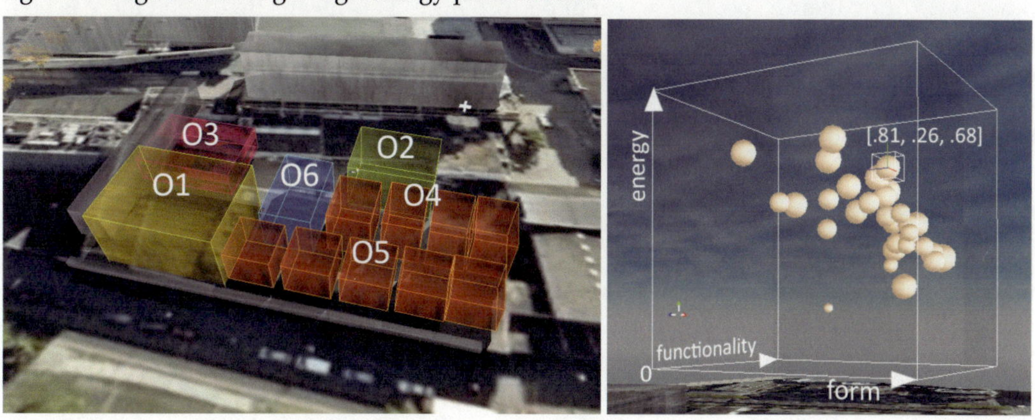

Fig. 16. Design D3 having a high form performance

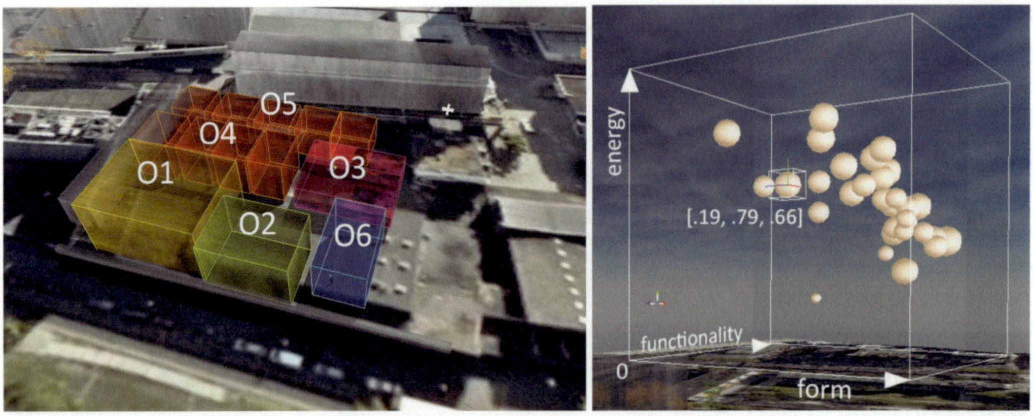

Fig. 17. Design D4 having a high functionality performance

Design D3 has a high form related performance (.81), while functionality is low (.26) and energy performance moderate (.68). Its maximal design performance is *p=.67*. The form related performance is high, because the building body is rather long and its façade to the west side consists of an office and the hotel building, which is fulfilling the form related preferences in this task. Functionality is low, for instance because the lobby O2 is located far from the street in the west, which is undesirable according to the requirements.

Design D4 has a high *functionality* (.79), while the form related performance is low (.19) and energy performance is moderate (.66). It design performance is *p=.67*. The high functionality is due to proximity among several objects, while hotel O1 and conference O3 are still quite distant from each other, as required. The low performance as to form is due to the square-like shape of the building.

From the results we note that all four Pareto solutions investigated, although being located at different extremities of the front, have shared properties. Namely the hotel object O1 is always located at the street corner. This means that this feature is desirable for any optimal solution, revealing a principle applicable to this design task. This discovery is referred to as *innovization* principle in the literature (Deb & Srinivasan, 2006).

From the results we note that design D1 has a maximal performance that is higher than the other Pareto optimal designs described by factor 1.15. That is, D1 clearly outperforms the others regarding their respective maximal performance. This means that when there is no a-priori bias for any of the three objectives, it is more proficient to be less concerned with energy, but to aim for maximal functionality and form qualities instead in the particular design task at hand. That is, in absence of second-order preferences, design D1 should be built, rather than the other designs.

4. Conclusions

A novel adaptive approach for formation of the Pareto front in multi-objective optimization is presented. The approach is an adaptive stochastic search, where a relaxed dominance concept is introduced, and the relaxation angle is adapted during the search. This approach is a dual counterpart of gradient-based stochastic adaptive algorithms. In this duality the fitnessfunction is the dual of stochastic gradient, and the degree of relaxation is the dual of the step-size parameter. The adaptation is found to be significantly favorable for convergence and diversity in the multi-objective optimization. This is demonstrated in an application from architectural design, where a building consisting of several volumes is obtained. In this design the location of the volumes relative to each other is subject to optimization. This is accomplished by identifying an optimal sequence of arranging the volumes, so that three objectives pertaining to the building are satisfied. These objectives are functionality, energy aspects, and form related aspects. The linguistic nature of these requirements is treated by using a fuzzy neural tree approach, that is able to handle the imprecision and complexity inherent to the concepts, forming a model. This model plays the role of fitness function in the adaptive MOEA, so that the search is endowed with some human like reasoning during the search. The designs obtained are diverse, and have a high design performance. This performance is the maximum suitability one can attribute to a solution without preference for any objectives. The location where this maximal performance is constant in objective space constitutes a circle for two objectives, and a sphere for three or more objectives etc. Using this location information and associating it with the Pareto front, it is shown that a solution satisfying each objective approximately equally yields a minimal performance among the Pareto solutions. A Pareto solution deviating from this equality is preferred. This situation in two dimensional cases can metaphorically be referred to the preference for the *golden section* concept in design, in comparison to square shape. Namely a square is considered to be visually less appealing, whereas the golden section is more interesting having some directionality in it. In general this means that designs can have a better performance if some measured extremity in one way or other is exercised, provided there is no preference. The results from the application show that in the particular task at hand one should look for designs with outstanding functionality, rather than a design with outstanding energy performance. This is due to the shape of the Pareto front. The results have shown that the goal of adaptive formation of the Pareto front is satisfactorily achieved, and this is demonstrated.

Appendix - Coordinate Transform

Let us consider the elements of an n-dimensional numerical vector $x=[x_1,x_2, \dots ,x_n]$ whose components represent the directions of the n basic mutually orthogonal unit vectors

$$i_1 = [1,0,0..,0], \; ..... \; ,i_n = [0,0, \; .... \; ,1] \tag{I}$$

which lie along the axes of reference rectangular coordinates x_1, x_2, ..., x_n in n-dimensional space. The numerical vector x can be expressed by

$$x = [x_1, x_2, \; .... \; , x_n] = \sum_{k=1}^{n} x_k i_k \tag{II}$$

Let a new coordinate system in n-dimensional space is choisen whose geometrical unit vectors i_1', i_2', ... ,i_n' in the directions of axes of the new coordinates x_1', x_2', ..., x_n' are linearly independent and are related to the original unit vectors by the equations

$$\begin{aligned} i_1^{'} &= q_{11}i_1 + q_{21}i_2 + \dots , q_{n1}i_n \\ &\dots\dots\dots\dots\dots\dots\dots\dots \\ i_n^{'} &= q_{1n}i_1 + q_{2n}i_2 + \dots , q_{nn}i_n \end{aligned} \tag{III}$$

which can be expressed as a matrix equation

$$\begin{bmatrix} i_1^{'} \\ \dots \\ i_n^{'} \end{bmatrix} = \begin{bmatrix} q_{11} \; q_{21} \; \dots\dots \; q_{n1} \\ \dots\dots\dots\dots \\ q_{1n} \; c_{2n} \; \dots\dots \; q_{nn} \end{bmatrix} \begin{bmatrix} i_1 \\ \dots\dots \\ i_n \end{bmatrix} \tag{IV}$$

From (III), one can write the set of equation in the following form.

$$i_k^{'} = \sum_{p=1}^{n} q_{pk} i_r \tag{V}$$

The geometrical vector determined by the components of the numerical vector x can be expressed by the components of the numerical vector x′ as follows

$$x^{'} = x_1^{'} i_1^{'} + x_2^{'} i_2^{'} + \dots , x_n^{'} = \sum_{k=1}^{n} x_k^{'} i_k^{'} \tag{VI}$$

Substitution of (IV) into (V) yields

$$x = \sum_{k=1}^{n} \sum_{p=1}^{n} x_k^{'} q_{pk} i_p = \sum_{p=1}^{n} \left(\sum_{k=1}^{n} q_{pk} x_k^{'} \right) i_p \tag{VII}$$

Comparison of (II) and (VII) yields

$$x_p = \sum_{k=1}^{n} q_{rk} x_k^{'} \tag{VIII}$$

The matrix equation form of (VIII) is given by

$$x = Q x^{'} \tag{IX}$$

where Q is the transformation matrix which is

$$Q = \begin{bmatrix} q_{11} \; q_{12} \; \dots\dots \; q_{1n} \\ \dots\dots\dots\dots \\ q_{n1} \; q_{n2} \; \dots\dots \; q_{nn} \end{bmatrix} \tag{X}$$

One should note that, Q is the transpose of the coefficient matrix of the equations in (IV). In order that the new unit vectors be linearly independent, and hence span n-dimensional space, the matrix Q must be non-singular. In this case from (IX) we can write

$$x^{'} = Q^{-1} x \tag{XI}$$

It may be interesting to note that, if the new unit vectors are mutually orthogonal, we obtain

$$Q^T Q = I \qquad or \qquad Q^T = Q^{-1} \tag{XII}$$

This result implies that Q is an *orthogonal matrix*.

5. References

Bazaraa, M. S.; Sherali, H. D. & Shetty, C. M. (1993), *Nonlinear Programming,* John Wiley & Sons, Inc, ISBN. 0-471-55793-5, New York

Branke, J.; Kaussler, T. & Schmeck, H. (2000), Guiding multi-objective evolutionary algorithms towards interesting regions, *Technical Report No: 399,* Institute AIFB University of Karlsruhe, Germany

Branke, J.; Kaussler, T. & Schmeck, H. (2001). Guidance in evolutionary multi-objective optimization, *Advances in Engineering Software,* vol. 32, pp. 499-507

Ciftcioglu, Ö. & Bittermann, M. S. (2008). Solution diversity in multi-objective optimization: A study in virtual reality, *Proc. World Congress on Computational Intelligence WCCI 2008,* Hong Kong, 2008,

Coello, C. A. C. (1999). An updated survey of GA-based multi-objective optimization techniques, *ACM Computing Surveys,* vol. 32, no. 2, pp. 109-143

Coello, C. A. C., Veldhuizen, D. A. & Lamont, G. B. (2003). *Evolutionary Algorithms for Solving Multiobjective Problems,* Kluwer Academic Publishers, Boston

Deb, K., Pratap, A., Agarwal, S. & Meyarivan, T. (2000). A fast and elitist multi-objective genetic algorithm: NSGA-II, *IEEE Transactions on Evolutionary Computation,* vol. 6, pp. 182-197

Deb, K. (2001). *Multiobjective Optimization Using Evolutionary Algorithms*, John Wiley & Sons

Deb, K., Zope, P. & Jain, A. (2003). Distributed computing of Pareto-optimal solutions with evolutionary algorithms, *Proc. 9th annual conference on Genetic and evolutionary computation,* pp. 532-549, 978-1-59593-697-4 London, England, ACM New York

Deb, K. & Srinivasan, A. (2006). Innovization: Innovating design principles through optimization, *Proc. of GECCO '06,* pp. 1629-1636, Seattle, Washington, July 8-12, 2006

Deb, K., Sundar, J., Bhaskara, U. & Chaudhuri, S. (2006). Reference point based multi-objective optimization using evolutionary algorithm, *Int. J. Comp. Intelligence Research,* vol. 2, no. 3, pp. 273-286

Eiben, A. E., Hinterding, R. & Michaelwicz, Z. (1999). Parameter control in evolutionary algorithms, *IEEE Trans. Evolutionary Computation,* vol. 3, no. 2, pp. 124-141

Farhang-Boroujeny, B. (1998), *Adaptive Filters,* John Wiley & Sons, New York

Horn, J., Nafploitis, N. & Goldberg, D. E. (1994). A niched pareto genetic algorithm for multiobjective optimization, *Proc. First IEEE Conf. on Evolutionary Computation,* pp. 82-87, 1994, IEEE Press

Hughes, E. J. (2005). Evolutionary many-objective optimisation: Many once or one many? *Proc. IEEE Congress on Evolutionary Computation CEC'2005,* pp. 222-227, Edinburgh, Scotland, 2005, IEEE Service Center

Jaszkiewicz, A. (2004). On the computational efficiency of multiple objective metaheuristics: The knapsack problem case study, *European Journal of Operational Research,* vol. 158, no. 2, pp. 418-433

Kuester, J. (1973). *Optimization Techniques with FORTRAN,* McGraw-Hill College, 0070356068

Laumanns, M., Thiele, L., Deb, K. & Zitzler, E. (2002). Combining convergence and diversity in evolutionary multiobjective optimization, *Evolutionary Computation,* vol. 10, no. 3, pp. 262-282

Mitra, S., Pal, S. K. & Mitra, P. (2002). Data mining in soft computing framework: A survey, *IEEE Trans. on Neural Networks,* vol. 13, no. 1, pp. 3-14

Sato, H., H.E. Aguirre, and K. Tanaka (2007). Controlling dominance area of solutions and its impact on the performance of MOEAs, *Lecture Notes in Computer Science, Evolutionary Multi-Criterion Optimization,* ISSN 0302-9743, Springer Berlin/Heidelberg, pp. 5-20, May

Yao, X., Liu, Y. & Lin, G. M. (1999). Evolutionary programming made faster, *IEEE Trans. Evolutionary Computation*, vol. 3, pp. 82-102

Zitzler, E. & Thiele, L. (1999). Multiobjective evolutionary algorithms: A comparative case study and the strength Pareto approach, *IEEE Trans. Evolutionary Computation*, vol. 3, no. 4, pp. 257-271

24

An Empirical Study of Graph Grammar Evolution

Martin Luerssen and David Powers
Flinders University
Australia

1. Introduction

Finding an optimal topology for a graph is relevant to many problem domains, as graphs can be used to model a variety of systems. Evolutionary algorithms (EAs) constitute a popular class of heuristic optimization algorithms, but have mainly been applied to what constitutes just a small subset of graphs, namely string and trees. Methods for evolving graphs typically involve the interpretation of a string or tree into a graph (e.g. Shirakawa et al., 2007). Accordingly, they rely on classical variation operators that are proven and easy to implement, but were fundamentally never designed for graphs and may struggle with their intrinsically greater complexity. Yet operating directly on graphs does not necessarily address this problem either. What is needed is a representation that facilitates the discovery and reuse of design dependencies within graphs. Graph grammars are the key to this, and their application to evolutionary graph building will be the focus of this chapter.
Grammars have mainly performed two distinct roles in the context of evolutionary comptuation: (1) as a means of establishing search bias, both declarative and preferential, which restrict and guide the search process, respectively; and (2) as a scalable representation that separates the complexity of the genotype from that of the phenotype. Both of these are eminently useful capabilities that are rarely found in conjunction. We therefore start by reviewing past research and trends in these fields and then describe the technique of Shared Grammar Evolution (SGE), which synergistically combines both roles into one coherent framework. SGE is subsequently applied to evolve a Cellular Graph Grammar, a graph representation tailored for evolutionary change. We experimentally explore the impact of diversity and spatial separation on evolutionary convergence, and propose a new evolutionary model inspired by swarm intelligence. Finally, the issue of graph bloat and the efficacy of the representational model are analysed so as to provide a practical insight into this unique scheme.

2. Grammar-Based evolution

For clarity, let us establish some introductory concepts first. In formal terms, a grammar G is a quadruple (N, T, P, A), where N is a finite set of nonterminal symbols, T is a finite set of terminal symbols (disjoint from N), P is a set of production rules, and $A \in N$ is the axiom (or starting symbol). Each production rule is an ordered pair $p = (P, S)$, where predecessor $P \in (N \cup T)^*$ denotes a string of symbols to be replaced by the successor $S \in (N \cup T)^*$.

Context-free grammars (CFGs) are a popular class of grammars constrained to $P \in N$, so that the predecessor can only be formed by a single nonterminal. A derivation involves applying a sequence of productions, starting from the axiom and typically generating a string.

2.1 Grammatical bias

Grammatical Evolution (GE) is a well-studied method for guiding evolution with a grammar (Ryan et al., 1998). The evolved genome in GE is a linear sequence of choices that are applied to a pre-defined CFG, which acts as a declarative bias, i.e. it restricts the search space to a limited set of predetermined, "sensible" possibilities. The GE grammar can itself be evolved using the meta-Grammar Genetic Algorithm (mGGA) (O'Neill, 2005). It thereby models a preferential bias, which dynamically adapts to the search process, i.e. produces better derivations with each generation. For this purpose, a pre-defined universal CFG is employed from which GE grammars are derived that then generate the actual solutions.

The use of a linear representation makes GE straightforward to implement, but a major drawback is the lack of guarantee that a sequence of choices will end in a terminal. The standard solution is to wrap the genome and repeat the choice sequence, but this can lead to never-ending derivations. CFG-GP is an alternative scheme based on Genetic Programming (GP) does not have this drawback as it derives trees rather than strings from a CFG (Whigham, 1995; Koza, 1992). CFG-GP is also capable of evolving its grammar by creating new productions from subtrees of the fittest solutions in the population. Grammatical GP (Augusto et al., 2008) is a recent, simplified variant of CFG-GP, where subtrees can be replaced only by other type-compatible subtrees. The grammar is not directly modified here, but subtree quantities will implicitly affect derivation probabilities.

Hoai et al. (2003) further formalize the tree-based approach by employing Lexicalized Tree-Adjunct Grammars (LTAGs). Each production in an LTAG consists of elementary trees, each of which must have at least one terminal node. The broad objective of this work is to extend the notion of probabilistic model building from string representations to trees (Mühlenbein & Paaá, 1996). Grammar Model-based Program Evolution (GMPE) correspondingly performs a hill-climbing search to learn a stochastic CFG from the best solutions in an existing population (Shan et al., 2004). A grammar that specifically describes only the fittest population members is established at each generation and then generalized by merging rules with the goal of minimizing the minimum description length of the grammar. A fraction of the next generation is then sampled using this grammar, and the procedure repeated, with novelty arising from the intermediate addition of random solutions.

2.2 Grammatical development

Grammars have also found popular use as models of developmental processes in biology and as such can provide further benefits to evolutionary search. A developmental process, or embryogeny, separates the representation of what is modified during evolution (the genotype) from the actual solution (the phenotype). If one merely applies a one-to-one mapping from genotype to phenotype, then the complexity of the former has to match the complexity of the latter. Large solutions therefore become difficult to optimize, even if they exhibit symmetry, which is common in many useful designs. Biological designs exploit symmetries by employing a highly indirect, developmental representation that has DNA transcribed into RNA, translated into polypeptides, and then processed into proteins which self-organize into phenotypic traits (Futuyma, 1998). Complex feedback loops within this system produce iterative and recursive algorithms of development that are characterized by polygeny (multiple genes define a single phenotypic variable) and pleiotropy (changes to a single gene affect multiple phenotypic variables). Two desirable properties in evolutionary search are facilitated by this: neutrality and modularity. Neutrality is defined by genotypic variations that fail to affect the phenotype, which may lead to a build-up of hidden genetic variation that, once exposed, may produce a more rapid directional change than would otherwise be expected to occur. Neutral variations therefore allow distinct exploration strategies to be encoded in - and ultimately evolved with - the genotype (Toussaint, 2003). Modularity concerns the effective partition of sets into distinct subsets that are more tightly coupled internally than externally (Simon, 1996). The indirection of embryogeny enables the encoding of modules and of graph designs in terms of these modules, thus potentially reducing the configuration space that must be searched.

Embryogenic models that wish to be faithful to the biological archetype must establish detailed developmental mechanisms based on chemical, mechanical, and genetic regulatory factors. Yet the complexity of such a system implies not only a considerable computational cost, but also a general difficulty in analyzing it. In comparison, modelling embryology as a grammar can combine much of the power of a realistic model with the practicality of something simpler. A popular instance thereof is the L-system, which uses a grammar to rewrite all the symbols in a string in parallel and was originally introduced by Lindenmayer (1968) for replicating the growth characteristics of plants. Kitano (1990) evolved neural networks using a matrix L-system, where each production rewrites a node or edge symbol within a node or edge matrix into a 2 × 2 node or edge matrix. Boers and Sprinkhuizen-Kuyper (2001) used a string L-system to likewise evolve neural networks by interpreting a rewritten string as a graph. The grammar of GENRE (Hornby, 2003), an evolutionary design framework based on a parametric L-system, is evolved by a simple EA with specialized operators. Strings are rewritten and then translated into solutions, with successful applications to table designs, neural networks, and robot controllers.

In most instances of grammatical development the grammar generates a string that is interpreted as some solution construct. Data structures other than strings are less common; a notable exception is Cellular Encoding (CE) (Gruau, 1995). CE represents graph rewriting rules as a list of grammar trees, which can be evolved by GP. The nodes of the tree are references to graph operators applied successively to develop a single ancestor cell into a neural network or circuit design (Koza, 1999). Yet whether it is the choice of graph operators or the interpretation function for strings, a bias is imposed on the evolvable outcomes that is usually not well understood. It would therefore be desirable to operate as directly as possible on the graph itself - without necessarily abandoning the benefits of a grammar.

3. Graph operations

A directed graph is a quadruple (V, E, s, t) where V is a finite set of vertices, E is a finite set of edges, and $s, t: E \to V$ assign a source $s(e)$ and a target $t(e)$ to each $e \in E$. Natural and artificial instances of systems that can be represented as graphs are ubiquitous, and many problems of practical interest may be formulated as questions about graphs. Some graphs, such as the circuit of a microprocessor, need to be designed, and this is where EAs can assist. EAs traditionally operate on strings, with more recent methods such as GP operating on trees, a larger subset of graphs. For proper graph evolution we need a way to manipulate graphs. Just like sets of strings can be characterised by string grammars, sets of graphs can be characterised by graph grammars. Graph grammars therefore provide an intuitive description for the manipulation of graphs and graphical structures in any applicable domain. Over the last 30 years a great many graph rewriting mechanisms have been devised; a comprehensive review is provided by Rozenberg (1997).

3.1 Hyperedge replacement

Hyperedge replacement constitutes one of the most elementary and frequently used concepts of graph rewriting (Habel, 1992). Edges in a graph normally have arity two, that is, they connect two vertices. A hyperedge may instead have multiple sources and targets, $s, t: E \rightarrow V^*$, connecting several vertices via a set of incoming tentacles and a set of outgoing tentacles. A graph with hyperedges is known as a hypergraph. Formally, a directed, labelled hypergraph over a label set C is a quintuple (V, E, s, t, l) where V is a finite set of nodes, E is a finite set of hyperedges, $s: E \rightarrow V^*$ assigns a sequence of sources $s(e)$ to each $e \in E$, $t: E \rightarrow V^*$ assigns a sequence of targets $t(e)$ to each $e \in E$, and $l: E \rightarrow C$ labels each hyperedge.

A multi-pointed hypergraph H is a hypergraph with additional *begin* and *end* nodes, which are also referred to as the external nodes of H. Let H_C be the set of all multi-pointed hypergraphs. A hypergraph production is an ordered pair $p = (A, R)$ with predecessor $A \in N$ and successor $R \in H_C$. A hyperedge replacement grammar *HRG* is a quadruple (N, T, P, Z) where $N \in C$ is a finite set of nonterminal symbols, $T \in C$ is a finite set of terminal symbols, P is a finite set of hypergraph productions, and $Z \in H_C$ is the axiom.

Hyperedges of a hypergraph may be replaced by other hypergraphs according to hypergraph productions. Given a hyperedge e in a hypergraph H, if there is a hypergraph production $p = (e, R)$ and the begin and end nodes of the multi-pointed hypergraph R match the available attachments in H, then e may be replaced by R. This occurs by removing the hyperedge and adding the hypergraph R, except for the begin and end nodes; each tentacle of a hyperedge within R that is attached to a begin or end node is handed over to the corresponding source or target attachment node of the replaced hyperedge e.

3.2 Cellular graph grammars

Evolution of graphs implies directed change, which can be perceived as either a change to the graph, compliant with a grammar; or as a change to the grammar itself, as is common in grammatical development models. These two choices are not exclusive, as graph operations can be defined as graph replacements, i.e. grammatical operations, which can be evolved like any other graph. However, in graph grammar theory it is generally presumed that a replacement is well-typed, so that the hyperedge being replaced matches the external nodes of the multi-pointed hypergraph. The classic handover operation fuses the i-th source with the i-th begin node and the j-th target with the j-th end node, assuming these exist. In this context, not fusing any nodes beyond those that are present can lead to ripple effects on the topology of the final graph. Position independence resolves this problem and can be achieved by allowing the ordering of nodes to evolve (Goldberg et al., 1989). An identifying label $l \in C$ is assigned to each external and internal node, so that $l(v)$ is the label of node v. Additionally, we extend the mappings s and t so that the label l of the external node of the multi-pointed hypergraph is specified; the mappings hence become $s: E(l) \rightarrow V^*$ and $t: E(l) \rightarrow V^*$, respectively.

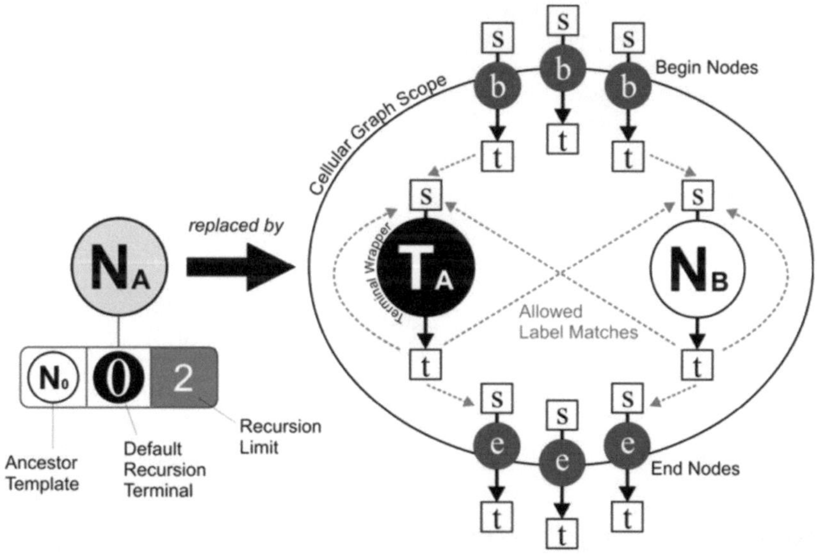

Fig. 1. A cellular production where nonterminal N_A is replaced by a cellular graph; T_A is a terminal, N_B is a nonterminal, *b* and *e* are begin and end nodes, and *s* and *t* are source labels and target labels.

A directed hypergraph can be described by an incidence structure, which contains a point for each vertex or hyperedge of the hypergraph and a line (i,j) if vertex i of the hypergraph is in hyperedge j. Storing these structures in an adjacency list has the drawback that adding or deleting a single structure would rarely be sufficient to substantially change the graph, as e.g. adding a hyperedge does not imply that it connects to anything. We address this by encapsulating those parts of a hyperedge or vertex that define how it attaches to other components into a descriptive unit referred to as a cellular graph, illustrated in Figure 1. A cellular production is a production with a cellular graph as its successor. It can be treated as a simplified hypergraph production in a hyperedge replacement system, except that all edges must be defined by cellular graphs, including those of the terminals. A graph is constructed from a grammar of cellular productions by replacing each nonterminal (or terminal wrapper) by the associated cellular graph, as shown in Figure 2. Fusion between begin and end nodes is established by finding target labels that match source labels.

We previously argued that a system that can be decomposed into modules may be more easily optimized. A module is expected to have minimal dependences with components external to the module. These dependencies usually relate to a well-specified interface of the module that acts as a dependency bottleneck. This way a successful design can be protected from being affected by changes to other components of the system. In the graph domain, achieving structural modularity translates into restricting the number of vertices inside a module that have edges to vertices outside the module. The begin and end nodes of the multi-pointed hypergraph provide a natural feature for restricting such edges, since it is only these nodes that allow binding to components external to the hypergraph.

When matching labels, we thus restrict ourselves to a specific scope for each label type. No label outside the scope boundary is visible from within the cellular graph, which, for a graph composed of many cellular graphs, greatly reduces the number of possible sources and targets for which labels must be matched. Labels are selected from a very large set (e.g.

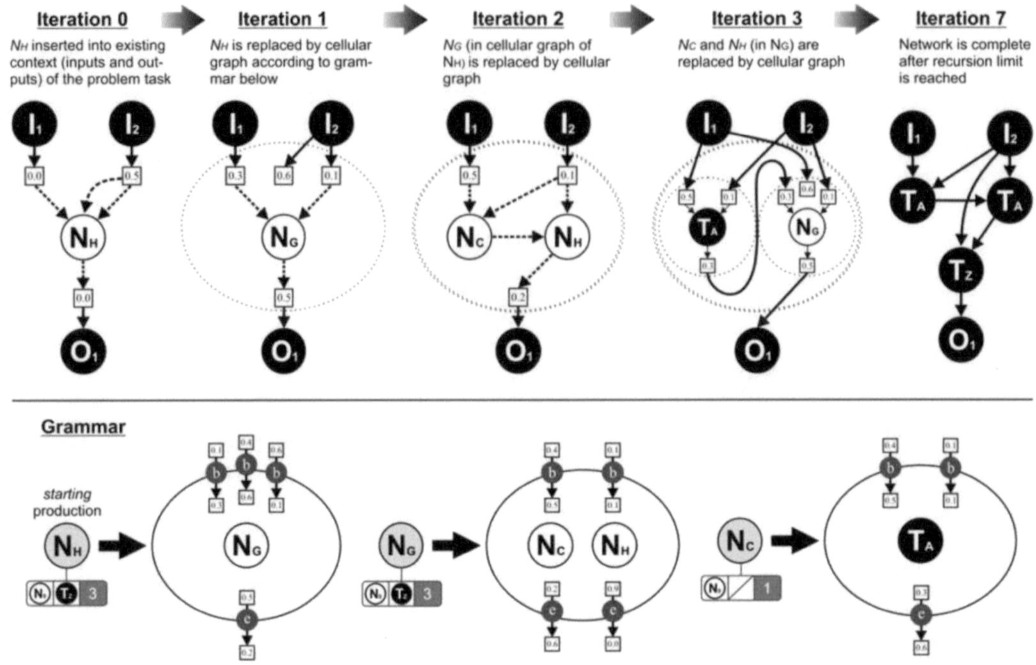

Fig. 2. A graph is derived from a cellular graph grammar over several iterations of replacement.

real numbers) and matched with the nearest, not necessarily identical, label - arithmetic difference is used here as the distance metric. Offset labels, which add to all the labels of associated cellular graphs, can also be applied to terminals and nonterminals. Labels may therefore change and combine in various ways without affecting the final solution. Subgraphs can be partially or fully disconnected from the host graph, allowing building blocks to neutrally accumulate and later be activated through possibly minor label changes.

4. Shared Grammar Evolution

Shared Grammar Evolution (SGE) provides a framework for evolving grammars such as the above (Luerssen & Powers, 2008). Each solution graph is described by its own individual grammar, referred to as an *i*-grammar, which is composed of a set of productions from which this graph (and only this graph) can be derived. Productions within an *i*-grammar may refer to each other, leading to recursion and a high degree of pleiotropy, as individual productions can trigger many other productions. This is comparable to the L-system evolution discussed previously, but instead of representing each solution by a separate set of productions, SGE combines these sets into a single set, the *p*-grammar. Productions with identical successors can be eliminated from the *p*-grammar, as only one instance of a particular production has to exist, even if it is involved in the derivation of different programs. Depending on the reuse of productions, the total number of productions in the population may thus be reduced, as shown in Figure 3.

Since a grammar with alternatives cannot uniquely represent - that is, describe deterministically - a specific solution, no productions with identical predecessors are

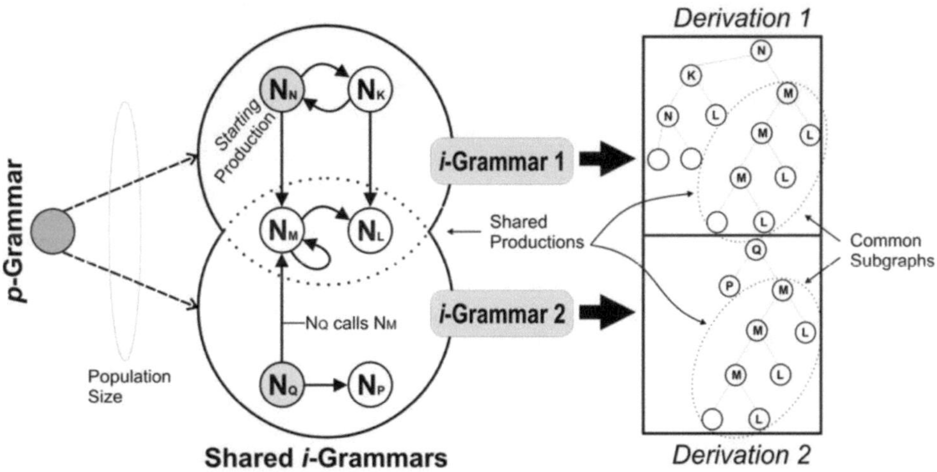

Fig. 3. Each graph is derived from an associated grammar, but grammars may share productions.

permitted in *i*-grammars. *i*-grammars are initially generated from a user-defined set of template productions, which define the cellular graphs and terminals that are permissible. Template productions can have alternatives, since their role is not as a representation, but as a declarative bias. They delimit the range of graphs that can evolve, as every new production is a variation of a template production. In case *a priori* knowledge about an optimal static template grammar is poor, cellular graphs can also be mutated directly during evolution. For this, the components of a cellular graph are organized into a list of nonterminal symbols (hyperedges of the graph), a list of terminal symbols (terminal nodes of the graph), and a list of *(source, target, direction)* label triples (begin and end nodes of the graph). Three operators may be applied to each list:

- *insert*, which adds a new element into a random position in the list, where the new element is defined by randomly selecting a new symbol and new labels from a global set of all possible choices, including the template grammar
- *remove*, which randomly selects an element from the list and deletes it
- *change*, which combines the insert and remove operator

A probability is assigned to each *(operation, list)* pair, so that all probabilities sum to 1. A mutation involves randomly selecting a pair from these probabilities. If an inserted label is obtained from the template grammar, it is changed to point to a new production instance (and its associated subgraph) generated from the template grammar. The above operators are supplemented by the *increase recursion* and *decrease recursion* operators, which increase or decrease the recursion limit of the cellular production by one. During derivation, a production is redirected to an associated default terminal if it calls itself, directly or indirectly, more often than specified by this limit.

SGE can be viewed as a repeated growing and pruning of the *p*-grammar; an illustration of this is given in Figure 4. For every graph derived from its associated starting production, a single expressed production is spontaneously replaced by a mutated variant. After testing all the mutated graphs, the least fit solutions, both from the mutated set and the previously evaluated graphs, are discarded by eliminating all associated productions that are not involved in any fitter solutions. Conversely, if a mutation survived, the *p*-grammar is modified so that the mutated graph becomes one of the graphs derivable from it.

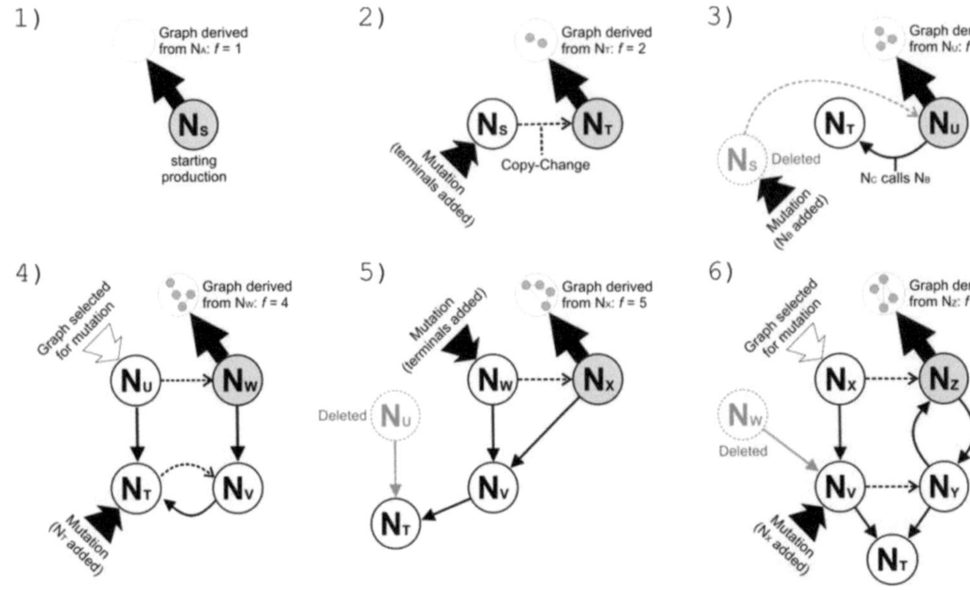

Fig. 4. Illustration of SGE with a maximum population of two graphs. Starting with an empty production/graph N_S in generation (1), terminals are added to a copy N_T of this production in (2), then N_T is added to itself, producing N_U in (3), while the graph of N_S has least fitness *f* and is thus removed. N_T in the graph of N_U is then mutated in (4), producing N_V and a copy of N_U, N_W, with a reference to N_V. The graph of N_T is now uncompetitive, but remains as a production used by N_U. Further offspring is created in (5) and (6), leading to N_Z, which exhibits a recursive self-reference.

5. Promoting diversity

Diversity refers to the differences between members of a population. Genotypic diversity is the diversity among genomes in the population, whereas phenotypic diversity is the diversity among fitness values in the population. Since genetic lineages often reduce to one lineage early in the evolutionary process (McPhee & Hopper, 1999), maintaining diversity in a population is necessary for the long-term success of any evolutionary system, as it allows the population to continue searching for productive regions of the search space and thus avoid becoming trapped by local optima. Several methods have been proposed to improve diversity and combat premature convergence in EAs; we will investigate two of these in the context of graph grammar evolution: phenotypic diversity objectives and spatial separation.

5.1 Phenotypic diversity objectives

The principal drawback of any genotypic diversity measure is its limited applicability to a grammar, as the extensive neutrality intrinsic to this representation would allow it to improve diversity while remaining isomorphic. A possible solution is to employ a phenotypic diversity objective instead (Luerssen, 2005). The error returned by the objective function is the most available phenotypic trait of a solution and hence a solid basis for measuring phenotypic diversity. To reduce any bias attributable to the nature of the specific objective function used, the solutions can be ranked against each other on this function;

distances are then computed as differences of ranks. The mean distance of solution i is the absolute difference between ranks,

$$D_i = \frac{\sum_{j=0}^{N} |R_i - R_j|}{N} \tag{5.1}$$

where N is the number of other solutions. A measure less biased towards rewarding poor performance is to compare whether two solutions i and j show non-identical performance,

$$S_{ij} = \begin{cases} 1 \; if \; R_i \neq R_j \\ 0 \; otherwise \end{cases} \tag{5.2}$$

The diversity of solution i can be defined as the proportion of solutions that are different in performance,

$$D_i = \frac{\sum_{j=0}^{N} S_{ij}}{N} \tag{5.3}$$

This 'difference' measure is logarithmically related to the phenotypic entropy of the solution:

$$H(i) = -\log(1 - \frac{\sum_{j=0}^{N} S_{ij}}{N}) \tag{5.4}$$

but since the diversity objective will also be ranked for selection purposes, we can use the simpler difference measure while obtaining the same effect.

Solutions with equal mean performance can still be different, and the measures presented so far do not recognise this. Distinguishing these solutions without comparing their genotypes is only feasible if there are multiple fitness cases that can be compared separately. Then the mean rank distance can be averaged across each case c,

$$D_i = \frac{\sum_{c=0}^{C} \sum_{j=0}^{N} |R_{ci} - R_{cj}|}{C \times N} \tag{5.5}$$

where C is the number of fitness cases. Two solutions perform identically if

$$S_{ij} = \begin{cases} 1 \; if \; \sum_{c=0}^{C} |R_{ci} - R_{cj}| > 0 \\ 0 \; otherwise \end{cases} \tag{5.6}$$

so that diversity may again be defined as the proportion of non-identical solutions,

$$D_i = \frac{\sum_{j=0}^{N} S_{ij}}{C \times N} \tag{5.7}$$

5.1.1 Handling multiple objectives

Having both a performance and a diversity objective implies that there is not one optimal solution, but a set of compromises known as a Pareto-optimal set. Multiobjective evolutionary algorithms (MOEAs) are typically based on Pareto-domination, where a solution S_1 is said to dominate another solution S_2 if S_1 is no worse than S_2 in all objectives and better than S_2 on at least one objective (Deb, 2001). If the population size is smaller than the size of the Pareto-optimal set, then the MOEA is meant to return solutions spread evenly along the Pareto boundary. Most MOEAs apply some form of phenotypic niching to achieve this: if individual S_1 is more nondominated than S_2, S_1 is preferred regardless of niching, whereas if S_1 and S_2 have the same degree of nondominatedness, the one residing in the most sparsely populated region of the search-space is preferred. In the multi-objective implementation of SGE, we assess population density as simply the distance between a chosen solution and its nearest neighbour, with a bias towards the lowest error solution in case of a tie (or the newest solution, if this fails). Otherwise the MOEA for SGE matches the NSGA-II presented by Deb et al. (2000).

	Binomial-3 Regression	**Random Bit Sequence (RBS)**	**Pole Balancing**	**Computer Network Topology (CNT)**
Objective	Infer the mapping $y = f(x)$, where $f(x)$ is the binomial-3 polynomial $(x+1)^3$	Reproduce a binary time sequence	Optimize topology and weights of a neural network balancing 2 poles fixed to a cart moving on a finite track	Create a virtual computer network that efficiently connects data sinks with sources
Terminals	0/1/2-ary: +, -, ×, % (protected division)	0/1/2-ary: AND, XOR	Neurons with transfer function: $\varphi(x) = \frac{1}{1+e^{-4.9x}}$	Virtual sinks, sources, and switches
Fitness Case(s)	21 equidistant points generated by the objective function over $x = [-1, 1]$	16-bit sequence given by a 4-bit de Bruijn Counter (with seed 0000)	Pole balancing setup and simulation, see Stanley & Miikkulainen (2002)	10 randomly pregenerated unit/data stream configurations
Simulation	Graph relaxed for 10 cycles	Simulation for 32 simulation cycles (+4 cycles lead-in), sampled every 2 cycles; to allow many different designs to be synchronized with the sampling rate, line delays are assigned to edges with a geometric probability of 0.5 of longer delays	Relaxed for 3 cycles; weights are assigned to edges by randomization with a standard Gaussian distribution ($\mu = 0$, $\sigma = 1$), at 0.3 prob., or by DE (Price, 1999), at 0.7 prob., with parameter $F = 0.2$ and a crossover prob. of 0.9	Simplified network simulation, see Luerssen (2009)
Error Measure	Mean squared error	Proportion of incorrectly reproduced bits	Reciprical number of cycles both poles remain balanced	Fraction of data requests not satisfied
Mutation	A single production is selected for mutation and a single mutation is applied at a time, with a geometric probability of 0.5 that further mutations are applied to the same production			
Population	20 graphs, each defined by a maximum of 1000 productions and 1000 terminals per production			
Generations	1000			

Table 1. Description and default parameters for all experimental problem tasks.

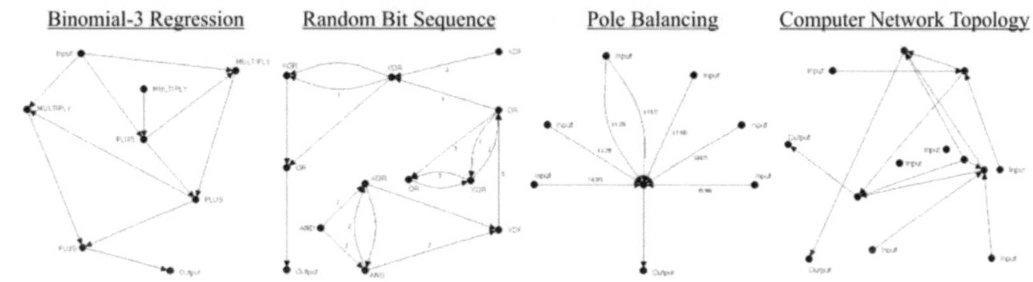

Fig. 5. A sample of graphs evolved by SGE on the four problem tasks. Connection weights are shown for the pole balancing ANN and line delays for the sequence circuit.

5.1.2 Experiment

To evaluate the effect of diversity on graph grammar evolution, we selected four problem tasks, which are described in Table 1. They are quick to evaluate, yet also challenging, and encompass different natural requirements of the representation. Sample solutions for each problem are shown in Figure 5. Solution candidates are evolved with a MOEA applied to three objectives: the function error, the solution size (see also section 8), and one of four diversity measures: entropy, fitness case entropy, distance, and fitness case distance. Results are averaged over 100 runs. Statistical significance is determined using a Z-test or non-parametric Wilcoxon rank sum test on the best solutions of the final generation of each run.

5.1.3 Results

The performance outcomes of using the different diversity measures are listed in tables 2 and 3 later in the chapter. On the Binomial-3 regression, the best results are obtained with the simple entropy measure, which gives a mean error of 0.0155 for the best solutions. Without a diversity measure, the mean error is 0.054, which appears a lot worse, yet the difference is only borderline significant ($p < 0.03$). The success rates for both the simple distance measure and fitness case Pareto are 57%, which is significantly worse than the 71% without a diversity measure ($p < 0.005$) and also significantly worse on the less sensitive non-parametric test than any of the entropy measures (all below $p < 0.003$).

All diversity measures improve performance on the RBS evolution, and this improvement is significant except with the simple distance objective. The distance objective is significantly better on the MSE if applied to fitness cases than otherwise ($p < 4 \times 10^{-13}$), but solutions obtained by use of any distance measure are also very large in size, typically more than 20 times of what is obtained otherwise. Only a single fitness case is used for pole balancing, so the fitness case-based diversity measure is inapplicable. MSEs are generally low, but not all solutions manage to balance the pole for the entire cycle sequence. The entropy measure leads to an improvement, but this is not significant, whereas the distance measure (with only 71% success rate) is significantly worse on the success rate ($p < 0.02$). The CNT design problem benefits significantly from every diversity measure except the simple distance objective, which had a negative, but not significant, influence on performance.

Overall, using phenotypic difference (i.e. entropy) as a diversity measure is generally quite effective, particularly if differences between fitness cases are taken into account. Mean distance measures are less effective; performance reductions are observed with the simple phenotypic distance, but computing distance over fitness cases produces better results. However, solutions arising from these measures are frequently much larger than otherwise, with a correspondingly negative impact on evaluation time (not shown).

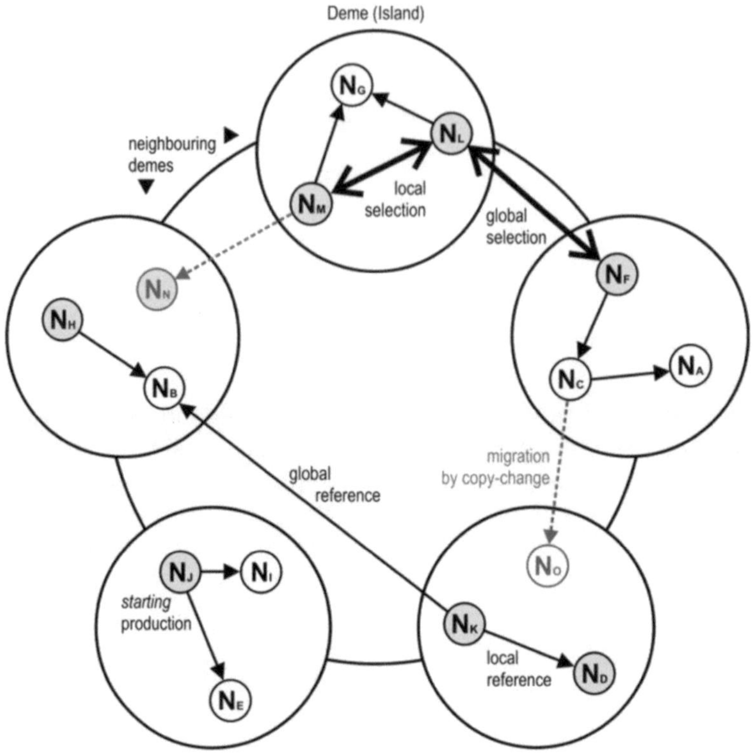

Fig. 6. The island model as applied to graph grammar evolution: islands are arranged in a ring, with offspring being allowed to move to neighbouring islands.

5.2 Island models

Separating individuals spatially may promote their diversity by allowing them to evolve more independently of other parts of the population. The most popular model of this, the island model, coarsely divides the population into several smaller subpopulations, called demes (Martin et al., 1997). An EA evolves each deme independently, but, periodically, information is exchanged by migrating individuals from one deme to another. The migration rate is an important parameter here, as high rates cause global mixing, reducing the isolation advantage, whereas a low rate may lead to each deme converging prematurely. Production sharing in SGE complicates this migration of an individual - and all its associated productions - to a different deme, so the island model will be applied to the selection process alone: solutions compete only against those on the same deme, but productions can refer to any others globally. There is no effect on the choice of productions for new solutions, i.e. the mating aspect of the island model.

This latter aspect may be included by making production choices dependent on the deme. Production choice matters only in two instances: when we choose a production for mutation, and when we add a production to another production. Choosing a production for mutation by a deme that matches that of the solution does not achieve any sort of localisation; it just modifies the effective mutation rate for each production. Consequently, we only explore choosing productions for insertion according to deme, which we will refer to as *local* mating. The deme to match in this case is the deme of the production that is being mutated, as this causes localisation along the call chain between productions - neighbouring productions will tend be on the same deme and so will alternative choices for these productions, which focuses the search along these choices. The various interactions of productions across islands are visualised in Figure 6.

5.2.1 Experiment

Our model is based on a simple 2-neighbour cellular space forming a ring, where transition is possible from any island to any of its two neighbours. We compare the island model with local selection but a fully global production pool against the island model with local selection and local mating. The number of demes in this case is fixed at 5, and there is no limit to how many solutions or productions may exist in a deme. The population starts with a single empty starting production in the first deme. The choice of mutations will be expanded so that productions can transit randomly to one of the two neighbouring demes. This *transition* mutation is applied at the same probability as any *insert* or *remove* mutation. These models are tested against running 5 populations (of 4 members) in complete seclusion to each other to establish whether there is any benefit to transitions at all. Each deme starts with a single empty production, and productions are exclusive to each deme. Finally, the effect of different deme numbers is also evaluated, but only on the model without local mating. Rings with 2, 5, and a more fine-grained 20 demes are used. Note that multiobjetive niching will be applied globally across all islands, so that being on a different island only affects domination, not niching.

5.2.2 Results

Dividing the population into any configuration of islands leads to an improved MSE on every problem - there are no instances in which the performance is actually diminished. The improvements are not always significant, however, and the number of islands appears to matter. For the Binomial-3 regression and the pole balancing, the best results are obtained with 5 islands (with a significance of $p < 0.009$ and $p < 0.0002$, respectively, against the single island). On the CNT design, the success rate of 35% is also best with 5 islands ($p < 0.02$). Choosing productions locally from an island rather than from a global repository appears to have no significant impact on the tested 5 island configuration. Since solutions that migrate from one island to another can still refer to the original, but now remote, productions, the practical differences to a fully global production repository are rather minor, so this is perhaps not a surprise. On the other hand, evolving populations on 5 isolated islands leads to worse performance than with the standard island model. Migration between islands is clearly essential for gaining performance benefits from the island model.

6. Adaptive search

Ant Colony Optimization (ACO) is perhaps the best-known implementation of swarm intelligence (Dorigo et al., 1999). It is inspired by the ability of ants to establish shortest route paths between their colony and food sources. In ACO, a set of simple computational agents - artificial ants - explore a graph of states corresponding to partial solutions of the problem. A solution to the problem is incrementally constructed by the ants moving between these states. Ants lay down a pheromone trail that indicates how beneficial a move was, which affects the probability distribution of future moves.

EAs differ from ACO in that the former represents the knowledge about the problem as a population of solutions, whereas the latter maintains a memory of past performance in the form of pheromone trails. For graph grammar evolution, such a memory may provide useful guidance in exploring the grammar. Productions can only survive if they are useful in some existing solution - thus, unlike any random construct, such productions also have a higher probability of being useful in a new solution. Naturally, this probability diminishes if there are niches for many different solutions in the population, because we might randomly pick a production and use it in a context for which it was not evolved. Reinterpreted for ACO, each production is a partial solution, and the addition of a production constitutes a move. Unlike ACO, SGE has no explicit probabilities assigned to each move. Consequently, production choice is highly random and depends solely on the composition of the grammar. Having an adaptable probability distribution as with ACO would provide superior guidance, but partial solutions in SGE are exceedingly short-lived: productions are added and removed with every generation. The path that one ant builds can rarely be followed by another. SGE thus does not appear easy to adapt to swarm intelligence, but a more limited model is possible and will be presented next.

6.1 Graph grammar swarms

At least two choices must be made when generating offspring from a graph. First, we must choose one of the productions expressed during derivation of this graph. Instead of randomly choosing from a uniform distribution, as in the existing framework, the following heuristic inspired by PBIL (Baluja & Caruana, 1995) is implemented. The chance of a production being chosen is decreased if it rarely results in successful offspring. A real value θ is stored with each production. When choosing a production to mutate, the chance of a specific production R_i being chosen from m productions is

$$P(R_i) = \frac{\theta_i}{\sum_{j=1}^{m} \theta_j}$$

θ is multiplied or divided by a user-defined factor $\rho > 1$ depending on whether the new offspring of this production survives into the next generation or is eliminated, respectively. No evaporation of θ occurs here. θ is simply reset to 1 for every new production, as the expected success of mutating a new production may be independent of the success of mutating the original production. The presented mechanism should globally reduce the mutation of productions that rarely lead to good offspring (e.g. productions fully optimized for their context) and focus on other productions that do.

Some of the graph grammar mutations involve novel choices, such as a choice of label and a choice of production being added, all from potentially very large sets. As, in some cases, multiple variations may be needed to produce fit offspring, a highly specific sequence of such variations is not likely to occur. Yet if it does occur, it never needs to occur again, as it will be stored as a new production. Our second proposal therefore is to make use of the genetic lineage when applying variation. Recording a lineage from a production to all its descendants provides a list of moves that are known to be successful. A descendant is likely to be located in a context similar to its ancestors, so replacing an ancestor with a descendant seems a promising move. Following this line, we replace a production, once chosen for mutation, by one of its descendants - and then apply additional variations. The descendant is chosen according to the above system of preferred mutation targets, as illustrated in Figure 7. The upshot of this is that the replacement effectively applies previously successful variations immediately, so the search can emphasise the neighbourhood of productions with high offspring ratios.

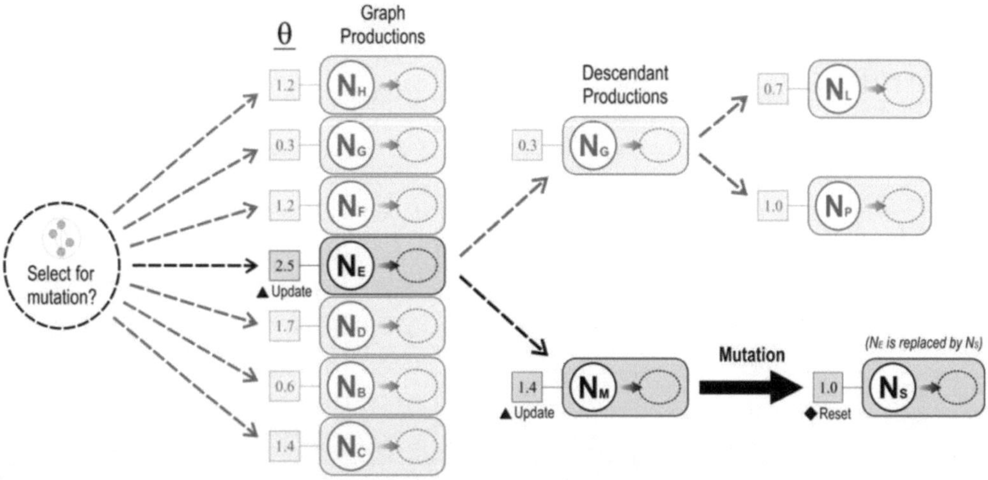

Fig. 7. Adaptive production search: The probability of a production being chosen for mutation is dependent on $\boldsymbol{\theta}$; it is then replaced by a descendant also determined by $\boldsymbol{\theta}$ before mutation is applied.

6.1.1 Experiment

We apply the above extensions separately and in combination. Choosing a production for mutation according to real value θ will be referred to as the *target* choice; replacing a production by a descendant is the *lineage* choice. The pheromone factor is ρ = 1.2 and the probability of replacement by a descendant is φ = 0.9. These values were chosen *a priori*: ρ should be set so that a production's respective θ is substantially different - but not excessively different - after several successful (or failed) mutations, whereas φ should allow for some cases where no descendant is chosen, but also have a large value so as to increase the experimental effect here.

6.1.2 Results

No evident trend can be observed across the different problem tasks. Applying lineage replacement results in better performance on all tasks compared to the default configuration, but the difference is not significant. It is likely that characterising a production through a single parameter θ is an oversimplification, as it fails to take the dynamic context into account. Furthermore, most of the productions in the grammar do not have many descendants, or in fact any: only 29.8% (averaged across all problem tasks) of final generation productions had at least one descendant present in the grammar. Graph evolution is characterised by a punctuated equilibrium, and only a few offspring survive each generation, often to replace their parents in the same niche. Under these conditions any production not replaced by a descendant is equal or better than its descendants. Although the descendants are the only known successful mutation transitions, the results suggest that a preference for offspring over parent is indeed not very beneficial to overall performance.

Problem		Parameters	Success Rate	MCE ×1000	Min MSE		Size	
					Min	Mean	Mean	Min Err.
Binomial-3 Regression		Default	71%	55	0.000	0.054±0.106	18±7	25±7
	Diversity	Entropy	*82%*	46	0.000	*0.016*±0.039	21±16	30±28
		Case Entropy	*79%*	45	0.000	0.029±0.074	19±5	30±11
		Distance	*57%*	104	0.000	0.064±0.100	41±79	29±11
		Case Distance	64%	84	0.000	0.060±0.107	72±110	39±64
	Island Model	2 Islands	76%	62	0.000	0.035±0.086	15±3	25±8
		5 Islands	*84%*	51	0.000	*0.015*±0.043	20±6	39±21
		20 Islands	71%	77	0.000	0.030±0.103	30±9	46±22
		5 Isl. (Local)	78%	63	0.000	0.020±0.047	20±5	35±15
		5 Isl. (Isolated)	66%	83	0.000	0.051±0.130	17±4	28±10
	Adaptive Search	Target	64%	77	0.000	0.079±0.126	18±5	24±7
		Lineage	79%	50	0.000	0.035±0.086	20±5	28±8
		Target+Lineage	74%	53	0.000	0.043±0.094	19±5	26±9
	Size Objective	Size Shared	*21%*	360	0.000	*0.451*±0.644	9±6	51±54
		No Primary Size	*31%*	399	0.000	*0.189*±0.246	47±37	47±37
		C.Entr.+No Size	*86%*	20	0.000	*0.009*±0.033	378±850	360±900
Random Bit Sequence Circuit		Default	1%	36390	0.000	0.134±0.057	13±5	14±7
	Diversity	Entropy	4%	7874	0.000	*0.109*±0.057	13±4	14±6
		Case Entropy	*21%*	1442	0.000	*0.065*±0.044	16±6	17±13
		Distance	2%	12522	0.000	0.119±0.051	375±230	32±36
		Case Distance	*24%*	1321	0.000	*0.063*±0.045	342±240	27±17
	Island Model	2 Islands	4%	6970	0.000	0.124±0.058	15±9	17±11
		5 Islands	*6%*	4687	0.000	0.116±0.058	16±9	17±11
		20 Islands	*10%*	2944	0.000	*0.102*±0.060	20±8	21±13
		5 Isl. (Local)	*6%*	5046	0.000	*0.109*±0.059	16±7	16±8
		5 Isl. (Isolated)	*8%*	4395	0.000	0.119±0.065	14±8	16±20
	Adaptive Search	Target	3%	8044	0.000	0.123±0.053	14±7	14±8
		Lineage	4%	8416	0.000	0.113±0.055	14±7	15±8
		Target+Lineage	3%	9685	0.000	0.134±0.063	12±5	13±5
	Size Objective	Size Shared	*0%*	N/A	0.063	*0.156*±0.061	18±9	27±38
		No Primary Size	*18%*	1376	0.000	*0.084*±0.061	23±19	23±19
		C.Entr.+No Size	*96%*	79	0.000	*0.003*±0.012	89±73	79±43

Table 2. Performance statistics for experiments, averaged over 100 runs. MCE denotes minimum computational effort for a success probability of 99% (see Koza, 1992).

Problem		Parameters	Success Rate	MCE ×1000	Min MSE		Size	
					Min	Mean	Mean	Min Err.
Pole Balancing		Default	82%	40	0.001	0.002±0.002	8±1	9±3
	Diversity	Entropy	*90%*	32	0.001	0.001±0.001	7±1	8±2
		Distance	*71%*	71	0.001	0.002±0.002	6±1	9±2
	Island Model	2 Islands	*96%*	26	0.001	*0.001*±0.001	7±1	9±2
		5 Islands	*98%*	20	0.001	*0.001*±0.001	8±2	10±4
		20 Islands	*95%*	23	0.001	*0.001*±0.001	12±9	13±10
		5 Isl. (Local)	*100%*	20	0.001	*0.001*±0.000	8±1	10±3
		5 Isl. (Isolated)	*96%*	32	0.001	*0.001*±0.000	8±2	9±2
	Adaptive Search	Target	77%	48	0.001	0.002±0.002	8±1	8±2
		Lineage	86%	34	0.001	0.002±0.002	7±0	7±2
		Target+Lineage	84%	37	0.001	0.002±0.002	8±1	8±2
	Size Objective	Size Shared	87%	46	0.001	0.002±0.002	8±1	8±2
		No Primary Size	*42%*	76	0.001	*0.003*±0.003	35±42	36±43
		C.Entr.+No Size	*51%*	47	0.001	*0.003*±0.003	91±119	31±36
ComputerNetwork Topology Design		Default	23%	1366	0.000	0.180±0.167	5±2	7±7
	Diversity	Entropy	32%	932	0.000	*0.127*±0.133	6±4	8±8
		Case Entropy	39%	1051	0.000	*0.112*±0.127	6±2	8±4
		Distance	20%	1463	0.000	0.141±0.120	6±4	9±13
		Case Distance	25%	1293	0.000	*0.134*±0.133	6±3	8±6
	Island Model	2 Islands	21%	1570	0.000	0.169±0.149	6±3	8±8
		5 Islands	*35%*	722	0.000	*0.126*±0.143	6±4	9±14
		20 Islands	28%	935	0.000	*0.102*±0.108	6±5	10±14
		5 Isl. (Local)	30%	1041	0.000	0.144±0.161	6±5	8±9
		5 Isl. (Isolated)	27%	1081	0.000	0.131±0.128	6±3	8±7
	Adaptive Search	Target	*26%*	1281	0.000	0.145±0.176	5±3	7±5
		Lineage	21%	1506	0.000	0.172±0.152	5±3	7±6
		Target+Lineage	24%	1378	0.000	0.161±0.154	6±2	7±3
	Size Objective	Size Shared	*1%*	30882	0.000	*0.400*±0.176	0±1	6±3
		No Primary Size	*37%*	450	0.000	*0.089*±0.108	13±24	12±17
		C.Entr.+No Size	*54%*	202	0.000	*0.047*±0.068	120±133	42±63

Table 3. (Continued from Table 2) Standard deviations are listed after each ±. *Italic* success rates are signifantly different from default (Z-test, $\boldsymbol{p} < 0.05$); *italic* MSEs are significantly different from default (Wilcoxon rank sum test, $\boldsymbol{p} < 0.05$)

7. Complexity growth

Solutions may grow during evolution more so than necessary, a phenomenon referred to as bloat (Langdon & Poli, 1997). Targeting solution size as an evolutionary objective is an effective means of addressing this and also leaves the user with a Pareto-optimal set of solutions balancing performance and size. This has been our default setup so far. In most instances this is desirable; in others only the best performing solution is acceptable and searching the entire Pareto boundary would then seem a disproportionate effort. A viable alternative is provided by having size become a secondary objective: only solutions with equal performance will compete on the size objective, so any solution with better performance will dominate another solution independent of its size.

Size is defined here as the sum of the terminals, nonterminals, and external nodes (i.e. label triples) of each cellular production expressed during the derivation of the graph. This is not the same as a node + edge count of the graph, but any less inclusive measure would permit bloat. With any form of size constraint, however, some degree of redundancy will be needed to balance exploitation, i.e., greedy search, against exploration, i.e., diversity in the population. Hidden variation can accumulate within redundant code and, once revealed, fuel the kind of rapid adaptation needed to escape from any suboptima that have trapped the search (Hansen, 2006). We suggest to accommodate this by sharing the size of a production among all the solutions in the population that make use of this production (excluding recurrency, which is still scored cumulatively). A production contributing to many graphs therefore becomes in effect cheaper, which facilitates its reuse.

7.1 Experiment

Experiments are performed using our standard set of problem tasks and parameters, with four variations being tested: 1) size is targeted as an evolutionary objective (the experimental default); 2) size is shared among that solutions that utilize it; 3) size is consulted only on equally performing solutions (denoted *No Size* for brevity); and 4) fitness case entropy is included as a primary objective when size is secondary (see reasons below).

7.2 Results

Allowing production size to be shared among solutions triggers a significant decline in performance across all tasks where reuse would be expected to matter (i.e. all except pole balancing, which is structurally trivial). At first this may seem puzzling, but analysis of the solutions provides a clue. Using shared size causes the evolution of a grammar where some productions call on many more (10+) other productions than is otherwise typical. A coevolution appears to happen where solutions minimise their effective size by maximising references to each other's productions. Part of the population is thus optimized on the size objective at the expense of actual task performance.

Significant performance differences are also observed when making size a secondary objective, with the Binomial-3 regression and the pole balancing performing worse ($p < 5 \times 10^{-8}$), yet the RBS and the CNT design performing better ($p < 3 \times 10^{-8}$). These contradictory results reflect a problem-dependent trade-off between the general benefit of not selecting against size and the detriment of losing diversity as a consequence of this. In line with this, both the Binomial-3 regression and the pole balancing have a relatively much lower diversity than the RBS and CNT design when using a secondary size objective.

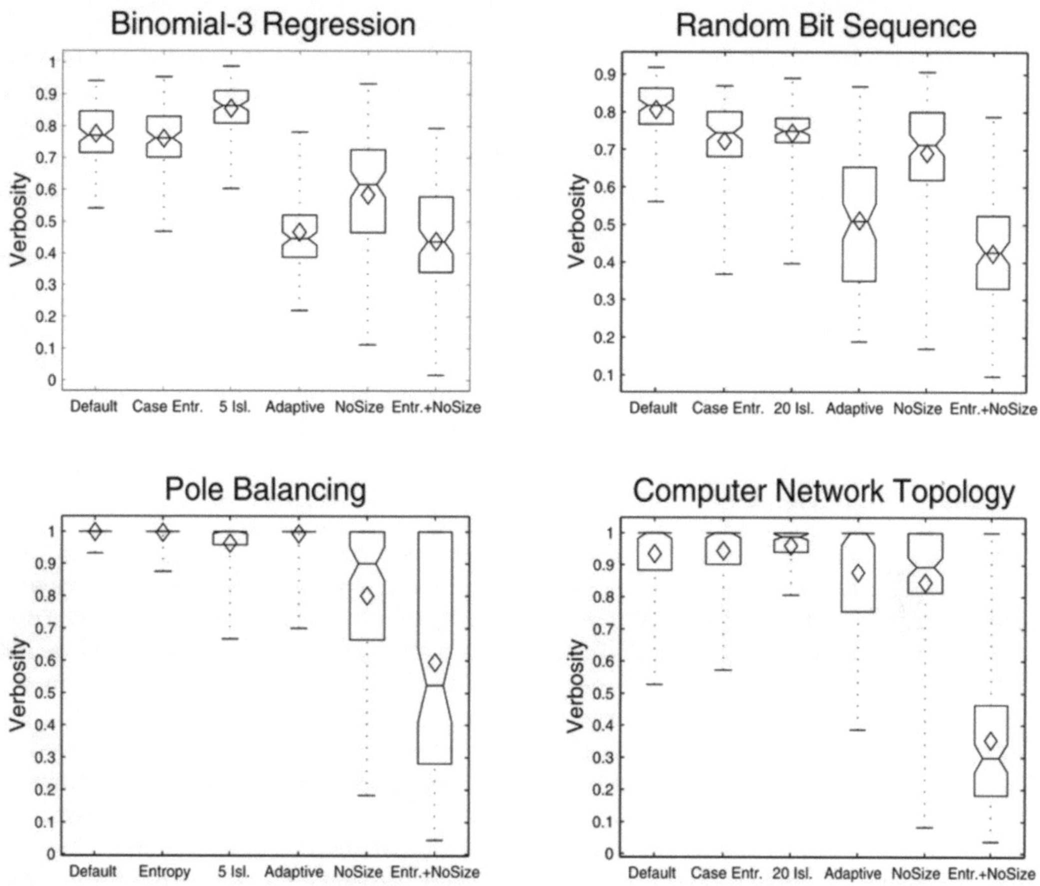

Fig. 8. Verbosity box plots for final generation that show median, quartiles, and outliers. Verbosity is defined as the ratio of the total production number expressed when deriving all graphs over the total production number in the population. If verbosity is 1, each production would belong to a single graph and there is no recursion, whereas low verbosity indicates high reuse.

Presumably, if a diversity objective were to be employed in conjunction with a secondary, rather than primary, size objective, performance improvements should be observed for any problem where size might be constraining factor.

Results indeed corroborate this hypothesis. Performance on the Binomial-3 regression, RBS, and CNT design improves significantly compared to the default configuration and also compared to the previous outcomes of using diversity measures (except for the regression, where $p = 0.11$). Particularly noteworthy is the improvement with the RBS, where the success rate rises to 96% from just 1% for the default. The disadvantage of this setup is the increase in solution size and hence computational cost: while using a secondary size objective approximately doubles the mean solution size, in combination with the diversity objective it increases almost 7× on the RBS – and more than 20× for the regression and CNT design. The large mean size is caused by a small number of very big solutions, as suggested by the large standard deviation.

7.3 Reuse

SGE is unique in sharing productions between multiple solutions. A measure of this reuse is shown in Figure 8. Problems previously identified as making more use of multiple productions – the Binomial-3 regression and the RBS – exhibit a moderate degree of reuse, while pole balancing shows very little. Some extreme outliers are noted; the occurrence of a small number of large recursive solutions in the population could be a possible explanation for this. We noted earlier that the use of adaptive search (target + lineage in this experiment) has little impact on performance, but this figure reveals that it encourages reuse on the problems where reuse should matter, resulting in much smaller grammars for the same graph size. Also noteworthy is the significant increase in reuse associated with removing the size objective as a primary objective. Reuse appears to scale with the size of the evolved solutions, which indicates that the efficiency of the grammar representation would be most evident with problems that require larger solutions than the ones evaluated here.

8. Generational trends

Figures 9 to 12 depict the changes of various population and solution statistics over 1000 generations for the major different configurations. The individual plots show, in clockwise order starting from the legend: the MSE of the best performing solution; the mean entropy of all population members (across all different fitness cases); the proportion of solutions that are replaced by new solutions each generation; the total number of productions in the population; the mean size of all solutions; and the size of the best performing solution.

Graph evolution without a primary size objective but with a diversity objective (denoted *C. Entr. + No Size*) converges most quickly among all alternative configurations and produces the best outcome on the majority of problem tasks, with the exception of pole balancing, where the small size of the optimal solution actually penalises any relaxation of the size constraint. Without either a primary size or a diversity objective the growth of solution size is much more contained, but solutions also exhibit inferior performance. Reductions in size during evolution seem to be uncommon, particularly when applying the primary size objective, which suggests that either the optimization towards a minimum size is quite ineffective, or, more likely, that solutions much larger than the current performance optimum have a propensity to do poorly on the performance objective. Nevertheless, it is apparent from the success of the *C. Entr. + No Size* configuration that the best outcomes are obtained when such solutions make up part of the population.

The total production numbers are dependent on solution size and the extent of reuse. The smallest grammars are obtained with the adaptive production search model, which encourages reuse without penalty to performance, although there seem to be no practical benefits to this. It was originally expected that adaptive search could accelerate convergence, yet as the plots indicate, adaptive search behaves very similarly to the default configuration.

On the entropy statistic, we note that using the entropy as an objective improves average entropy of the solutions, but also not nearly as much as the island model does. An explanation for this may be found in the comparatively low rate of solution replacement that we observe with the entropy objective. It suggests that not much opportunity is given for introducing the kind of structural novelty into the population that is not directly reflected in phenotypic diversity. However, it is not clear why the replacement ratio for the island

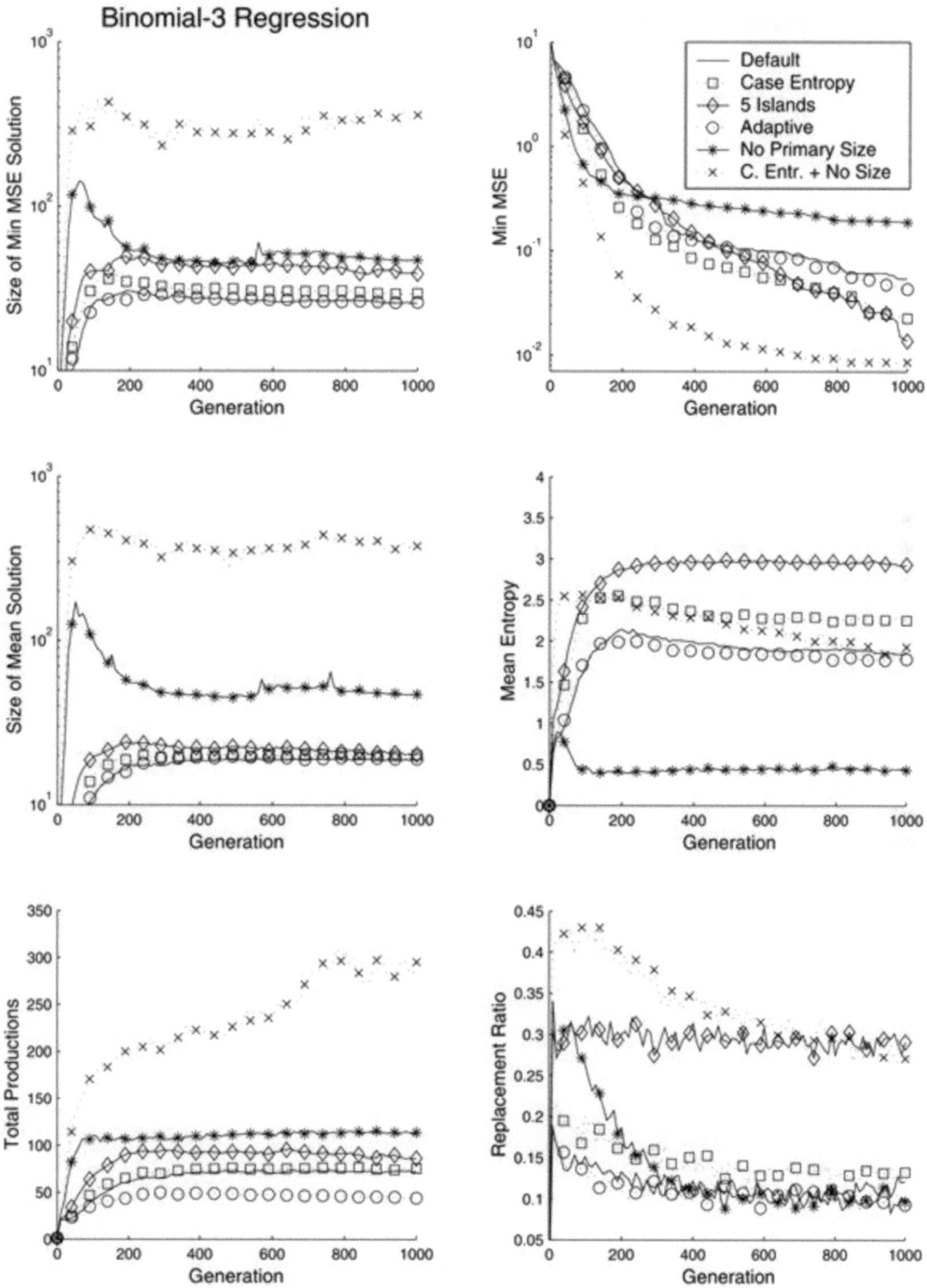

Fig. 9. Generational development for the Binomial-3 regression problem. (MSE and size are shown on a logarithmic Y-axis to improve readability.)

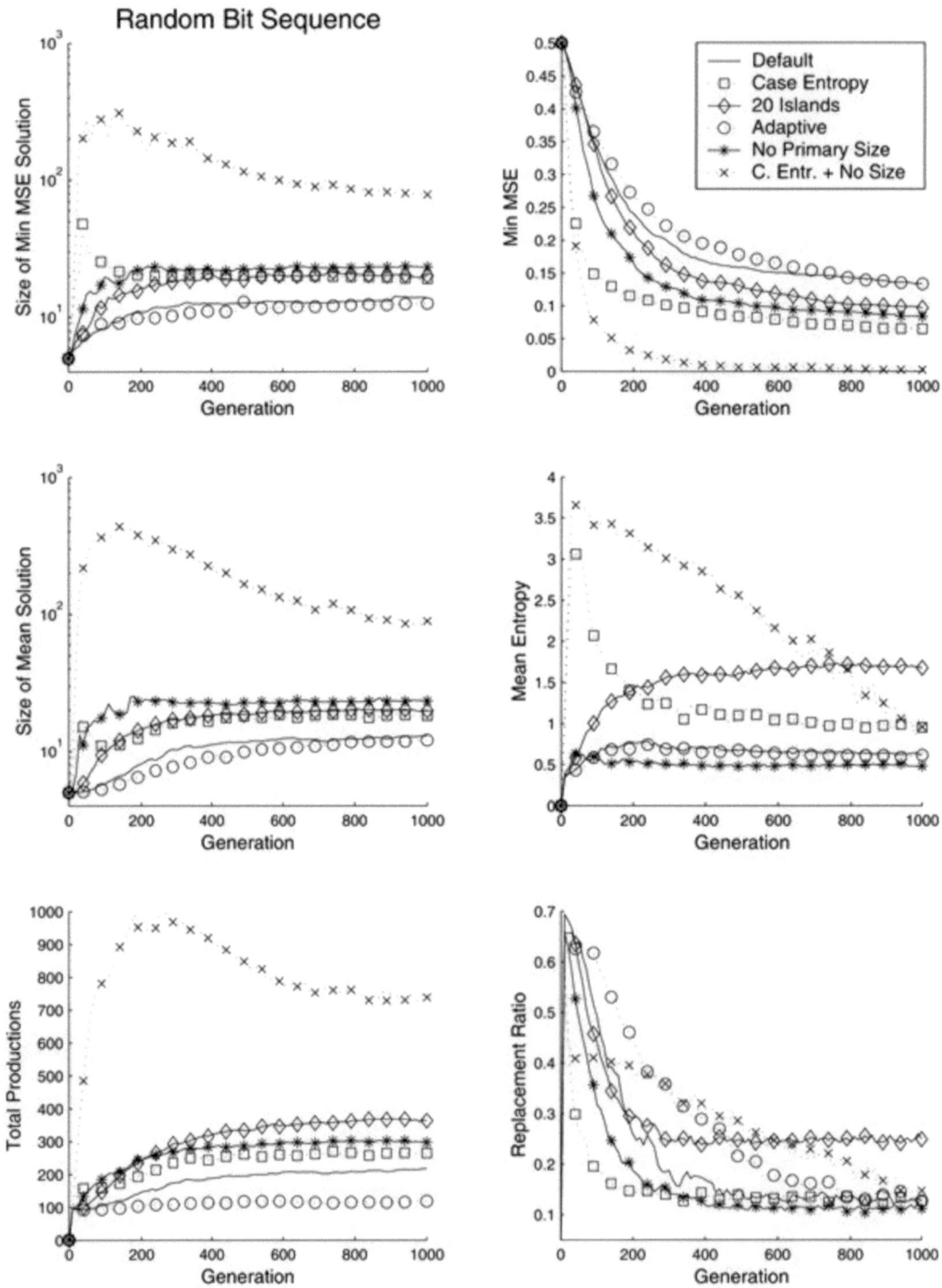

Fig. 10. Generational development for the RBS circuit problem. (Size is shown on a logarithmic Y-axis to improve readability.)

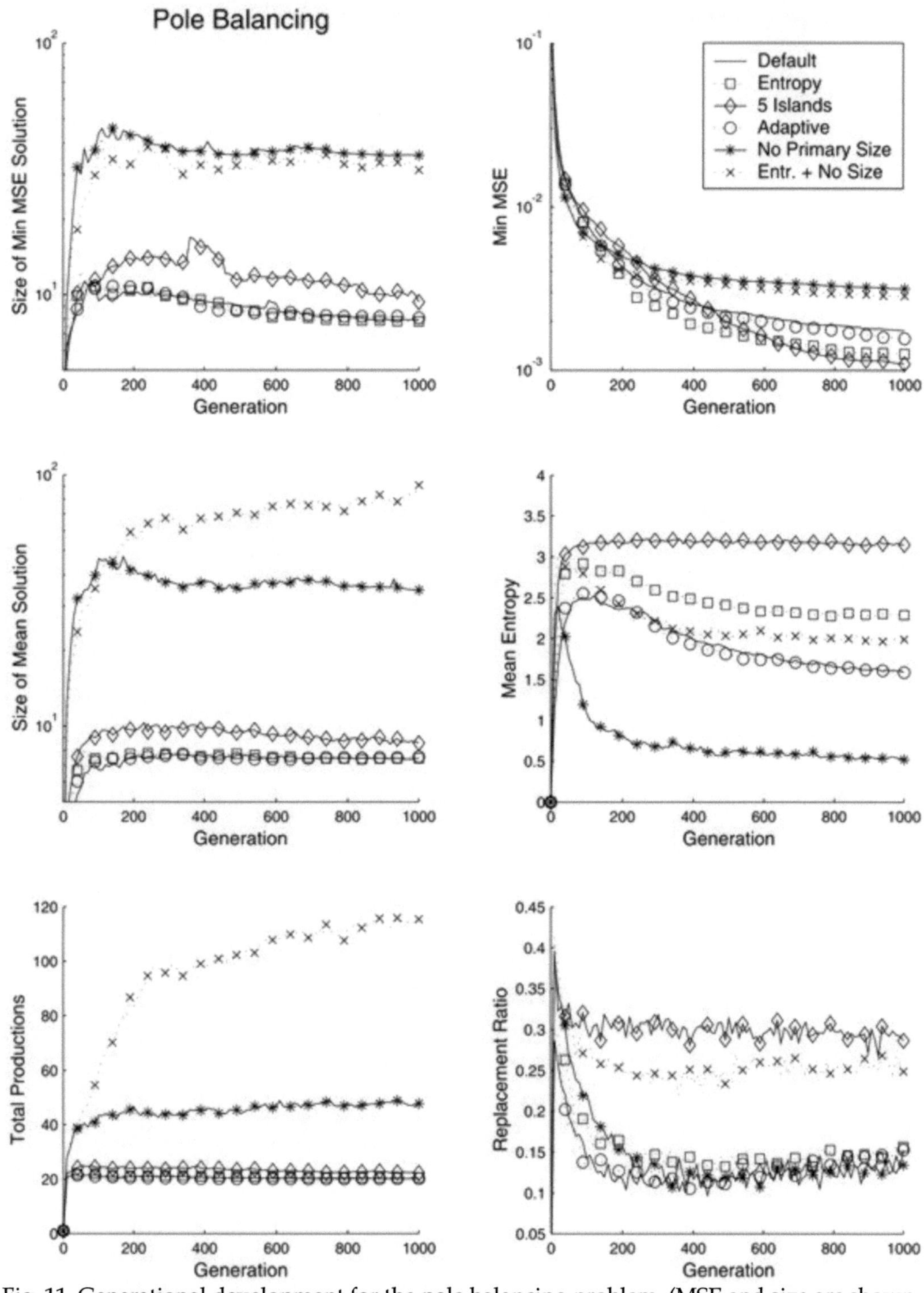

Fig. 11. Generational development for the pole balancing problem. (MSE and size are shown on a logarithmic Y-axis to improve readability.)

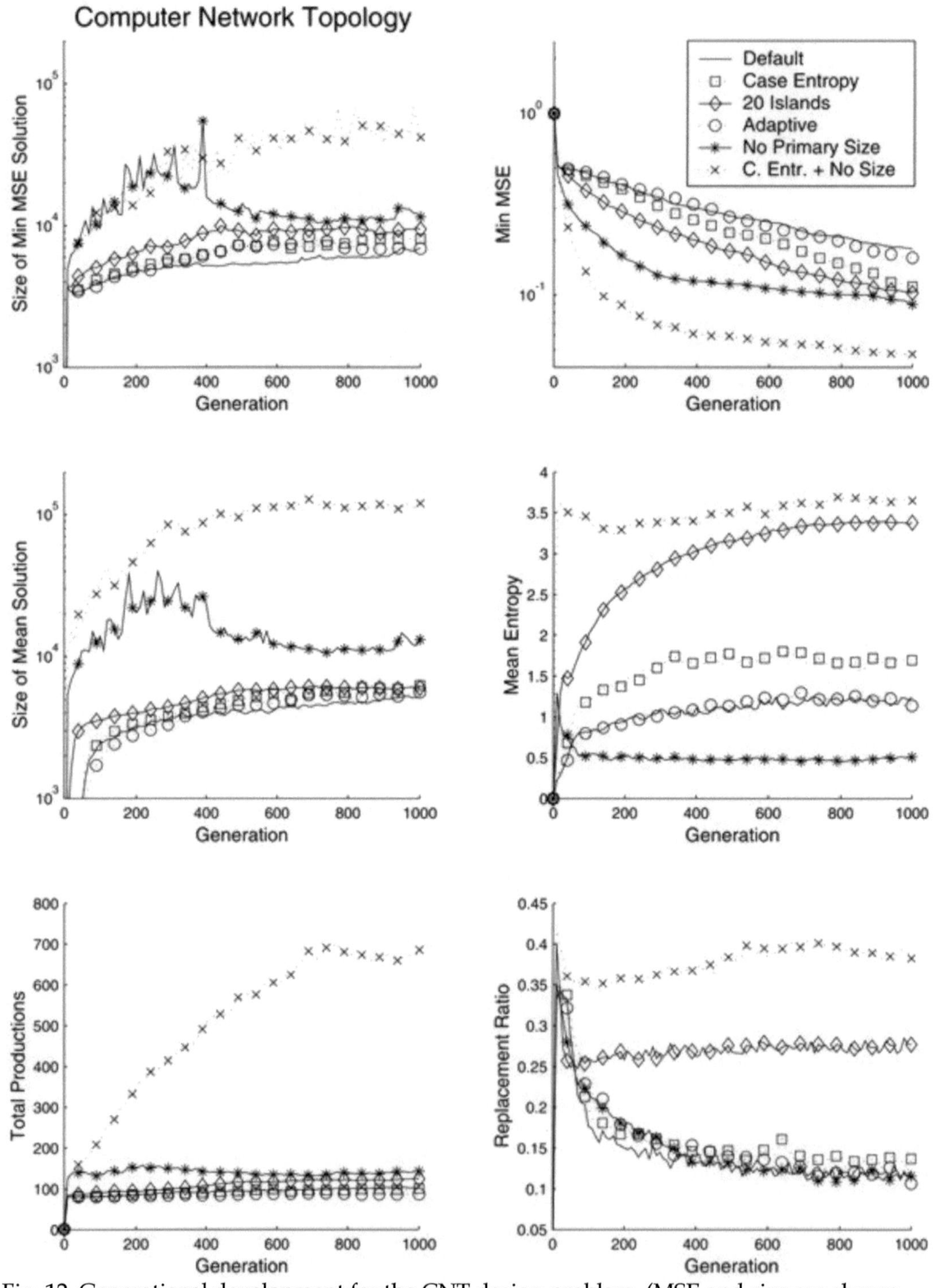

Fig. 12. Generational development for the CNT design problem. (MSE and size are shown on a logarithmic Y-axis to improve readability.)

model is so high - this may have nothing to do with the island model par se, but with our attempt at establishing a Pareto frontier across the islands. The resultant asymmetric elimination of solutions from the islands should cause new niches (in the shape of underpopulated islands) to arise with each generation, allowing otherwise unfit, but potentially novel, solutions to survive for more than one generation.

At any rate, the phenotypic entropy is not a reliable indicator of performance. The least entropy is observed with the secondary size objective on its own, which reflects the loss of the diversity that was provided by having a Pareto frontier of different solutions, but this configuration is not the worst performer. However, in the Binomial-3 regression and the CNT design it is inclined to flatten out early, which is indicative of a premature convergence of many runs. Adding the diversity objective raises entropy (and, of course, greatly raises performance), but in both the Binomial-3 regression and pole balancing tasks the entropy still remains below the corresponding configuration with a primary size objective.

9. Conclusion

The system presented in this chapter is a significant step towards achieving a simple, formal, comprehensive basis for graph evolution. Its main significance arises from simplifying hypergraph grammars for the purpose of evolutionary optimization, which avoids many of the complexity pitfalls of "biologically realistic" models. Yet unlike other simpler models, the graph transformations are not predefined and fixed here, but fully evolvable, allowing for an automatic optimization of the graph design bias and thus a greater degree of domain independence. It assumes, however, that we have a method for evolving such grammar. Shared grammar evolution unites several aspects of grammatical bias and developmental systems into an effective method that can evolve anything derivable from a CFG, including graphs. The success of this approach is governed by a number of factors, and through application to a diverse set of design problems, we have gained some perspective on these. Firstly, significant performance improvements can be obtained when emphasizing diversity in the grammar population. This can be accomplished most effectively by adding an entropy measure of phenotypic diversity as an evolutionary objective. Further significant improvements are obtained in combination with a less restrictive size objective, but notable increases in solution size become an issue here. Alternatively, we have also presented a multi-objective island model that exhibits performance benefits comparable to the entropy method. We further propose the application of concepts from swarm intelligence to accelerate convergence, but associated experiments fail to produce significant performance improvement, although they reveal significant increases in production reuse that lead to a more compact grammar. In relation to this, we ascertained that the search process is severely constrained by co-optimization towards a size objective, yet excessive bloat occurs as soon as the effective importance of size is reduced. The representational effectiveness of graph grammars becomes evident with the latter, but at great computational cost; a proper balance has not yet been found. Future performance improvements should arise from a better understanding of how the grammar establishes a preferential bias. We need to develop a more intelligent selection scheme that makes exploratory mutations into distant search regions viable, which, in combination with ACO-like exploitation, could ultimately improve the convergence characteristics of graph grammar evolution.

10. References

Augusto, D. A.; Barbosa, H. J. C. & Ebecken, N. F. F. (2008). Coevolution of data samples and classifiers integrated with grammatically-based genetic programming for data classification. *Proceedings of the 10th annual conference on Genetic and evolutionary computation (GECCO'08)*, Atlanta, USA, pp. 1171-1178, ACM Press.

Baluja, S. & Caruana, R. (1995). Removing the genetics from the standard genetic algorithm. *Proceedings of the Twelfth International Conference on Machine Learning, ML-95*, pp. 38-46, Morgan Kaufmann.

Boers, E. & Sprinkhuizen-Kuyper, I. (2001). Combined biological metaphors. *Advances in the evolutionary synthesis of intelligent agents*, pp. 153-183, MIT Press.

Deb, K.; Agrawal, S.; Pratab, A. & Meyarivan, T. (2000). A fast elitist non-dominated sorting genetic algorithm for multi-objective optimization: NSGA-II. *Proceedings of the Parallel Problem Solving from Nature VI Conference*, LNCS 1917, pp. 849-858, Springer-Verlag.

Deb, K. (2001). *Multi-Objective Optimization using Evolutionary Algorithms*. Wiley.

Dorigo, M.; Di Caro, G. & Gambardella, L. (1999). Ant algorithms for discrete optimization. *Artificial Life*, vol. 5, no. 2, pp. 137-172.

Futuyma, D. (1998). *Evolutionary biology* (3rd ed.), Sinauer Associates, Inc.

Gruau, F. (1995). Automatic definition of modular neural networks. *Adaptive Behaviour*, vol. 3, no. 2, pp. 151-183.

Goldberg, D.; Deb, K. & Korb, B. (1989). Messy genetic algorithms: motivation, analysis, and first results. *Complex Systems*, vol. 3, pp. 493-530.

Habel, A. (1992). *Hyperedge Replacement: Grammars and Languages*. LNCS 643, Springer-Verlag.

Hansen, T. F. (2006). The evolution of genetic architecture. *Annual Review of Ecology Evolution and Systematics*, vol. 37, no. 1, pp. 123-157.

Hoai, N.; McKay, R. & Abbass, H. (2003). Tree adjoining grammars, language bias, and genetic programming. *Proceedings of the 6th European Conference on Genetic Programming (EuroGP 2003)*, LNCS 2610, pp. 335-344, Springer-Verlag.

Hornby, G. (2003). *Generative representations for evolutionary design automation*. Ph.D. thesis, Dept. of Computer Science , Brandeis University.

Kitano, H. (1990). Designing neural networks using genetic algorithms with graph generation systems. *Complex Systems*, vol. 4, no. 4, pp. 461-476.

Koza, J. (1992). *Genetic Programming: on the programming of computers by means of natural selection*. MIT Press.

Koza, J.; Bennett III, F.; Andre, D. & Keane, M. (1999). *Genetic Programming III: Darwinian invention and problem solving*, Morgan Kaufmann.

Langdon, W. & Poli, R. (1997). Fitness causes bloat. *Second On-line World Conference on Soft Computing in Engineering Design and Manufacturing*, pp. 13-22, Springer-Verlag.

Lindenmayer, A. (1968). Mathematical models for cellular interaction in development, parts I and II. *Journal of Theoretical Biology*, vol. 18, pp. 280-315.

Luerssen, M. (2005). Phenotype diversity objectives for graph grammar evolution. *Recent Advances in Artificial Life*, vol. 3, pp. 159-170, World Scientific.

Luerssen, M. & Powers, D. (2008). Evolving encapsulated programs as shared grammars. *Genetic Programming and Evolvable Machines*, vol. 9, no. 3, pp. 203-228.

Luerssen, M. (2009). *Experimental Investigations into Graph Grammar Evolution: A novel approach to evolutionary design*. VDM Verlag Dr. Müller.

Martin, W.; Lienig, J. & Cohoon, J. (1997). Island (migration) models: evolutionary algorithms based on punctuated equilibria. *Handbook of Evolutionary Computation*, pp. 1-16, Oxford University Press.

McPhee, N. & Miller, J. (1995). Accurate replication in genetic programming. *Proceedings of the Sixth International Conference on Genetic Algorithms (ICGA'95)*, pp. 303-309, Morgan Kaufmann.

McPhee, N. & Hopper, N. (1999). Analysis of genetic diversity through population history. *Proceedings of the Genetic and Evolutionary Computation Conference*, pp. 1112-1120, Morgan Kaufmann.

Miller, J. (2001). What bloat? Cartesian Genetic Programming on Boolean problems. *Proceedings of the Genetic and Evolutionary Computation Conference (GECCO'01) Late Breaking Papers*, pp. 295-302, ISGEC Press.

Mühlenbein, H. & Paaá, G. (1996). From recombination of genes to the estimation of distributions I, binary parameters. *Parallel Problem Solving from Nature (PPSN IV)*, LNCS 1411, pp. 178-187, Springer-Verlag.

O'Neill, M. (2005). mGGA: The meta-Grammar Genetic Algorithm. *Proceedings of the 8th European Conference on Genetic Programming*, Lausanne, Switzerland, LNCS 3447, pp. 311-320, Springer-Verlag.

Price, K. (1999). An introduction to differential evolution. *New Ideas in Optimization*, pp. 79–108, McGraw-Hill.

Rozenberg, G. (1997). *Handbook of Graph Grammars and Computing by Graph Transformation: volume I. Foundations*. World Scientific.

Ryan, C.; Collins, J. & O'Neill, M. (1998). Grammatical evolution: evolving programs for an arbitrary language. *Proceedings of the First European Workshop on Genetic Programming (EuroGP'98)*, pp. 83-95, Springer-Verlag.

Shan, Y.; McKay, R.; Baxter, R.; Abbass, H.; Essam, D. & Nguyen, H. (2004). Grammar model-based program rvolution. *Proceedings of the 2004 IEEE Congress on Evolutionary Computation (CEC 2004)*, Portland, Oregon, vol. 1, pp. 478-485.

Shirakawa, S.; Ogino, S. & Nagao, T. (2007). Graph structured program evolution. *Proceedings of the Genetic and Evolutionary Computation Conference (GECCO'07)*, pp. 1686-1693, ACM Press.

Simon, H. (1996). *The Sciences of the Artificial* (3rd ed.), MIT Press.

Stanley, K. O. & Miikkulainen, R. (2002). Evolving neural networks through augmenting topologies. *Evolutionary Computation*, vol. 10, no. 2, pp. 99-127.

Toussaint, M. (2003). On the evolution of phenotypic exploration distributions. *Foundations of Genetic Algorithms 7 (FOGA VII)*, pp. 169-182, Morgan Kaufmann.

Whigham, P. (1995). Rosca, J. (ed.) Grammatically-based genetic programming. *Proceedings of the Workshop on Genetic Programming: From Theory to Real-World Applications*, Tahoe City, USA, pp. 33-41, Morgan Kaufmann Publishers.

25

A Dialectical Method to Classify Alzheimer's Magnetic Resonance Images

Wellington Pinheiro dos Santos[1], Francisco Marcos de Assis[2], Ricardo Emmanuel de Souza[3], Priscilla Batista Mendes[1], Henrique Specht de Souza Monteiro[1] and Havana Diogo Alves[1]
[1]*Escola Politécnica de Pernambuco, Universidade de Pernambuco*
[2]*Departamento de Engenharia Elétrica, Universidade Federal de Campina Grande*
[3]*Departamento de Física, Universidade Federal de Pernambuco*
Brazil

1. Introduction

It is largely known that a great amount of current methods of analysis in image analysis and processing is based on parametric statistics. Alternatively, several approaches in Computational Intelligence, and particularly in Evolutionary Computation, are inspired by biology and other social-based sciences, like the ones based on the movement of flocks and birds, particularly particle swarm optimization, that tend to approximate this basic social behaviour present in inferior animals to the searching process to find a global optimum in a determined objective functions. However, it notorious that just a few approaches, to be optimistic, and almost none to be realistic, are inspired in Philosophy.

Herein this work we claim that Philosophy can be also considered as a source of inspiration to build new tools for analysis in Computational Intelligence, in particular, and in image processing and analysis, in general. This chapter presents the Objective Dialectical Method (ODM): an evolutionary method for classification based on the Philosophy of Praxis, a philosophical approach that considers parts of reality as complex systems composed by basic units called poles, where such units are involved in conflict, affecting each other and generating more poles or eliminating others, as this dynamics proceeds.

Alzheimer's disease is the most common cause of dementia, both in senile and presenile individuals, observing the gradual progress of the disease as the individual becomes older (Ewers et al., 2006). The major manifestation of Alzheimer's disease is the diminution of the cognitive functions with gradual loss of memory, including psychological, neurological and behavioral symptoms indicating the decline of the daily life activities as a whole. Alzheimer's disease is characterized by the reduction of gray matter and the growth of cerebral sulci. However, the white matter is also affected, although the relation between Alzheimer's disease and white matter is still unknown (Friman et al., 2006).

Acquisition of diffusion-weighted magnetic resonance images (DW-MR images) turns possible the visualization of the dilation of the lateral ventriculi temporal corni, enhancing the augment of sulci, related to the advance of Alzheimer's disease (Haacke et al., 1999). Therefore, volumetrical measuring of cerebral structures is very important for diagnosis and evaluation of the progress of diseases like Alzheimer's (Ewers et al., 2006), especially the measuring of the volumes occupied by sulci and lateral ventriculi, turning possible the addition of quantitative information to the qualitative information expressed by the DW-MR images (Hayasaka et al., 2006).

Usually, the evaluation of the progress of Alzheimer's disease using image analysis of DW-MR images is performed after acquiring at least three images of each slice of interest, generated using the sequence spin-echo Stejskal-Tanner with different diffusion exponents, where one of the exponents is 0 s/mm^2, that is, a T2-weighted spin-echo image (Haacke et al., 1999). Then, a fourth image is calculated: the Apparent Diffusion Coefficient Map, or ADC map, where each pixel is associated to the corresponding apparent diffusion coefficient of the associated voxel: the brighter the pixels, the greater the corresponding apparent diffusion coefficients (Haacke et al., 1999).

The dialectical conception of reality is a kind of philosophical investigative method for analyzing processes present in nature and in human societies. Its origins are connected to the philosophy of the ancient civilizations of Greece, China and India, closely connected to the thoughts of Heraclite, Plato, and the philosophies of Confucionism, Buddhism, and Zen. As a general analysis method, dialectics has experienced considerable progress due to the development of German Philosophy in the 19th century, with Hegel's dialectics and, in the 20th century, the works of Marx, Engels, and Gramsci. All those philosophers produced seminal works on the dynamics of contradictions in nature and class-based societies, giving rise to the Historical Materialism (Marx, 1980; Engels, 1975; Gramsci, 1992a; Gramsci1992b; Bobbio, 1990).

The dialectical method of Historical Materialism is a tool for studying systems by considering the dynamics of their contradictions, as dynamic processes with intertwined phases of *evolution* and *revolutionary crisis*. It has inspired us to conceive an evolutionary computational intelligent method for classification that is able to solve problems commonly approached by neural networks and genetic algorithms.

Each of the most common paradigms of Computational Intelligence, namely neural networks, evolutionary computing, and culture-inspired algorithms, has its basis in a kind of theory intended to be of general application, but in fact very incomplete; e.g. the neural networks approach is based on a certain model of the brain; evolutionary computing is based on Darwin's theory; and cultural-inspired algorithms are based on the study of populations, such as those of ant colonies.

However, it is important to notice that it is not necessarily the case (and indeed it may be impossible) that the theories an algorithm are based on have to be complete. For example, neural networks utilize a well-known incomplete model of the neurons. This is a strong reason for investigating the use of Philosophy as a source of inspiration for developing computational intelligent methods and models to apply in several areas, such as pattern recognition.

Thornley and Gibb discussed the application of Dialectics to understand more clearly the paradoxical and conceptually contradictory discipline of information retrieval (Thornley & Gibb, 2007), while Rosser Jr. attempted to use some aspects of Dialectics in nonlinear dynamics, comparing some aspects of Marx and Engel's dialectical method with concepts of Catastrophe Theory, Emergent Dynamics Complexity and Chaos Theory (Rosser Jr., 2000). However, there are no works proposing a mathematical approach to establish the fundamentals of Dialectics as a tool for constructing computational intelligent methods.

This work presents the Objective Dialectical Method (ODM), which is an evolutionary computational intelligent method, and the Objective Dialectical Classifier (ODC), an instance of ODM that operates as a non-supervised self-organized map dedicated to pattern recognition and classification. ODM is based on the dynamics of contradictions among dialectical poles. In the task of classification, each class is considered as a dialectical pole. Such poles are involved in pole struggles and affected by revolutionary crises, when some poles may disappear or be absorbed by other ones. New poles can emerge following periods of revolutionary crisis. Such a process of pole struggle and revolutionary crisis tends to a stable system, e.g. a system corresponding to the clusterization of the original data.

This chapter presents a relatively new approach to evaluate the progress of Alzheimer's disease: once the ADC map usually presents pixels with considerable intensities in regions not occupied by the head of patient, a degree of uncertainty can also be considered in the pixels inside the sample. Furthermore, the ADC map is very sensitive to noisy images (Haacke et al., 1999; Santos et al., 2007a). Therefore, in this case study, images are used to compose a multispectral image, where each diffusion-weighted image is considered as a spectral band in a synthetic multispectral image. This multispectral image is classified using the Objective Dialectical Classifier, a new classification method based on Dialectics as defined in the Philosophy of Praxis.

Herein this chapter ODM is used to generate an adaptative image classifier able to start the classification process with a determined initial number of classes and, after a determined period of evolution, to find a suboptimum number of classes according to classification performance. These results were generated using an image database composed by real Alzheimer's magnetic resonance images, to get synthetic multispectral images. The classification results were compared with results generated using image classifiers based on Kohonen's self-organized maps, fuzzy c-means and k-means. ODM demonstrated to be instrumental in assembling evolutionary mathematical tools for the analysis of multispectral images. A 2-degree polynomial network with supervised training is used to generate the ground truth image. The classification results are used to improve the usual analysis of magnetic resonance images based on diffusion tensors in clinical analysis of Alzheimer's disease. The results are compared to ground-truth images produced by polynomial networks using a morphological similarity index.

2. Materials and methods

2.1 DW-MR images and ADC maps

The DW-MR images used in this work were acquired from the clinical images database of the Laboratory of MR Images, at the Department of Physics of Universidade Federal de Pernambuco, Recife, Brazil. This database is composed by clinical images acquired from Alzheimer's volunteers, using clinical 1.5 T MR imaging systems. We used 60 cerebral DWMR images corresponding to male patients with Alzheimer's disease. To perform the training of the proposed analysis, we chose the MR images corresponding to the 13th slice, showing the temporal corni of the lateral ventriculi, to furnish a better evaluation for specialists and facilitate to stablish correlations between data generated by the computational tool and *a priori* specialist knowledge.

An image can be considered as a mathematical function, where its domain is a region of the plane of the integers, called grid, and its counterdomain is the set of the possible values occupied by the pixels corresponding to each position on the grid.

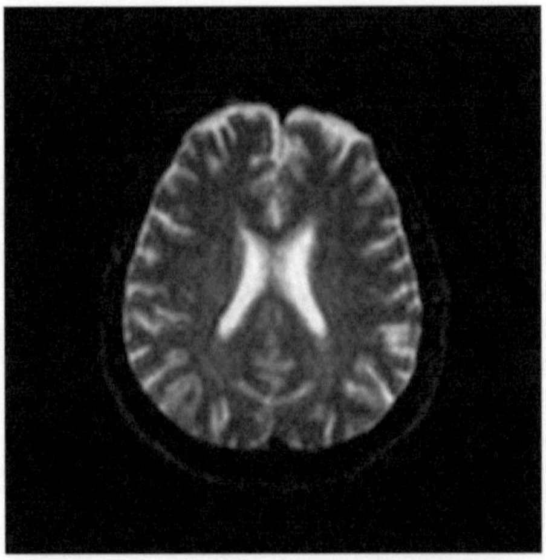

Fig. 1. Axial diffusion-weighted image with exponent diffusion of 0 s/mm^2

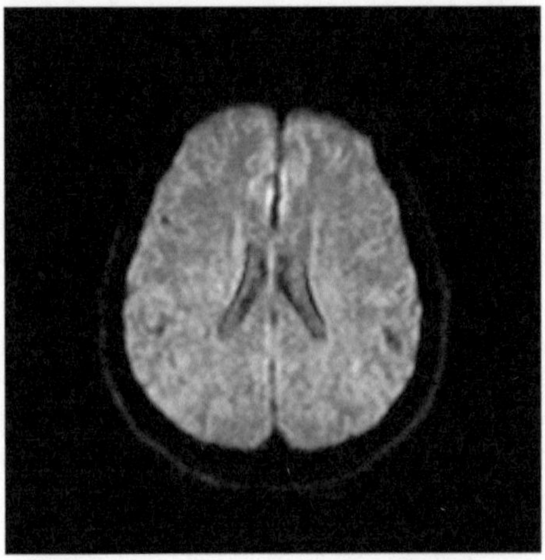

Fig. 2. Axial diffusion-weighted image with exponent diffusion of 500 s/mm^2

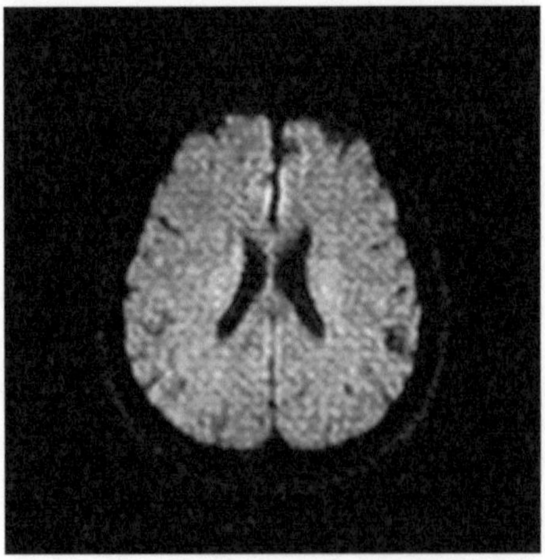

Fig. 3. Axial diffusion-weighted image with exponent diffusion of 1000 s/mm^2

Let $f_i : S \to W$ be the set of the diffusion-weighted MR images, where $1 \leq i \leq 3$,, $S \subseteq \mathbf{Z}^2$ is the grid of the image f_i, where $W \subseteq \mathbf{R}$ is its codomain. The synthetic multispectral image $f : S \to W^3$ composed by the MR images of the figures 1, 2 and 3 is given by:

$$f(\mathbf{u}) = (f_1(\mathbf{u}), f_2(\mathbf{u}), f_3(\mathbf{u}))^T \tag{1}$$

where $\mathbf{u} \in S$ is the position of the pixel in the image f, and f_1, f_2 and f_3 are the diffusion-weighted MR images. Considering that each pixel $f_i(\mathbf{u})$ is approximately proportional to the signal of the corresponding voxel as follows (Castano-Moraga et al., 2006):

$$f_i(\mathbf{u}) = K\rho(\mathbf{u})e^{-T_E/T_2(\mathbf{u})}e^{-b_i D_i(\mathbf{u})}, \tag{2}$$

where $D_i(\mathbf{u})$ is the nuclear spin diffusion coefficient measured after the i-th experiment, associated to the voxel mapped in the pixel in position $\mathbf{u}$; $\rho(\mathbf{u})$ is the nuclear spin density in the voxel; K is a constant of proportionality; $T_2(\mathbf{u})$ is the transversal relaxation time in the voxel; T_E is the echo time and b_i is the diffusion exponent, given by (Haacke et al., 1999):

$$b_i = \gamma^2 G_i^2 T_E^3/3, \tag{3}$$

where γ is the gyromagnetic ratio and G_i is the gradient applied during the experiment . Figures 1, 2 and 3 show images with diffusion exponents 0 s/mm^2, 500 s/mm^2 and 1000 s/mm^2, respectively.

The analysis of DW-MR images is often performed using the resulting ADC map f_{ADC}: $S \to W$, which is calculated as follows (Basser, 2002):

$$f_{\mathrm{ADC}}(\mathbf{u}) = \frac{C}{b_2}\ln\left(\frac{f_1(\mathbf{u})}{f_2(\mathbf{u})}\right) + \frac{C}{b_3}\ln\left(\frac{f_1(\mathbf{u})}{f_3(\mathbf{u})}\right), \tag{4}$$

where C is a constant of proportionality.

Considering n experiments, we can generalize equation 4 as follows:

$$f_{\mathrm{ADC}}(\mathbf{u}) = \sum_{i=2}^{n} \frac{C}{b_i}\ln\left(\frac{f_1(\mathbf{u})}{f_i(\mathbf{u})}\right). \tag{5}$$

Thus, the ADC map is given by:

$$f_{\mathrm{ADC}}(\mathbf{u}) = C\bar{D}(\mathbf{u}), \tag{6}$$

where $\bar{D}(\mathbf{u})$ is an ensemble average of the diffusion coefficient $D(\mathbf{u})$ (Fillard et al., 2006). Therefore, pixels of the ADC map are proportional to diffusion coefficients in the corresponding voxels. In figure 4 can be seen several artifacts associated to presence of noise. In regions of image where signal-to-noise ratio is poor (let us say, $s/n \approx 1$), the ADC map produces artifacts as consequence of the calculation of logarithms (see equations 4 and 5). Consequently, pixels of the ADC map not necessarily correspond to diffusion coefficients but *apparent* diffusion coefficients, once several pixels indicate high diffusion rates in voxels in empty areas or in very solid areas, e.g. bone in the cranial box, as can be seen in figure 4. This fact generates a considerable degree of uncertainty about the values inside brain area.

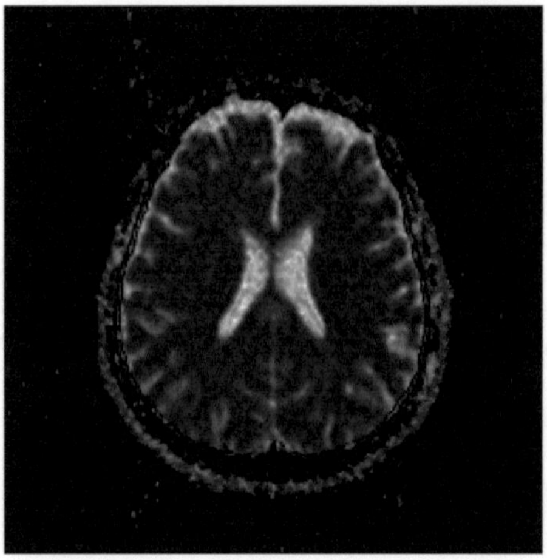

Fig. 4. ADC map calculated from the three diffusion images

In this work we present an alternative to the analysis of the ADC map: the multispectral analysis of the image $f: S \to W^3$ using methods based on neural networks as an alternative that could be easily extended to other diffusion-weighted images than cerebral ones. The proposed analysis is performed using the Objective Dialectical Classifier, presented in the following section.

2.2 Classification using the Objective Dialectical Method

Objective Dialectical Classifiers (ODC) are an adaptation of Dialectics, as defined in the Philosophy of Praxis, to tasks of classification (Gramsci, 1992a; Gramsci, 1992b). This means that the feature vectors are mounted and considered as vectors of conditions. Specifically, once they are applied to the inputs of the dialectical system, their coordinates will affect the dynamics of the contradictions among the integrating dialectical poles. Hence, the integrating poles model the recognized classes at the task of non-supervised classification (Santos et al., 2008a).

Therefore, an ODC is in fact an adaptable and evolutionary-based non-supervised classifier where, instead of supposing a predetermined number of classes, we can set an initial number of classes (dialectical poles) and, as the historical phases happen (as a result of pole struggles and revolutionary crises), some classes are eliminated, others are absorbed, and a few others are generated. At the end of the training process, the system presents a number of statistically significant classes present in the training set and, therefore, a feasible classifier associated to the final state of the dialectical system (Santos et al., 2008a).

To accelerate the convergence of the dialectical classifier, we have removed the operator of pole generation, present at the revolutionary crises. However, it could be beneficial to the classification method, once such operator is a kind of diversity generator operator. The solution found can then be compared to other sort of evolutionary-based image classifiers (Santos et al., 2008a).

The following algorithm is a possible implementation of the training process of the objective dialectical classifier, used in this work (Santos et al., 2008a):

1. Set the following initial parameters:
   1.1 Number of historical phases, n_P;

1.2 Length of each historical phase, n_H;
1.3 Desired final number of poles, $n_{C,f}$;
1.4 Step of each historical phase $0<\eta(0)<1$;
1.5 Maximum crisis, $0 \leq \chi_{\max} \leq 1$;
1.6 Initial number of poles $\# \Omega(0) = n_C(0)$, defining the initial set of poles:

$$\Omega(0) = \{C_1(0), C_2(0), \ldots, C_{n_C(0)}(0)\}.$$

2. Set the following thresholds:
   2.1 Minimum force, $0 \leq f_{\min} \leq 1$
   2.2 Minimum contradiction, $0 \leq \delta_{\min} \leq 1$
3. Initialize the weights $\omega_{i,j}(0)$, where $1 \leq i \leq n_C(0)$ and $1 \leq j \leq n$.
4. Let $\# \Omega(t)$ be the cardinality of $\Omega(t)$, repeat until n_P iterations or $\# \Omega(t) = n_{C,f}$:
   4.1 Repeat until n_H iterations:
      4.1.1 Initialize the measures of force $f_i=0$, for $1 \leq i \leq n_C(t)$.
      4.1.2 For all vectors of conditions
      $\mathbf{x} = (x_1, x_2, \ldots, x_n)^T$
      of the input set $\Psi = \{\mathbf{x}^{(l)}\}_{l=1}^{L}$, repeat:
      4.1.2.1 Compute the values of the anticontradiction functions:
      $$g_i(\mathbf{x}) = e^{-||\mathbf{x}-\mathbf{w}_i||}$$
      where $1 \leq i \leq n_C(t)$.
      4.1.2.2 Calculate $g_{\max}$:
      $$g_{\max} = \max\{g_1(\mathbf{x}), g_2(\mathbf{x}), \ldots, g_{n_C(t)}(\mathbf{x})\}.$$
      4.1.2.3 Calculate the index $k(t)$ of the winner class:
      $$g_i = g_{\max} \Rightarrow k(t) = i.$$
      4.1.2.4 Adjust the weights of the winner pole:
      $$w_{i,j}(t+1) = \begin{cases} w'_{i,j}(t), & i = k(t) \\ w_{i,j}(t), & i \neq k(t) \end{cases}$$
      where
      $$w'_{i,j}(t) = w_{i,j}(t) + \eta(t)(x_j(t) - w_{i,j}(t)).$$
      4.1.2.5 Update the measure of force of the integrating poles:
      $$f_i(t+1) = \begin{cases} f_i(t) + 1, & i = k(t) \\ f_i(t), & i \neq k(t) \end{cases}.$$
      4.1.3 Quantitative changing: $\Omega(t+1) = \Omega(t)$,
   4.2 Calculate the normalized measures of force:

$$\bar{f}_i(t) = \frac{f_i(t)}{\max\{f_j(t)\}_{j=1}^{n_C(t)}},$$

for $1 \leq i \leq n_C(t)$.

4.3 Compute the contradictions:

$$\delta_{i,j} = 1 - g_i(\mathbf{w}_j),$$

where $2 \leq j \leq n_C(t)$, $1 \leq i \leq j$ and find the maximum contradiction

$$\delta_{\max} = \max\{\delta_{i,j}, i \neq j\},$$

for $j = 2,3,\ldots, n_C(t)$ and $i = 1,2,\ldots, j-1$.

4.4 Qualitative changing: compute the new set of poles, $\Omega\ (t+1)$:

$$\bar{f}_i(t) > f_{\min} \Rightarrow C_i(t) \in \Omega(t+1),$$

where $1 \leq i \leq n_C(t)$ and

$$\delta_{i,j} \geq \delta_{\min} \Rightarrow C_i(t), C_j(t) \in \Omega(t+1),$$
$$\delta_{i,j} < \delta_{\min} \Rightarrow C_i(t) \in \Omega(t+1),$$
$$\delta_{i,j} = \delta_{\max} \Rightarrow C_q \in \Omega(t+1),$$

where $2 \leq j \leq n_C(t)$, $1 \leq i \leq j$, $q = n_C(t)+1$, and

$$w_{q,k}(t+1) = \begin{cases} w_{i,k}(t+1), & k \bmod 2 = 1 \\ w_{j,k}(t+1), & k \bmod 2 = 0 \end{cases},$$

for $k = 1,2,\ldots, n$.

4.5 Add the crisis effect to the weights of the new integrating poles of the dialectical system:

$$w_{i,j}(t+2) = w_{i,j}(t+1) + \chi_{\max} G(0,1),$$
for $1 \leq i \leq n_C(t+1), 1 \leq j \leq n$ and $\Omega(t+2) = \Omega(t+1)$.

Once the training process is complete, ODC behavior occurs in the same way as any non-supervised classification method. This is clear if we analyze the training process when $n_P = n_H = 1$. This transforms the ODC into a k-means method (Santos et al., 2008a).

The classification is performed in the following way: given a set of input conditions

$$\mathbf{x} = (x_1, x_2, \ldots, x_n)^T,$$

if the dialectical system reaches stabilization when $\Omega = \{C_1, C_2, \ldots, C_n\}$, then we apply the following classification rule:

$$g_k(\mathbf{x}) = \max\{g_1(\mathbf{x}), g_2(\mathbf{x}), \ldots, g_{n_C}(\mathbf{x})\} \Rightarrow \mathbf{x} \in C_k,$$

where $1 \leq k \leq n_C$.

2.3 Classification using neural networks

Let the universe of classes of interest be defined as $\Omega = \{C_1, C_2, C_3\}$, C_1 represents the cerebrospinal fluid; C_2, the white and the gray matter, as they cannot be distinguished using diffusion images, because their diffusion coefficients are very similar; and C_3 corresponds to the image background.

For the multispectral analysis using neural nets, the inputs are associated with the vector $\mathbf{x} = (x_1, x_2, x_3)^T$, where $x_i = f_i(\mathbf{u})$, for $1 \leq i \leq 3$. The net outputs represent the classes of interest and are associated with the vector $\mathbf{y} = (y_1, y_2, y_3)^T$, where each output corresponds to the class with the same index. The decision criterion employed in this analysis was the Bayes criterion: the output with greater value indicates the most probable class (Duda et al., 2001; Duda & Hart, 1972; Sklansky & Wassel, 1981). The training set and the test set were built using specialist knowledge during the selection of the regions of interest (Haykin, 1999). The synthetic multispectral image was classified using the following methods:

- Kohonen Self-Organized Map (SOM) classifier: 3 inputs, 3 outputs, maximum of 200 iterations, initial learning rate $\eta_0 = 0.1$, circular architecture, Gaussian function of distance;
- Fuzzy c-means classifier: 3 inputs, 3 outputs, maximum of 200 iterations, initial learning rate $\eta_0 = 0.1$;
- Radial Basis Function (RBF) network: layer 1: a k-means clustering map with 3 inputs, 18 outputs, maximum of 200 iterations, initial learning rate $\eta_0 = 0.1$; layer 2: an one-layer perceptron with 18 inputs, 3 outputs, 75 iterations, training error of 5%, initial learning rate $\eta_0 = 0.1$.

To make comparisons between the proposed multispectral approach and the ADC map, we performed a monospectral non-supervised classification of the ADC map using a clustering-based method (Li et al., 2006; Bartesaghi & Nadar, 2006). We chose a Kohonen SOM classifier (KO-ADC) with 3 inputs, 3 outputs, maximum of 200 iterations, and initial learning rate $\eta_0 = 0.1$.

These methods were chosen in order to evaluate the behavior and performance of a classical neural network (RBF network) and well-known clustering-based networks (Kohonen SOM and fuzzy c-means) executing the task of classification of the synthetic multispectral image. Their initial learning rates and number of iterations were empirically determined.

3. Discussion and results

The ground-truth image was built by the use of a two-degree polynomial network to classify the multispectral image. The training set was assembled using anatomic information obtained from T1, T2 and spin density MR images.

The ODC was trained using an initial system of 10 integrating classes, affected by 3 input conditions, studied during 5 historical 100-length phases, with an initial historical step $\eta_0 = 0.1$. At the stages of revolutionary crisis we considered a minimum measure of force of 0.01, minimum contradiction of 0.25 and maximum crisis of 0.25. The stop criterion was the final number of classes, in our case, 4 classes. The input conditions are the values of pixels on each of the 3 bands.

ODC training resulted in 6 classes, reduced to 4 classes after a manual post-labeling that merged the 3 classes external to the cranium, i.e. background, noise and cranial box, into a single class, namely background. This post-labeling was performed manually because the 3 populations are statistically different and only conceptually can they be reunited in a unique class. Figures 5 and 6 show the resulting classification by ODC before and after manual post-labeling, respectively.

From Figure 6 we can see that ODC was able to make a distinction between white and gray matter, the latter present in the interface between cerebrospinal fluid and white matter. Notice that an increased damaged area is highlighted. The classification fidelity was measured using the morphological similarity index, with structure element square 3×3, and Wang's index (Wang & Bovik, 2002), yielding 0.9877 and 0.9841, respectively.

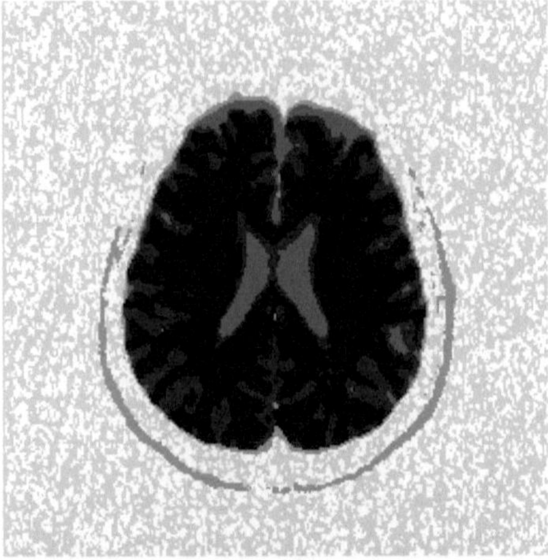

Fig. 5. Classification result by ODC before manual post-labeling

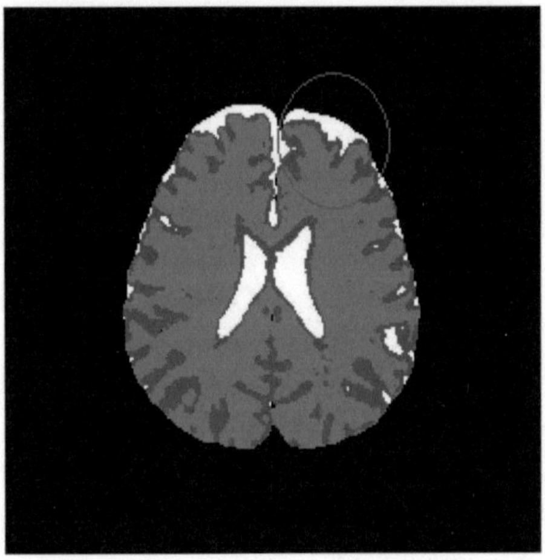

Fig. 6. Classification result by ODC after manual post-labeling. White areas are indication of cerebrospinal fluid, once gray and dark gray areas indicate white and gray matter, respectively. The damaged area is emphisized.

Figures 7, 8, and 9 show classification results obtained by the use of classifiers based on Kohonen SOM (KO), RBF networks (RBF), and fuzzy c-means (CM), respectively, considering a fixed number of classes, namely white and gray matter, cerebrospinal fluid and background (Santos et al., 2008b; Santos et al., 2007a; Santos et al., 2007b; Santos et al., 2007c; Santos et al., 2007d). Figure 10 shows the result of the classification of the ADC map using the Kohonen SOM classifier (KO-ADC) (Santos et al., 2007d). However, these visual results are evidence that, using such an approach, it is not possible to distinguish between white and gray matter in multispectral DW-MR Alzheimer's images.

The objective dialectical classifier could identify statistically significant classes in situations where the initial number of classes is not well known. It makes possible the detection of relevant classes and even singularities beyond the initial prediction made by the medical specialist. It is also able to aid the medical specialist to measure the volumes of interest, in an attempt to establish a correlation of such measuring with the advance of

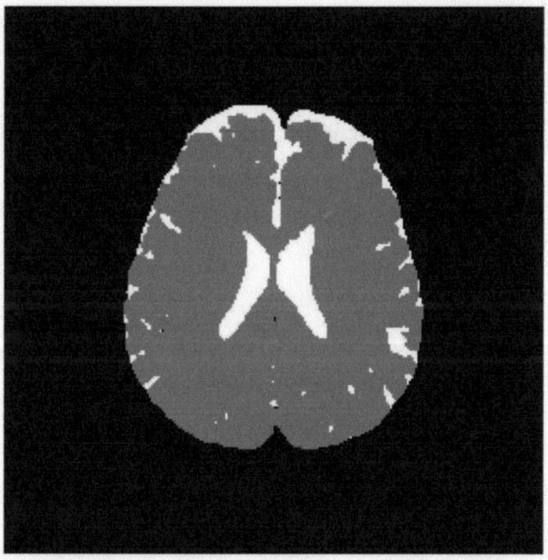

Fig. 7. Classification result by Kohonen SOM after manual post-labeling

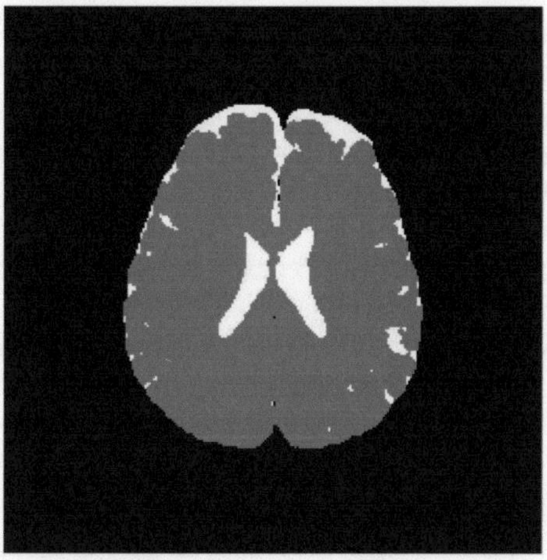

Fig. 8. Classification result by the RBF network classifier

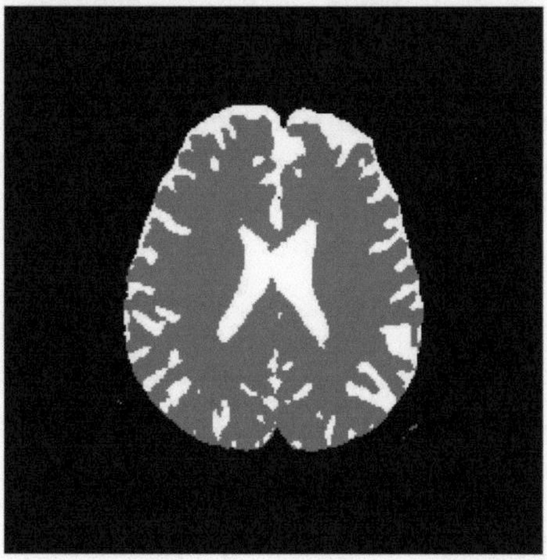

Fig. 9. Classification result by fuzzy c-means after manual post-labeling

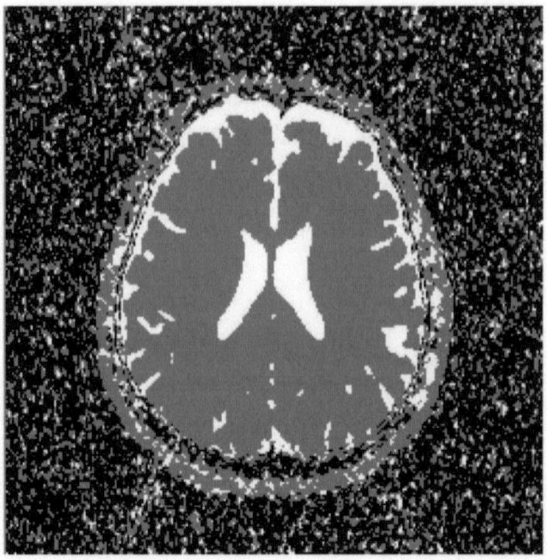

Fig. 10. Classification of ADC map by Kohonen SOM

neurodegenerative diseases, such as Alzheimer's, and to differentiate significant alterations in the values of the measured diffusion coefficients. ODC can qualitatively and quantitatively improve the analysis of the human medical specialist.

In summary, the objective dialectical classifier can be used in problems where the number of statistically significant classes is not well known, or in problems where we need to find a sub-optimum clustering map to be used for classification. The task of finding a suboptimum clustering map is empirical, once it is necessary to analyze the behavior of the training process as a function of the several parameters of the method, namely the minimum force, the minimum contradiction, the initial number of classes, the number of historical phases, the duration and the historical step of each historical phase, that is, all the initial parameters of the proposed segmentation algorithm. Nevertheless, it is important to emphasize that, as the number of initial parameters is given, the classification performance of the dialectical classifiers is highly dependent on these initial parameters.

The objective dialectical method inaugurates a new family of evolutionary methods inspired in the Philosophy, especially the Philosophy of Praxis, which can be used to solve both classical and new image analysis problems, such as the one presented in our case study, that is, biomedical image analysis and processing.

We conclude by stating that philosophical thought is a great source of inspiration for constructing new computational intelligent methods highly applicable to Biomedical Engineering problems, since we are simply returning to our original source of knowledge: Philosophy as an important tool to a better understanding of nature and ourselves in a larger sense.

4. References

Ewers, M.; Teipel, S.J.; Dietrich, O.; Schönberg, S.O.; Jessen, F.; Heun, R.; Scheltens, P.; van de Pol, L.; Freymann, N.R.; Moeller, H.J. & Hampela, H. (2006). Multicenter assessment of reliability of cranial MRI. *Neurobiology of Aging*, 27, 1051-1059

Friman, O.; Farnebäck, G. & Westin, C.F. (2006). A bayesian approach for stochastic white matter tractography. *IEEE Transactions on Medical Imaging*, 25, 8, 965-978

Haacke, E.M.; Brown, R.W.; Thompson, M.R. & Venkatesan, R. (1999). *Magnetic Resonance Imaging: Physical Principles and Sequence Design,* Wiley-Liss

Marx, K. (1980). Critique of Hegel's dialectics and philosophy. In *Economic and Philosophic Manuscripts of 1844,* International Publishers

Engels, F. (1975). The role played by labor in the transition from ape to man. In *Collected Works of Karl Marx and Frederik Engels,* International Publishers

Gramsci, A. (1992). Introduction to the Study of Philosophy and Historical Materialism. In *Prison Notebooks,* Columbia University

Gramsci, A. (1992). Some Problems in the Study of the Philosophy of Praxis. In *Prison Notebooks,* Columbia University

Bobbio, N. (1990). *Saggi su Gramsci,* Feltrinelli, Milano Thornley, C. & Gibb, F. (2007). A dialectical approach to information retrieval. *Journal of Documentation,* 63, 5, 755-764

Rosser Jr, J.B. (2000). Aspects of dialectics and nonlinear dynamics. *Cambridge Journal of Economics,* 24, 3, 311-324

Hayasaka, S.; Du, A.T.; Duarte, A.; Kornak, J.; Jahng, G.H.; Weiner, M.W. & Schuff, N. (2006). A non-parametric approach for co-analysis of multi-modal brain imaging data: Application to Alzheimer's disease. *NeuroImage,* 30, 768-779

Santos, W.P.; Souza, R.E. & Santos-Filho, P.B. (2007a). Evaluation of Alzheimer's disease by analysis of MR images using multilayer perceptrons and Kohonen SOM classifiers as an alternative to the ADC maps. In *29th Annual International Conference of the IEEE Engineering in Medicine and Biology Society,* Lyon, France, EMBS-IEEE

Santos, W.P.; Assis, F.M.; Souza, R.E. & Santos-Filho, P.B. (2008a). Evaluation of Alzheimer's Disease by Analysis of MR Images using Objective Dialectical Classifiers as an Alternative to ADC Maps. In *30th Annual International Conference of the IEEE Engineering in Medicine and Biology Society,* Vancouver, Canada, EMBS-IEEE

Castano-Moraga, C.A.; Lenglet, C.; Deriche, R. & Ruiz-Alzola, J. (2006). A Fast and Rigorous Anisotropic Smoothing Method for DT-MRI. In *Proceedings of the ISBI 2006,* CSIEEE

Basser, P.J. (2002). Diffusion-Tensor MRI: Theory, Experimental Design, and Data Analysis. In *Procedings of the 2nd Joint EMBS BMES Conference,* 1165-1166, Houston, USA,, EMBS-IEEE-BMES

Fillard, P.; Arsigny, V.; Pennec, X. & Ayache, N. (2006). Clinical DT-MRI estimations, smoothing and fiber tracking with log-Euclidean metrics. In *Proceedings of the ISBI 2006,* CS-IEEE

Duda, R.; Hart, P. & Stork, D.G. (2001). *Pattern Classification,* John Wiley and Sons

Duda, R. & Hart, P. (1972). *Pattern Classification and Scene Analysis,* John Wiley and Sons

Sklansky, J. & Wassel, G.N. (1981). *Pattern Classifiers and Trainable Machines,* Springer-Verlag, 1st edition

Haykin, S. (1999). Neural Networks: A Comprehensive Foundation, Prentice Hall, New York

Li, H.; Liu, T.; Young, G.; Guo, L. & Wong, S.T.C. (2006) Brain Tissue Segmentation Based on DWI/DTI Data. In *Proceedings of the ISBI 2006,* CS-IEEE

Bartesaghi, A. & Nadar, M. (2006). Segmentation of Anatomical Structure from DTMRI. In *Proceedings of the ISBI 2006,* CS-IEEE

Wang, Z. & Bovik, A.C. (2002). A universal image quality index. *IEEE Signal Processing Letters,* 9

Santos, W.P.; Souza, R.E.; Silva, A.F.D. & Santos-Filho, P.B. (2008b). Evaluation of Alzheimer's disease by analysis of MR images using multilayer perceptrons and committee machines. *Computerized Medical Imaging and Graphics*, 32(1):17–21

Santos, W.P.; Souza, R.E.; Silva, A.F.D.& Santos-Filho, P.B. (2007b). Evaluation of Alzheimer's disease by analysis of MR images using multilayer perceptrons, polynomial nets and Kohonen LVQ classifiers. In *Lecture Notes in Computer Science: Computer Vision / Computer Graphics Collaboration Techniques and Applications (MIRAGE 2007)*, volume 2, pages 12–22, Rocquencourt, France, INRIA & CS-IEEE

Santos, W.P.; Souza, R.E.; Silva, A.F.D. & Santos-Filho, P.B. (2007c). Avaliação da Doença de Alzheimer pela Análise Multiespectral de Imagens DW-MR por Mapas Auto-Organizados de Kohonen como Alternativa aos Mapas ADC. In *IV Congreso Latino-Americano de Engenharia Biomédica*, Porlamar, Venezuela, IFMBE

Santos, W.P.; Souza, R.E.; Silva, A.F.D. & Santos-Filho, P.B. (2007d). Avaliação da doença de Alzheimer pela análise multiespectral de imagens DW-MR por redes RBF como alternativa aos mapas ADC. In *VIII Congresso Brasileiro de Redes Neurais*, Florianópolis, Brasil, SBRN

26

Simultaneous Topology, Shape and Sizing Optimisation of Skeletal Structures Using Multiobjective Evolutionary Algorithms

Chaid Noilublao and Sujin Bureerat
Applied Mathematics and Optimisation Research Unit, Department of Mechanical Engineering, Faculty of Engineering, Khon Kaen University, 4000 Thailand

1. Introduction

A framework or skeletal structure is one of the most used structures in engineering applications. Using such a structure is said to be advantageous since they are simple and inexpensive to construct. It can be employed in many engineering purposes e.g. transmission towers, wind turbine towers, communication towers, civil engineering structures, and mechanical parts. In the past, the design of such a structure was usually carried out in such a way that the conceptual design stage was somewhat ignored and the initial shape of a structure had been formed by an experienced engineering designer. The classical civil engineering design approach is then applied in the preliminary and detailed design stages.

Recently topology optimisation, an efficient tool for structural conceptual design, has been studied and used in a wide range of engineering applications. Considerable research work on the conceptual design of truss and frame structures by means of topology optimisation has been conducted in the last two decades (e.g. Hajela & Lee,1995; Ohsaki, 1995; Zhou, 1996; Yunkang & Xin, 1998; Hasancebi & Erbatur, 2002; Kawamura et al., 2002; Stolpe & Svanberg, 2003; Ohsaki & Katoh, 2005; Achtziger & Stolpe, 2007; Svanberg & Werme, 2007; Hagishita & Ohsaki, 2009). By the use of such design technology, the optimised layout of a skeletal structure can be accomplished. Having a structural layout from this design process, the shape and sizing design processes are then implemented. Nevertheless, a more efficient design approach can be achieved if a design problem is posed to have topological, shape, and sizing design variables at the same time. Much research work has been conducted towards combining and performing topology, shape, and sizing optimisation at the same optimisation run (e.g. Wang et al., 2004; Zhou et al., 2004; Tang et al., 2005; Shea & Smith, 2006; Achtziger, 2007; Martínez et al., 2007; Chan & Wong, 2008; Noiluplao & Bureerat, 2008; Zhu et al., 2008). The optimum design problem of the simultaneous topology/shape/sizing optimisation is usually structural weight minimisation subject to stress and other safety constraints. The optimisers employed can be a derivative-based method (Martínez et al., 2007), an evolutionary algorithm (Tang et al., 2005; Shea & Smith, 2006; Noiluplao & Bureerat, 2008), and a hybrid method (Chan & Wong, 2008). From the literature, most if not all of the optimisation problems are formulated to have one objective function, whereas in a practical design of an engineering system, there usually are several design objectives for decision making. If we have an optimiser that can deal with the design problem with such multiple design objectives, it could be useful and beneficial for designers.

Evolutionary algorithms (EAs) have been developed and used for several decades. The methods can be viewed as optimisation methods that search for optimum solutions by imitating some kinds of natural behaviours, and relying on a random process. Most EA searches are based upon using a population or a group of design solutions; consequently, they are often called population-based optimisers. Compared to their gradient-based counterparts, the EAs have advantages in that their searching process can be performed without using function derivatives. The methods are robust and simple to use, and can deal with almost all kinds of optimum design problems. As they are dependent on randomisation, EAs however have some drawbacks since they have low convergence rates and lack search consistency.

Evolutionary algorithms can deal with both single- and multiple-objective optimisation problems. The best known single-objective evolutionary optimiser is the genetic algorithm. Some other established single-objective EAs are: evolution strategies, particle swarm optimisation, and population-based incremental learning. EAs that can deal with multiple objective functions are called multiobjective evolutionary algorithms (MOEAs). As they use a set of design solutions for searching, on each generation those solutions can be sorted to find the so-called non-dominated design solutions. The set of non-dominated design solutions are improved iteratively, and the final set is taken as an approximate Pareto optimal set. This is the most outstanding and attractive ability of MOEAs as they can search for a group of non-dominated design solutions within one optimisation run. While the other conventional gradient-based optimisers need to be run as many times as the number of Pareto optimal solutions required.

The use of EAs for structural optimisation has been investigated and studied by many researchers around the world. By using EAs, any kind of design variables, constraints, as well as objective function can be defined. With additional strong points i.e. the capability of reaching near global optima of EAs and their robustness, they are even more popular than their gradient-based counterparts. The methods can be used for structural weight or cost minimisation (Benage & Dhingra, 1994, Bureerat & Cooper, 1988), passive vibration alleviation (Keane, 1995; Ton et al., 1998; Moshrefi-Torbati et al., 2003; Alkhatib et al., 2004; Kanyakam & Bureerat, 2007), and other performance maximisation (Xu et al., 2003; Achtziger & Kocvara, 2007).

The work in this chapter, consisting of two parts, is concerned with the demonstration of implementing MOEAs on the optimisation of skeletal structures. In the first part, the performance comparison of a number of MOEAs including non-dominated sorting genetic algorithm (NSGAII), strength Pareto evolutionary algorithm (SPEA2), population-based incremental learning (PBIL), Pareto archive evolution strategy (PAES), and multiobjective particle swarm optimisation (MPSO) are employed to solve seven simultaneous shape and sizing design problems of two structures. The comparative studies are carried out by using the so-called *C*-indicator. Also, a new indicator *C'* is proposed to be used along with the *C* parameter. The Pareto optimum results obtained from using the various MOEAs are compared and discussed while some of the best performers are obtained. The second part involves the application of MOEAs to a simultaneous topology/shape/sizing optimisation of a skeletal structure. The design demonstrations are performed and illustrated.

2. Multiobjective evolutionary algorithms

A typical multiobjecitve optimisation problem can be defined as:

$$\text{find } \mathbf{x} \text{ such that} \quad \text{Min: } \mathbf{f} = \{f_1(\mathbf{x}),\ldots,f_m(\mathbf{x})\} \quad \text{Subject to} \quad g_i(\mathbf{x}) \le 0, \quad h_i(\mathbf{x}) = 0 \tag{1}$$

where $\mathbf{x}$ is a vector of n design variables, f_i are the m objective functions, g_i are inequality constraints, and h_i are equality constraints.

If the problem has one objective, there will be one (global) optimum solution. In cases that the problem has more than one objective function, there will be a set of optimal solutions, which is called a Pareto optimum set. Figure 1 illustrates a particular 2-objective design problem where all the feasible solutions are plotted in the objective domain. The Pareto optimal solutions are the points on the bold frontier, which is called a Pareto frontier or Pareto front. Similarly to the 2-objective case, the Pareto front of a 3-objective design problem is a 3-dimensional surface and so on.

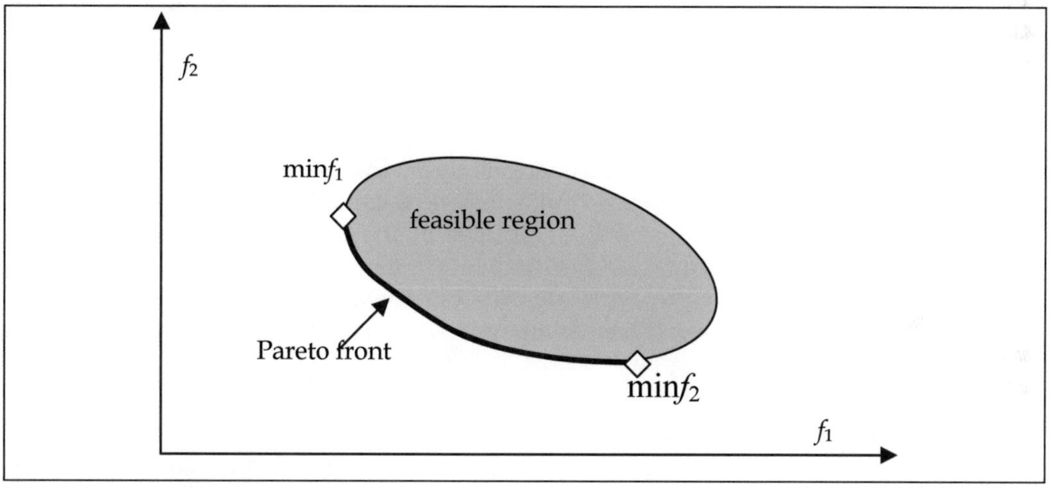

Fig. 1. Pareto front

The basic concept of exploring Pareto optimum points via MOEA search is that, in each generation while a new population is created, non-dominated solutions are classified and carried on to the next generation. The term non-dominated solutions define the local Pareto solutions among the members of the current population during evolutionary search. The definitions associated with non-domination (for minimisation) are given as:

Definition 1 **Dominance** Given $f_i(\mathbf{x})$ for $i = 1,\ldots m$ are objective functions, if $f_i(\mathbf{x}_1) \le f_i(\mathbf{x}_2)$ for every $i \in \{1,\ldots,m\}$ and there is j such that $f_j(\mathbf{x}_1) < f_j(\mathbf{x}_2)$, then $\mathbf{x}_1$ dominates $\mathbf{x}_2$.

Definition 2 **Non-Dominated Solutions (Approximate Pareto Set)** Given a set of solutions or population $\mathbf{G}$ size N, a solution $\mathbf{x}_e \in \mathbf{G}$ is a non-dominated solution in $\mathbf{G}$ if there does not exist $\mathbf{x} \in \mathbf{G}$ such that $\mathbf{x}$ dominate $\mathbf{x}_e$.

Figure 2 displays the plot of 7 design solutions on a 2-objective domain. The non-dominated solutions are $\mathbf{x}_1$, $\mathbf{x}_3$, and $\mathbf{x}_7$.

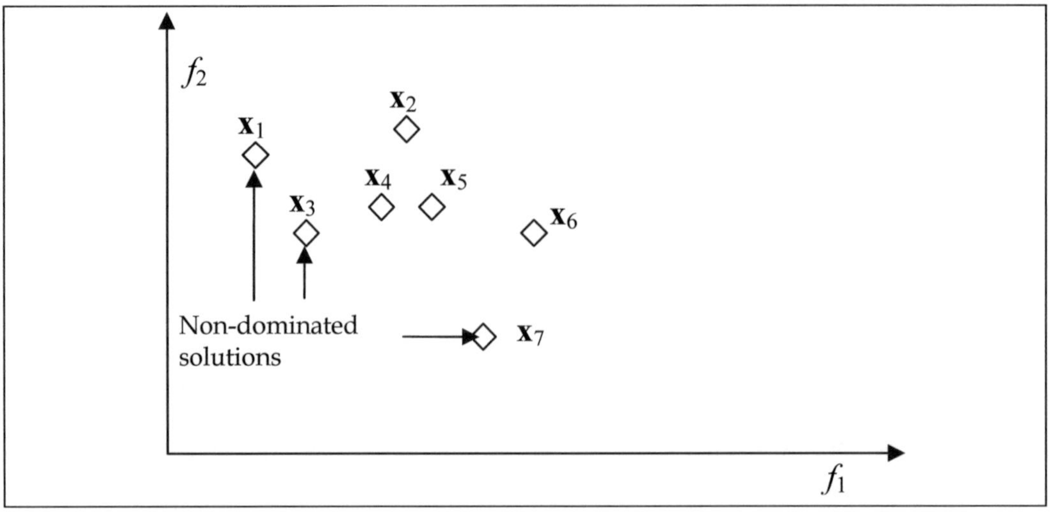

Fig. 2. non-dominated solutions

In this work, five MOEAs are used including PAES, NSGAII, SPEA2, PBIL and MPSO. The methods are briefly reviewed as follows:

2.1 Pareto archive evolution strategy

PAES was proposed by Knowles & Corne, 2000. The simplest version of PAES is the combination of (1+1)-ES with a Pareto archiving strategy. The algorithm starts with an initial solution called a parent and an external Pareto archive. A candidate solution is then created by mutating the parent. The parent will be replaced by the candidate based on a selection strategy. The decision to discard or add the candidate to the Pareto archive is made. In cases that the archive is full, the adaptive grid algorithm is activated to remove one of the non-dominated solutions from the archive. As the procedure continues, the Pareto archive is iteratively updated until reaching the termination criterion.

2.2 Non-dominated sorting genetic algorithm

NSGA was proposed by Srinivas & Deb, 1994, and later the upgraded version NSGAII was presented by Deb et al., 2002. Starting with an initial population, selection, crossover and mutation operators are then used for exploring Pareto solutions. After crossover and mutation are operated with the given probabilities, the children are obtained and a new population is selected by performing non-dominated and crowding distance sorting algorithms on a union set of the parents and their children. The population is updated iteratively until the termination criterion is met.

2.3 Strength Pareto evolutionary algorithm

SPEA was proposed by Zitzler & Thiele, 1999, whereas its second version SPEA2 was presented in Zitzler et al., 2002. The search procedure starts with an initial population and an external Pareto set. Fitness values are assigned to the population based upon the level of domination. A set of solutions are then selected to a mating pool by performing the binary tournament selection operator. The new population are created by means of crossover and mutation on those selected solutions. The new external Pareto solutions are the non-dominated solutions of the combination of the old external Pareto set and the new population. In cases that the number of non-dominated solutions in the Pareto archive exceeds its predefined size, the truncation operator also known as the nearest neighbourhood technique is executed to delete some design solutions from the archive. The Pareto archive is updated repeatedly until the termination criterion is met.

2.4 Multiobjective particle swarm optimisation

The particle swarm optimisation method uses real codes and searches for an optimum by mimicking the movement of a flock of birds, which aim to find food (Reyes-Sierra & Coello Coello, 2006). The search procedure herein is based on the particle swarm concepts combining with the use of an external Pareto archiving scheme. Starting with an initial set of design solutions as well as their corresponding particle velocities and objective function values, an initial Pareto archive is filled with the non-dominated solutions obtained from sorting the initial population. A new population is then created by using the particle swarm updating strategy where the global best solution is randomly selected from the external Pareto archive. Afterwards, the external archive is updated by the non-dominated solutions of the union set of the new population and the previous non-dominated solutions. In cases that the number of non-dominated solutions is too large, the adaptive grid algorithm (Knowles & Corne, 2000) is employed to properly remove some solutions from the archive. The Pareto archive is repeatedly improved until fulfilling the termination criteria.

2.5 Population-based incremental learning

Population-based incremental learning, probably the simplest form of an estimation of distribution algorithm (EDA), was first proposed by Beluja, 1994, for single-objective optimisation. The method was then extended for multiobjective optimisation (Bureerat & Sriworamas, 2007; Kanyakam & Bureerat, 2007). The algorithm of multiobjective PBIL starts with an external Pareto archive and initial probability matrix having all elements set to be 0.5. A set of binary design solutions are then created corresponding to the probability matrix while their function values are evaluated. The Pareto archive is updated by replacing its members with the non-dominated solutions of the new population and the previous Pareto archive. In cases that the number of non-dominated solutions exceeds the predefined archive size, the normal line method is activated to remove some members from the archive. The probability matrix and the Pareto archive are iteratively updated until the termination criteria are fulfilled.

3. Structural modelling

A structural dynamic model can be described as a structure being in a dynamic equilibrium state. It is the state at which the system has minimum potential energy (potential energy herein includes structural elastic potential energy, the work done by external forces, and the work due to inertial forces). The equations of motion basically comprise of kinetic energy, structural restoration (spring and damping) and external dynamic forces. By using the finite element approach, the structural dynamic model is represented by

$$\mathbf{M}\ddot{\boldsymbol{\delta}} + \mathbf{K}\boldsymbol{\delta} = \mathbf{F}(t) \tag{2}$$

where $\boldsymbol{\delta}$ is the vector of structural displacements, $\mathbf{M}$ is a structural mass matrix, $\mathbf{K}$ is a structural stiffness matrix, and $\mathbf{F}$ is the vector of dynamic forces acting on the structure.
The computation is traditionally achieved by means of finite element analysis. With the given boundary conditions (say $\boldsymbol{\delta}_b = \mathbf{0}$) being given, Equation (2) can be partitioned as

$$\begin{bmatrix} \mathbf{M}_{aa} & \mathbf{M}_{ab} \\ \mathbf{M}_{ba} & \mathbf{M}_{bb} \end{bmatrix} \begin{bmatrix} \ddot{\boldsymbol{\delta}}_a \\ \ddot{\boldsymbol{\delta}}_b \end{bmatrix} + \begin{bmatrix} \mathbf{K}_{aa} & \mathbf{K}_{ab} \\ \mathbf{K}_{ba} & \mathbf{K}_{bb} \end{bmatrix} \begin{bmatrix} \boldsymbol{\delta}_a \\ \boldsymbol{\delta}_b \end{bmatrix} = \begin{bmatrix} \mathbf{F}_a \\ \mathbf{F}_b \end{bmatrix} \tag{3}$$

where the subscript b indicates the known displacements and unknown reactions at the boundary conditions, and the subscript a denotes unknown displacements and predefined external forces.
Equation (3) can be rearranged leading to 2 systems of differential equations as:

$$\mathbf{M}_{aa}\ddot{\boldsymbol{\delta}}_a + \mathbf{K}_{aa}\boldsymbol{\delta}_a = \mathbf{F}_a \tag{4}$$

and

$$\mathbf{M}_{ba}\ddot{\boldsymbol{\delta}}_a + \mathbf{K}_{ba}\boldsymbol{\delta}_a = \mathbf{F}_b\,. \tag{5}$$

In the cases of free vibration analysis, Equation (4) can be written as

$$\mathbf{M}_{aa}\ddot{\boldsymbol{\delta}}_a + \mathbf{K}_{aa}\boldsymbol{\delta}_a = \mathbf{0}\,. \tag{6}$$

By substituting $\boldsymbol{\delta}_a = \bar{\boldsymbol{\delta}}_a e^{i\omega t}$ to (6), we have an eigenvalue problem

$$(\mathbf{K}_{aa} - \omega^2\mathbf{M}_{aa})\bar{\boldsymbol{\delta}}_a = \mathbf{0}\,. \tag{7}$$

Solving such a system of equations leads to N natural frequencies $\boldsymbol{\omega} = \{\omega_1, \omega_2, \ldots, \omega_N\}$ and their corresponding eigenvectors $\boldsymbol{\Phi} = [\boldsymbol{\varphi}_1, \boldsymbol{\varphi}_2, \ldots, \boldsymbol{\varphi}_N]$, where N is the size of the square mass and stiffness matrices. The orthogonality conditions can be written as

$$\boldsymbol{\Phi}^T\mathbf{M}_{aa}\boldsymbol{\Phi} = diag(\mu_i) \tag{8}$$

$$\boldsymbol{\Phi}^T\mathbf{K}_{aa}\boldsymbol{\Phi} = diag(\mu_i\omega_i^2)\,.$$

By using the proportional (Rayleigh) damping concept, a damping matrix can be introduced to the model yielding

$$\mathbf{M}_{aa}\ddot{\boldsymbol{\delta}}_a + \mathbf{C}_{aa}\dot{\boldsymbol{\delta}}_a + \mathbf{K}_{aa}\boldsymbol{\delta}_a = \mathbf{F}_a \tag{9}$$

where $\mathbf{C}_{aa} = \alpha\mathbf{M}_{aa} + \beta\mathbf{K}_{aa}$, and α and β are damping coefficients to be defined.
From equation (9), by substituting $\boldsymbol{\delta}_a = \bar{\boldsymbol{\delta}}_a e^{i\omega t}$ and $\mathbf{F}_a = \bar{\mathbf{F}}_a e^{i\omega t}$, a frequency response function (FRF) matrix can be determined from the relation (Preumont, 2001)

$$\mathbf{H}(\omega) = \left[-\omega^2\mathbf{M}_{aa} + j\omega\mathbf{C}_{aa} + \mathbf{K}_{aa}\right]^{-1} = \boldsymbol{\Phi}diag\left\{\frac{1}{\mu_i(\omega_i^2 - \omega^2 + 2j\xi_i\omega_i\omega)}\right\}\boldsymbol{\Phi}^T \tag{10}$$

where ω is the frequency of the input force and its output displacement, and $\xi_i = \frac{1}{2}\left(\frac{\alpha}{\omega_i} + \beta\omega_i\right)$ is a damping ratio. FRF can be defined as the ratio of steady-state harmonic output to steady-state harmonic input, and here is the ratio of response displacement to input force or *receptance*. To reduce computational time in the optimisation process, the frequency response function matrix can be approximated using the first m modes as (Preumont, 2001)

$$\mathbf{H}(\omega) \approx \sum_{i=1}^{m} \frac{\boldsymbol{\varphi}_i \boldsymbol{\varphi}_i^T}{\mu_i(\omega_i^2 - \omega^2 + 2j\xi_i\omega_i\omega)} + \mathbf{K}_{aa}^{-1} - \sum_{i=1}^{m} \frac{\boldsymbol{\varphi}_i \boldsymbol{\varphi}_i^T}{\mu_i \omega_i^2}. \quad (11)$$

The relation between displacement response and input force can be expressed as

$$\bar{\boldsymbol{\delta}}_a = \mathbf{H}(\omega)\bar{\mathbf{F}}_a. \quad (12)$$

Figure 3 illustrates how to measure $H(r,s)$ which represents the ratio of a displacement response at the rth degree of freedom to a harmonic excitation at the sth degree of freedom. Furthermore, by defining force transmissibility (FT), denoted by $\mathbf{T}(\omega)$, as the ratio of output harmonic reaction forces to the input external harmonic forces, it can be written as

$$\bar{\mathbf{F}}_b = \mathbf{T}(\omega)\bar{\mathbf{F}}_a. \quad (13)$$

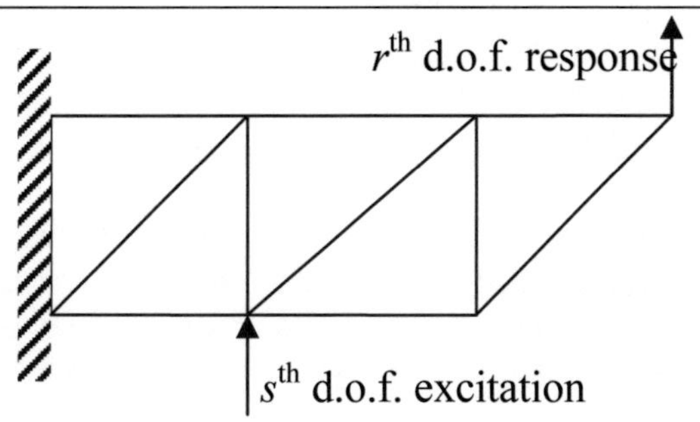

Fig. 3. Measurement of FRF

By letting the reaction force be $\mathbf{F}_b = \bar{\mathbf{F}}_b e^{i\omega t}$, and substituting (12) & (13) in (5), force transmissibility can be obtained as

$$\mathbf{T}(\omega) = \left(-\omega^2\mathbf{M}_{ba} + \mathbf{K}_{ba}\right)\mathbf{H}. \quad (14)$$

In structural vibration design, FRF and FT determine structural merit. The lower FRF or FT at a particular frequency means the better structural vibration suppression design. Therefore, a design objective can be assigned in such a way that frequency responses at a frequency range of interest are minimised. Moreover, maximising structural natural frequency is an alternative criterion for design of structures under dynamic loadings.

Apart from dynamic analysis, structural static analysis can be carried out by using Equation (3) ignoring the structural kinetic energy or the mass matrix. The system of equations then becomes

$$\begin{bmatrix} \mathbf{K}_{aa} & \mathbf{K}_{ab} \\ \mathbf{K}_{ba} & \mathbf{K}_{bb} \end{bmatrix} \begin{bmatrix} \boldsymbol{\delta}_a \\ \boldsymbol{\delta}_b \end{bmatrix} = \begin{bmatrix} \mathbf{F}_a \\ \mathbf{F}_b \end{bmatrix}. \tag{15}$$

The solutions of (15) are

$$\boldsymbol{\delta}_a = \mathbf{K}_{aa}^{-1}(\mathbf{F}_a - \mathbf{K}_{ab}\boldsymbol{\delta}_b) \tag{16}$$

and

$$\mathbf{F}_b = \mathbf{K}_{ba}\boldsymbol{\delta}_a - \mathbf{K}_{bb}\boldsymbol{\delta}_b. \tag{17}$$

The displacement vector δ is used for displacement constraints as well as for computing stresses on structural elements. The reaction $\mathbf{F}_b$ is also an important factor since the reaction force can affect a structural foundation. In an optimisation process, it is also common to use many load cases since, in real-world problems, there are many aspects of applied loads acting on one structure.

4. Numerical experiment

4.1 Design problems

The optimisation problems assigned in this study are to find a Pareto optimal set that optimises multiple objective functions subject to stress constraints, which can be expressed as

$$\min_{\mathbf{x}} \mathbf{f} \tag{18}$$

subject to

$$\sigma_i \leq \sigma_a, \ i = 1, \ldots, N_e$$

where σ_i is a stress on the ith element, σ_a is an allowable stress, and N_e is the total number of elements.

The multiobjective design problems presented here are similar to the work in Kanyakam & Bureerat, 2007, where the objective functions include structural mass, a natural frequency, an FRF crest parameter, and an FT crest parameter. Figure 4 displays the term FRF crest parameter, which determines the shaded area in a frequency range of interest. As we need

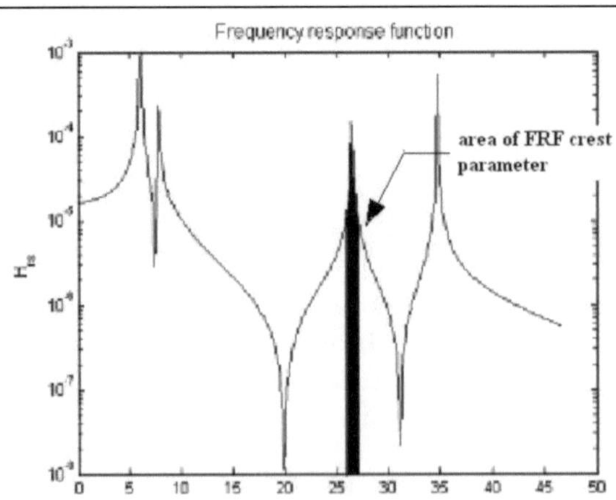

Fig. 4. FRF crest parameter

to reduce the magnitude of the FRF for vibration suppression, the frequency range is thus the interval that bounds a particular natural frequency. Seven design criteria are defined as:

f_1: structural mass

f_2: $1/\omega_1^2$

f_3: $1/(\omega_1^2+\omega_2^2+\omega_3^2)$

f_4: FRF crest parameter at ω_1

f_5: mean value of FRF crest parameters at ω_1, ω_2 and ω_3

f_6: FT crest parameter at ω_1

f_7: mean value of FT crest parameters at ω_1, ω_2 and ω_3

where ω_i is the ith natural frequency.

The sets of objective functions can be arranged as:

P1: min f_1, min f_2
P2: min f_1, min f_3
P3: min f_1, min f_4
P4: min f_1, min f_5
P5: min f_1, min f_6
P6: min f_1, min f_7
P7: min f_1, min f_5, min f_7.

As a result, we have seven multiobjective design problems with the above sets of objective functions and stress constraints. It should be noted that some of these objective function sets have been implemented and examined in Kanyakam & Bureerat, 2007, and it is shown that using P2, P4 and P6 leads to a more effective design based on vibration alleviation. All seven design problems are however used to benchmark the performance of the MOEAS.

We apply the above-mentioned problems to design three frame structures made of material with $E = 209\times10^9$ N/m^2, and $\rho = 7000$ kg/m^3. The structures are named as:

ST1: a 2D bridge (Figure 5). The structure has 12 nodes and 21 elements where nodes 1 and 12 are fixed. The vertical loads are applied to nodes 2, 4, 6, 8, and 10. The design variables consist of element diameters, and the vertical positions of nodes 3, 5, 7, 9, and 11. Both shape and sizing design variables are treated as being symmetric; as a result, there are 14 continuous design variables. The FRF used as design criteria is the point receptance in the vertical direction of node 7. The FT is the vertical direction transmission from node 7 to the fixed support node 1.

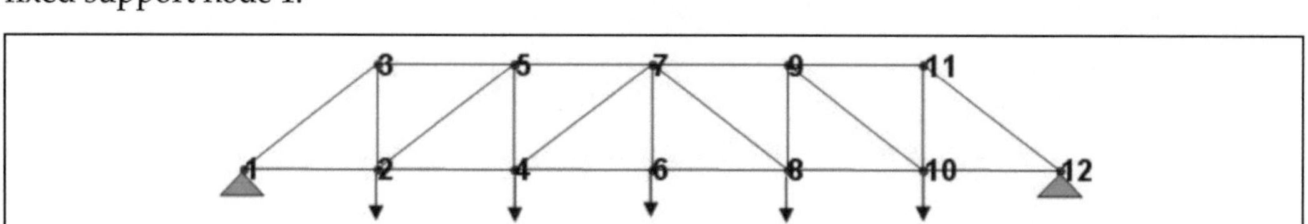

Fig. 5. 2D bridge ST1

ST2: a walking tractor handlebar (Figure 6). The finite element model of the handlebar structure (Kanyakam & Bureerat, 2007) consists of 16 nodes and 27 elements with four nodes being fixed. The structure is subjected to two static load cases, one is the load for turning the tractor and the other is the load for balancing and controlling the tractor. The total number of continuous shape and sizing design variables is 24. The FRF being used is the point receptance in the vertical direction of node 6. The FT is the vertical direction transmission from node 6 to the fixed support node 1.

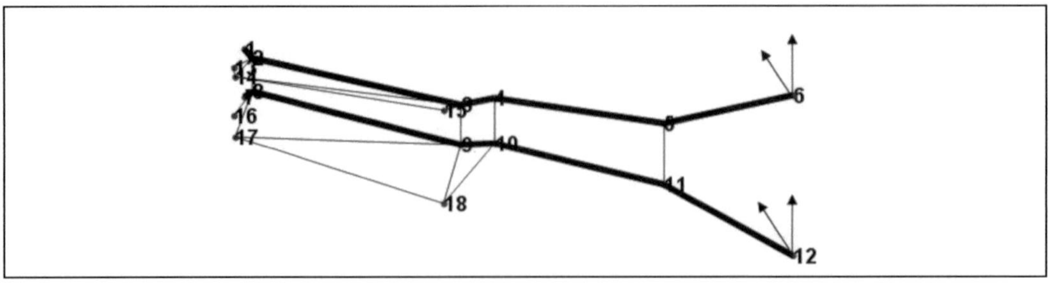

Fig. 6. Walking tractor handlebar structure ST2

ST3: a 2D bridge (Figure 7). The ST3 structure is modified from ST1 for the demonstration of simultaneous topology/shape/sizing optimisation. The structure in Figure 7, which is set as a ground structure for topology optimisation, has 12 nodes and 25 elements. The design variables are element diameters, and the vertical and horizontal positions of nodes 3, 5, 7, 9, and 11, which have a total of 18 variables after symmetry treatment. The diameters are discrete and allowed to have nearly zero size so that we can have various structural topologies. The position of FRF and FT measures are the same as that of ST1.

Finite element analysis is carried out by using the 2-node 3-dimensional 12 d.o.f. beam element. The ST1 and ST2 structures are used for the investigation of a comparative performance of MOEAs, while the ST3 structure is assigned for the demonstration of performing topology/shape/sizing optimisation at the same time.

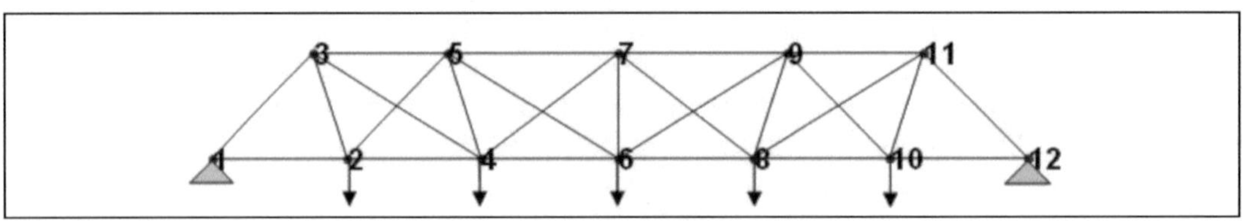

Fig. 7. 2D bridge's ground structure for simultaneous topology/shape/sizing optimisation ST3

4.2 Performance assessment

Seven multiobjective evolutionary strategies are employed in this study, which are designated as:

BPBIL: PBIL using binary codes with 0.05 mutation rate, and 0.2 mutation shift

BPAES: PAES using binary codes

BNSGA: NSGAII using binary codes with crossover and mutation rates as 1.0 and 0.5 respectively

BSPEA: SPEA2 using binary codes with crossover and mutation rates as 1.0 and 0.5 respectively

RSPEA: SPEA2 using real codes (Sirsomporn & Bureerat, 2008) with crossover and mutation rates as 1.0 and 0.5 respectively

RNSGA: NSGAII using real codes with crossover and mutation rates as 1.0 and 0.5 respectively

RMPSO: MPSO (Reyes-Sierra & Coello Coello, 2006) using real codes with a starting inertia weight, an ending inertia weight, a cognitive learning factor, and a social learning factor as 0.5, 0.01, 0.5, and 0.5 respectively.

For the comparative performance study of optimising ST1 and ST2, starting with the same initial population, the number of generations of MOEAs is set to be 100 while both the population and archive size are set as 50. Each optimiser is applied to solve each design problem for designing each structure with 10 optimisation runs. The last updated Pareto archive is set to be a Pareto optimal set. For the design of ST3, one of the best MOEAs obtained from the first two design case studies is employed to solve the P2, P4, and P6 design problems with the number of generations being 150 while the population and the external archive are sized 100. The non-dominated sorting scheme proposed in Deb et al. (2001) is used to handle the stress constraints.

The performance assessment is accomplished by using the *C*-parameter (Zitzler et al., 2000). Having two particular non-dominated fronts {*A*} and {*B*}, $C_{A,B}$ determines the number of solutions in {*B*} that are dominated or equal to some solution in {*A*} divided by the total number of solutions in {*B*}. On the other hand, $C_{B,A}$ determines the number of solutions in {*A*} that are dominated or equal to some solution in {*B*} divided by the total number of solutions in {*A*}. From the definition, if $C_{A,B} > C_{B,A}$, we can say that front {*A*} is better than front {*B*} or vice versa. Figure 8 displays two approximate Pareto fronts {*A*} and {*B*} where $C_{A,B}$ = 0.5000 and $C_{B,A}$ = 0.4000. This implies that {*A*} is better than {*B*}. However, we can observe from the shaded areas between the two fronts dominating each other that the dominating area of {*B*} is larger than {*A*}. These shaded areas are also meaningful for front comparison. Nevertheless, it is difficult or even impossible to calculate such areas of hundred pairs of Pareto fronts directly. We can laterally calculate them and define a new performance indicator as:

$$C'_{A,B} = \frac{V_A}{V_A + V_B} \tag{19}$$

$$C'_{B,A} = 1 - C'_{AB}$$

where

$$V_A = \sum_{\mathbf{a} \in \hat{A}_1} \min\left\{\|\mathbf{a} - \mathbf{b}\|; \mathbf{b} \in \hat{B}_1\right\}$$

and

$$V_B = \sum_{\mathbf{b} \in \hat{B}_2} \min\left\{\|\mathbf{b} - \mathbf{a}\|; \mathbf{a} \in \hat{A}_2\right\}.$$

If $V_A = V_B = 0$, $C'_{A,B} = C'_{B,A} = 0.5$.

$\hat{A}_1$ is the set of some members of {*A*} that dominate the set of $\hat{B}_1 \subseteq \{B\}$ and $\hat{B}_2$ is the set of some members of {*B*} that dominate $\hat{A}_2 \subseteq \{A\}$. Similarly to the *C* parameter, if $C'_{A,B} > C'_{B,A}$, it means {*A*} is better than {*B*}. From the definition, the *C*′-indicator also has the effects of front extension and the number of dominant points.

From Figure 8, we have $C'_{A,B}$ = 0.4556 and $C'_{B,A}$ = 0.5444, which means {B} is the better front than {A}. Based on these two indicators, we have two different views of comparing approximate Pareto fronts. The special characteristic of the *C*′ parameter is illustrated in Figure 9, which shows three particular non-dominated fronts {A_1}, {A_2}, and {A_3}. The C and

C' comparisons of the three fronts are given in Table 1. In the Table, the value in the ith row and j^{th} column represents $C_{Ai,Aj}$. From the C comparison, it can be concluded that the front $\{A_3\}$ is the best method while the second best is $\{A_1\}$. However, in cases of C' comparison, we can see that $\{A_2\}$ is better than $\{A_1\}$, $\{A_1\}$ is better than $\{A_3\}$, and $\{A_3\}$ is better than $\{A_2\}$. This scenario can be called a scissor-paper-stone situation, which can happen in comparing approximate Pareto fronts obtained from using MOEAs. The two indicators, in fact, are not always conflicting to each other but they should be used together to provide different aspects of front comparing.

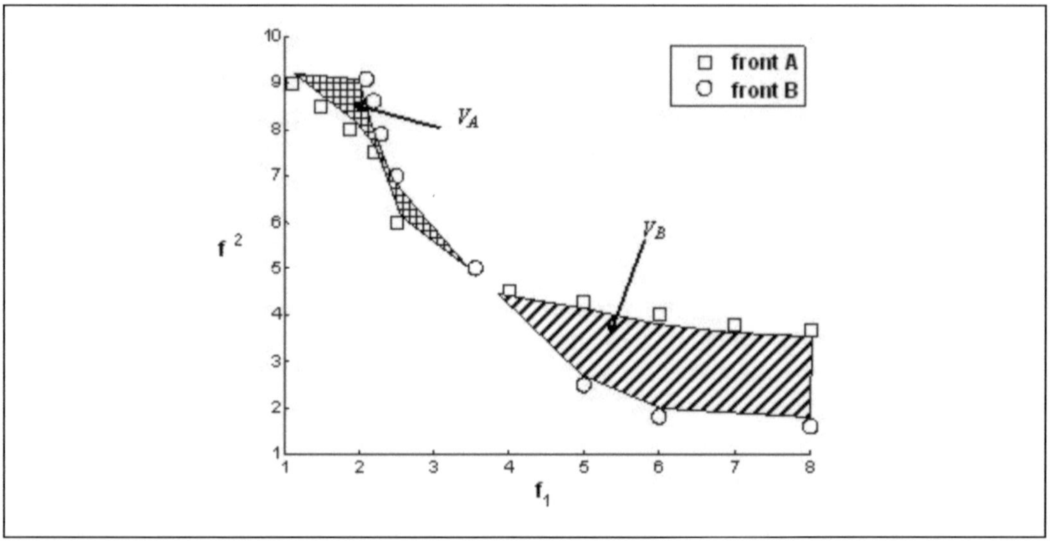

Fig. 8. Comparing two non-dominated fronts

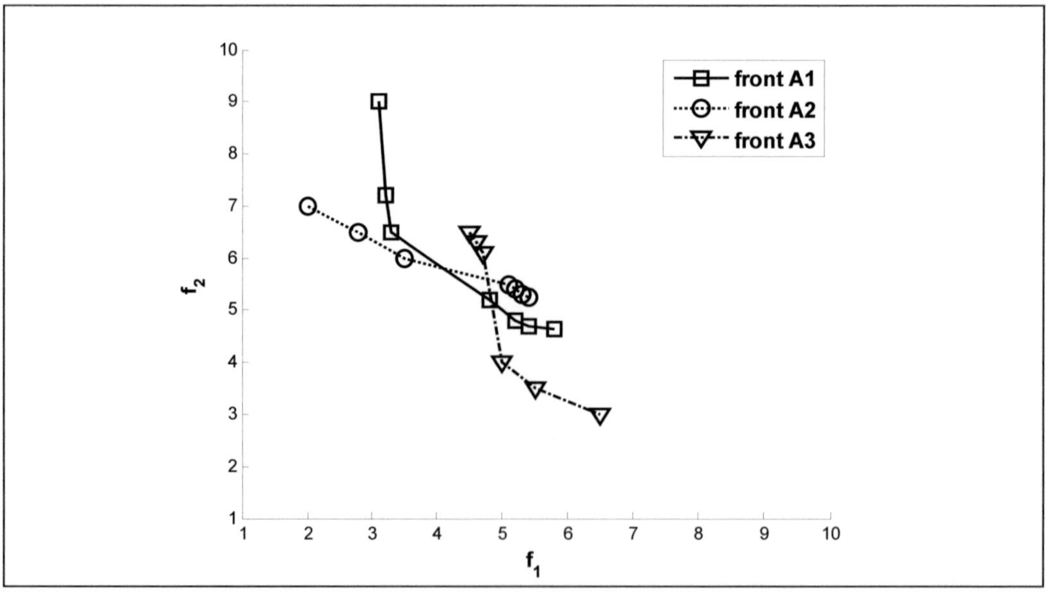

Fig. 9. Scissors-paper-stone situation

C-indicator			*C′*-indicator		
$\{A_1\}$	0.5714	0.1667	$\{A_1\}$	0.4929	0.5029
0.4286	$\{A_2\}$	0.5000	0.5076	$\{A_2\}$	0.4908
0.4286	0.5714	$\{A_3\}$	0.4971	0.5092	$\{A_3\}$

Table 1. *C* and *C′* indicators of $\{A_1\}$, $\{A_2\}$, and $\{A_3\}$

5. Design results

The performance comparison of 7 MOEAs is displayed in Figures 10 – 17. In Figure 10, the box-plots of *C* parameters comparing the various MOEAs when solving the P1-P7 design problems for the case of ST1 are illustrated. Each box-plot represents 10×10 *C* values of comparing 10 fronts obtained from using a method X to 10 fronts obtained from using a method Y when solving a particular design problem. The box-plots at the ith row and j^{th} column display the *C* values comparing non-dominated fronts of the seven design problems obtained from the ith optimiser with respect to those obtained from using the jth optimiser. For example the box-plots at the first row and second column in the figure present the *C* values of the fronts obtained from using BNSGA to those obtained from using BSPEA. We also need the box-plots in the second row and first column to compare these two optimisers. From the Figure, it can be concluded that BPBIL is the best for all the design problems. The *C′* comparison of these four methods is given in Figure 11. It can be shown that BPBIL is the best method except for the P7 design problem, which BNSGA gives the best results.
The best multiobjective evolutionary algorithm using binary codes BPBIL is taken to be compared with the methods using real codes as shown in Figures 12-13. From the *C* comparison in Figure 12, the overall best method is BPBIL with RSPEA being the second best. In Figure 13, it can be seen that RSPEA is as good as BPBIL based on *C′* comparison. This occurrence is probably similar to that illustrated in Figure 8. However, when taking an account of both indicators, the best method for designing ST1 is BPBIL.

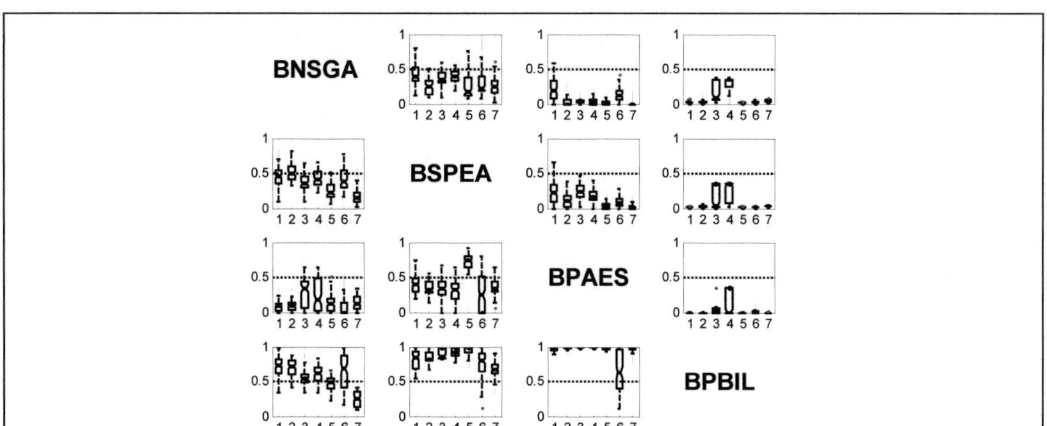

Fig. 10. Box-plot of *C* indicator of ST1 – I

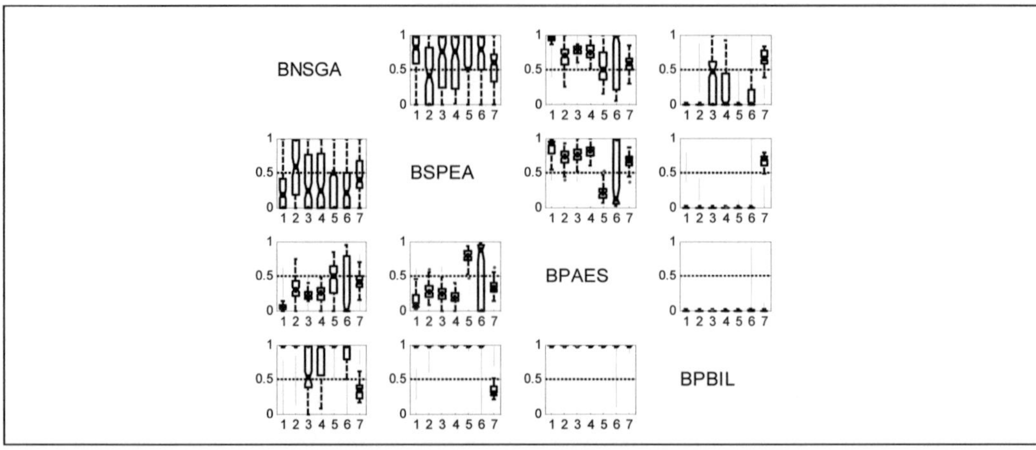

Fig. 11. Box-plot of C' indicator of ST1 – I

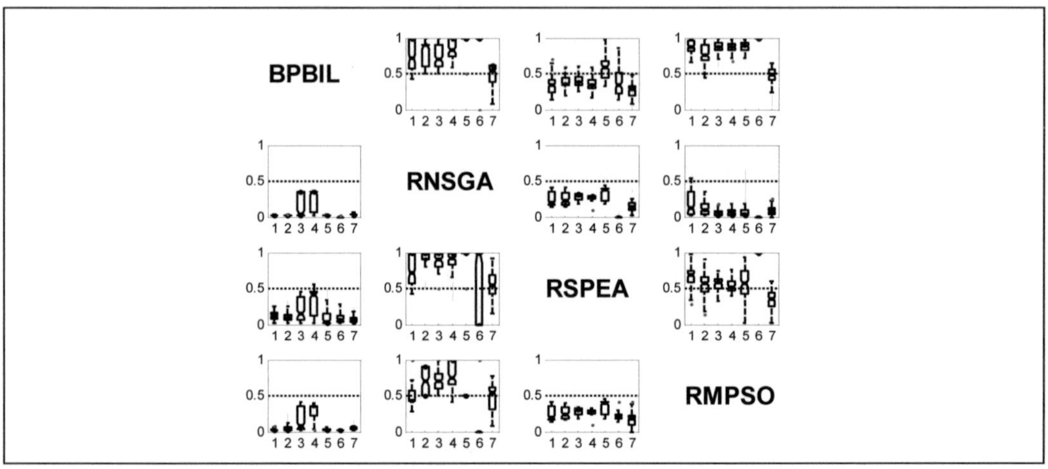

Fig. 12. Box-plot of C indicator of ST1 – II

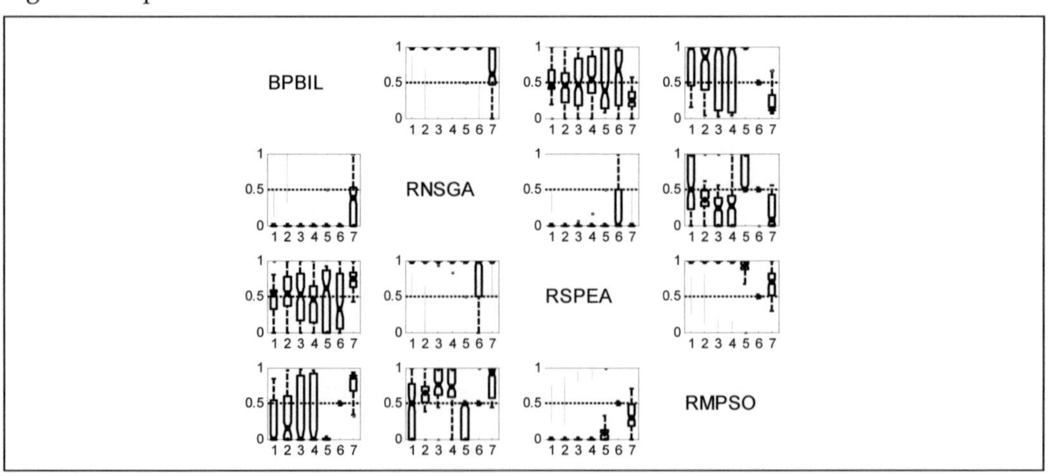

Fig. 13. Box-plot of C' indicator of ST1 - II

The comparative performance of MOEAs for solving the P1-P7 optimisation problems for the case of ST2 is illustrated in Figures 14-17. The best method that use binary codes based on the C indicator is BPBIL whereas the second best method is BNSGA as shown in Figure 14. Based on the C' indicator, the best method is BPBIL while the close second best is BNSGA. BNSGA even outperforms BPBIL in cases of the P3 and P4 design problems. This situation is similar to that displayed in Figure 8.

The best evolutionary optimiser among the methods using binary codes (BPBIL) is taken to be compared with the optimisers using real codes as shown in Figures 15 and 16. Based on the C indicator, the best optimiser is RSPEA whereas the second best is BPBIL. For the C' comparison, the best optimiser is still RSPEA with BPBIL being the second best. From both ST1 and ST2 case studies, it can be concluded that BPBIL tends to be more efficient when dealing with design problems with a smaller number of design variables while RSPEA is the better optimiser for the design problems with a greater number of design variables.

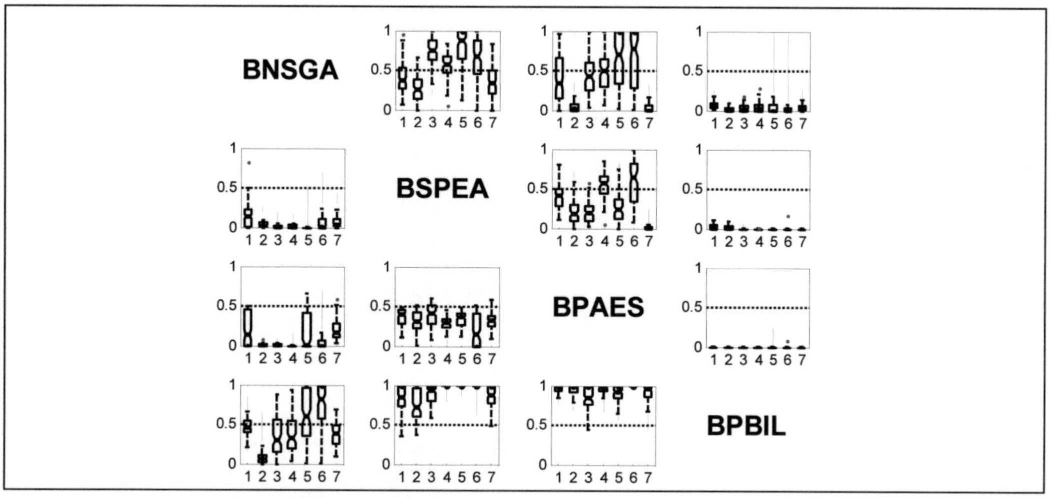

Fig. 14. Box-plot of C indicator of ST2 – I

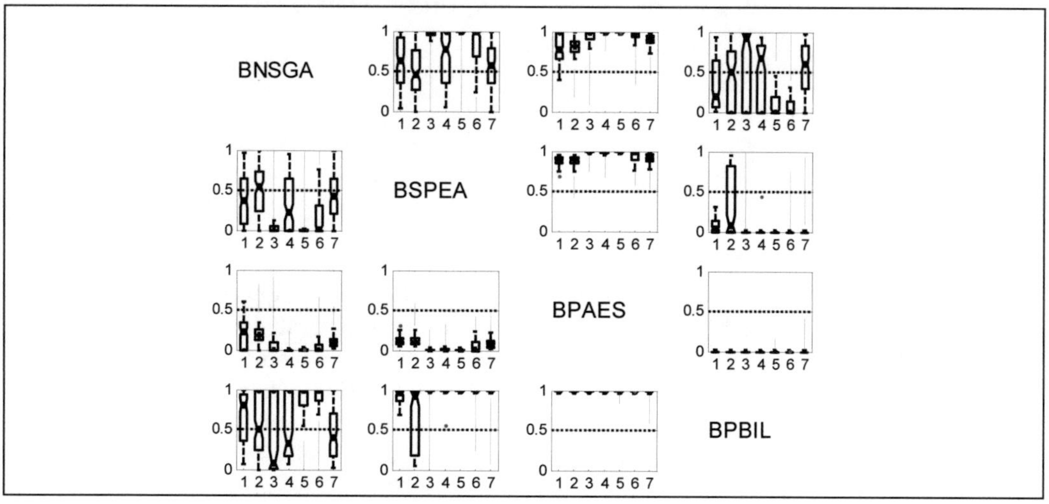

Fig. 15. Box-plot of C'indicator of ST2 - I

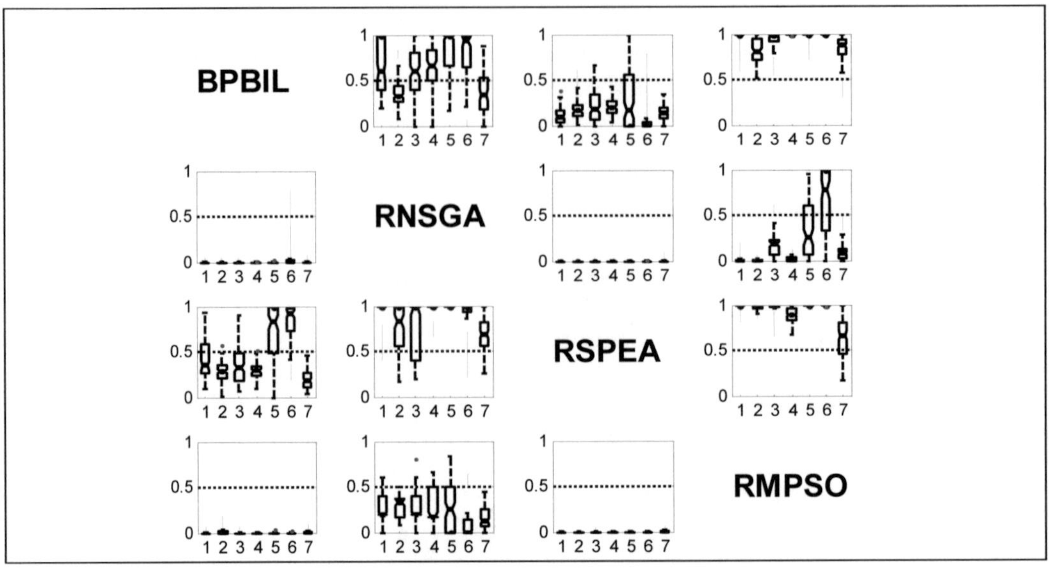

Fig. 16. Box-plot of C indicator of ST2 – II

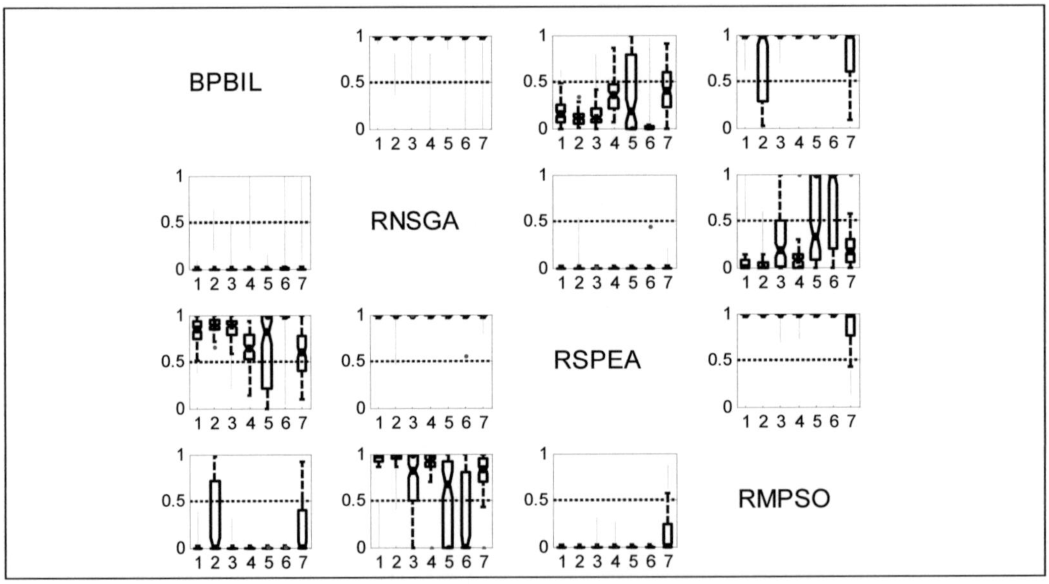

Fig. 17. Box-plot of C′ indicator of ST2 - II

The BPBIL algorithm is chosen to solve the P2, P4 and P6 design problems where the structure to be optimised is ST3. In this design case, some structural elements are allowed to be removed if their diameters are too small. The Pareto optimum results of P2 for optimising ST3 obtained from using BPBIL are plotted in Figure 18. Some selected non-dominated solutions are labelled whereas their corresponding structures are given in Figure 19. It can be seen that the structures have various layouts and shapes as well as various element sizes. The approximate Pareto front of P4 is plotted in Figure 20 whereas some selected structures from the front are illustrated in Figure 21. Similarly to the P2 design case, there consist of various structural topologies, shape and element sizes. The non-dominated front of P6 obtained from using BPBIL is given in Figure 22 whilst the selected solutions are shown in Figure 23. Similarly to the first two cases, the structures have various topologies, shapes, and element sizes. The obvious advantage of using MOEA for solving the simultaneous topology/shape/sizing optimisation is that they are robust and simple to use, and we can have a set of Pareto optimal solutions for decision making within one simulation run.

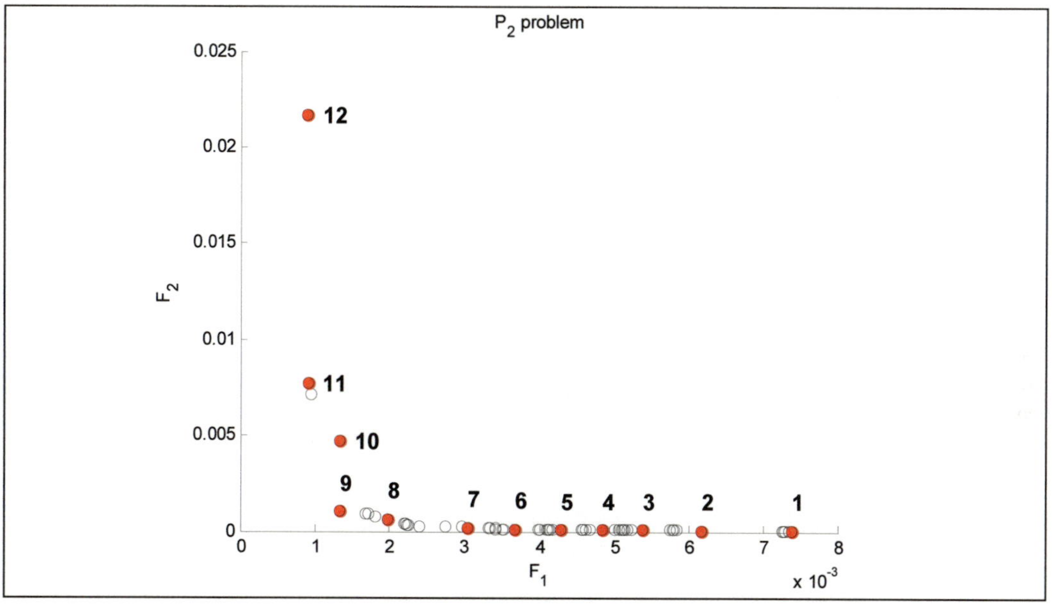

Fig. 18. Pareto front of P2 problem and ST3 structures

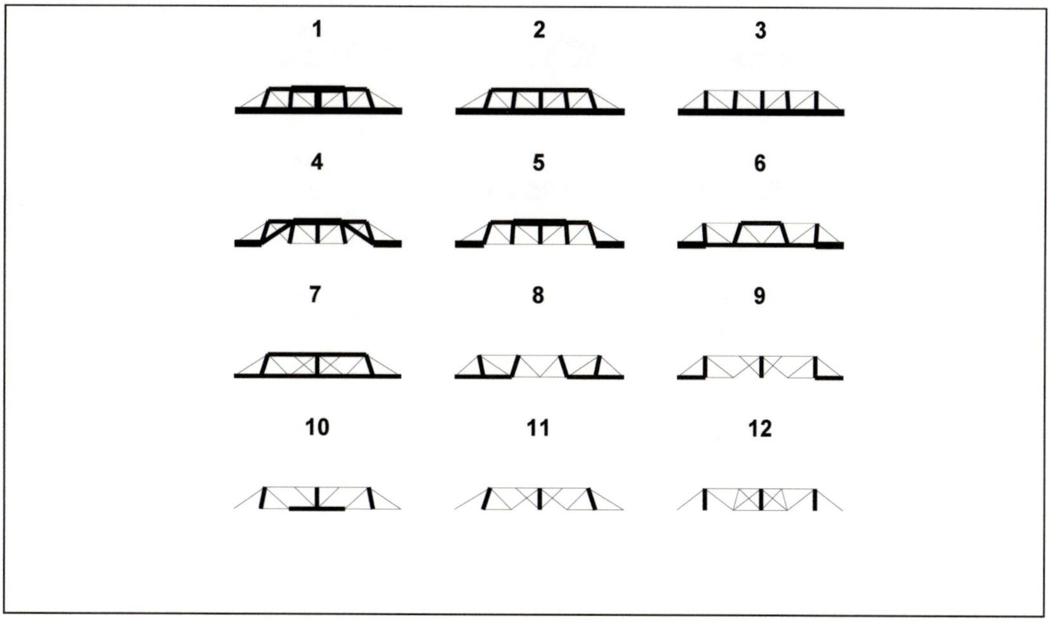

Fig. 19. Some selected structures of P2

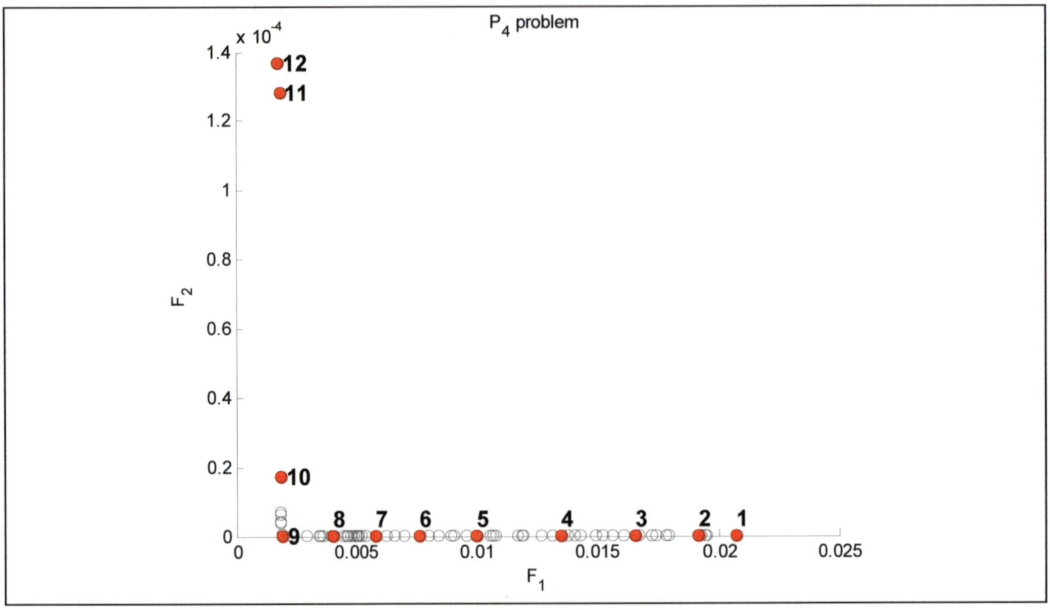

Fig. 20. Pareto front of P4 problem and ST3 structures

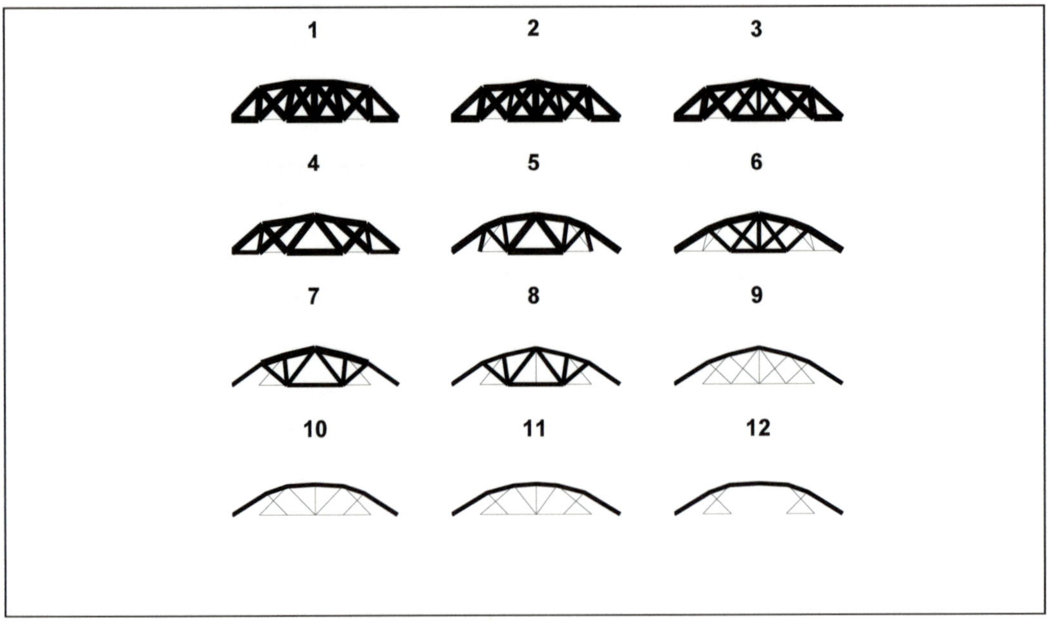

Fig. 21. Some selected structures of P4

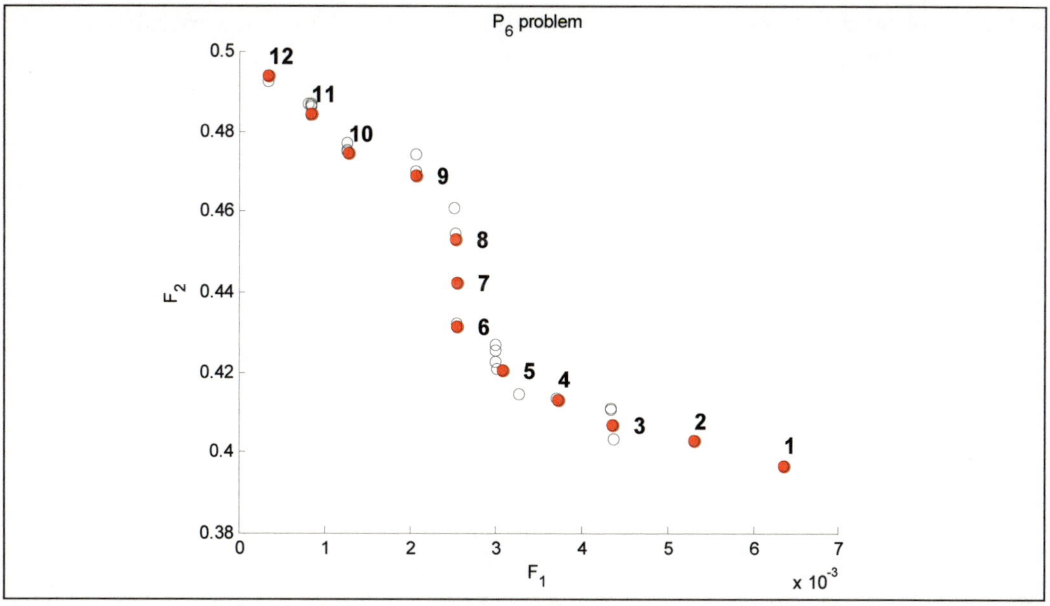

Fig. 22. Pareto front of P6 problem and ST3 structures

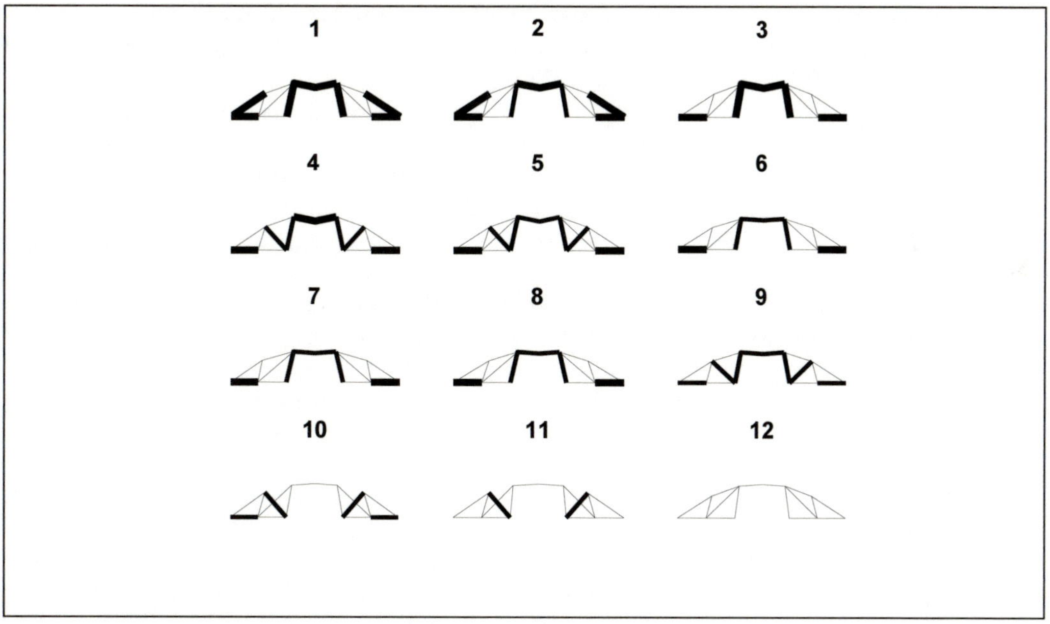

Fig. 23. Some selected structures of P6

5. Conclusions and discussion

The search procedures of the various MOEAs as well as the static and dynamic analysis of skeletal structures are briefly detailed. Seven multiobjective optimum design problems are posed for benchmarking the performance of the MOEAs. The design problems are applied to three skeletal structures. The first two structures have simultaneous shape/sizing design variables while the third structure is used for design demonstration of simultaneous topology/shape/sizing optimisation. From the optimum results, it can be concluded that SPEA2 using real codes is the best performer for the ST2 structure which has greater number of design variables. The PBIL using binary string is said to be the best method for ST1, which has a smaller number of design variables. From the design demonstration of using topological, shape, and sizing design variables at the same time, it is shown that BPBIL is an efficient and effective optimisation tool for such a type of structural optimum design. The C and C′ indicators should be used together to provide some insight that is missing from using either of them solely. The application of MOEAs for design optimisation of skeletal structures is said to be advantageous since they are robust and simple to use. The method can cope with all kind of design criteria as demonstrated in this work. Most importantly, we can have a set of non-dominated solutions for decision making within one optimisation.

6. References

Achtziger, W. (2007). On simultaneous optimization of truss geometry and topology. *Structural and Multidisciplinary Optimization*, Vol. 33, 285–304

Achtziger, W. & Kocvara, M. (2007). On the maximization of the fundamental eigenvalue in topology optimization. *Structural and Multidisciplinary Optimization*, Vol. 34,181–195

Achtziger, W. & Stolpe, M.(2007). Truss topology optimization with discrete design variables—Guaranteed global optimality and benchmark examples. *Structural and Multidisciplinary Optimization*, Vol. 34,1–20

Alkhatib, R.; Jazar, G. N. & Golnaraghi, M. F. (2004). Optimal design of passive linear suspension using genetic algorithm. *Journal of Sound and Vibration*, Vol. 275, 665-691

Baluja, S. (1994). Population-Based Incremental Learning: A Method for Integrating Genetic Search Based Function Optimization and Competitive Learning. In: *Technical Report CMU_CS_95_163*, School of Computer Science, Carnagie Mellon University, Pittsburgh

Benage, W.A. & Dhingra, A.K. (1994). Single and multiobjective structural optimization in discrete-continuous variables using simulated annealing. *International Journal of Numerical Methods in Engineering*, Vol. 38, 2753-2773

Bureerat, S. & Cooper, J. E. (1998). Evolutionary methods for the optimisation of engineering systems. *IEE Colloquium Optimisation in Control: Methods and Applications*, pp. 1/1-1/10, IEE, London, UK

Bureerat, S. & Sriworamas K. (2007). Population-based incremental learning for multi-objective optimisation. *Advances in Soft Computing*, Vol. 39, 223-232

Chan, C.M. & Wong, K.M. (2008). Structural topology and element sizing design optimization of tall steel frameworks using a hybrid OC–GA method. *Structural and Multidisciplinary Optimization*, Vol. 35, 473–488

Deb, K.; Pratap, A.; Agarwal, S. & Meyarivan, T. (2002). A fast and elitist multiobjective genetic algorithm: NSGAII. IEEE *Transactions on Evolutionary Computation*, Vol. 6, No. 2, 182-197

Deb, K.; Pratap, A. & Meyarivan, T. (2001). Constrained test problems for multi-objective evolutionary optimisation. *Lecture Notes in Computer Science*, Vol. 1993/2001, 284-298

Hagishita, T. & Ohsaki, M. (2009). Topology optimization of trusses by growing ground structure method. *Structural and Multidisciplinary Optimization*, Vol. 37, 377-393

Hajela, P. & Lee, E. (1995). Genetic algorithms in truss topology optimization. *International Journal of Solids and Structures*, Vol. 32, No. 22, 3341-3357

Hasancebi, O. & Erbatur, F. (2002). Layout optimisation of trusses using simulated annealing. *Advances in Engineering Software*, Vol. 33, 681–696

Kanyakam, S. & Bureerat, S. (2007). Passive vibration suppression of a walking tractor handlebar structure using multiobjective PBIL. *IEEE Congress on Evolutionary Computation (CEC 2007)*, pp. 4162-4169, Singapore

Kawamura, H.; Ohmori, H. & Kito, N. (2002). Truss topology optimization by a modified genetic algorithm. *Structural and Multidisciplinary Optimization*, Vol. 23, 467–472

Keane, A. J. (1995). Passive vibration control via unusual geometries: the applications of genetic algorithm optimization to structural design. *Journal of Sound and Vibration*, Vol. 185, No.30, 441-453

Knowles, J.D. & Corne, D.W. (2000) Approximating the non-dominated front using the Pareto archive evolution strategy. *Evolutionary Computation*, Vol. 8, No. 2, 149-172

Martínez, P.; Martí, P. & Querin, O.M. (2007). Growth method for size, topology, and geometry optimization of truss structures. *Structural and Multidisciplinary Optimization*, Vol. 33, 13–26

Moshrefi-Torbati, M.; Keane, A.J.; Elliott, J.; Brennan, M. J. & Rogers, E. (2003). Passive vibration control of a satellite boom structure by geometric optimization using genetic algorithm, *Journal of Sound and Vibration*, Vol. 276, 879-892.

Noiluplao, C. & Bureerat, S. (2008). Simultaneous topology and shape optimisation of a 3D framework structure using simulated annealing. *Technology and Innovation for Sustainable Development Conference (TISD2008)*, Faculty of Engineering, Khon Kaen University, Thailand, 28-29 January 2008

Ohsaki, M. (1995). Genetic algorithms for topology optimization of trusses. *Computers and Structures*, Vol. 57, No. 2, 219-225

Ohsaki, M. & Katoh, N. (2005). Topology optimization of trusses with stress and local constraints on nodal stability and member intersection. *Structural and Multidisciplinary Optimization*, Vol. 29, 190–197

Preumont, A. (2001). *Vibration control of active structures: an introduction*, Kluwer Academic Publishers

Reyes-Sierra, M. & Coello Coello, C.A.(2006) Multi-objective particle swarm optimizers: a survey of the state-of-the-art. *International Journal of Computational Intelligence Research*, Vol. 2, No. 3, 287-308

Shea, K. & Smith, I.F.C. (2006). Improving full-scale transmission tower design through topology and shape optimization. *Journal of Structural Engineering*, Vol. 132, No. 5, 781–790

Srinivas, N. & Deb, K. (1994). Multiobjective optimization using non-dominated genetic algorithms. *Evolutionary Computation*, Vol. 2, No. 3, 221-248

Srisomporn, S. & Bureerat, S. (2008). Geometrical design of plate-fin heat sinks using hybridization of MOEA and RSM. *IEEE Trans on Components and Packaging Technologies*, Vol. 31, 351-360.

Stolpe, M. & Svanberg, K. (2003). A note on stress-constrained truss topology optimization. *Structural and Multidisciplinary Optimization*, Vol. 25, 62–64

Svanberg, K. & Werme, M. (2007). Sequential integer programming methods for stress constrained topology optimization. *Structural and Multidisciplinary Optimization*, Vol. 34, 277–299

Tang, W.; Tong, L. & Gu, Y. (2005). Improved genetic algorithm for design optimization of truss structures with sizing, shape and topology variables. *International Journal for Numerical Methods in Engineering*, Vol. 62, No. 13, 1737 - 1762

W. H. Tong, J. S. Jiang and G. R. Liu, "Dynamic Design of Structures under Random Excitation," *Computational Mechanics*, vol. 22, 1998, pp. 388-394.

Wang, X.; Wang, M.Y. & Guo, D. (2004). Structural shape and topology optimization in a level-set-based framework of region representation. *Structural and Multidisciplinary Optimization*, Vol. 27, 1–19

Xu, B.; Jiang, J.; Tong, W. & Wu, K. (2003). Topology group concept for truss topology optimization with frequency constraints. *Journal of Sound and Vibration*, Vol. 261, 911–925

Yunkang, S. & Xin, Y. (1998). The topological optimization for truss structures with stress constraints based on the exist-null combined model. *ACTA MECHANICA SINICA (English Series)*, Vol.14, No.4, 363-370

Zhou, M. (1996). Difficulties in truss topology optimization with stress and local buckling constraints. *Structural Optimization*, Vol. 11,134-136

Zhou, M.; Pagaldipti, N.; Thomas, H.L. & Shyy, Y.K. (2004). An integrated approach to topology, sizing, and shape optimization. *Structural and Multidisciplinary Optimization*, Vol. 26, 308–317

Zhu, J.; Zhang, W.; Beckers, P.; Chen, Y. & Guo Z. (2008). Simultaneous design of components layout and supporting structures using coupled shape and topology optimization technique. *Structural and Multidisciplinary Optimization*, Vol. 36, 29–41

Zitzler, E.; Deb, K. & Thiele, L. (2000). Comparison of multiobjective evolutionary algorithms: empirical results. *Evolutionary Computation*, Vol. 8, No. 2, 173-195

Zitzler, E.; Laumanns, M. & Thiele, L. (2002). SPEA2: improving the strength Pareto evolutionary algorithm for multiobjective optimization. *Evolutionary Methods for Design, Optimization and Control*, Barcelona, Spain

Zitzler, E. & Thiele, L. (1999). Multiobjective evolutionary algorithms: a comparative case study and the strength Pareto approach. *IEEE Transactions On Evolutionary Computation*, Vol. 3, No. 4, 257-271

27

EC Application in Speech Processing - Voice Quality Conversion Using Interactive Evolution of Prosodic Control

Yuji Sato
Hosei University
Japan

1. Introduction

This chapter outlines Interactive Evolutionary Computation (IEC) and IEC application in speech processing. IEC is an optimization method that adapts evolutionary computation (EC) based on subjectively human evaluation. EC is a biologically inspired general computational algorithm and includes genetic algorithms (GA), genetic programming (GP), evolution strategies (ES), and evolutionary programming (EP) (Bäck et al., 1997). These algorithms are a heuristic search technique based on the ideas of natural selection and work with a population of solutions that undergo modifications under the influence of genetic manipulations and finally converge to the optimal solution. Here, the selection will be processed based on an explicit evaluative function prepared by human designer beforehand. EC has been widely used to engineering applications and effective for a variety of complex large sized combinational problems such as the travelling salesman problem, the job-shop scheduling problem, the machine-loading problem, etc. On the other hand, it is difficult, or even impossible, to design human evaluation explicit functions for interactive systems. For example, to obtain the most favorable outputs from interactive systems that create or retrieve graphics or music, such outputs must be subjectively evaluated. IEC is the technology that EC optimizes the target systems based on subjective human evaluation as fitness values for system outputs and effective for such kind of interactive systems. IEC research conducted during 1990s originated from the work of Dawkins (Dawkins, 1986) and two major research streams developed during the 1990s. The first research stream (Sims, 1991; Biles, 1994; Unemi, 2002) is Artificial Life (Dawkins, 1989) and the second research stream comes from the increase of researchers who are interested in humanized technology or human-related systems and have applied the IEC to engineering fields (Watanabe & Takagi, 1995; Takagi & Ohya, 1996; Sato, 1997; Parmee & Bonham, 1999; Kim & Cho, 2000). In the following, as a concrete example, we describe about voice quality conversion using IEC.

In section 2 we briefly explain about a basic voice conversion technique and application. In section 3 we show voice elements and our voice quality conversion systems. In section 4 we describe prosodic coefficient fitting by IEC. In section 5 we describe the simulations we performed to evaluate this technique, and in the final sections we discuss our results and finish with a conclusion.

2. Voice conversion techniques and applications

With the sudden arrival of the multimedia era, the market for multimedia information devices centered about the personal computer has been growing rapidly. The market for multimedia application software has likewise taken off providing an environment where users can manipulate images and sound with ease. At the same time, new markets are appearing using voice conversion (processing) technology.

Voice conversion is a technique for transforming the timbre and other characteristics of voices. Research into voice conversion has so far been centered on techniques for transforming the voice of one speaker (A) into the voice of another (B), principally with the aim of making synthetic speech sound more natural by giving it some sort of personality. For example, since personality parameters are difficult to specify, voice conversion between designated speakers A and B is performed by associating the voice patterns with VQ codebooks for each speaker (Shikano et al., 1991; Moulines & Sagisaki, 1995; Levent & David, 1997). These VQ codebooks are made by quantizing the feature space of the speaker's vocal characteristics as a set of vectors which are then encoded. Research is also being carried out into voice morphing techniques (Slaney et al., 1996) that can achieve a continuous transformation from speaker A to speaker B. Voice morphing is implemented by continuously varying the correspondence between speakers A and B with regard to some attribute such as a spectral envelope. Techniques associated with voice conversion are summarized in the reference by Puterbaugh (Puterbaugh, 2009).

However, these voice conversion and voice morphing techniques often have residual problems with the resulting speech quality due to the large transformation that results from converting speech characteristics down to the parameter level. Effort must also be put into preliminary tasks such as acquiring speech data from the target speaker of the conversion, and having a speech specialist generate a VQ codebook from this data. If a technique can be found to enable ordinary users to convert freely between voices of their own choosing without any particularly noticeable audio degradiation and without being limited to conversion between specific pre-registered speakers or having to prepare resources such as a VQ codebook, then a much wider range of marketable applications would be opened up to voice conversion techniques.

These include multimedia-content editing, computer games, and man-personal machine interfaces. In multimedia-content editing, adding narration to business content such as presentation material and digital catalogs or to personal content such as photo albums and self-produced video can enhance content. It is not necessarily easy, however, for the general user to provide narration in a clear and intelligible voice, and the need for voice conversion can be felt here. Technology for converting raw speech to clear and easily understand speech can also be effective for people that are required to give public speeches. In this regard, we can cite the example of Margaret Thatcher, the former U.K. prime minister, who took voice training so that she could give speeches in a clear, resonant voice that could provide more impact (Sample, 2002). Voice conversion technology can also be useful in the world of computer games, especially for multiplayer configurations. For example, a player puts on a headphone set and speaks into a microphone, and the input speech is conveyed to other players in the game as the voice of the game character representing the incarnation of that player. Voice conversion technology could be used here to convert raw input speech to an extremely clear voice rich in intonation and emotion making for a more compelling game. Finally, in the world of man-personal machine interfaces, voice-based interfaces have been considered for some time, and big markets are now anticipated for a wide range of voice-based applications from the reading out of e-mail and World Wide Web text information to the voice output of traffic reports and other text information by car-navigation equipment. It is essentially impossible, though, to set a voice favorable to all users beforehand on the manufacturer's side, and if technology existed that could enable the user to convert speech to a voice of his or her liking, it might have a great effect on such applications.

There are still some issues, however, that must be overcome in products using the voice processing technologies described above. To begin with, only qualitative know-how has so far been acquired with respect to voice processing technologies that convert raw speech to a clear voice or a voice that one desires, and specific parameter setting is performed on a trial and error basis. Optimal parameter values for voice conversion are also speaker dependent, which makes parameter adjustment difficult. Nevertheless, in voice output equipment targeting the readout of e-mail and World Wide Web text information, products using speech synthesis technology are beginning to be developed. Mechanically synthesized speech using rule-based synthesis, however, suffers from various problems, including an impression of discontinuity between phoneme fragments, degraded sound quality due to repeated signal processing, and limitations in sound-source/articulation segregation models. In short, speech synthesis that can produce a natural sounding voice is extremely difficult to achieve. Current speech-synthesis technology tends to produce mechanical or even unintelligible speech, and voice-quality problems such as these are simply delaying the spread of speech synthesis products.

Against the above background, this research aims to establish technology for converting original human speech or speech mechanically synthesized from text to clear speech rich in prosodic stress. As the first step to this end, we have proposed the application of interactive evolutionary computation to parameter adjustment for the sake of voice quality conversion using original speech recorded by a microphone as input data, and have reported on several experimental results applicable to the fitting of prosodic coefficients (Sato, 1997). It has also been shown that the use of evolutionary computation for parameter adjustments can be effective at improving the clarity not only of natural speech that has been subjected to voice quality conversion but also of synthetic speech generated automatically from text data (Sato, 2002). This chapter shows those experimental results and discuss why parameter adjustment using evolutionary computation is more effective than that based on trial and error by an experienced designer.

3. Voice elements and their relationship to voice quality conversion

3.1 Voice elements

In human speech production, the vocal cords serve as the sound generator. The vocal cords, which are a highly flexible type of muscle located deep in the throat, are made to vibrate by breath expelled from the lungs, thereby causing acoustic vibrations in the air (sound waves). The waveform of this acoustic signal is approximately triangular or saw-tooth in form and consists of harmonic components that are integer multiples of the fundamental frequency of the sound wave. This acoustic signal that has a broad range of harmonic components of a constant interval propagates through the vocal tract from the vocal cords to the lips and acquires resonances that depend on the shape of the vocal tract. This transformations results in the production of phonemes such as /a/ or /i/, which are finally emitted from the lips as speech. That is to say, the human voice characteristics are determined by three factors: sound generation, propagation in the vocal tract, and emission. The vocal cords control the pitch of the voice and the shape of the vocal tract controls prosody. If we define voice quality in terms of properties such as timbre, we can consider voice quality to be determined by both the state of the vocal cords and the state of the vocal tract (Klatt & Klatt, 1990). In other words, we can consider prosodic information and spectral information as feature quantities for the control of voice quality. Prosody consists of three main elements—pitch information, amplitude information, and temporal structure—described as follows. First, pitch is the basic frequency of the speech waveform, that is, the frequency at which the vocal chords vibrate to generate sound, and it carries information related to voice modulation. The accent in a word and intonation in a sentence are formed by fluctuation in pitch information. In human speech, average pitch is about 130 Hz in men and 250 Hz in women. Next, amplitude information refers to the actual amplitude of the speech waveform, that is, the vibrational energy of the vocal chords, and it carries information related to vocal strength. Amplitude information is used to control stress placed on a word and emphasis placed at various levels when speaking. While there are several methods for expressing amplitude information, we will here use the "short-interval average power" method. Finally, temporal structure corresponds to the temporal operation of the vocal chords, and this structure is responsible for forming rhythm in speech and generating pauses, for example. Temporal structure is thought to contribute to detection of important words.

3.2 Modification of voice quality through prosodic adjustment

Research on the features of the voices of professional announcers has clarified to some extent the qualitative tendencies that are related to highly-intelligible speech. It is known, for example, that raising the overall pitch slightly and increasing the acoustic power of consonants slightly increases intelligibility (Kitahara & Tohkura, 1992). It remains unclear, however, to what specific values those parameters should be set. Moreover, it is generally difficult to control dynamic spectral characteristics in real time. In other words, it is difficult to even consider adjusting all of the control parameters to begin with. Therefore, sought to achieve voice quality conversion by limiting the data to be controlled to pitch data, amplitude data, and temporal structure prosodic data.

Figure 1 shows the pitch modification method. Pitch modification is not performed by modifying temporal length. Rather, when raising pitch, for example, the procedure is to repeat the waveform partially cut from one pitch unit and then insert the same waveform as that of the prior interval every so many cycles of the above process. This does not change temporal length. Then, when lowering pitch, the procedure is to insert a mute portion into each pitch unit and then curtail the waveform every so many cycles of the above process so that again temporal length does not change. Next, Fig. 2 shows the method for converting temporal length. In this method, temporal length is converted by extension or contraction without changing pitch by the time-domain-harmonic-scaling (TDHS) (Malah, 1979) enhancement method. In Fig. 2(a), where one pitch period (autocorrelation period) is denoted as Tp and the extension rate as γ, shift Ls corresponding to the extension rate can be expressed by Eq. (1) below.

$$Ls = \frac{Tp}{\gamma - 1} \tag{1}$$

Likewise, in Fig. 2(b), where the contraction rate is denoted as γ, shift Lc corresponding to the contraction rate can be expressed by Eq. (2).

$$Lc = \frac{\gamma Tp}{\gamma - 1} \tag{2}$$

Amplitude is controlled by converting on a logarithmic power scale. Letting W_i denote the current value and β the modification coefficient, the modification formula is given by Eq. (3) below.

$$\log_{10} W_{i+1}^2 = \log_{10} W_i^2 + \beta \tag{3}$$

The modification coefficient-learning unit is provided with qualitative objectives, such as terms of emotion, and the modification coefficients used for prosodic modification targeting those objectives are acquired by learning. As the learning algorithm, this unit employs evolutionary computation.

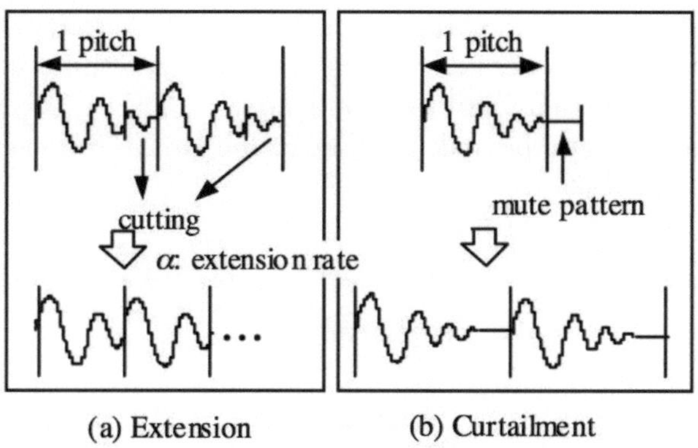

Fig. 1. Extension and curtailment of pitch period. Pitch is raised by cutting out of the waveform within one pitch unit. Pitch is lowered by inserting silence into pitch unit.

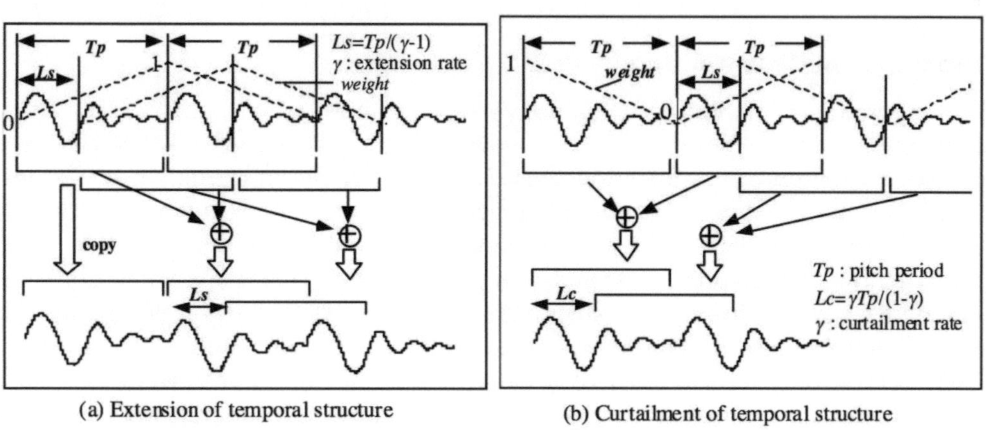

Fig. 2. Extension and curtailment of temporal structure. The continuation length is accomplished by using the TDHS enhancement method to extend or contract the sound length without changing the pitch.

3.3 Formulation of the voice quality conversion problem

First, the objective function f is unknown, and the optimal solutions of α, β and γ are speaker-dependent. For example, the algorithm for specifically determining the value of α is unknown, and the optimal value of α changes depending on the speaker of the speech waveform to be transformed. Second, the optimal values of variables α, β and γ are not entirely independent, and are weakly correlated to one another. For example, experiments have shown that when an attempt is made to find an optimal solution for α with fixed values of β and γ, this optimal solution for α will change slightly when the value of β is subsequently altered. Third, since the evaluation is performed at the level of the objective function f instead of the variables α, β and γ, the solution of this problem involves the use of implicit functions. At last, we consider the problem of multimodality accompanied by time fluctuation. For example, it often happens that a subject may not necessarily find an optimum solution from a voice that has already been subjected to several types of conversion. It has also been observed that optimum solutions may vary slightly according to the time that experiments are held and the physical condition of subjects at that time. In other words, we can view the problem as being one of determining a practical semi-optimum solution in as short a time as possible from a search space having multimodality and temporal fluctuation in the difficulty of prediction.

The voice quality conversion problem is therefore formulated as follows:

$$\left.\begin{array}{ll} \textit{Minimize} & f(\alpha,\beta,\gamma,t) \\ \textit{subject to} & \alpha = g_1(\beta,\gamma),\ \beta = g_2(\gamma,\alpha),\ \gamma = g_3(\alpha,\beta) \\ & (\alpha,\beta,\gamma) \in X = R^n \end{array}\right\} \tag{4}$$

where α, β and γ are conversion coefficients for pitch, power and time duration, respectively. Here, $X = R^n$ is an n-dimensional real space, and $f(\alpha, \beta, \gamma, t)$ is a real-value function of multimodality accompanied by time fluctuation. And f, g_1, g_2, g_3 are unknown (and probably non-linear) functions.

4. Prosodic coefficient fitting by IEC

4.1 Configuration of the voice quality conversion system

The configuration of the voice quality conversion system is illustrated in Fig. 3. The system comprises a voice processing part and prosody control coefficient learning part. The voice modification unit changes voice quality, targeting terms that express emotional feelings, such as "clear," and "cute." The modification of prosodic information is done by the prosodic control unit. To prevent degradation of voice quality, the processing is done at the waveform level as described above rather than at the parameter level, as is done in the usual analysis-synthesis systems. The modification coefficient learning unit is provided with qualitative objectives, such as terms of emotion, and the modification coefficients used for prosodic modification targeting those objectives are acquired automatically by learning. As the learning algorithm, this unit employs evolutionary computation, which is generally known as an effective method for solving problems that involve optimization of a large number of combinations.

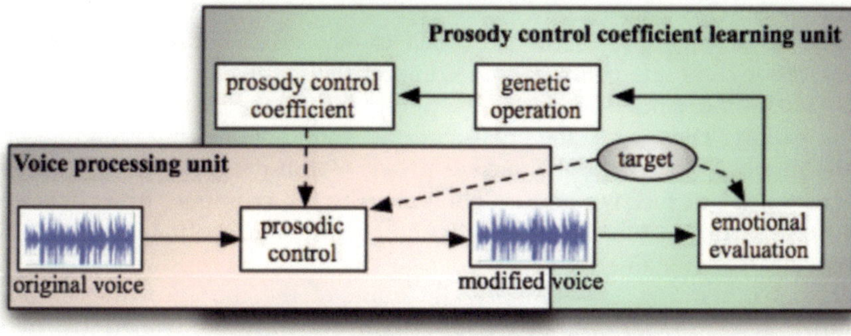

Fig. 3. Block diagram of proposed voice quality conversion system. The system comprises a voice processing part and prosody control coefficient learning part.

4.2 Overview of interactive evolution of prosodic control

The first step in this IEC procedure is to define chromosomes, i.e., to substitute the search problem for one of determining an optimum chromosome. In this procedure, we define a chromosome as a one-dimensional real-number array corresponding to a voice-modification target (an emotive term) and consisting of three prosody modification coefficients. Specifically, denoting the pitch modification factor as α, the amplitude modification factor as β, and the continuation time factor as γ, we define a chromosome as the array $[\alpha, \beta, \gamma]$.

The next step is to generate individuals. Here, we generate 20, and for half of these, that is, 10 individuals, chromosomes are defined so that their prosody modification coefficients change randomly for each voice-conversion target. For the remaining 10, chromosomes are defined so that their coefficients change randomly only within the vicinity of prosody-modification-coefficient values determined from experience on a trial and error basis. In the following step, evaluation, selection, and genetic manipulation are repeated until satisfactory voice quality for conversion is attained. Several methods of evaluation can be considered here, such as granting points based on human subjectivity or preparing a target speech waveform beforehand and evaluating the mean square difference between this target waveform and the output speech waveform from voice-conversion equipment. In the case of evolutionary computation, a designer will generally define a clear evaluation function beforehand for use in automatic recursion of change from one generation to another. It is difficult to imagine, however, a working format in which an end user himself sets up a clear evaluation function, and in recognition of this difficulty, we adopt a system of interactive evolution (Takagi, 2001) in which people evaluate results subjectively (based on feelings) for each generation.

4.3 Genetic manipulation

4.3.1 Selection rule

The population is replenished by replacing the culled individuals with a new generation of individuals picked by roulette selection (Holland, 1975; Goldberg, 1989) based on human evaluation.

Although the method used here is to assign a fitness value to each individual and cull the individuals that have low values, it is also possible to select the individuals to be culled by a tournament system. In that case, we do not have access to the fitness values, so we considered random selection of the parent individuals.

4.3.2 Crossover and mutation

Figure 4 presents an example of the proposed crossover and mutation operation. In the crossover operation, any one column is chosen and the values in that column are swapped in the two parent individuals. Here, it is thought that the search performance can be improved by making changes to the crossover and spontaneous mutation operations so as to reduce the number of generations needed to arrive at a practical quasi-optimal solution. In this operation, one of the two entities generated by the crossover operation is randomly subjected to crossovers in which the average value of each coefficient in the two parent entities (Bäck, 2000) are obtained.

For spontaneous mutations, the standard deviation of the mutation distribution was set small as shown in Eq. (5) for entities where crossovers were performed just by swapping coefficients as in the conventional approach. In this equation, C_i represents a modification coefficient for generation i, I is a unit matrix, and N is a normal distribution function with a mean vector of 0 and a covariance of $0.000025I$.

$$C_{i+1} = C_i + N(0, 0.000025I) \tag{5}$$

Conversely, a larger standard deviation was set for entities where crossovers were performed by taking the average of two coefficients as shown in Eq. (6).

$$C_{i+1} = C_i + N(0, 0.01I) \tag{6}$$

That is, the emphasis is placed on local search performance for entities where crossovers are performed in the same way as in earlier systems, and the emphasis is placed on increasing diversity and searching new spaces for entities where crossovers are performed by obtaining the average of two coefficients.

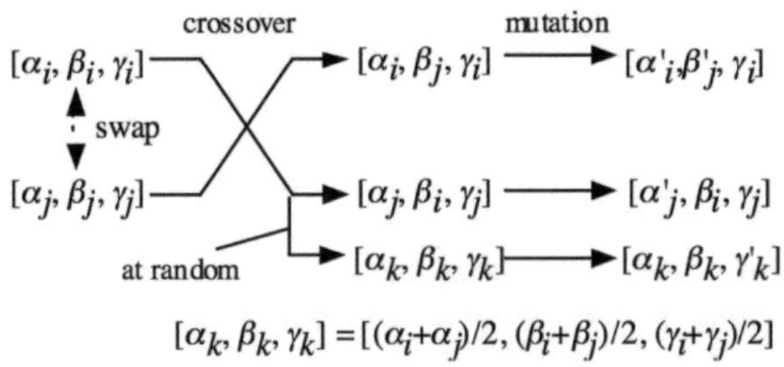

Fig. 4. Example of the proposed genetic manipulation. In this operation, one of the two entities generated by the swap operation is randomly subjected to crossovers in which the average value of each coefficient in the two parent entities are obtained.

5. Evaluation experiments

5.1 Experiment with original speech as input data

5.1.1 Voice stimuli

The original voice sample, $S0$, was the sentence, "Let me tell you about this company." spoken by a female in Japanese. Five modified samples, $SA1$ through $SA5$, that correspond to the five emotive terms, "intelligible," "childish," "joyful," "calm," and "angry," were produced by applying prosody modification coefficients obtained by the evolutionary computation learning scheme described above. In addition, five modified samples, $SB1$ through $SB5$, that correspond to the same five emotive terms, "intelligible," "childish," "joyful," "calm," and "angry," were produced by applying prosody modification coefficients obtained by trial and error based on the experience of a designer.

5.1.2 Experimental method

The subjects of the experiments were 10 randomly selected males and females between the ages of 20 and 30 who were unaware of the purpose of the experiment. Voice sample pairs $S0$ together with SA_i (i = 1 to 5) and $S0$ together with SB_i (i = 1 to 5) were presented to the test subjects through speakers. The subjects were instructed to judge for each sample pair whether voice modification corresponding to the five emotive terms specified above had been done by selecting one of three responses: "Close to the target expressed by the emotive term," "Can't say," and "Very unlike the target." To allow quantitative comparison, we evaluated the degree of attainment (how close the modification came to the target) and the degree of good or bad impression of the sample pairs on a nine-point scale for the childish emotive classification. Subjects were allowed to hear each sample pair multiple times.

5.1.3 Experimental results

The results of the judgments of all subjects for voice sample pairs $S0$ - SA_i (i = 1 to 5) and $S0$ - SB_i (i = 1 to 5) are presented in Fig. 5 as a histogram for the responses "Close to the target" and "Very unlike the target". From those results, we can see that although the trial and error approach to obtaining the modification coefficients was successful for the "childish", "intelligible", and "joyful" classifications, the modification results were judged to be rather unlike the target for the "calm" and "angry" classifications. In contrast to those results, the samples produced using the modification coefficients obtained by the evolutionary computation approach were all judged to be close to the target on the average.

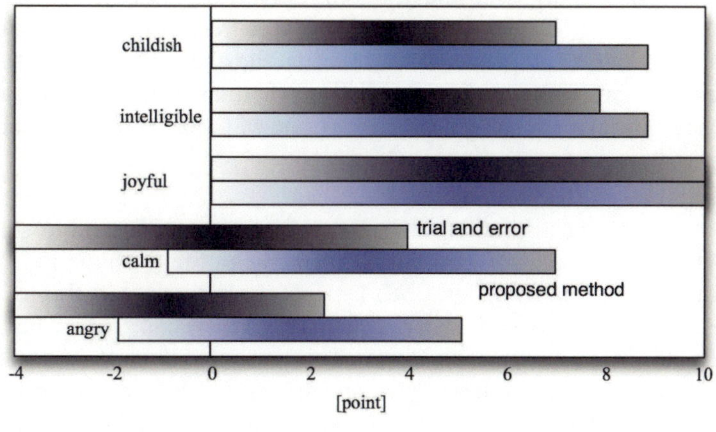

Fig. 5. The results of the judgment of all subjects for voice sample pairs. The results are presented as a histogram for the responses "Close to the target" and "Very unlike the target"

Next, this section shows the results of the evaluation of target attainment and good/bad impression. The values averaged for all subjects are presented in Fig. 6. Relative to an attainment rate of +1.2 for the prosody modification coefficient combination obtained by a designer according to experience, the attainment rate for the evolutionary approach was 1.8, or an improvement of 0.6. For the impression evaluation, the scores were -0.6 for the human design approach and +0.8 for the evolutionary computation approach, or an improvement of 1.4. The reason for these results is that there was a strong tendency to raise the pitch in the adjustment by the designer to achieve the "childish voice" modification, resulting in a mechanical quality that produced an unnatural impression. The evolutionary computation approach, on the other hand, resulted in a modification that matched the objective without noticeable degradation in sound quality, and thus did not give the impression of processed voice.

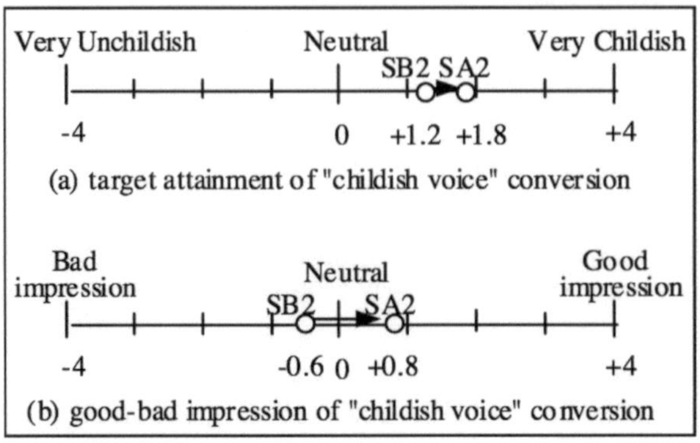

Fig. 6. The results of the evaluation of target attainment and good-bad impression. The values averaged for all subjects are presented.

5.2 Experiment with synthesized speech as input data

5.2.1 Voice stimuli

The voice stimuli used in this experiment were as follows. Voice sample *S*1 consisted of the words "voice conversion using evolutionary computation of prosodic control" mechanically synthesized from text using Macintosh provided software (Macin Talk3). Voice samples *SC*1 to *SC*3 were obtained by performing voice conversion on the above sample for the three emotive terms of "childish," "intelligible," and "masculine" applying prosody modification coefficients obtained by the learning system using evolutionary computation as described above.

5.2.2 Experimental method

As in the experiment using original speech, the subjects were 10 randomly selected males and females between the ages of 20 and 30 knowing nothing about the purpose of the experiment. Voice sample pairs *S*1 and SC_i (i= 1-3) were presented through a speaker to these 10 subjects who were asked to judge whether voice conversion had succeeded in representing the above three emotive terms. This judgement was made in a three-level manner by selecting one of the following three responses: "close to the target expressed by the emotive term," "can't say," and "very unlike the target." Furthermore, for the sake of obtaining a quantitative comparison with respect to the emotive term "intelligible," we also had the subjects perform a nine-level evaluation for both degree of attainment in voice conversion and good/bad impression for this voice sample pair. Subjects were allowed to hear each sample pair several times.

5.2.3 Experimental results

The judgments of all subjects for voice sample pairs *S*1 and SC_i (i = 1-3) are summarized in Fig. 7 in the form of a histogram for the responses "close to the target" and "very unlike the target." These results demonstrate that voice conversion is effective for all emotive terms on average.

Figure 8 shows the results of judging degree of attainment and reporting good/bad impression averaged for all subjects. These results demonstrate that degree of attainment improved by +1.2 from a value of +0.0 before conversion by determining an optimum combination of prosody modification coefficients using evolutionary computation. We also see that good/bad impression improved by +0.8 changing from +0.6 to +1.4.

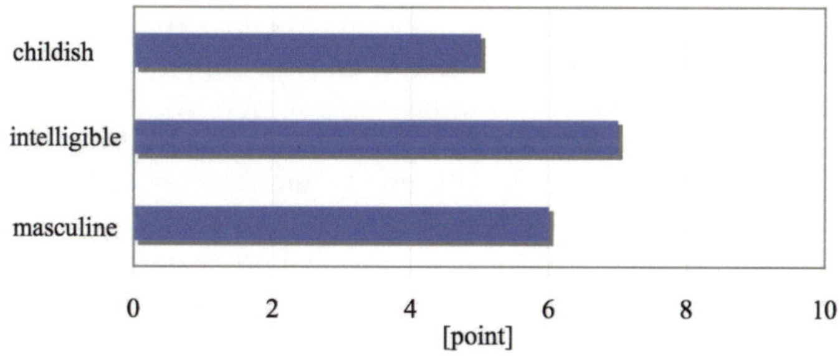

Fig. 7. The results of the judgment of all subjects for voice sample pairs. The results are presented as a histogram for the responses "Close to the target" and "Very unlike the target"

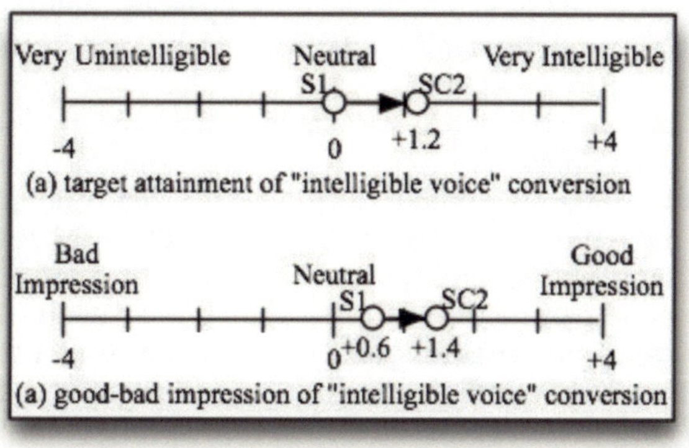

Fig. 8. The results of the evaluation of target attainment and good-bad impression. The values averaged for all subjects are presented.

6. Discussion

The above experiments have shown that voice quality conversion using evolutionary computation can get closer to a target than parameter adjustment based on a designer's experience or trail and error. They have also shown that degradation in sound quality is relatively small and that listeners are not given a strong impression of a processed voice in the case of evolutionary computation. We here examine the question as to why evolutionary computation is superior. First, we consider the problem of accuracy in prosody modification coefficients. In the past, coefficients have been adjusted manually using real numbers of two or three significant digits such as 1.5 and 2.14. Such manual adjustment, however, becomes difficult if the search space becomes exceedingly large. On the other hand, it has been observed that a slight modification to a prosody modification coefficient can have a significant effect on voice quality conversion. For example, while raising pitch is an effective way of making a voice "childish," increasing the pitch modification factor gradually while keeping the amplitude modification factor and continuation time factor constant can suddenly produce an unnatural voice like that of a "spaceman." This can occur even by making a slight modification to the fourth or fifth decimal place. In other words, there are times when the accuracy demanded of prosody modification coefficients will exceed the range of manual adjustment.

Second, we consider the fact that each type of prosody information, that is, pitch, amplitude, and time continuation, is not independent but related to the other types. When manually adjusting coefficients, it is common to determine optimum coefficients one at a time, such as by first adjusting the pitch modification factor while keeping the amplitude modification factor and continuation time factor constant, and then adjusting the amplitude modification factor. However, as pitch, amplitude, and time continuation are not independent of each other but exhibit correlation, it has been observed that changing the amplitude modification factor after setting an optimum value for the pitch modification factor will consequently change the optimum solution for pitch. This suggests that the modification coefficients for pitch, amplitude, and continuation time must be searched for in parallel.

Third, we consider the problem of multimodality accompanied by time fluctuation. For example, it often happens that a subject may not necessarily find an optimum solution from a voice that has already been subjected to several types of conversion. It has also been observed that optimum solutions may vary slightly according to the time that experiments are held and the physical condition of subjects at that time. In other words, we can view the problem as being one of determining a practical semi-optimum solution in as short a time as possible from a search space having multimodality and temporal fluctuation in the difficulty of prediction.

On the basis of the above discussion, we can see that the problems of voice quality conversion are indeed complex. For one, a practical semi-optimum solution must be determined in as short a time as possible from a search space having multimodality and temporal fluctuation in the difficulty of prediction. For another, high accuracy is demanded of modification coefficients and several types of modification coefficients must be searched for in parallel. In these experiments, we have shown that evolutionary computation is promising as an effective means of voice quality conversion compared to the complex real-world problems associated with finding an explicit algorithm and a solution based on trail and error by a designer.

Because the current system employs an interactive type of evolution, a real-time search for optimal modification coefficients for prosodic control cannot be performed. The system also suffers from various limitations, such as input data taken to be the utterance of one sentence within a fixed period of time. On the other hand, when conducting an experiment to check for sentence dependency of optimal modification coefficients when targeting the emotive terms of "intelligible," "childish," and "masculine" no particular sentence dependency was found for the same speaker. In other words, optimal modification coefficients for voice quality conversion, while being speaker dependent, are considered to be sentence independent, or any text dependency that exists is within a range that can be ignored for the most part. Thus, once optimal modification coefficients for converting raw speech to intelligible speech can be found for a certain sentence, the values of those coefficients can be applied to other sentences as long as the speaker remains the same. In addition, voice quality conversion after optimal modification coefficients have been determined can be executed in real time from stored input data, which points to the feasibility of applying current technology to real products in fields like addition of narration in multimedia-content editing, computer games, recorded TV soundtracks, and man-personal machine interfaces given that appropriate procedures for use are established. Please refer to http://www.h3.dion.ne.jp/~y-sato/demo/demo1.html for an example of voice quality conversion.

7. Conclusion

We have proposed the application of interactive evolutionary computation to the adjustment of prosodic modification coefficients for the purpose of voice quality conversion. To examine the effectiveness of the technique described, we performed voice quality conversion experiments on both original human speech recorded by a microphone and speech mechanically synthesized from text, and evaluated results from the viewpoint of target attainment and good or bad impression. It was found that the application of interactive evolutionary computation could convert speech more efficiently than manual adjustment of prosodic modification coefficients. Furthermore, on comparing speech obtained by the proposed technique with that obtained by manual determination of prosodic modification coefficients, it was found that the former exhibited relatively little deterioration in voice quality and no impression of processed speech. Given, moreover, that the values of optimal parameters, while speaker dependent, are sentence independent, and that voice quality conversion can be executed online from stored input data once optimal parameters have been determined, we expect this technique to be applicable to products in fields such as addition of narration in multimedia-content editing, computer games, and man-personal machine interfaces even with current technology. Future studies must take up means of improving the accuracy of voice quality conversion by adding the conversion of spectral information and the application of evolutionary computation to parameter adjustment for synthesizing natural speech from continuously input text.

8. Acknowledgments

The author would like to express their gratitude to Dr. Y. Kitahara and Mrs. H. Ando of Hitachi, Ltd., Central Research Laboratory, and Dr. M. Sato of Tokyo University of Agriculture & Technology for their valuable discussions on experimental results.

9. References

Bäck, T.; U. Hammel, U. & Schwefel, H.-P. (1997). Evolutionary Computation: Comments on the History and Current State, *IEEE Trans. on Evolutionary Computation*, Vol.1, No.1, pp.3-17, 1997.

Bäck, T.; Fogel, D.B. & Michalewicz, Z. (2000). *Evolutionary Computation 1: Basic Algorithms and Operators*, 2000, Institute of Physics Publishing, Bristol, UK.

Biles, J.A. (1994). GenJam: A Genetic Algorithm For Generating Jazz Solos, In: *Proceedings of the 1994 International Computer Music Conference* (ICMC-94), pp.131-137, Aarhus, Denmark, 1994.

Dawkins, R. (1986). *The Blind Watchmaker*, Long-man, Essex, 1986.

Dawkins, R. (1989). The Evolution of Evolvability, Langton, C.G. (ed.), *Artificial Life*, pp.201-220, 1989, Addison-Wesley, Reading, MA.

Goldberg, D.E. (1989). *Genetic Algorithms in Search, Optimization, and Machine Learning*, 1989, Addison-Wesley, Reading, MA.

Holland, J.H. (1975). *Adaptation in Natural and Artificial Systems*, 1975, University of Michigan Press (Second edition: 1992, MIT Press, Cambridge, MA).

Kim, H.-S. & Cho, S.-B. (2000). Knowledge-based encoding in interactive genetic algorithm for a fashion design aid system, In: *Proceedings of the 2000 Genetic and Evolutionary Computation Conference*, p. 757, Las Vegas, July 2000, Morgan Kaufmann Publishers.

Kitahara, Y. and Tohkura, Y. (1992). Prosodic Control to Express Emotions for Man-Machine Speech Interaction", *IEICE Trans. Fundamentals.*, Vol. E75, No. 2, pp. 155-163, 1992.

Klatt, D.H. & Klatt, L.C. (1990). Analysis, Synthesis, and Perception of Voice Quality Variations Among Female and Male Talkers, *Journal of Acoustic Society America*, 87(2), pp. 820-856, 1990.

Koza, J.R. (1992). *Genetic Programming: On the Programming of Computers by Means of Natural Selection*, 1992, MIT Press, Cambridge, MA.

Levent, M.A. & David, T. (1997). Voice Conversion by Codebook Mapping on Line Spectral Frequencies and Excitation Spectrum, In: *Proceedings of the EuroSpeech97*, 1997.

Malah, J.D. (1979). Time-domain algorithms for harmonic bandwidth reduction and time scaling of speech signals, *IEEE Trans. Acoust. Speech, Signal Processing*, Vol. ASSP-27, pp. 121-133, 1979.

Moulines, E. & Sagisaka, Y. (1995). Voice Conversion: State of Art and Perspectives, *Speech Communication 16*, pp. 125-126, 1995.

Parmee, I.C. & Bonham, C.R. (1999). Cluster-oriented genetic algorithms to support interactive designer/evolutionary computing systems, In: *Proceedings of the Congress on Evolutionary Computation*, pp. 546-553, 1999.

Puterbaugh, J. (2009). Dr. John Puterbaugh homepage at the Department of Music, Princeton University. <http://silvertone.princeton.edu/~john/voiceconversion.htm> Accessed on: June 9, 2009.

Sample, I. (2002). Darwinian boost for public speakers, *NewScientist*, Vol. 175, No. 2352, p. 18, 2002, New Science Publications, London.

(http://www.newscientist.com/news/news.jsp?id=ns99992560)

Sato, Y. (1997). Voice Conversion Using Evolutionary Computation of Prosodic Control, In: *Proceedings of the Australasia-Pacific Forum on Intelligent Processing and Manufacturing of Materials* (IPMM-97), pp. 342-348, Gold Coast, Australia, July 1997.

Sato, Y. (2002). Voice Conversion Using Interactive Evolution of Prosodic Control, In: *Proceedings of the 2002 Genetic and Evolutionary Computation Conference* (GECCO-2002), pp. 1204-1211, New York, July 2002, Morgan Kaufmann Publishers, San Francisco, CA.

Shikano, K.; Nakamura, S. & Abe, M. (1991). Speaker Adaptation and Voice Conversion by Codebook Mapping, In: *Proceedings of the IEEE Symposium on Circuits and Systems*, Vol. 1, pp. 594-597, 1991.

Sims, K. (1991). Interactive Evolution of Dynamical Systems, Varela, F.J. & Bourgine, P. (eds.), Toward a Practice of Autonomous Systems, In: *Proceedings of the First European Conference on Artificial Life*, pp.171-178, 1991, MIT Press, Cambridge, MA.

Slaney, M.; Covell, M. & Lassiter, B. (1996). Automatic Audio Morphing, In: *Proceedings of the ICASSP*, pp. 1001-1004, 1996.

Takagi, H. (2001). Interactive Evolutionary Computation: Fusion of the Capabilities of EC Optimization and Human Evaluation, In: *Tutorial Book of the 2001 Congress on Evolutionary Computation*, 2001, IEEE Press, NJ.

Takagi, H. & Ohya, K. (1996). Discrete Fitness Values for Improving the Human Interface in an Interactive GA, In: *Proceedings of the IEEE 3rd Inter. Conf. on Evolutionary Computation*, pp. 109-112, Nagoya, May 1996, IEEE Press.

Unemi, T. (2002). SBEAT3: A Tool for Multi-part Music Composition by Simulated Breeding, In: *Proceedings of the A-LIFE VIII*, pp. 410-413, Sydney, NSW, Australia, 2002.

Watanabe, T. & Takagi, H. (1995). Recovering System of the Distorted Speech Using Interactive Genetic Algorithms, In: *Proceedings of the IEEE Inter. Conf. on Systems, Man and Cybernetics*, Vol. 1, pp. 684-689, 1995.

28

Multi-Ring Particle Swarm Optimization

Carmelo J. A. Bastos-Filho, Danilo F. Carvalho, Marcel P. Caraciolo, Péricles B. C. Miranda and Elliackin M. N. Figueiredo
Department of Computing and Systems, University of Pernambuco
Brazil

1. Introduction

Many real world problems are quite expensive to be solved by using exhaustive computation. Because of this, many metaheuristics have been proposed recently to deal with optimization and search problems. Although many approaches have been proposed based on local search, the current research in Evolutionary Computation (EC) is mainly focused on algorithms that are based on populations and inspired in nature (Schwefel, 1981; Bäck, 1996; Fogel, 1996; Beyer, 2001; Beyer, 2002).

In this context, Swarm intelligence techniques, mainly Particle Swarm Optimization (PSO), have been widely applied to solve many different types of optimization problems. PSO was proposed by Kennedy and Eberhart (Kennedy & Eberhart, 1995) and the main idea is to explore the intelligence originated by the social knowledge disseminated by the agents during the search process. Due to its great performance in difficult optimization tasks and its simplicity, PSO became a popular, easy-to-use and extendable technique (Abido, 2001; Eberhart & Shi, 2001; Parsopoulos & Vrahatis, 2001; Agrafiotis & Cedeno, 2002; Coello Coello & Lechuga, 2002; Parsopoulos et al., 2002; Shi & Krohling, 2002; Praveen et al., 2007; Santana-Quintero ET AL., 2008).

By applying PSO to problems where the feasible solutions are too much difficult to find, more sophisticated approaches are required, mainly for hyper dimensional spaces. Many variations on the basic PSO form have been explored, most of them proposing different velocity update equations (Shi & Eberhart, 1998; Clerc & Kennedy, 2002; Kennedy, 2005; Jiao, et al., 2008). Other approaches attempt to change the structure of the swarm (Kennedy & Mendes, 2002; Suganthan, 1999) and its communication schema (Engelbrecht, 2005; Sutton et al., 2006).

To disseminate information within the swarm is the key of any swarm intelligence based algorithm. PSO, like others swarm algorithms, makes use of its own information exchange methods to distribute the best positions found during the algorithm execution (Engelbrecht, 2005). The way used by the swarm to distribute this information lies in the social structure formed by the particles. Variations in this structure can improve the algorithm performance.

By using local communication, each particle of the swarm has its own neighborhood. Many papers (Engelbrecht, 2005; Carvalho & Bastos-Filho, 2008; Carvalho & Bastos-Filho, 2009) have shown that it improves the exploration capacity of the entire swarm but decreases the convergence speed of the algorithm. It means that the algorithm obtains better solutions, but it needs more iterations to reach the convergence.

Other important and already known PSO algorithm variation is the Cooperative Particle Optimizer (CPSO) (van den Bergh & Engelbrecht, 2001; van den Bergh & Engelbrecht, 2004) which is based on the cooperative GA proposed by Potter and De Jong (Potter & De Jong, 1994). This approach proposes a performance improvement of the PSO algorithm by splitting the solution vector into different components that will be optimized by different sub-swarms cooperatively. CPSO inserts another parameter called *split factor* which can be interpreted as the number of sub-swarms that compose the entire swarm.

By using the ring structure as an inspiration, a novel PSO topology called Multi-ring PSO (MRPSO) based on coupling different rings was recently proposed (Bastos-Filho *et al.* 2008). This novel approach makes use of a diversity mechanism provided by ring rotations in order to improve the exploration of the search space. The structure of the proposed topology is formed by ring layers connected by axis that cross the layers trough the particles. Each single particle, which belongs to a specific layer, is automatically connected to other particles in neighbour ring layers. These connections establish the communication between neighbour particles which is a peculiar neighbourhood scenario based on local communication. The ring layers increase the capacity to avoid stagnation states making use of a process and an attribute called rotation skill and trigger criterion, respectively, also described in the chapter. Furthermore, we included a novel concept proposed by Cai *et al.* (Cai *et al.* 2008) that assigns a grade to the particles based on their fitness. This information is used to switch the neighbourhood inside the rings.

The rest of this paper is organized as follows. Section 2 shows a brief review about PSO. It also describes some well known topologies. In Section 3 the proposed Multi-ring topology and its features are described. Section 4 is devoted to the Dispersed based Multi-ring approach. The simulation setup used by the experiments and the chosen benchmark functions are presented in Section 6. In section 7 the analysis of Multi-ring and Multi-ring Dispersed are shown. The results of a comparison with some well-known topologies are presented too.

2. Background

2.1 Particle Swarm Optimization - PSO

The basic form of the PSO algorithm is composed by a group particles, where each particle represents a possible solution to the problem. Each particle maps the attributes of a solution, *i. e.*, the position of one particle represents exactly the values of the attributes of a solution. Besides, particles move inside the search space reaching new positions. After some iterations, particles tend to a global optimum based on two basic components: the cognitive component and the social component. The first one considers the best position already found by the particle itself (***pbest***). The second one use the best position attained by all the particles of the swarm (***gbest***) in order to guide the swarm to a common spot in the search space. Based on these two information components, each particle updates its own velocity. The velocity is a vector that directs the particle to the next position.

As the original PSO is based on the global knowledge of the swarm, it has a low capacity for local search. Thus, other approaches were proposed in order to avoid this disadvantage. Shi and Eberhart (Shi & Eberhart, 1998) proposed a velocity update equation that uses an inertia factor w (see equation 1). This factor balances the exploration-exploitation trade-off by controlling the contribution of the previous velocity in the evaluation of the current velocity of each particle. For each iteration of the PSO algorithm the velocity $\vec{v}_i(t)$ contribution is decreased. Thus, the exploitation level of the swarm is increased.

$$\vec{v}_i(t+1) = \omega\vec{v}_i(t) + c_1 r_1(\vec{p}_i(t) - \vec{x}_i(t)) + c_2 r_2(\vec{p}_g(t) - \vec{x}_i(t)), \quad (1)$$

where w is the inertia factor, $\vec{x}_i(t)$ is the current position of particle i in time step t, c_1 and c_2 are positive acceleration constants, and $r1$ and $r2$ are two random numbers generated by a uniform distribution in the interval [0,1].

Recently, Jiao *et al.* (Jiao *et al.*, 2008) proposed a dynamic inertia weight for the particle swarm optimization algorithm. They showed that it can improve the quality of the solutions obtained by the algorithm.

Another popular approach for the PSO velocity update equation involves a constriction factor which implies a velocity value reduction at each time step (Clerc & Kennedy, 2002). Under some peculiar conditions, it can guarantee both convergence and a high degree of exploration.

Both inertia and constriction approaches balance exploration and exploitation abilities and improve the convergence speed and the quality of the solutions found by the algorithm (Bratton & Kennedy, 2007).

2.2 Topologies

The communication between particles inside a swarm is one of the most important mechanisms of PSO. This mechanism distributes information already achieved by the

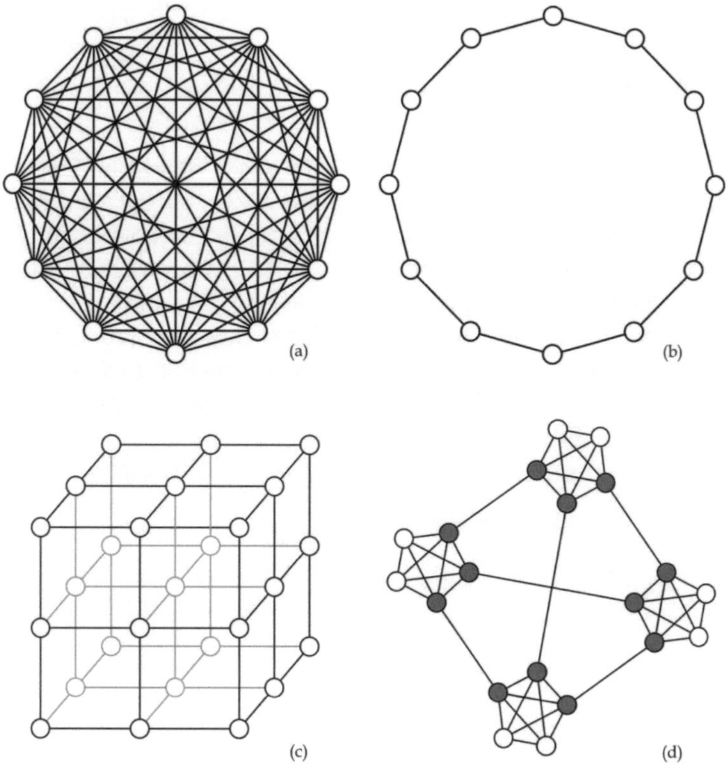

Fig. 1. Commonly used particle topologies: (a) Star topology used in ***gbest***, (b) Ring topology used in ***lbest***, (c) Von Neumann topology and (d) Four clusters topology.

swarm through all particles, updating the swarm status. Global and local communication structures are the two main structures used for particles' communication. Considering that particles share information acquired through a structured swarm, this model of communication can be seen as a topology. Some of the well-known topologies are depicted in Figure 1.

Each topology shown in Figure 1 has its own way to spread information through the swarm (Kennedy, 1999; Kennedy & Mendes, 2002).

Star and *ring* topologies are shown in Figure 1(a) and Figure 1(b), respectively. *Star* topology is composed by a fully-connected structure (***gbest***) that allows each particle of the swarm to share information globally. In a global neighbourhood, information is instantaneously disseminated to all particles, quickly attracting the entire swarm to the same swarm region. To avoid local minima, *ring* topology (Figure 1(b)) make use of local neighbourhoods (***lbest***), *i. e.*, particles just communicate with its immediate neighbours. Therefore, the swarm needs a great number of iterations to converge, but higher quality solutions can be found.

In Figure 1(c), a grid of particles forming a peculiar social structure is shown. This structure is very useful for many optimization problems (Kennedy & Mendes, 2002; Peer et al., 2003) and is known as *Von Neumann* topology.

Based on clusters of particles, the *four clusters* topology is shown in Figure 1(d). Each cluster communicates with the others by connections previous defined between the particles (Mendes et al., 2003; Engelbrecht, 2005). The number of connections originated from a cluster is equal to the number of neighbour clusters.

3. Multi-ring topology

3.1 Multi-ring concepts

Multi-Ring is a novel PSO topology that uses the *ring* structure as an inspiration. By using local communication, each particle of the swarm has its own neighbourhood. Many papers have shown that it improves the explorarion capacity of the entire swarm but decreases the convergence time of the algorithm (Engelbrecht, 2005; Carvalho & Bastos-Filho, 2008; Carvalho & Bastos-Filho, 2009). A topology based on coupling different rings with dynamic commutation of the neighbourhood is proposed, which aims to obtain better solutions as the benefit of the local communication. At the same time, we expect to reduce the number of iterations to reach a convergence as the benefit of the dynamic neighbourhood mechanism.

The proposed topology is formed by particles arranged in multiple rings layers, where each particle of the ring can communicate with some particles of neighbour rings. In order to

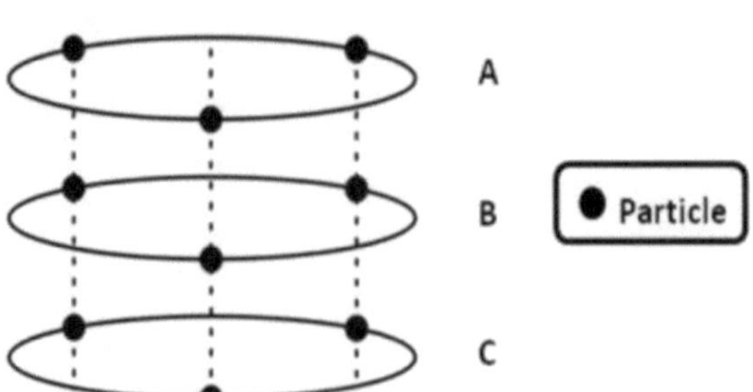

Fig. 2. Multi-Ring Topology.

couple different ring layers, the number of particles in each ring must be the same. Therefore, each single particle, which belongs to a specific layer, is automatically connected to other particles from neighbour ring layers, as shown in Figure 2. The structure in Figure 2 illustrates an example of the multi-ring topology with 3 rings (A, B and C) of 3 particles.

3.2 Communication between different rings

The particles from different ring layers communicate with each other by using a peculiar neighbourhood scenario. The Figure 3 can be used to illustrate this scenario. Considering a ring layer $rl_{(k)}$, each particle $rl_{(k)(i)}$ is directly connected with the particles $rl_{(k-1)(i)}$ and $rl_{(k+1)(i)}$ of the next and previous ring layers. During the algorithm execution, one particle $rl_{(k)(i)}$ will exchange information with a neighbourhood composed by { $rl_{(k)(i-1)}$, $rl_{(k)(i+1)}$, $rl_{(k-1)(i)}$, $rl_{(k+1)(i)}$ }.

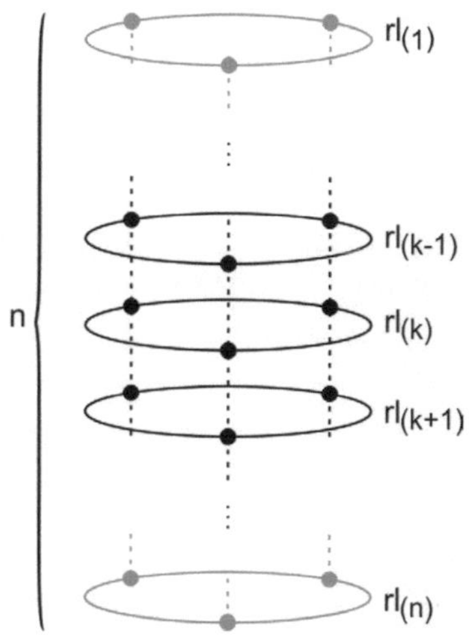

Fig. 3. Ring layers structure.

One special observation must be considered for the first and last ring layers of the topology. The communication between the particles located at those two rings is partially limited, since both do not have a complete ring neighbourhood, it means that they only have a unique ring layer directly connected to them. Therefore, the information exchange for one particle belonging to a ring $rl_{(1)}$ is limited by the set { $rl_{(1)(i-1)}$, $rl_{(1)(i+1)}$, $rl_{(2)(i)}$ }. The same restriction must be considered for the ring $rl_{(n)}$, which the neighbourhood is composed by the set { $rl_{(n)(i-1)}$, $rl_{(n)(i+1)}$, $rl_{(n-1)(i)}$ }.

One particle which belongs to a ring layer $rl_{(k)}$ exchange information with other layers $rl_{(k-1)}$ and $rl_{(k+1)}$ in order to make use of the social information achieved by the other layers. If one particle just exchanges information with the same neighbourhood through the entire execution of the algorithm, the neighbourhood would be static. In this case, the topology is just a simple *local* approach. To avoid this static possibility, one important process was added to the proposed topology, called *rotation skill.*

3.3 Ring layer rotation skill

One of the biggest problems of PSO is the stagnation. In nonlinear multimodal problems, which have many local minima regions, the swarm can be stagnated in one those regions of the search space during the algorithm execution. In those regions, the particles can spend

many time steps without varying the value of the best position found by their neighbourhoods. It can cause a stagnation state in the entire swarm. Hence, the proposed strategy to avoid stagnation is to add the ability of rotation to each ring layer. By adding the rotation skill, the position of the particles in the ring can be altered. Hence, the neighbourhood is changed. It can move the swarm from one region to another, increasing the exploration of the space search by considering different local minima regions.
In the Multi-Ring approach, the particles of different rings exchange information between themselves using local communication. The particle that belongs to a ring $rl_{(k)}$ exchanges information with other rings $rl_{(k-1)}$ and $rl_{(k+1)}$ aiming to transmit its previous experience.
Each ring layer of the Multi-Ring has the ability to self-rotate. It means that if the ring layer $rl_{(k)}$ does not improve its own best position, defined as *ringbest,* it will be rotated. In the rotation process, each particle in the ring layer has its index changed to $i = (i+d) \ mod \ (nl)$, where d is the rotation distance and nl is the number of particles in a layer. Thus, the new neighbourhood will be composed by $\{ rl_{(k)(i-1)}, rl_{(k)(i+1)}, rl_{(k-1)(i+d)}, rl_{(k+1)(i+d)} \}$. One can note that the main difference is the communication replacement between the neighbour ring layers.
Figure 4 shows an example of the rotation process. Initially, the particle E communicates with {D,F,B,H}. After the rotation, the neighbourhood of the particle E is changed to {D,F,A,G}. This process improves the social information exchange. Besides, it also improve the convergence capacity of the swarm. One can note that all the particles of the same ring layer change its neighbourhood.

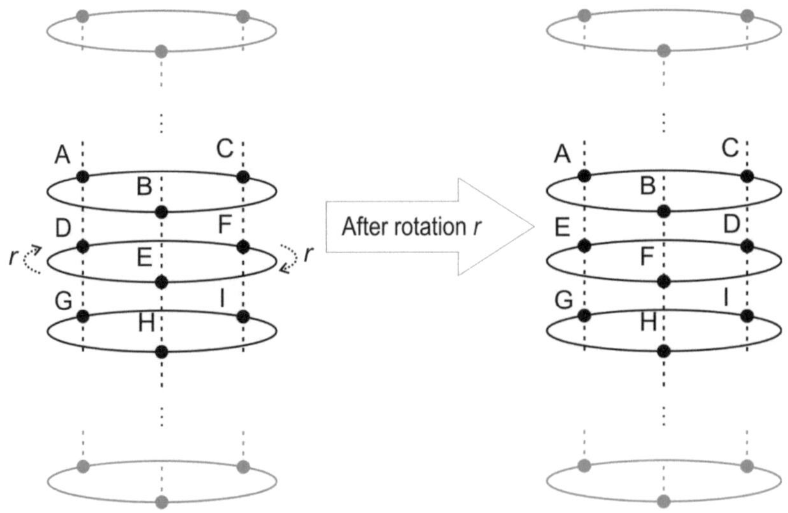

Fig. 4. Rotation skill example.

The main mechanism of the rotation process is the trigger criterion that will be used to invoke the rotation skill. It is based on the idle status of the best solution found in a specific ring layer, i.e. the number of iterations that the best solution found by a specific ring does not change. To clarify the process described above, consider a ring layer $rl_{(k)}$. If the best solution found remains with the same value during t_r iterations, so this ring layer will be rotated after t_r iteration.
Therefore, the use of the exploration capacity provided by the local communication combined with rotation mechanisms helps to avoid the stagnation of the solution found by the swarm during the execution of the PSO algorithm.

3.4 Multi-ring PSO algorithm

Inspired by the entity described in the previous section, the PSO algorithm with this novel topology has some new specific steps that must be considered in the execution process of the algorithm. Figure 5 illustrates the Multi-Ring topology containing an example with two ring layers ($rl_{(1)}$ and $rl_{(2)}$) of three particles.

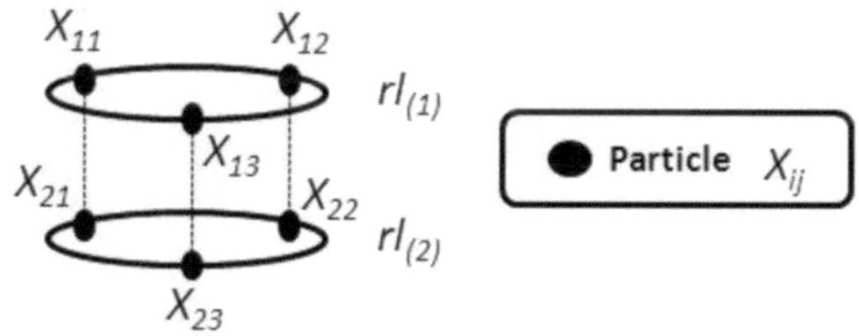

Fig. 5. Multi-Ring topology of 2 ring layers with 3 particles.

In the basic PSO algorithm, one of the steps is the definition of the initial *pbest* and *gbest,* which represent the best position found by the particle and swarm, respectively. The manner how the value of *pbest* is updated or chosen is not influenced by the use of Multi-Ring topology, since it is related to the individual experience of the particle. Therefore, all the particles of the swarm define the *pbest* in the same way.

For each iteration, each ring layer performs a search and marks the particle that reached the best position of the entire ring layer. Different from *gbest,* in the Multi-Ring approach, the definition of this new position called *ringbest,* considers only the particles within the respective ring layer. Therefore, each ring layer will have its own *ringbest.* After that, the *ringbests* of each ring layer are compared with each other, and the best one will be selected as the best solution. The pseudo-code of the algorithm is presented in Figure 6.

Algorithm 1: Multi-Ring based particle swarm updating position, velocity and cognitive and social information during the search process.

```
initializeSwarm()
while step <= numberOfSteps do
  foreach ring of the swarm do
      rotate();
      foreach particle of the ring do
          updateVelocityAndPosition();
          calculateFitness();
          updateInformation();
      end
// marks the best particle of each ring
      defineRingBest ();
  end
  evaluateBestRing();
end
return bestPositionFound
```

Fig. 6. Multi-Ring particle swarm optimization algorithm.

After the *pbest* evaluation, the algorithm performs the selection of the best particle of the respective ring layer. This process is repeated for all the ring layers that compose the Multi-

Ring topology (see Line 10 in Figure 6). Line 12 of Figure 6 shows that the selection of the best *ringbest* for the topology occurs at the end of each algorithm iteration.
The **updateVelocityAndPosition()** and **updateInformation()** processes are the core of any PSO algorithm. These two processes are described in the pseudo-codes of Algorithms 2 and 3 that are shown in Figures 7 and 8, respectively.

Algorithm 2: Position of one particle being updated based on PSO velocity update equation.

```
foreach dimension do
    newVelocity ← currentVelocity +c1 * r1 * (bestIndividualPosition −
    currentPosition ) + c2 * r2 * (neighborhoodBestPosition − newPosition )
    newPosition ← currentPosition + velocity
end
```

Fig. 7. Particle swarm position and velocity updating algorithm.

Algorithm 3: Particle information update method.

```
if currentFitness < bestIndividualFitness then
    bestIndividualFitness ← currentFitness
end
if currentFitness < neighborhoodBestFitness then
    neighborhoodBestFitness ← currentFitness
end
```

Fig. 8. Particle information updating algorithm.

The other process involved in Algorithm 1 execution is **rotate()** (see Line 4), which belongs only to the multi-ring topology approach proposed here. One can note that this step is done before the *fitness* evaluation. Figure 9 can be used to represent this process. Consider that the rotation trigger criterion used is the number of successive iterations that the best solution found (*ringbest)* by the ring layer has not improved and d is the number of positions that the ring will be rotated. Using t_r to represent the trigger mechanism and X_i to represent the particle i of the ring layer X, the ring layer X will be rotated if the value of its best position has not improved after t_r iterations. Otherwise, if the respective number of iterations is below t_r, the algorithm does not rotate the ring layer X and the number of iterations is incremented. This process is done for all ring layers of the Multi-ring topology.
When the trigger criterion is satisfied, the ring layer is rotated by d particles and the number of iterations that the *ringbest* did not improved is reset. It implies in a new neighbourhood for each particle of the rotated ring and, as a result, it improves the social information exchange. One can note that there is a trigger criteria $t_{r(k)}$ for each ring layer $rl_{(k)}$. The figure 10 illustrates the rotation algorithm process described above.

4. Dispersed particle swarm optimization

4.1 Dispersed PSO concepts

In particle swarm optimization (PSO) literature, the published social coefficients settings aims to increase the search around the swarm memory. However, few approaches

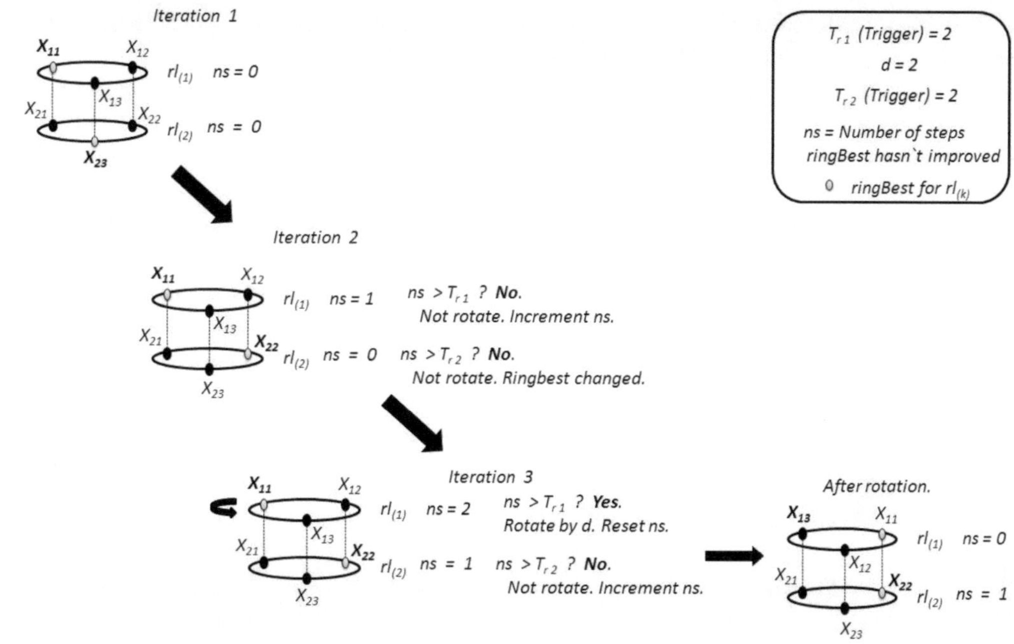

Fig. 9. Rotation simulation process.

Algorithm 4: Multi-Ring rotation process.

```
trigger ← getRingTriggerCriteria(ring);
//check if the ringbest of the ring did not improved.
if ringBest == lastRingBest then
    if numberOfStepsRingStagnated >= trigger then
        // rotate the ring by d particles
        d ← getRingRotationDistance();
        rotateRing(d);
        numberOfStepsRingStagnated ← 0
    else then
        numberOfStepsRingStagnated ← numberOfStepsRingStagnated + 1
    end
else then
    //reset the number of steps ring stagnated.
    numberOfStepsRingStagnated ← 0
end
```

Fig. 10. Multi-Ring rotation process.

take into account the useful information inside the particle's memories. Thus, to improve the convergence speed, a new approach considering the social coefficient was proposed (Cai et

al, 2008) by introducing an explicit selection pressure, in which each particle decides its search direction toward the personal memory or swarm memory.
The fitness value of the current position of each particle represents its adaptive capability, and it can be selected to distinguish between search modes. In this approach, the better the fitness of the current position is, more adaptation this particle can get to enhance its survival ratio.
Since the literature consider the extreme situations such as *global* or *local* approaches, they neglect the differences between the particles in the search process. These settings lose some information that can be useful to find the global optima or escape from local optima.
To minimize this problem, Cai *et al.* (Cai *et al.*, 2008) proposed a new index to indicate performance differences, named $Grade_i(t)$. The definition of the index is provided as follows:

$$Grade_i(t) = \frac{f_{worst}(t) - f[\vec{x}_i(t)]}{f_{worst}(t) - f_{best}(t)}, \tag{2}$$

where $f_{worst}(t)$ and $f_{best}(t)$ are the worst and the best fitness values of the swarm at time step t, respectively.
Occasionally, the swarm can converge onto one point, that means $f_{worst}(t) = f_{best}(t)$. In this case, the value $Grade_i(t)$ of an arbitrary particle i is set to 1. $Grade_i(t)$ represents the performance of particle i at time t, according to its fitness value of the current position. The better particle is, the larger $Grade_i(t)$ is, and vice-versa.
In most cases, if the fitness value of particle i is better than the fitness of particle u, the probability of i's neighbourhood falls into a global optima is higher than the particle u. Thus, the particle i should give more attentions to exploit its neighbourhood. On the contrary, it may tend to explore other regions with a larger probability. Therefore, the best solution should perform a complete search around its historical best position and the worst solution should perform a global search around the best solution found so far.
Then, the dispersed social coefficient of particle i at time t is set as follows:

$$c_{2,i}(t) = c_{low} + (c_{up} - c_{low})Grade_i(t), \tag{3}$$

where c_{up} and c_{down} are two predefined numbers, and $c_{2,i}(t)$ represents the social coefficient of particle j at time t. One can note that better particles will present higher values for c_2.

4.2 Multi-ring dispersed particle swarm optimization

Based on the new manner to determine the acceleration coefficients, the dispersed PSO approach was included into the Multi-Ring Topology. By applying the $Grade_i(t)$ to determine the communication rules inside each ring, we expect that it will improve the performance of the search made by the Multi-Ring PSO algorithm.
The grade criterion, which is calculated by evaluating a fitness comparison, will make the best solutions perform searches around its vicinities and the worst solutions look for the history of a larger part of the swarm, in order to increase its experience.
Figure 11 illustrates the grade strategy in action. If the $Grade_i(t)$ is above a threshold (good solutions), we reduce the neighbourhood of the particle. In this case, the neighbourhood of the particle i is defined as { $rl_{(k)(i-1)}$, $rl_{(k)(i+1)}$, $rl_{(k-1)(i)}$, $rl_{(k+1)(i)}$ }. Otherwise, the particle should expand its communication range to achieve more information, which it would get

information from all particles in the same ring in order to increase its experience. One can note that rings which the *ringbest* are below the threshold will perform searches using a more connected structure in order to achieve better regions in the search space. In spite of this, one should note that the communication between the ring layer remains local.

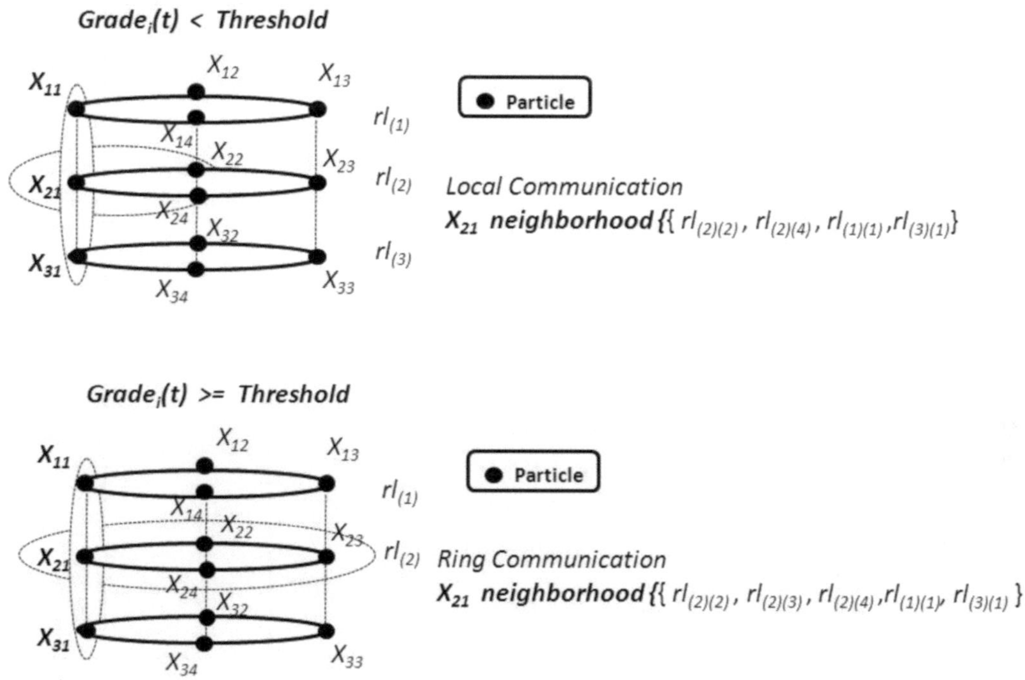

Fig. 11. Grade criteria at Multi-Ring PSO.

5. Simulation setup

In Table 1, seven commonly used benchmark functions are presented. Their names, definitions, search space, initialization range, and optimum compose the columns of Table 1. All the functions described are used as minimization problems classified as unimodal (f_1) or multimodal (f_2, f_3, f_4, f_5, f_6 and f_7) containing many local minima and a high level of complexity. For the simulations, each function was tested with 30 dimensions.

Each simulation was performed using PSO with inertia factor. The reduction of w is linear and starts at 0.9 decreasing to 0.4 along the iterations. The number of rings was varied based on a swarm with 30 particles. Thus, the number of ring layers is defined as $nl = 30 / n$. The rotation distance is equal to a half of the ring layer size ($d = nl / 2$) and the trigger criterion was $t_r = 15$.

We used c_1 and c_2 equal to 2.05. In the MRDPSO, we used $c_{low} = 1.5$ and $c_{up} = 2.5$.

The number of iterations used in a single simulation was 10,000. After 30 executions, the mean and standard deviation were stored. The initial positions of the entire swarm are defined randomly inside the initialization range of the benchmark function used. Comparisons with other topologies were also provided for convergence performance validation in both inertia and dispersed approaches.

Function	Equation	Search space	Init.	Opt.
Rosenbrock (f_1)	$f_1 = \sum_{i=1}^{n-1}\left[100\left(x_{i+1} - x_i^2\right)^2 + (1 - x_i)^2\right]$	$(-30, 30)^D$	$(15, 30)^D$	1.0^D
Ackley (f_2)	$f_4 = -20\exp\left(-0.2\sqrt{\frac{1}{n}\sum_{i=1}^{n} x_i^2}\right)$ $-\exp\left(\frac{1}{n}\sum_{i=1}^{n}\cos(2\pi x_i)\right) + 20 + e$	$(-32, 32)^D$	$(16, 32)^D$	0.0^D
Griewank (f_3)	$f_3 = 1 + \sum_{i=1}^{n}\frac{x_i^2}{4000} - \prod_{i=1}^{n}\cos\left(\frac{x_i}{\sqrt{i}}\right)$	$(-600, 600)^D$	$(300, 600)^D$	0.0^D
Penalized P8 (f_4)	$f_7 = \frac{\pi}{n}\{10\sin^2(\pi y_i)$ $+\sum_{i=1}^{n-1}(y_i - 1)^2\{1 + 10\sin^2(\pi y_{i+1})\}$ $+(y_n - 1)^2\} + \sum_{i=1}^{n}\mu(x_i, 10, 100, 4)$ $y_i = 1 + \frac{1}{4}(x_i + 1)$ $\mu(x_i, a, k, m) = \begin{cases} k(x_i - a)^m, & x_i > a \\ 0, & -a \le x_i \le a \\ k(-x_i - a)^m, & x_i < a \end{cases}$	$(-50, 50)^D$	$(25, 50)^D$	-1.0^D
Penalized P16 (f_5)	$f_8 = 0.1\{\sin^2(3\pi x_i) + \sum_{i=1}^{n-1}(x_i - 1)^2\{1 + \sin^2(3\pi x_{i+1}$ $+(x_n - 1)^2 \times \{1 + \sin^2(2\pi x_n)\}\} + \sum_{i=1}^{n}\mu(x_i, 5, 100, 4)$	$(-50, 50)^D$	$(25, 50)^D$	1.0^D
Rastrigin (f_6)	$f_2 = 10n + \sum_{i=1}^{n}\left[x_i^2 - 10\cos(2\pi x_i)\right]$	$(-5.12, 5.12)^D$	$(2.56, 5.12)^D$	0.0^D
Schwefel 2.6 (f_7)	$f_6 = -\sum_{i=1}^{n} x_i \sin\left(\sqrt{x_i}\right)$	$(-500, 500)^D$	$(-500, -250)^D$	420.96^D

Table 1. Benchmark functions used in the experiments.

6. Results

This section shows the results of the experiments involving the benchmark functions described previously. In the first section (Section 6.1) of the simulation results, we vary the number of ring layers. The second one (Section 6.2) presents a comparison between each Multi-ring approach and the topologies already mentioned in Section 2 of this paper.

6.1 Ring layer variation

Table 2 shows the results of MRPSO varying the number of ring layers in simulations involving each benchmark function. For function f_6, the structure composed by 3 ring layers behaved better. The 5-ring MRPSO achieved a better performance for functions f_1, f_2 and f_3, and the 10-ring behaves better for f_4, f_5, and f_7.

One can note that the best choice for function f_6 was 3-ring layers followed by the 5-rings configuration. Thus, in general, the 5-rings configuration achieved the most satisfactory fitness values. This is due to the fact that maintaining a balance between the degree of

Function	MRPSO					
	3 ring layers		5 ring layers		10 ring layers	
	Mean	SD	Mean	SD	Mean	SD
(f_1)	17.48	9.39	**15.05**	**7.87**	29.48	29.33
(f_2)	3.19E-9	3.40E-9	**2.28E-9**	**3.53E-9**	2.56E-10	3.41E-10
(f_3)	0.0097	0.01	**0.00509**	**0.0063**	0.0062	0.00902
(f_4)	2.56E-32	3.1E-32	2.72E-32	4.26E-32	**1.62E-32**	**2.23E-32**
(f_5)	2.72	2.82	3.56	4.94	**0.56**	**1.03**
(f_6)	**16.3**	**5.19**	17.36	7.41	19.57	5.85
(f_7)	3305.57	577.24	2963.11	498.9	**2686.44**	**456.16**

Table 2. Number of ring layers variation of MRPSO.

communication inside a ring and through different rings, the MRPSO can reach regions with better solutions.

For the dispersed approach for the proposed topology (MRDPSO) (see Table 3) the 5-rings configuration achieved the best overall performance.

Function	MRDPSO					
	3 ring layers		5 ring layers		10 ring layers	
	Mean	SD	Mean	SD	Mean	SD
(f_1)	12.99	19.05	9.84	14.42	**8.44**	**5.97**
(f_2)	**6.83E-15**	**1.44 E-15**	7.31E-15	9.01E-16	7.54E-15	1.61E-15
(f_3)	**0.70E-4**	**0.01**	0.80E-4	0.80E-4	0.01	0.01
(f_4)	4.08E-32	5.40E-32	4.55E-32	5.36E-32	**8.37E-33**	**7.96E-33**
(f_5)	**0.28**	**0.42**	0.29	0.41	0.37	0.78
(f_6)	14.725	4.008	**13.929**	**3.102**	20.39	7.54
(f_7)	4063.20	543.16	**3969.54**	**563.79**	3975.34	356.32

Table 3. Number of ring layers variation of MRDPSO.

For functions f_2, f_3 and f_5 the 3-rings configuration achieved the best fitness values. The configuration with 10 ring layers achieved better performance in functions f_1 and f_4. Again, we can consider that a configuration with 5-rings is enough to reach satisfactory fitness values in complex and different search spaces.

The dispersed coefficient improves the convergence speed, thus is clearly expected that MRDPSO will converge fast than MRPSO. Therefore, the 5-rings configuration can be considered the best configuration choice in both MRPSO and MRDPSO.

Varying the number of rings, both MRPSO and MRDPSO can fit to different kind of problems. Hence, the number of rings can be varied according to the problem to be solved.

6.2 Topologies comparison

The results between the comparison of MRPSO and MRDPSO and other topologies are shown in Table 4 and Table 5, respectively. For all the functions, the fitness values presented by the Multi-ring approaches are the ones that achieved the best performance or similar performance to the best performance.

f	MRPSO		Global		Local		Von Neumann		Four Clusters	
	Mean	SD	Mean	SD	Mean	SD	Mean	SD	Mean	SD
(f_1)	**15.05**	**7.87**	17.712	6.3686	18.215	12.995	39.54	29.36	88.15	44.51
(f_2)	2.28E-9	3.53E-9	**1.26E-14**	**3.04E-15**	9.61E-8	8.70E-8	1.81E-10	1.86E-10	0.16	0.51
(f_3)	0.00509	0.0063	0.01	0.02	**0.0031**	**6.4E-3**	0.008	0.01	0.04	0.03
(f_4)	1.62E-32	2.23E-32	5.02E-32	5.52E-32	**6.22E-33**	**7.82E-33**	9.94E-33	1.27E-32	9.42E-32	5.05E-32
(f_5)	**0.56**	**1.03**	4.46	8.31	1.33	1.47	1.00	1.64	52.67	39.25
(f_6)	16.3	5.19	**15.35**	**5.93**	21.94	5.33	19.58	4.89	19.58	7.37
(f_7)	2686.44	456.16	**2164.17**	**368.74**	2964.79	389.31	2898.37	347.01	3633.34	519.53

Table 4. Comparison between MRPSO and other topologies.

f	MRDPSO		Global Dispersed		Local Dispersed		Von Neumann Dispersed		Four Clusters Dispersed	
	Mean	SD	Mean	SD	Mean	SD	Mean	SD	Mean	SD
(f_1)	**8.44**	**5.97**	32.8099	33.7074	15.3180	18.0088	10.8321	13.8913	83.8264	54.0686
(f_2)	**6.83E-15**	**1.44 E-15**	1.13E-14	3.60E-15	9.73E-13	5.43E-13	7.54E-15	9.01E-16	0.2947	0.6127
(f_3)	0.70E-4	0.01	0.0134	0.0137	**4.09E-11**	**2.24E-10**	0.0103	0.014	0.0529	0.0498
(f_4)	8.37E-33	7.96E-33	4.86E-32	4.81E-32	**5.23E-33**	**7.53E-33**	2.72E-32	4.1436	9.10E-32	5.09E-32
(f_5)	0.28	0.42	0.7080	1.5170	**0.1375**	**0.22**	0.16	0.401	63.50	40.47
(f_6)	**13.929**	**3.102**	13.99	3.66	20.96	4.6	21.16	6.84	36.92	6.86
(f_7)	3969.54	563.79	**2320.08**	**355.31**	3610.09	461.8253	3889.64	503.86	3750.91	334.53

Table 5. Comparison between MRDPSO and other topologies.

For function f_1 and f_5 MRPSO reaches the best fitness values (F = 15.05 and F = 0.56). For all the other functions used, it reaches values close to the best performance achieved by some well known topologies. A good example is the performance for functions f_6 and f_7, in which

the only topology that achieved fitness values better than the ones achieved by MRPSO was the global topology. Hence, considering that MRPSO is a local communication topology, the results presented by Table 4 are strongly satisfactory.
Table 5 shows the results of the MRDPSO and topologies enabled with the dispersion grade strategy. For function f_1, f_2, and f_6 the MRDPSO achieves the best fitness values (F=8.44, F=6.83E-15 and F=13.929). For the functions f_3 and f_5, it reaches a good value for the mean fitness with low standard deviation, close to the best performance achieved by well known topologies. For the function f_7, MRDPSO achieves a value for the mean fitness in the same order of magnitude of Dispersed PSO with local, Von Neumann and Four Clusters topologies. Therefore, considering all results shown at the Table 5, the MRDPSO achieves good solutions for both unimodal and multimodal problems.

7. Conclusions

This paper has proposed a novel topology for Particle Swarm Optimization based on a multi layer structure based on local communication (***lbest***). The Multi-ring PSO (MRPSO) and also its combination with the Dispersed PSO approach (MRDPSO) are thoroughly described. The first one introduces a new feature called *rotation skill* that minimizes the stagnation probability of the PSO algorithm. In the second one, some changes in the communication rules inside the rings were made by using the dispersion grade attribute of Dispersed PSO approach.
The Multi-ring approaches achieved better performance or close to well-known topologies used for comparison. This fact exalts how satisfactory the results involving MRPSO and MRDPSO were. By varying the number of rings, the size of each ring and how the rotation skill work, the proposed approach could be used to reach good quality solutions for both unimodal and multimodal problems. Besides, it helps to avoid the swarm of being trapped at local minima regions, making it moves to new regions of space search in order to help the PSO algorithm to converge to the best solution.
Due to its peculiar features, the proposed PSO topology is an interesting approach able to be applied in different kind of optimization problems.

8. References

Abido, M.A. (2001). Optimal design of power system stabilizers using particle swarm optimization. *IEEE Trans. Energy Conversion,* Vol. 17, No. 3, (September 2002) Pages: 7 (406–413), ISSN 0885-8969

Agrafiotis, D.K. & Cedeno, W (2002). Feature selection for structure-activity correlation using binary particle swarms. *J. Medicinal Chem.,* Vol. 45, No. 5, (February 2002) Pages: 9 (1098–1107)

Bäck, T. (1996). *Evolutionary Algorithms in Theory and Practice,* Springer-Verlag, ISBN 0-19-509971-0, Berlin, Germany

Bastos-Filho, C. J. A.; Caraciolo, M. P. ; Miranda, P. B. C. ; Carvalho, D. F. . Multi Ring Particle Swarm Optimization. *In: SBRN'2008 (the 10th Brazilian Symposium on Neural Networks),* pp. 111-116, 2008, Salvador/BA. *Proceedings of* SBRN'2008 (the 10th Brazilian Symposium on Neural Networks), 2008

Beyer, H.-G. (2001). *The Theory of Evolution Strategies,* Springer-Verlag New York, Inc., ISBN 3-540-67297-4, New York, NY, USA

Beyer, H.-G. (2002). Evolution strategies: A comprehensive introduction. *Nat. Comput.,* Vol. 1, No. 1, (March 2002) Pages: 49 (3-52), ISSN 1567-7818

Bratton, D. & Kennedy, J. (2007). Defining a standard for particle swarm optimization, *Proceedings of Swarm Intelligence Symposium SIS 2007,* pp. 120–127, ISBN 1-4244-0708-7, Honolulu, HI, April 2007, IEEE Service

Cai, X., Cui, Z., Zeng, J. & Tan, Y. (2008). Dispersed particle swarm optimization. *Information Processing Letters,* Vol. 105, No. 6, (February 2008) Pages: 4 (231-235), ISSN 0020-0190

Carvalho, D.F. & Bastos-Filho, C.J.A. (2008). Clan particle swarm optimization, *Proceedings of IEEE Congress on Evolutionary Computation CEC 2008 (IEEE World Congress on Computational Intelligence),* pp. 3044-3051, ISBN 978-1-4244-1822-0, Hong Kong, June 2008

Carvalho, D.F. & Bastos-Filho, C.J.A. (2009). Clan particle swarm optimization. *International Journal of Intelligent Computing and Cybernetics,* Vol. 2, No. 2, (June 2009) Pages: 31 (197 - 227), ISSN 1756-378X

Clerc, M. & Kennedy, J. (2002). The particle swarm - explosion, stability, and convergence in a multidimensional complex space. *IEEE Transactions on Evolutionary Computation,* Vol. 6, No. 1, (February 2002) Pages: 5 (58-73), ISSN 1089-778X

Coello Coello, C.A. & Lechuga, M.S. (2002). MOPSO: A proposal for multiple objective particle swarm optimization, *Proceedings of 2002 IEEE Congr. Evolutionary Computation CEC 2002,* pp. 1051–1056, ISBN 0-7803-7282-4, Honolulu, HI, May 2002, IEEE Computer Society, Washington, DC, USA

Eberhart, R.C. & Shi, Y. (2001). Tracking and optimizing dynamic systems with particle swarms, *Proceedings of 2001 IEEE Congr. Evolutionary Computation CEC 2001,* pp. 94–100, ISBN 0-7803-6657-3, Seoul, South Korea, May 2001

Engelbrecht, A.P. (2005). *Fundamentals of Computational Swarm Intelligence,* John Wiley & Sons, ISBN 0470091916

Fogel, D. (1996). *Evolutionary Computation: Toward a New Philosophy of Machine Intelligence,* Wiley-IEEE Press, ISBN 978-0-471-66951-7

Jiao, B., Lian, Z. & Gu, X. (2008). A dynamic inertia weight particle swarm optimization algorithm. *Chaos, Solitons and Fractals,* Vol. 37, No. 3, (August 2008) Pages: 7 (698–705), ISSN 0960-0779

Kennedy, J. & Eberhart, R.C. (1995). Particle swarm optimization, *Proceedings of the IEEE Int. Conf. on Neural Networks,* pp. 1942-1948, ISBN 0-7803-2768-3, Perth, WA, Australia, December 1995, IEEE Service Center, Piscataway, NJ

Kennedy, J. (1999). Small worlds and mega-minds: effects of neighborhood topology on particle swarm performance, *Proceedings of 1999 Congress on Evolutionary Computation CEC 99,* pp. -1938, ISBN 0-7803-5536-9, Washington, DC, USA, July 1999, IEEE Service

Kennedy, J. & Mendes, R. (2002). Population structure and particle swarm performance, *Proceedings of the 2002 Congress on Evolutionary Computation CEC 2002,* pp. 1671-1676, ISBN 0-7803-7282-4, Honolulu, HI, USA, May 2002, IEEE Press

Kennedy, J. (2005). Why does it need velocity?, *Proceedings of the Swarm Intelligence Symposium SIS 2005*, pp. 38-44, ISBN 0-7803-8916-6, Pasadena, California, June 2005

Mendes, R., Kennedy, J. & Neves, J. (2003). Watch thy neighbor or how the swarmcan learn from its environment, *Proceedings Swarm Intelligence Symposium SIS 2003*, pp. 88-94, ISBN 0-7803-7914-4, Indianapolis, Indiana, USA, April 2003, IEEE Service

Parsopoulos, K.E. & Vrahatis, M.N. (2001). Particle swarm optimizer in noisy and continuously changing environments, *Proceedings of Artificial Intelligence and Soft Computing*, pp. 289–294, Cancun, Mexico, 2001, IASTED/ACTA Press

Parsopoulos, K.E., Laskari, E.C. & Vrahatis, M.N. (2002). Recent approaches to global optimization problems through particle swarm optimization. *Natural Computing,* Vol. 1, No. 2-3, (June 2002) Pages: (235–306), ISSN 1572-9796

Peer, E.S., van den Bergh, F. & Engelbrecht, A.P. (2003). Using neighbourhoods with the guaranteed convergence PSO, *Proceedings of 2003 IEEE Swarm Intelligence Symposium SIS '03*, pp. 235-42, ISBN 0-7803-7914-4, Indianapolis, Indiana, USA, April 2003, IEEE Service

Potter, M.A. & De Jong, K.A. (1994). A cooperative coevolutionary approach to function optimization, In: *The Third Parallel Problem Solving From Nature,* Pages: 8 (249–257), Springer Berlin / Heidelberg, ISBN 978-3-540-58484-1, Berlin, Germany

Praveen, K.; Sanjoy, D. & Stephen, M.W. (2007). Multi-objective hybrid PSO using μ-fuzzy dominance, *Proceedings of 9th annual conference on Genetic and evolutionary computation GECCO '07*, pp. 853–860, ISBN 978-1-59593-697-4, London, England, July 2007, ACM, New York, NY, USA

Santana-Quintero, L.V.; Coello Coello, C.A.; Hernandez-Diaz, A.G. & Velazquez, J.M.O. (2008). Surrogate-based Multi-Objective Particle Swarm Optimization, *Proceedings of Swarm Intelligence Symposium SIS 2008*, pp. 1-8, ISBN 978-1-4244-2704-8, St. Louis, Missouri, September 2008, IEEE

Schwefel, H.-P. (1981). Numerical Optimization of Computer Models, John Wiley & Sons, Inc, ISBN 0471099880, New York, NY, USA

Shi, Y. & Eberhart, R.C. (1998). A modified particle swarm optimizer, *Proceedings of the IEEE International Conference on Evolutionary Computation*, pp. 69-73, ISBN 0-7803-4869-9, Anchorage, AK, USA, May 1998, IEEE Press, Piscataway, NJ

Shi, Y. & Krohling, R.A. (2002). Co-evolutionary particle swarm optimization to solve min-max problems, *Proceedings of 2002 IEEE Conf. Evolutionary Computation CEC 2002*, pp. 1682–1687, ISBN 0-7803-7282-4, Honolulu, HI, May 2002, IEEE Computer Society, Washington, DC, USA

Suganthan, P.N. (1999). Particle swarm optimiser with neighbourhood operator, *Proceedings of the 1999 Congress on Evolutionary Computation CEC 99*, pp. -1962, ISBN 0-7803-5536-9, Washington, DC, USA, June 1999

Sutton, A.M.; Whitley, D., Lunacek, M. & Howe, A. (2006). PSO and multi-funnel landscapes: how cooperation might limit exploration, *Proceedings of 8th Annual Conference on Genetic and Evolutionary Computation GECCO '08*, pp. 75–82, ISBN 1-59593-186-4, Seattle, Washington, USA, July 2008, ACM, New York, NY, USA

van den Bergh, F. & Engelbrecht, A.P. (2001). Training product unit networks using cooperative particle swarm optimisers, *Proceedings of International Joint Conference on*

Neural Networks IJCNN '01, pp. 126–131, ISBN 0-7803-7044-9, Washington, DC, USA, July 2001

van den Bergh, F. & Engelbrecht, A.P. (2004). A Cooperative approach to particle swarm optimization. *IEEE Transactions on Evolutionary Computation,* Vol. 8, No. 3, (June 2004) Pages: 14 (225–239), ISSN 1089-778X

29

Agent-Based Multi-Objective Evolutionary Algorithms with Cultural and Immunological Mechanisms

Leszek Siwik and Rafał Dreżewski
AGH University of Science and Technology
Poland

1. Introduction

Evolutionary algorithms are heuristic techniques for finding (sub)optimal solutions for hard global optimization problems. Evolutionary algorithms may be also applied to multimodal and multi-objective problems (for example compare (Deb, 2001)). In these cases however some special techniques must be used in order to obtain multiple high-quality solutions. Most important of these mechanisms are techniques that maintain population diversity because we are interested in finding the whole set of solutions—it would be a set of non-dominated solutions in the case of multi-objective optimization (all notions and ideas of multi-objective optimization may be found in (Deb, 2001)) and a set of individuals located within basins of attraction of different local optima in the case of multi-modal optimization problems.
Agent-based evolutionary algorithms result from mixing two paradigms: evolutionary algorithms and multi-agent systems. Two approaches are possible when we try to mix these two paradigms. In the first one we can use agent-based layer of the computing system as a "manager" of the computations. In this case each agent has sub-population of individuals inside of it. Agent tries to utilize computational resources in a best way—it observes the computational environment and tries to migrate to nodes which have free computational resources. In this approach evolving individuals are processed with the use of standard evolutionary algorithm.
In the second approach individuals are agents which live within the environment composed of computational nodes, compete for resources, reproduce, die, observe the environment and other agents, communicate with other agents, and can change the environment. The selection is realized in the decentralized way: there are some resources defined in the system and "worse" agents (which have "worse" solutions encoded within their genotypes) give some amount of their resources to "better" agents. These resources are needed for all activities, like reproduction, migration, etc. When an agent runs out of resources it dies and is removed from the system.
The example of the second approach is *evolutionary multi-agent system (EMAS)* model (Cetnarowicz et al., 1996), and *co-evolutionary multi-agent system (CoEMAS)* model (Dreżewski, 2003), which additionally allows for existence of many species and sexes of agents—it is also possible to define interactions between them and introduce co-evolutionary interactions.

The two mentioned approaches can be mixed in such a way that we use agent-based layer for managing the computations and each evolving individual is also an agent which can compete for resources, migrate within the environment, reproduce, and die.
Agent-based evolutionary algorithms have some distinguishing features, among which the most interesting seem to be:

1. The possibility of constructing hybrid systems. In such a case we can use many different bio-inspired techniques together, within one coherent agent-based computational model.
2. Relaxation of computational constraints—computations are decentralized and asynchronous because we use agent-based approach.
3. The possibility of introducing new biologically and socially inspired operators, which were hard or impossible to introduce in the case of "classical" evolutionary computations.

In this chapter we mainly focus on the first and third of the mentioned above issues. The main objective is to introduce two new mechanisms for EMAS model: cultural, and immunological. These mechanisms are applied in agent-based multi-objective evolutionary algorithm.
Following (Deb, 2001)—*multi-objective optimization problem*—*MOOP* in its general form is being defined as follows:

$$MOOP \equiv \begin{cases} Minimize/Maximize & f_m(\bar{x}), \quad m = 1,2\ldots,M \\ Subject\ to & g_j(\bar{x}) \geq 0, \quad j = 1,2\ldots,J \\ & h_k(\bar{x}) = 0, \quad k = 1,2\ldots,K \\ & x_i^{(L)} \leq x_i \leq x_i^{(U)}, \quad i = 1,2\ldots,N \end{cases}$$

Authors assume that readers are familiar with at least fundamental concepts and notions regarding multi-objective optimization in the Pareto sense (relation of domination, Pareto frontier and Pareto set etc) and because of space limitation their explanation is omitted in this chapter (interested readers can find definitions and deep analysis of all necessary concepts and notions of Pareto MOO for instance in (Coello et al., 2007; Deb, 2001)).
The chapter is organized as follows:

- in section 2 shortcomings of naive application of EMAS model for solving multi-objective optimization problems are discussed and concluded with motivation for further research on advanced mechanisms that could be introduced into EMAS and overcome defined problems;
- in section 3 short introduction into immune and cultural mechanisms is given and next our realization of immune-cultural Evolutionary Multi-Agent System for multi-objective optimization *ic*-EMAS is presented and discussed;
- in section 4 we discuss shortly test suite, performance metric and noising algorithm used during experiments, and next we glance at obtained results;
- in section 5 the most important remarks, conclusions and comments are given.

2. Shortcomings of naive application of EMAS model for solving MOOPs

Evolutionary Multi-Agent System (EMAS) discussed for instance in (Dobrowolski & Kisiel-Dorohinicki, 2002; Cetnarowicz et al., 1996; Socha & Kisiel-Dorohinicki, 2002; Dreżewski & Siwik, 2008*b*; Dreżewski et al., 2009) proved to be very promising computational model. Unfortunately, at the same time, results obtained during solving multi-objective optimization problems (MOOPs) by distributed and decentralized agent-based evolutionary heuristic approach turned out to be not as high-quality as results obtained by *classical* equivalents and state-of-the-art algorithms.

During testing EMAS on various optimization problems, two core issues that could have great negative influence on obtained results have been identified i.e. algorithm stagnation and non-uniform distribution of agents over (approximation of) the Pareto frontier.

The crucial activities of agents in EMAS environment are interactions with another agents. In particular it means meetings with another agents and comparing with each other represented by them solutions. According to the *domination principle* when one of agents dominates the other one—*life energy* is transferred from dominated agent to the dominating one. Because almost any activity of EMAS agents depends on the amount of their resources (*life energy*)—it is now obvious why agents' interactions and flows of resources are so important.

Unfortunately, with time (during our experiments after ca. six hundreds of steps—see fig. 1b) the number of non-dominated agents is (almost) equal to the number of agents in environment. In the consequence, there are almost only mutually non-dominated individuals, so the probability that the solution represented by agent randomly selected from the whole population, will be dominating or dominated one is quite low.

From the point of view of Agent A in fig. 1a (Siwik et al., 2008) flow of energy takes place only when met agent is located in the Area A or in the Area C—so only if it meets Agents B and C or Agents F, G and H). In the consequence the process of evolution falls into stagnation. It implies that during meetings among agents the flow of energy disappears, so agents can neither reproduce nor die.

In the case of classical algorithms (like NSGA-II) such problem is not so significant, since individual is compared with all the others in each iteration. Similar solution (meetings and comparisons with the whole population in each step/iteration) is not possible in the case of EMAS-based approach since it is distributed and decentralized system and one of the main assumption in this case is lack of the global knowledge and lack of the global management of the whole population as well.

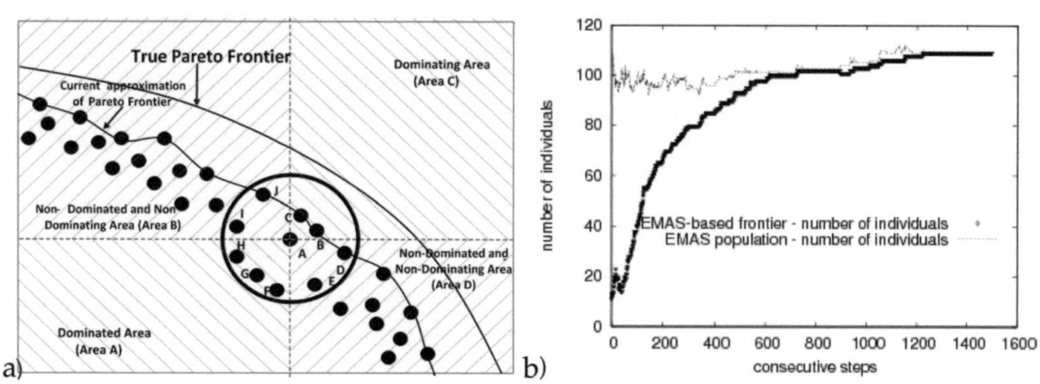

Fig. 1. Stagnation process in EMAS-based multi-objective optimization

Since in the basic implementation of EMAS there are no mechanisms responsible for even distribution of non-dominated solutions over the whole (approximation of the) Pareto frontier, there is also one more difficulty with effective applying "plain" EMAS for solving *MOOPs*— often non-dominated agents are grouped within some areas while other parts of the Pareto frontier are not covered at all. Such situation is absolutely undesirable since main goals of multi-objective optimization is to find non-dominated solutions located as close to the true Pareto frontier as it is possible but simultaneously none of the objectives should be preferred. So, in other words, all found non-dominated solutions should be evenly dispersed over the whole Pareto frontier. The reason of mentioned problem is often associated with the fact that the probability of locating agents in some areas of the Pareto frontier is pretty low. Often large area in problem domain is mapped into relatively small function value range. EMAS should take such a situation into account and cover such problematic areas.

To recapitulate, it has to be said that introducing evolutionary mechanisms into the population of (autonomous) agents and proposed in this way distributed and decentralized model of evolution seemed to be very promising and attractive. On the other hand simultaneously however, direct and naive applying of such model for solving multi-objective optimization problems turned out to be fruitless to some extent—and that has been the reason and the motivation for researching on additional (advanced) mechanisms that could be introduced into EMAS to eliminate mentioned shortcomings.

Our research on such advanced mechanisms includes inter alia:

- elitist and semi-elitist mechanisms (Siwik & Natanek, 2008*b*; Siwik & Natanek, 2008*a*; Siwik & Kisiel-Dorohinicki, 2006; Siwik & Kisiel-Dorohinicki, 2005);
- flock-based mechanisms (Kisiel-Dorohinicki, 2004; Siwik et al., 2008);
- mechanisms dedicated for solving constrained MOOPs (Siwik & Sikorski, 2008);
- responsible mainly for diversity maintaining co-evolutionary mechanisms and techniques. In this group, the following approaches should be mentioned:
    - co-evolutionary multi-agent system with predator-prey interactions (Dreżewski & Siwik, 2007*b*; Dreżewski & Siwik, 2007*a*);
    - co-evolutionary multi-agent system with host-parasite interactions (Dreżewski & Siwik, 2006*b*);
    - co-evolutionary multi-agent system with sexual selection (Dreżewski & Cetnarowicz, 2007; Dreżewski & Siwik, 2006*a*; Dreżewski & Siwik, 2008*a*);

During further research it has turned out that also mechanisms borrowed from immunological as well as from cultural algorithms can be introduced into EMAS and improve significantly its effectiveness taking solving MOOPs into account. One of possible realization of immune-cultural Evolutionary Multi-Agent System *ic*-EMAS (which in particular allows for overcoming mentioned in this section shortcomings of simple EMAS) is presented in the next section.

3. Immune-cultural Evolutionary Multi-Agent System—*ic*-EMAS

The idea of artificial immune systems comes from the observation of natural, human-being immune system which is responsible—in general—for identification and destroying or neutralization of any kind of pathogens like viruses, bacteria, parasites, tumor-cells etc. Computer models of immune system are a subject of quite intensive research since 90s (Hunt & Cooke, 1995; Dasgupta, 1999; Forrest & Hofmeyr, 2000) and the most important and interesting features of (artificial) immune systems are self-organizing as well as adaptability and learning capabilities. In the consequence, artificial immune systems are very interesting computational approach providing fault tolerance, robustness, dynamism and adaptability (Frank, 1996; Hunt & Cooke, 1995; Castro & Timmis, 2002).

In immunology, there are two crucial concepts i.e. antigens and antibodies (Wierzchon, 2001). Antigens it is such kind of pathogen which can be recognized by immune system and can trigger off so-called immune response. Antigens activate immune cells—lymphocytes. Lymphocytes are producing antibodies which are able to destroy or to neutralize antigens. Lymphocytes posses so-called pattern recognition receptors so they are able to discover not-known so far antigens. Apart from that, immune system possesses also so-called immune memory and it is able to discover in more and more effective way antigens it has been in contact previously. It turns out, that computer model of natural immune systems can improve significantly multi-objective optimization algorithms (Coello & Nareli, 2005).

Immune system, like agent system, is autonomous so applying immune mechanisms within the agent system seems to be natural and smooth. Like in a real immune systems also here the most important issue and responsibility of "immune agents" is recognizing and neutralizing pathogens i.e. dominated specimen.

The most natural way to model immune system within agent system was introducing agents behaving like lymphocytes. Their antibodies can vary, with time, depending on met agents—it is a kind of equivalent of learning feature mentioned and observed in natural immune systems.

Lymphocyte-agent is a kind of EMAS agent so it possesses a genotype. It is also able to gather resources ("life energy") however, in this case, it does not need life energy to perform its activities—it can be said so that "lympho-agents" are immortal. During their life in EMAS environment lympho-agents are able to meet with ordinary agents only and during such meetings relation of domination is evaluated. If lympho-agent dominates met ordinary-agent it means that it meets antigen. According to the ideas and principles of immune systems it triggers an immune response i.e. antigen neutralization. In our realization the process of neutralization consists of two parts. First of all, lympho-agent takes 60% of ordinary-agent's life-energy (the value of 60% was taken on the basis of experiments performed). The second part of neutralization process consists in crossing over genotypes of ordinary- and lympho-agent and if better genotype is created it replaces the genotype of ordinary agent.

It is obviously possible that during the meeting between ordinary- and lympho-agent ordinary-agent dominates lympho-agent. In such a case the process of adaptation of lympho-agent takes place which is realized as taking over by lympho-agent mutated genotype of ordinary-agent. In the consequence lympho-agent is now able to recognize all of that antigens which so far it hasn't been able to dominate and to recognize as antigens (it is similar to some extent to so-called clonal selection known from natural immune systems (Castro & von Zuben, 2002)). During this process, lympho-agent transfers all of its life-energy to dominating ordinary-agent.

Very important parameter from the effectiveness of proposed agent-based artificial immune system point of view is the proper number of lympho-agents. In our realization the number of lympho-agents should be correlated (should be equal to) with the number of ordinary-agents located on the particular island.

Cultural algorithm proposed by R. G. Reynolds from Wayne State University (Reynolds, 1994) has been developed as a kind of supplement of classical genetic algorithm. Such kind of algorithms are making the use of sociological (and archaeological) theories to propose a model of cultural evolution. It is realized by introducing to the system a kind of common (available for all individuals) consciousness which allows for determining the set of expected features and for steering the process of evolution and the behavior of specimens in such a way to maximize the number of specimens possessing such features. On the other hand, the state of consciousness (so called belief space) depends on the knowledge and experience of individuals, so any change in the population can influence on it causing changes of preferred features. Cultural algorithm works on two levels, i.e.:

- on genome level with the use of mutation, crossover and selection mechanisms as usual in genetic algorithms;
- on the level of belief space being the representation of common consciousness storing the knowledge gathered by all individuals and influencing their behavior.

Both of these levels are able to communicate each other. A given number (fulfilling given conditions) of (best) individuals influences the belief space. Specimens belonging to such a group are chosen with the use of *acceptation*() function. Function *direction*() works in a different way—it influences genetic operators in such a way to maximize the number of individuals with expected features—where "expected features" are defined on the basis of the knowledge stored in the belief space.

Approaches utilizing ideas of cultural algorithm have been successfully applied to solving many optimization problems (Jin & Reynolds, n.d.; Jin & Reynolds, 2000). And what is more important from our point of view, cultural-like approaches have been also successfully applied to solving MOOPs (Coello & Becerra, 2003; Becerra & Coello, 2006).

In our EMAS-based realization of cultural mechanisms, belief space has been introduced on the level of each island. Similarly, to some extent, to solutions proposed in (Coello & Becerra, 2003) as the knowledge stored in the belief space—localization of (non-dominated) individuals in particular areas of search space was chosen. During the initialization, extreme values of each objective function for initial population is determined. Next, each found interval is divided into N_d subintervals. Those subranges divide belief space into $c = N_d^k$ cells. Each cell stores the number of non-dominated individuals representing the given area of search space.

Cultural mechanisms are used during crossover process. In simple EMAS, during reproduction one single offspring is created which is automatically added to the population. Now, after introducing cultural-oriented mechanisms, the process of reproduction looks as follows. First of all, making the use of crossover and mutation operators the number of $N_{\mathcal{P}}$ pretenders are being created. For each of them, their localization in belief space is being determined but in this moment they are not added to the belief space. First the tournament is being performed and only its winner is being added to the belief space and to the population—the rest of pretenders are destroyed. During the tournament each pretender meets all the others. During each meeting (compare Alg. 1) firstly relation of domination is evaluated. If one of them dominates the other, the value of p_v counter is being increased. If pretenders are mutually non-dominated their localization in the belief space is being checked. If one of them is located outside the borders of the belief space—it wins, else the numbers of individuals located in represented by both agents cells are being checked and the winner is the one representing less crowded cell. After performing such a tournament pretender with the highest number of victories becomes the descendant (the rest—as it was mentioned—is being destroyed).

As one may notice, belief space and cultural-oriented mechanisms address the second problem mentioned in previous section i.e. even distribution of non-dominated solution over the whole approximation of the Pareto frontier.

Algorithm 1. `duelCultural`($\mathcal{P}$) - tournament in *ic*-EMAS

```
for all p_i ∈ P do
  for all p_j ∈ P ∧ p_i ≠ p_j do
    if p_i ≻ p_j then
      p_i.v = p_i.v + 1
    else if p_j ≻ p_i then
      p_j.v = p_j.v + 1
    else
      if (p_i.C = ∅ ∧ p_j.C ≠ ∅) ∨ (‾p_i.C‾ > ‾p_j.C‾ ∧ ‾p_i.C‾ > 0) then
        p_i.v = p_i.v + 1
      else if (p_i.C ≠ ∅ ∧ p_j.C = ∅) ∨ (‾p_i.C‾ < ‾p_j.C‾ ∧ ‾p_j.C‾ > 0) then
        p_j.v = p_j.v + 1
      end if
    end if
  end for
end for
return rand({p_x : (p_x ∈ P) ∧ (∀p_y ∈ P : p_x.v ≥ p_y.v)})
```

Now, keeping in mind both: immune and cultural-oriented mechanisms, interactions between lympho-agents and ordinary-agents with the use of belief space look as follows (compare Alg. 2): In our realization of immune-cultural EMAS (*ic*-EMAS) also lympho-agents posses information about their localization in belief space. Now, modified lympho-agent is able to recognize not only dominated agent but also agents located in more crowded cell in belief space. If lympho- and ordinary-agent are mutually non-dominated the one located in less crowded cell is being considered as the better alternative. In such a case immune response is different than in the case of domination, because in such a situation it is more important to neutralize antigen by transferring it to less crowded cell. That is why its genotype is replaced by mutated genotype of lympho-agent. Simultaneously, ordinary-agent transfers 40% of its life energy to lympho-agent. In Alg. 2 the complete algorithm of interaction between lympho-agent (l) and ordinary-agent (s) is presented where:

- *l,s* means lympho- and ordinary-agent respectively;
- $l.\mathcal{E}$ and $s.E$ means energy possessed by lympho- and ordinary-agent respectively;
- $\mathcal{P}$ means the set of pretenders and $N_{\mathcal{P}}$ means the number of pretenders;
- $x.\mathcal{E}$ means genotype of particular agents;
- $l.C$ and $s._C$ means the content of the cell in the belief space where particular agents belongs to;

4. Experimental results

To compare *classical*, i.e. non agent-based algorithms, with proposed in this chapter immune-cultural Evolutionary Multi-Agent System, at least two aspects have to be taken into consideration, since the effectiveness of optimization algorithm can be analyzed as the function of (algorithm's) step and as the function of time. *Decision maker* (algorithm's user) is interested obviously in time aspects (it is important for him how fast it is possible to obtain valuable results) and how precisely given algorithm is able to approximate the model (ideal)

Algorithm 2. `immunoCulturalAction`(l, s) - interaction between lympho-agent and ordinary agent in *ic*-EMAS

if $l > s$ **then**
  $l.\mathcal{E} = l.\mathcal{E} + 0.6 \cdot s.\mathcal{E}$
  $s.\mathcal{E} = 0.4 \cdot s.\mathcal{E}$
  while $\overline{\mathcal{P}} < N_{\mathcal{P}}$ **do**
    $t.\mathcal{G} = \texttt{crossover}(l.\mathcal{G}, s.\mathcal{G})$
    $t.\mathcal{G} = \texttt{mutate}(t.\mathcal{G})$
    $\mathcal{P} = \mathcal{P} \cup t$
  end while
  $c = \texttt{duelCultural}(\mathcal{P})$
  $s.\mathcal{G} = c.\mathcal{G}$
else if $s > l$ **then**
  if $s.nonDominated = true$ **then**
    $l.\mathcal{G} = \texttt{mutate}(s.\mathcal{G})$
  end if
  $s.\mathcal{E} = s.\mathcal{E} + l.\mathcal{E}$
  $s.\mathcal{E} = 0$
else if $(l.C = \emptyset \wedge s.C \neq \emptyset) \vee (\overline{l.C} < \overline{s.C} \wedge \overline{l.C} > 0)$ **then**
  $s.\mathcal{G} = \texttt{mutate}(l.\mathcal{G})$
  $l.\mathcal{E} = l.\mathcal{E} + 0.4 \cdot s.\mathcal{E}$
  $s.\mathcal{E} = 0.6 \cdot s.\mathcal{E}$
else if $(l.C \neq \emptyset \wedge s.C = \emptyset) \vee (\overline{l.C} > \overline{s.C} \wedge \overline{s.C} > 0)$ **then**
  if $s.nonDominated = true$ **then**
    $l.\mathcal{G} = \texttt{mutate}(s.\mathcal{G})$
  end if
  $s.\mathcal{E} = s.\mathcal{E} + l.\mathcal{E}$
  $s.\mathcal{E} = 0$
end if

solution (in the case of multi-objective optimization it is of course true Pareto frontier). On the other hand, researchers, during the process of algorithm development should keep in mind also its effectiveness per computational step. Because of its significance for the *Decision Maker* in this chapter time aspects and comparisons will be presented. It is important to notice in this place that all experiments have been performed with the use of one single hardware and software environment and if it was only possible with the same value of particular parameters. There is also one more important disclaimer that has to be underlined here. The goal of this chapter is to present, for the first time, the general idea of introducing both: immune and cultural mechanisms into EMAS with explanation of shortcomings of applying simple EMAS for solving MOOPs and it is not the goal of this chapter to present detailed and deep experimental analysis and comparisons. Therefore, in this section only general—it can be said: from bird's eye view—results are presented. Detailed discussion of obtained results not only for ZDT but also for CTP and DTLZ test suites, values of particular parameters and their influence on the behavior of proposed *ic*-EMAS are presented and discussed in (Goik et al., 2007).

4.1 Test suite, performance metric, state-of-the-art algorithms and noise

As it was mentioned, in the course of this chapter there are presented only selected, general results obtained during solving the Zitzler-Deb-Thiele test suite which in the literature is known and identified as the set of test problems ZDT1-ZDT6 ((Zitzler, 1999, p. 57–63), (Zitzler et al., 2000), (Deb, 2001, p. 356–362), (Coello et al., 2007, p. 194–199)).

Two main distinguishing features of high-quality solution of MOOPs are: closeness to the true Pareto frontier as well as dispersion of found non-dominated solution over the whole (approximation) of the Pareto frontier (see fig. 2).

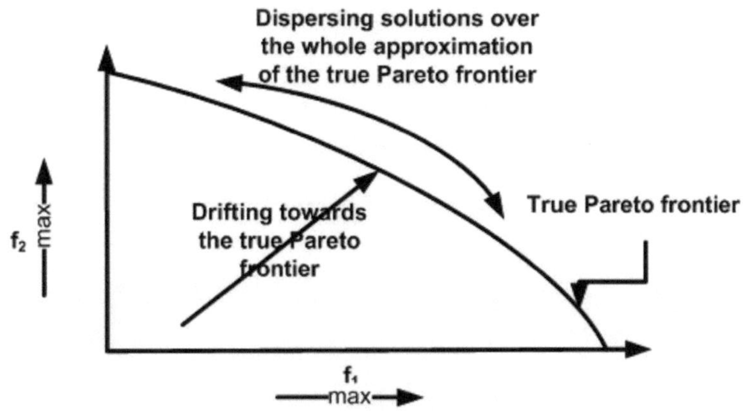

Fig. 2. Two goals of multi-objective optimization

In the consequence, despite that using only one single measure during assessing the effectiveness of (evolutionary) algorithms for multi-objective optimization is not enough (Zitzler et al., 2003), since Hypervolume Ratio measure (HVR) (Zitzler & Thiele, 1998) allows for estimating both of these aspects—in this chapter discussion and presentation of obtained results is based on this very measure.

Hypervolume or Hypervolume ratio (HVR), describes the area covered by solutions of obtained result set. For each solution, hypercube is evaluated with respect to the fixed reference point. In order to evaluate hypervolume ratio, value of hypervolume for obtained set is normalized with hypervolume value computed for true Pareto frontier. HV and HVR are defined as follows:

$$\mathrm{HV} = v\left(\bigcup_{i=1}^{N} v_i\right) \quad \mathrm{HVR} = \frac{\mathrm{HV}(PF^*)}{\mathrm{HV}(PF)} \tag{1a}$$

where v_i is hypercube computed for i - th solution, PF^* represents obtained Pareto frontier and PF is the true Pareto frontier.

To assess (in a quantitative way) proposed *ic*-EMAS, the comparison with results obtained with the use of state-of-the-art algorithms has to be made. That is why we are comparing results obtained by *ic*-EMAS with results obtained by NSGA-II (Deb et al., 2002) and SPEA2 (Zitzler & Thiele, 1999) algorithms since these very algorithms are the most efficient and most commonly used evolutionary multi-objective optimization algorithms.

When one considers applying proposed optimization method for solving real-life problems its effectiveness in noisy environment has to be considered and assessed since in real-life problems noise can not be avoided.

To assess the behavior of algorithm solving multi-objective optimization problem(s)—several forms of noise can be considered and introduced (in order to simulate real situations). So, the noise can be considered at the level of objective function evaluation, as well as at the level of decision variables and finally the noise can be introduced as the—so called— environmental noise (Bui et al., 2004; Miller, 1997; Siwik et al., 2008).

Since several forms of noise can be considered—to omit such considerations as: how strong and how often repeating noise at the level of decision variables results in noise at the level of objective function evaluation (especially that it depends on the particular problem that is being solved)—in this chapter authors focus on objective function evaluation noise (see Algorithm 3).

Such kind of noise simulation directly affects fitness value, and directly influences the quality of obtained result set, and allows in the consequence for direct observation of algorithm's ability for coping with noise occurrences.

Algorithm 3. Noising algorithm

if Agent *A* dominates Agent *B* **then**
  Assume that Agent *B* dominates Agent *A* with the probability of NoiseRisk parameter
end if
if Agent *B* dominates Agent *A* **then**
  Assume that Agent *A* dominates Agent *B* with the probability of NoiseRisk parameter
end if
if Agents *A* and *B* are mutually non-dominated **then**
  the result of assessing the relation of domination is not affected
end if

4.2 A glance at obtained results

In figures fig. 3 and fig. 4 there are presented results obtained by NSGA-II, SPEA2, *ic*- EMAS and EMAS approaches solving ZDT1 to ZDT6 problems in environment with no occurrence of noise.

As one may see, on all five diagrams from fig. 3 and fig. 4 presenting values of HVR metric for ZDT problems—introducing into EMAS, discussed in this chapter cultural and immunological mechanisms significantly positively influence evolutionary agent-based systems, however in the comparison to state-of-the-art algorithms (SPEA2 and NSGA-II) it can not be said that *ic*-EMAS is better alternative—since in the case of ZDT4 problem (see fig.4a) it is better than classical algorithms but in the case of ZDT6 (see fig.4b) it is worse and in the case of ZDT1, ZDT2 and ZDT3 problems (see fig.3abc) it allows for obtaining only as valuable results as mentioned well-known referencing algorithms.

The situation is completely different when experiments are conducted in noisy environment. In fig. 5 and fig. 6 there are presented results obtained by *ic*-EMAS as well as by NSGA-II and SPEA2 algorithms during solving ZDT1–ZDT6 problems with the simulation of noisy environment with the probability of the occurrence of noise equal to 20%. As one may see, only in the case of ZDT1 problem all three approaches allow for obtaining similar results

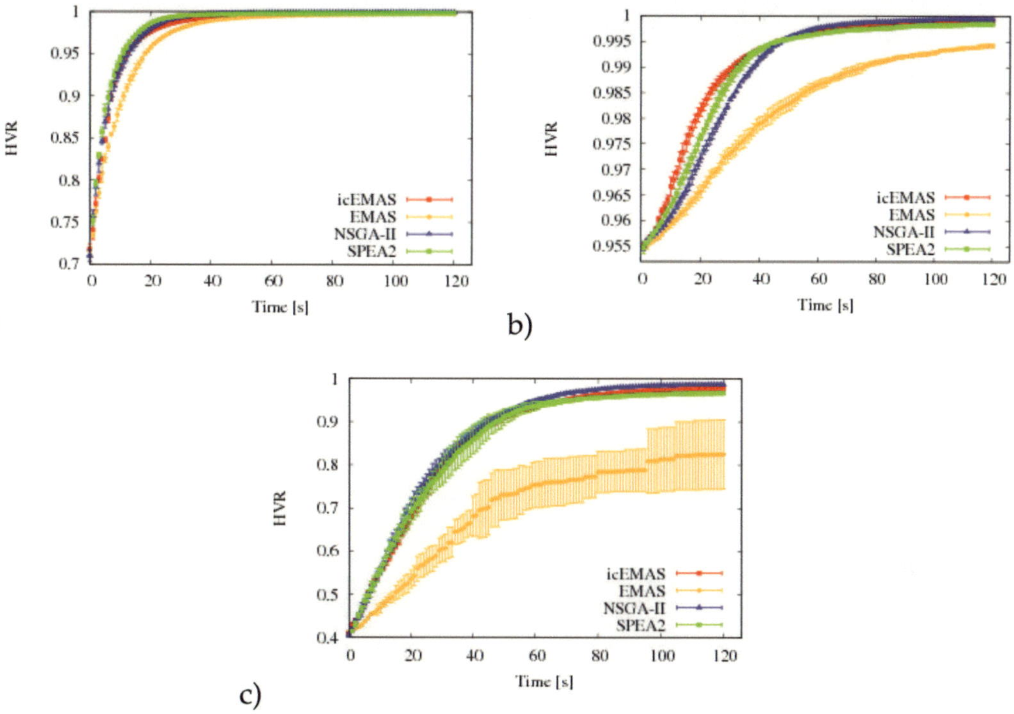

Fig. 3. HVR values obtained solving ZDT1 (a), ZDT2 (b) and ZDT3 (c) in environment without noise

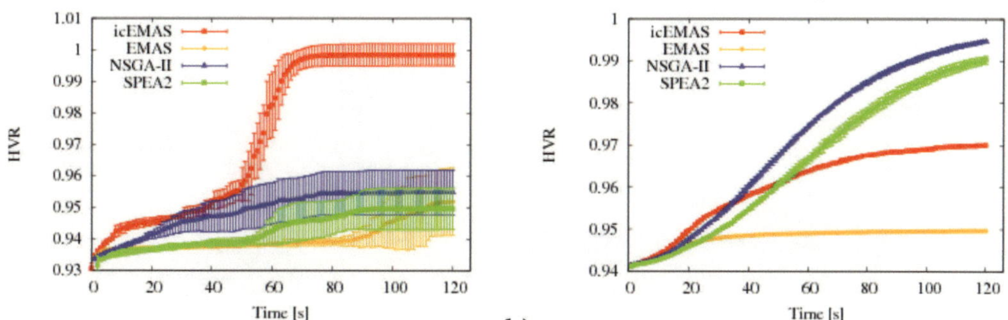

Fig. 4. HVR values obtained solving ZDT4 (a) and ZDT6 (b) problems in environment without noise

(see fig. 5a) whereas in the case of ZDT2, ZDT3, ZDT4 and ZDT6 problems (see fig. 5bc and fig. 6ab)—proposed in this chapter immune-cultural Evolutionary Multi-Agent Systems is definitely the best alternative. In fig. 7 there are presented visualizations of Pareto frontiers' approximations obtained by *ic*-EMAS, NSGA-II and SPEA2 algorithms in noisy environment after 15 (a), 30 (b), 60 (c) and 120 (d) seconds solving ZDT3 problem. It is obviously coherent with the values of HVR measure presented in figures 5 and 6 and confirms that in noisy environment *ic*-EMAS is better alternative than state-of-the-art NSGA-II and SPEA2 algorithms.

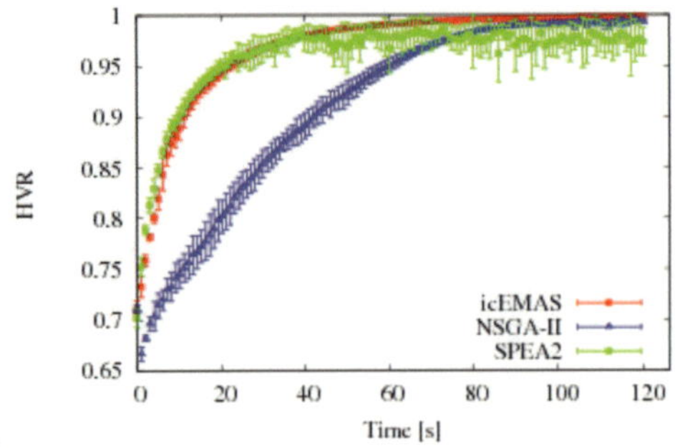

a)

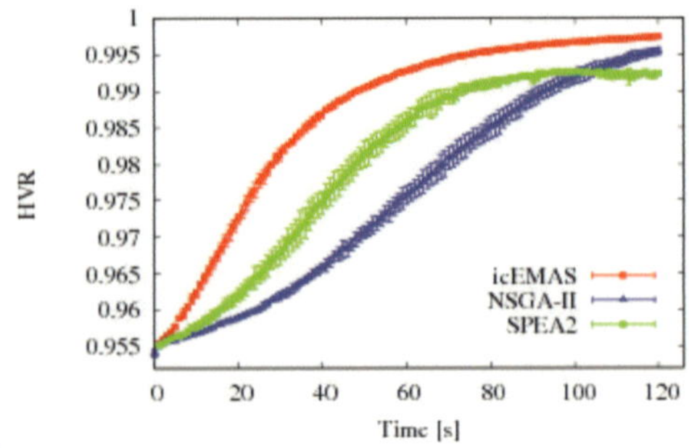

b)

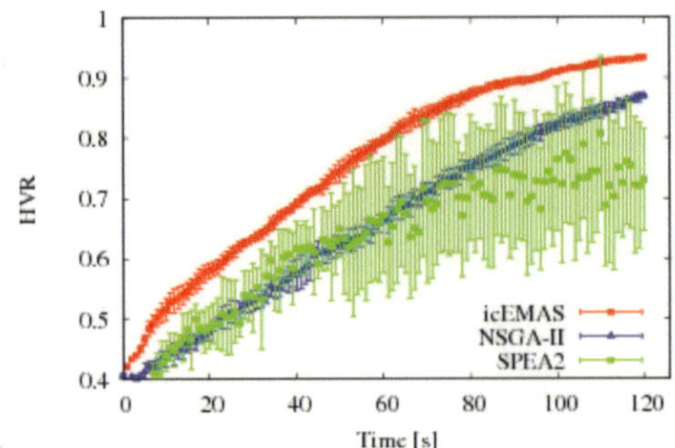

c)

Fig. 5. HVR values obtained solving ZDT1 (a), ZDT2 (b) and ZDT3 (c) problems in noisy environment with the probability of noise occurrence equal to 20%

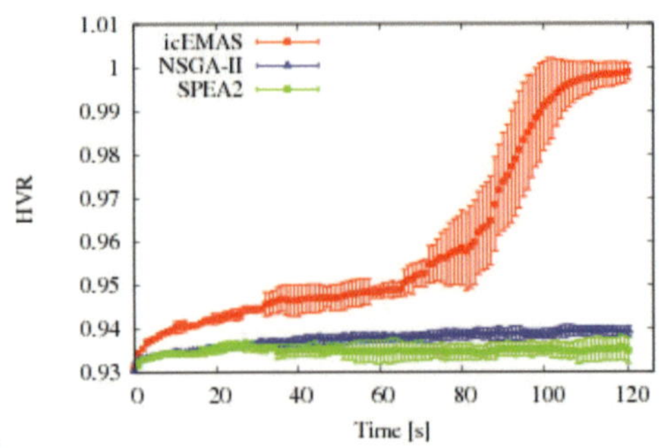

a)

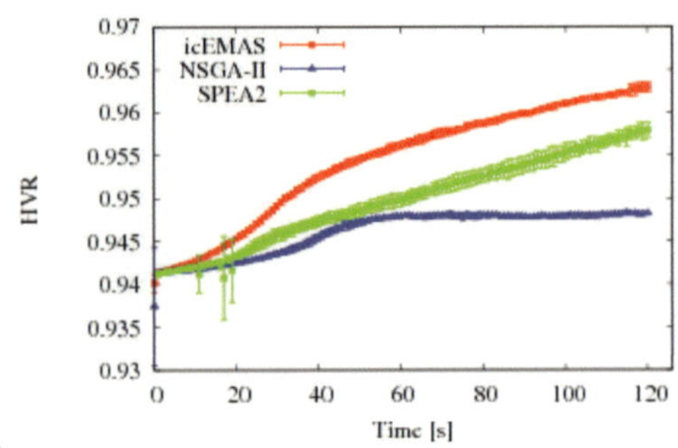

b)

Fig. 6. HVR values obtained solving ZDT4 (a) and ZDT6 (b) problems in noisy environment with the probability of noise occurrence equal to 20%

5. Conclusions

To recapitulate considerations presented in the course of this chapter, it is worth to say, that:

- in this chapter, for the first time, the general idea of realization of cultural and immune mechanisms in decentralized way within the confines of EMAS model is presented;
- EMAS model turns out to be so flexible that introducing considered mechanisms was possible, moreover, as it was discussed, it can be done in elegant, smooth and fully consistent with distributed, autonomous and decentralized agent-oriented way;

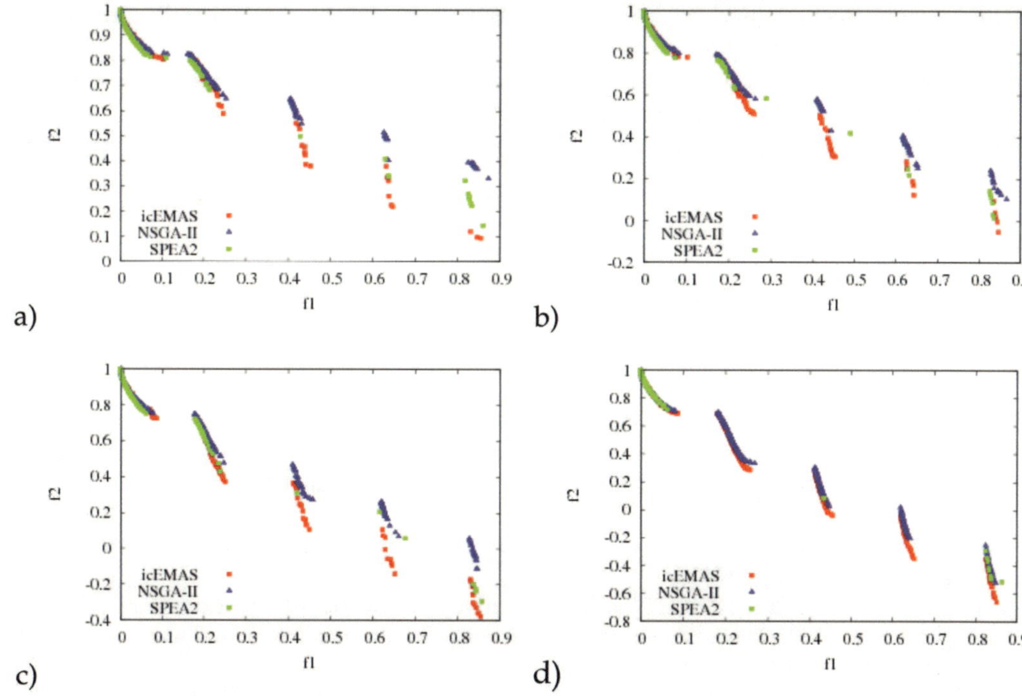

Fig. 7. Approximation of Pareto frontiers obtained by *ic*-EMAS, NSGA-II and SPEA2 in noisy environment after 15 (a), 30 (b), 60 (c) and 120 (d) seconds solving ZDT3 problem

- introduced cultural and immune mechanisms significantly improved the effectiveness of simple EMAS taking the quality of obtained approximations of the Pareto frontier into account as well as time needed for obtaining such high-quality results;
- as it was stated in section 2, there are two shortcomings when applying simple EMAS for solving MOOPs i.e. stagnation and lack of mechanisms responsible for dispersing individuals over the whole approximation of the Pareto frontiers. Proposed in this chapter immune mechanisms address the first problem whereas cultural mechanisms address the second one;
- in the consequence, in the function of time, *ic*-EMAS i.e. presented in this chapter realization of immune-cultural Evolutionary Multi-Agent System allows for obtaining as high quality results as it is possible with the use of state-of-the-art algorithms like NSGA-II and SPEA2;
- what is more, in noisy environment *ic*-EMAS turns out to be even significantly more effective than mentioned state-of-the-art EMOAs;
- significant superiority of *ic*-EMAS over NSGA-II and SPEA2 comes from the phenomenon that can be called *soft* selection. Even, if in a given step strong agent (individual) because of the noise turns out to be dominated—the only consequence is the lost (the part) of its energy. But still—on the contrary to classical algorithms where in such a situation individual is usually removed from the population – it can operate in the environment and during the next meeting(s) with another agents, when only the noise disappears it dominates another agents, so it gains energy and it can reproduce etc. etc. So, to recapitulate in a *soft* model of selection represented by evolutionary

multi-agent systems (and by *ic*-EMAS in particular)—temporary noise does not cause losing strong/promising (often non dominated in fact) individuals;

- because proposed immune-cultural agent-based approach seems to be very promising one, further research on hybridization of EMAS and cultural and immune systems will be conducted with special attention to real-life optimization and decision-supporting applications.

6. References

Becerra, R. & Coello, C. (2006). Solving hard multiobjective optimization problems using econstraint with cultured differential evolution, In: *Parallel Problem Solving from Nature - PPSN IX, 9th International Conference,* Vol. 4193 of *LNCS,* Reykjavik, Iceland, pp. 543–552

Bui, L. T., Essam, D., Abbas, H. A. & Green, D. (2004). Performance analysis of evolutionary multi-objective optimization methods in noisy environments, In: *8th Asia Pacific Symposium on Intelligent and Evolutionary Systems,* Monash University, Melbourne, Australia

Castro, L. & Timmis, J. (2002). Artificial immune systems: a new computational intelligence approach, Spronger-Verlag

Castro, L. & von Zuben, F. (2002). Learning and optimization using the clonal selection principle, *IEEE Transactions on Evolutionary Computation, Special Issue on Artificial Immune Systems* 6(3), 239–251

Cetnarowicz, K., Kisiel-Dorohinicki, M. & Nawarecki, E. (1996). The application of evolution process in multi-agent world (MAW) to the prediction system, In: M. Tokoro, (Ed.), *Proc. of the 2nd Int. Conf. on Multi-Agent Systems (ICMAS 96),* AAAI Press

Coello, C. & Becerra, R. (2003). Evolutionary multiobjective optimization using a cultural algorithm, In: *IEEE Swarm Intelligence Symposium Proceedings,* IEEE Service Center, Indianapolis, Indiana, USA, pp. 6–13

Coello, C., Lamont, G. & Van Veldhuizen, D. (2007). *Evolutionary Algorithms for Solving Multi-Objective Problems,* second edn, Springer, New York. ISBN 978-0-387-33254-3

Coello, C. & Nareli, C. (2005). Solving multiobjective optimization problems using an artificial immune system, *Genetic Programming and Evolvable Machines* 6(2), 163–190

Dasgupta, D. (1999). Artificial Immune Systems and Their Applications, Springer-Verlag

Deb, K. (2001). Multi-Objective Optimization using Evolutionary Algorithms, John Wiley & Sons

Deb, K., Pratap, A., Agarwal, S. & Meyarivan, T. (2002). A Fast and Elitist Multiobjective Genetic Algorithm: NSGA-II, *IEEE Transactions on Evolutionary Computation* 6(2), 182–197

Dobrowolski, G. & Kisiel-Dorohinicki, M. (2002). Management of evolutionary mas for multiobjective optimisation, In: T. Burczynski & A. Osyczka, (Ed.), *Proceedings of symposium on Evolutionary methods in mechanics,* Kluwer Academic Publishers, Cracow, pp. 81–90

Dreżewski, R. (2003). A model of co-evolution in multi-agent system, In: V. Mařík, J. Müller & M. Pěchouček, (Ed.), *Multi-Agent Systems and Applications III,* Vol. 2691 of *LNCS,* Springer-Verlag, Berlin, Heidelberg, pp. 314–323

Dreżewski, R. & Cetnarowicz, K. (2007). Sexual selection mechanism for agent-based evolutionary computation, In: Y. Shi, G. D. van Albada, J. Dongarra & P. M. A. Sloot, (Ed.), *Computational Science – ICCS 2007,* Vol. 4488 of *LNCS,* Springer-Verlag, Berlin, Heidelberg, pp. 920–927

Dreżewski, R., Sepielak, J. & Siwik, L. (2009). Classical and agent-based evolutionary algorithms for investment strategies generation, In: A. Brabazon & M. O Neill, (Ed.), *Computational Intelligence in Finance*, Vol. 2, Springer-Verlag, Berlin, Heidelberg

Dreżewski, R. & Siwik, L. (2006*a*). Co-evolutionary multi-agent system with sexual selection mechanism for multi-objective optimization, In: *Proceedings of the IEEE World Congress on Computational Intelligence (WCCI 2006)*, IEEE

Dreżewski, R. & Siwik, L. (2006*b*). Multi-objective optimization using co-evolutionary multiagent system with host-parasite mechanism, In: V. N. Alexandrov, G. D. van Albada, P. M. A. Sloot & J. Dongarra, (Ed.), *Computational Science – ICCS 2006*, Vol. 3993 of *LNCS*, Springer-Verlag, Berlin, Heidelberg, pp. 871–878

Dreżewski, R. & Siwik, L. (2007*a*). The application of agent-based co-evolutionary system with predator-prey interactions to solving multi-objective optimization problems, In: *Proceedings of the 2007 IEEE Symposium Series on Computational Intelligence*, IEEE

Dreżewski, R. & Siwik, L. (2007*b*). Co-evolutionary multi-agent system with predator-prey mechanism for multi-objective optimization, In: B. Beliczynski, A. Dzielinski, M. Iwanowski & B. Ribeiro, (Ed.), *Adaptive and Natural Computing Algorithms*, Vol. 4431 of *LNCS*, Springer-Verlag, Berlin, Heidelberg, pp. 67–76

Dreżewski, R. & Siwik, L. (2008a). Agent-based multi-objective evolutionary algorithm with sexual selection, In: Proceedings of 2008 IEEEWorld Congress on Computational Intelligence (WCCI 2008), 2008 IEEE Congress on Evolutionary Computation (CEC 2008), number IEEE Catalog Number: CFP08ICE-CDR, ISBN: 978-1-4244-1823-7, IEEE, Research Publishing Services, Hong Kong, pp. 3680–3685

Dreżewski, R. & Siwik, L. (2008*b*). Co-evolutionary multi-agent system for portfolio optimization, In: A. Brabazon & M. O Neill, (Ed.), *Natural Computation in Computational Finance*, Vol. 1, Springer-Verlag, Berlin, Heidelberg, pp. 271–299

Forrest, S. & Hofmeyr, S. (2000). *Design principles for the immune system and other distributed autonomous systems*, Oxford University Press, chapter Immunology as information processing, pp. 361–387

Frank, S. (1996). The Design of Natural and Artificial Adaptive Systems, Academic Press: New York

Goik, P., Siwik, L. & Kisiel-Dorohinicki, M. (2007). Applying of immune and cultural algorithms for solving multiobjective optimization problems, Internal report 9/07, Department of computer Science, University of Science and Technology, Krakow, Poland

Hunt, J. & Cooke, D. (1995). An adaptive, distributed learning systems based on the immune system, In: *Proceedings of the IEEE International Conference on Systems, Man and Cybernatics*, pp. 2494–2499

Jin, X. & Reynolds, R. (2000). Mining knowledge in large-scale databases using cultural algorithms with constraint handling mechanisms, In: *Congress on Evolutionary Computation*, IEEE Service Center., New Jersey

Jin, X. & Reynolds, R. (n.d.). Using knowledge-based evolutionary computation to solve nonlinear constraint optimization problems: a cultural algorithm approach, In: *Congress on Evolutionary Computation*, IEEE Service Center, pp. 1672–1678

Kisiel-Dorohinicki, M. (2004). Flock-based architecture for distributed evolutionary algorithms, In: L. Rutkowski, J. Siekmann, R. Tedeusiewicz & L. Zadeh, (Ed.), *Artificial Intelligence and Soft Computing – ICAISC 2004*, Vol. 3070 of *Lecture Notes in Artificial Intelligence*, Springer-Verlag

Miller, B. L. (1997). Noise, Sampling, and efficient genetic Algorithms, PhD thesis, University of Illinois at Urbana-Champaign, Urbana, IL. IllIGAL Report No. 97001

Reynolds, R. (1994). An introduction to cultural algorithms, In: *Proceedings of the Annual Conference on Evolutionary Programming*, World Scienfific Publishing

Siwik, L. & Kisiel-Dorohinicki, M. (2005). Elitism in agent-based evolutionary multiobjective optimization, *Inteligencia Artificial* 9(28). Special issue: New trends on Multiagent systems and soft computing

Siwik, L. & Kisiel-Dorohinicki, M. (2006). Semi-elitist evolutionary multi-agent system for multiobjective optimization, In: V. N. Alexandrov, G. D. van Albada, P. M. A.

Sloot & J. Dongarra, (Ed.), *Computational Science – ICCS 2006*, Vol. 3993 of *LNCS*, Springer-Verlag, Reading,UK, pp. 831–838

Siwik, L. & Natanek, S. (2008*a*). Elitist evolutionary multi-agent system in solving noisy multiobjective optimization problems, In: *Proceedings of 2008 IEEE World Congress on Computational Intelligence (WCCI 2008), 2008 IEEE Congress on Evolutionary Computation (CEC 2008)*, number IEEE Catalog Number: CFP08ICE-CDR, ISBN: 978-1- 4244-1823-7, IEEE, Research Publishing Services, Hong Kong, pp. 3318–3325

Siwik, L. & Natanek, S. (2008*b*). Solving constrained multi-criteria optimization tasks using elitist evolutionary multi-agent system, In: *Proceedings of 2008 IEEEWorld Congress on Computational Intelligence (WCCI 2008), 2008 IEEE Congress on Evolutionary Computation (CEC 2008)*, number IEEE Catalog Number: CFP08ICE-CDR, ISBN: 978- 1-4244-1823-7, IEEE, Research Publishing Services, Hong Kong, pp. 3357–3364

Siwik, L., Psiuk, M. & Sroka, P. (2008). Flock-based evolutionary multi-agent system in solving noisy multi-objective optimization problems, In: *Proceedings of 2008 IEEE World Congress on Computational Intelligence (WCCI 2008), 2008 IEEE Congress on Evolutionary Computation (CEC 2008)*, number IEEE Catalog Number: CFP08ICECDR, ISBN: 978-1-4244-1823-7, IEEE, Research Publishing Services, Hong Kong, pp. 3403–3411

Siwik, L. & Sikorski, P. (2008). Efficient constrained evolutionary multi-agent system for multi-objective optimization, In: Proceedings of 2008 IEEE World Congress on Computational Intelligence (WCCI 2008), 2008 IEEE Congress on Evolutionary Computation (CEC 2008), number IEEE Catalog Number: CFP08ICE-CDR, ISBN: 978-1-4244- 1823-7, IEEE, Research Publishing Services, Hong Kong, pp. 3211–3218

Socha, K. & Kisiel-Dorohinicki, M. (2002). Agent-based evolutionary multiobjective optimisation, In: *Proc. of the 2002 Congress on Evolutionary Computation*, IEEE

Wierzchon, S. T. (2001). Artificial immune systems theory and applications, EXIT

Zitzler, E. (1999). Evolutionary Algorithms for Multiobjective Optimization: Methods and Applications, PhD thesis, ETH Zurich, Switzerland

Zitzler, E., Deb, K. & Thiele, L. (2000). Comparison of Multiobjective Evolutionary Algorithms: Empirical Results, *Evolutionary Computation* 8(2), 173–195

Zitzler, E. & Thiele, L. (1998). An evolutionary algorithm for multiobjective optimization: The strength pareto approach, Technical Report 43, Swiss Federal Institute of Technology, Zurich, Gloriastrasse 35, CH-8092 Zurich, Switzerland

Zitzler, E. & Thiele, L. (1999). Multiobjective Evolutionary Algorithms: A Comparative Case Study and the Strength Pareto Approach, *IEEE Transactions on Evolutionary Computation* 3(4), 257–271

Zitzler, E., Thiele, L., Laumanns, M., Fonseca, C. & da Fonseca, V. (2003). Performance assessment of multiobjective optimizers: An analysis and review, *IEEE Transactions on Evolutionary Computation* 7(2), 117–132

30

Mobile Robot Navigation using Alpha Level Fuzzy Logic System: Experimental Investigations

S.Parasuraman[1], Bijan Shirinzadeh[2] and Velappa Ganapathy[1]
[1]Monash University
[2]Monash University
[1]Malaysia
[2]Australia

1. Introduction

The interest in investigating and developing mobile robots is very largely motivated by a need and a desire to have robots that can work with and for people in their normal work. The field of the autonomous mobile robot is a fascinating research topic for many reasons. In this research, some problems associated with mobile robot navigation are identified and described, and the new methodologies are established and verified with real world experiments. The problem description and importance are given in section 2. Numerous behavior rule selection and/or behavior coordination mechanisms can be found in the earlier literatures. Saffiotti A, and Leblanc K (2000) suggest dividing action selection mechanisms into two groups that he calls arbitration and command fusion which correspond to [Mackenzie D.C, Arkin R.C, and Cameron J.M (1997)] state-based and continuous classes respectively. Arbitration or state-based mechanisms are suitable in situations where only a relevant subset of the robot's behavior repertoire needs to be activated in a given state.
Behavior arbitration schemes [Pattie Maes (1991)] emphasized the testing of hypotheses of behavior rather than solving real-life tasks. Konolige, et al [Kurt Konolige, Karen Meyers, and Alessandro Saffiotti (1992),] used fuzzy control in conjunction with modeling and planning techniques to provide reactive guidance of their robot. Computer simulations [Song K.Y. and Tai J. C (1992)] feature a mobile robot that navigates using a planned path based on fuzzy logic. Song et.al.[Pin F.G(1992)] presented a scheme for independent control of two drive wheels on their simulated robot. When an obstacle is detected by one of the robot's proximity sensors, the fuzzy controller increases the speed of the respective wheel to turn away from it. Another approach [Arbib M. A (1992)] is more strongly motivated by the biological sciences which appeared on the heels of the subsumption architecture. Arkin [Arkin R. C (1989)] addressed the implications of schema theory for autonomous robotics [Arkin R. C. and D. Mackenzie (1994)]. A neural network [Petru Rusu, Thom E. Whalen, Aurel Cornell and HansJ.W Spoelder (2003)], [C.T. Lin and C.S.G. Lee (1991)] relies on training to relate inputs to outputs. Although observing the weights gives us an idea about the input –output relations, the governing rules cannot be explicitly stated.

The shortcomings of the above approaches are explored and resolved using the proposed approach named as the Alpha Level Fuzzy Logic System (ALFLS).

2. Important

The problems identified for the mobile robot navigation are (i) Behavior rule selection without rule conflict while more than one rule receives equal activation strength as the robot encountered multiple obstacles in the environment and (ii) Finding a near optimal path for the robot to reach the target from the starting point.

In the application of mobile robot navigation in real life situations such as explorations, searching for objects, sign of life in the event of accident and/or natural disasters, etc., the robot is required to navigate and reach the target in the quickest possible time using the shortest path. The capability of AI based control techniques can be used to achieve these types of navigation task. In the fuzzy logic based mobile robot navigation techniques as stated in the literatures in section 1, the input and output fuzzy sets are scaled to larger intervals. As a result of this, the robot deviates from the encountered obstacles much earlier before reaching the obstacles. Due to these situations, the deviations between the robot and the obstacles are quite large. Therefore, the robot takes more time and longer distance to reach the given target position during robot navigation. Also, as the interval of fuzzy set becomes larger, the possibilities of behaviour conflict situations are more. In order to resolve these issues, the proposed methodology ALFLS has been established.

In the proposed method, the environmental perceptual field is well defined by a set of control parameters through alpha level intervals of fuzzy sets. Similarly, the expected control output parameters are partitioned by alpha level intervals. An alpha level threshold is set at each critical fuzzy set and this maximizes the truth value for a particular behavior rule that needs to be fired at a time. In ALFLS, an alpha level makes all the truth membership functions between the threshold intervals to be true and the remaining values to be zero. When an alpha level threshold is applied to the truth of a rule's predicate, it determines whether or not the truth is sufficient to fire the rule. The effectiveness of ALFLS has been demonstrated through experimental studies using Khepera II Robots.

The effectiveness of the proposed ALFLS is demonstrated through experimental results and analysis and has shown the improved performance as compared with the previous methods in the aspect of (i) the time taken for the robot to reach the given target, (ii) the distance traveled to reach the given target position and (iii) resolving behavior rule conflicts in situations, where the obstacles appear with equal preferences in the environment.

As the outcome of the research, a new deterministic methodology was established and implemented. A comprehensive mathematical framework of decision-making procedure incorporating alpha-level fuzzy logic was established and discussed. The performance of ALFLS was demonstrated using the navigation rules which are obtained by varying the fuzzy intervals such as 3-alpha interval and 2-alpha interval. The comparative results have showed that the 3-alpha interval method has significantly improved the performance with respect to the issues highlighted as objectives.

3. Theoretical work

The behavior rule conflict situation is illustrated in Figure 1. In this illustration, the environment consists of several obstacles which are represented in a fuzzy scale called Small

(S), Medium (M) and Big (B) with the measure of (0-2 meters), (2-3.5 meters) and (3.5 -5.0 meters) respectively. In the above environment, there are two obstacles appear in Small fuzzy set (0 to 2 meters) at two different distance ranges as detected by front sensors S3 and S4. Similarly another two obstacles appear in the Medium fuzzy set. In these situations the active navigation rules are presented as below.

If S3 Small and S4 Medium Then Z SN (1)
If S3 Small and S4 Big Then Z SN (1)
If S3 Medium and S4 Medium Then Z Zero (1)
If S3 Small and S4 Small Then Z MP (1)

The activation strength of each rule appears as '1'at a particular instant. In this situation, a particular rule needs to be activated. This type of situation is resolved by defining each of the input fuzzy set into alpha-intervals and the limits are established. The corresponding output membership grade is estimated as a truth membership value and referred to as alpha or truth-value.

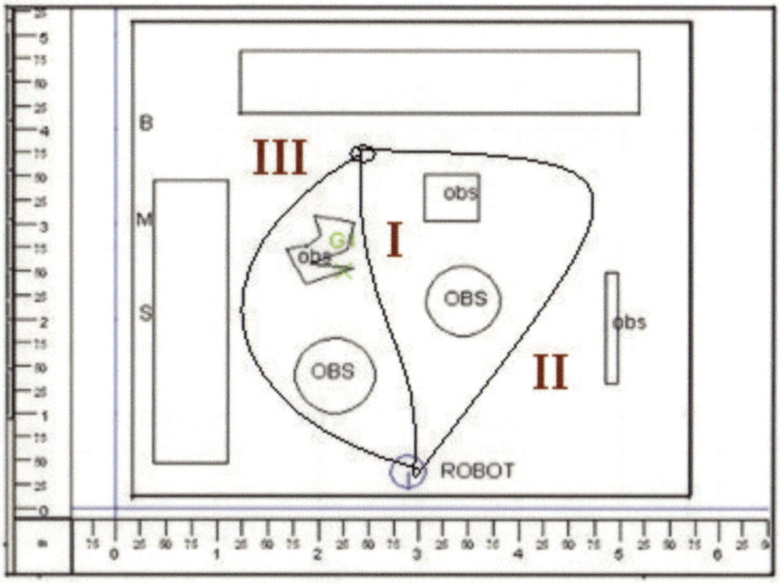

I -Near optimal path, II and III - Wide path, OBS and obs- obstacles, S-Small set, M-Medium set and B-Big set.

Fig. 1. Environment with multiple Obstacles showing the Conflict Situations.

When an alpha threshold is applied to the truth of a rule's predicate, it determines whether or not the truth is sufficient to fire the rule. And as a result of single behavior rule activation in the above context, the navigation path must be optimized with minimum deviation from obstacles. When there are no behavior conflicts, the formulation established using fuzzy logic approach [S.Parasuraman, V.Ganapathy, Bijan Shirinzadeh, (2006)] is good enough to navigate in the complex environment. The following section presents the mathematical formulation of ALFLS. The output membership of the navigation system consists of output of normal and behavior conflicting environmental context. The control system chooses the output membership function between the above two contexts based on the maximization of the truth-values. Based on Table 1, the possible rule activations of the present illustration as given in Figure 1 is expressed mathematically and given in Table 2. In this table only two input X1 and input X2 (front sensor data (S1 and S2)) are considered, which are used to detect obstacles that appear in the front region of the robot as illustrated in Figure 1.

C Output	$X_{1,2}$	....	$X_{j,2}$	$X_{1,j+1}$	.....	$X_{m,2}$
$X_{1,1}$	$C_{1,1}$		$C_{j,1}$	$C_{1,j+1}$	.....	$C_{1,m}$
....	.....		.....	.....	.....	.....
$X_{i,1}$	$C_{i,1}$		$C_{i,j}$	$C_{1,j+1}$	.....	$C_{1,m}$
$X_{i+1,1}$	$C_{i+1,1}$		$C_{i+1,j}$	$C_{i+1,j+1}$	.....	$C_{i+1,m}$
....	....		....	....	.....	....
$X_{n,1}$	$C_{n,1}$		$C_{n,j}$	$C_{n,j+1}$	.....	$C_{n,m}$

Table 1. Decision Table: if and then Rules.

$X_{1,1}$, $X_{1,2}$, ……$X_{n,1}$, $X_{m,2}$ are fuzzy inputs and $C_{1,1}$ $C_{i,1}$, $C_{j,1}$, ….. $C_{n,m}$ are corresponding fuzzy outputs.

Considering the fuzzy set of the above two sensors, the possible behavior rule sets are shown in the Table.2.

Inputs	Sensor X2 (S2)			
Sensor X1 (S1)	Membership/Output	Small(s)	Medium(M)	Big (B)
	Small (S)	0	SP	SP
	Medium (M)	SN	Z	Z
	Big (B)	SN	Z	Z

Table 2. If and Then rule

MP: Medium Positive, SP: Small Positive, SN: Small Negative, Z: Zero, SN, Z, MP: conflicting rules

The behavior rules shown by row-column (2,10,(2,1),(2,2) and (1,3) cells are conflict rules as discussed in the illustration. The measurement values of input parameters X1 and X2 obtained from the sensors S1 and S2 have to be translated to the corresponding linguistic variables. Normally any reading has a crisp value, which has to be matched against the appropriate membership function representing the linguistic variable. The matching is necessary because of the overlapping of terms as shown in Figures 2 (a) and (b), and this matching is called, coding the inputs or fuzzification.

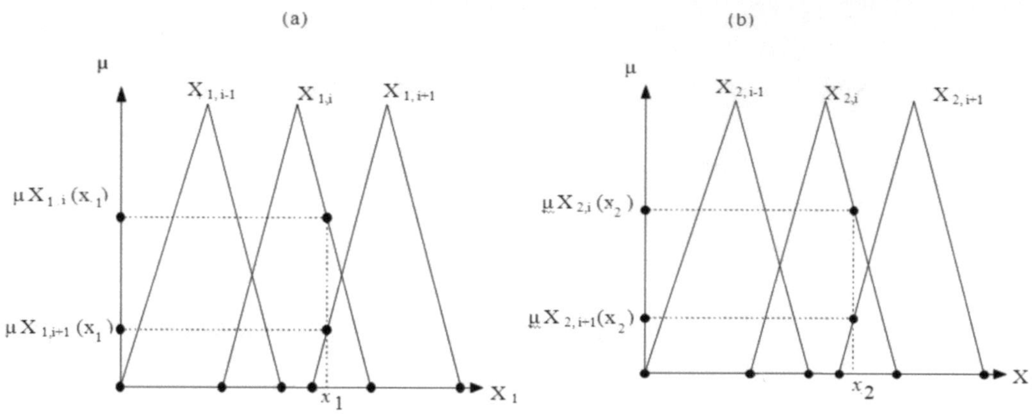

Fig. 2. Crisp values from Fuzzy sets corresponding to the fuzzy inputs x1 (a) and x2 (b)

In Figure 2, the sensor input x1 ∊ U1, $\alpha_i \leq x_1 \leq \alpha_{i+1}$ that corresponds to two values μX1, i (x1) and μX1, i+1 (x1) of the input X1. where α is the interval of the fuzzy set X1, i and X1, i+1. They can be interpreted as the truth-values of x1 related to fuzzy set Xi and to Xi+1, correspondingly. In the same way the fuzzy inputs are obtained corresponding to the reading x2 ∊ U2 and $\alpha_i^{'} \leq x_2 \leq \alpha_{i+1}^{'}$. In both the Figures, only a few terms of the fuzzy set X1 and X2 are presented. The straight line passing through xo parallel to $\mu \in [0,1]$ intersect only the terms X1i and X1i+1 of X1 thus reducing the fuzzy terms to crisp values denoted as shown below.

$$X_{1,i}(x_1) = \{\mu_{X1,i}(x_1), \mu_{X1,i+1}(x_1)\} \tag{1a}$$

Similarly the line passing through x2 intersects only the terms X2i and X2i+1 of X2 giving the crisp values as shown below:

$$X_{2,i}(x_2) = \{\mu_{X2,i}(x_2), \mu_{X2,i+1}(x_2)\} \tag{1b}$$

The active rules shown in the Table 2 are redefined and are shown in Table 3 as a generalized formulation to resolve the conflicting behavior rule selection. Four cells in Table 3 contain nonzero terms. These cells are called active cells. Table 3 shows only four rules that are active as illustrated in the present example shown in Figure 1. The rest of the rules will not produce any output.

Inputs	Sensor X2 (S3)			
Sensor X1 (S4)	Membership/Output	$\mu(X_{2,j-1}(x_2))$	$\mu(X_{2,j}(x_2))$	$\mu(X_{2,j+1}(x_2))$
	$\mu(X_{1,i-1}(x_1))$	0	0	0
	$\mu(X_{1,i}(x_1))$	$\mu(C_{i,j}(Z))$	$\mu(C_{i,j+1}(Z))$	0
	$\mu(X_{1,i+1}(x_1))$	$\mu(C_{i+1,j}(Z))$	$\mu(C_{i+1,j+1}(Z))$	0

Table 3. Decision table with active cell.

where $\mu(_{Ci,j}(Z))$, $\mu(_{Ci,j+1}(Z))$, $\mu(_{Ci+1,j}(Z))$, $\mu(_{Ci+1,j+1}(Z))$ are conflicting outputs. The conflict rules as illustrated in the example are presented mathematically as below.

$$\text{Rule 1: If X1 is X1, i}(x_1) \text{ and X2 is X2, j}(x_2) \text{ then Z is Ci, j}$$

$$\text{Rule 2: If X1 is X1, i}(x_1) \text{ and X2 is X2,j+1}(x_2) \text{ then Z is Ci, j + 1},$$

$$\text{Rule 3: If X1 is X1, i + 1}(x_1) \text{ and X2 is X2,j}(x_2) \text{ then Z is Ci + 1, j} \quad \text{and}$$

$$\text{Rule 4: If X1 is X1, i + 1}(x_1) \text{ and } X_2 \text{ is X2,j+1}(x_2) \text{ then Z is Ci + 1, j + 1} \qquad (2)$$

In the equation (2), the then part of each rule is called the strength of the rule and the strength is denoted as 'α'. The strengths α_{ij} of the rules are obtained using the fuzzy rule conjunction [S.Parasuraman V.Ganapathy, Bijan Shirinzadeh,(2006)] and given in the Table 4 and equation (3).

Inputs	Sensor X2 (S3)			
Sensor X1 (S4)	Membership/Output	$\mu(_{X2,j-1}(x_2))$	$\mu(_{X2,j}(x_2))$	$\mu(_{X2,j+1}(x_2))$
	$\mu(_{X1,i-1}(x_1))$	0	0	0
	$\mu(_{X1,i}(x_1))$	α_{ij}	$\alpha_{i,j+1}$	0
	$\mu(_{X1,i+1}(x_1))$	$\alpha_{i+1,j}$	$\alpha_{i+1,j+1}$	0

Table 4. Active Rule

Where

$$\alpha_{ij} = \mu_{X1,i}(x_1) \wedge \mu_{X2,j}(x_2) = \min(\mu_{X1,i}(x_1), \mu_{X2,j}(x_2)),$$

$$\alpha_{i,j+1} = \mu_{X1,i}(x_1) \wedge \mu_{X2,j+1}(x_2) = \min(\mu_{X1,i}(x_1), \mu_{X2,j+1}(x_2)),$$

$$\alpha_{i+1,j} = \mu_{X1,i+1}(x_1) \wedge \mu_{X2,j}(x_2) = \min(\mu_{X1,i+1}(x_1), \mu_{X2,j}(x_2)), \text{ and}$$

$$\alpha_{i+1,j+1} = \mu_{X1,i+1}(x_1) \wedge \mu_{X2,j+1}(x_2) = \min(\mu_{X1,i+1}(x_1), \mu_{X2,j+1}(x_2)) \qquad (3)$$

The numbers αij, αij+1, αi+1,j and αi+1, j+1 are called rule strengths, and are shown in Table.4. Table 4 is similar to Table 3 with the difference that the active cells in Table 4 are the numbers expressing the strength of the rules while the same cells in Table 3 are occupied by fuzzy output. Control output (CO) of each rule is defined by operation conjunction applied, based on the strength of the rules (number expressing the strength) and the fuzzy output and are given as below. This is equivalent to performing max operation on the corresponding elements in the active cells and are shown in the Table 5

Inputs		Sensor X2 (S3)		
Sensor X1 (S4)	Membership/Output	$\mu(X_{2,j-1}(x_2))$	$\mu(X_{2,j}(x_2))$	$\mu(X_{2,j+1}(x_2))$
	$\mu(X_{1,i-1}(x_1))$	0	0	0
	$\mu(X_{1,i}(x_1))$	$\alpha_{ij} \vee \mu_{Cij}(Z)$	$\alpha_{i,j+1} \vee \mu_{Ci,j+1}(Z)$	0
	$\mu(X_{1,i+1}(x_1))$	$\alpha_{i+1,j} \vee \mu_{Ci+1,j}(Z)$	$\alpha_{i+1,j} \vee \mu_{Ci+1,j}(Z)$	0

Table 5. Control output rules

$$\text{CO rule 1} : \alpha_{ij} \vee \mu_{Cij}(Z) = \max(\alpha_{ij}, \mu_{Cij}(Z)),$$

$$\text{CO rule 2} : \alpha_{i,j+1} \vee \mu_{Ci,j+1}(Z) = \max(\alpha_{i,j+1}, \mu_{Cij+1}(Z)),$$

$$\text{CO rule 3} : \alpha_{i+1,j} \vee \mu_{Ci+1,j}(Z) = \max(\alpha_{i+1,j}, \mu_{Ci+1,j}(Z)) \text{ and}$$

$$\text{CO rule 4} : \alpha_{i+1,j} \vee \mu_{Ci+1,j}(Z) = \max(\alpha_{i+1,j}, \mu_{Ci+1,j}(Z)) \quad (4)$$

The output of four rules, located in the active cells in Table 5, have to be combined or aggregated in order to produce one control output with membership function μagg (Z) as shown below.

$$\mu_{agg}(Z) = (\alpha_{ij} \vee \mu_{Cij}(Z)) \wedge (\alpha_{i,j+1} \vee \mu_{C\,i,j+1}(Z)) \wedge (\alpha_{i+1,j} \vee \mu_{Ci+1,j}(Z)) \wedge (\alpha_{i+1,j+1} \vee \mu_{Ci+1,j+1}(Z)) \quad (5)$$

The ∨ (max) operation is performed on a number and a membership function of an output fuzzy set. Number of linguistic fuzzy set on each sensor input i = j. In this context, the real number α and the output membership function μ C (Z) can be obtained as shown below. A max operation is performed on a number and a membership function of the output fuzzy sets.

$$\mu_\alpha \wedge \mu_C(Z) = \max(\mu_\alpha(Z), \mu_C(Z)) \quad (6)$$

The final ith output of the fired rule μ'Ci (Z) is expressed as

$$\mu'_{Ci}(Z) = \max(\mu_{\alpha i}(Z), \mu_{Ci} Z)) \quad (7)$$

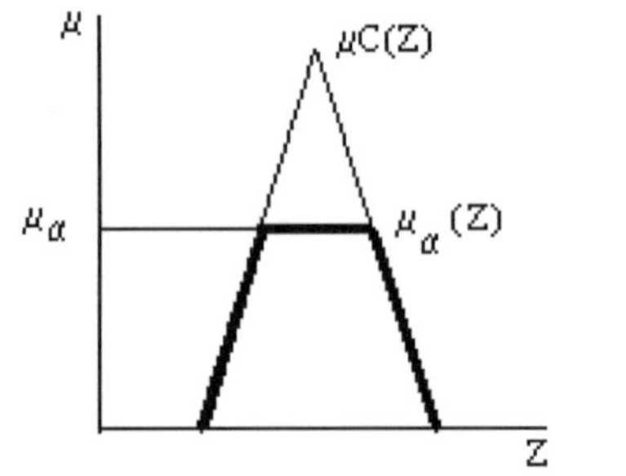

Fig. 3. Output membership using alpha level threshold

where $\mu_{\alpha i}(Z) = \{Z,\ Z \in U,\ \text{and}\ \alpha_i \le Z \le \alpha_{i+1}\}$, $\alpha \in [0,1]$ and μCi (Z) is the ith output membership function based on normal environmental context.

μCi (Z) = max (min ((X1i+1) ∘ (X1i → Zi)), ((X1i+1) ∘ (X1i and X2i → Zi)), ((X2i+1) ∘ (X2i → Zi)), (X2i+1) ∘ (X1i and X2i → Zi)).

3.1 Implementation of ALFLS

The programming procedures are provided in the flow chart shown in Figure 4. In the proposed ALFLS method, a control rule is activated, when the measurement of the obstacle distance exactly matches the rule conditional part ('if' part of the rule). Each conditional part of the rule is formulated using the alpha interval fuzzy sets. The final decision made is based on the corresponding action part ('then' part of the rule) of the matched rule. In order to match the input data of the sensor with the ALFLS rules, the following control procedures are formulated and adapted for the experiments.

The programming procedures are provided in the flow charts shown in Figure 2.

i. Consider the first rule, i = 1. Initialize μCo (Z) = 0.

ii. For ith rule, read the membership value of each of the variables in the antecedent part as per the equation 3.

iii. Take the minimum value of step 2, then find the output membership value using the equation 3.

iv. If i = final rule, set μC' (Z) = μC i (Z) then stop. Otherwise set i = i+1 and go to step2.

4. Experimental investigations

The 3-alpha Intervals: In order to illustrate the capability and performance of ALFLS techniques, the experimental studies are carried out as follows. Firstly, the obstacle distances of the environment from the robot represented by 'Small' fuzzy set are well defined by dividing the corresponding distance ranges into three intervals and referred to as 3-alpha intervals. The navigation rules are established using the three alpha intervals and experimental studies are carried out. Secondly, in order to demonstrate the variations of the performance of the ALFLS techniques, the experimental studies are repeated using two intervals of the 'small' fuzzy set and are referred to as 2-alpha intervals.

The real world environment consists of real obstacles such as blocks, walls, and curved walls etc., which are situated in an unstructured manner as shown in Figure 5. The experiments were repeated several times in the same environment with the same starting and the target positions and for different alpha intervals.

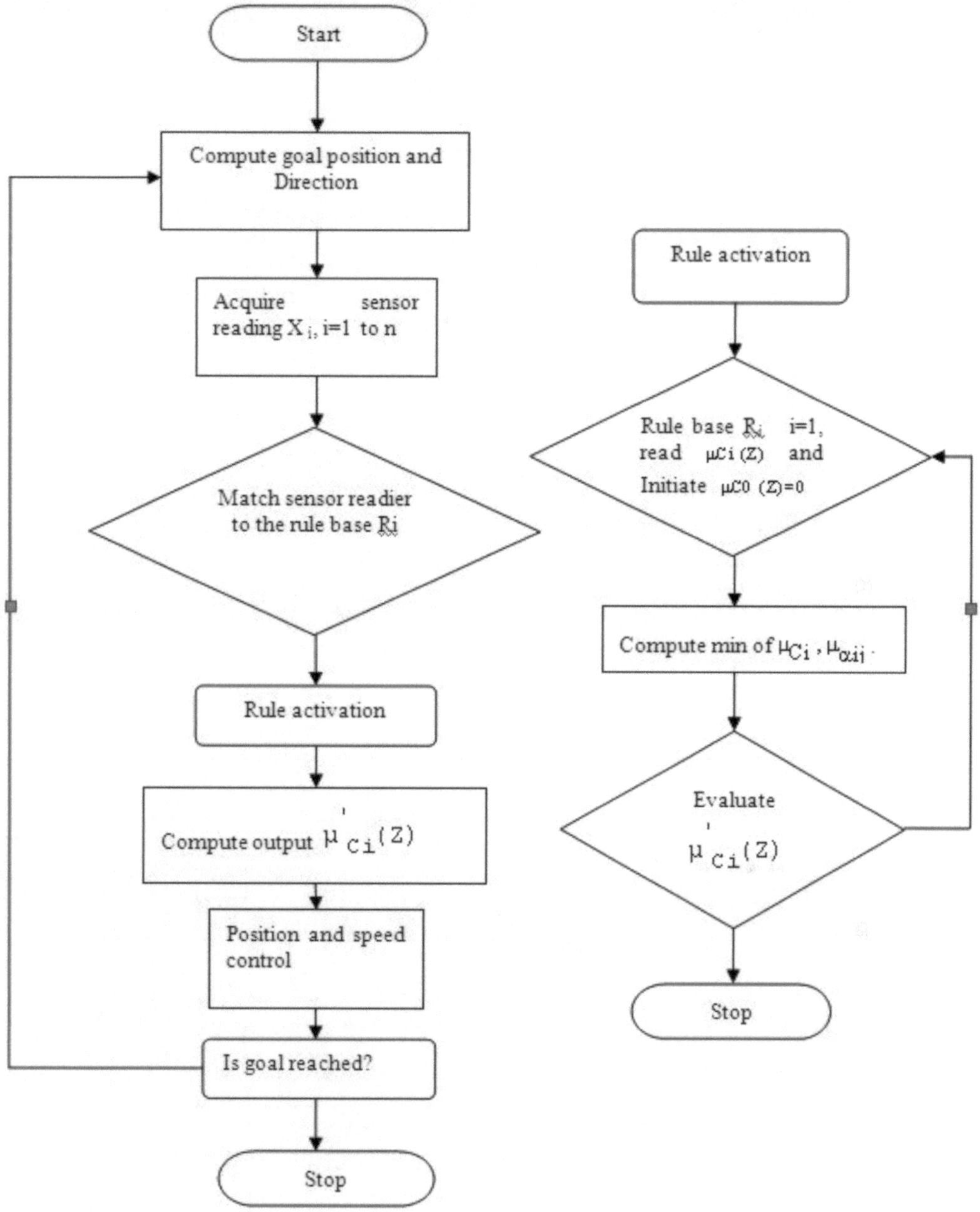

Fig. 4. Flow charts showing the procedures of the program

The behavior rules obtained from ALFLS are fed into the robot control system and the experimental results are obtained and evaluated to show the performance of the proposed methodology. It is observed from the experiment that the robot moves through the optimized path and deviates from the encountered obstacles and reaches the target. The results of the experiments are shown in the graph and given in Figures 6 and 7. These Figures are the graphs showing cycle time plotted against the obstacle distances from

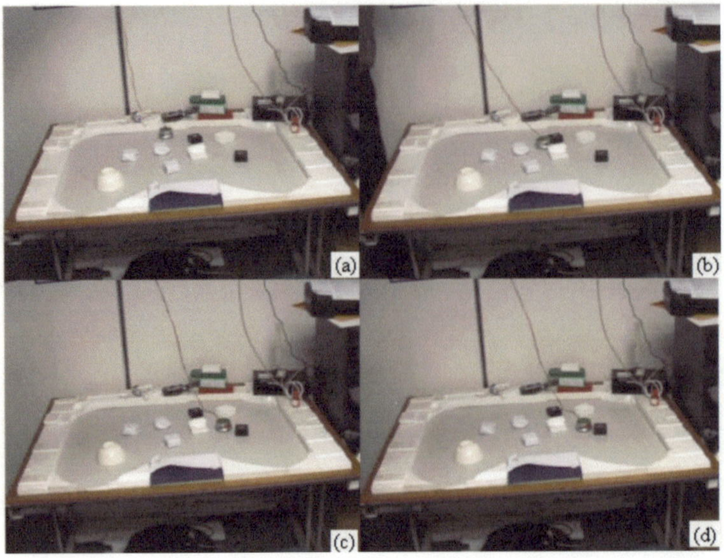

Fig. 5(a)-(d). Real world experiments using Khephera II to validate the ALFLS.

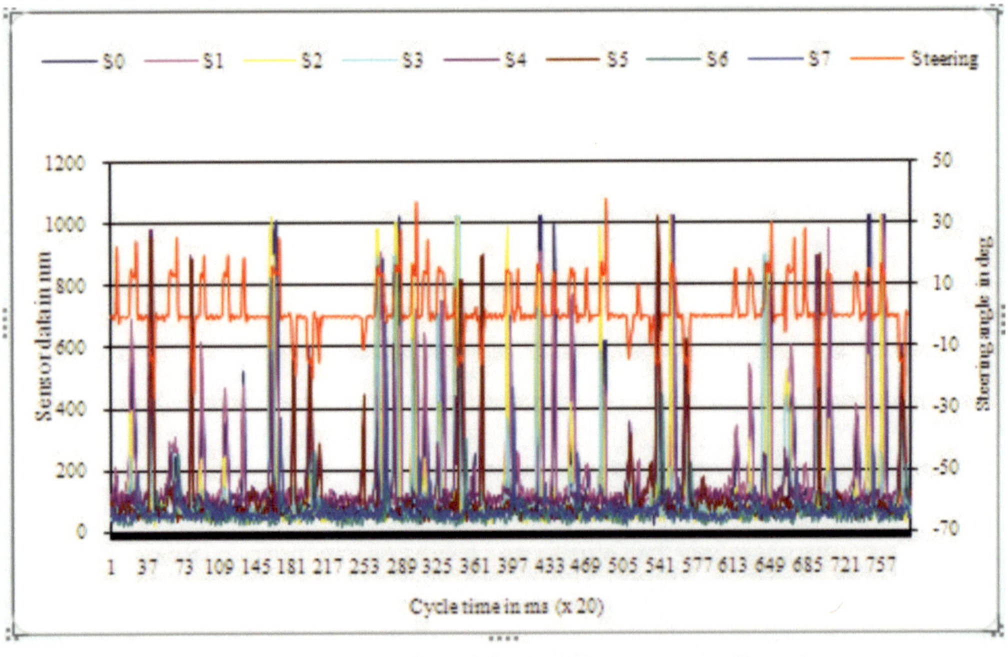

Fig. 6. Graph showing the cycle time plotted against the sensor readings in mm

sensors S0 to S7and steering angle. The final path travel is computed from the total control cylce time and the speed of the robot, which kept as same value in all experiements. The near optimal path is achieved by behaviour rule selection using the 3- alpha fuzzy intervals when more than one behaviour rules of the same kind is present in the environment during navigation. A small portion (period around 280 x20 ms, 300 x 20 ms and 345 x 20 ms) of the output results of Figure 6 are enlarged and shown in Figure 7.

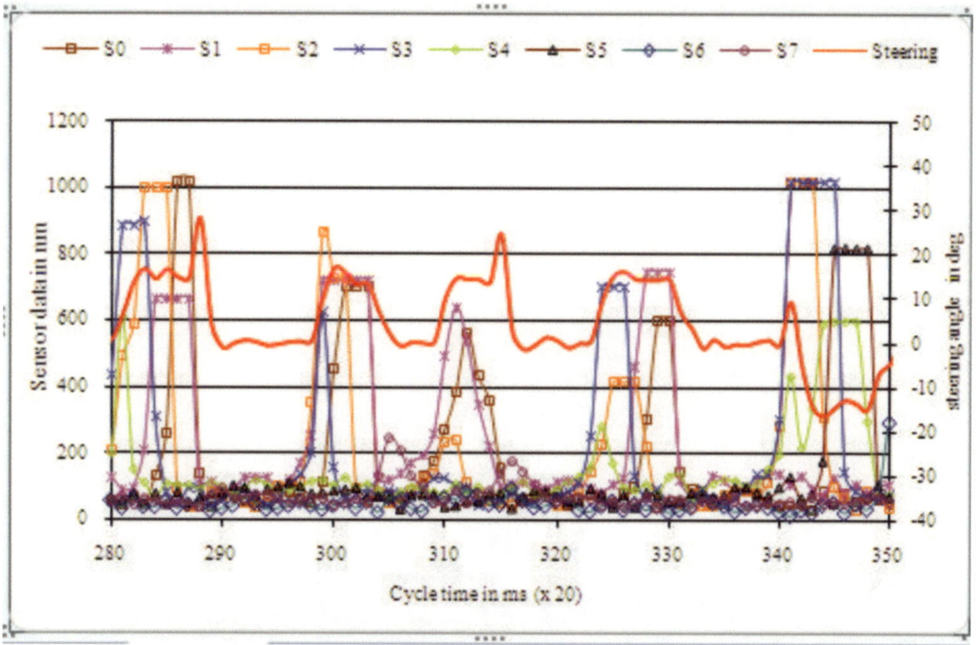

Fig. 7. Graph showing the enlarged section of Figure 6 between cycle times 280 to 350 x 20 ms plotted against obstacle distances.

As illustrated in Figure 7, the sensor reading shows the obstacles which have appeared at various distances. As defined in ALFLS, these obstalce distances are partitioned as alpha level and the corresponding rule predicates maximizes the truth value for particular rule to be fired in the conflicting sitaution. As a result of ALFLS (3 alpha intervals), the robot deviates from the encountered obstacles with the turn angles deviations from +30 to -20 deg for the entire control cycle. This is illustrated in the enlarged portion of the graph in Figure 6. From the above experiment, it has been observed that due to the 3- alpha intervals used in establishing behaviour rules, the robot deviates from obstacles (as perceived by sensors) in close vicinity and navigate towards the target. The navigation path deviations are as close to as ± 30 degrees. As a result of the close deviation, the time taken that the robot reaches the target is faster with optimum path when multiple obstacles are present close to the robot.

The significant variations of the results of ALFLS methodology are illustrated by changing the alpha intervals to two ranges (2-alpha intervals) and are discussed in this section. The experiments have been conducted similar to the above method without changing the environment. The range of the input fuzzy set small is changed into two intervals and the corresponding navigations rules are established and tested with experiments. The navigation path in this experiment is shown by a series of Figures 8 from (a) to (f). The experimental results are discussed and shown in Figure 9 and the enlarged portion of Figure 9 is given in Figure 10. It can be seen from the graph shown in Figure 10, that the robot deviations due to the encountered obstacles are more than the deviations illustrated in the 3-alpha intervals while the robot moved towards the target. The robot turn angle deviations are ± 70 degrees for the similar obstacle environment as done in 3-alpha intervals. Due to the larger turn angle from encountered obstacles, the navigation path of the robot is longer to reach the target.

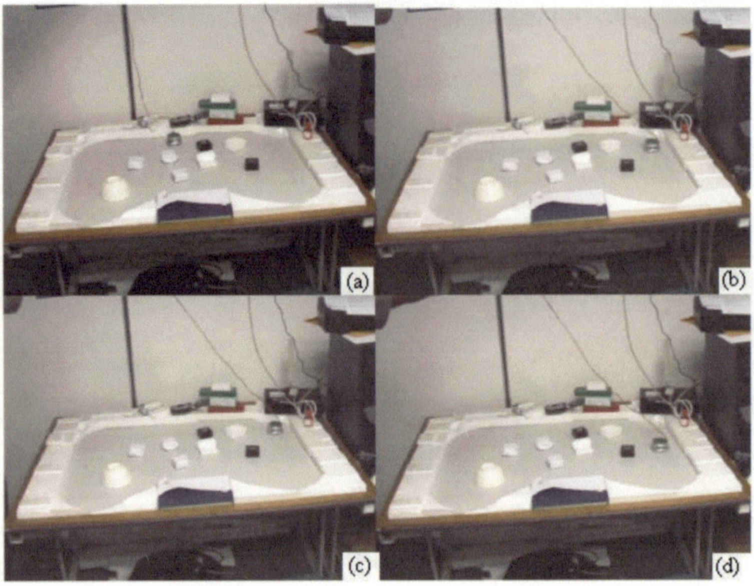

Fig. 8. (a) -(d): Real world experiments using Khepera II to validate the ALFLS by means of 2-alpha intervals.

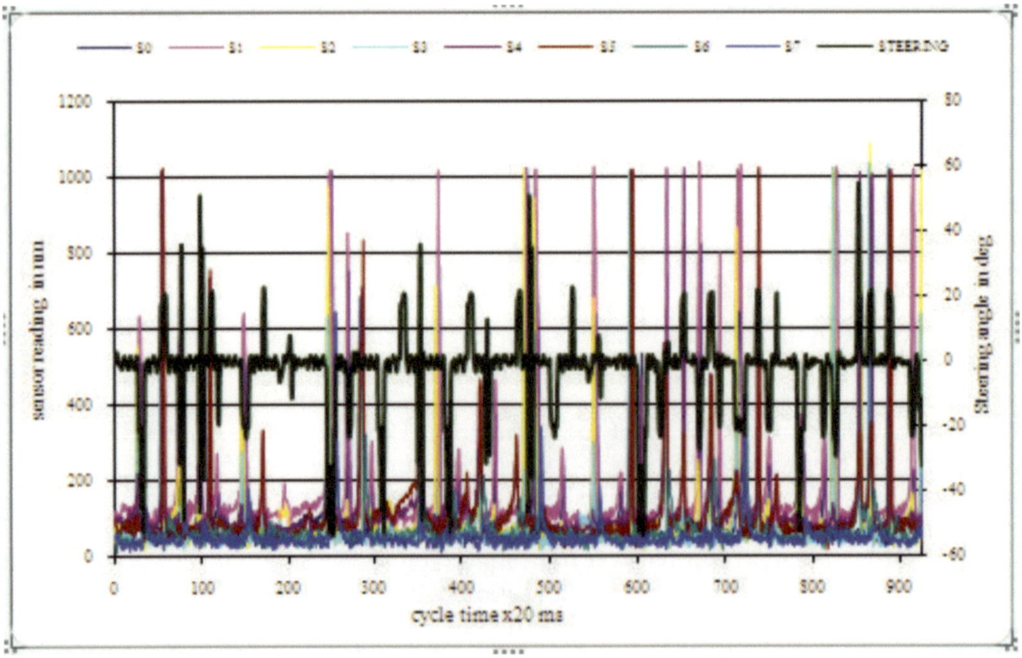

Fig. 9. Plot showing the cycle time drawn against the sensor readings in mm.

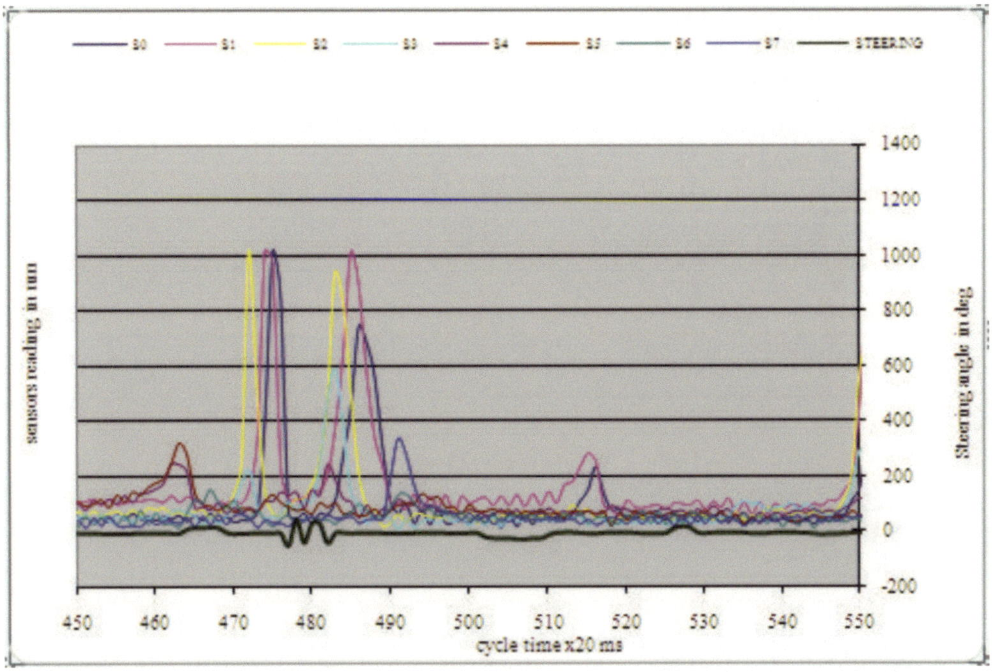

Fig. 10. Plot showing the enlarged section of Figure 9 between cycle times 400 to 650 x 20 ms plotted against obstacle distances.

5. Results and discussions

The effectiveness of ALFLS is demonstrated using the real world experimental results of Khepera II. The comparative results of obstcale deviations from 3 and 2 alpha intervals are shown against the control cycle time in Figure 11. As observed from the graph, the navigation path deviations are as close to ± 30 degrees while using 3 alpha intervals and ± 70 degrees while using the 2-alpha intervals navigation rules. As a result of wider deviation using 2-alpha fuzzy set, the robot takes a longer path to reach the target. It can be found from the experiments that the robot reached the target with an optimum path using minimum deviation from obstacles while using navigation rules obtained from 3-alpha intervals as established in ALFLS. The effectiveness of ALFLS is demonstrated and found that the navigation rules obtained from 3-alpha intervals have shown significant improvements during navigation.

The existing Fuzzy logic approaches used larger interval of input, output fuzzy sets, and build the navigation rules. Due to the larger intervals, the robot turns over wider angle and avoided obstacles during navigation. Some times this also affects the behavior selection, when more than one obstacles are present at the same intervals with two different distances closer to the robot. In this situation the proposed ALFLS is more suitable to map the sensor's

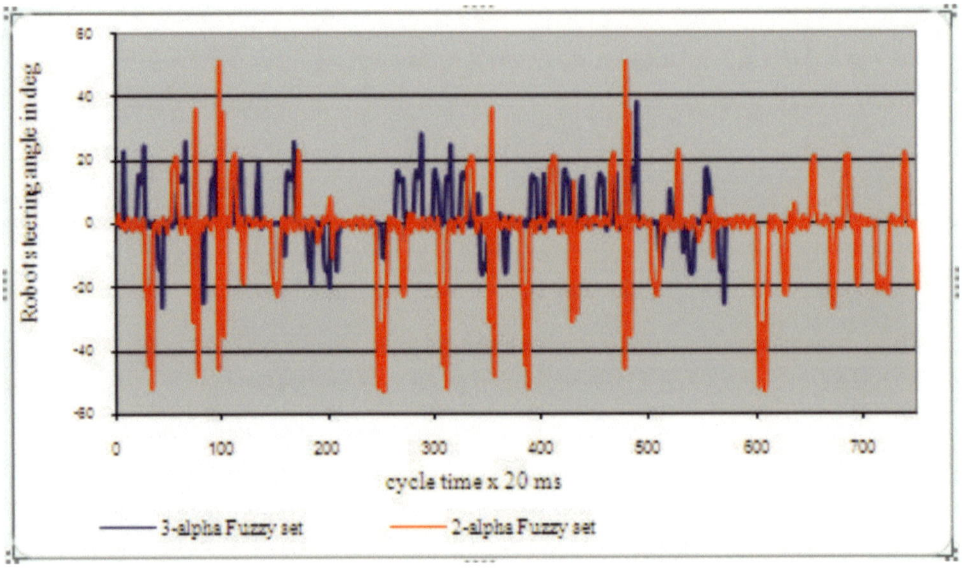

Fig. 11. Graph showing the cycle time plotted against robot steering angle for 3-alpha fuzzy outputs and 2- alpha fuzzy outputs

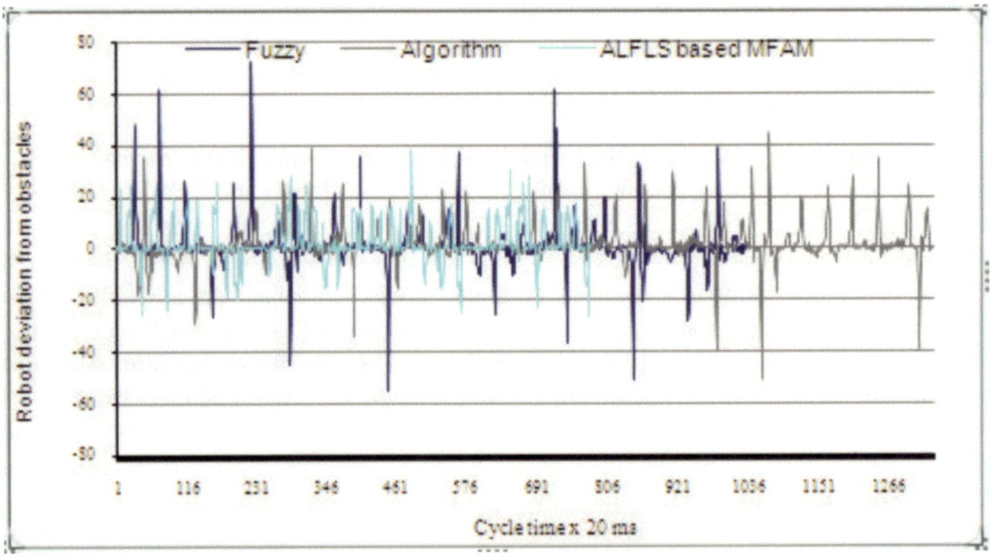

Fig. 12. Comparison of the proposed ALFLS based MFAM with the existing methodologies Mathematical model, Fuzzy logic and Algorithm based approaches.

inputs and behavior rule selection. The graph shown in Figure 12 shows significant improvements using ALFLS than the existing fuzzy logic approaches for mobile robot navigation.

7. Conclusion

The experimental study was conducted to investigate the proposed ALFLS methodology for mobile robot navigation using Khepera II mobile robot. The Experimental investigations show that the proposed formulation reduces the complexity of building the navigation system in a complex environment. The proposed methodology demonstrated improved performance of mobile robot navigation in terms of (i) behaviour rule selection without conflicting (ii) smaller time taken of the robot to reach the target and (iii) the distance traveled to reach the target position, which is shorter compared to the other accepted methods

8. References

Saffiotti A, and Leblanc K (2000). "Active PERCEPTUAL anchoring of Robot Behavior in a Dynamic Environment" Proceedings of the IEEE Int. Conf. On Robotics and Automation (ICRA-2000) SanFrancisco, CA.

Mackenzie D.C, Arkin R.C, and Cameron J.M (1997), "specification and Execution of Multiagent Missions" Autonomous Robots 4 (1), pg. 29-57.

Pattie Maes (1991) "A Bottom-Up Mechanism for Behavior Selection in an Artificial Creature," From Animals to Animats, MIT Press.

Kurt Konolige, Karen Meyers, and Alessandro Saffiotti (1992), "FLAKEY, an Autonomous Mobile Robot," technical document, Stanford Research Institute International.

Song K.Y. and Tai J. C (1992), "Fuzzy Navigation of a Mobile Robot," Proceedings of IEEE/RSJ International Conference on Intelligent Robots and Systems, Raleigh, North Carolina.

Pin F.G(1992) "Using Custom-Designed VLSI Fuzzy Inferencing Chips for the Autonomous Navigation of a Mobile Robot" Proceedings of IEEE/RSJ Intl. Conf. on Intel. Robots and Systems, North Carolina.

Arbib M. A (1992) "Schema Theory" in the Encyclopedia of Artificial Intelligence 2nd ed. Wiley-Inderscience, pg 1427-43, New York.

Arkin R. C (1989)."Motor Schema Based Mobile Robot Navigation" international Journal of Robotics Research, pg. 92-112, vol 18.

Arkin R. C.. and D. Mackenzie(1994), "Temporal Coordination of Perceptual Algorithms for Mobile Robot Navigation", *IEEE Transactions on Robotics and Automation*, vol 10, No. 3, pg 276-286.

Petru Rusu, Thom E. Whalen, Aurel Cornell and HansJ.W Spoelder (2003) "Behavior based Neuro-Fuzzy Controller for Mobile Robot Navigation IEEE Transaction on Instrumentation and measurement", vol. 52, No. 4.

C.T. Lin and C.S.G. Lee (1991)"Neural network based fuzzy logic control and decision systems," IEEE Transaction on Computations. vol 40, pg 120-1336.

S.Parasuraman V.Ganapathy, Bijan Shirinzadeh,(2006)."Behavior rule selection using α-level FIS for mobile robot navigation during multiple rule conflicts in the complex environments" Inderscience, International Journal of Automation and Control (IJAAC), pg.342-361, vol1, No.4.